Lecture Notes in Computer Science 16898

Founding Editors

Gerhard Goos
Juris Hartmanis

The series Lecture Notes in Computer Science (LNCS), including its subseries Lecture Notes in Artificial Intelligence (LNAI) and Lecture Notes in Bioinformatics (LNBI), has established itself as a medium for the publication of new developments in computer science and information technology research, teaching, and education.

LNCS enjoys close cooperation with the computer science R & D community, the series counts many renowned academics among its volume editors and paper authors, and collaborates with prestigious societies. Its mission is to serve this international community by providing an invaluable service, mainly focused on the publication of conference and workshop proceedings and postproceedings. LNCS commenced publication in 1973.

Simin Nadjm-Tehrani · Andreas Ekelhart ·
Buse Atli · Mikael Asplund
Editors

Availability, Reliability and Security

21st International Conference, ARES 2026
Linköping, Sweden, August 24–27, 2026
Proceedings, Part I

Springer

Editors
Simin Nadjm-Tehrani
Department of Computer and Information Science
Linköping University
Linköping, Sweden

Buse Atli
Department of Computer and Information Science
Linköping University
Linköping, Sweden

Andreas Ekelhart
SBA Research and University of Vienna
Vienna, Austria

Mikael Asplund
Department of Computer and Information Science
Linköping University
Linköping, Sweden

ISSN 0302-9743 ISSN 1611-3349 (electronic)
Lecture Notes in Computer Science
ISBN 978-3-032-36873-7 ISBN 978-3-032-36874-4 (eBook)
https://doi.org/10.1007/978-3-032-36874-4

This Springer imprint is published by the registered company Springer Nature Switzerland AG
The registered company address is: Gewerbestrasse 11, 6330 Cham, Switzerland

Preface

The Program Chairs for the 21st International Conference on Availability, Reliability, and Security (ARES) had the pleasure of putting together the main track of the conference for 2026. The conference program benefited from close coordination between the main track and the 23 co-located workshops led by General Chair Mikael Asplund and Workshop Chairs Zeeshan Afzal, Patrick Kochberger, Florian Skopik and Peter Kieseberg.

The program for the main track consisted of three Keynotes, 35 full papers, 2 SoK papers and 9 short papers selected among all the submitted papers after undergoing at least three double-blind program committee reviews for each accepted paper.

We received 225 paper submissions, of which 22 were desk-rejected because they did not comply with the submission requirements, including anonymity violations, excessive length, formatting issues, hallucinated references, problematic use of AI or withdrawal by the authors. Of the 203 papers that underwent review, 170 were full papers, 10 were SoK papers, and 23 were short papers. The main track accepted all in all 46 papers to be presented. For full and SoK papers, this yields an acceptance rate of 18.8%. This selection would not have been possible without the help of the members of the Program Committee. We are deeply grateful to the PC members and their numerous subreviewers for their careful reviews, constructive feedback, and active participation in the discussion phase and, in some cases, for shepherding papers through the final revision process. Thank you!

The keynote speakers for this year's ARES brought the key discussions of our field to Linköping to engage all the participants from near and far. Roberto Baldoni brought both his scholarly experience and political advisory engagement to discuss a very current topic for our times: why democracies need trusted technologies. Erik Hemberg linked threat intelligence to understanding how systems can be exposed to threats and how the threats are to be mitigated. Last but not least, Elena Dubrova brought the audience up to date with the field of quantum cryptography and how security as we know it today will be impacted by the quantum revolution. We wholeheartedly thank the speakers for giving us their time and wisdom.

Finally, we thank all authors for submitting their work and all participants for contributing to the exchange that makes ARES a vibrant scientific community. We were pleased to welcome you to ARES 2026 in Linköping!

August 2026

Simin Nadjm-Tehrani
Andreas Ekelhart

Organization

General Chair

Mikael Asplund	Linköping University, Sweden

Program Committee Chairs

Simin Nadjm-Tehrani	Linköping University, Sweden
Andreas Ekelhart	SBA Research and University of Vienna, Austria

Steering Committee

Abdelmalek Benzekri	University of Toulouse, France
Francesco Buccafurri	Università Mediterranea di Reggio Calabria
Dominik Engel	Salzburg University of Applied Sciences, Austria
Mathias Fischer	University of Hamburg, Germany
Steven Furnell	University of Nottingham, UK
Stefanie Rinderle-Ma	University of Vienna, Austria
Shujun Li	University of Kent, UK
Christian Doerr	Delft University of Technology, Netherlands
Pierangela Samarati	Università degli Studi di Milano, Italy
Melanie Volkamer	Karlsruhe Institute of Technology, Germany

Steering Committee Chairs

Edgar Weippl	SBA Research, Austria
A Min Tjoa	TU Vienna, Austria

Workshop Chairs

Zeeshan Afzal	Linköping University, Sweden
Patrick Kochberger	St. Pölten University of Applied Sciences, Austria

EU Projects Symposium Workshop Chairs

Florian Skopik	AIT Austrian Institute of Technology, Austria
Peter Kieseberg	St. Pölten University of Applied Sciences, Austria

Proceedings Chair

Buse Atli	Linköping University, Sweden

Publicity Chair

Gurjot Singh	Linköping University, Sweden

Website Chair

Sebastian Schrittwieser	SBA Research and University of Vienna, Austria

Industry Track Chair

Beatrice Magnusson	Linköping Science Park, Sweden

Program Committee

Isaac Agudo	University of Málaga, Spain
Magnus Almgren	Chalmers University of Technology, Sweden
Saed Alrabaee	United Arab Emirates University, United Arab Emirates
Todd Andel	University of South Alabama, USA
Ingmar Baumgart	Karlsruhe Institute of Technology, Germany
Monowar Bhuyan	Umeå University, Sweden
Gregory Blanc	Institut Mines-Télécom, Télécom SudParis, Institut Polytechnique de Paris, France
Olivier Blazy	École Polytechnique, France
Aymen Boudguiga	CEA LIST, France
Nora Boulahia-Cuppens	Polytechnique Montréal, Canada
Alessandro Brighente	University of Padua, Italy
Francesco Buccafurri	Università Mediterranea di Reggio Calabria, Italy

Krzysztof Cabaj	Warsaw University of Technology, Poland
Jordi Castellà-Roca	Universitat Rovira i Virgili, Spain
Marta Catillo	Università del Sannio, Italy
Luca Caviglione	CNR-IMATI, Italy
Mariano Ceccato	University of Verona, Italy
Sherman S. M. Chow	Chinese University of Hong Kong, China
Marijke Coetzee	North-West University, South Africa
Emilio Coppa	LUISS University, Italy
Tiago Cruz	University of Coimbra, Portugal
Michel Cukier	University of Maryland, College Park, USA
Frederic Cuppens	Polytechnique Montréal, Canada
Laurens D'hooge	Ghent University, Belgium
Mila Dalla Preda	University of Verona, Italy
Bjorn De Sutter	Ghent University, Belgium
Nicolás E. Díaz Ferreyra	Hamburg University of Technology, Germany
Pavlos Efraimidis	Democritus University of Thrace, Greece
Günther Eibl	Salzburg University of Applied Sciences, Austria
Christian Engelmann	Oak Ridge National Laboratory, USA
Santiago Escobar	Universitat Politècnica de València, Spain
Hannes Federrath	University of Hamburg, Germany
Panagiotis Fouliras	University of Macedonia, Greece
Ulrik Franke	Swedish Defence University, Sweden
Virginia Franqueira	University of Kent, UK
Steven Furnell	University of Nottingham, UK
Golden G. Richard III	Louisiana State University, USA
Christian Gehrmann	Lund University, Sweden
Giorgio Giacinto	University of Cagliari, Italy
Karl M. Goeschka	Vienna University of Technology, Austria
Lorena González Manzano	Universidad Carlos III de Madrid, Spain
Thomas Gross	Newcastle University, UK
Rene Rydhof Hansen	Aalborg University, Denmark
Péter Hegedűs	University of Szeged, Hungary
Dominik Herrmann	University of Bamberg, Germany
Dorjan Hitaj	Sapienza University of Rome, Italy
Zhen Huang	DePaul University, USA
Michele Ianni	University of Calabria, Italy
Pedro Inácio	Universidade da Beira Interior, Portugal
Martin Gilje Jaatun	SINTEF Digital, Norway
Nesrine Kaaniche	Télécom SudParis, France
Liina Kamm	Cybernetica AS, Estonia
Stylianos Karagiannis	Ionian University, Greece

Sokratis Katsikas	Norwegian University of Science and Technology, Norway
Stefan Katzenbeisser	University of Passau, Germany
Hyoungshick Kim	Sungkyunkwan University, South Korea
Marina Krotofil	Maersk, Denmark
Oksana Kulyk	IT University of Copenhagen, Denmark
Romain Laborde	Université de Toulouse, France
Costas Lambrinoudakis	University of Piraeus, Greece
Jorn Lapon	KU Leuven, Belgium
Maryline Laurent	Télécom SudParis, France
Olivier Levillain	Télécom SudParis/IP Paris, France
Shujun Li	University of Kent, UK
Jens Lindemann	Universität Hamburg, Germany
Leandros Maglaras	Edinburgh Napier University, UK
Lukas Malina	Brno University of Technology, Czech Republic
Keith Martin	Royal Holloway, University of London, UK
Barbara Masucci	University of Salerno, Italy
Raimundas Matulevičius	University of Tartu, Estonia
Rudolf Mayer	SBA Research/TU Wien, Austria
Wojciech Mazurczyk	Warsaw University of Technology, Poland
Michael Meier	University of Bonn/Fraunhofer FKIE, Germany
Per Håkon Meland	SINTEF Digital, Norway
Weizhi Meng	Lancaster University, UK
Francesco Mercaldo	University of Molise, Italy
Massimo Merro	University of Verona, Italy
Joachim Meyer	Tel Aviv University, Israel
Rodrigo Miani	Federal University of Uberlândia, Brazil
Aleksandra Mileva	Goce Delčev University, North Macedonia
Stephan Neumann	SaarLB, Germany
Zhenyu Ning	Hunan University, China
Christoforos Ntantogian	Ionian University, Greece
Rolf Oppliger	eSECURITY Technologies, Switzerland
Federica Paci	University of Verona, Italy
Marc-Oliver Pahl	IMT Atlantique, France
Miguel Pardal	Universidade de Lisboa, Portugal
Sergio Pastrana	Universidad Carlos III de Madrid, Spain
Günther Pernul	University of Regensburg, Germany
Marie-Laure Potet	Verimag Laboratory, France
Md Masoom Rabbani	Chalmers University of Technology, Sweden
Silvio Ranise	University of Trento/FBK, Italy
Christian Reuter	TU Darmstadt, Germany
Junghwan Rhee	University of Central Oklahoma, USA

Thomas Rosenstatter	Salzburg University of Applied Sciences, Austria
Michael Rossberg	TU Ilmenau, Germany
Christoph Saatjohann	FH Münster, Germany
Morteza Safaei Pour	San Diego State University, USA
Pierangela Samarati	University of Milan, Italy
Luis Enrique Sánchez Crespo	University of Castilla-La Mancha, Spain
Riccardo Scandariato	Hamburg University of Technology, Germany
Jörn-Marc Schmidt	IU Internationale Hochschule, Germany
Jan Seedorf	HFT Stuttgart, Germany
Hervais Simo	Fraunhofer SIT, Germany
Nazatul Haque Sultan	University of Newcastle, Australia
Shamik Sural	IIT Kharagpur, India
Oliver Theel	University of Oldenburg, Germany
Simon Tjoa	St. Pölten University of Applied Sciences, Austria
Jacob Torrey	Thinkst Applied Research, South Africa
Katja Tuma	Eindhoven University of Technology, Netherlands
Andreas Unterweger	Salzburg University of Applied Sciences, Austria
Emmanouil Vasilomanolakis	Technical University of Denmark, Denmark
Umberto Villano	University of Sannio, Italy
Corrado Aaron Visaggio	University of Foggia, Italy
Christos Xenakis	University of Piraeus, Greece
Koen Yskout	KU Leuven, Belgium
Nicola Zannone	Eindhoven University of Technology, Netherlands
Jose Maria de Fuentes	Universidad Carlos III de Madrid, Spain

Additional Reviewers

Sedat Akleylek
Mehbub Alam
Buse Atli
Marvin Banse
Stefan Bavendiek
Andreas Brandhøj
Tobias Bøgedal
Andrew Case
Arcangelo Castiglione
Stelvio Cimato
Arthur Cordeiro
Ioannis Chouchoulis
Dairo de Ruck
Minxin Du
Martin Dukek
Jules Dumezy
Karina Elzer
Eleftherios Eleftheriadis
Christian Esposito
Reyhane Falanji
Clemente Galdi
Thrasyvoulos Giannakopoulos
Labani Halder
Wouter Hellemans
Markus Henkel
Maya Herrscher
Nazrul Hoque
Thodoris Ioannidis
Jef Jacobs
Andes Y. L. Kei

Peter Kieseberg
Emil Larsson
Madeleine Lindström
Jack P. K. Ma
Majid Mollaeefar
Alberto Mongardini
Laurent Mounier
Meghali Nandi
Christos Chrysanthos Nikolaidis
Lauren Pace
Ying-Yu Pan
Cecilia Pasquini
Rui Pinto
Pille Pullonen-Raudvere
Aikaterini Psychogyiou
Matteo Rizzi
Tiago Roxo
Atif Rizwan
Christoph Sanders
Olaf Saßnick
Bernardo Sequeiros
Charilaos Skandylas
Akim Stark
Ioannis Stylianou
Arturo Hernandez Sanchez
Theodoros Tsiolakis
Johannes Wilson
Nicolas Ye
Ricardo Yaben
Niklas Zapatka

ARES 2026 Keynotes

Proactive Cyber Defense with Artificial Intelligence

Erik Hemberg

ALFA Lab at Massachusetts Institute of Technology, USA
hembergerik@csail.mit.edu

Proactive cyber defense could improve security, e.g. through cyber hunting. Defending against diverse, dynamic threats requires linked knowledge of threats, vulnerabilities, and mitigations. Cyber analysts and hunters use this knowledge to trace threats from observed indicators—and, conversely, to identify likely indicators from known threats. Threat modelers rely on it to explore and prioritize mitigations. We have aggregated public cyber threat knowledge into a property graph, enriching sources that currently expose only limited, unidirectional links. This property graph could make it easier for analysts and automated systems to answer key questions. To further increase utility, we apply Artificial Intelligence both to enhance the data and to inform testing and evaluation of computer networks. This talk exposes the insights gained from my studies of adversarial engagements in multiple different environments, from tax avoidance to malware detection, and also discusses how it affects current and future challenges.

Strategic Autonomy in the Age of AI: Why Democracies Need Trusted Technologies

Roberto Baldoni

Università degli Studi di Roma La Sapienza, Italy
roberto.baldoni@uniroma1.it

As artificial intelligence becomes a critical resource, digital sovereignty is evolving from a question of data control into a broader challenge of controlling the technological infrastructures that generate intelligence. In a multipolar world increasingly shaped by geopolitical competition, the technology stack underlying AI systems - from critical minerals, semiconductors, and cloud infrastructures to models, orchestration layers, and digital platforms - is becoming a key determinant of economic power, resilience, and strategic autonomy.

This talk examines why democracies need trusted technologies to remain free, competitive, and sovereign in the age of AI. Using the AI technology stack as an analytical framework, it explores how dependencies across critical layers are reshaping the balance between states, firms, and alliances. These dependencies can create innovation and scale, but they can also become instruments of coercion, hidden leverage, or private concentration when they are not governable, contestable, and aligned with democratic values. The talk argues that democracies cannot preserve sovereignty through autarky, as this would leave them vulnerable to coercion either by autocracies or by a handful of tech giants. They must instead build trusted interdependence: a model of technological cooperation in which supply chains, infrastructures, models, and platforms are transparent, secure, resilient, and accountable. Preserving strategic autonomy in the age of AI will require like-minded countries to rethink industrial policy, procurement, standards, and governance so that technology advances freedom rather than control.

Physical Attacks on Implementations of Post-Quantum Cryptographic Algorithms

Elena Dubrova

Royal Institute of Technology (KTH), Sweden
dubrova@kth.se

The emergence of quantum computing poses a threat to today's widely deployed public-key cryptographic systems, driving the urgent adoption of post-quantum cryptography (PQC). Over the past few years, PQC has rapidly progressed from academic research to standardization and real-world deployment. In August 2024, the U.S. National Institute of Standards and Technology (NIST) finalized its first PQC standards, standardizing the CRYSTALS-Kyber key encapsulation mechanism and the CRYSTALS-Dilithium digital signature scheme as ML-KEM and ML-DSA, respectively. The transition to these new cryptographic standards is now underway across industry and government.

Achieving secure and efficient implementations of PQC algorithms, however, remains a significant challenge. Beyond mathematical security, practical implementations must also withstand physical attacks that exploit unintended information leakage. Side-channel attacks exploit timing variations, power consumption, or electromagnetic emissions to recover secret information, while fault attacks deliberately induce errors during cryptographic computations to compromise security.

This talk presents recent advances in physical attacks on implementations of ML-KEM and ML-DSA. Through representative case studies, we examine how side-channel and fault attacks expose implementation vulnerabilities and discuss their implications for the secure deployment of post-quantum cryptography.

Contents

Privacy I

A Unified Evaluation Framework for Privacy-Preserving Data Publication Techniques

Jenno Verdonck[1], Qianying Liao[1(✉)], Michiel Willocx[1], Wouter Joosen[1], Vincent Naessens[1], and Dimitri Van Landuyt[2(✉)]

[1] DistriNet, KU Leuven, Leuven, Belgium
liao.qianying@kuleuven.be
[2] LIRIS, KU Leuven, Leuven, Belgium
vanlanduyt.dimitri@kuleuven.be

Abstract. Privacy-preserving data publication (PPDP) aims to reduce privacy risks before releasing datasets. As alternative techniques, (i) *data de-identification* alters original data values through generalization or suppression to weaken their link to data subject identities; whereas (ii) *synthetic data generation* produces artificial datasets that do not contain any original data yet preserve statistical similarity to the original data. Given that their outcomes lack direct comparability, it remains unclear which technique leads to better privacy protections while retaining data utility. To address this gap, we present (i) a novel quantitative evaluation framework for comparing privacy and utility across synthetic and de-identified datasets, and (ii) a comparative study based on a location optimisation task and a predictive machine learning application. Our results reveal a nuanced trade-off. De-identified datasets perform better on traditional statistical privacy metrics but are more vulnerable to adversarial attacks such as attribute inference. Conversely, utility outcomes vary widely by use case, indicating that the selection of a PPDP technique remains highly dependent on the application context.

Keywords: data privacy · privacy-preserving data publishing · synthetic data · data de-identification · generative model · anonymized data

1 Introduction

Privacy concerns and regulations such as the GDPR in Europe, HIPAA in the United States, and POPIA in South Africa can restrict the sharing of sensitive data, despite the importance of such data for scientific and technological advancement. To address this challenge, privacy-enhancing technologies such as *Federated Learning* and *Secure Multi-party Computation* reduce the

J. Verdonck and Q. Liao—Equal contribution; order determined by coin flip.

S. Nadjm-Tehrani et al. (Eds.): ARES 2026, LNCS 16898, pp. 3–25, 2027.
https://doi.org/10.1007/978-3-032-36874-4_1

need for direct data sharing through decentralised computation. However, these approaches rely on pre-specified computations and lack the flexibility and robustness of direct data access. Consequently, techniques for privacy-preserving data publication (PPDP) remain essential for enabling practical and accountable data sharing.

There are two main PPDP strategies for tabular and structured data: (i) de-identification via generalising and suppressing personally identifiable information; or (ii) synthetic data generation via multivariate distribution modelling and sampling. While the former method is well-studied [3,15,38], it requires expertise and data-domain transformations, and still poses residual privacy risks upon data release. While the latter method breaks direct links to the original data and provides "first glance" similarity, its production is strongly dependent on generative algorithms and is costly, especially for high-dimensional data.

The relative effectiveness of these strategies remains actively debated in the literature. Cynthia Dwork, often regarded as the godmother of *Differential Privacy*, argues against data de-identification [8], suggesting that this strategy fails to achieve a satisfactory privacy–utility trade-off. In contrast, some researchers describe synthetic data as the '*holy grail of data sharing*' [9]. However, other scholars argue that synthetic data is not necessarily a superior alternative [36,37], as its performance is not deterministic and the resulting privacy gains are often insufficient to justify the computational overhead.

Resolving this debate requires a rigorous comparative evaluation of the privacy and utility outcomes of both PPDP techniques, which is lacking in the literature. This is in part because the evaluation practices commonly used for PPDP techniques differ substantially, making their privacy results difficult to compare directly. For synthetic data, holdout-based assessment [29] is widely used to estimate privacy and utility by comparing released data with unseen original records. The holdout set serves as a useful, principled reference point for both privacy and utility, enabling more consistent comparisons across different PPDP approaches. On the other hand, evaluations of de-identified data typically focus on quasi-identifiers (QIDs), reflecting their central role in re-identification risk. However, holdout-based evaluation is rarely applied to de-identified data [21,26], while QID-specific analyses are not considered when evaluating synthetic data [36,37].

We present a common task framework that incorporates both evaluation practices. By combining holdout-based assessment with QID-aware analysis under consistent threat models, our framework enables the principled, comparative evaluation between data de-identification and synthetic data release.

We evaluate the framework through a controlled comparative study involving two complementary and realistic PPDP applications: (i) processing patient and location data (the *Patients* dataset) to determine the optimal placement of pharmacy outlets [41]; (ii) performing regression and classification tasks to predict individuals' annual income based on attributes such as occupation and education (the *ACSIncome* dataset [7]). Our results show that de-identified datasets appear more privacy-preserving under traditional statistical metrics, yet are more susceptible to attribute inference attacks than synthetic data. In terms of utility, we demonstrate that synthetic data and de-identified data achieve optimal utility in different use cases. While these insights aid practitioners in better understanding trade-offs, reaching a definitive conclusion requires a greater variety of settings and a joint effort from the research community.

Contribution/Novelty Statement. Our main contributions are twofold:

1. We establish a novel framework for the systematic and comparative evaluation of both PPDP approaches. The framework integrates relevant privacy and utility metrics, ensures applicability to both synthetic and de-identified datasets, and combines QID-based assessment with holdout-based evaluation. As secondary contributions, we conduct a qualitative analysis of metric applicability (presented in Tab. 1) and develop a distance formulation grounded in prior research [14,41]. The framework implementation is open-sourced [1].
2. We report the main results of a comparative study across two relevant application cases, demonstrating that the choice of a PPDP strategy depends strongly on the application context and the acceptable level of privacy risk.

The remainder of this paper is structured as follows. Section 2 discusses the background. Then, Sect. 3 introduces the evaluation framework. Section 4 then discusses the experimental setup, and Sect. 5 presents the main results. Section 6 provides discussion, and Sect. 7 discusses related work. Finally, Sect. 8 concludes this paper.

2 Background

2.1 Privacy-Preserving Data Publication (PPDP)

Data publication poses significant privacy risks, especially when conducted with consolidated, large datasets involving many data subjects. We articulate the privacy threats relevant to this context using the LINDDUN privacy threat modelling framework [23]. The undue sharing of raw datasets is often considered *excessive* or *unnecessary* (*Data disclosure* threats in LINDDUN), and may lead to loss of plausible deniability (*Non-repudiation*), of user control in the overall proliferation of personal data (*Unintervenability*), and the overall sharing may be considered unlawful (*Non-compliance*). Furthermore, the shared data may be used to infer the data subject's involvement (*Detecting*), to infer specific attributes (*Linking*), or to learn the data subject's identity (*Identification*). PPDP refers to the deliberate use of proactive measures —such as de-identification[1] and synthetic data generation— to mitigate or reduce such privacy risks.

Data De-identification. Data de-identification protects individuals' private information through targeted modification of the dataset. This is achieved using techniques such as generalisation, suppression, swapping, noise addition, and

[1] In literature, 'de-identified data' is also referred to as '*anonymised data*' [37]. In this paper, we consistently use 'de-identification' to refer to a broader class of techniques that reduce the risk of identifiability through generalisation and suppression.

bucketization, which are applied to meet specific privacy criteria, such as k-anonymity [35]. Various tools, such as ARX [31], and sdcMicro [40] implement these techniques. User-defined hierarchies are used to support data generalisation. An optimal combination of generalisation and suppression for each attribute is typically found using heuristic search methods [6].

Synthetic Data Generation. The generation of tabular synthetic data follows a two-step process: (i) a statistical model or machine learning (ML) model (such as a *Generative Adversarial Network* [42], or *Diffusion model* [18]) is trained to approximate the properties of the original data; and (ii) a synthetic dataset is sampled from the resulting model. Privacy is achieved by providing a computer-generated surrogate representation of real data records. Existing libraries and tools, such as Synthcity [32] and SDV [28], provide these capabilities.

2.2 Privacy and Utility Evaluation

Ensuring the privacy and utility is a prerequisite for PPDP [24]. Privacy involves protecting sensitive information by actively preventing re-identification and other disclosures. Moreover, utility refers to the ability of PPDP data to remain useful for its intended applications. Owing to a fundamental incompatibility between both types of outcomes, the state of the art in de-identification and synthetic data generation uses different privacy and utility metrics.

Evaluating De-Identified Data. Privacy metrics are used to define the criteria for creating de-identified data. Most notably, k-anonymity [35] is a widely used metric. It states that each record is indistinguishable from at least $k-1$ other records based on quasi-identifiers (QIDs) (e.g., attributes such as *age* or *gender*), that, when combined, could uniquely identify an individual. These groups of indistinguishable records, known as equivalence classes, are often obtained by combining techniques such as generalisation, suppression, swapping, noise addition, and bucketisation. Over time, l-diversity, t-closeness, and δ-disclosure, as extensions of k-anonymity, have been proposed to enhance privacy protection.

On the other hand, widely recognized utility metrics such as *Precision* [39], *Loss* [16], *Non-uniform entropy* [30], and *Average class size* [20] are often used to derive a utility score that is independent of specific use cases. Despite their popularity, these theoretical metrics have two significant limitations. First, they often do not correlate directly with practical, use-case-specific utility. Second, these metrics assume that data can be partitioned into equivalence classes, or that generalisations have been applied using hierarchy-based methods. These assumptions fail *under realistic threat models*, in which adversaries may exploit information irrespective of data partitions, and *under practical utility settings*, where practitioners use the data as provided for specific downstream tasks.

Evaluating Synthetic Data. Unlike de-identified data, the level of privacy protection for synthetic data cannot be estimated upfront, due to the stochastic nature of the training and sampling processes in the generative model. The generative model learns to approximate the distribution of real data using objective functions based on the similarity between the approximated and real distributions. While similarity-based metrics, such as *Nearest Neighbor Distance* [25], *Closest Value Ratio* [28], *Similarity Ratio* [44], and *Nearest Neighbor Accuracy* [19], can be considered privacy metrics, research shows that the results of similarity tests do not indicate the model's robustness to inference attacks. Hence, attack-based evaluation, such as *Attribute Inference Attack* (AIA) [11] and *Membership Inference Accuracy* (MIA) [37], may be better suited for estimating obscurity of sensitive properties [27].

Utility metrics for synthetic data are often scenario-based and depend on the specific task [12,13]. The usefulness of synthetic data is measured by how well it retains essential properties, typically quantified as the performance loss relative to using the original datasets. This is evaluated in terms of the overall suitability for downstream applications, such as machine learning tasks [5].

3 Evaluation Framework and Metrics

Figure 1 depicts the unified evaluation framework that addresses the following key challenges: (i) **Establishing unified privacy and utility evaluation protocols:** we define protocols for consistently comparing the *privacy* and *utility* of synthetic and de-identified datasets (Sect. 3.1); (ii) **Establishing a standard suite of privacy metrics:** privacy metrics used in literature for synthetic data and de-identified data differ. We therefore survey privacy metrics, assess their applicability to both synthetic and de-identified data (Sect. 3.2), and adapt existing metrics where possible (Sect. 3.3). The resulting suite covers *similarity-based*, *model-based*, and *attack-based* privacy metrics. (iii) **Defining downstream task-based utility metrics:** finally, we introduce utility metrics grounded in downstream analytical tasks[2], as detailed in Sect. 3.4.

3.1 Evaluation Protocols

Privacy Evaluation Protocol. We extended a hold-out-based assessment [29] that uses the original dataset (R) and a complementary hold-out set ($R_{holdout}$) drawn from the exact same statistical distribution as R. R is subjected to active privacy preservation, either by performing de-identification (leading to variant A), or synthetic data generation (leading to S). Hence, privacy evaluation is conducted using three types of datasets: (i) R, which represents the worst-case privacy baseline; (ii) $R_{holdout}$, which serves as an achievable privacy reference; and (iii) $M \in \{S, A\}$ which is a privacy-enhanced dataset obtained by applying a PPDP technique.

De-identification modifies only the quasi-identifiers (QIDs) while leaving other attributes unchanged. To enable a more nuanced comparison of the privacy guarantees associated with QIDs, we evaluate privacy along two attribute

[2] The privacy metric suite is comprehensive and exhaustive; however, we argue that utility metrics should depend on the specific application. Our utility evaluation protocol is designed to be metric-agnostic and can be extended to any new utility metric.

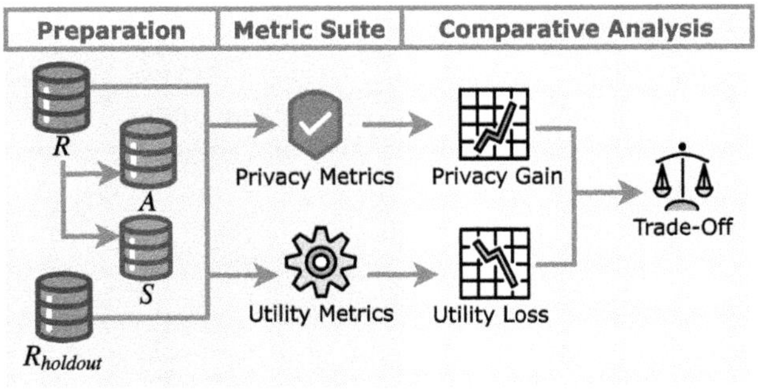

R Original dataset
$R_{holdout}$ Hold-out dataset
A De-identified datasets
S Synthetic datasets

Fig. 1. Overall evaluation framework.

dimensions: (i) *QID-columns*: privacy metrics are computed using only QIDs. (ii) *All-columns*: privacy metrics are computed using all available attributes, representing a stronger privacy evaluation.

Privacy Gain. Assuming that all privacy metrics are defined such that *higher values correspond to better privacy*, let $\mathcal{P}_d(\cdot)$ denote a privacy metric evaluated under the dimension $d \in \{qid, all\}$, we define the *privacy gain* PG_d of $M \in \{S, A\}$ under $\mathcal{P}$ and d as:

$$\mathcal{PG}_{\mathcal{P},d}(M) = \frac{\mathcal{P}_d(M) - \mathcal{P}_d(R)}{\mathcal{P}_d(R_{holdout}) - \mathcal{P}_d(R)} \tag{1}$$

This formulation anchors privacy measurements between R and $R_{holdout}$. Hence, the resulting privacy gain can be interpreted as:

- $\mathsf{PG}(M) < 0$: privacy is worse than the original dataset.
- $\mathsf{PG}(M) = 0$: privacy is on par with the original dataset.
- $\mathsf{PG}(M) = 1$: privacy matches that of the holdout dataset.
- $\mathsf{PG}(M) > 1$: privacy exceeds the holdout baseline (preferable).

Because the same original and holdout datasets are used as anchors, privacy gains are directly comparable across PPDP techniques in different dimensions.

Utility Evaluation Protocol. To evaluate downstream utility, we adopt a fixed protocol across all datasets. For each released dataset variant $M \in \{S, A\}$, we apply a utility metric derived from a downstream utility task. As a reference baseline, we apply the same utility metric to R. This baseline represents the preferred utility under the chosen downstream utility task.

Utility Loss. Assuming all utility metrics are defined such that *higher values correspond to better utility*, let $\mathcal{U}(\cdot)$ denote a utility metric. *Utility loss* UL of $M \in \{S, A\}$ is then defined as:

$$\mathsf{UL}(M) = \mathcal{U}(R) - \mathcal{U}(M). \tag{2}$$

A positive $\mathsf{UL}(M)$ value indicates a degradation in utility relative to the original-data baseline, while $\mathsf{UL}(M) = 0$ indicates no utility loss. Because all methods are evaluated on the same holdout set, $\mathsf{UL}(M)$ provides a directly comparable measure of utility degradation across PPDP techniques.

3.2 Privacy Metrics

We argue that privacy evaluation should not rely on arbitrarily selected metrics without proper justification or quality assessment. Therefore, we conduct a comprehensive qualitative analysis of the feasibility and relevance of privacy metrics for both PPDP techniques. This analysis is grounded on an explicit attacker model, which informs the selection and interpretation of the privacy metrics.

Privacy Threat Model or Attacker Model. We assume that an adversary has unrestricted access to the complete released dataset (A or S), and we evaluate two complementary attacker assumptions. Under the maximum-knowledge intruder model [34], the attacker can apply a wide range of transformations and inference techniques in an attempt to reverse the privacy-preserving mechanism, and evaluate the quality of each outcome with R (e.g., in terms of likelihood or similarity to real data)[3]. Under the public knowledge model [29], the attacker is assumed to have access to auxiliary data sampled from the same underlying distribution as the original dataset R, which is represented as $R_{holdout}$. A practical example of such public knowledge is census data, where newly released datasets may coexist with historical releases sharing the same attributes.

Selected Privacy Metrics. The results of metric selection are listed in Table 1. For each metric, we assess its applicability and portability to de-identified data and make a grounded selection for inclusion in our evaluation framework. The final column of Table 1 provides explicit rationale for inclusion or exclusion. Privacy metrics commonly used to evaluate de-identified data, such as k-anonymity, l-diversity, and t-closeness, essentially quantify the level of ambiguity within the released data set. However, in the case of synthetic data, such ambiguity is inherent, as all released data records are artificially generated without any direct, one-on-one link to records in the original data set. For this reason, we exclude such metrics from our study. To ensure diversity, we include applicable metrics of each class: (i) *similarity-based*, (ii) *model-based*, and (iii) *attack-based* or adversarial privacy metrics.

To ensure consistent interpretation across privacy metrics, we harmonise their directions (shown in the third column of Table 1) such that higher values always indicate stronger privacy protection.

3.3 Privacy Metric Adaptations

In de-identification, (i) categorical attributes *QID columns* are generalized to higher-level concepts (e.g., 'Six-Grade' becomes 'Primary School'), and (ii) numerical *QID columns* replace exact values with ranges (e.g., 25 becomes [20–30]).

[3] This represents a worst-case assumption and may be unrealistic in practice.

Table 1. Overview of the privacy metrics considered for this study, with motivations for including or excluding them.

Name	Abbrv.	↕	Description		Motivation
SIMILARITY-/DISTANCE-BASED PRIVACY METRICS					
Nearest Neighbor Distance	NND	↑	The mean distance of the released records to their closest records in the original dataset [25, 29, 32].	•••	Similarity-based metrics remain relevant because they quantify how closely released data resembles the original data, providing a proxy for the amount of information preserved. Higher similarity indicates that more information about the original data is retained, which may increase the risk of privacy leakage.
Close Value Ratio	CVR	↓	The percentage of released records that are similar to records in the original dataset (with a fixed threshold) [32].	•••	
Similarity Ratio	SR	↓	The percentage of released records that are similar to records in the original dataset (where the statistics of the original dataset define the threshold) [32, 44].	•••	
Nearest Neighbor Accuracy	NNA	↑	The sum of the dissimilarity percentages between the released dataset and the original dataset, and the released dataset to itself [43].	•••	
Hitting Ratio	HR	↓	The percentage of identical records between the released dataset and the original dataset [25, 28, 32].	🗑	De-identified data are real data with modified QIDs. This disadvantages de-identified data and skews results.
MODEL-/DISTRIBUTION BASED PRIVACY METRICS					
Detection Rate	DR	↑	The classification accuracy measures how accurately a classifier can distinguish records in the original dataset from those in a released dataset [28, 32].	🔧	A higher detection rate indicates greater deviation from the original dataset's distribution and, thus, potentially stronger privacy protection.
Structural Similarity	SS	↓	The similarity of the multivariate correlations between the released dataset and the original dataset. The multivariate distribution is derived through both structure learning and parameter learning of a Bayesian network.	🔧	Measuring how well the released data preserves the multivariate distribution of the original data can provide insights into its privacy strength.
Data Likelihood	DL	↓	The fidelity and similarity of the privacy-enhanced records by fitting the privacy-enhanced dataset to the distribution of the original dataset [28].	🔧	Measuring how much the distribution of the released dataset deviates from the original dataset helps quantify privacy.
ATTACK-BASED/ADVERSARIAL PRIVACY METRICS					
Attribute Inference Attack:			The accuracy or error of an active inference attack to derive or deduce sensitive values in the original dataset [13, 28, 32, 36, 37].		The extent to which a released dataset limits its sensitive attribute inference reflects its privacy protection. AIA-based evaluation provides a model-agnostic framework applicable to both PPDP approaches.
- Accuracy	AIA-C	↓	- the target sensitive value is categorical.	•••	
- Regression error	AIA-R	↑	- the target sensitive value is numerical.	🔧	
Membership Inference Attack	MIA	↓	The accuracy of successfully deducing whether a particular record is contained in the original dataset used to generate the released data [11, 27, 32, 34, 36, 37].	🗑	In de-identification, membership is a given: without record suppression, any original record will also appear in the de-identified dataset.
Reconstruction Attack	RA	↓	The error and accuracy of an adversary's reverse-engineered data records using synthetic data and auxiliary information [17].	🗑	Different variants rely on different threat assumptions [4, 10]. Finding a single assumption that applies to both cases is difficult, so they are incomparable.
Singling Out	SO	↓	The accuracy of uniquely identifying records through unique combinations of column values [11].	🗑	Under k-anonymity, the success rate is bounded by $\frac{1}{k}$, whereas in synthetic data, plausible deniability depends on the specific generative process. These differing assumptions make singling out comparisons across data types difficult to interpret and incompatible.
Record Linkage	RL	↓	The accuracy of establishing linkage to an external public dataset (that does not share the same distribution as the original dataset) through the released dataset [11, 25].	🗑	Assuming the availability of different external public datasets may lead to various outcomes.

••• Adaptation 1: Customized Distance calculation
🔧 Adaptation 2: Domain transformation
🗑 Excluded
↑ higher values indicate stronger privacy protection
↓ lower values indicate stronger privacy protection

In consequence, the QIDs in A have different domains from those in S and R, which hinders direct comparability. To address this, we apply two types of adaptations, which are both based on established methods for distance computation and transformation in mixed-domain data using pre-defined hierarchies [14, 41]:

Adaptation 1: Distance Calculation. Similarity-based metrics such as NND, CVR, SR, NNA, and AIA-C require distance computations between records. Distance hierarchies represent categorical and numerical values within a hierarchical structure and measure similarity as the path length between nodes. For numerical attributes, distances are computed using the L_1 distance[4] in the original domain. Identical generalized ranges yield a distance of 0, whereas mismatched ranges are assigned the maximum distance. When comparing an original value with a generalized range, a normalized thresholded distance is used: values within the range are computed using L_1 distances among the possible values in the generalized domain, while values outside the range receive the maximum distance[5]. For categorical attributes, distances are computed using the generalization hierarchy, where the distance equals the number of edges between nodes. Matching generalizations yield a distance of 0, whereas mismatched generalizations receive the maximum number of edges. Attribute-level distances are normalized and aggregated to obtain a record-level distance.

Our distance evaluation does not favor any PPDP approach, because distance hierarchies provide a unified representation in which original and generalized values are comparable within the same distance space. Hence, distances between records from R, S, and A are computed under identical assumptions.

Adaptation 2: Domain Transformation. Model-based metrics such as DR, SS, AIA-R, and MIA require datasets to share the same domain. To achieve this, generalized QID values in A are mapped back to the original domain through random sampling [41]. Each generalized value is replaced with a value uniformly sampled from the original values it represents (e.g., range $[1-5]$ is replaced with a random value from $\{1, 2, 3, 4, 5\}$). This yields a plausible realization of the original data that is consistent with the generalization, without assuming a specific distribution.

3.4 Utility Metrics

Statistical utility metrics can be applied to evaluate the utility of any PPDP method. We use random count queries, as they provide a clearer sense of practical utility than summary statistics. Because downstream task utility is typically scenario-dependent, we evaluate predictive and optimisation tasks as representative downstream utilities.

[4] Our hierarchical and threshold-based distance calculation can be readily extended to other distance norms.

[5] Assigning the maximum distance to dissimilar values does not affect the final computation; rather, it acts as an effective filter because the privacy metrics consider only the nearest neighbours.

Statistical Utility (Random Count Queries). Statistical utility is assessed using random count queries, a widely adopted approach for evaluating how well low-order statistics and attribute correlations are preserved under privacy transformations [22,33]. Each query computes aggregate statistics of the form

```
COUNT(*) WHERE x IN R_x AND y IN R_y AND ....
```

on A or S, and the results are compared against those obtained from the original dataset R. The resulting *Count Query Error* (CQE) quantifies deviations in statistical correlations induced by the privacy mechanism. For generalised attributes, we assume that original values are uniformly distributed within each generalisation interval, allowing estimated counts to be derived. CQE directly reflects statistical utility loss.

Downstream Task Utility. Utility is evaluated by assessing how well the privacy-enhanced datasets support downstream analytical tasks. We consider two representative settings: (i) **Machine learning analytics.** A common application of PPDP is enabling machine learning (ML) analysis. Predictive performance is evaluated by training an ML model on A or S and measuring its test accuracy on $R_{holdout}$. The resulting accuracy, referred to as *ML Efficacy* (MLE), quantifies how well predictive performance is preserved. When attributes are generalised, the same generalisation procedure is applied to $R_{holdout}$ to ensure that the training and testing data reside in the same attribute domain [41]. (ii) **Optimisation tasks.** Optimisation utility is measured using the Resource Allocation Utility (RAU) metric [6]. An optimisation solution is derived from A or S and applied to the original dataset R. The resulting score is then normalised against the score obtained when optimising directly on R. Because RAU directly captures optimisation-related utility loss, we report RAU without further transformation. Higher RAU values indicate greater performance degradation and therefore lower utility.

4 Experimental Setup

We perform an experimental validation of the established evaluation framework over two different use case. These experiments are conducted on a system equipped with an AMD Ryzen 9 5950X CPU and 128 GB of memory. This section provides a detailed description of the experimental setup.

4.1 Experiment Datasets

We selected two datasets: (i) the *Patients* dataset and (ii) the *ACSIncome* dataset. The *Patients* dataset has previously been used to study the effects of de-identification in an optimisation use case [6]. It contains heart disease health records and demographic information (e.g., gender, age, income, and zip code) for 33,268 U.S. citizens. The 2018 *ACSIncome* dataset, extracted using Folktables [7], contains attributes similar to those of the widely used Adult dataset [2] while offering greater customizability. This dataset contains 1,664,500 records with 10 attributes and is suitable for training ML models to predict individuals' income. Table 2 summarises both datasets, highlighting quasi-identifiers (QIDs) with underlining and sensitive attributes with dotted underlining[6].

Table 2. Dataset descriptions of *Patients* and *ACSIncome*.

Dataset	Size (n)	Categorical	Numerical
Patients	33 268	*gender*, *stroke*, *ZIP*, *hypertension*, *heart_disease*	*smoking_status*, *age*, *bmi*, *Income*, *glucose_level*
ACSIncome	1 664 500	*COW*, *SCHL*, *MAR*, *OCCP*, *POBP*, *SEX*, *RAC1P*	*AGEP*, *WKHP*, *PINCP*

underline Quasi-identifier (QID)
dotted underline Sensitive attribute

4.2 Preparation and Preprocessing

Dataset Preparation. We first preprocess the *Patients* dataset by imputing missing data. As a result, 32.9% of the rows are modified to impute values for the *smoking_status* and/or *bmi* attributes. The input dataset (i.e., *ACSIncome* or *Patients*) is then split into (i) a data set R containing 80% of the data and (ii) a hold-out set $R_{holdout}$ containing the remaining 20%. As shown in Fig. 1, R is used to create S or A, while $R_{holdout}$ is utilised for validation.

Generation of Privacy-Enhanced Datasets. Each de-identified dataset A is created using the ARX [31] library. Within this library, three parameters must be specified: (i) QIDs, as highlighted in Table 2; (ii) generalization hierarchies, which are adopted from [6] for the *Patients* and [41] for the *ACSIncome* dataset; and (ii) the k-anonymity privacy model, with k set to 5, 10, and 20. ARX provides utility heuristics to help practitioners select the optimal de-identified dataset from the available outputs. However, since we aim to evaluate privacy and utility using our chosen metrics, we assess all available de-identified datasets to ensure a fair comparison that is not influenced by such heuristics. These settings lead to 502 unique de-identified versions of the *Patients* dataset and 69 470 unique de-identified versions of the *ACSIncome* dataset.

Synthetic datasets S are generated using the SDV [28] and Synthcity [32] libraries. Three distinct generative models are applied: (i) CTGAN [42], (ii) TVAE [42], and (iii) TabDDPM [18]. The model parameters are set to ensure that model training is completed within a reasonable time. Specifically, the CTGAN and TVAE models from the SDV library are used with default parameters, except that the batch size was set to 1 000. Similarly, the TabDDPM model is used with default settings, except that the number of hidden layers is increased to 8 and the dataset-specific targets are set to *heart_disease* for *Patients* and *PINCP* for

[6] In the *ACSIncome* dataset, only the *PINCP* representing an individual's exact income is labeled as a sensitive attribute. For *Patients*, these include medical attributes (*hypertension*, *heart_disease*, *avg_glucose_level*, *bmi*, and *stroke*) and *Income*.

ACSIncome. To avoid uncertainty and sampling bias, five synthetic datasets, each matching the size of R, are generated for each trained model, resulting in a total of 15 synthetic datasets.

4.3 Performing Evaluation

Privacy Evaluation. We calculate all privacy metrics selected in Table 1 by applying the protocols described in Sect. 3.1. The AIA targets are restricted to the sensitive attributes within each dataset, i.e., those highlighted as such in Table 2. The AIA metric is implemented with k-nearest neighbours and XGBoost.

Utility Evaluation. We evaluate utility using the protocol described in Sect. 3.1. The *Count Query Error* (CQE) metric (Sect. 3.4) is dataset-agnostic and applied to both *ACSIncome* and *Patients*.

In addition, each dataset is evaluated using a task-specific utility metric aligned with its application. For *ACSIncome*, ML models predict individual income (*PINCP*) using (i) a binary classifier distinguishing incomes above or below \$50,000 and (ii) a multiclass classifier predicting the ranges [0 − 20,000[, [20,000 − 100,000[, and > 100,000. Both models use XGBoost, with categorical attributes one-hot encoded and numerical features standardised. To train on A and evaluate on $R_{holdout}$, we align the domains by applying the same generalisation to $R_{holdout}$; numerical ranges are represented by their means, and unseen categorical values are replaced with '*'. The pipeline is implemented using Scikit-learn. Utility is measured as predictive accuracy using *ML Efficacy* (MLE).

For *Patients*, utility is evaluated through a optimisation model following [6], implemented using Pyomo with the Gurobi solver. Instead of averaging generalised values as in [6], we apply a tailored domain transformation technique.

5 Quantitative Results

5.1 Privacy Evaluation and Comparison

We first evaluate the diversity of our metric suite, specifically by investigating the extent to which their results are statistically correlated. Then, we present the overall results expressed in term of privacy gains ($\mathsf{PG}(M)$ with $M \in \{A, S\}$).

Privacy Metric Correlations. Figure 2 illustrates the pairwise correlations, specifically Spearman's ρ, between the pairs of privacy metrics[7]. We observe strong correlations within families of similarity-based metrics (such as SR, NNA, NND) and within attack-based metrics (such as AIA-C and AIA-R) across all settings. A key distinction emerges between synthetic and de-identified data. For synthetic datasets, similarity-based metrics exhibit less or even negative correlation with attack-based metrics, suggesting that similarity to the original data

[7] The conclusions drawn from the privacy metric correlation analysis are consistent across the *ACSIncome* and *Patient* datasets, as well as across the All-columns and QID attribute dimensions. Due to space limitations, we report results for *ACSIncome* only; the complete results are provided in the supplementary materials [1].

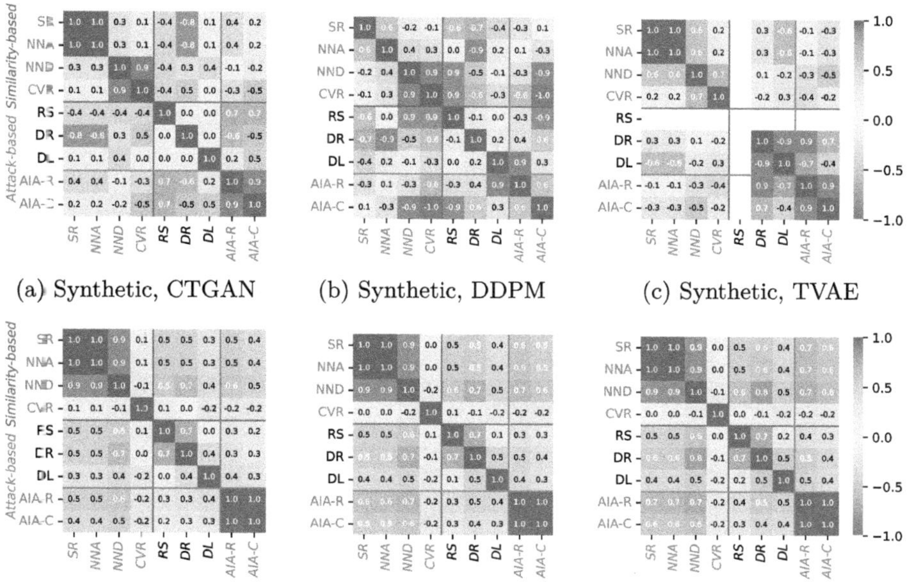

(a) Synthetic, CTGAN (b) Synthetic, DDPM (c) Synthetic, TVAE

(d) De-identified, K=5 (e) De-identified, K=10 (f) De-identified, K=20

Fig. 2. Spearman correlation heatmaps of privacy metrics across three scenarios for synthetic and de-identified datasets (All Columns, *ACSIncome* dataset)

does not directly translate into increased vulnerability to inference attacks. In contrast, for de-identified data, similarity-based metrics are consistently correlated with AIA, indicating that greater similarity to the original data is associated with higher attack success rates. This occurs because generalized attribute values can still serve as predictors of sensitive attributes in AIA.

This difference reflects the fundamentally distinct privacy mechanisms of the two approaches. De-identification operates directly on original records, such that residual similarity preserves information exploitable by inference attacks. As a result, similarity serves as a proxy for attack risk in de-identified datasets. Synthetic generation, by contrast, decouples record-level similarity from downstream privacy leakage, breaking the direct link between similarity-based estimators and attack effectiveness. Consequently, similarity-based metrics are less predictive of attack vulnerability for synthetic data.

Privacy Gains. We select representative metrics from each privacy metric family[8] and present their results. Specifically, we report $\mathsf{PG}_{\mathrm{NND}}$ (nearest-neighbour distance) as the primary similarity-based metric, together with $\mathsf{PG}_{\mathrm{DR}}$ (detection rate) as the primary model-based privacy metric, and $\mathsf{PG}_{\mathrm{AIA\text{-}R}}$ (attribute inference attack, regression) as a representative attack-based metric. Table 3 presents the privacy gains under both QID-only and all-columns attribute dimensions.

[8] The results of the complete metric suite can be found in the supporting materials [1].

Table 3. Privacy gain comparison (values are printed as 'mean±standard dev.').

	ACSIncome					
	PG_{NND}		PG_{DR}		$PG_{AIA\text{-}R}$	
Method	QID	ALL	QID	ALL	QID	ALL
CTGAN	1.23 ± 0.00	1.21 ± 0.00	0.98 ± 0.00	1.03 ± 0.00	1.46 ± 0.04	1.61 ± 0.01
DDPM	$\mathbf{2.01 \pm 0.01}$	$\mathbf{1.93 \pm 0.01}$	$\mathbf{1.32 \pm 0.00}$	$\mathbf{1.31 \pm 0.00}$	$\mathbf{1.97 \pm 0.03}$	$\mathbf{2.23 \pm 0.08}$
TVAE	1.49 ± 0.00	1.44 ± 0.00	1.30 ± 0.00	1.30 ± 0.00	1.30 ± 0.01	1.37 ± 0.06
k = 5	2.39 ± 0.34	2.25 ± 0.32	1.23 ± 0.04	1.22 ± 0.04	1.29 ± 0.12	1.40 ± 0.12
k = 10	2.49 ± 0.34	2.35 ± 0.32	1.24 ± 0.04	1.23 ± 0.03	1.33 ± 0.11	1.44 ± 0.12
k = 20	$\mathbf{2.57 \pm 0.32}$	$\mathbf{2.42 \pm 0.30}$	$\mathbf{1.25 \pm 0.03}$	$\mathbf{1.24 \pm 0.03}$	$\mathbf{1.36 \pm 0.10}$	$\mathbf{1.47 \pm 0.11}$
	Patients					
	PG_{NND}		PG_{DR}		$PG_{AIA\text{-}R}$	
Method	QID	ALL	QID	ALL	QID	ALL
CTGAN	1.12 ± 0.00	1.12 ± 0.00	0.75 ± 0.01	0.91 ± 0.00	1.51 ± 0.01	1.81 ± 0.01
DDPM	$\mathbf{1.67 \pm 0.01}$	$\mathbf{1.50 \pm 0.01}$	$\mathbf{1.24 \pm 0.00}$	$\mathbf{1.33 \pm 0.00}$	$\mathbf{2.65 \pm 0.06}$	$\mathbf{3.72 \pm 0.18}$
TVAE	1.18 ± 0.00	1.12 ± 0.00	1.14 ± 0.00	1.28 ± 0.00	1.23 ± 0.01	1.45 ± 0.01
k = 5	2.59 ± 0.58	1.77 ± 0.40	$\mathbf{0.81 \pm 0.14}$	0.86 ± 0.14	1.32 ± 0.13	1.75 ± 0.14
k = 10	2.61 ± 0.56	1.77 ± 0.38	0.81 ± 0.13	0.86 ± 0.13	1.34 ± 0.11	1.78 ± 0.11
k = 20	$\mathbf{2.62 \pm 0.53}$	$\mathbf{1.78 \pm 0.36}$	0.81 ± 0.13	$\mathbf{0.86 \pm 0.13}$	$\mathbf{1.36 \pm 0.10}$	$\mathbf{1.80 \pm 0.09}$

De-identified datasets consistently achieve higher PG_{NND} than synthetic datasets across all scenarios. This outcome is expected, as de-identification techniques explicitly apply generalisation and suppression to QIDs, thereby increasing the distance between protected records and their nearest neighbours in the original data (this is also reflected in the $k = 20$ setting, which represents the most significant distortion). In contrast, synthetic data generation does not significantly disturb QIDs' values, resulting in more moderate gains under similarity-based metrics.

For the *ACSIncome* case, PG_{DR} are comparable for synthetic and de-identified data, with synthetic data exhibiting a slightly higher gain. This suggests that, in this setting, both approaches yield a similar level of distributional separation from the original data. In contrast, for the *Patient* case, synthetic data achieves substantially higher PG_{DR} than de-identified data. This can be attributed to the stronger cross-attribute correlations present in the *Patient* dataset, where generative models introduce more pronounced distributional changes than QID-based generalisation. As a result, the distribution of synthetic data is more skewed than that of the original and de-identified datasets.

Synthetic datasets generally yield higher attack-based privacy gains, as measured by $PG_{AIA\text{-}R}$, than de-identified datasets. This indicates that although de-identified data may exhibit more distortion according to similarity-based metrics; Residual attribute dependencies remain exploitable by inference attacks.

Synthetic data generation, by decoupling records from the original dataset, effectively disrupts attribute-level inference and distribution-based signals.

Discussion. These results indicate that similarity-based privacy gains and attack-based privacy gains capture fundamentally different aspects of privacy. While stronger dissimilarity may indicate compliance with legislative privacy requirements (e.g., anonymity requirements under the GDPR), it does not necessarily imply stronger resistance to inference attacks. This distinction highlights the importance of reporting privacy metrics that align with the intended threat model and the actual privacy goals (i.e., protecting anonymity or sensitive values), rather than relying on aggregate scores across heterogeneous measures.

5.2 Utility Evaluation and Comparison

We first present the utility loss results, and then discuss the trade-offs between utility and privacy.

Table 4. Utility loss comparison.

Method	*ACSIncome*		*Patients*	
	UL_{MLE}	CQE	RAU	CQE
CTGAN	0.35 ± 0.01	0.74 ± 0.00	$\mathbf{1.00 \pm 0.00}$	1.20 ± 0.06
DDPM	0.41 ± 0.02	1.53 ± 0.02	1.09 ± 0.03	5.61 ± 0.04
TVAE	$\mathbf{0.29 \pm 0.01}$	$\mathbf{0.71 \pm 0.01}$	1.01 ± 0.00	$\mathbf{0.75 \pm 0.01}$
k = 5	$\mathbf{0.25 \pm 0.03}$	$\mathbf{3.30 \pm 1.43}$	$\mathbf{1.01 \pm 0.01}$	16.64 ± 10.13
k = 10	0.26 ± 0.03	3.58 ± 1.40	1.01 ± 0.01	16.45 ± 10.17
k = 20	0.26 ± 0.03	3.79 ± 1.35	1.01 ± 0.01	$\mathbf{16.30 \pm 10.22}$

Utility Loss Comparison. Table 4 compares the utility losses across the synthetic and de-identified datasets. RAU exhibits comparable values across the synthetic and de-identified datasets, whereas UL_{MLE} and CQE results diverge.

For the *ACSIncome* dataset, de-identified data consistently yields lower machine-learning (ML) loss than synthetic data. This result could be attributed to the fact that supervised ML models are designed to learn *generalizable patterns* rather than to memorise individual records[9]. De-identification techniques based on generalisation transform fine-grained attributes into coarser representations, thereby reducing noise and variance in the training data and facilitating the learning of robust decision boundaries.

[9] This advantage, however, relies on the assumption that practitioners know the applied generalisation scheme. We note that this assumption does not introduce additional privacy risks, as such generalisation rules can typically be inferred from released data or prior deployments.

In contrast, CQE reveals that query utility is substantially better preserved in synthetic data than in de-identified data across both datasets. This gap can be explained by generative models' ability to capture multivariate joint distributions and attribute correlations. De-identification methods based on generalisation implicitly assume uniformity within equivalence classes and therefore discard fine-grained distributional information, leading to higher query distortion, especially for conjunctive or range-based queries.

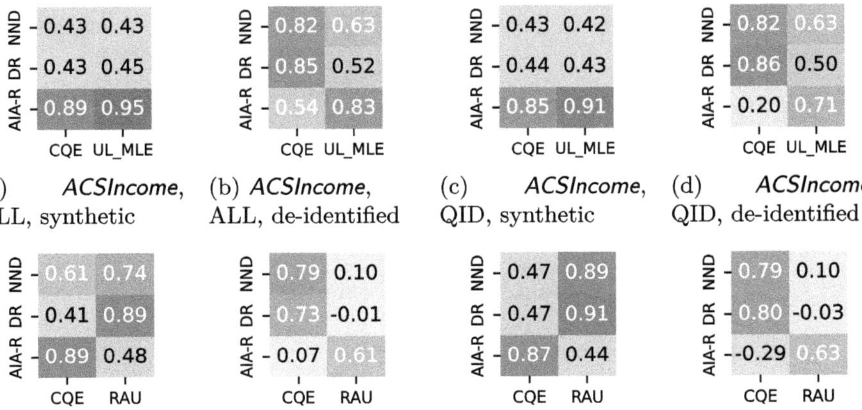

(a) *ACSIncome*, ALL, synthetic (b) *ACSIncome*, ALL, de-identified (c) *ACSIncome*, QID, synthetic (d) *ACSIncome*, QID, de-identified

(e) *Patients*, ALL, synthetic (f) *Patients*, ALL, de-identified (g) *Patients*, QID, synthetic (h) *Patients*, QID, de-identified

Fig. 3. Privacy–utility cross-correlation matrices.

Privacy-Utility Tradeoff. We construct cross-correlation matrices between privacy and utility metrics to analyse how privacy–utility trade-offs differ between de-identified and synthetic datasets for the *ACSIncome* and *Patients* cases. Figure 3 reports Spearman correlations between privacy metrics (where higher values indicate stronger privacy protection) and utility loss metrics (where higher values indicate lower utility). Positive correlations indicate privacy-utility trade-offs, with larger coefficients reflecting a tighter coupling between privacy gains and utility degradation.

For de-identified datasets, both the similarity-based metric NND and the model-based metric DR exhibit consistently strong correlations with count query error CQE across both datasets ($0.73 \le \rho \le 0.86$). In contrast, synthetic datasets show only moderate correlations ($0.41 \le \rho \le 0.61$). This indicates that, under de-identification, increases in record-level dissimilarity or distributional distortion are more directly coupled with degradation in query accuracy. The stronger coupling can be explained by the fact that generalisation-based de-identification directly alters attribute ranges and frequency structure, which are precisely the features exploited by count queries.

The privacy–utility trade-off for machine learning tasks is comparatively consistent across synthetic and de-identified datasets. In both cases, privacy metrics associated with resistance to attribute inference (e.g., AIA-R) exhibit stronger correlations with ML utility loss than similarity/model-based metrics such as NND or DR. This suggests that degrading attribute predictability, rather than merely increasing record-level dissimilarity, has a more pronounced impact on downstream predictive performance, regardless of whether privacy is achieved through synthesis or de-identification.

For resource allocation optimisation tasks, data synthesis and de-identification exhibit markedly different trade-off patterns. In synthetic datasets, optimisation utility loss correlates strongly with both NND and DR ($0.74 \leq \rho \leq 0.91$), indicating that increased value-level and distributional distortion substantially degrade optimisation performance. By contrast, correlations are weak or negligible for de-identified datasets. A likely explanation is that de-identified data remain grounded in real records, such that optimisation solutions derived from generalised but authentic locations are less sensitive to privacy-induced distortion than those derived from fully synthetic data.

Discussion. The utility results presented above indicate that the optimal PPDP strategy, from a utility perspective, strongly depends on the targeted use case. De-identified datasets outperform synthetic datasets in terms of *ML Utility*, provided that suitable generalisation hierarchies can be defined; otherwise, synthetic data may be preferable, as it does not require additional, use-case-specific pre-processing or post-processing for machine learning tasks. In contrast, synthetic datasets consistently achieve lower *Count Query Error*, indicating better preservation of statistical query utility. For *Optimisation Utility*, both techniques can deliver comparable and satisfactory performance.

Across both datasets, the strength and nature of the observed privacy-utility trade-offs depend critically on the *family of privacy metrics* considered. Similarity-based metrics primarily capture distortion at the record level and are therefore most informative for de-identified data. In contrast, attack-based metrics capture inference resistance and are more indicative of utility degradation in synthetic datasets. Taken together, these findings demonstrate that conclusions about privacy-utility trade-offs are susceptible to the choice of privacy metrics.

6 Discussion

6.1 Threats to Validity

Our study is subject to several potential threats to validity:

- **Metric selection:** Bias may have been introduced by excluding some privacy metrics (cf, Table 1). Metric selection is based on three criteria: (i) applicability to both outcomes, (ii) diversity, and (iii) enabling fair comparison.
- **Exclusion of differential privacy:** Differential privacy, as a privacy definition, is often used in combination with PPDP techniques, i.e., de-identification and synthetic data generation. To study the *isolated effects*, we have excluded differential privacy mechanisms from our evaluation.

- **Sampling bias:** Because domain transformation involves sampling, individual trials may yield different results, potentially affecting reproducibility. However, sampling bias is mitigated by the large dataset size and by drawing attribute values from the set of possible offspring of each generalised value.
- **No optimisations:** We adopted a best-effort approach to generating synthetic datasets, primarily relying on default parameters. We acknowledge that tailored optimisations performed by experts may yield better results.
- **External validity:** While the use cases in our study (i.e., the pharmacy outlet optimisation problem and the ML income prediction case) are indicative of typical PPDP scenarios, we refrain from generalising the findings more broadly.

6.2 Other Relevant Aspects of PPDP

We further compare the two PPDP approaches along four dimensions: required effort, flexibility, maturity, and hardware requirements.

Required Effort. Both PPDP techniques require substantial effort and expertise. De-identification requires domain knowledge and understanding of the intended use case, in which practitioners must identify QIDs, identifiers, and sensitive attributes, define generalisation hierarchies, and manually select an appropriate privacy level. Synthetic data generation requires knowledge of statistical and AI modelling, as practitioners must select suitable generative models, carefully define hyperparameters, and tune model parameters.

Flexibility. De-identification techniques offer limited flexibility: adding rows or columns requires re-evaluating privacy levels, reassessing potential quasi-identifiers, and updating generalisation hierarchies when new attribute values are introduced. In contrast, synthetic data generation is more flexible, as models can be updated incrementally and new records can be sampled on-demand.

Technological Maturity. De-identification tools are mature and user-friendly. Established systems such as ARX [31], and sdcMicro [40] support a wide range of de-identification methods, with ARX being the most mature and comprehensive. In contrast, synthetic data generation is more recent and rapidly evolving. Actively maintained libraries such as Synthcity [32] and the Synthetic Data Vault Project [28] integrate data generators with evaluation metrics, but remain largely primarily developer-oriented: they lack the beginner-friendly graphical interfaces and documentation of current de-identification tools.

Hardware Requirements. Throughout our experiments, we have recorded the memory usage and processing time statistics of the applied de-identification and synthetic data generation techniques, which can be consulted in supporting materials [1]. Data de-identification proved substantially more efficient, typically completing within seconds, whereas training of the generative models ranged from minutes to days, depending on the model and dataset. Memory usage of generative models also varied considerably across datasets. While de-identification algorithms are often executed over a single core, generative models can exploit multi-core CPUs and GPUs to improve performance, at the cost of substantially higher RAM and VRAM requirements.

7 Related Work

We first discuss related studies on the efficacy of PPDP methods, and then we compare our framework with other tools.

Quantitative Evaluation of PPDP Methods. To the best of our knowledge, only two existing studies in the literature [36,37] directly compare PPDP techniques on structure and tabular datasets. The first [36] assesses whether the publication of synthetic data rather than original data reduces information leakage. The second [37] directly compares the privacy and utility of synthetic and de-identified datasets. Both studies adopt similar evaluation methodologies by simulating MIA and AIA on released datasets and reporting privacy gains relative to the original or de-identified data, alongside utility assessments based on ML performance and summary statistics. [36,37] find that synthetic data is not a superior alternative to de-identification due to highly stochastic and unpredictable privacy and utility outcomes.

In contrast to [37] who facilitated k-anonymity via record removal, we adopt a representative de-identification strategy based on generalisation, leading to a more realistic and methodologically sound comparison. Moreover, our evaluation explicitly distinguishes between privacy effects at QID level and at the full-dataset level. This dual-granularity analysis provides more comprehensive insights into how de-identification impacts privacy.

Table 5. Comparison of open source privacy evaluation tools.

	[28]	[32]	[36]	[37]	[11]	Our framework
Nearest Neighbor Distance	✦	✦				✦●
Close Value Ratio	✦	✦				✦●
Similarity Ratio		✦				✦●
Nearest Neighbor Accuracy						✦●
Data Likelihood	✦					✦●
Detection Rate						✦●
Structural Similarity						✦●
Attribute Inference Attack	✦	✦	✦	✦●	✦	✦●
Membership Inference Attack		✦	✦	✦●		
Singling out					✦	
Record Linkage					✦	
Hitting Ratio	✦	✦				

✦ Evaluation of synthetic data
● Evaluation of de-identified data

Open Source Privacy Evaluation Frameworks. Table 5 outlines the different open-source tools that support the privacy evaluation of PPDP techniques. As shown in the final column, our framework provides the most comprehensive and diverse privacy metric suite. These privacy metrics were selected based on their applicability and relevancy to both synthetic and de-identified datasets.

8 Conclusions

Data de-identification and synthetic data generation are widely used yet fundamentally different PPDP techniques. Their respective privacy evaluations rely on disparate metrics and assumptions, which makes a direct comparison difficult. To address this gap, we introduce a unified, novel privacy evaluation framework that applies to both synthetic and de-identified data and integrates widely used privacy notions from both domains. Developing this framework involved re-conceptualising and adapting existing metrics to ensure fair and consistent applicability of both PPDP techniques.

We evaluate the framework on two complementary use cases: a location optimisation task using the *Patients* dataset, and a predictive learning task using the *ACSIncome* dataset. Our results show that de-identified data performs better under similarity-based privacy metrics, whereas synthetic data offers stronger protection against adversarial evaluations such as attribute inference (AIA), while both approaches achieve comparable utility.

Overall, neither synthetic data nor de-identified data is universally superior, and rather than drawing a definitive conclusion on the superiority of a PPDP technique, we emphasise the importance of comprehensive, multi-metric evaluation. Their suitability strongly depends on the intended use case and risk tolerance. This key insight further highlights the importance of our unified evaluation framework, which enables practitioners to assess privacy-utility trade-offs in a principled and reproducible manner and to make informed decisions about appropriate PPDP strategies in an application-aware context.

Acknowledgement. This research is partially funded by the Research Fund KU Leuven, by the Cybersecurity Research Program Flanders and by the AIDE project funded by the Belgian SPF BOSA under the programme "Financing of projects for the development of artificial intelligence in Belgium" with reference number 06.40.32.33.00.10.

Disclosure of Interests. The authors have no competing interests to declare that are relevant to the content of this article.

Open Science Statement. The framework implementation, including the ported and adapted privacy and utility metrics, and the *ACSIncome* dataset has been made available in the supporting materials [1]. Note that we exclude the *Patients* dataset as it was retracted from Kaggle during this research.

References

1. Anonymous: Supplementary material for "A Comparative Evaluation of Privacy-Preserving Data Publication Techniques" (2026). https://doi.org/10.5281/zenodo.18134089
2. Becker, B., Kohavi, R.: Adult. UCI Machine Learning Repository (1996). https://doi.org/10.24432/C5XW20
3. Ciriani, V., Di Vimercati, S.D.C., Foresti, S., Samarati, P.: k-anonymous data mining: A survey. Privacy-Preserving Data Mining: Models and Algorithms, pp. 105–136 (2008)
4. Cohen, A.: Attacks on deidentification's defenses. In: 31st USENIX security symposium (USENIX Security 22), pp. 1469–1486 (2022)
5. Dankar, F.K., Ibrahim, M.: Fake it till you make it: guidelines for effective synthetic data generation. Appl. Sci. **11**(5), 2158 (2021)
6. Boeck, D., Verdonck, K., Willocx, J., Lapon, M., Naessens, J., V.: Dataset anonymization with purpose: a resource allocation use case. In: 2021 International Symposium on Computer Science and Intelligent Controls (ISCSIC), pp. 202–210. IEEE (2021)
7. Ding, F., Hardt, M., Miller, J., Schmidt, L.: Retiring adult: New datasets for fair machine learning. Adv. Neural. Inf. Process. Syst. **34** (2021)
8. Dwork, C., Smith, A., Steinke, T., Ullman, J.: Exposed! a survey of attacks on private data. Ann. Rev. Stat. Appl. **4**(1), 61–84 (2017)
9. Figueira, A., Vaz, B.: Survey on synthetic data generation, evaluation methods and gans. Mathematics **10**(15), 2733 (2022)
10. Ganev, G., De Cristofaro, E.: On the inadequacy of similarity-based privacy metrics: Reconstruction attacks against truly anonymous synthetic data (2023). arXiv preprintarXiv:2312.05114
11. Giomi, M., Boenisch, F., Wehmeyer, C., Tasnádi, B.: A unified framework for quantifying privacy risk in synthetic data. In: Proceedings on Privacy Enhancing Technologies, (2023)
12. Hittmeir, M., Ekelhart, A., Mayer, R.: Utility and privacy assessments of synthetic data for regression tasks. In: 2019 IEEE International Conference on Big Data (Big Data), pp. 5763–5772. IEEE (2019)
13. Hittmeir, M., Mayer, R., Ekelhart, A.: A baseline for attribute disclosure risk in synthetic data. In: Proceedings of the Tenth ACM Conference on Data and Application Security and Privacy, pp. 133–143. CODASPY '20, ACM, New York (2020)
14. Hsu, C.C., Chen, C.L., Su, Y.W.: Hierarchical clustering of mixed data based on distance hierarchy. Inf. Sci. **177**(20), 4474–4492 (2007)
15. Inan, A., Kantarcioglu, M., Bertino, E.: Using anonymized data for classification. In: IEEE 25th International Conference on Data Engineering, pp. 429–440. IEEE (2009)
16. Iyengar, V.S.: Transforming data to satisfy privacy constraints. In: Proceedings of the Eighth ACM SIGKDD International Conference on Knowledge Discovery and Data Mining, pp. 279–288 (2002)
17. Kasiviswanathan, S.P., Rudelson, M., Smith, A.: The power of linear reconstruction attacks. In: Proceedings of the Twenty-Fourth Annual ACM-SIAM Symposium on Discrete Algorithms, pp. 1415–1433. SIAM (2013)
18. Kotelnikov, A., Baranchuk, D., Rubachev, I., Babenko, A.: Tabddpm: modelling tabular data with diffusion models. In: International Conference on Machine Learning, pp. 17564–17579. PMLR (2023)

19. Kuppa, A., Aouad, L., Le-Khac, N.A.: Towards improving privacy of synthetic datasets. In: Annual Privacy Forum, pp. 106–119. Springer (2021)
20. LeFevre, K., DeWitt, D.J., Ramakrishnan, R.: Mondrian multidimensional k-anonymity. In: 22nd International Conference on Data Engineering (ICDE'06), pp. 25–25. IEEE (2006)
21. Li, N., Li, T., Venkatasubramanian, S.: t-closeness: Privacy beyond k-anonymity and l-diversity. In: 2007 IEEE 23rd International Conference on Data Engineering, pp. 106–115. IEEE (2006)
22. Li, T., Li, N.: On the tradeoff between privacy and utility in data publishing. In: Proceedings of the 15th ACM SIGKDD International Conference on Knowledge Discovery and Data Mining, pp. 517–526 (2009)
23. Liao, Q., et al.: Ai've got a bad feeling about this: a privacy threat modeling framework for genai
24. Loukides, G., Shao, J.: Data utility and privacy protection trade-off in k-anonymisation. In: Proceedings of the 2008 international workshop on Privacy and anonymity in information society, pp. 36–45 (2008)
25. Lu, P.H., Wang, P.C., Yu, C.M.: Empirical evaluation on synthetic data generation with generative adversarial network. In: Proceedings of the 9th International Conference on Web Intelligence, Mining and Semantics, pp. 1–6 (2019)
26. Machanavajjhala, A., Kifer, D., Gehrke, J., Venkitasubramaniam, M.: l-diversity: privacy beyond k-anonymity. Acm Trans. Knowl. Discovery Data (tkdd) **1**(1), 3–es (2007)
27. Meeus, M., Guepin, F., Creţu, A.M., de Montjoye, Y.A.: Achilles' heels: vulnerable record identification in synthetic data publishing. In: European Symposium on Research in Computer Security, pp. 380–399. Springer (2023)
28. Patki, N., Wedge, R., Veeramachaneni, K.: The Synthetic Data Vault (SDV). In: IEEE International Conference on Data Science and Advanced Analytics (DSAA), pp. 399–410 (2016)
29. Platzer, M., Reutterer, T.: Holdout-based empirical assessment of mixed-type synthetic data. Front. Big Data **4**, 679939 (2021)
30. Prasser, F., Bild, R., Kuhn, K.A.: A generic method for assessing the quality of de-identified health data. MIE, pp, 312–316 (2016)
31. Prasser, F., Eicher, J., Spengler, H., Bild, R., Kuhn, K.A.: Flexible data anonymization using arx—current status and challenges ahead. Software: Practice and Experience **50**(7), 1277–1304 (2020)
32. Qian, Z., Cebere, B.C., van der Schaar, M.: Synthcity: facilitating innovative use cases of synthetic data in different data modalities (2023)
33. Rastogi, V., Suciu, D., Hong, S.: The boundary between privacy and utility in data publishing. In: Proceedings of the 33rd International Conference on Very Large Data Bases, pp. 531–542 (2007)
34. Ruiz, N., Muralidhar, K., Domingo-Ferrer, J.: On the privacy guarantees of synthetic data: a reassessment from the maximum-knowledge attacker perspective. In: Privacy in Statistical Databases: UNESCO Chair in Data Privacy, International Conference, PSD 2018, Valencia, Spain, September 26–28, 2018, Proceedings, pp. 59–74. Springer (2018)
35. Samarati, P.: Protecting respondents identities in microdata release. IEEE Trans. Knowl. Data Eng. **13**(6), 1010–1027 (2001)
36. Stadler, T., Oprisanu, B., Troncoso, C.: Synthetic data-a privacy mirage (2020). arXiv preprint arXiv:2011.07018

37. Stadler, T., Oprisanu, B., Troncoso, C.: Synthetic data-anonymisation groundhog day. In: 31st USENIX Security Symposium (USENIX Security 22), pp. 1451–1468 (2022)
38. Stalla-Bourdillon, S., Knight, A.: Anonymous data v. personal data-false debate: an eu perspective on anonymization, pseudonymization and personal data. Wis. Int'l LJ **34**, 284 (2016)
39. Sweeney, L.: Achieving k-anonymity privacy protection using generalization and suppression. Internat. J. Uncertain. Fuzziness Knowledge-Based Systems **10**(05), 571–588 (2002)
40. Templ, M., Kowarik, A., Meindl, B.: Statistical disclosure control for micro-data using the r package sdcmicro. J. Stat. Softw. **67**, 1–36 (2015)
41. Verdonck, J., De Boeck, K., Willocx, M., Lapon, J., Naessens, V.: A hybrid anonymization pipeline to improve the privacy-utility balance in sensitive datasets for ml purposes. In: Proceedings of the 18th International Conference on Availability, Reliability and Security, pp. 1–11 (2023)
42. Xu, L., Skoularidou, M., Cuesta-Infante, A., Veeramachaneni, K.: Modeling tabular data using conditional gan. Adv. Neural. Inf. Process. Syst. **32** (2019)
43. Yale, A., Dash, S., Dutta, R., Guyon, I., Pavao, A., Bennett, K.P.: Generation and evaluation of privacy preserving synthetic health data. Neurocomputing **416**, 244–255 (2020)
44. Yoon, J., Drumright, L.N., Van Der Schaar, M.: Anonymization through data synthesis using generative adversarial networks (ads-gan). IEEE J. Biomed. Health Inform. **24**(8), 2378–2388 (2020)

Preserving Socio-Connective Diversity in Locally Private Social Graph Synthesis

Manel Jerbi(✉), Reynaldo Gil Pons, and Sjouke Mauw

University of Luxembourg, Luxembourg, Luxembourg
manel.jerbi@uni.lu, reynaldo.gilpons@uni.lu, sjouke.mauw@uni.lu

Abstract. In decentralised social networks, users typically hold only partial views of the overall network structure. Synthesising a global social graph from such distributed data, while protecting user privacy, remains an open challenge. We present DHSG-LDP, a framework and reference architecture for privacy-preserving heterogeneous graph synthesis in decentralised settings. Each client perturbs locally held ego-network information before sharing it with an untrusted aggregator, which reconstructs a synthetic user–user graph for downstream analysis without collecting raw relationship data. DHSG-LDP preserves *socio-connective diversity*, capturing both homophilous and heterophilous interaction patterns. Privacy is enforced locally: individual user connections cannot be reliably inferred from reported information, even when multiple reports are combined. We implement a prototype and evaluate it on real-world datasets using link prediction and community detection tasks. Results show that synthesised graphs retain several structural properties, with performance varying across datasets, metrics, and privacy budgets. At moderate privacy levels, utility approaches that of the original graph while meaningful privacy protection is maintained.

Keywords: Heterogeneous social graph synthesis · Socio-connective diversity · Decentralised heterogeneous graphs · Local Differential Privacy

1 Introduction

Social networks capture diverse relationships between individuals, communities, and content. *Heterogeneous graphs* provide a flexible modelling framework for representing such interactions through multiple node and edge types [11]. As social data becomes increasingly decentralised across platforms, system resilience improves, but privacy risks intensify [15]. While decentralisation reduces reliance on trusted central storage, it complicates privacy-preserving analysis because global structure must be inferred from locally held data. To address these challenges, *Differential Privacy (DP)* [2] introduces controlled randomness to limit information leakage about individuals. For graph data, DP-based approaches typically either (i) release aggregate statistics under privacy guarantees or

S. Nadjm-Tehrani et al. (Eds.): ARES 2026, LNCS 16898, pp. 26–48, 2027.
https://doi.org/10.1007/978-3-032-36874-4_2

(ii) generate synthetic graphs via privacy-preserving model estimation and sampling. We adopt the latter approach. We propose *DHSG-LDP* (*Decentralised Heterogeneous Social Graphs under Local Differential Privacy*), a decentralised synthesis framework that reconstructs heterogeneous synthetic social graphs from locally perturbed ego-network information while preserving structural fidelity and socio-connective diversity under local privacy guarantees. Synthetic generation is particularly important when downstream tasks require explicit relational structure, such as link prediction or community detection, which cannot be supported by summary statistics alone. DHSG-LDP targets practical decentralised scenarios in which users retain control over their local data while contributing to a global structure. Such scenarios arise in federated social platforms (e.g., Mastodon), privacy-sensitive decentralised infrastructures [21], and graph learning settings in which centralised aggregation must be avoided. In these environments, protecting the existence of specific user connections and shared content is critical, even against an honest-but-curious aggregator. In decentralised settings, *Local Differential Privacy (LDP)* is particularly suitable, as perturbation occurs on the client side before any data transmission [6]. Prior work on privacy-preserving graph synthesis spans statistical network models, such as ERGMs and actor-oriented approaches, which capture reciprocity, homophily, and transitivity but assume centralised access to the full graph, and DP-based methods addressing degree distribution estimation [13] and graph modelling under LDP [17]. More directly related, LDPGen [13] and LDPGM [20] generate synthetic graphs from locally perturbed statistics or neighbourhood structures, while PrivGraph [19] exploits community information for DP graph synthesis but assumes centralised access and does not target heterogeneous decentralised settings. Existing LDP-based synthesis methods often struggle to preserve higher-order structural properties under strong noise, and none explicitly targets socio-connective diversity in heterogeneous decentralised settings. A central limitation of prior approaches is their limited ability to preserve *socio-connective diversity*, encompassing both *homophily*—the tendency of similar users to connect—and *heterophily*—links between dissimilar users [9]. DHSG-LDP addresses this limitation by jointly targeting structural fidelity and semantic fidelity, which together support socio-connective diversity. Structural fidelity concerns degree distribution, clustering, and connectivity patterns, while semantic fidelity captures meaning-bearing relationships derived from text-based similarity signals [5]. This dual objective enables preservation of both homophilous and heterophilous interaction patterns, which we evaluate through structural mixing proxies such as assortativity, clustering, and community structure. Concretely, DHSG-LDP operationalises this objective through a utility-driven ego-graph selection mechanism that balances structural consistency with similarity-based compatibility. The global graph is reconstructed from locally perturbed *ego graphs*, each centred on a user and their direct connections. Unlike approaches that treat content purely as attributes, we introduce *text nodes* as structural entities linking users through shared content. These nodes enable similarity estimation even without direct user–user edges. Text nodes and user–text edges remain strictly client-side and are never transmitted to the curator; they serve only as anchors for similarity estimation within ego graphs. Ego-graph selection is performed using the Exponential Mechanism (EM) [10], favouring higher-utility structures while maintaining formal privacy guarantees. We evaluate DHSG-LDP on multiple real-world datasets, averaging results over repeated runs to account for stochasticity in perturbation and selection. The framework supports downstream tasks including link prediction and community detection in privacy-sensitive decentralised environments. Our contributions are threefold: (1) We introduce a decentralised LDP-based framework for synthesising heterogeneous social graphs while preserving structural properties and socio-connective diversity. (2) We design an ego-graph mechanism that combines local semantic perturbation with utility-driven structural selection under formal privacy guarantees. (3) We empirically demonstrate that the resulting synthetic graphs retain competitive utility for downstream tasks under local differential privacy.

2 Preliminaries

This section introduces heterogeneous and ego graphs, the Edge Local Differential Privacy (ELDP) model adopted in this work, and the Laplace and Exponential mechanisms used to enforce it.

2.1 Heterogeneous Graphs and Ego Graphs

Heterogeneous social graphs extend traditional networks by incorporating multiple node and edge types. In decentralised settings, users observe partial views through *ego graphs*, i.e., subgraphs centred on individual nodes.

Definition 1 (Heterogeneous graph [15]**).** *Let $\mathcal{T}_V$ and $\mathcal{T}_E$ denote sets of vertex and edge types, respectively. A heterogeneous graph is $G = (\mathcal{V}, \mathcal{E}, \phi, \psi)$ where:*

- *$\mathcal{V}$ is the vertex set,*
- *$\mathcal{E} \subseteq \mathcal{V} \times \mathcal{V}$ is the edge set,*
- *$\phi : \mathcal{V} \to \mathcal{T}_V$ assigns a type to each vertex,*
- *$\psi : \mathcal{E} \to \mathcal{T}_E$ assigns a type to each edge,*
- *$|\mathcal{T}_V| + |\mathcal{T}_E| > 2$.*

$\mathcal{G}$ denotes the universe of such graphs.

Definition 2 (Heterogeneous ego graph [12]*).* *For $v \in \mathcal{V}$, the ego graph g_v is the subgraph $g_v = (\mathcal{V}_{g_v}, \mathcal{E}_{g_v}, \phi_{g_v}, \psi_{g_v})$ where:*

- *$\mathcal{V}_{g_v} = \{v\} \cup \{w \in \mathcal{V} \mid (v, w) \in \mathcal{E}$ or $(w, v) \in \mathcal{E}\}$,*
- *$\mathcal{E}_{g_v} = \{(v, w) \in \mathcal{E} \mid w \in \mathcal{V}_{g_v}\}$,*
- *ϕ_{g_v} and ψ_{g_v} are restrictions of ϕ and ψ.*

The set of ego graphs in G is $\mathrm{Ego}(G) = \{g_v \mid v \in \mathcal{V}\}$.

Domain of Ego Graphs. For privacy analysis, we consider the domain $\mathcal{D}_{\text{ego}}$ consisting of *all feasible* heterogeneous ego graphs consistent with $(\mathcal{T}_V, \mathcal{T}_E)$. Each user's input to the local mechanism is an ego graph $g_v \in \mathcal{D}_{\text{ego}}$ containing only edges incident to the ego node. The local randomisation mechanisms operate over $\mathcal{D}_{\text{ego}}$, not only over the observed ego graphs $\text{Ego}(G)$ of a fixed underlying graph.

2.2 Edge Local Differential Privacy

Definition 3 (ε-Local Differential Privacy (ε-LDP) [6]). *A randomised mechanism $\mathcal{M}$ with domain $\mathcal{D}$ satisfies ε-LDP if for all $d, d' \in \mathcal{D}$ and all $r \in$* Range($\mathcal{M}$),

$$\Pr(\mathcal{M}(d) = r) \leq e^{\varepsilon} \Pr(\mathcal{M}(d') = r).$$

In graph settings, protection may target nodes or edges [13]. We adopt an edge-level notion tailored to ego graphs.

Definition 4 (Neighbouring ego graphs). *Two ego graphs $g, g' \in \mathcal{D}_{ego}$ are neighbouring, denoted $g \sim g'$, if they differ by the presence or absence of exactly one edge incident to the ego node.*

Formally, there exists a unique edge (v, w) such that it belongs to exactly one of $\mathcal{E}_g$ or $\mathcal{E}_{g'}$.

Definition 5 (ε-Edge Local Differential Privacy (ε-ELDP)). *A mechanism $\mathcal{M}$ with domain $\mathcal{D}_{ego}$ satisfies ε-ELDP if for all neighbouring $g \sim g'$ and all outputs r,*

$$\Pr(\mathcal{M}(g) = r) \leq e^{\varepsilon} \Pr(\mathcal{M}(g') = r).$$

The neighbouring relation covers both user–user and user–text edges incident to the ego node. Consequently, user–text associations are protected under ELDP, although such edges are never released by our protocol.

2.3 Mechanisms for Enforcing LDP

Laplace Mechanism

Definition 6 (Global sensitivity). *Let $f : \mathcal{D}_{ego} \to \mathbb{R}$. The global sensitivity of f under the ELDP neighbouring relation is*

$$\Delta f = \max_{g \sim g'} |f(g) - f(g')|.$$

Definition 7 (Laplace Mechanism [2]). *Given a query f with global sensitivity Δf, the Laplace mechanism outputs*

$$\mathcal{M}_L(g) = f(g) + Y,$$

where $Y \sim \text{Lap}\left(\frac{\Delta f}{\varepsilon}\right)$.

Exponential Mechanism

Definition 8 (Exponential Mechanism [10]**).** *Let $\mathcal{Y}$ be a fixed finite output space and $U : \mathcal{D}_{ego} \times \mathcal{Y} \to \mathbb{R}$ a utility function with sensitivity*

$$\Delta U = \max_{g \sim g'} \max_{y \in \mathcal{Y}} |U(g, y) - U(g', y)|.$$

The mechanism selects $y \in \mathcal{Y}$ with probability

$$\Pr[\mathcal{M}_E(g) = y] \propto \exp\left(\frac{\varepsilon U(g, y)}{2\Delta U}\right).$$

We denote the probability of selecting g' given g by $\Pr_{\text{select}}(g' \mid g)$.

2.4 Sequential Composition

Lemma 1 (Sequential Composition [6]**).** *If mechanisms $\{\mathcal{M}_i\}_{i=1}^{n}$ satisfy ε_i-differential privacy, then their sequential composition satisfies $\sum_{i=1}^{n} \varepsilon_i$-differential privacy.*

3 Threat Model

We specify the adversarial capabilities, protection scope, and assumptions under which DHSG-LDP provides privacy guarantees. The protocol operates under the ε-ELDP definition introduced in Sect. 2.

Scope of the Guarantee. The privacy guarantee is defined at the level of each user's ego graph. Two ego graphs are neighbouring if they differ by the presence or absence of a single edge incident to the reporting user. The mechanism therefore protects whether a user is connected to a specific alter (user or text node) in that user's local view. The guarantee is strictly per-user: each output satisfies ELDP with respect to the reporting user's ego graph. The protocol does not provide global differential privacy for the entire underlying social graph. Since only ego–alter edges are reported, any user–user edge can influence at most the reports of its two endpoints.

Adversary Model. We assume an *honest-but-curious* data curator whose goal is to infer whether a specific edge incident to a reporting user exists. The adversary follows the protocol, observes the released noised similarity scores and selected ego graphs, and knows the public parameters and privacy budgets. The curator receives only outputs of the local randomisation mechanisms (e.g., noised similarity scores or selected ego graphs), and never raw edges, text identifiers, or user–text associations. Under ε-ELDP, the probability of any output changes by at most a multiplicative factor e^{ε} when a single protected edge is added or removed. Because each user reports only on edges incident to themselves, a user–user edge (u_i, u_j) may appear in at most two independent reports: one from u_i and one from u_j. No third party reports this edge, as alter–alter edges are never released. Consequently, any protected edge contributes to at most two local randomisation events.

Assumptions. We assume that: (i) users trust the correctness of their local mechanism implementation; (ii) there is no collusion between users and the curator; (iii) the curator has no auxiliary information beyond the perturbed outputs; (iv) side-channel and timing attacks are out of scope; (v) text features and preference vectors used in Phase 1 are computed locally and are not observable by the curator. The curator never receives text-node identifiers, raw text content, or user–text edges; only differentially private summaries are shared. Consequently, similarity computations cannot be exploited to infer unreported edges via shared text access. This threat model applies to all phases of the DHSG-LDP framework described in Sect. 4.

4 DHSG-LDP

Reconstructing a coherent global graph from locally perturbed ego graphs is challenging: decentralised views prevent direct neighbourhood alignment, and privacy-induced noise can break connectivity and distort degree distributions. We introduce DHSG-LDP, a framework for synthesising decentralised social graphs under LDP while preserving structural fidelity and *socio-connective diversity*. DHSG-LDP supports privacy sensitive settings (e.g., online communities, collaborative learning platforms, and decentralised recommendation) where direct user–user relationships are sensitive.

4.1 Framework Objectives

DHSG-LDP is designed to: (1) capture key structural features (e.g., degree distributions and clustering) while preserving socio-connective diversity through both homophilous and heterophilous links; (2) protect individual relationships via local randomisation without requiring a trusted aggregator; and (3) generate synthetic graphs that retain analytical utility under formal ε-ELDP guarantees. For each user u_i, one execution of DHSG-LDP satisfies $(\varepsilon_1 + \varepsilon_2)$-ELDP with respect to u_i's ego graph. Since only ego–alter edges are reported, any user–user edge (u_i, u_j) can affect at most the two independent reports produced by its endpoints, yielding a $2(\varepsilon_1 + \varepsilon_2)$-ELDP bound at the edge level. This distinction is important: the per-user guarantee bounds what the curator can infer about a single user's connections, while the edge-level bound bounds what can be inferred about any specific pair of users. Formal proofs and privacy accounting are provided in Sect. 8. The framework operates on decentralised ego graphs centred on a user ("ego") and their direct connections ("alters"). Text nodes are used *strictly locally* as structural evidence of shared content to derive preference vectors and compatibility signals; text nodes are never released. This supports the modelling of thematic similarity and indirect ties, which is particularly important in sparse or decentralised networks. The synthesis process proceeds in three phases: *Phase 1* computes preference vectors and similarity scores from locally accessible text; *Phase 2* perturbs these scores under ε_1-ELDP before transmission to an honest-but-curious curator; and *Phase 3* selects and integrates noised ego graphs via the EM to construct the final synthetic global graph. Figure 1 summarises this process.

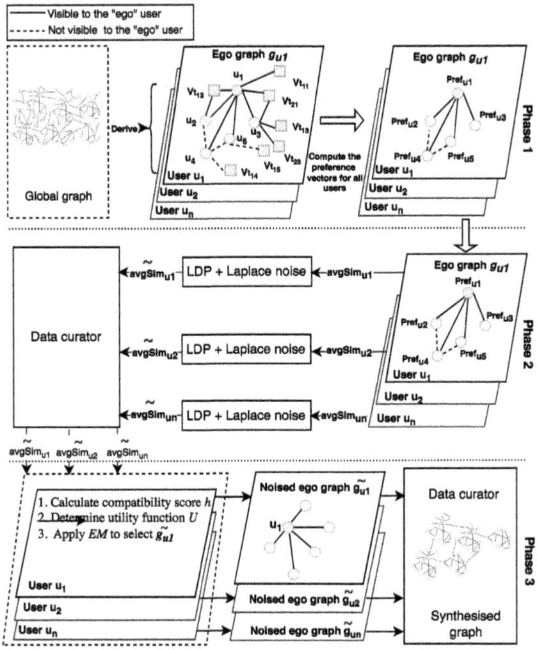

Fig. 1. General workflow of DHSG-LDP from decentralised ego graphs to a synthetic global graph.

4.2 Problem Formulation and Design

Synthesising decentralised social graphs under privacy constraints requires addressing three interrelated challenges: (1) balancing privacy and utility; (2) preserving structural consistency without central oversight; and (3) maintaining socio-connective diversity despite noise and sparsity.

Optimisation Objective. Formally, our objective is to construct a synthetic graph $G_{\text{synthetic}}$ that maximises structural and compatibility-based utility with respect to the decentralised ego graphs, while satisfying LDP constraints. Let $\{g_{u_i}\}_{u_i \in U}$ denote the set of observed ego graphs, each held locally by user u_i. We seek to approximate the solution of:

$$\max_{G'} \mathcal{F}\big(G', \{g_{u_i}\}_{u_i \in U}\big) \quad \text{subject to } (\varepsilon_1 + \varepsilon_2)\text{-ELDP},$$

where $\mathcal{F}$ captures: (i) structural retention (e.g., degree preservation, clustering consistency), and (ii) compatibility consistency induced by similarity scores. The privacy constraint follows from sequential composition of ε_1-ELDP (Phase 2) and ε_2-ELDP (Phase 3), as formalised in Sect. 2.

Input Model. The input is a heterogeneous graph

$$G = (\mathcal{V}, \mathcal{E}, \phi, \psi),$$

decentralised across user nodes

$$U = \{u_i \in \mathcal{V} \mid \phi(u_i) = \tau_{\text{user}}\}, \quad \tau_{\text{user}} \in \mathcal{T}_V.$$

Each user u_i holds an observed ego graph $g_{u_i} \in \text{Ego}(G)$. For privacy analysis, we view g_{u_i} as an element of the domain $\mathcal{D}_{\text{ego}}$ of all feasible ego graphs consistent with the allowed node and edge types $(\mathcal{T}_V, \mathcal{T}_E)$ (cf. Sect. 2).

The ego graph g_{u_i} consists of:

- user neighbours $\mathcal{N}_{\text{user}}(u_i) = \{u_j \in \mathcal{V}_{g_{u_i}} \mid \phi(u_j) = \tau_{\text{user}}\}$,
- text nodes $T_{u_i} = \{t_{1i}, t_{2i}, \ldots, t_{li}\}$, where $\phi(t_{ji}) = \tau_{\text{text}}$.

Bounded-Degree Assumption. For sensitivity analysis in Phase 3, we assume that ego degrees are uniformly bounded by a finite constant $D_{\max}$ over the domain $\mathcal{D}_{\text{ego}}$, i.e.,

$$|\mathcal{N}_{\text{user}}(u_i)| \leq D_{\max} \quad \text{for all feasible } g_{u_i} \in \mathcal{D}_{\text{ego}}.$$

This assumption ensures that the EM utility function admits a finite global sensitivity.

Compatibility Lower Bound. Since similarity scores are clipped to $[0,1]$ in Phase 2, the difference between any two scores lies in $[-1,1]$, and its square is at most 1. The compatibility functions therefore satisfy

$$h_{u_i u_j} = \exp\Big(-(\text{avgSim}_{u_i} - \widetilde{\text{avgSim}}_{u_j})^2\Big) \geq \exp(-1),$$
$$\widetilde{h}_{u_k u_j} = \exp\Big(-(\widetilde{\text{avgSim}}_{u_k} - \widetilde{\text{avgSim}}_{u_j})^2\Big) \geq \exp(-1).$$

Consequently, whenever $\mathcal{N}_{\text{user}}(u_i) \neq \emptyset$, each term $\widetilde{h}_{u_k u_j} d_{u_k}$ in the denominator is at least $\exp(-1)$, since $d_{u_k} \geq 1$ for existing neighbours. Hence the denominator is bounded below by $\exp(-1) > 0$, and the finite upper bound C_u exists.

Neighbouring Relation. Two ego graphs $g, g' \in \mathcal{D}_{\text{ego}}$ are *neighbouring* (denoted $g \sim g'$) if they differ by the presence or absence of a single edge incident to the ego node (user–user or user–text), consistent with the ε-ELDP definition introduced in Sect. 2. We assume G is undirected for clarity of exposition, although the framework extends to directed or weighted graphs without altering the privacy guarantees. For undirected graphs, we treat edges as ordered pairs stored once, so (v, w) and (w, v) refer to the same edge and membership checks such as $(u_i, u_j) \in \mathcal{E}_{\tilde{g}_{u_i}}$ are interpreted accordingly.

Phase 1: Calculating Preference Vectors and Similarity Scores. Each user constructs a preference vector by aggregating topic and sentiment features from their locally accessible text nodes. To reduce semantic loss under subsequent perturbation, we adopt topic-based vectorization. For users with few interactions, aggregation is performed via averaging, ensuring scale-invariance with respect to interaction volume [5]. This phase estimates compatibility between connected users based solely on locally available information, without introducing any structural modification.

Text Node Processing. For each text node t_{ji} associated with user u_i (Algorithm 1, lines 3–8), a text vector is computed as:

$$V_{t_{ji}} = [\Gamma_{ji}, S_{ji}],$$

where:

- $\Gamma_{ji} = [\gamma_{1ji}, \ldots, \gamma_{mji}]$ is the topic distribution vector of dimension m, where γ_{kji} denotes the probability that t_{ji} belongs to topic k;
- $S_{ji} \in [-1, 1]$ is the sentiment score of t_{ji}.

Preference Vector Calculation. The preference vector of user u_i is defined as:

$$\text{Pref}_{u_i} = [p_{1i}, p_{2i}, \ldots, p_{mi}, p_{(m+1)i}],$$

where:

$$p_{wi} = \begin{cases} \frac{1}{l} \sum_{j=1}^{l} \gamma_{wji}, & 1 \leq w \leq m, \\ \frac{1}{l} \sum_{j=1}^{l} S_{ji}, & w = m + 1, \end{cases}$$

and $l = |T_{u_i}|$. Aggregation via averaging ensures that the magnitude of the preference vector does not depend on the number of text interactions.

Similarity Score Calculation. For each explicit user–user connection, we assume that the associated text nodes are locally accessible to both endpoints. The similarity score is computed using cosine similarity. Let $N_i := \mathcal{N}_{\text{user}}(u_i)$.

$$\text{avgSim}_{u_i} = \begin{cases} \frac{1}{|N_i|} \sum_{u_j \in N_i} \text{CosSim}(\text{Pref}_{u_i}, \text{Pref}_{u_j}), & |N_i| > 0, \\ 0, & |N_i| = 0. \end{cases}$$

All computations rely exclusively on locally accessible information; if $|N_i| = 0$ we set $\text{avgSim}_{u_i} = 0$.

At the end of this phase, each user holds their own similarity score avgSim_{u_i}, computed exclusively from locally accessible content and ready for privacy-preserving perturbation in Phase 2.

Phase 2: Privacy-Preserving Data Collection. In Phase 2 (Algorithm 2), each user perturbs their locally computed similarity score before transmission, ensuring ε_1-ELDP.

Algorithm 1 Calculate_Similarity_Scores (CSS)

Input: Set of users $U = \{u_1, u_2, \ldots, u_n\}$, text nodes T_{u_i} for each u_i, neighbours $\mathcal{N}_{\text{user}}(u_i)$ for each u_i
Output: Average similarity scores avgSim_{u_i} for all users
for each user $u_i \in U$ **do**
  for each text node $t_{ji} \in T_{u_i}$ **do**
    Compute topic distribution $\Gamma_{ji} = [\gamma_{1ji}, \ldots, \gamma_{mji}]$
    Compute sentiment score S_{ji}
    Form text vector $V_{t_{ji}} = [\Gamma_{ji}, S_{ji}]$
  end for
  Compute preference vector:
  For $w = 1, \ldots, m$,
  $p_{wi} = \frac{1}{l} \sum_{j=1}^{l} \gamma_{wji}$
  Sentiment component:
  $p_{(m+1)i} = \frac{1}{l} \sum_{j=1}^{l} S_{ji}$
  Assemble:
  $\text{Pref}_{u_i} = [p_{1i}, p_{2i}, \ldots, p_{mi}, p_{(m+1)i}]$
  Compute similarity score:
  $\text{avgSim}_{u_i} = \frac{1}{|\mathcal{N}_{\text{user}}(u_i)|} \sum_{u_j \in \mathcal{N}_{\text{user}}(u_i)} \text{CosSim}(\text{Pref}_{u_i}, \text{Pref}_{u_j})$
end for
return avgSim_{u_i} for all u_i

Local Perturbation. Let avgSim_{u_i} denote the similarity score of user u_i computed in Phase 1. User u_i applies the Laplace mechanism:

$$\widetilde{\text{avgSim}}_{u_i} = \text{avgSim}_{u_i} + \text{Lap}\left(\frac{\Delta\text{Sim}}{\varepsilon_1}\right).$$

The global sensitivity ΔSim is defined with respect to the ELDP neighbouring relation. Adding or removing one ego-incident edge affects at most one term in the average and may change the normalising degree. Since cosine similarity values lie in $[0,1]$ and we define $\text{avgSim}_{u_i} = 0$ when $|\mathcal{N}_{\text{user}}(u_i)| = 0$, it follows that $\text{avgSim}_{u_i} \in [0,1]$ for all feasible ego graphs in $\mathcal{D}_{\text{ego}}$, including boundary cases $d_{u_i} \in \{0,1\}$. Therefore, for any neighbouring $g \sim g'$, $|\text{avgSim}_{u_i}(g) - \text{avgSim}_{u_i}(g')| \leq 1$, and we set $\Delta\text{Sim} = 1$ as a valid, degree-independent sensitivity bound.

Because noise may move the value outside the valid similarity range, we apply deterministic post-processing: $\widetilde{\text{avgSim}}_{u_i} \leftarrow \text{clip}\big(\widetilde{\text{avgSim}}_{u_i}, 0, 1\big)$.

Aggregation. The perturbed scores $\widetilde{\text{avgSim}}_{u_i}$ are transmitted to the curator, which redistributes the set $\{\widetilde{\text{avgSim}}_{u_j} \mid u_j \in U\}$ to all users. No raw similarity scores or text features are ever shared.

At the end of this phase, all users hold a complete set of noised similarity scores $\{\widetilde{\text{avgSim}}_{u_j} \mid u_j \in U\}$, ready for compatibility-based ego graph selection in Phase 3.

Algorithm 2 DHSG-LDP (Phases 2–3 client-side + curator-side synthesis)

Input: Users U, local ego graphs $\{g_{u_i}\}$, privacy budgets $(\varepsilon_1, \varepsilon_2)$
Output: Synthetic graph $G_{\text{synthetic}} = (U, \mathcal{E}_{\text{synthetic}})$
Phase 2 (client u_i): send noised similarity score

$$\widetilde{\text{avgSim}}_{u_i} \leftarrow \text{clip}\left(\text{avgSim}_{u_i} + \text{Lap}\left(\tfrac{\Delta\text{Sim}}{\varepsilon_1}\right), 0, 1\right)$$

Curator: broadcast $\{\widetilde{\text{avgSim}}_{u_j}\}_{u_j \in U}$ to all users
Phase 3 (client u_i): define fixed output space $\mathcal{Y}_{u_i}$, compute utilities $U(g_{u_i}, g'_{u_i})$ select $\tilde{g}_{u_i} \in \mathcal{Y}_{u_i}$ using the EM with budget ε_2
Client u_i: send selected ego graph $\tilde{g}_{u_i}$ (user–user edges only)
Curator synthesis: $\mathcal{E}_{\text{synthetic}} \leftarrow \emptyset$
for each unordered pair $\{u_i, u_j\} \subseteq U$ **do**
  $p \leftarrow \frac{1}{2}\left(\mathbb{I}[(u_i, u_j) \in \mathcal{E}_{\tilde{g}_{u_i}}] + \mathbb{I}[(u_i, u_j) \in \mathcal{E}_{\tilde{g}_{u_j}}]\right)$
  draw $b \sim \text{Bernoulli}(p)$
  if $b = 1$ **then**
    $\mathcal{E}_{\text{synthetic}} \leftarrow \mathcal{E}_{\text{synthetic}} \cup \{(u_i, u_j)\}$
  end if
end for
return $G_{\text{synthetic}} = (U, \mathcal{E}_{\text{synthetic}})$

Phase 3: Ego Graph Selection and Global Synthesis. In Phase 3 (Algorithm 2), users select a perturbed ego graph via the EM, and the curator integrates the selected ego graphs into a synthetic global graph. The objective is to preserve structural properties and compatibility patterns while satisfying ε_2-ELDP.

Candidate Ego Graphs (Finite Range of the EM). Fix a user u_i. Let $\mathcal{A}_{u_i}$ denote the set of *eligible alters* (user-type nodes) that u_i may connect to when constructing candidates. We assume $\mathcal{A}_{u_i}$ is finite and determined independently of the realised private ego-edge set, for example from a locally known user list, a sampled pool, or a public directory. Let

$$E_i = \{(u_i, u_j) \mid u_j \in \mathcal{A}_{u_i}\}$$

be the set of all feasible ego–alter user–user edges for u_i over $\mathcal{A}_{u_i}$. We define the fixed finite output space of the EM as

$$\mathcal{Y}_{u_i} = \left\{ g'_{u_i} \in \mathcal{D}_{\text{ego}} \;\middle|\; \mathcal{E}_{g'_{u_i}} \subseteq E_i \;\wedge\; |\mathcal{E}_{g'_{u_i}}| \le D_{\max} \right\}.$$

The EM selects one noised ego graph $\tilde{g}_{u_i} \in \mathcal{Y}_{u_i}$ according to the utility function below. The output space is therefore fixed for neighbouring inputs; the private ego graph g_{u_i} only affects the utility values, not the set of possible outputs. We restrict $\mathcal{A}_{u_i}$ to alters whose content features are locally accessible to u_i, so that Pref_{u_j} is computable for all $u_j \in \mathcal{A}_{u_i}$.

Compatibility Score. For a candidate alter u_j, user u_i computes

$$h_{u_i u_j} = \exp\Big(-(\mathrm{avgSim}_{u_i} - \widetilde{\mathrm{avgSim}}_{u_j})^2\Big),$$

where avgSim_{u_i} is local to u_i and $\widetilde{\mathrm{avgSim}}_{u_j}$ is the noised score received from Phase 2. For an existing neighbour $u_k \in \mathcal{N}_{\text{user}}(u_i)$, the compatibility with u_j is computed using noised scores:

$$\widetilde{h}_{u_k u_j} = \exp\Big(-(\widetilde{\mathrm{avgSim}}_{u_k} - \widetilde{\mathrm{avgSim}}_{u_j})^2\Big).$$

Thus, user u_i uses only its own raw similarity score and the noised scores received in Phase 2.

Edge Utility (Inspired by [5].) For an edge $e_{u_i u_j}$ incident to u_i:

$$u(g_{u_i}, e_{u_i u_j}) = \begin{cases} \dfrac{h_{u_i u_j}\, d_{u_i}}{\sum_{u_k \in \mathcal{N}_{\text{user}}(u_i)} \widetilde{h}_{u_k u_j}\, d_{u_k}} & \text{if } \mathcal{N}_{\text{user}}(u_i) \neq \emptyset, \\ 0 & \text{otherwise.} \end{cases}$$

where d_{u_i} is the degree of u_i in g_{u_i}. The denominator sums $\widetilde{h}_{u_k u_j} \cdot d_{u_k}$ over all current user-neighbours u_k of u_i, normalising the weight of edge $e_{u_i u_j}$ relative to how compatible each existing neighbour u_k is with u_j. This scores each candidate edge against the competitive landscape of u_i's current neighbourhood, so that edges to alters who are more compatible with u_i's existing neighbours receive lower relative weight, promoting connective diversity. When $\mathcal{N}_{\text{user}}(u_i) = \emptyset$, the utility defaults to 0.

Ego-Graph Utility. For a candidate ego graph $g'_{u_i} \in \mathcal{Y}_{u_i}$, define

$$U(g_{u_i}, g'_{u_i}) = \sum_{e \in \mathcal{E}_{g_{u_i}} \cap \mathcal{E}_{g'_{u_i}}} u(g_{u_i}, e)\, W(g_{u_i},\ \mathrm{e}) + S(g_{u_i}, g'_{u_i}),$$

where the edge-retention weight is

$$W(g_{u_i},\ \mathrm{e}) = 1 - \frac{1}{\max(1, |\mathcal{E}_{g_{u_i}}|)},$$

and we define the candidate-based similarity score. Let $N'_i := \mathcal{N}'_{\text{user}}(u_i)$.

$$\mathrm{avgSim}'_{u_i} = \begin{cases} \frac{1}{|N'_i|} \sum_{u_j \in N'_i} \mathrm{CosSim}\big(\mathrm{Pref}_{u_i}, \mathrm{Pref}_{u_j}\big), & |N'_i| > 0, \\ 0, & |N'_i| = 0. \end{cases}$$

Here $\mathcal{N}'_{\text{user}}(u_i)$ denotes the user-neighbour set of u_i in g'_{u_i}. The structural consistency term is then

$$S(g_{u_i}, g'_{u_i}) = -\left|\mathrm{avgSim}_{u_i} - \mathrm{avgSim}'_{u_i}\right|.$$

This utility promotes (i) retention of important ego–alter edges, (ii) compatibility consistency, and (iii) bounded distortion of similarity scores.

Utility Sensitivity Bound. We assume the bounded-degree condition $|\mathcal{N}_{\text{user}}(u_i)| \leq D_{\max}$ over $\mathcal{D}_{\text{ego}}$.

Bound on Edge-Level Utility. For any edge $e = (u_i, u_j)$ with $\mathcal{N}_{\text{user}}(u_i) \neq \emptyset$, the edge utility is

$$u(g_{u_i},\ \mathrm{e}) = \frac{h_{u_i u_j}\, d_{u_i}}{\sum_{u_k \in \mathcal{N}_{\text{user}}(u_i)} \widetilde{h}_{u_k u_j}\, d_{u_k}}.$$

The numerator $h_{u_i u_j}\, d_{u_i}$ is bounded above by $D_{\max}$, since $h_{u_i u_j} \in (0, 1]$ and $d_{u_i} \leq D_{\max}$. The denominator is bounded below by $\exp(-1) > 0$: since the sum runs over $u_k \in \mathcal{N}_{\text{user}}(u_i)$, each u_k is an existing neighbour of u_i, so $d_{u_k} \geq 1$ holds by construction, and each $\widetilde{h}_{u_k u_j} \geq \exp(-1)$ by the compatibility lower bound. Since the numerator is bounded above by $D_{\max}$ and the denominator is bounded away from zero, the ratio is finite. We denote by $C_u < \infty$ a finite upper bound on $u(g_{u_i}, e)$ over all feasible ego graphs. Explicitly, the denominator has $|\mathcal{N}_{\text{user}}(u_i)| \geq 1$ terms each at least $\exp(-1)$, so denominator $\geq |\mathcal{N}_{\text{user}}(u_i)| \cdot \exp(-1) \geq \exp(-1)$. The worst case is $|\mathcal{N}_{\text{user}}(u_i)| = 1$, giving $C_u \leq D_{\max}/\exp(-1) = D_{\max} \cdot e$. When $\mathcal{N}_{\text{user}}(u_i) = \emptyset$, the utility is 0 by definition. In both cases,

$$0 \leq u(g_{u_i}, e) \leq C_u < \infty.$$

Change Under ELDP Adjacency. Under the ELDP neighbouring relation, two ego graphs differ by one incident edge. This change may affect d_{u_i}, the denominator of the edge utility, and the edge-retention weight. Since the selected ego graph has at most $D_{\max}$ user–user edges and each edge-level term is bounded by C_u, the whole edge-level component of U is bounded in $[0, D_{\max} C_u]$. Hence the change in this component between neighbouring inputs is at most $2 D_{\max} C_u$.

Structural Term. Since $\text{avgSim}_{u_i}, \text{avgSim}'_{u_i} \in [0, 1]$, $|S(g_{u_i}, g'_{u_i})| \leq 1$.

Global Sensitivity. Let $\mathcal{Y}$ denote the fixed finite output space of candidate ego graphs. The global sensitivity of U under the ELDP neighbouring relation is defined as

$$\Delta U = \max_{g \sim g'} \max_{y \in \mathcal{Y}} |U(g, y) - U(g',\ \mathrm{y})|.$$

Under the bounded-degree assumption $|\mathcal{N}_{\text{user}}(u_i)| \leq D_{\max}$, two neighbouring ego graphs differ by exactly one ego–incident edge. This may affect the edge-level component of the utility, while the structural term remains bounded by 1. Since the edge-level component is bounded in $[0, D_{\max} C_u]$, it follows that

$$\Delta U \leq 2 D_{\max} C_u + 1.$$

Selection Probability. The EM selects $g'_{u_i} \in \mathcal{Y}_{u_i}$ with probability

$$\Pr_{\text{select}}(g'_{u_i} \mid g_{u_i}) = \frac{\exp\left(\frac{\varepsilon_2\, U(g_{u_i}, g'_{u_i})}{2\Delta U}\right)}{\sum_{g''_{u_i} \in \mathcal{Y}_{u_i}} \exp\left(\frac{\varepsilon_2\, U(g_{u_i}, g''_{u_i})}{2\Delta U}\right)},$$

where ΔU is the global sensitivity of U under the ELDP neighbouring relation. By construction, this mechanism satisfies ε_2-ELDP because the output space $\mathcal{Y}_{u_i}$ is fixed for neighbouring ego graphs.

Synthesising the Global Graph After EM selection, each user transmits their selected ego graph $\tilde{g}_{u_i}$ to the curator. The curator constructs the synthetic graph $G_{\text{synthetic}} = (U, \mathcal{E}_{\text{synthetic}})$ by merging the received ego graphs. For each unordered pair $\{u_i, u_j\} \subseteq U$, the edge is sampled according to the agreement between the two selected ego graphs. Text nodes and user–text edges are never transmitted. At the end of this phase, the curator outputs $G_{\text{synthetic}}$, a privacy-preserving synthetic social graph that preserves both structural properties and socio-connective diversity under $(\varepsilon_1 + \varepsilon_2)$-ELDP per user by sequential composition (Theorem 3).

4.3 Discussion

DHSG-LDP targets decentralised settings where users retain control over their ego graphs and raw relational data cannot be centralised. A distinctive design choice is the use of text nodes as local structural anchors: topic- and sentiment-based compatibility signals guide edge selection while text nodes and user–text edges remain strictly client-side. In the absence of direct user–user edges, these nodes provide the only locally available signal for estimating compatibility. Removing them would reduce DHSG-LDP to a homogeneous setting, which is precisely the limitation of prior approaches such as LDPGen and LDPGM. Privacy operates in two stages. The Laplace mechanism perturbs similarity scores under ε_1-ELDP, while the EM selects ego graphs under ε_2-ELDP. The statistic avgSim_{u_i} is bounded with sensitivity at most 1 (Lemma 2), so ε_1 fully accounts for any structural signal it may convey. Although evaluated on undirected, unweighted graphs, the framework extends naturally to directed or weighted settings. Aggregate LDP statistics alone cannot support link prediction or community detection, which require explicit edge-level structure; this motivates full graph synthesis rather than standalone privatised metrics.

5 Experimental Setup and Data Processing

This section describes the experimental design, datasets, and processing steps used to evaluate DHSG-LDP in synthesising structurally realistic and socio-connectively diverse graphs under LDP.

5.1 Research Questions

We address the following research questions:

- **RQ1:** To what extent does our decentralised ego-graph-based approach generate structurally realistic social graphs from locally observed data?

- **RQ2:** How well does the synthesised graph preserve socio-connective diversity, including both homophily and heterophily in user interactions?
- **RQ3:** How does the use of LDP mechanisms affect the privacy–utility trade-off?
- **RQ4:** How effectively does the synthesis preserve structural connectivity patterns?
- **RQ5:** How does our method compare with state-of-the-art approaches?

5.2 Experimental Setup

Our evaluation follows established practices in privacy-preserving graph synthesis [13,20]. Structural metrics are aligned with the research questions and widely used in graph analytics.

Metrics

- *Degree distribution and degree standard deviation*: evaluation of structural realism (**RQ1**)
- *Degree assortativity, clustering coefficient, and modularity*: assessment of socio-connective diversity and structural connectivity patterns (**RQ2, RQ4**)
- *Maximum Mean Discrepancy (MMD)*: evaluation of the privacy–utility trade-off (**RQ3**)
- *Mean relative errors*: benchmarking across datasets and comparison with prior work (**RQ5**)

Each experiment is repeated ten times with different random seeds, and mean values are reported.

Datasets. We use three real-world datasets: Enron email [7], DBLP citation [18], and Yelp social network [1] (Table 1).

Table 1. Dataset statistics

Dataset	Nodes	Edges	Type
Enron	36,692	183,831	Email
DBLP	317,080	1,049,866	Citation
Yelp	716,847	13,954,819	Social

Downstream-Task Protocol. We use temporal splits (train $\leq t$, test $(t, t + \Delta]$) to avoid leakage [8]. For link prediction, positives are edges first observed in $(t, t + \Delta]$; negatives are node pairs that are non-edges at time t. Metrics: AUC and AP. For community detection, communities on the synthetic graph (data $\leq t$) are compared to those on the original graph at time t using NMI and ARI. We also report the original-graph baseline.

6 Results Analysis

Degree Distribution. Wasserstein Distance (WD) [14] values indicate strong degree preservation for Enron and DBLP, while Yelp shows higher divergence due to scale and heterogeneity. As expected, WD decreases as ε increases, reflecting the privacy–utility trade-off (Table 2).

Table 2. WD for degree preservation across datasets

Epsilon	Enron	DBLP	Yelp
0.1	11.7	4.8	225.6
0.3	8.4	8.4	185.9
0.6	9.4	3.7	176.2
1.0	8.3	3.8	190.4
3.0	10.2	5.3	154.5
5.0	8.1	5.9	172.4
9.0	7.5	6.6	192.5
10.0	10.3	4.4	169.5

Clustering Coefficient Yelp achieves a low relative error (10.81%), suggesting strong preservation of local triadic structure. Enron and DBLP exhibit higher deviations but remain stable across privacy budgets. Overall, DHSG-LDP retains substantial clustering behaviour under privacy constraints.

Degree Standard Deviation. Low relative errors for Enron (1.16%) and Yelp (1.05%) demonstrate preservation of structural heterogeneity and central–peripheral balance. DBLP shows higher error (14.02%), reflecting its denser and more overlapping community structure.

Degree Assortativity. DBLP exhibits the lowest relative error (26.10%), indicating reasonable preservation of degree–degree correlations. Enron and Yelp show larger deviations (60% and 65% respectively), likely due to their flatter, less structured mixing patterns which amplify noise sensitivity under ego-level perturbation. These results indicate that socio-connective diversity is partially preserved, with stronger preservation for some metrics than for assortativity-sensitive structures.

Maximum Mean Discrepancy. Maximum Mean Discrepancy (MMD) [3] increases as ε decreases, confirming the privacy–utility trade-off. DBLP remains comparatively stable, suggesting robustness to local perturbations.

Modularity. Yelp yields the lowest modularity error (23.62%), DBLP shows moderate deviation (37.70%), and Enron the highest (52.16%), consistent with its sparse hub-dominated topology where community boundaries are less stable under LDP noise (Fig. 2).

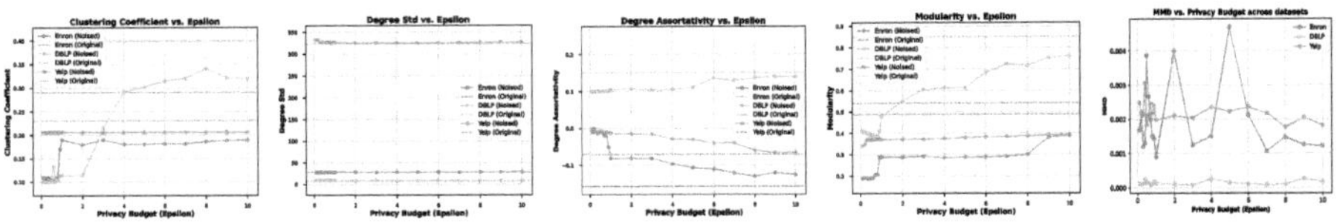

(a) Clust. coeff. (b) Degree std. (c) Assortativity (d) Modularity (e) MMD

Fig. 2. Structural metrics across privacy budgets for synthetic vs. original graphs.

Mean Relative Errors. Table 3 summarises aggregated performance across datasets. Degree standard deviation is most accurately preserved. This table establishes a consolidated view of structural fidelity and serves as a basis for state-of-the-art comparison (**RQ5**) (Table 3).

Table 3. Mean relative errors across datasets

Dataset	Clustering coefficient	Degree std	Degree assortativity	Modularity
Enron	0.5020	0.0116	0.6038	0.5216
DBLP	0.5232	0.1402	0.2610	0.3770
Yelp	0.1081	0.0105	0.6502	0.2362

7 Applicability to Downstream Tasks

We evaluate link prediction (LP) and community detection (CD) across privacy budgets $\varepsilon \in [0.1, 10]$.

Link Prediction. Enron approaches its original-graph baseline as ε increases. DBLP stabilises near $\varepsilon \approx 2$. Yelp improves gradually but remains below baseline, reflecting higher structural heterogeneity (Fig. 3).

Community Detection. DBLP achieves the highest NMI and ARI values and remains comparatively stable. Yelp shows a slight upward trend with increasing ε. Enron decreases at larger budgets. All synthetic graphs remain below their respective original baselines, reflecting the inherent privacy–utility trade-off.

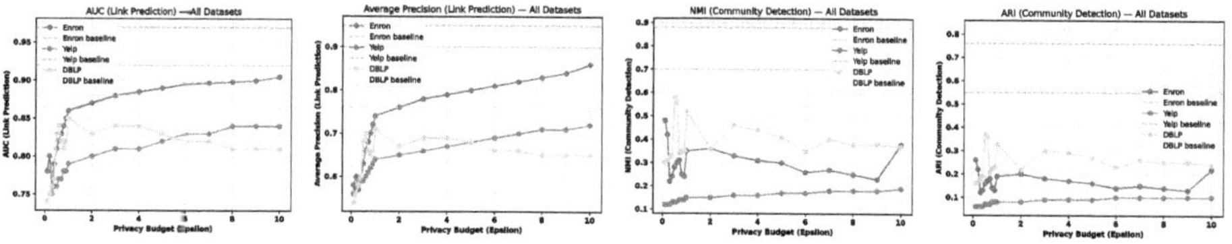

(a) AUC (b) AP (c) NMI (d) ARI

Fig. 3. Link prediction and community detection performance across datasets and privacy budgets.

Comparison to State-of-the-Art. We compare DHSG-LDP with LDPGen [13] and LDPGM [20], the closest LDP graph synthesis methods. PrivGraph [19] is not included in the quantitative comparison because it assumes centralised graph access. The comparison is limited to Enron and to the metrics reported by prior work. LDPGen obtains lower modularity and clustering errors, while DHSG-LDP obtains a lower reported degree-distribution error than LDPGM and supports heterogeneous ego graphs with local text-derived compatibility signals. For instance, for $\varepsilon \in [1, 10]$, DHSG-LDP achieves approximately 17% modularity error, 16% clustering error, and 0.016 L1 degree error on Enron (Tables 4 and 5).

Table 4. Comparison of DHSG-LDP, LDPGen, and LDPGM on Enron

Method	Privacy Budget (ε)	Metric	Performance
DHSG-LDP	$1.0 \leq \varepsilon \leq 10.0$	Modularity	Relative error: ~17%
		Clustering coefficient	Relative error: ~16%
		Degree distribution	L1 error: ~0.016
LDPGen	$2 \leq \varepsilon \leq 7$	Modularity	Relative error: 9–14%
		Clustering coefficient	Relative error: 8–12%
LDPGM	$1 \leq \varepsilon \leq 6$	Clustering coefficient	Relative error: 40–60%
		Degree distribution	L1 error: ~0.038

DHSG-LDP is slower than LDPGen on Enron, mainly due to heterogeneous feature construction and EM-based ego-graph selection. For DBLP and Yelp, only DHSG-LDP runtimes are reported because comparable values for LDPGen and LDPGM were not available under the same setting.

8 Proofs of ELDP and Privacy Budget Allocation

We show that DHSG-LDP satisfies ε-ELDP under the neighbouring relation defined in Sect. 2, and we justify the privacy budget allocation across phases.

Table 5. Runtime comparison (seconds)

Dataset	LDPGen	LDPGM	DHSG-LDP
Enron	61.41	Not reported	79.57
DBLP	Not reported	Not reported	118.06
Yelp	Not reported	Not reported	138.41

Neighbouring Relation (ELDP Adjacency). Fix a user u_i. Two feasible ego graphs $g_{u_i}, g'_{u_i} \in \mathcal{D}_{\text{ego}}$ are neighbouring, denoted $g_{u_i} \sim g'_{u_i}$, if they differ by the presence or absence of exactly one edge incident to the ego node u_i (either a user–user or user–text edge). This is the adjacency relation used throughout the analysis.

Released Information. DHSG-LDP releases (i) noised similarity scores $\widetilde{\text{avgSim}}_{u_i}$ (Phase 2) and (ii) a selected ego–alter *user–user* edge set encoded in $\tilde{g}_{u_i}$ (Phase 3). User–text edges and raw text features remain local and are never transmitted. Restricting the output to user–user edges can only reduce leakage by the post-processing property of differential privacy.

8.1 Phase 2: Similarity Reporting via the Laplace Mechanism

Each user computes a similarity statistic avgSim_{u_i} from the local ego graph and reports $\widetilde{\text{avgSim}}_{u_i} = \text{avgSim}_{u_i} + \text{Lap}\left(\frac{\Delta\text{Sim}}{\varepsilon_1}\right)$, followed by clipping to $[0, 1]$.

Lemma 2 (Sensitivity of the similarity statistic). *Let $f(g_{u_i}) = avgSim_{u_i}$. Then $f(g_{u_i}) \in [0, 1]$ for all feasible inputs, and under ELDP adjacency*

$$\Delta Sim = \max_{g_{u_i} \sim g'_{u_i}} |f(g_{u_i}) - f(g'_{u_i})| \leq 1.$$

Proof The statistic is an average of cosine similarities in $[0, 1]$, or 0 when the ego has no neighbours. Hence $f(g_{u_i}) \in [0, 1]$, implying $|f(g_{u_i}) - f(g'_{u_i})| \leq 1$ for any neighbouring pair.

Theorem 1 (Phase 2 satisfies ε_1-ELDP). *For each user u_i, the clipped Laplace mechanism*

$$\mathcal{M}^{(2)}_{u_i}(g_{u_i}) = \text{clip}\left(avgSim_{u_i} + \text{Lap}\left(\frac{\Delta Sim}{\varepsilon_1}\right), 0, 1\right)$$

satisfies ε_1-ELDP under ELDP adjacency.

This follows from Lemma 2 and the standard Laplace mechanism guarantee [2]. Clipping is deterministic post-processing and does not affect privacy.

8.2 Phase 3: Ego-Graph Selection via the Exponential Mechanism

User u_i privately selects a perturbed ego graph using the EM. The mechanism operates over the fixed finite output space $\mathcal{Y}_{u_i}$ of feasible noised ego graphs, defined by public feasibility constraints such as type compatibility, the eligible alter set, and the bound $D_{\max}$. The private input g_{u_i} affects only the utility values $U(g_{u_i}, y)$, not the output space.

Utility Sensitivity. Assume a bounded ego degree $|\mathcal{N}_{\text{user}}(u_i)| \le D_{\max}$. Edge-level utility terms are bounded by a constant C_u, and each selected ego graph has at most $D_{\max}$ user–user edges. Hence the edge-level component of U is bounded in $[0, D_{\max}C_u]$. Since the structural consistency term is bounded by 1, we obtain

$$\Delta \mathrm{U} = \max_{g_{u_i} \sim g'_{u_i}} \max_{y \in \mathcal{Y}_{u_i}} |U(g_{u_i}, y) - U(g'_{u_i}, y)| \le 2D_{\max}C_u + 1.$$

Theorem 2 (Phase 3 satisfies ε_2-ELDP). *Let $\mathcal{M}^{(3)}_{u_i}$ select $y \in \mathcal{Y}_{u_i}$ with probability*

$$\Pr[\mathcal{M}^{(3)}_{u_i}(g_{u_i}) = y] = \frac{\exp\left(\frac{\varepsilon_2}{2\Delta U} U(g_{u_i}, y)\right)}{\sum_{z \in \mathcal{Y}_{u_i}} \exp\left(\frac{\varepsilon_2}{2\Delta U} U(g_{u_i}, z)\right)}.$$

Then $\mathcal{M}^{(3)}_{u_i}$ satisfies ε_2-ELDP.

This follows from the standard EM guarantee [10] with sensitivity ΔU.

Lemma 3 (No edge replication via mutual neighbours). *For any user–user edge (u_i, u_j) and any third user $u_k \notin \{u_i, u_j\}$, the output of DHSG-LDP for u_k is independent of the presence or absence of (u_i, u_j).*

Proof The ego graph g_{u_k} contains only edges incident to u_k. Since (u_i, u_j) is not incident to u_k, it does not appear in g_{u_k} and cannot influence similarity computation or candidate utilities. Hence it cannot affect $\tilde{g}_{u_k}$.

8.3 Overall Privacy Guarantee

Theorem 3 (Per-user guarantee). *One execution of Phase 2 and Phase 3 satisfies $(\varepsilon_1 + \varepsilon_2)$-ELDP for each user.*

Proof Both mechanisms operate on the same underlying ego graph g_{u_i}: Phase 2 releases a differentially private function of g_{u_i}, and Phase 3 takes g_{u_i} as direct input. Phase 2 satisfies ε_1-ELDP by Theorem 1, and Phase 3 satisfies ε_2-ELDP by Theorem 2. Sequential composition therefore yields $(\varepsilon_1 + \varepsilon_2)$-ELDP [6].

Curator-Side Synthesis. The curator receives only $\{\widetilde{\text{avgSim}}_{u_i}\}$ and $\{\tilde{g}_{u_i}\}$. All reconstruction and redistribution steps use only these differentially private outputs and therefore incur no additional privacy loss by post-processing.

Repeated participation If user u_i participates in r_i reporting rounds,

$$\varepsilon_{\text{total},i} = r_i(\varepsilon_1 + \varepsilon_2).$$

Choosing $\varepsilon_1 + \varepsilon_2 = \varepsilon / r_{\max}$ with $r_{\max} = \max_i r_i$ ensures $\varepsilon_{\text{total},i} \leq \varepsilon$.

Edge-Level Composition. By Lemma 3, a user–user edge (u_i, u_j) affects at most the two reports of u_i and u_j. The edge-level privacy loss per execution is therefore bounded by $2(\varepsilon_1 + \varepsilon_2)$.

Summary. Phase 2 protects semantic information via the Laplace mechanism with budget ε_1, while Phase 3 protects structural edge decisions via the EM with budget ε_2. Curator-side synthesis is post-processing and incurs no additional privacy cost. The overall guarantee is $(\varepsilon_1 + \varepsilon_2)$-ELDP per user per execution and $2(\varepsilon_1 + \varepsilon_2)$-ELDP at the edge level. User–text edges remain local and are protected under ε_1-ELDP.

9 Limitations and Future Directions

Limitations. Our evaluation considers undirected, unweighted graphs under an ELDP adjacency that varies a single ego–alter edge in an honest-but-curious curator model. The framework does not address collusion, auxiliary side information beyond the stated threat model, or side-channel attacks. We evaluate two downstream tasks, i.e., link prediction and community detection, using temporal splits. Privacy accounting follows standard sequential composition; budget allocation and reporting frequency are configurable but not optimised.

Future Directions. The framework can be extended to dynamic, weighted, or directed graphs with corresponding ELDP analyses [4,16]. Structural protection could be complemented with attribute-level perturbation [20]. Broader evaluations across tasks such as recommendation, anomaly detection, influence modelling, and fairness-aware analysis would further assess applicability. Integration with privacy-enhancing infrastructures (e.g., secure aggregation or trusted execution environments) may reduce curator visibility while remaining complementary to local privacy guarantees. Long-term deployments also motivate adaptive privacy budgeting and policy-driven privacy management.

10 Conclusion

We introduced DHSG-LDP, a decentralised framework for synthesising privacy-preserving heterogeneous social graphs while preserving *socio-connective diversity*, combining Laplace-based semantic perturbation [2] with private ego-graph selection via the EM [10] under ELDP. Experiments on three real-world datasets show competitive performance for link prediction and community detection at moderate privacy levels. Privacy composition is formally bounded per user and at the edge level, with curator-side reconstruction incurring no additional privacy cost as pure post-processing. DHSG-LDP provides a practical foundation for privacy-preserving graph synthesis in decentralised environments.

Acknowledgments. This research was funded in whole by the Luxembourg National Research Fund (FNR), grant reference C21/IS/16281848/HETERS.

Ethics and open science. This study uses only publicly available datasets and involves no human subjects, private data collection, or re-identification attempts. Code and datasets are publicly available: Code: https://github.com/anonymous-main-user/synthetic-graphs; Enron: https://www.cs.cmu.edu/enron/; DBLP: https://dblp.org/; Yelp: https://www.yelp.com/dataset.

Disclosure of Interests. The authors have no competing interests to declare that are relevant to the content of this article.

References

1. Deep Graph Library (DGL): Yelp Dataset (2021). https://docs.dgl.ai/en/latest/api/python/dgl.data.YelpDataset.html. Accessed 2025-03-08
2. Dwork, C., Roth, A.: The algorithmic foundations of differential privacy. Found. Trends Theoret. Comput. Sci. **9**(3–4), 211–407 (2014)
3. Gretton, A., Borgwardt, K.M., Rasch, M.J., Schölkopf, B., Smola, A.: A kernel two-sample test. J. Mach. Learn. Res. **13**(25), 723–773 (2012)
4. Hou, L., Ni, W., Zhang, S., Fu, N., Zhang, D.: Ppdu: dynamic graph publication with local differential privacy. Knowl. Inf. Syst. **65**(7), 2965–2989 (2023)
5. Karimi, F., Génois, M., Wagner, C., Singer, P., Strohmaier, M.: Homophily influences ranking of minorities in social networks. Sci. Rep. **8**(1), 11077 (2018)
6. Kasiviswanathan, S.P., Lee, H.K., Nissim, K., Raskhodnikova, S., Smith, A.: What can we learn privately? SIAM J. Comput. **40**(3), 793–826 (2011)
7. Leskovec, J., Chakrabarti, D., Kleinberg, J., Faloutsos, C., Ghahramani, Z.: Kronecker graphs: an approach to modeling networks. J. Mach. Learn. Res. **11**(2) (2010)
8. Lichtenwalter, R.N., Lussier, J.T., Chawla, N.V.: New perspectives and methods in link prediction. In: Proceedings of the 16th ACM SIGKDD International Conference on Knowledge Discovery and Data Mining, pp. 243–252 (2010)
9. McPherson, M., Smith-Lovin, L., Cook, J.M.: Birds of a feather: homophily in social networks. Ann. Rev. Sociol. **27**, 415–444 (2001)
10. McSherry, F., Talwar, K.: Mechanism design via differential privacy. In: 48th IEEE Symposium on Foundations of Computer Science (FOCS), pp. 94–103 (2007)
11. Newman, M.E.J.: Fast algorithm for detecting community structure in networks. Phys. Rev. E **69**(6), 066133 (2004)
12. Newman, M.: Networks: An Introduction. Oxford University Press (03 2010). https://doi.org/10.1093/acprof:oso/9780199206650.001.0001, https://doi.org/10.1093/acprof:oso/9780199206650.001.0001
13. Qin, Z., Yu, T., Yang, Y., Khalil, I., Xiao, X., Ren, K.: Generating synthetic decentralized social graphs with local differential privacy. In: ACM SIGSAC Conference on Computer and Communications Security (CCS), pp. 425–438 (2017)
14. Villani, C.: Optimal Transport: Old and New, vol. 338. Springer (2009)

15. Wang, X., Bo, D., Shi, C., Fan, S., Ye, Y., Yu, P.S.: A survey on heterogeneous graph embedding: methods, techniques, applications and sources. IEEE Trans. Big Data **9**(2), 415–436 (2022)
16. Xu, W., Li, Z., Liu, H., Gao, Y., Liao, X., Li, K.: Differentially private weighted graphs publication under continuous monitoring. IEEE Trans. Mob. Comput. (2024)
17. Xu, W., Qiao, P., Liu, S., Zheng, Z., Cao, Y., Li, Z.: Continuous publication of weighted graphs with local differential privacy. Proc. VLDB Endowment **18**(11), 4214–4226 (2025)
18. Yang, J., Leskovec, J.: Defining and evaluating network communities based on ground-truth. Knowl. Inf. Syst. **42**(1), 181–213 (2015)
19. Yuan, Q., Zhang, Z., Du, L., Chen, M., Cheng, P., Sun, M.: {PrivGraph}: Differentially private graph data publication by exploiting community information. In: 32nd USENIX Security Symposium (USENIX Security 23), pp. 3241–3258 (2023)
20. Zhang, Y., Wei, J., Zhang, X., Hu, X., Liu, W.: A two-phase algorithm for generating synthetic graph under local differential privacy. In: International Conference on Communication and Network Security, pp. 84–89 (2018)
21. Zyskind, G., Nathan, O.: Decentralizing privacy: Using blockchain to protect personal data. In: IEEE security and privacy workshops, pp. 180–184. IEEE (2015)

A Robust and Privacy Preserving Crowd Monitoring Framework: Short Paper

Raphael Ritz, Marc Damie, Thijs van Ede, and Fatemeh Marzani(✉)

University of Twente, Enschede, The Netherlands
r.ritz@student.utwente.nl, {m.f.d.damie,t.s.vanede,f.marzani}@utwente.nl

Abstract. A key aspect of crowd monitoring is quantifying crowd size. While determining the size of a crowd in a single location at a specific moment is straightforward, measuring crowd flow across locations or over extended periods requires estimating the intersection of unique individuals observed at different points in space or time. In this work, we look at the re-identification of facial data, which inherently poses significant privacy risks. We propose a privacy-preserving framework for crowd flow estimation providing both robustness against variations in images captured at different cameras (using LSH) and privacy protection to ensure biometric data is not visible outside the camera (using garbled circuits). Facial embeddings are first transformed into binary representations (LSH), ensuring that embeddings belonging to the same individual (intra-class) have low Hamming distances, while embeddings from different individuals (inter-class) are well separated. This design enables robust matching in the presence of biometric noise. To compute the crowd flow, we compare the hashes using garbled circuits, allowing collaborating camera nodes to jointly estimate crowd flow without revealing raw facial data or intermediate representations. Experimental results show that a 128-bit configuration achieves an average F1-score of 96.18% with an amortized execution time of 10.21 ms per comparison, demonstrating the practicality of the proposed approach for privacy-compliant crowd monitoring.

Keywords: Crowd monitoring · Biometric privacy · Garbled Circuits · Multiparty Computation · Locality-Sensitive Hashing · Privacy By Design

1 Introduction

Automated crowd monitoring systems play an important role in smart cities, supporting applications such as urban planning, public safety, and large-scale event management by quantifying human movement patterns. Two fundamental tasks are commonly distinguished in this domain: *footfall* and *crowd flow*. Footfall refers to counting the number of individuals observed at a single location within a given time window. Crowd flow measures how many individuals move between different locations over time [21].

S. Nadjm-Tehrani et al. (Eds.): ARES 2026, LNCS 16898, pp. 49–60, 2027.
https://doi.org/10.1007/978-3-032-36874-4_3

While such operations are valuable in practice, crowd monitoring raises privacy concerns because access to raw observation data (e.g., camera footage) can enable mass surveillance. To address these concerns, several works have proposed privacy-preserving solutions that enable these measurement tasks without revealing raw observation data to a central party. The level of privacy risk depends strongly on the task. Footfall estimation is less privacy-sensitive because it can be computed directly from local observations. In contrast, crowd-flow estimation is inherently more privacy-sensitive because it requires linking observations made at different locations or times. This linking step introduces significant privacy risks since it enables tracking individuals across space and time.

Related Work. For *footfall* estimation, existing solutions mainly rely on camera data processed locally. Chan et al. [4] estimate crowd density using visual features without explicit tracking and report only footfall statistics. Similarly, edge-based systems such as CaCTUs [2] process visual data directly on the camera, discard raw frames, and export only aggregate statistics.

For *crowd-flow* estimation, two main approaches have emerged in the literature: re-identification and Private Set Intersection (PSI).

Camera-based re-identification techniques estimate crowd flow by matching individuals across multiple camera views. Mazzon et al. [15] and Narayan et al. [16] show that high-dimensional facial embeddings enable reliable cross-camera matching. However, these approaches rely on storing and comparing biometric representations, which raises important privacy concerns. Facial embeddings have been shown to be partially invertible, enabling reconstruction of facial images or inference of sensitive attributes [12]. This property complicates compliance with privacy regulations such as the GDPR.

Several recent solutions [13,14,18] instead rely on a cryptographic protocol called Private Set Intersection (PSI) [8]. PSI enables two parties to compute the intersection, or only its size, of two private sets without revealing the individual sets. In crowd-flow estimation, PSI is used to compute the intersection size of two sets of biometric identifiers without revealing the identifiers themselves. The size of the intersection between two cameras corresponds to the crowd flow. Stanciu et al. [18] build a PSI protocol based on homomorphic encryption and Bloom filters to compare facial embeddings. Marzani et al. [13] enhance privacy in sparsely populated regions through controlled uncertainty using sampling, and later introduce formal differential privacy guarantees in [14]. However, these solutions rely on exact matching of stable identifiers and therefore cannot support inherently noisy data sources such as facial embeddings (Table 1).

Gap in the Literature. While existing footfall estimation systems provide accurate and privacy-preserving solutions, current approaches for crowd-flow estimation still present major limitations.

Camera-based solutions [15,16] provide no privacy guarantees because they require exchanging facial embeddings from which private information can be extracted [12]. Hence, these approaches cannot be considered privacy-preserving.

PSI-based solutions provide strong privacy guarantees but rely on exact matching of biometric information. Biometric data is inherently noisy because

Table 1. Comparison of crowd monitoring systems.

Work	Task	Privacy-Preserving	Robust to Biometric Noise
Chan et al. [4]	Footfall	✔	✔
CaCTUs [2]	Footfall	✔	✔
Stanciu et al. [18]	Both	✔	✘
Marzani et al. [13,14]	Both	✔	✘
Camera Re-ID [15,16]	Both	✘	✔
This work	**Crowd-flow**	✔	✔

a face can be captured from different positions or under different lighting conditions. As a result, the extracted representations can vary between locations and time windows. Exact matching therefore leads to many false negatives and biases the estimation toward lower values. Consequently, these solutions lack robustness to biometric noise.

In summary, there is currently no crowd-flow estimation framework that provides both strong privacy guarantees and robustness to biometric noise.

Our Contributions. We introduce a crowd monitoring framework that estimates the crowd flow between two cameras in a privacy-preserving and robust manner. Our solution combines facial vector embeddings, locality-sensitive hashing (LSH), and garbled circuits (GCs). LSH is a hashing technique that is insensitive to small variations in the input. We use this property to ensure robustness to biometric noise. GCs are a cryptographic protocol that enables two parties to evaluate a function without revealing their private inputs. We use GCs to compare the hashes produced by two cameras without revealing the hashes themselves. The GC evaluation directly outputs the number of matching hashes, which corresponds to the crowd-flow estimation. The protocol ensures that no information about biometric data is revealed beyond the crowd-flow statistic in the semi-honest adversarial model.

To demonstrate the practicality of our approach, we implement[1] our protocol using the MPC4J framework and evaluate it on the FERET Color and SCFace datasets [10,17]. Our experiments reach an average F1-score of 96.18% for 128-bit hashes and an amortized execution time of 10.21 ms per comparison.

[1] The implementation of the proposed system is publicly available at: https://github.com/utwente-scs/FPSI-for-crowd-monitoring.

2 Our Crowd Monitoring Framework

System Presentation. In crowd flow monitoring, cameras are deployed at different locations, and the objective is to measure the flow of individuals between two locations. This requires comparing the images captured by two cameras in order to identify individuals observed at both sites. As in previous work [13,18], our solution relies on a two-party protocol that enables two cameras to measure the flow between their respective locations without relying on an external party. This protocol can be executed in a peer-to-peer manner between each pair of locations. The output of the two-party protocol, namely the flow measurement, can then be transmitted to a client that centralizes these statistics. With this peer-to-peer design, the images captured by the cameras never leave the devices.

Threat Model. Our two-party protocol involves two camera nodes C_A and C_B, that observe disjoint locations. We assume a semi-honest adversarial model in which both cameras follow the protocol but may attempt to infer *passively* additional information about the other party's data from the exchanged messages. We make two additional assumptions that are standard in this setting. First, a secure communication channel exists between the nodes, which can for instance be instantiated using TLS. Second, the parties do not collude, meaning that they are not simultaneously corrupted. If both parties were corrupted, no secure protocol could protect their data, since corruption already reveals the data to the adversary.

Solution Overview. Our framework consists of three main steps. First, each camera extracts biometric data from the raw image frames. This step outputs vector embeddings that encode the facial or biometric features of each individual observed at the location. Second, each camera applies locality-sensitive hashing (LSH) to transform each vector embedding into a compact binary hash. LSH is a class of hashing functions designed to preserve similarity, meaning that small variations in the input result in similar hash values. This property provides robustness to noise in the captured images. Third, the two cameras jointly execute a cryptographic protocol to compute the Hamming distance between their hashes without revealing the hashes themselves. For this purpose, we rely on Garbled Circuits (GC), a standard framework for such secure computations. Figure 1 illustrates the overall protocol. The following paragraphs describe each step in more detail.

Facial Data Embedding. This step is straightforward, as it relies on existing tools for face detection and facial embedding extraction. In our implementation, faces are detected using VOLO [20], and embeddings are computed using a ResNet-50 model pre-trained on VGGFace2 [3]. These components are modular and can be replaced with alternative detection or embeddings, provided that the resulting embeddings are high-dimensional real-valued vectors.

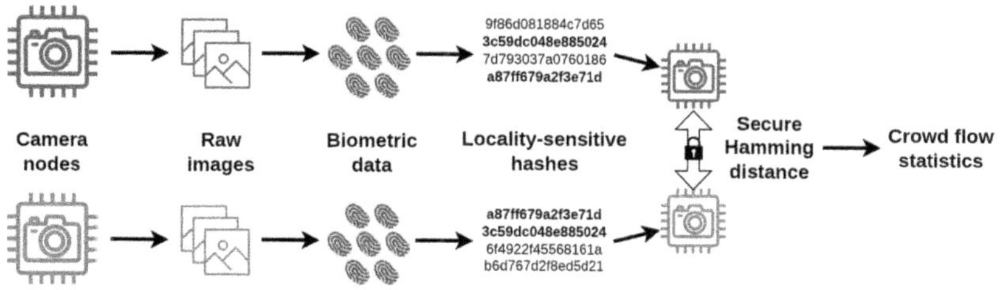

Fig. 1. High-level overview of our framework

Hashing. Facial embeddings exhibit two main limitations. First, they are high-dimensional real-valued vectors, which makes storage and pairwise comparison costly in large-scale deployments where cameras may observe thousands of individuals. Second, their real-valued structure is not well suited for most secure computation protocols, which are typically designed for binary or finite-field inputs. For this reason, directly processing real-valued embeddings within cryptographic protocols is inefficient.

To address this issue, prior work such as [18] has relied on classical hashing to obtain compact binary representations that are easy to store and compatible with secure computation. However, standard cryptographic hash functions are highly sensitive to input variations. Even a small perturbation in the facial embedding produces a completely different hash value. As a consequence, two embeddings corresponding to the same individual may be mapped to unrelated hashes, leading to false mismatches.

To achieve robustness to biometric noise, we instead rely on LSH, designed so that similar inputs are likely to produce similar hash values. More specifically, we use the scheme proposed by [5]. In this construction, each embedding is projected onto k random hyperplanes, and one bit is assigned per projection according to the sign of the dot product, that is $h_i(\mathbf{x}) = 1$ if $\mathbf{x} \cdot r_i \geq 0$, and 0 otherwise. Charikar et al. [5] show that the expected Hamming distance between two hashes is proportional to the angular distance between the corresponding embeddings. Consequently, embeddings of the same individual are likely to lie on the same side of most hyperplanes, resulting in a small Hamming distance between their binary representations. We therefore define a similarity threshold δ such that two hashes are considered to correspond to the same individual if their Hamming distance is at most δ, and to different individuals otherwise.

Secure Hamming Distance. Binary hashes are less privacy-sensitive than raw images or facial embeddings. However, an adversary may still infer private information from these hashes, in particular with LSH. To provide stronger privacy guarantees, the Hamming distance should therefore be computed using a cryptographic protocol that keeps the hashes secret and reveals only the output, namely the number of matching elements between the two sets.

To enable such secure computations between multiple parties, the cryptographic literature has developed protocols known as multi-party computations

(MPC). Among the many existing MPC constructions, we rely on one of the most established approaches: GC [19].

GC is a cryptographic protocol that enables two parties to evaluate a function $f(x_A, x_B)$ on their respective private inputs x_A and x_B. At the end of the protocol execution, only the output $f(x_A, x_B)$ is revealed, while x_A and x_B remain secret. Any function that can be expressed as a Boolean or arithmetic circuit can be evaluated using GC. In the protocol, one party acts as the garbler and the other as the evaluator. The garbler constructs a garbled version of the circuit corresponding to f and encoding its input x_A. The garbled circuit is then transmitted to the evaluator. To obtain the encoded input corresponding to x_B, the parties execute an Oblivious Transfer protocol. The evaluator can then evaluate the garbled circuit and obtain an encoded output. Finally, the parties combine their information to recover the value of $f(x_A, x_B)$. This paragraph provides only a brief GC overview and we refer the reader to [19] for a detailed description.

Complete Circuit. In our framework, each camera owns a set of hashes, so our GC implements a more complex function able to batch process sets of hashes. The function f takes as input two sets of k-bit hashes and outputs the number of elements from one set that have at least one match within Hamming distance δ in the other set. The hashes of one set are encoded as packed bit vectors and compared simultaneously against the elements of the other set, allowing many Hamming-distance computations to be performed in parallel within the circuit. The underlying circuit is composed of XOR gates, comparisons with the threshold δ, OR gates for per-element match accumulation, and an adder tree for the final match count. All these operations are easily supported by GC.

It is essential for privacy to reveal only the total number of matches and not the individual matches. Revealing individual matches would allow the cameras to know which individuals were present in both locations. Thus, the batch processing is necessary to preserve the expected privacy of the computation.

At the end of the GC evaluation, only the evaluator learns the number of similar hashes; the garbler learns nothing. This value corresponds to the crowd-flow estimate and can be transmitted to a client or a central database. The use of LSH ensures robustness to variations in image capture and feature extraction. Under the semi-honest adversarial model, GC ensures that no information about the hashes is revealed beyond the crowd-flow statistic.

Exactness of the Secure Computation. Note that our GC-based protocol implements the Hamming distance computation exactly. In other words, a plaintext (i.e., non-privacy-preserving) execution of the same Hamming distance computation would produce exactly the same output as our GC protocol. This property may appear trivial, but it is not always present in cryptographic protocols. Some privacy-preserving constructions approximate certain operations, which can lead to small differences compared to plaintext executions. In our case, the computation remains exact because LSH produces binary representations. This representation allows the Hamming distance to be computed exactly using Boolean operations supported by GC.

3 Evaluation

We evaluate the proposed framework in three aspects: (i) selection of the Hamming-distance threshold δ, (ii) accuracy of biometric matching, and (iii) computation and communication cost of the secure similarity protocol. The evaluation is performed on the FERET Color and SCFace datasets [10,17], where faces are detected using VOLO [20], and embedded using a ResNet-50 model.

In this experimental setup, we randomly assign images of 50 people to camera C_A and 50 people to camera C_B. To emulate cross-camera observations, embeddings of the same individual on different cameras are always selected from different camera angles, ensuring that identical embeddings never appear in both sets. Within the experiments, we vary the number of individuals appearing in both sets from 0 to 50, conducting 5 trials at each level (255 trials in total). The experimental pipeline consists of two stages: threshold selection followed by evaluation of the secure protocol implemented in Java using MPC4J.

Threshold Selection. To understand if two LSH hashes represent the same individual we compute the Hamming distance d_H between these representations and check if this distance is lower than a threshold, i.e., $d_H \leq \delta$. To determine δ, we split the FERET dataset into 20% for threshold selection and 80% for the remaining evaluation. Of this threshold selection dataset, we randomly sample two sets of 50 identities representing observations at C_A and C_B. The number of identities appearing in both sets defines the ground-truth intersection size $GT \in [0, 50]$. Facial embeddings are transformed into binary hashes using LSH with k random hyperplanes ($k = 64$ and $k = 128$). For each candidate threshold δ, we compare the detected matches with the ground-truth correspondences and compute the corresponding precision, recall, and F1-score. The experiment is repeated 100 times for each value of GT to obtain stable averages. Figure 2 reports the resulting mean precision, recall, and F1-score as a function of the threshold. The F1-score reaches its maximum at $\delta = 13$ for $k = 64$ and at $\delta = 28$ for $k = 128$. These values provide the best balance between precision and recall and are therefore selected for the subsequent experiments.

Secure Crowd-Flow Simulation. We simulate two camera nodes C_A and C_B observing different locations, each receiving a set of facial embeddings. The embeddings are transformed into binary hashes using LSH with $k = 64$ and $k = 128$ random hyperplanes. Two camera instances are created: C_A, responsible for constructing the garbled circuit, and C_B, responsible for executing it. The circuit computes pairwise Hamming distances and checks whether $d_H \leq \delta$. The output is the total number of matching embeddings observed at both C_A and C_B, thereby not leaking additional information. The estimated crowd-flow statistics is obtained by counting embeddings from C_A that have at least one match in C_B, counting multiple matches only once to avoid overestimation. Figure 3 shows the resulting matching performance (F1-score) as a function of the ground-truth

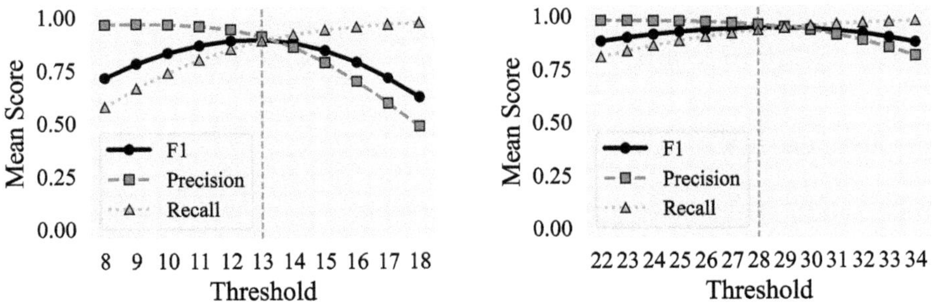

(a) $k = 64$ (b) $k = 128$

Fig. 2. Threshold selection for LSH with $k = 64$ and $k = 128$.

overlap for both datasets. Furthermore, Table 2 shows the average matching performance in terms of precision, recall and F1-score. Here we find that increasing the hash length from $k = 64$ to $k = 128$ consistently improves performance.

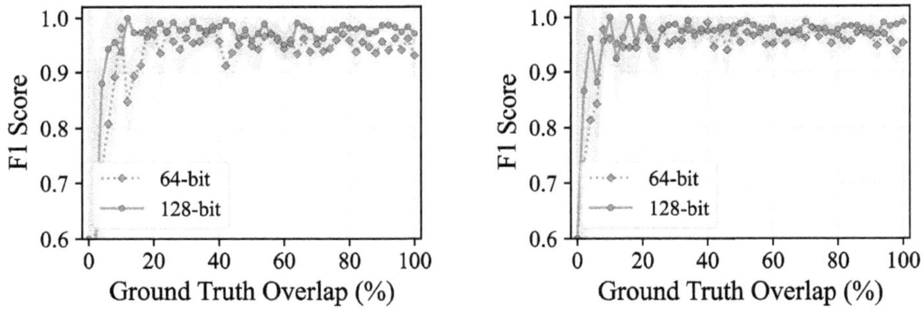

(a) SCFace dataset (b) FERET dataset

Fig. 3. Matching accuracy (F1-score) for $k = 64$ and $k = 128$ on SCFace and FERET.

Protocol Costs. Table 2 reports the average matching accuracy and protocol overhead. Computation time reflects the cost of generating and evaluating the garbled circuit, while communication time measures the data exchanged between the parties. The communication cost (KB) denotes the total amount of data transmitted per comparison.

As explained in Sect. 2, our GC processes two sets of hashes at a time. The cost of the overall protocol is therefore proportional to the sizes of the two sets. For clarity, we report amortized costs obtained by dividing the total protocol cost by the number of comparisons (i.e., pairs of hashes). These amortized values are easier to interpret and to extrapolate to real-world deployments.

Increasing the hash length improves accuracy but increases both computation and communication costs due to larger GCs.

Table 2. Average matching performance and protocol cost per comparison.

Dataset	k	Performance			Protocol Cost (ms)		
		Precision	Recall	F1	Computation	Communication	Total*
FERET	64	96.0%	94.8%	94.5%	2.06	2.90 (9.2KB)	5.00
	128	97.7%	96.6%	96.5%	4.17	5.91 (19.0KB)	10.12
SCFace	64	94.8%	92.4%	92.0%	2.09	2.92 (9.2KB)	5.06
	128	97.0%	96.0%	95.8%	4.26	5.99 (19.0KB)	10.29

*Total includes minor system and initialization overhead

4 Extensions

The experimental results presented in Sect. 3 show that our framework provides robustness and privacy while maintaining high efficiency. These findings indicate that the combination of LSH and garbled circuits (GC) is a promising direction for designing trustworthy crowd monitoring systems. To further advance this research direction, we identify three possible research directions.

Security against Malicious Parties. Our threat model assumes semi-honest parties, meaning that the cameras follow the prescribed protocol but may attempt to infer private information passively. This assumption is a common starting point in the secure computation literature. However, it naturally leads to a stronger security notion, namely security against malicious parties that may deviate arbitrarily from the protocol in order to reconstruct private input data.

Designing a variant of our framework that achieves malicious security is therefore a relevant direction for future work. Our GC construction relies only on basic arithmetic and Boolean operations, namely XOR, addition, and comparison. For such operations, the cryptographic literature already provides GC protocols with malicious security guarantees [11]. Extending our framework to the malicious setting would therefore require re-implementing the Hamming distance computation using recent improvements of Yao's GC that ensure security against malicious adversaries.

Enhancing the Output Privacy. Our framework ensures that the crowd monitoring process does not reveal information about the inputs. However, the monitoring output itself may still leak sensitive information. For example, if the matching procedure is executed between two cameras and one camera holds only a single image, a positive match would imply with certainty that a specific individual appeared at both locations. Since the objective of crowd monitoring is to estimate population flow rather than to track individuals, it is desirable to further mitigate such risks. A simple mitigation strategy is to allow matching between two cameras only if each holds a sufficiently large batch of observations. Enforcing a minimum batch size prevents the extreme scenario described above. In the presence of malicious adversaries, compliance with this requirement could be enforced using cryptographic mechanisms such as zero-knowledge proofs [9]. A more formal mitigation can be achieved using Differential Privacy (DP) [7]. This statistical framework requires adding calibrated noise to computation results in order to limit the influence of any single individual. More precisely, DP ensures that the distribution of the output remains statistically similar whether or not a specific (input) data point is included. Consequently, the presence of a particular individual cannot be reliably inferred from the released crowd flow statistics.

Three-Party Protocols. Our framework relies on garbled circuits to implement a two-party secure computation. However, the cryptographic literature shows that three-party protocols can achieve significantly lower communication and computation costs. For example, a vector dot product can be computed with $O(1)$ communication complexity in certain three-party protocols, whereas two-party constructions typically require $O(n)$ communication [6]. Introducing a third party in our secure Hamming distance protocol could therefore enable the use of more efficient constructions.

More generally, this observation indicates that exploring alternative threat models may lead to more efficient variants of our framework. Future work could also investigate cryptographic primitives such as (Fuzzy) Private Set Intersection [1] as an alternative to our secure Hamming distance protocol.

5 Conclusion

Crowd-flow estimation is important for many smart-city applications but raises significant privacy concerns because it requires linking observations of individuals across locations. In this work, we proposed a privacy-preserving framework that enables robust matching of detected faces without revealing sensitive information. Our approach combines locality-sensitive hashing with garbled circuits to support robust biometric matching while revealing only the final crowd-flow statistic. Experiments on the FERET and SCFace datasets show that the approach achieves high matching accuracy with practical performance. In particular, the 128-bit configuration reaches F1-scores above 96% while requiring only about 10 ms per comparison, demonstrating that privacy-preserving and efficient crowd-flow estimation can be achieved.

Acknowledgements. The authors have no competing interests to declare that are relevant to the content of this article. This work was supported by Netherlands National Science Foundation (NWO) through the PERSPECTIEF Program P21-08 'XCARCITY'

References

1. van Baarsen, A., Pu, S.: Fuzzy private set intersection with large hyperballs. In: Annual International Conference on the Theory and Applications of Cryptographic Techniques, pp. 340–369. Springer (2024)
2. Beugin, Y., et al.: Building a privacy-preserving smart camera system (Jan 2022). arXiv:2201.09338 [cs]
3. Cao, Q., Shen, L., Xie, W., Parkhi, O.M., Zisserman, A.: VGGFace2: a dataset for recognising faces across pose and age . In: 2018 13th IEEE International Conference on Automatic Face & Gesture Recognition (FG 2018), pp. 67–74. IEEE Computer Society, Los Alamitos (2018)
4. Chan, A.B., Liang, Z.S.J., Vasconcelos, N.: Privacy preserving crowd monitoring: counting people without people models or tracking. In: 2008 IEEE Conference on Computer Vision and Pattern Recognition, pp. 1–7 (Jun 2008), iSSN: 1063-6919
5. Charikar, M.S.: Similarity estimation techniques from rounding algorithms. In: Proceedings of the thirty-fourth annual ACM symposium on Theory of computing (STOC) (2002)
6. Damie, M., Hahn, F., Peter, A., Ramon, J.: Secure sparse matrix multiplications and their applications to privacy-preserving machine learning
7. Dwork, C.: Differential privacy. In: International Colloquium on Automata, Languages and Programming, pp. 1–12. Springer (2006)
8. Freedman, M.J., Nissim, K., Pinkas, B.: Efficient private matching and set intersection. In: Kanade, T., et al. (eds.) Advances in cryptology - EUROCRYPT 2004, vol. 3027, pp. 1–19. Springer, Heidelberg (2004)
9. Goldreich, O., Oren, Y.: Definitions and properties of zero-knowledge proof systems. J. Cryptol. **7**(1), 1–32 (1994)
10. Grgic, M., Delac, K., Grgic, S.: Scface - surveillance cameras face database. Multimed. Tools Appl. **51**(3), 863–879 (2011)
11. Lindell, Y., Pinkas, B.: Secure two-party computation via cut-and-choose oblivious transfer. J. Cryptol. **25**(4), 680–722 (2012)
12. Mai, G., Cao, K., Yuen, P.C., Jain, A.K.: On the reconstruction of face images from deep face embeddings. In: IEEE Trans. Pattern Anal. Mach. Intell. (T-PAMI) (2019)
13. Marzani, F., van Ede, T., Heijenk, G., van Steen, M.: Stop watching me! moving from data protection to privacy preservation in crowd monitoring. In: Dalla Preda, M., Schrittwieser, S., Naessens, V., De Sutter, B. (eds.) Availability, Reliability and Security, pp. 46–67. Springer Nature Switzerland, Cham (2025)
14. Marzani, F., van Ede, T., Heijenk, G., van Steen, M.: Differentially private crowd monitoring over encrypted bloom filters. In: Proceedings of the 41st ACM/SIGAPP Symposium on Applied Computing (SAC '26), pp. 1–8. Association for Computing Machinery (2026)
15. Mazzon, R., Tahir, S.F., Cavallaro, A.: Person re-identification in crowd. Pattern Recogn. Lett. **33**(14), 1828–1837 (2012)
16. Narayan, N., Sankaran, N., Setlur, S., Govindaraju, V.: Re-identification for online person tracking by modeling space-time continuum. In: IEEE/CVF Conference on Computer Vision and Pattern Recognition Workshops (CVPRW), pp. 1519–151909. IEEE, Salt Lake City, UT, USA (2018)
17. Phillips, P., Moon, H., Rizvi, S., Rauss, P.: The feret evaluation methodology for face-recognition algorithms. IEEE Trans. Pattern Anal. Mach. Intell. **22**(10), 1090–1104 (2000)

18. Stanciu, V.D., Steen, M.v., Dobre, C., Peter, A.: Privacy-preserving crowd-monitoring using bloom filters and homomorphic encryption. In: Proceedings of the 4th International Workshop on Edge Systems, Analytics and Networking, EdgeSys '21, pp. 37–42. Association for Computing Machinery, New York, April 2021
19. Yao, A.C.C.: How to generate and exchange secrets. In: 27th Annual Symposium on Foundations of Computer Science (sfcs 1986), pp. 162–167 (1986)
20. Yuan, L., Hou, Q., Jiang, Z., Feng, J., Yan, S.: Volo: Vision outlooker for visual recognition. IEEE Trans. Pattern Anal. Mach. Intell. **45**(5), 6575–6586 (2023)
21. Zhan, B., Monekosso, D.N., Remagnino, P., Velastin, S.A., Xu, L.Q.: Crowd analysis: a survey. Mach. Vis. Appl. **19**(5–6), 345–357 (2008)

Privacy II

SPiRiT: Verifiable Contact Tracing for Balanced Security, Privacy, and Safety

Reyhaneh Rabaninejad[1(✉)], Azra Abtahi[2,3], Antonis Michalas[1], and Amir Aminifar[3]

[1] Tampere University, Tampere, Finland
rabaninejad@gmail.com, antonios.michalas@tuni.fi
[2] Malmö University, Malmö, Sweden
[3] Lund University, Lund, Sweden

Abstract. Digital contact tracing systems play a pivotal role in mitigating the spread of infectious diseases during pandemics by identifying individuals exposed to confirmed cases. In decentralized privacy-preserving contact tracing protocols, users broadcast pseudo-random IDs and, upon infection, upload the relevant IDs to a cloud server. Other users can then download these IDs to determine if they have been in proximity to infected individuals. However, existing protocols often lack verifiability, implicitly assuming honest user behavior when uploading data to the server. This gap creates vulnerabilities, including false positives and false negatives, which hinder the widespread adoption crucial for the effectiveness of contact tracing apps. This paper introduces SPiRiT, a secure and privacy-preserving verifiable contact tracing protocol, designed to address these shortcomings by introducing verifiability, ensuring the legitimacy of uploaded IDs, while still maintaining user privacy. Verifiability ensures whether an upload contains a valid set of pseudo-random IDs with respect to the contagious period of the infected individual, and that the individual claiming those IDs is the legitimate owner, in a privacy-preserving manner. The goal of our design is to maintain a balance between the competing objectives of privacy, security, and decentralization while fostering greater public trust and adoption by addressing the aforementioned vulnerabilities. Through rigorous evaluation using a face-to-face individual interaction dataset, we demonstrate that SPiRiT not only reduces false alarms but also can be on par with or even outperform existing protocols in detecting high-risk contacts.

Keywords: Digital Contact Tracing · False Alarm · Pandemic Risk Mitigation · Privacy · Security · Verifiability

1 Introduction

Digital contact tracing protocols serve the fundamental purpose of alerting individuals who have spent a significant time in close physical proximity to a confirmed case of a fast-spreading, highly-contagious pathogen. Notifications of

S. Nadjm-Tehrani et al. (Eds.): ARES 2026, LNCS 16898, pp. 63–87, 2027.
https://doi.org/10.1007/978-3-032-36874-4_4

this type alert us for potential exposure to the virus, prompting precautionary actions, such as testing or quarantine, as recommended by public health authorities. Confidentiality regarding the diagnosed individual's identity and the specifics of when and where the contact occurred is crucial in this process. In our smartphone-dominated society, individuals carry these devices throughout the day, presenting an opportunity for a mobile application to collect data on close physical interactions. This application could play a crucial role in tracing contacts potentially infected through the spread period of the pathogen. The app keeps track of contacts when personal smartphones are in close physical proximity for a predefined duration and distance. Utilizing proximity tracing, the app identifies individuals who should be notified of a potential high-risk exposure without disclosing specific details about the diagnosed person or the location of the contact [10].

A substantial body of research has explored proximity-based contact tracing, producing a diverse range of protocol designs and analysis (e.g. [6,7,9,14,25,32,35]). A cutting-edge protocol for contact tracing is the Decentralized Privacy-Preserving Proximity Tracing (DP-3T) [36,37], which also heavily influenced the Apple/Google-API (GAEN) developed for COVID-19 contact tracing [5]. In the DP-3T protocol, a user's digital device continuously transmits ephemeral pseudo-random IDs using Bluetooth Low Energy (BLE) while concurrently recording the pseudo-random IDs received from other users' devices in close proximity. When a user gets infected, they can disclose the pseudo-random IDs previously broadcasted by their device during the contagious period by uploading them to a central server. All user applications periodically download these pseudo-random IDs from the cloud. Subsequently, they cross-check these IDs against locally recorded IDs to identify high-risk contacts. Users with high-risk contacts receive an alert from the application, advising them to enter quarantine and undergo testing, facilitating prompt preventive measures.

Recent work [3] first introduces A/P DP-3T, an extended version of the DP-3T protocol. This protocol empowers users to control their privacy by enabling participation as either active or passive users, enhancing privacy and utility compared to previous work [36]. Specifically, passive users, embodying a more conservative approach, choose not to broadcast BLE beacons. Meanwhile, active participants continue to broadcast BLE beacons with pseudo-random IDs (employing the same mechanism as DP-3T). Passive participants do not broadcast BLE beacons but actively listen for broadcasted BLE beacons. Consequently, passive participants become aware of their potential exposure and can take appropriate action. Then, [3] introduces DP-ACT, where passive participants who become infected disclose their list of high-risk contacts based on the *received* pseudo-random IDs. Using this information, active participants can undergo home quarantine if their pseudo-random IDs are reported by passive participants. The authors emphasize that it is necessary to have at least one active participant in each contact group (defined as groups of users in close proximity for a considerable duration) in order to identify all high-risk contact groups with at least one infected participant.

However, there are some security risks associated with DP-ACT as also discussed in their paper [3]: *(I)* Malicious passive users possess the ability to actively manipulate the protocol by uploading IDs broadcasted by other active users, potentially leading to *false positive* outcomes. This vulnerability arises because passive users are granted the right to claim another's pseudo-random ID upon infection. This feature may be maliciously exploited to generate false positives. *(II)* An attacker, such as a malicious active user, has the capability to execute *flooding* and *replay* attacks by generating a substantial number of contact events, potentially overwhelming a user's phone memory, creating a vulnerability to trigger *false alerts*. Notably, this attack is also viable in DP-3T protocol [18,36]. It is crucial to recognize that these identified security shortcomings can also impact the system's utility. Users may find it challenging to trust the protocol's alerts, ultimately impeding widespread adoption by the public [4,13,27,30].

We argue that the root cause of false alert attacks lies in the inability to *verify* both *(I)* the legitimacy of an individual claiming a set of pseudo-random IDs, and *(II)* the validity of those IDs with respect to the contagious period. While some existing works partially address aspect *(I)*, as discussed below, there is– to the best of our knowledge– a surprising lack of solutions that fully address verifiability, encompassing both *(I)* and *(II)*.

Authorization in Prior Systems. Existing systems such as DP-3T [36] and its derivatives implement basic user authorization schemes to prevent arbitrary uploads. Typically, users are issued authorization codes alongside positive COVID-19 test results, which must be presented to upload their broadcasted pseudo-random IDs. While this ensures that only diagnosed users can upload data, it has two major limitations: *(a)* There is no cryptographic binding between the uploaded pseudo-random IDs and the persistent identities of the users. As a result, while authorized DP-3T [36] provides *user authorization*, it does not *verify the trace information* itself, leaving the system vulnerable to false alerts. *(b)* Moreover, such authorization mechanisms unfortunately introduce privacy risks by creating identifiable links between the meant-to-be-anonymous database of pseudo-random IDs and unique identities in public health registries. The approach proposed by Silde and Strand [34] addresses the latter issue and takes a step toward more private contact tracing by employing a direct extension of Privacy Pass tokens. In their design, the verification and backend services hold a master secret key k (in a designated verifier setting) and derive daily keys using a key derivation function: $\mathsf{KDF}(k, \mathsf{date})$. The corresponding public keys are published by the verification service. However, a fundamental limitation remains: there is no secret key associated with the users that can cryptographically bind the broadcasted pseudo-random IDs to the users. Consequently, issue *(a)* remains unresolved. Furthermore, the interactive nature of the design (user are required to obtain fresh keys and tokens from the verification service on a daily basis), the designated verifier setting, and the lack of support for threshold issuance, collectively lead to a more centralized architecture. The protocol also does not support passive users.

Given these observations in prior work, we ask the following question: "*Is it possible to develop an efficient contact tracing protocol that enables the verification of uploads, all while preserving user privacy?*"

Before presenting our contributions, it is crucial to clarify that in this paper, we solely focus on advocating for a cryptographic solution to the verifiable digital contact tracing problem, while electromagnetic side channels or BLE tracking mechanisms [23] are orthogonal to this work. Notably, there exist parallel advancements in the practical obfuscation of BLE tracking mechanisms [24], a topic beyond the scope of this paper.

1.1 Contributions

In this work, we aim to incorporate verifiability into digital contact tracing and propose a practical, secure, and privacy-preserving protocol grounded in well-established cryptographic assumptions. Our ultimate goal is to foster widespread acceptance by effectively addressing the notable concerns outlined above. Following we present our contributions:

Definitions. We formalize SPiRiT (**S**ecure and **Pri**vacy-Preserving Ve**Ri**fiable Contact **T**racing) (Sect. 3.1), where users perform a one-time registration to obtain a unique token under a privacy-preserving distributed trust model. The token enables users to broadcast unlinkable yet verifiable pseudo-random IDs. When diagnosed, a user submits the pseudo-random IDs generated during the contagious period to the Public Health Authority (PHA) together with an efficient zero-knowledge proof showing *(I)* that the IDs correspond to the contagious period and *(II)* legitimate ownership of those IDs. User devices periodically query the PHA for published IDs and check for matches with stored observations. From a privacy perspective, all stages–registration, ID broadcasting, and trace disclosure–must remain unlinkable to the user's identity and across broadcasts (unlinkability). From a security perspective, the system must prevent adversaries from producing valid proofs for IDs not derived from a registered key (upload integrity) and from rebroadcasting previously observed IDs (replay security).

Efficient Construction. We put forth an efficient construction of SPiRiT that realizes our formal model under standard cryptographic assumptions (Sect. 4). For token issuance during registration, we leverage Anonymous Counting Tokens (ACTs) [8] in a threshold setting (tACT) [1] (Sect. 2), enabling anonymous user registration and deduplication. Each user obtains a unique token that is stored together with a commitment to the user's key after verification against redeemed tokens. During verification, the PHA checks a zero-knowledge proof on the uploaded trace information using the ACT token and the committed key, ensuring legitimate ownership while mitigating false alerts. Our design is compatible with A/P DP-3T, allowing users to operate in active or passive modes depending on their privacy and security preferences. The system preserves decentralization while enabling zero-knowledge verification, balancing privacy, security, and deployability, mitigating the aforementioned vulnerabilities.

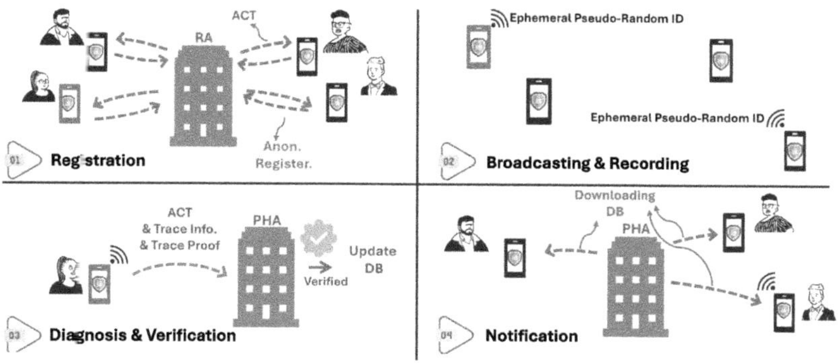

Fig. 1. SPiRiT system flow. ① Users partake in a one-time registration process to obtain a unique Anonymous Counting Token (ACT) from a committee of Registration Authorities (RAs) within a privacy-preserving and distributed trust framework. ② During the broadcast phase, active users generate ephemeral pseudo-random IDs tied to the user's registered key and the current epoch number, in an unlinkable and yet verifiable manner. ③ Upon a positive diagnosis, the infected active user generates trace information (pseudo-random IDs), along with a zero-knowledge proof which is used by Public Health Authority (PHA) to verify the validity of claimed IDs. The PHA runs the SPiRiT verification algorithm to confirm both the authenticity of the trace information with respect to the user's ACT and its validity with respect to the contagious period. These IDs are then stored in PHA database for efficient querying. If registered as passive, the user only listens for broadcasted IDs (Step 2) and does not upload trace data if infected (Step 3). ④ During the trace phase, user devices regularly check for updates in the server DB and alerts the user of any matches found within the locally stored database of pseudo-random IDs.

Evaluation. We evaluate SPiRiT using the face-to-face interaction InVS15 dataset [22] (Sect. 5) under two scenarios. First, we consider attackers who maliciously reveal IDs of non-infected users as those of infected individuals. SPiRiT prevents this attack and maintains a zero false-alarm rate, while existing protocols accumulate high false alarms over time. In addition, SPiRiT outperforms DP-3T and achieves performance comparable to A/P DP-3T in detecting high-risk contacts. Second, we study the case where diagnosed users withhold a fraction of their broadcasted IDs during the contagious period. While this behavior significantly degrades the performance of existing protocols, SPiRiT remains robust. Benchmark results from an unoptimized implementation show that user registration completes in approximately 2.6 s, and proof generation for trace verification takes about 173 ms on the slowest tested device. The implementation is publicly available at SPiRiT GitHub.

Figure 1 outlines a high-level architecture of the SPiRiT system, while Table 1 compares contact tracing protocols across key aspects.

Table 1. Comparison of contact tracing protocols across key aspects. $\mathbb{CP}$ and id_U denote contagious period and unique user identifier, respectively.

Aspect	DP-3T (2020) [36]	Slide & Strand (2022) [34]	A/P DP-3T & DP-ACT (2024) [3]	This Work
Verify User Legitimacy (I)	Full (authorization codes)	Full (tokens)	Not Addressed	Full (tokens)
w.r.t. $\mathbb{CP}$ Verify Uploads (II) w.r.t. id_U	Not Addressed	Not Addressed	Not Addressed	Full (cryptographic binding)
	Not Addressed	Not Addressed	Not Addressed	Full (cryptographic binding)
Preserve User Privacy	Partial (linkability issue)	Partial (improved)	Full (no formal proof provided)	Full (strong unlinkability, formal definition and rigorous proof)
Support Passive Users	Not Addressed	Not Addressed	Full	Full
Prevent False Alarms	Not Addressed	Not Addressed	Not Addressed (vulnerable)	Effectively Reduced (verified uploads)

1.2 Applications Beyond Contact Tracing

Our primary motivation stems from decentralized privacy-preserving contact tracing protocols such as DP-3T [36], and we believe that preparedness for future pandemics remains a critical global priority. However, our design approach extend to a broader set of applications where privacy, integrity, and decentralization are essential. These include:

- **Crowd density monitoring without tracking individuals' movements:** Users can anonymously broadcast ephemeral identifiers when present in a physical location (e.g., a café, public transport hub, or event venue), to contribute to aggregate crowd size estimations, enabling services like *Crowd Alerts* that inform users about how busy a place is *before* they head out—without revealing individual presence or movement patterns.
- **Secure check-in systems for events or shared spaces:** Powered by SPiRiT's verifiability feature, users can anonymously *prove* their presence in locations such as co-working spaces or libraries, enabling capacity management or access tracking without storing identifiable data.

2 Foundation of SPiRiT: Anonymous Counting Tokens

In the next lines, we revisit anonymous counting tokens (ACT) and review their security properties. ACT primitive recently introduced in [8] allows users to acquire tokens for private messages while enabling issuers or verifiers to enforce rate limits on the number of tokens obtained or redeemed per message. One of the basic challenges in ACT system design is balancing anonymity. This prevents mapping tokens to user identities, with the need to limit individual user contributions. Benhamouda et al. [8] propose two ACT constructions. The first uses PRF evaluation for token issuance with keyed verification. It is suitable when the issuer and verifier are the same entity. The second leverages equivalence class signatures (EQS) [20,21] to build an ACT scheme. These two approaches operate in a centralized setting, where a single issuer issues tokens for users. A recent proposal in this field [2] further enhances the action by operating in a distributed-trust environment and proposes a publicly verifiable threshold issuance ACT scheme. The proposed construction is also accompanied by full implementations demonstrating its practicality. To ensure trust among issuers and avoid single points of failure, we leverage the threshold ACT scheme referred to as tACT [1] in our final SPiRiT implementation. Nevertheless, it is important to mention that, any ACT scheme may serve as a building block in SPiRiT design allowing anonymous user deduplication during the registration phase.

Consider a private unique user attribute denoted as $\mathsf{id_U}$, such as social security number (SSN). ACT mainly aims at allowing users to obtain a deterministic high-entropy token corresponding to $\mathsf{id_U}$ and ensuring issuers remain oblivious to $\mathsf{id_U}$ (oblivious issuance). Furthermore, the token must be *anonymously* verifiable. This means that a public verifier can authenticate the token without learning anything about $\mathsf{id_U}$. In the following, we describe a high-level abstract interface of tACT algorithms. For technical details on concrete instantiations, we refer to [1].

Definition 1. (tACT). *A threshold anonymous counting token scheme consists of the following algorithms (public parameters* pp *are implicit inputs):*

- $(\mathsf{pp}, \{\mathsf{prv}_j\}_{j\in[1,N]}) \leftarrow \mathsf{Setup}(1^\lambda, t, N)$: *Generates system public parameters* pp *and issuer secret keys* prv_j *for* N *issuers with threshold* t.
- $(\mathsf{st_{Rg}}, \mathsf{cm}) \leftarrow \mathsf{Register}(\mathsf{id_U})$: *The user commits to identifier* $\mathsf{id_U}$ *by computing* $\mathsf{cm} = \mathsf{Commit}(\mathsf{id_U}; r)$ *and stores registration state* $\mathsf{st_{Rg}} = (\mathsf{id_U}, r)$.
- $(\mathsf{blindRequest}, \mathsf{rand_{id_U}}) \leftarrow \mathsf{TokenRequest}(\mathsf{st_{Rg}}, \mathsf{cm})$: *Generates a blinded token request and corresponding state information.*
- $\mathsf{blindToken}_j \leftarrow \mathsf{tIssue}(\mathsf{blindRequest}, \mathsf{prv}_j)$: *Issuer* I_j *produces a partial blind token.*
- $\mathsf{blindToken} \leftarrow \mathsf{Aggregate}(\{\mathsf{blindToken}_j\}_{j\in[t]})$: *The user combines* t *partial tokens into a blinded token.*
- $\mathsf{token} \leftarrow \mathsf{Unblind}(\mathsf{blindToken}, \mathsf{rand_{id_U}})$: *The user derives the final token embedding attribute* $\mathsf{id_U}$.
- $\pi \leftarrow \mathsf{Prove}(\mathsf{token}, \mathsf{aux}, \mathsf{rand_{id_U}})$: *Generates a proof of token validity.*
- $\{0, 1\} \leftarrow \mathsf{Verify}(\mathsf{token}, \pi, \mathsf{blindRequest})$: *Verifies the token with respect to the blinded request, outputting* 1 *if valid and* 0 *otherwise.*

This scheme provides: *(I)* Unforgeability (Theorem 2, [1]), *(II)* Unlinkability (Theorem 3, [1]), and *(III)* Threshold issuance. Loosely speaking, unforgeability ensures that an adversary controlling less than a threshold of issuers cannot create tokens for more attributes than requested, nor can it generate more than one token for a specific attribute per user. Unlinkability ensures that even issuers cannot link a user's token requests to the corresponding unblinded tokens.

3 Building a Verifiable Contact Tracing System

3.1 Definitions and Properties

Subsequently, we formalize a **S**ecure and **Pri**vacy-Preserving Ve**Ri**fiable Contact **T**racing (SPiRiT) system and provide a precise definition of its essential properties. SPiRiT consists of the following actors.

Registration Authorities. Registration authorities denoted as $\mathbb{I} = \{I_1, \ldots, I_N\}$, form a committee of N entities that run a distributed key generation protocol [31] to generate a secret key sk where party $j \in [1, N]$ receives the share sk_j of sk such that t shares of the secret reconstruct sk. These authorities attest to the binding between users U and their identifiers id_U and issue unique tokens to users who aim to join the system during registration process.

User. A user denoted as U, owns a private unique human-readable identifier, such as SSN, denoted as id_U. U interacts with registration authorities in a registration process to obtain a unique token within a privacy-preserving and distributed trust framework. This token empowers U, who wishes to be discoverable to other close-proximity SPiRiT users, to emit verifiable ephemeral pseudo-random IDs all while protecting U's privacy.

Public Health Authority. This authority denoted as PHA acts during the protocol's diagnostic and tracing phases. When a user is diagnosed with the virus, they are required to submit the pseudo-random IDs emitted from their device to the PHA, while contagious. Additionally, the infected individual is tasked with computing an efficient zero-knowledge proof that the PHA can use to verify (I) the authenticity of the pseudo-random IDs corresponding to the contagious period and, (II) verify the individual's legitimate ownership of those IDs. During tracing, each user's device periodically queries the PHA server for newly published pseudo-random IDs and alerts the user of any matches found within the locally stored database of pseudo-random IDs.

Definition 2. (SPiRiT). *A verifiable contact tracing scheme consists of the following algorithms (public parameters* pp *are implicit inputs):*

- $(\mathsf{pp}, \{\mathsf{prv}_j\}_{j\in[1,N]}) \leftarrow \mathsf{Setup}(1^\lambda, t, N)$: *Generates system public parameters* pp *and issuer secret keys* prv_j *for* N *issuers with threshold* t.
- $(\mathsf{pp}_\mathsf{U}, \mathsf{prv}_\mathsf{U}, \mathsf{T}_\mathsf{Rgstr}) \leftarrow \mathsf{Register}(\mathsf{id}_\mathsf{U}, \{\mathsf{prv}_j\}, \mathsf{T}_\mathsf{Rgstr})$: *Interactive protocol between user (with identifier* id_U*) and issuers. Outputs user parameters* $(\mathsf{pp}_\mathsf{U}, \mathsf{prv}_\mathsf{U})$*, where* pp_U *includes a* $tACT$ token*, and updates the registration table* $\mathsf{T}_\mathsf{Rgstr}$.
- $\mathsf{T}_\mathsf{eID} \leftarrow \mathsf{Broadcast}(i, \mathsf{prv}_\mathsf{U}, \mathsf{T}_\mathsf{eID})$: *At epoch* i*, the user derives an epoch-specific pseudo-random ID from* prv_U *and broadcasts it. Received beacons and exposure scores are stored locally in* T_eID*, which is periodically pruned.*
- $(\mathsf{pp}_\mathsf{U}, \mathsf{tr}, \pi_\mathsf{tr}) \leftarrow \mathsf{Diagnosis}(\mathsf{pp}_\mathsf{U}, \mathsf{prv}_\mathsf{U}, \mathbb{CP})$: *A diagnosed user generates trace information* tr *for contagious period* $\mathbb{CP}$ *and a zero-knowledge proof* π_tr *attesting to its authenticity.*
- $(\mathsf{db}, \mathsf{bit}) \leftarrow \mathsf{Verify}(\mathsf{tr}, \pi_\mathsf{tr}, \mathsf{pp}_\mathsf{U}, \mathsf{T}_\mathsf{Rgstr}, \mathbb{CP})$: *The* PHA *verifies token validity and proof* π_tr*, ensuring* tr *corresponds to* $\mathbb{CP}$ *and belongs to the user. If valid (*$\mathsf{bit} = 1$*),* tr *is added to backend database* db*; otherwise* $\perp$ *is returned.*
- $(\mathsf{intCnt}, \mathsf{alrmBit}) \leftarrow \mathsf{Trace}(\mathsf{db}, \mathsf{T}_\mathsf{eID})$: *The user device compares local records* T_eID *with backend database* db*. If matches exist (*$\mathsf{intCnt} > 0$*), it outputs* $\mathsf{alrmBit} = 1$ *to signal potential exposure.*

Security and Privacy Properties. SPiRiT presents the following core features. In terms of security, we require that an adversary should not be able to upload inauthentic trace information that does not embed a key registered by the presenting user (upload integrity). Furthermore, it must be infeasible for an adversarial user to rebroadcast pseudo-random IDs that were previously sent or received (replay security). The properties of correctness, upload integrity, and replay security collectively ensure that the adversary is unable to trigger a false alarm for an honest SPiRiT user. More precisely, an adversary cannot cause SPiRiT users not in contact with a diagnosed person to receive an alarm (false positive) or cause users who were in contact not to receive an alarm (false negative). From a privacy perspective, the protocol ensures that the entire process— from registration and ID broadcasting to the disclosure of pseudo-random IDs during the trace phase— preserves the user's information such as the real-world identity of the user, locations, relationships between users, or any information beyond what is available without the use of the exposure notification system, and prevents the linkage of different broadcasts from the same user (unlinkability). Next, we formally define upload integrity, replay security, and unlinkability. To establish upload integrity, we consider an adversary capable of corrupting up to $t-1$ out of N issuers, while also potentially compromising any number of users. For the strongest unlinkability guarantee, we assume an adversary with the power to corrupt any number of issuers and verifiers. The adversary may also corrupt multiple users. However, even with access to multiple compromised devices, the adversary should not be able to gain any additional information beyond what could be obtained by compromising each device individually. Our model excludes adversaries who tamper with the contact tracing app on devices belonging to general users, such as by generating false notifications. We also consider out-of-scope side-channel attacks, such as those exploiting signal strength or power levels to link different transmissions from the same user, as well as physical attacks, like surveillance or the implantation of hidden listening devices. The backend server maintains a publicly available database and is operated by an honest but curious administrator.

Definition 3. (Correctness). *A SPiRiT scheme is correct if for any parameters* $(\mathsf{pp}, \{\mathsf{prv}_j\}_{j\in[1,N]}) \leftarrow \mathsf{Setup}(1^\lambda)$ *and any user* id_U*, after registration* $(\mathsf{pp}_\mathsf{U}, \mathsf{prv}_\mathsf{U}, \mathsf{T}_\mathsf{Rgstr}) \leftarrow \mathsf{Register}(\mathsf{id}_\mathsf{U}, \{\mathsf{prv}_j\}_{j\in[1,N]}, \mathsf{T}_\mathsf{Rgstr})$ *and broadcast* $\mathsf{T}_\mathsf{elD} \leftarrow \mathsf{Broadcast}(\mathsf{prv}_\mathsf{U}, \mathsf{T}_\mathsf{elD})$*, the trace information* $(\mathsf{tr}, \pi_\mathsf{tr}) \leftarrow \mathsf{Diagnosis}(\mathsf{pp}_\mathsf{U}, \mathsf{prv}_\mathsf{U}, \mathbb{CP})$ *produced by an honest user is accepted by* $(\mathsf{db}, \mathsf{bit}) \leftarrow \mathsf{Verify}(\mathsf{tr}, \pi_\mathsf{tr}, \mathsf{pp}_\mathsf{U}, \mathsf{T}_\mathsf{Rgstr}, \mathbb{CP})$ *with overwhelming probability (*$\mathsf{bit} = 1$*). Furthermore, any user whose device previously received pseudo-random IDs from the diagnosed user obtains* $(\mathsf{intCnt}, \mathsf{alrmBit}) \leftarrow \mathsf{Trace}(\mathsf{db}, \mathsf{T}_\mathsf{elD})$ *with* $\mathsf{alrmBit} = 1$.

Upload Integrity. Informally, this property describes the infeasibility of a malicious uploader submitting inauthentic trace information. Specifically, an adversary controlling issuing entities in corrupted set CS has a negligible chance of deceiving an honest verifier into believing that the user possesses a list of pseudo-random IDs, if, in reality, presented IDs do not embed a key registered by the presenting user. Figure 2 outlines the detailed game setup, where the adversary begins by registering users of its choice, each possessing a unique identifier. The adversary succeeds by outputting authentic trace information that does not correspond to any of the users it controls. In interactive Register algorithm, subscripts U and I denote interactions on the user side and the issuer side, respectively.

Definition 4. (Upload Integrity). *A SPiRiT scheme achieves upload integrity if for any PPT adversary $\mathcal{A}$ and any $R \geq 0$*

$$\mathbf{Adv}^{UI}_{SPiRiT,\mathcal{A},R}(\lambda) := \Pr[UI_{SPiRiT,\mathcal{A},R}(\lambda) \to 1] \leq \mathsf{negl}(\lambda),$$

where $UI_{SPiRiT,\mathcal{A},R}(\lambda)$ is defined in Fig. 2.

Game $\mathrm{UI}_{SPiRiT,\mathcal{A},R}(\lambda)$	$\mathcal{O}_{\mathsf{Register(pp)}}$
$(\mathsf{pp}, \{\mathsf{prv}_j\}_{j\in[1,N]})$ $\leftarrow \mathsf{SPiRiT.Setup}(1^\lambda)$ $\mathsf{CS} = \emptyset, \mathcal{Q} = \emptyset, \mathsf{T_{Rgstr}} = \emptyset$ $\mathsf{CS}, \{\mathsf{tr}^*, \pi^*_{\mathsf{tr}}, \mathsf{pp}^*_{\mathsf{U}}\} \leftarrow \mathcal{A}^{\mathcal{O}}(\mathsf{pp})$ **return** $(\lvert\mathsf{CS}\rvert < t \wedge$ $\mathsf{pp}^*_{\mathsf{U}} \notin \mathcal{Q} \ \wedge \ \mathsf{SPiRiT.Verify}($ $\mathsf{tr}^*, \pi^*_{\mathsf{tr}}, \mathsf{pp}^*_{\mathsf{U}}, \mathsf{T_{Rgstr}}, \mathbb{CP}) = (*, 1))$	$(\mathsf{pp_U}, \mathsf{prv_U}, \mathsf{T_{Rgstr}}) \leftarrow$ $(\mathsf{SPiRiT.Register_U}(\mathsf{id_U}),$ $\mathsf{SPiRiT.Register_I}(\mathsf{prv}_j, \mathsf{T_{Rgstr}}))$ **if** $\mathsf{pp_U} = \perp$ **then abort** **else** $\mathcal{Q} = \mathcal{Q} \cup \mathsf{pp_U}$ **return** $\top$ $\mathcal{O}_{\mathsf{Corrupt}(k)}$ **if** $k \in \mathsf{CS}$ **then abort** **else** $\mathsf{CS} = \mathsf{CS} \cup \{k\} \wedge$ $\mathsf{HS} = \mathsf{HS} \setminus \{k\}$ **return** prv_k

Fig. 2. SPiRiT upload integrity experiment.

Replay Security. This property concerns the integrity of contacts. It captures the infeasibility of an adversary to rebroadcast pseudo-random IDs that were either *sent* or *received* at an earlier time. The definition is based on the replay security game $\mathrm{Replay}_{SPiRiT,\mathcal{A},\Delta}(\lambda)$ as depicted in Fig. 3 and follows the same intuition as described in [11,26]. The game is parameterized by a delay $\Delta \in \mathbb{N}$. Adversary $\mathcal{A}$ selects a time t and honest users $\mathsf{U}_1, \mathsf{U}_2$ to perform a delayed replay attack. Then, $\mathcal{A}$ interacts with U_1 during the period $[0, t-\Delta-1]$. It then waits for Δ time steps before interacting with U_2. $\mathcal{A}$ wins the game if it causes U_2, which was not in proximity to U_1, to receive false alarms. The notation $\mathsf{SPiRiT}.\Pi_{\mathsf{U}}$, refers to the execution of algorithm $\mathsf{SPiRiT}.\Pi$ on the user U's side.

Definition 5. (Replay Security). *A SPiRiT scheme is replay secure if for any PPT adversary $\mathcal{A}$ and $\Delta \in \mathbb{N}$*

$$\mathbf{Adv}^{Replay}_{SPiRiT,\mathcal{A},\Delta}(\lambda) := \Pr[Replay_{SPiRiT,\mathcal{A},\Delta}(\lambda) \rightarrow 1] \leq \mathsf{negl}(\lambda),$$

where $Replcy_{SPiRiT,\mathcal{A},\Delta}(\lambda)$ is defined in Fig. 3.

Game $\mathrm{Replay}_{SPiRiT,\mathcal{A},\Delta}(\lambda)$

$(\mathsf{pp}, \{\mathsf{prv}_j\}_{j\in[1,N]}) \leftarrow \mathsf{SPiRiT.Setup}(1^\lambda)$
$\mathsf{T}_{\mathsf{Rgstr}} = \emptyset, t \leftarrow\$ (\Delta, T]$
$\mathsf{T}_{\mathsf{eID}_{\mathsf{U}_1}} = \emptyset, \mathsf{T}_{\mathsf{eID}_{\mathsf{U}_2}} = \emptyset, \mathsf{T}_{\mathsf{eID}_{\mathcal{A}}} = \emptyset$
$(\mathsf{pp}_{\mathsf{U}_1}, \mathsf{prv}_{\mathsf{U}_1}, \mathsf{T}_{\mathsf{Rgstr}}) \leftarrow \mathsf{SPiRiT.Register}(\mathsf{id}_{\mathsf{U}_1}, \{\mathsf{prv}_j\}_{j\in[1,N]}, \mathsf{T}_{\mathsf{Rgstr}})$
$(\mathsf{pp}_{\mathsf{U}_2}, \mathsf{prv}_{\mathsf{U}_2}, \mathsf{T}_{\mathsf{Rgstr}}) \leftarrow \mathsf{SPiRiT.Register}(\mathsf{id}_{\mathsf{U}_2}, \{\mathsf{prv}_j\}_{j\in[1,N]}, \mathsf{T}_{\mathsf{Rgstr}})$
$\forall i \in [0, t - \Delta):$
  $\mathsf{T}_{\mathsf{eID}_{\mathsf{U}_1}}, \mathsf{eID}^{\mathsf{U}_1}_i \leftarrow \mathsf{SPiRiT.Broadcast}_{\mathsf{U}_1}(i, \mathsf{prv}_{\mathsf{U}_1}, \mathsf{T}_{\mathsf{eID}_{\mathsf{U}_1}})$
  $\mathsf{T}_{\mathsf{eID}_{\mathcal{A}}} \leftarrow \mathsf{T}_{\mathsf{eID}_{\mathcal{A}}} \cup \mathsf{eID}^{\mathsf{U}_1}_i$
$\forall i \in [t, T]:$
  $\mathsf{T}_{\mathsf{eID}_{\mathcal{A}}}, \mathsf{eID}^{\mathsf{U}_1}_{i-\Delta} \leftarrow \mathsf{SPiRiT.Broadcast}_{\mathcal{A}}(i - \Delta, *, \mathsf{T}_{\mathsf{eID}_{\mathcal{A}}})$
  $\mathsf{T}_{\mathsf{eID}_{\mathsf{U}_2}} \leftarrow \mathsf{T}_{\mathsf{eID}_{\mathsf{U}_2}} \cup \mathsf{eID}^{\mathsf{U}_1}_{i-\Delta}$
$(\mathsf{tr}_{\mathsf{U}_1}, \pi_{\mathsf{tr}_{\mathsf{U}_1}}) \leftarrow \mathsf{SPiRiT.Diagnosis}_{\mathsf{U}_1}(\mathsf{pp}_{\mathsf{U}_1}, \mathsf{prv}_{\mathsf{U}_1}, \mathbb{CP})$
$\mathsf{db}_2 := \mathsf{db}_1 \cup \mathsf{tr}_{\mathsf{U}_1}$ ▷ $\mathtt{db}_1$: database extracted from backend server
$(\mathsf{intCnt}_\mathsf{b}, \mathsf{alrmBit}_\mathsf{b}) \leftarrow \mathsf{SPiRiT.Trace}_{\mathsf{U}_2}(\mathsf{db}_\mathsf{b}, \mathsf{T}_{\mathsf{eID}_{\mathsf{U}_2}}), \mathsf{b} \in \{1, 2\}$
$\mathsf{n}_{\mathsf{U}_1\mathsf{U}_2} \leftarrow \mathsf{numCntct}(\mathsf{U}_1, \mathsf{U}_2)$ ▷ number of epochs of $\mathtt{U}_1 - \mathtt{U}_2$ vicinity
return
$(\mathsf{SPiRiT.Verify}(\mathsf{tr}_{\mathsf{U}_1}, \pi_{\mathsf{tr}_{\mathsf{U}_1}}, \mathsf{pp}_{\mathsf{U}_1}, \mathsf{T}_{\mathsf{Rgstr}}, \mathbb{CP}) = (\mathsf{db}_2, 1) \wedge$
$\mathsf{intCnt}_2 - \mathsf{intCnt}_1 > \mathsf{n}_{\mathsf{U}_1\mathsf{U}_2})$

Fig. 3. SPiRiT replay security experiment.

Unlinkability. This property captures two distinct privacy features: pseudo-random ID unlinkability and positive user unlinkability. It ensures that an adversarial verifier, potentially colluding with multiple issuers and verifiers, cannot link the execution of $\mathsf{Broadcast}$ with either another execution of $\mathsf{Broadcast}$ (pseudo-random ID unlinkability for all users, including healthy and positive ones), or with the executions of $\mathsf{Register}$ algorithm for a specific user identifier id_U (positive-user unlinkability). This is defined by $\mathrm{UNLINK}_{SPiRiT,\mathcal{A}}(\lambda)$ as illustrated in Fig. 4. The adversary $\mathcal{A}$, can corrupt a subset CU of users registered through the $\mathcal{O}_{\mathsf{Register}}$ oracle and get access to their private parameters prv_U. Then, $\mathcal{A}$ selects and presents two identifiers $(\mathsf{id}_{\mathsf{U}_0}, \mathsf{id}_{\mathsf{U}_1})$ provided they do not belong to corrupted users. Next, one of them is randomly picked to generate trace information via the $\mathsf{Chl}_{\mathsf{Diagnosis}}$ oracle. The adversary's task is to distinguish eID for the same user across two different $\mathsf{Broadcast}$ sessions (pseudo-random ID unlinkability); or to link trace information with the private user identifier (positive-user unlinkability). It is important to note that we do not consider indirect methods of data extraction (side-channel attacks) in our model, such as those exploiting Received Signal Strength Indicator (RSSI) or Bluetooth Low Energy (BLE) tracking mechanisms to link different eIDs from the same user. There exist recent advancements in addressing such vulnerabilities including [24].

Game $\text{UNLINK}_{SPiRiT,\mathcal{A}}(\lambda)$	$\mathsf{Chl}_{\mathsf{Broadcast}}(\mathsf{ppu}_{\mathsf{U}_0}, \mathsf{ppu}_{\mathsf{U}_1}, i_0, i_1)$
$(\mathsf{pp}, \{\mathsf{prv}_j\}_{j\in[1,N]})$ $\leftarrow \mathsf{SPiRiT.Setup}(1^\lambda)$ $R = 0, \mathsf{CU} = \emptyset, \mathsf{HU} := [R] \setminus \mathsf{CU}$ $\mathcal{Q} = \emptyset, \mathcal{Q}' = \emptyset, \mathsf{T}_{\mathsf{Rgstr}} = \emptyset$ $\mathsf{b} \leftarrow_{\$} \{0,1\}$ $\mathsf{b}' \leftarrow \mathcal{A}^{\mathcal{O}}(\mathsf{pp}, \{\mathsf{prv}_j\}_{j\in[1,N]})$ **return** $(\mathsf{b}' == \mathsf{b})$	**if** $(*, \mathsf{ppu}_{\mathsf{U}_0}) \notin \mathcal{Q}$ **then abort** **if** $(*, \mathsf{ppu}_{\mathsf{U}_1}) \notin \mathcal{Q}$ **then abort** $\mathsf{eID}_0 \leftarrow \mathsf{SPiRiT.Broadcast}($ $i_0, \mathsf{prv}_{\mathsf{U}_b}, *)$ $\mathsf{eID}_1 \leftarrow \mathsf{SPiRiT.Broadcast}($ $i_1, \mathsf{prv}_{\mathsf{U}_b}, *)$ **return** eID_b
$\mathcal{O}_{\mathsf{Register(pp)}}$	$\mathsf{Chl}_{\mathsf{Diagnosis}}(\mathsf{id}_{\mathsf{U}_0}, \mathsf{id}_{\mathsf{U}_1})$
$(\mathsf{ppu}_{\mathsf{U}}, \mathsf{prv}_{\mathsf{U}}, \mathsf{T}_{\mathsf{Rgstr}}) \leftarrow$ $(\mathsf{SPiRiT.Register}_{\mathsf{U}}(\mathsf{id}_{\mathsf{U}}),$ $\mathsf{SPiRiT.Register}_{\mathsf{I}}(\mathsf{prv}_j, \mathsf{T}_{\mathsf{Rgstr}}))$ **if** $\mathsf{ppu}_{\mathsf{U}} = \perp$ **then abort** **else** $\mathcal{Q} = \mathcal{Q} \cup (\mathsf{prv}_{\mathsf{U}}, \mathsf{ppu}_{\mathsf{U}})$ $\mathcal{Q}' = \mathcal{Q}' \cup \mathsf{id}_{\mathsf{U}}$ $R = R + 1$ **return** $\top$	**if** $\mathsf{id}_{\mathsf{U}_0} \notin \mathcal{Q}' \vee \mathsf{id}_{\mathsf{U}_0} \notin \mathsf{HU}$ **then abort** **if** $\mathsf{id}_{\mathsf{U}_1} \notin \mathcal{Q}' \vee \mathsf{id}_{\mathsf{U}_1} \notin \mathsf{HU}$ **then abort** **if** $\exists k \in \mathsf{CU} : \mathsf{numCntct}(\mathsf{U}_k, \mathsf{U}_0) \neq$ $\mathsf{numCntct}(\mathsf{U}_k, \mathsf{U}_1)$ **then abort** $(\mathsf{ppu}_{\mathsf{U}_0}, \mathsf{tr}_0, \pi_{\mathsf{tr}_0}) \leftarrow \mathsf{SPiRiT.Diagnosis}($ $\mathsf{ppu}_{\mathsf{U}_0}, \mathsf{prv}_{\mathsf{U}_0}, \mathbb{CP})$ $(\mathsf{ppu}_{\mathsf{U}_1}, \mathsf{tr}_1, \pi_{\mathsf{tr}_1}) \leftarrow \mathsf{SPiRiT.Diagnosis}($ $\mathsf{ppu}_{\mathsf{U}_1}, \mathsf{prv}_{\mathsf{U}_1}, \mathbb{CP})$ **if** $\mathsf{Verify}(\mathsf{tr}_0, \pi_{\mathsf{tr}_0}, \mathsf{ppu}_{\mathsf{U}_0}, \mathsf{T}_{\mathsf{Rgstr}}, \mathbb{CP}) = (*, 0)$ $\vee$ $\mathsf{Verify}(\mathsf{tr}_1, \pi_{\mathsf{tr}_1}, \mathsf{ppu}_{\mathsf{U}_1}, \mathsf{T}_{\mathsf{Rgstr}}, \mathbb{CP}) = (*, 0)$ **then abort** **return** $(\mathsf{ppu}_{\mathsf{U}_b}, \mathsf{tr}_b, \pi_{\mathsf{tr}_b})$
$\mathcal{O}_{\mathsf{Corrupt}(k)}$	
if $k \in \mathsf{CU}$ **then abort** **else** $\mathsf{CU} = \mathsf{CU} \cup \{k\} \wedge$ $\mathsf{HU} = \mathsf{HU} \setminus \{k\}$ **return** $\mathsf{prv}_{\mathsf{U}_k}$	

Fig. 4. SPiRiT unlinkability experiment.

Definition 6. (Unlinkability). *A SPiRiT system achieves unlinkability if for PPT adversary $\mathcal{A}$ the advantage defined as*

$$\mathbf{Adv}^{UNLINK}_{SPiRiT,\mathcal{A}}(\lambda) := |2\Pr[UNLINK_{SPiRiT,\mathcal{A}}(\lambda) \rightarrow 1] - 1| \leq \mathsf{negl}(\lambda).$$

where $UNLINK_{SPiRiT,\mathcal{A}}(\lambda)$ is defined in Fig. 4.

Algorithm 1 SPiRiT Construction. Σ denotes tACT scheme from Section 2.

$\mathsf{SPiRiT.Setup}(1^\lambda, t, N)$

Run $(\mathsf{pp}', \{\mathsf{prv}_j\}_{j=1}^N) \leftarrow \Sigma.\mathsf{Setup}(1^\lambda, t, N)$ and let $\mathsf{H}'' : \{0,1\}^* \rightarrow \mathbb{F}_p$ and $\mathsf{h} : \mathbb{G}_1 \rightarrow \mathbb{F}_p$ be secure hash functions.
Let $\mathsf{I} = \{I_1, \ldots, I_N\}$ denote the set of authorized issuers. Issuers initialize a shared table $\mathsf{T}_{\mathsf{Rgstr}} := \emptyset$. Each user device initializes a bit $\mathsf{alrmBit} \leftarrow 0$ and a local table $\mathsf{T}_{\mathsf{eID}} := \emptyset$.
Output: System public parameters $\mathsf{pp} = (\mathsf{pp}', \mathsf{H}'', \mathsf{h}, \mathsf{T}_{\mathsf{Rgstr}})$, issuers' private parameters $\{\mathsf{prv}_j\}_{j \in [1,N]}$

$\mathsf{SPiRiT.Register}(\mathsf{id}_\mathsf{U}, \{\mathsf{prv}_j\}_{j\in[1,N]}, \mathsf{T}_{\mathsf{Rgstr}})$ [a user U and issuers I]:

U on input private unique identifier id_U runs $(\mathsf{blindRequest}, \mathsf{rand}_\mathsf{U}) \leftarrow \Sigma.(\mathsf{Register}, \mathsf{TokenRequest})(\mathsf{id}_\mathsf{U})$. I_j runs $\mathsf{blindToken}_j \leftarrow \Sigma.\mathsf{tIssue}(\mathsf{blindRequest}, \mathsf{prv}_j)$
U runs $\mathsf{token} \leftarrow \Sigma.(\mathsf{Aggregate}, \mathsf{Unblind})(\{\mathsf{blindToken}_{jk}\}_{j\in[t]}, \mathsf{rand}_\mathsf{U})$, and $\pi \leftarrow \Sigma.\mathsf{Prove}(\mathsf{token}, \mathsf{rand}_\mathsf{U})$
U samples a key $\mathsf{k} \leftarrow\$\ \mathbb{F}_p$ and outputs $\mathsf{cm}_\mathsf{k} \leftarrow \mathsf{Ped.Commit}(\mathsf{k}, r_\mathsf{k})$, where $r_\mathsf{k} \leftarrow\$\ \mathbb{F}_p$
I check $\mathsf{bit} \leftarrow \Sigma.\mathsf{Verify}(\mathsf{token}, \pi)$: **if** $(\mathsf{bit} = 0 \vee (\mathsf{bit} = 1 \wedge \mathsf{token} \in \mathsf{T}_{\mathsf{Rgstr}}))$, abort. **Else**, $\mathsf{T}_{\mathsf{Rgstr}} \leftarrow \mathsf{T}_{\mathsf{Rgstr}} \cup \{\mathsf{token}, \mathsf{cm}_\mathsf{k}\}$.
Output: $\mathsf{pp}_\mathsf{U} \leftarrow \{\mathsf{token}, \mathsf{cm}_\mathsf{k}\}, \mathsf{prv}_\mathsf{U} \leftarrow \{\mathsf{id}_\mathsf{U}, \mathsf{k}\}$, $\mathsf{T}_{\mathsf{Rgstr}}$

$\mathsf{SPiRiT.Broadcast}(i, \mathsf{prv}_\mathsf{U}, \mathsf{T}_{\mathsf{eID}})$ [a user U]:

At each epoch with unique epoch number i, U's device does the following:
a: Broadcast pseudo-random ID– Generate $\mathsf{eID}_i = \mathsf{PRF}(\mathsf{k}, i)$ and broadcast eID_i via BLE.
b: Log received BLE beacons– Compute an exposure score es_i for each received eID_i, record $(\mathsf{eID}_i, \mathsf{es}_i)$ in $\mathsf{T}_{\mathsf{eID}}$.
Output: $\mathsf{T}_{\mathsf{eID}}$

$\mathsf{SPiRiT.Diagnosis}(\mathsf{pp}_\mathsf{U}, \mathsf{prv}_\mathsf{U}, \mathbb{CP})$ [a user U]:

if U receives a positive diagnosis test result **then**
a: Parse $\mathsf{pp}_\mathsf{U} = \{\mathsf{token}, \mathsf{cm}_\mathsf{k}\}$, $\mathsf{prv}_\mathsf{U} = \{\mathsf{id}_\mathsf{U}, \mathsf{k}\}$. ▷ token : unique anonymous token acquired during registration phase.
b: Re-computes the following vector as the trace information $\mathsf{tr} \leftarrow \{\mathsf{eID}_i = \mathsf{PRF}(\mathsf{k}, i)\}_{i\in\mathbb{CP}}$ ▷ pseudo-random IDs broadcasted from U's device during $\mathbb{CP}$.
c: Generates $\pi_{\mathsf{tr}} = \mathsf{ZKPoK}\{(\mathsf{k}, r_\mathsf{k}) : \mathsf{cm}_\mathsf{k} = \mathsf{Ped.Commit}(\mathsf{k}, r_\mathsf{k}), \{\mathsf{eID}_i = \mathsf{PRF}(\mathsf{k}, i)\}_{i\in\mathbb{CP}}\}$
Output: $(\mathsf{pp}_\mathsf{U}, \mathsf{tr}, \pi_{\mathsf{tr}})$ to PHA.

$\mathsf{SPiRiT.Verify}(\mathsf{tr}, \pi_{\mathsf{tr}}, \mathsf{pp}_\mathsf{U}, \mathsf{T}_{\mathsf{Rgstr}}, \mathbb{CP})$ [public health authority PHA]:

The PHA, upon receiving input from a positively diagnosed U, does the following:
a: Parse $\mathsf{pp}_\mathsf{U} = \{\mathsf{token}, \mathsf{cm}_\mathsf{k}\}$
b: **if** $\{\mathsf{token}, \mathsf{cm}_\mathsf{k}\} \in \mathsf{T}_{\mathsf{Rgstr}} \wedge \mathsf{ZKVerify}(\mathsf{cm}_\mathsf{k}, \pi_{\mathsf{tr}}) = 1$ **then** $\mathsf{bit} \leftarrow 1 \wedge \forall i \in \mathbb{CP} : \mathsf{CF} \leftarrow \mathsf{CF.Insert}(\mathsf{tr}[i])$. **Else**, $\mathsf{bit} \leftarrow 0$. ▷ insert items $\{\mathsf{tr}[i] = \mathsf{eID}_i\}_{i\in\mathbb{CP}}$ into CF.
Output: $(\mathsf{CF}, \mathsf{bit})$ to the backend server database.

$\mathsf{SPiRiT.Trace}(\mathsf{CF}, \mathsf{T}_{\mathsf{eID}})$ [all system users]:

Each user device periodically queries the backend server for updated CF and does the following:
for $i \in [1, |\mathsf{T}_{\mathsf{eID}}|]$ **do**
a: $\mathsf{bit} \leftarrow \mathsf{CF.Check}(\mathsf{T}_{\mathsf{eID}}[i])$ ▷ Compute the set intersection of CF and user's local database $\mathsf{T}_{\mathsf{eID}}$ through the lookup operation.
b: **if** $\mathsf{bit} = 1 \wedge \mathsf{es}_i \geq$ **exposurelimit then** $\mathsf{intCnt} \leftarrow \mathsf{intCnt} + 1$
Output: $\mathsf{intCnt}, \mathsf{alrmBit} \leftarrow (\mathsf{intCnt} \geq 1)?1 : 0$

4 SPiRiT Design

We now introduce SPiRiT, our verifiable contact tracing scheme outlined in Algorithm 1. This protocol is grounded on the tACT system, which facilitates anonymous user registration, thereby ensuring privacy and verifiability in the contact tracing process. In SPiRiT.Register algorithm, token generated in the underlying tACT algorithm serves as a distinctive high-entropy function derived from the private unique identifier $\mathsf{id_U}$–such as SSN–, allowing for anonymous user deduplication and registration. Upon successful verification of token the issuers proceed by comparing the token against their database of redeemed tokens and reject the token, if the value already appears. Otherwise, they update the database by adding the registered token to $\mathsf{T_{Rgstr}}$. In $\mathsf{T_{Rgstr}}$, alongside the redeemed token token, issuers also keep a commitment $\mathsf{cm_k}$ to the unique key k registered by a user.

In the SPiRiT.Broadcast algorithm, a user's digital device periodically transmits ephemeral pseudo-random IDs while concurrently logging the received pseudo-random IDs from nearby user devices. Specifically, during each epoch with unique epoch number i, the user's device generates an ephemeral pseudo-random ID, denoted as eID, by evaluating a pseudo-random function (PRF) under the user's registered key k and the epoch number i. Hence, $\mathsf{eID}_i = \mathsf{PRF}(\mathsf{k}, i)$ is unique per user and per epoch. The selected PRF must possess a structural design enabling efficient integration with Sigma protocols [15,16]. Two potential instantiations include the Naor-Pinkas-Reingold PRF [33] $\mathsf{PRF}(\mathsf{k}, i) = \mathsf{H}(i)^{\mathsf{k}}$ or the Dodis-Yampolskiy PRF [17] $\mathsf{PRF}(\mathsf{k}, i) = g^{(\mathsf{k}+i)^{-1}}$, where g is a generator of a group $\mathbb{G}$. Later in the SPiRiT.Diagnosis algorithm, the user efficiently computes a zero-knowledge proof π_{tr} to prove the correct computation of trace information tr with respect to epoch numbers i during the contagious period, and the user's key k committed to during the registration phase. This reinforces the non-transferability of pseudo-random IDs among users as each user must demonstrate the consistency of claimed IDs with their registered key k. Finally, the user broadcasts the ephemeral pseudo-random ID eID_i via BLE. Concurrently, the user's device listens for BLE beacons broadcasted by other users' devices in close proximity and records them in a table denoted by $\mathsf{T_{eID}}$. Additionally, the device computes an exposure score es_i and records it in $\mathsf{T_{eID}}$, which is a function of *proximity* and *contact duration* for each received eID_i, determined based on the latest policies provided by the public health authority (PHA). The algorithm's output comprises the updated database $\mathsf{T_{eID}}$, which is stored locally on each user's device.

In the SPiRiT.Diagnosis algorithm, following a positive diagnosis, the infected user with public parameter $\mathsf{pp_U}$, computes the tracing information consisting of pseudo-random IDs broadcasted from their device during the contagious period $\mathbb{CP}$[1], denoted as $\mathsf{tr} = \{\mathsf{eID}_i = \mathsf{PRF}(\mathsf{k}, i)\}_{i \in \mathbb{CP}}$. Furthermore, the user computes a zero-knowledge proof π_{tr} to demonstrate the accurate computation of tr across

[1] The contagious period denoted as $\mathbb{CP}$, encompasses epoch indices defining the duration considered infectious for a particular virus in accordance with health policies.

epoch numbers $i \in \mathbb{CP}$, relative to the key k committed to during the registration phase. This process ensures that malicious users cannot claim somebody else's eID as their own, thereby maintaining the integrity of uploads. Subsequently, the user transmits $(\mathsf{pp_U}, \mathsf{tr}, \pi_{\mathsf{tr}})$ to the PHA for verification.

In the $\mathsf{SPiRiT.Verify}$ algorithm, the PHA, upon receiving input $(\mathsf{pp_U}, \mathsf{tr}, \pi_{\mathsf{tr}})$, first checks whether the user is already registered by checking if $\mathsf{pp_U} = \{\mathsf{token}, \mathsf{cm_k}\} \in \mathsf{T_{Rgstr}}$. If $\mathsf{token} \notin \mathsf{T_{Rgstr}}$, the user is directed to undergo the registration phase. Else, the PHA uses the commitment $\mathsf{cm_k}$ to the user-specific registered key k and verifies the zero-knowledge proof π_{tr}, ensuring the authenticity of the returned eIDs with regard to: *(I)* the key k *(II)* the epoch numbers in contagious period $i \in \mathbb{CP}$, all while maintaining anonymity. More precisely, first, the verification ensures that only the true owner can release the eIDs (non-transferability). This is achieved by tethering the eIDs to the committed unique user key k. Second, this verification prevents malicious users from revealing a different set of eIDs instead of the ones corresponding to the contagious period (replay attack). This is made possible due to the design of eIDs which are bound to epoch numbers i. Upon successful verification, the PHA inserts the list $\{\mathsf{eID}_i\}_{i \in \mathbb{CP}}$ into a Cuckoo filter CF for compact representation, which is subsequently stored on the backend server. A Cuckoo filter (CF) is a probabilistic data structure with a compact set representation facilitating fast membership testing [19]. We rely on standard definitions of Cuckoo filter [19].

In the $\mathsf{SPiRiT.Trace}$ algorithm, each user device periodically queries the backend server for updates in CF. The user device then cross-references its local database $\mathsf{T_{eID}}$ with CF to determine the intersection. More precisely, the algorithm looks up all pseudo-random ID in $\mathsf{T_{eID}}$, checking if each one of them belongs to the filter CF through the lookup operation $\mathsf{CF.Check}$. It then assesses an exposure score es for all matching pseudo-random IDs. If the exposure score exceeds a threshold denoted as `exposurelimit` determined by the PHA, a bit $\mathsf{alrmBit}$ is set to 1, triggering the device to display a notification that alerts the user of potential exposure to the virus due to prolonged close proximity to the infected individual(s). The notification offers guidance on necessary actions including staying in quarantine and getting tested for the viral infection and directs the user to additional information resources. Furthermore, to save storage space and improve trace lookup efficiency, applications automatically delete records that are no longer relevant for epidemiological purposes, e.g., those that exceed a 10-day timeframe. Similarly, the backend server can remove old items from the Cuckoo filter using the $\mathsf{CF.Delete}$ operation. This deletion capability allows the filter to accommodate new items without necessitating reconfiguration or expansion.

Remark. Here we describe minor modifications to Algorithm 1 necessary to accommodate passive users. First, the PHA must establish an upper limit on the percentage of users who can opt for passive participation. This is essential to maintain a balance between accommodating user preferences and ensuring the SPiRiT system's effectiveness in detecting high-risk cases. Increasing the number of passive users will inevitably reduce the overall detection probability, as these users refrain from broadcasting pseudorandom IDs. During registration, users are required to specify their participation mode—either active or passive. Consequently, $\mathsf{T_{Rgstr}}$ will also reflect the mode chosen by the user. The Broadcast, Diagnosis, and Trace algorithms for passive users, which follow same intuition as the A/P DP-3T protocol [3], are as follows:

- SPiRiT.Broadcast: Passive users do not broadcast pseudo-random IDs; they only listen for broadcasts from others.
- SPiRiT.Diagnosis: If a passive user becomes infected, and the PHA confirms their passive status based on registration data, they are not required to upload tracing information. Consequently, SPiRiT.Verify algorithm is not executed for passive users.
- SPiRiT.Trace: This algorithm for passive users operates in the same way as it does in Algorithm 1 for active users.

4.1 Security Analysis of the Proposed Scheme

Theorem 1. *[Upload Integrity] If* (ZKSetup, ZKPoK, ZKVerify) *is a* NIZK *with knowledge soundness property, and the* tACT *scheme is an unforgeable threshold anonymous counting token, then, the* SPiRiT *scheme described in Algorithm 1 satisfies upload integrity as in Definition Definition 4.*

Proof. Assume an adversary $\mathcal{A}$ can successfully cheat the upload integrity game in Fig. 2 with non-negligible probability. We construct two efficient adversaries $\mathcal{B}_1$ and $\mathcal{B}_2$. $\mathcal{B}_1$ can break the unforgeability of the tACT system, while $\mathcal{B}_2$ can compromise the soundness of the NIZK argument. We will show that:

$$\mathbf{Adv}^{\mathsf{UI}}_{\mathsf{SPiRiT},\mathcal{A}} \leq \mathbf{Adv}^{\mathsf{UF}}_{\mathsf{tACT},\mathcal{B}_1}((\lambda)) + \mathbf{Adv}^{\mathsf{zksound}}_{\mathsf{NIZK},\mathcal{B}_2}((\lambda)). \tag{1}$$

Construction of $\mathcal{B}_1$. $\mathcal{B}_1$ interacts with a challenger C in the unforgeability game for tACT and $\mathcal{B}_1$ simulates the upload integrity game for $\mathcal{A}$.

- C runs $(\mathsf{pp}, \mathsf{prv}) \leftarrow \mathsf{tACT.Setup}(1^\lambda)$ and gives public parameters pp to $\mathcal{B}_1$. Then $\mathcal{B}_1$ provides pp to $\mathcal{A}$.
- $\mathcal{B}_1$ simulates the environment and oracles for $\mathcal{A}$. When oracles $\mathcal{O}_{\mathsf{Corrupt}}$ and $\mathcal{O}_{\mathsf{Register}}$ are called, $\mathcal{B}_1$ queries $\mathcal{O}_{\mathsf{Corrupt}}$ and $(\mathcal{O}_{\mathsf{Register}}, \mathcal{O}_{\mathsf{tIssue}})$ of the tACT scheme, respectively. $\mathcal{B}_1$ answers register queries $\mathsf{blindRequest}_i$ from $\mathcal{A}$ as follows. $\mathcal{B}_1$ queries C and provides the answer tok_i. In addition, $\mathcal{B}_1$ runs Ext, extractor algorithm of the underlying ZKPoK to extract the values r_i and $\mathsf{id_U}_i$. Subsequently, $\mathcal{B}_1$ sets $\mathcal{Q} = \mathcal{Q} \cup \{\mathsf{id_U}_i, r_i, \mathsf{bR}_i, \mathsf{tok}_i, \pi_{\mathsf{tok}_i}\}$.
- Upon game completion, $\mathcal{A}$ generates the output $(\mathsf{tr}^*, \pi^*_{\mathsf{tr}}, \mathsf{pp_U}^* = (\mathsf{tok}^*, \pi^*_{\mathsf{tok}}, \mathsf{cm_k}^*)) \notin \mathcal{Q}$. $\mathcal{B}_1$ submits $((\mathsf{id_U}^*_i, r^*_i, \mathsf{bR}^*_i, \mathsf{tok}^*, \pi^*_{\mathsf{tok}}) \cup \mathcal{Q})$ to the tACT challenger C as its forgery.

Construction of $\mathcal{B}_2$. $\mathcal{B}_2$ interacts with a challenger C' in the soundness game for NIZK. At the end of the game, $\mathcal{A}$ produces the outputs $(\mathsf{tr}^*, \pi^*_{\mathsf{tr}}, \mathsf{pp_U}^* =$

$(\mathsf{tok}^*, \pi^*_{\mathsf{tok}}, \mathsf{cn_k}^*))$ for which SPiRiT.Verify outputs 1. $\mathcal{B}_2$ returns $(\pi^*_{\mathsf{tr}}, \mathsf{pp_U}^* = (\mathsf{tok}^*, \pi^*_{\mathsf{tok}}, \mathsf{cn_k}^*))$ to the NIZK challenger C' as proof of an incorrect statement. Notably, neither $\mathcal{B}_1$ nor $\mathcal{B}_2$ can determine in polynomial time if their submissions to the respective challengers tACT/NIZK will be successful, i.e., whether they will win the $\mathsf{tACT}_{\mathcal{B}_1}((\lambda))$ and $\mathsf{zkSND}_{\mathcal{B}_2}((\lambda))$ games. Nonetheless, this does not hinder the proof that at least one of adversaries $\mathcal{B}_1$ and $\mathcal{B}_2$ must have a non-negligible advantage if the adversary $\mathcal{A}$ can breach upload integrity experiment with non-negligible probability. Our proof strategy involves defining two events, namely $\mathsf{E_{tACT}}$, and $\mathsf{E_{zkSND}}$ with the following conditions:

- Only one of these events must occur if the adversary $\mathcal{A}$ wins.
- If either event happens, either adversary $\mathcal{B}_1$, or $\mathcal{B}_2$ will successfully break unforgeability or soundness, respectively.

Definition of Events. Consider the experiment $\mathsf{UI}_{\mathsf{SPiRiT},\mathcal{A}}(\lambda)$ for which we define the following two events:

- Event $\mathsf{E_{tACT}}$: The adversary $\mathcal{A}$ terminates and produces a $\mathsf{pp_U} = (\mathsf{token}, \ldots)$ and π_{tok} that are not in the Register query list (while computing a valid trace tr and its associated NIZK proof π_{tr}).
- Event $\mathsf{E_{zkSND}}$: The adversary $\mathcal{A}$ terminates and produces an invalid trace tr accompanied by a valid proof π_{tr} (while presenting a valid token). Specifically, π_{tr} is valid but proves a wrong tr as NIZK statement, and, and the conditions for event $\mathsf{E_{tACT}}$ must not be met.

Conclusion of the Proof. Given that exactly one of the events $\mathsf{E_{tACT}}$ and $\mathsf{E_{zkSND}}$ must occur and these events are disjoint, by applying the total probability rule we can write:

$$\mathbf{Adv}^{\mathsf{UI}}_{\mathsf{SPiRiT},\mathcal{A}} = \Pr[\mathsf{UI}_{\mathcal{A}}((\lambda)) = 1] = \Pr[\mathsf{UI}_{\mathcal{A}}((\lambda)) = 1 \wedge \mathsf{E_{tACT}}] + \Pr[\mathsf{UI}_{\mathcal{A}}((\lambda)) = 1 \wedge \mathsf{E_{zkSND}}]$$

Furthermore, considering the construction of $\mathcal{B}_1$ and the fact that this reduction perfectly simulates the environment for $\mathcal{A}$, we have:

$$\Pr[\mathsf{UI}_{\mathcal{A}}((\lambda)) = 1 \wedge \mathsf{E_{tACT}}] = \Pr[\mathsf{UF}_{\mathsf{tACT},\mathcal{B}_1}((\lambda)) = 1 \wedge \mathsf{Event_{tACT}}] \leq \Pr[\mathsf{UF}_{\mathsf{tACT},\mathcal{B}_1}((\lambda)) = 1]$$

Likewise, we have, $\Pr[\mathsf{UI}_{\mathcal{A}}((\lambda)) = 1 \wedge \mathsf{E_{zkSND}}] \leq \Pr[\mathsf{zkSND}_{\mathsf{NIZK},\mathcal{B}_2}((\lambda)) = 1]$.
This proves Equation (1) and concludes the proof of Theorem 1.

Theorem 2. (Replay Security). *If* (ZKSetup, ZKPoK, ZKVerify) *is a* NIZK *with knowledge soundness property, then, the* SPiRiT *scheme described in Algorithm 1 satisfies replay security as in Definition Definition 5.*

Proof. Replay security aims to prevent false positives meaning that an adversary $\mathcal{M}$ cannot cause an honest SPiRiT user B not in contact with an honest diagnosed user A or corrupted diagnosed user C to receive an alarm. Consider the experiment $\mathsf{Replay}_{\mathsf{SPiRiT},\mathcal{M},\Delta}(\lambda)$ for which we define the following two events, where only one of these events must occur if the adversary $\mathcal{M}$ wins and it causes B, which was not in proximity to an infected user to receive false alarms.

- Event E_1: The adversary $\mathcal{M}$ has been in close proximity to honest user B. Also, $\mathcal{M}$ controls an infected corrupted user C. This event requires proximity of adversary $\mathcal{M}$ to B, while B and C have not been in contact with each other. The adversary $\mathcal{M}$ terminates at time t and rebroadcasts IDs that were sent by C (and known to $\mathcal{M}$) at time $t - \Delta$.
- Event E_2: The adversary $\mathcal{M}$ has been in close proximity to both honest users A and B, with A being infected, but B and A have not been in contact with each other. The adversary $\mathcal{M}$ terminates at time t and rebroadcasts IDs that it previously received from A at time $t - \Delta$.

For an honest user B to receive a false alarm, there must be an intersection between the set of announced IDs and the IDs stored on B's device. This can only happen if B's local database contains an ID associated with C (event E_1: warning triggered by a corrupted user C) or an ID associated with A (event E_2: warning triggered by an honest user A). Given that one of the events E_1 and E_2 must occur for the adversary to succeed in the experiment in Fig. 3, we can write:

$$\mathbf{Adv}^{\mathsf{Replay}}_{\mathsf{SPiRiT},\mathcal{M}} = \Pr[\mathsf{Replay}_{\mathcal{M}}((\lambda)) = 1] = \Pr[\mathsf{Replay}_{\mathcal{M}}((\lambda)) = 1 \wedge \mathsf{E}_1] + \Pr[\mathsf{Replay}_{\mathcal{M}}((\lambda)) = 1 \wedge \mathsf{E}_2]$$

If the conditions for event E_1 are met and the honest user B receives a false alarm, it implies that B's local database contains an ID associated with the corrupted user C, and that the epoch numbers corresponding to the matching IDs in both B's local database and the backend server's database must match. This matching is necessary because the epoch number is integrated into the ID generation process. For this to happen, the corrupted user C must produce an invalid trace tr accompanied by a valid proof π_{tr} (while presenting a valid token). Essentially, π_{tr} is valid but proves an incorrect trace tr as a NIZK statement, unless the backend server is compromised and updates the database with incorrect data and manipulated epoch numbers. Therefore, we conclude:

$$\Pr[\mathsf{Replay}_{\mathcal{M}}((\lambda)) = 1 \wedge \mathsf{E}_1] \leq \Pr[\mathsf{zkSND}_{\mathsf{NIZK},\mathcal{B}_2}((\lambda)) = 1].$$

where $\mathcal{B}_2$ is constructed similarly to Sect. 4.1. Likewise, we have,

$$\Pr[\mathsf{Replay}_{\mathcal{M}}((\lambda)) = 1 \wedge \mathsf{E}_2] \leq \Pr[\mathsf{zkSND}_{\mathsf{NIZK},\mathcal{B}_2}((\lambda)) = 1].$$

Hence, assuming the knowledge soundness property of NIZK, this concludes the proof of Theorem 2.

Theorem 3. (Unlinkability). *If the* tACT *scheme is an unlinkable threshold anonymous counting token, the* Ped.Commit *scheme provides hiding property, and* $\mathsf{NIZK} : (\mathsf{ZKSetup}, \mathsf{ZKPoK}, \mathsf{ZKVerify})$ *provides zero-knowledge property, then, the* SPiRiT *scheme described in Algorithm 1 satisfies unlinkability as in Definition Definition 6 in the random oracle model.*

Proof. We prove the theorem using a sequence of hybrid games.

G_0. The original game defined in Fig. 4.

G_1. Replace honest Diagnosis proofs with simulated proofs for the challenge token. By the zero-knowledge property of NIZK, G_0 and G_1 are computationally indistinguishable.

G_2. Replace PRF evaluations $\mathsf{eID}_i = \mathsf{PRF}(\mathsf{k}, i)$ in Broadcast queries with random values. Indistinguishability follows from PRF security.

G_3. This game is similar to its predecessor except that in any Register query, we change Ped.Commit evaluations for the key k as $\mathsf{cm_k} = \mathsf{Ped.Commit}(\mathsf{k}, r_\mathsf{k})$ to randomly sampled $\mathsf{cm_k}$. This change is indistinguishable due to the hiding property of Ped.Commit and the zero-knowledge property of NIZK.

G_4. Replace the user identifier $\mathsf{id_U}$ with a random string during registration. By the hiding property of Ped.Commit and the unlinkability of tACT, G_3 and G_4 are indistinguishable.

In G_4, Register queries are independent of $\mathsf{id_U}$, and $\mathsf{Chl_{Diagnosis}}$ returns fresh parameters and simulated proofs. Hence the adversary's advantage in guessing b is negligible under the security of PRF, the hiding property of Ped.Commit, the zero-knowledge property of NIZK, and the unlinkability of tACT.

Proof. To prove this theorem, we employ a hybrid argument where the games are defined as follows:

Game G_0 The original game as defined in Fig. 4.

Game G_1: This game is similar to its predecessor except now we change from honestly generated proofs for Diagnosis queries w.r.t. the challenge token to simulated proofs. Since the proof π_tr is now simulated, the key k is not needed as part of the witness anymore.

G_0-G_1: The games G_0 and G_1 are computationally indistinguishable. This is justified by the zero-knowledge property of the NIZK argument.

Game G_2: This game is similar to its predecessor except that in any Broadcast query, we change PRF evaluations for the pseudo-random ID $\mathsf{eID}_i = \mathsf{PRF}(\mathsf{k}, i)$ to randomly sampled eID_i.

G_1-G_2: The games G_1 and G_2 are computationally indistinguishable. This is justified by the security of the PRF scheme.

Game G_3: This game is similar to its predecessor except that in any Register query, we change Ped.Commit evaluations for the key k as $\mathsf{cm_k} = \mathsf{Ped.Commit}(\mathsf{k}, r_\mathsf{k})$ to randomly sampled $\mathsf{cm_k}$.

G_2-G_3: The games G_2 and G_3 are computationally indistinguishable. This is justified by the hiding property of the Ped.Commit scheme and the zero-knowledge property of the NIZK argument.

Game G_4: This game is similar to its predecessor except that in any Register query, we change user identifier $\mathsf{id_U}$ to a randomly sampled string.

G_3-G_4: The games G_3 and G_4 are computationally indistinguishable. This is justified by assuming Ped.Commit scheme provides the hiding property and tACT scheme provides unlinkability.

In game G_4, Register queries no longer depend on the user's $\mathsf{id_U}$. $\mathsf{Chl_{Diagnosis}}$ oracle returns fresh $\mathsf{pp_U}, \mathsf{tr}$ on random $\mathsf{id_U}$, and a simulated proof π_tr. Hence, assuming the unlinkablity of tACT, hiding property of Ped.Commit, zero-knowledge property of NIZK, and security of PRF, adversary $\mathcal{A}$ has a negligible advantage in guessing the bit b, and the theorem follows.

5 Evaluation

In this section, we evaluate the proposed protocol using a face-to-face individual interaction dataset, specifically the InVS15 dataset [22]. The InVS15 dataset comprises face-to-face interactions measured over 12 days in an office building in France in 2015. We assume all participants use COVID-19 contact tracing mobile applications. The median incubation period (time from exposure to symptom onset) for COVID-19 is reported to be 5 days, but it can range from 2 to 14 days [28]. Studies indicate that people can start transmitting the virus even before symptoms appear, typically around 1 to 2 days before they feel sick [12]. We assume that all users who had high-risk contact with infected individuals will become infected and can transmit the virus to others after 4 days from the high-risk contact. In addition, we assume that none of these newly infected users can be detected without receiving high-risk alarms due to the lack of symptoms. We consider several scenarios with varying percentages of initially infected users. The objective is to identify all users with high-risk contacts with both the initial infected users and the secondary high-risk users after 4 days. We update the set of infected users likely to transfer the virus to other users (after 4 days from having a high-risk contact) day by day. Here, a high-risk contact is defined as a face-to-face interaction lasting 5 min or more. In our simulations, we conduct 1,000 runs with randomly selected COVID-19-infected users and passive users. The *high-risk case detection probability* is the ratio of detected high-risk cases to the total number of high-risk cases, averaged over these 1,000 runs. A high-risk case is an individual, who had a high-risk contact with an infected person (either those initially revealed or those infected by the initially revealed and capable of transmitting the virus after 4 days). The *COVID-19%* is defined as the number of initially revealed COVID-19-infected users relative to the total number of users.

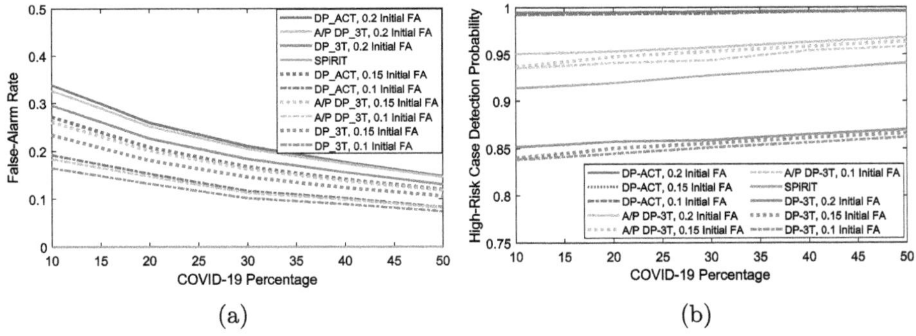

Fig. 5. (a) High-risk case detection probability versus the COVID-19%; (b) False-alarm rate versus the COVID-19%; for initial false-alarm rates of 0.1, 0.15, and 0.2, with 10% of users being passive.

5.1 False Positive

In the following, we explore the impact of attackers attempting to falsely reveal the IDs of the non-infected users as those of the infected ones. We define the *initial false-alarm rate* as the proportion of users falsely revealed as infected to the total number of users. We also define the *false-alarm rate* as the proportion of users falsely identified as infected (including those falsely revealed as infected) to the total number of users. In each run of our experiment, the users falsely revealed as infected are selected randomly. In Fig. 5a, we illustrate the false-alarm rate versus the COVID-19% for initial false-alarm rates of 0.1, 0.15, and 0.2, with 10% of users being passive. Figure 5b also shows the high-risk case detection probability versus the COVID-19% for initial false-alarm rates of 0.1, 0.15, and 0.2, with 10% of users being passive. As can be seen, having an initial false-alarm rate results in a slightly higher high-risk case detection probability. This is because some real high-risk cases have high-risk contact with the falsely identified users. However, as this initial false alarm propagates over our study period, it results to a significant false-alarm rate after 12 days according to Fig. 5a. The proposed SPiRiT protocol, however, is not affected by the initial false alarm due to integrating the verifiability mechanism. The false-alarm rate is 0 when using the proposed SPiRiT protocol, while our performance is better than DP-3T and on par with A/P DP-3T according to Fig. 5b.

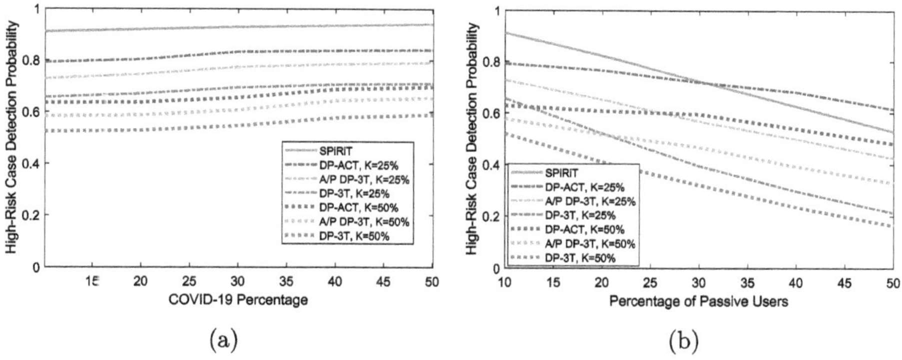

Fig. 6. (a) High-risk case detection probability versus the COVID-19% with 10% of users being passive; (b) High-risk case detection probability versus the percentage of passive users with 10% of users being diagnosed with COVID-19; assuming that 20% and 50% percentages of the broadcasted IDs during the contagious period are not revealed by the diagnosed users.

5.2 False Negative

We assume that diagnosed users tend not to reveal a certain percentage of their broadcasted IDs during their contagious period, denoted by K. Figure 6a illustrates the high-risk case detection probability versus the COVID-19% with 10%

of users being passive, assuming that 20% and 50% of the broadcasted IDs during the contagious period are not revealed by the diagnosed users. Furthermore, Fig. 6b shows the high-risk case detection probability versus the percentage of passive users with 10% of users being diagnosed with COVID-19 assuming that 20% and 50% percentages of the broadcasted IDs during the contagious period are not revealed by the diagnosed users. As can be seen from Fig. 6, if some percentage of the broadcasted IDs during the contagious period are not revealed by the diagnosed users, the performance of the COVID-19 contact tracing can decrease significantly. However, this issue is resolved in the proposed SPiRiT protocol.

5.3 Efficiency Analysis

We now provide a cost analysis of SPiRiT. We leverage the tACT proposed in [1] along with Naor-Pinkas-Reingold PRF [33] in our instantiation. Our implementation is developed in Rust using the `ark_bls12_381` library, compiled for cross-platform execution on ARM-based mobile devices (`aarch64-apple-ios` for iOS, `aarch64-linux-android` for Android) via the Rust toolchain, ensuring portability and near-native performance. The code is not optimized, leaving room for potential performance improvements in future iterations. The issuer runtime costs are measured on an Intel Core i7-1265U with 16 GB of RAM spanning high-performance, mid-range, and older hardware still in use. The overview of the runtime costs, broken down by individual algorithms, is presented in Table 2. With $t = \frac{N}{2} + 1$ as parameter of tACT, where N denotes the number of issuers, running $\mathsf{Register}$ on the user side requires approximately 359 ms for $N = 4$ on the iPhone 13 Pro, increasing to 2592.7 ms on the Huawei P10. We note that $\mathsf{Register}$ is a *one-time* operation executed as a single-round protocol, that can be run in parallel with all issuers. This mitigates the impact of $\mathsf{Register}$ on overall system performance. Also, $\mathsf{Diagnosis}$ is *only necessary to be run by a user once the user gets infected.* On the other hand, algorithms $\mathsf{Broadcast}$ and Trace are expected to be executed frequently by system users during the system's operation. As such, their runtime performance is critical for ensuring the schemenn's practical efficiency and scalability in real-world deployments.

The Trace algorithm follows the same operational steps as in prior works; thus, we expect its runtime performance to be comparable, since the verifiability features of our scheme do not impact the trace phase. For our implementation, the Cuckoo filter parameters follow the configuration in [29], with a bucket size of $b = 3$, tag length $v = 32$, and a maximum false positive rate of $\epsilon_{\text{max}} \approx 2^{-29}$. In Trace algorithm, the user device looks up the downloaded CF to determine the intersection. Consequently, the computational cost of the Trace is linear with respect to the size of the table $\mathsf{T}_{\mathsf{eID}}$ stored on the user device. Assuming a relevant epidemiological timeframe of 10 days and an epoch duration i of 15 min, we have $|\mathsf{T}_{\mathsf{eID}}| = 960$. This results in an average total lookup time of 346.2 ms on an iPhone 13 Pro and up to 2500 ms on the slowest tested device, demonstrating the practicality of the protocol for real-time usage.

The primary communication overhead arises from transmitting the CF from the server to the user. For instance, based on the database size considered in [29], a compressed CF representing a server database of size $|DB| = 2^{28}$ with a FPR of $\epsilon_{max} \approx 2^{-29}$, has a size of ≈ 1 GiB. Such a large transmission is impractical for mobile networks due to bandwidth limitations and data costs. To address this bottleneck, we refer to the techniques outlined in [29] to reduce the user-server communication complexity to logarithmic in the size of the server database DB. Additionally, any changes in the server database–such as insertions or deletions–trigger an update phase. Instead of retransmitting the entire CF, the server sends a small delta update to the user device, which reflects only the modified entries. This incremental update mechanism further minimizes the communication overhead.

Table 2. Estimated runtime of SPiRiT with $N = 4$, $n = 30$, $t = \frac{N}{2} + 1$, $b = 3$, $v = 32$, $\epsilon_{max} \approx 2^{-29}$. All runtimes are given in milliseconds. Register is a one-time process, and Diagnosis is only necessary to be run by a user once the user gets infected. Trace is executed on a daily basis (e.g., daily scanning). $\mathsf{Register_I}$ and Verify were obtained on an Intel Core i7-1265U, while user-side operations ($\mathsf{Register_U}$, Broadcast, Diagnosis, Trace) were obtained on the specified devices.

Algorithm	iPhone 13 Pro	Galaxy S10	Huawei P10
$\mathsf{Register_I}$	103.6	103.6	103.6
$\mathsf{Register_U}$	359.0	1333.4	2592.7
Broadcast	0.1	0.3	0.6
Diagnosis	23.9	88.9	172.8
Verify	50.0	50.0	50.0
Trace	346.2	1285.7	2500.0

6 Discussion and Conclusion

The effectiveness of contact tracing systems ultimately depends on user participation, as detection coverage increases approximately quadratically with the fraction of app users in the population [14]. By enhancing reliability through verifiable reporting and minimizing false alarms, SPiRiT strengthens user trust, an essential factor for widespread uptake. While our simulation results may not fully capture this dynamic, we anticipate that the protocol will achieve higher detection rates in the long run, as user adoption increases, ultimately enhancing its long-term efficacy.

Acknowledgments. This work received funding from the EU research project SWARMCHESTRATE (project no. 101135012).

Disclosure of Interests. The authors have no competing interests to declare that are relevant to the content of this article.

References

1. Abdolmaleki, B., Michalas, A., Rabaninejad, R., Ramacher, S., Slamanig, D.: Attribute-based threshold issuance anonymous counting tokens and its application to sybil-resistant self-sovereign identity. Cryptology ePrint Archive, Paper 2024/1024 (2024). https://eprint.iacr.org/2024/1024
2. Abdolmaleki, B., Michalas, A., Rabaninejad, R., Ramacher, S., Slamanig, D.: Attribute-based threshold issuance anonymous counting tokens and its application to sybil-resistant self-sovereign identity. IACR Commun. Cryptology **3**(1) (2026). https://doi.org/10.62056/ayivr-zn4
3. Abtahi, A.: Dp-act: decentralized privacy-preserving asymmetric digital contact tracing. In: Proceedings on Privacy Enhancing Technologies (2024)
4. Altmann, S., et al.: Acceptability of app-based contact tracing for covid-19: cross-country survey study. JMIR Mhealth Uhealth **8**(8), e19857 (2020)
5. Apple, Google: Privacy-Preserving Contact Tracing (2020). http://www.apple.com/covid19/contacttracing
6. Auerbach, B., Chakraborty, S., Klein, K., Pascual-Perez, G., Pietrzak, K., Walter, M., Yeo, M.: Inverse-sybil attacks in automated contact tracing. In: Cryptographers' Track at the RSA Conference, pp. 399–421. Springer (2021)
7. Ayalon, O.: Exploring privacy and incentives considerations in adoption of covid-19 contact tracing apps. In: USENIX Security Symposium (2023)
8. Benhamouda, F., Raykova, M., Seth, K.: Anonymous counting tokens. In: ASIACRYPT (2023)
9. Beskorovajnov, W., Dörre, F., Hartung, G., Koch, A., Müller-Quade, J., Strufe, T.: Contra corona: Contact tracing against the coronavirus by bridging the centralized-decentralized divide for stronger privacy. In: ASIACRYPT (2021)
10. California Health Care Foundation. https://www.chcf.org/blog/preliminary-research-suggests-covid-19-warning-app-slowed-transmission-virus/
11. Canetti, R., et al.: Privacy-preserving automated exposure notification. Cryptology ePrint Archive (2020)
12. Cevik, M., Kuppalli, K., Kindrachuk, J., Peiris, M.: Virology, transmission, and pathogenesis of sars-cov-2. bmj 371 (2020)
13. Chan, E.Y., Saqib, N.U.: Privacy concerns can explain unwillingness to download and use contact tracing apps when covid-19 concerns are high. Comput. Hum. Behav. **119**, 106718 (2021)
14. Cicala, F.: Pure: A framework for analyzing proximity-based contact tracing protocols. ACM Computing Surveys (CSUR) (2021)
15. Cramer, R.: Modular design of secure yet practical cryptographic protocols. CWI and U. of Amsterdam 2 (1996). Ph. D.-thesis
16. Cramer, R.: Proofs of partial knowledge and simplified design of witness hiding protocols. In: Annual International Cryptology Conference (1994)
17. Dodis, Y., Yampolskiy, A.: A verifiable random function with short proofs and keys. In: Public Key Cryptography-PKC (2005)
18. DP-3T GitHub: Privacy and security risk evaluation of digital proximity tracing systems (2024). https://github.com/DP-3T/documents/blob/master/
19. Fan, B., Andersen, D.G., Kaminsky, M., Mitzenmacher, M.D.: Cuckoo filter: practically better than bloom. In: Proceedings of the 10th ACM International on Conference on emerging Networking Experiments and Technologies, pp. 75–88 (2014)
20. Fuchsbauer, G., Gay, R.: Weakly secure equivalence-class signatures from standard assumptions. In: Public-Key Cryptography-PKC (2018)

21. Fuchsbauer, G.: Structure-preserving signatures on equivalence classes and constant-size anonymous credentials. J. Cryptol. (2019)
22. Génois, M., Barrat, A.: Can co-location be used as a proxy for face-to-face contacts? EPJ Data Sci. **7**(1), 1–18 (2018)
23. Givehchian, H., et al.: Evaluating physical-layer ble location tracking attacks on mobile devices. In: IEEE Symposium on Security and Privacy (SP) (2022)
24. Givehchian, H., et al.: Practical obfuscation of ble physical-layer fingerprints on mobile devices. In: IEEE Symposium on Security and Privacy (SP) (2023)
25. Griffy, S., Lysyanskaya, A.: Pacific: privacy-preserving automated contact tracing scheme featuring integrity against cloning. Cryptology ePrint Archive (2023)
26. Günther, C.U., Pietrzak, K.: Deniability in automated contact tracing: impossibilities and possibilities. In: Proceedings on Privacy Enhancing Technologies (2024)
27. Hassandoust, F., et al.: Individuals' privacy concerns and adoption of contact tracing mobile applications in a pandemic: a situational privacy calculus perspective. J. Am. Med. Inform. Assoc. **28**(3), 463–471 (2021)
28. Johansson, M.A., et al.: Sars-cov-2 transmission from people without covid-19 symptoms. JAMA Netw. Open **4**(1), e2035057–e2035057 (2021)
29. Kales, D., Rechberger, C., Schneider, T., Senker, M., Weinert, C.: Mobile private contact discovery at scale. In: 28th USENIX Security Symposium (2019)
30. Kaptchuk, G., et al.: How good is good enough? quantifying the impact of benefits, accuracy, and privacy on willingness to adopt covid-19 decision aids. Digital Threats: Res. Practice (DTRAP) **3**(3), 1–18 (2022)
31. Kate, A., Huang, Y., Goldberg, I.: Distributed key generation in the wild. Cryptology ePrint Archive (2012)
32. Morio, K., Esiyok, I., Jackson, D., Künnemann, R.: Automated security analysis of exposure notification systems. In: 32nd USENIX Security Symposium (2023)
33. Naor, M., Pinkas, B., Reingold, O.: Distributed pseudo-random functions and kdcs. In: Stern, J. (ed.) Advances in Cryptology - EUROCRYPT (1999)
34. Silde, T., Strand, M.: Anonymous tokens with public metadata and applications to private contact tracing. In: International Conference on Financial Cryptography and Data Security, pp. 179–199. Springer (2022)
35. Tedeschi, P., Bakiras, S., Di Pietro, R.: Spreadmenot: a provably secure and privacy-preserving contact tracing protocol. IEEE Trans. Dependable Secure Comput. **20**(3), 2500–2515 (2022)
36. Troncoso, C.: Decentralized privacy-preserving proximity tracing (2020). arXiv preprint arXiv:2005.12273
37. Troncoso, C.: Deploying decentralized, privacy-preserving proximity tracing. Commun. ACM (2022)

Beyond Theory: Identifying Barriers to Applied GDPR Compliance in a Privacy Range

Sophia Mittelbach(✉), Florian Seida, and Dominik Herrmann

University of Bamberg, Bamberg, Germany
{sophia.mittelbach,dh.psi}@uni-bamberg.de, mail@florianseida.de

Abstract. Prior work identifies insufficient GDPR knowledge as a main barrier to privacy-compliant software development and recommends formal education as a remedy. But does theoretical knowledge translate into applied competence? We investigate this question through a qualitative lab study (N = 10) in which IT students who had recently completed a dedicated GDPR lecture course attempted to identify privacy issues in the *Privacy Range*, a high-fidelity web environment with 13 intentional GDPR-related problems. Using thematic analysis, framework analysis, and qualitative content analysis, we examined participants' investigative behavior, translation successes and failures, and their perception of the environment as a training tool. Findings suggest that barriers arose less from absent conceptual knowledge than from difficulties in procedural application of that knowledge in context. Participants lacked systematic investigation routines, defaulted to trusting interface claims rather than verifying system behavior, and struggled to connect legal concepts to their technical manifestations. We further observed that habituated exposure to non-compliant web patterns could override formal knowledge, which led to normalizing problems instead of triggering detection. Post-session interviews indicate that participants valued the Privacy Range less as a knowledge delivery mechanism than as a diagnostic instrument that made their own competence gaps visible. These findings inform the development of practice-oriented GDPR training that targets procedural skills alongside conceptual understanding.

Keywords: GDPR · Privacy compliance · Training environment · Applied competence · Practitioner training

1 Introduction

Data protection regulations such as the General Data Protection Regulation (GDPR) [12] have made privacy compliance a central concern for software engineers and IT practitioners. However, empirical evidence suggests that even practitioners who are aware of privacy challenges struggle to apply them correctly in

S. Nadjm-Tehrani et al. (Eds.): ARES 2026, LNCS 16898, pp. 88–110, 2027.
https://doi.org/10.1007/978-3-032-36874-4_5

practice [4,17]. While legal background knowledge is highly relevant for successful GDPR implementation, the regulation leaves substantial room for interpretation and does not easily translate into concrete software requirements [8,16,19]. Compliance assessment thus depends on practitioners' ability to verify assumptions, interpret system behavior, and reason about ambiguous situations. In web contexts, integration decisions can increase privacy risks, especially the embedding of third-party services [33,34]. As these challenges affect more actors than developers alone (e. g., website operators), we frame our target group more broadly as "IT practitioners".

A substantial body of prior work has proposed tools, guidelines, methods, and frameworks to support privacy-aware software development across the lifecycle [22,23,29,36]. However, some of these solutions require existing privacy expertise or familiarity with specific regulations, which limits their practical applicability [35]. The prevailing recommendation remains formal GDPR education and training [3,35]. Our study therefore complements the existing line of work that documents persistent legal-technical translation gaps in operationalization of privacy principles in concrete technical contexts [3,17,18] by examining whether such gaps persist after participants have completed a dedicated, legally-focused GDPR lecture course. We treat this course as broadly representative of formal GDPR education for non-lawyers as we presume it to be delivered in IT-related curricula and professional settings.

In the field of cybersecurity education and training, hands-on exercises (e. g., Capture-The-Flag (CTF) challenges, vulnerability assessment, and pentesting) in realistic circumstances such as high-fidelity environments (Cyber Ranges) are well-established as they promote active learning and engagement [9]. This vulnerability-detection paradigm of learning by looking for flaws in situ has proven effective in building the kind of applied reasoning that bridging theory and practice demands [9].

We are not aware of a GDPR-focused high-fidelity web training environment that embeds realistic privacy violations for applied analysis. We therefore created the Privacy Range: an exploratory web environment that, analogous to cyber ranges in the security domain, embeds GDPR-relevant problems in a realistic application with authentic technical infrastructure, combining environmental fidelity with the vulnerability-detection paradigm described above.

Using this environment, we examine how IT students (as novice IT practitioners) with theoretical GDPR knowledge identify and reason about privacy issues in a realistic web application context. We recruited 10 students from IT-related degree programs who had recently completed a dedicated 1-week GDPR lecture course, which allows us to study participants who possess a shared, recent, and verifiable baseline of theoretical GDPR knowledge. Their diverse IT-related backgrounds reflect the range of roles involved in real-world website creation and maintenance [34], allowing us to examine whether legal knowledge is sufficient for individuals with a technical background to successfully analyze client-side GDPR issues.

Beyond investigating where and why theory-practice translation succeeds or fails in participants with a controlled theoretical knowledge baseline, the study serves as a preliminary evaluation of the Privacy Range as a novel training concept. Based on this, we address the following research questions:

1. How do novice IT practitioners who have completed a GDPR lecture course approach the task of identifying privacy issues in a realistic web environment?
2. How and why does translation of theoretical GDPR knowledge into hands-on privacy analysis succeed or fail?
3. How do participants perceive the value of the Privacy Range as a tool for applying and consolidating theoretical GDPR knowledge?

This paper makes three contributions. First, we introduce the Privacy Range, a high-fidelity training environment that confronts trainees with realistic GDPR-related problems requiring active investigation. Second, we characterize a procedural competence layer that mediates between conceptual GDPR knowledge and applied compliance analysis, challenging the implicit assumption that once legal concepts are understood, their technical manifestation follows. Third, we provide a preliminary evaluation of the Privacy Range as a GDPR training tool prototype for this procedural layer.

2 Related Work

In this section, we summarize prior research on the challenges IT practitioners face with translating legal privacy requirements into technical implementations. We further present existing attempts for privacy education environments and the OWASP Juice Shop [20], as it is the most relevant conceptual inspiration for our Privacy Range training environment.

2.1 Difficulties with Technical GDPR Implementation

Previous research has shown that developers face issues with embedding privacy principles into software. Senarath and Arachchilage [30] found that developers lacked formal privacy knowledge, deprioritized privacy as a non-functional requirement, and had difficulties validating the privacy-compliance of their designs. Alhazmi and Arachchilage [3] similarly found limited GDPR familiarity and ambiguity in technical guidance as main barriers to compliant implementation.

Utz et al. [34] investigated third-party adoption decisions for common use cases and the extent to which privacy and data collection issues were considered in these processes. It was found that ease of integration, features, and familiarity were the prevalent adoption drivers, while privacy rarely played any role in the decision process. Participants showed awareness of data collection tied to a service's core purpose but had limited understanding of incidental data exposure, particularly the transmission of IP addresses and device information inherent to any third-party HTTP(S) request. The study also found that privacy policies were rarely consulted, and that developers often trusted third parties or felt unable to change default data collection.

Horstmann et al. [17] studied how professional developers implement privacy requirements and the challenges they encounter in practice through a qualitative lab study involving GDPR-related programming tasks. They found that privacy-compliant solutions were rare across conditions, even when developers were explicitly prompted to implement a GDPR-compliant solution and had access to a privacy expert, who was infrequently consulted and had limited impact. Overall, the results indicate that developers tend to deprioritize privacy in favor of functionality and security, perceive privacy requirements as restrictive and complex, and often lack support or motivation to implement privacy effectively.

Subsequently, Horstmann et al. [18] further explored developer behavior and their use of and challenges with privacy information sources when identifying privacy issues and remedies in a GDPR-related fictional privacy-sensitive scenario. Participants were asked to pinpoint privacy issues, using their own knowledge first, followed by web search and AI assistants. Findings suggest that developers' personal knowledge was insufficient for detecting privacy issues as they heavily relied on external information sources. Participants frequently failed to identify critical privacy issues and, when they did recognize problems, proposed mitigation measures that were generic rather than context-sensitive and technically precise, which underpins the persistent gap between theoretical privacy knowledge and applied problem detection.

While this work highlights fundamental challenges in translating GDPR principles into practice, it primarily reflects situations in which practitioners lack prior formal GDPR education, their background knowledge level varies, or is unknown. In contrast, our study focuses on participants who have completed a dedicated GDPR lecture course, allowing us to examine challenges that persist despite conceptual familiarity with the regulation. This distinction enables a more fine-grained analysis of whether observed implementation gaps are primarily driven by missing legal knowledge or by difficulties in applying that knowledge in concrete technical contexts.

2.2 Training Environments for Privacy and Security

In subsequent work, Alhazmi and Arachchilage [2] proposed a serious game design framework for improving developers' ability to achieve GDPR-compliant implementation. The framework combines a learning taxonomy with the six GDPR principles, and a behavioral motivation model based on threat perception. The framework remains conceptual, as the game has not yet been implemented or empirically evaluated to date.

The Privacy Universe, created and evaluated by Christensen et al. [7], is an extension of a cybersecurity training platform (Haaukins [28]) aimed at increasing student competencies related to privacy, data protection and general risks of the online space. Trainees solve various CTF challenges focused on privacy in social media network contexts. The Privacy Universe differs from our approach as it addresses non-technical users and is not targeted to the GDPR.

In the domain of (web) security, realistic training environments are common and range from web security playgrounds and serious games to complex and sophisticated laboratory environments. The OWASP Juice Shop is an intentionally vulnerable web application designed as a training environment for web security [20]. It contains numerous hacking challenges of varying difficulty and requires users to actively exploit security flaws embedded in a realistic online shop setting. Progress is tracked via an in-application scoreboard, and players can look up hints for the challenges. We adopt the Juice Shop's core paradigm – providing bad rather than best practices and encouraging learning through detection of intentionally embedded flaws in a realistic application – but transfer it to the domain of privacy and the GDPR.

3 Methods

We conducted an exploratory qualitative lab study with 10 IT students, using interaction observation with the think-aloud method [21] to obtain detailed insights into participants' reasoning under controlled conditions. As the Privacy Range is conceptually new, we prioritized rich qualitative data for exploratory evaluation over quantitative generalization. We first describe the Privacy Range environment, followed by the study procedure, course details, participants and recruitment, and data analysis.

3.1 About the Privacy Range Environment

The training environment is designed as an online shop (Fig. 1), chosen because online shops involve many privacy-relevant functionalities (user accounts, reviews, payment data) and are familiar to most internet users. The shop contains 13 intentionally embedded GDPR-related problems that vary in legal clarity and discoverability, divided into three categories: problems visible in the UI (V1–V6), problems resulting from missing functionality or information (M1–M2), and problems hidden in source code or browser developer tools (H1–H5). Most problems are clear GDPR violations, but two problems can be seen as merely user-unfriendly choices that are not optimal from a GDPR or privacy perspective (M1, H4). These problems require weighing up the interests of users and operators/developers, as is often necessary in reality. Table 1 shows examples from each problem category. For designing the problems, we drew on the GDPR as well as various sources, such as the OWASP *Top 10 Privacy Risks* project https://owasp.org/www-project-top-10-privacy-risks/ and empirical analyses of prevalent issues of non-compliance on the web, e.g. [25]. The environment is built on a modern web stack (Nuxt, Strapi, Docker) and deployed as a self-contained containerized setup. Source code, full problem descriptions, design rationales and the mapping of problems to sources are provided in the supplementary material (https://doi.org/10.5281/zenodo.20285016).

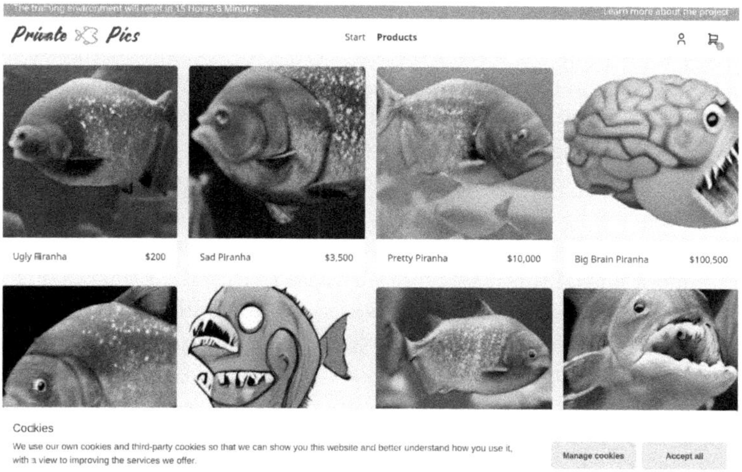

Fig. 1. Screenshot of the Privacy Range, which is designed as a fictitious online shop.

Table 1. Example implemented privacy-related problems

Type	Problem	Description
Visible	V2: Sneaky Custom Preferences	Consent toggles for non-essential cookies are pre-enabled by default.
	V4: Breaking Right to Erasure	Account deletion leaves username and email visible in public reviews and user pages.
Hidden	H1: Faulty Content Blocker	A hashtag button loads scripts and cookies without disclosure and consent.
	H5: Leaky Forms	Form inputs are sent to a third party before submission [31].
Missing	M2: Incomplete Privacy Policy	The privacy policy omits required information on data portability, storage duration, and processing purposes.

3.2 Study Setup and Procedure

After initial briefing and obtaining consent, each session followed five steps:

1. **Pre-Interview.** At the beginning of the session, a semi-structured interview was conducted assessing self-rated GDPR and web development proficiency and what participants would focus on when reviewing a web application for GDPR compliance.
2. **Exploration phase.** Participants engaged in a free, unstructured exploration of the Privacy Range with the instruction to identify privacy-related issues ("Find privacy problems. Whenever you think you found a problem, articulate what the problem is as clearly as possible."). They were informed about the three different categories of problems (*visible*, *hidden*, *missing*) and the

possibility for legal ambiguities, but received no further guidance. This phase ended when participants indicated that they had completed their exploration or after a maximum duration of 45 min. In the session introduction, the facilitator stated that the study examined both the training environment and how participants identified privacy issues based on the theoretical course content. To minimize performance pressure, the platform-evaluation aspect was emphasized.
3. **Hint phase.** For each problem not identified during the exploration phase, participants received up to two hints by the conducting researcher. First-level hints provided a subtle nudge, whereas second-level hints gave more explicit guidance. A second-level hint was given if, after the first hint, the participant explicitly stated that they were stuck, shifted their exploration to a different area of the website, or failed to demonstrate at least partial recognition of the problem within two minutes.
4. **Walkthrough phase.** After the exploration and hint phases, participants were presented with a structured walkthrough explaining each problem, regardless of whether they found it in the phases before. For every problem, they were asked to reflect on their ability to identify the problem and attention to or avoidance of similar issues in future development scenarios.
5. **Final interview.** The session concluded with a semi-structured interview for gathering qualitative feedback on the overall experience and the Privacy Range as a training tool and assessing participants' perceived learning outcomes.

Exploration lasted between 12 and 45 min ($M = 29$ min), the hint phase between 7 and 24 min ($M = 15$ min), and the walkthrough between 9 and 41 min ($M = 27$ min). Session duration, excluding briefing, pre- and post-interviews, ranged from 60 to 90 min.

This study procedure combines think-aloud observation [10] with elements of guided discovery learning [1] and stimulated recall [15]. Our sequential structure – free exploration followed by scaffolding through graduated hints and, finally, explicit instruction – follows the Problem Solving before Instruction (PS-I) paradigm [24], in which initial (guided) struggle with a problem activates prior knowledge, reveals misconceptions, and makes subsequent instruction more effective [32]. The exploration and hint phases yield situated data on reasoning processes and knowledge application (RQ1, RQ2). The hint phase both ensures coverage of relevant areas and supports guided discovery learning [1]. The walkthrough phase functions as a form of stimulated recall [15] and elicits retrospective reflection that makes unobservable gaps explicit. At the same time, the walkthrough ensures participants get the correct instruction in the end, which is an important element of PS-I [24].

Setup. All sessions were conducted using Mozilla Firefox with the default settings without any privacy-enhancing extensions enabled. A researcher was seated next to the participant to facilitate the think-aloud protocol, track problem discovery, and document handout usage and non-verbalized behavior. No feedback, confirmation, or guidance toward specific problems was provided during the exploration phase. The exploration and hint phases were conducted within the training environment. For the reflection phase, participants were instructed to navigate to a separate walkthrough page containing the official problem explanations. This page was separated from the training environment to prevent premature exposure to solutions.

Provided Resources. To mitigate disadvantages for participants unfamiliar with Firefox as a development browser and to balance variability in technical expertise, participants were provided with a printed handout explaining Firefox dev tools (how to use network and storage inspection to look for third-party requests and cookies). In addition, participants were allowed to consult a GDPR reference handout, provided as a bookmarked page in the browser toolbar. It summarized core GDPR principles, data subject rights, and background information on cookies and consent management. Both handouts were available throughout the entire session. Mock user data for an already registered account was provided for logging in. All provided resources, as well as interview questions, hints, and the full problem recognition rubric are made available in the supplementary material (see Sect. 3.1).

3.3 Piloting

We conducted three pilot sessions to refine the study protocol, one with a former student (Pilot1) and two with student assistants from our chair (Pilot2, Pilot3). All pilot participants had attended the same GDPR lecture course as our participants (see Sect. 3.4). Pilot2 and Pilot3 had completed the course recently, like the main study participants. As a result of the pilots, we replaced an initial task-based exploration design with free exploration, as pilot participants indicated that the shop's natural affordances provided sufficient navigational structure, and separated the hint phase from exploration, as hints interrupted exploration flow and reduced control over session progression. The third pilot followed the finalized protocol and data collection procedures. As this participant belonged to the target population, we included the session data in the analysis as P0.

3.4 Participants, Course Details, and Recruitment

Our study required participants with an IT background, ideally some experience with web development, a comparable level of theoretical knowledge about privacy and specifically the GDPR, who were available for a 90 min in-person session. To find participants who meet these criteria, we chose to recruit only among students who recently attended a one-week intensive GDPR lecture course. The course is taught by a practicing data-protection lawyer, comprises 14 lectures of 90 min, and is concluded by a 90-minute written exam. While tailored to IT practitioners (with case discussions and a Moot Court using software-engineering and web-context scenarios), the course is legally focused and does not include hands-on technical exercises such as browser developer tools, network inspection, or source-code review. It covers the legal foundations of European data-protection law, such as the scope of the GDPR; data-protection principles; lawful bases of processing; transparency obligations and data-subject rights; controller and processor obligations; third-country transfer; security of processing; incident handling, and liability and sanctions.

Participants were recruited via the course forum and a personal follow-up invitation in November 2025 after the final exam had been graded. The invitation described the study purpose as evaluation of a new training tool. While the invitation made the general study task transparent, it did not reference specific GDPR articles, problem types, or the number of problems to be found. Think-aloud sessions took place between November 17 and December 5, 2025. Of the 29 students registered for the final exam, 10 had volunteered by that point, of whom 9 were eligible for participation. We chose to not extend recruitment to keep the interval between course completion and study participation comparable. Together with P0 (Sect. 3.3), the final sample consisted of 10 students with different IT-related backgrounds (see Table 2). Participants were incentivized and compensated with a 20 € shopping voucher. We reflect on the limitations of our small student sample in Sect. 5.2. Although we did not assess theoretical saturation, we observed that core behavioral patterns recurred across participants from mid-sample onward, and code saturation was reached after the sixth participant.

Table 2. Participant overview. GDPR and web development (WebDev) expertise were self-rated on 7-point scales (1 = novice, 7 = expert). P0 served as the final pilot whose data was included in the analysis.

ID	Degree program	Semester	GDPR	WebDev
P0	Software Systems Science (B.Sc.)	6	5	7
P1	Computing in the Humanities (M.Sc.)	2	4	3
P2	Business Informatics (B.Sc.)	7	5	4
P3	Applied Computer Science (B.Sc.)	3	3	4
P4	Computing in the Humanities (M.Sc.)	3	2	3
P5	Applied Computer Science (B.Sc.)	6	3	4
P6	Computing in the Humanities (M.Sc.)	3	4	3
P7	Applied Computer Science (B.Sc.)	3	5	3
P8	Applied Computer Science (B.Sc.)	6	3	4
P9	Applied Computer Science (B.Sc.)	6	4	6

3.5 Ethical Considerations

Our institution does not require ethics board approval for studies of this type. All participants received a consent form explaining the types of data collected and data retention policies. Participants were informed that they could withdraw from the study at any time and were assured that participation had no professional or academic consequences. We de-personalized study data (e.g., by using pseudonyms and removing potentially identifying utterances from the transcript), and minimized data collection to what was deemed absolutely necessary, e.g., refraining from video-recording participants. Data handling was compliant with the GDPR, and recordings were deleted after completion of analysis. The full consent form, facilitator script, and interview questions are included in the supplementary material (see Sect. 3.1). None of the authors had personal connections to or grading authority over participants in the GDPR lecture course at the time of the study.

3.6 Data Collection and Analysis

Screen interactions and voice were recorded for analysis of interaction with the training environment and the problem walkthrough reflection. The pre- and postsession interviews were voice recorded. All recordings were transcribed locally with Whisper (https://github.com/openai/whisper) and the resulting transcripts were manually checked against the original recordings by the first researcher (R1). R1 also watched all session recordings end-to-end and annotated the time-stamped video transcripts with UI interactions and non-verbalized behavior to be available for coding. All analyzed sessions were conducted in German. Data analysis was performed on the original data, quotes were translated into English verbatim after the analysis was completed. Because the three research questions target different analytic goals – emergent behavioral patterns (RQ1), systematic cross-case comparison of recognition outcomes (RQ2), and participants' summarized perceptions (RQ3) – we applied a corresponding analytic method for each, as specified below. Data analysis was conducted with MAXQDA (https://www.maxqda.com/).

To explore participants' reasoning processes and behavioral patterns, we conducted an inductive reflexive thematic analysis following Braun and Clarke [6]. In line with the epistemological assumptions of reflexive thematic analysis, which foregrounds researcher reflexivity and does not require multiple independent coders [6,27], initial coding and theme development were carried out by the first researcher. To enhance analytic rigor and intersubjective transparency, the resulting candidate themes were subsequently reviewed through structured peer debriefing with a researcher experienced in qualitative analysis. Discussions were used to refine theme boundaries and clarify underlying analytic assumptions.

For RQ2, we followed a framework analysis procedure [14]. After familiarization, we developed an analytic framework with two dimensions: (i) problem recognition outcomes and (ii) the nature of translation failures (misconceptions, knowledge gaps, technical skill gaps). Translation failure categories were developed inductively during the indexing phase and charted across participants, problems, and session phases. For recognition coding, a rubric was developed prior to data collection to define when a privacy problem was considered not recognized, partially recognized, or fully recognized. Full recognition required articulating the core privacy and compliance implication specified for each problem (e.g., identifying third-party data exposure plus the resulting need for disclosure and consent), whereas partial recognition consisted of perceiving some aspects of the problem without the rubric-defined implication. A second researcher independently coded a subset of the data (40% of transcripts covering a range of participant profiles and recognition outcomes) using the rubric. Inter-coder agreement was substantial ($\kappa_w = .78$, quadratic weighted Cohen's kappa) [13]. Interpretive classifications regarding translation failures such as privacy-related and technical misconceptions were discussed with members of the research team with expertise in data protection and privacy to ensure domain plausibility. Answers to the final semi-structured interviews were analyzed using qualitative content analysis (QCA) according to Mayring [26]. QCA codes were applied independently to half of the interview transcripts by the second researcher, whereby inter-coder-reliability was substantial as well with $\kappa = .76$ and disagreements were refined through discussion.

4 Results

We first characterize how participants approached the task of identifying privacy issues (RQ1) based on thematic analysis of behavioral patterns observed during exploration and reflection. Second, we examine where and why translation of theoretical knowledge into applied analysis succeeded or failed (RQ2), using the results of framework analysis to map specific misconceptions, knowledge gaps, and skill-level barriers. Third, we report participants' perceptions of the Privacy Range as a training tool (RQ3). Our analysis uses data from all three interaction phases. The exploration and hint phases (EP, HP) contain participants' spontaneous behavior, reasoning, and reactions during interaction. The walkthrough phase (WP) captures retrospective reflection on the problems after their explanation. These phases constitute different analytical angles. In-situ data shows what participants did and said under realistic conditions, while walkthrough data reveals why participants believe they succeeded or failed. The latter can make otherwise unobservable gaps explicit but is also subject to hindsight bias. We therefore report the phase of origin for each analytic segment.

4.1 Behavioral Patterns During Investigation

We identified four themes that describe participants' investigation strategies and explain barriers to problem discovery.

Theme 1: Ad-Hoc Investigation Without Audit Infrastructure. Participants approached the exploration task without an established procedural script for conducting privacy audits. Rather than following a systematic workflow, investigation was ad hoc, reactive, and frequently marked by disorientation. Several participants explicitly expressed uncertainty about how to proceed (*"Well, to be honest, I don't really know what I'm looking for."* – P4:EP), indicating the absence of a mental checklist or investigative sequence. To compensate for this lack of structure, participants repeatedly relied on the provided GDPR handout, which was used as an improvised checklist by switching back and forth between the document and the website. In the absence of an audit-specific orientation, participants frequently applied their own user perspective as a fallback. This shaped how they navigated the system and, in some cases, led to entire features not being investigated at all when they were not deemed personally relevant or interesting (*"I'm someone who never really writes reviews, so [...] I didn't see the feature as particularly relevant to me."* – P5:WP). As a result, investigation paths remained opportunistic and fragmented rather than systematic. Contrasting cases show that more systematic investigation was possible, though observed far less frequently. In these instances, participants deliberately combined specific actions (e. g., login, form filling, checkout) with inspection of network traffic or storage, treating interactions as probes rather than mere use. This suggests an absence of a default audit procedure rather than an absolute inability.

Theme 2: Privacy Anchors – What Is Interpreted as Privacy-Relevant. Participants' investigations were guided by recurring privacy anchors that structured where they oriented their attention during exploration. These anchors functioned as focal points that made certain aspects of the system appear immediately privacy-relevant, while leaving others outside the scope of investigation. Importantly, these anchors were not incorrect, but limited in coverage due to their selective application.

Across sessions, participants most commonly oriented to privacy in terms of

- data minimization in forms (*"I'm currently looking at what data they want from me in order to do their thing, so if it's something obviously completely unnecessary, [...] I would say you don't need that to send me a product. That's why I'm looking at what they have, what they're asking for, and [...] whether it's necessary data collection."* – P1:EP)
- individual control through user rights such as rectification and deletion (*"But I think I'll see if I can delete my account, or rather, how I can delete it."* – P8:EP; *"It is definitely my right to delete this data."* – P6:EP)
- transparency and user-friendliness of disclosures (*"Cookies are displayed here for which there is no explanation. This means that there is simply a technical name here that does not mean much to users who are not technically savvy."* – P3:EP), and
- protection from potential harm (*"And I could misuse that if, I don't know, if I have an email address and then try to hack it or something, so that I could find out other information about that person and then misuse it."* – P2:EP; *"I actually just wanted to find out whether, anything is clearly evident, in terms of them transferring my data [...] in the URL or something to another site. That was important to me."* – P4:EP).

The Consent Management Platform (CMP) was also frequently inspected, as its visual prominence drew attention early in the exploration (*"The first thing I notice, of course, is the cookie banner, which I don't really approve of."* –

P7:EP). In contrast, elements that did not align with these anchors – such as background network traffic and third-party requests – were often overlooked or only superficially investigated.

Theme 3: The Verification Gap: Assumed Compliance Instead of Testing. Even when participants correctly identified privacy-relevant features, their investigation frequently remained superficial. For example, account and data deletion were typically accepted as successful based on immediate UI feedback, and most participants did not look for remaining user data, which was visible in the public reviews (*"Uh, again, because I, um, didn't do any proper pentesting. [...] because I didn't go out and check that when I delete my data, it happens everywhere on the site."* – P4:WP). As one participant reflected, *"[...] I somehow assume that when I delete my data and my account, everything will be deleted. But I can't verify that. Just like it was only when I got the hint that I realized, ah, you can log in again and check. It's a matter of believing rather than checking."* – P6:WP.

Trust in policy claims and interface signals (*"So they said the site is SSL encrypted, I'm assuming that's the case."* – P6:EP; *"But at least the data has been blocked for now, according to the UI at least."* – P1:EP) routinely replaced inspection of underlying system behavior. Only a small number of contrasting cases were observed, in which participants treated privacy claims as falsifiable, like verifying website encryption claims made in the privacy policy, inspecting API response payloads for remaining account data, revisiting the review page, or attempting to log in after account deletion.

Theme 4: Experience as a Double-Edged Sword. Participants' investigation strategies, expectations, and reasoning were strongly shaped by prior experiences with other websites. During inspection, participants frequently relied on comparisons with known interfaces and transferred established usage habits. Familiar patterns that are common on the web tended to remain unquestioned (*"Well, I'm actually already aware of that, but since it's relatively common for Google Fonts, for example, to be integrated somewhere, I didn't give it much thought, but the fact that this isn't okay because it's a third party didn't even occur to me at the time."* – P5:WP; *"I wouldn't know that you can do that directly – at least I don't know that from other websites, that you can do that directly in your profile. That's why it doesn't look unusual to me."* – P2:HP).

In some cases, experience transfer supported recognition, for instance when participants identified deceptive patterns precisely because of repeated exposure elsewhere (*"Well, it always annoys me when you see this on other websites, that you either can accept everything or you have this 'manage your cookies individually and please tell us for every single one whether this one is okay for this area after all.' And accordingly, it is then relatively visible.* – P7:WP). However, when experience transfer turned into habituation, it hindered detection (*"I could of course have had a Reject All button directly. [...] But honestly, I've gotten so used to it being this way that I don't even notice that it's actually rubbish."* – P6:HP) or rendered privacy issues effectively invisible (*"Okay, nothing strikes me as extremely negative so far, when I compare it to other websites I know."* – P5:EP).

A small number of participants explicitly noted that the ubiquity of such practices might even lead them to reproduce similar problems if they were responsible for implementing a website (*"I don't know if, because I'm so used to it being done that way, I'd do the same thing in my own application out of habit. Which is stupid. [...] I can't promise that I won't do the same stupid thing myself at some point."* – P5:WP). Prior web experience thus operates simultaneously as a resource and an obstacle.

4.2 Knowledge Gaps and Procedural Barriers

The following section examines recognition outcomes across problems and the specific knowledge-level breakdowns that contributed to translation failure.

Table 3. Problem recognition outcomes during exploration and after hints (N=10). Hint effectiveness reports participants who improved their recognition level (e. g., from none to partial or from partial to full) out of those who received hints for that problem. Example: For V2, 6 participants received hints and 5 of them improved their recognition level.

		Exploration		**After hints**		**Hint**
ID	**Short description**	**Partial**	**Full**	**Partial**	**Full**	**eff.**
Visible problems						
V1	CMP blocks privacy policy	–	1	1	9	9/9
V2	Optional cookies pre-enabled	2	2	4	5	5/6
V3	Hidden Deny All	–	3	3	7	7/7
V4	Incomplete account deletion	2	1	6	3	7/9
V5	Storage limitation violated	3	–	9	1	6/7
V6	Forced privacy policy agreement	4	3	4	5	3/6
Hidden problems						
H1	Hashtag button w/o consent	7	3	7	3	0/4
H2	Video cookie consent mislabeled[a]	1	1	1	1	0/6
H3	External font loading (IP exposure)	3	–	3	–	0/7
H4	Extensive third-party tracking	–	–	1	1	2/8
H5	Leaky Forms	3	–	7	1	5/7
Missing problems						
M1	Missing data export function	1	1	–	4	3/8
M2	Incomplete privacy policy	7	1	4	4	1/6

[a]Two participants did not face H2 during either phase because they did not notice the video, counts are therefore based on $n = 8$ for H2

Problem Recognition. Table 3 summarizes recognition outcomes across participants and problems during the exploration and hint phases. Participants rarely achieved full recognition of privacy problems during free exploration. Two extremes illustrate the spread: Network requests or cookies set by the unblocked hashtag button (H1) were at least partially recognized by all participants (7 partial; 3 full), whereas excessive tracking (H4) was not recognized by any participant. A recurring pattern was that some issues were salient enough to trigger concern but were rarely articulated in legally complete terms (e.g., the missing deny all option (V3), pre-enabled cookie consent (V2), or the incomplete privacy policy (M2)). By contrast, issues that depended on both inspecting background behavior and exploring alternative system states remained largely undetected in unstructured exploration (e.g., H2, and especially H4, where detection required accepting optional cookies which most participants never did purposefully).

Hints substantially improved recognition for *visible* and *missing* problems, but had little effect on *hidden* problems requiring technical interpretation. Also, hints were less effective for legally ambiguous problems that are not clear violations, but user-unfriendly choices (H4, M1).

Notably, alongside recognition failures, five participants made privacy-relevant observations about system aspects that were not among the 13 intended problems but could arguably constitute legitimate GDPR concerns: Two participants (P0, P7) noticed that account deletion was possible without additional user verification, P2 commented on missing password security requirements and the missing option to write anonymous reviews, and P6 claimed that automatically saving the address to the user profile after a purchase is illegitimate because it exceeds the legitimate purpose of data processing (the purchase).

Reasons for Translation Failures. While Table 3 captures whether problems were recognized, the following examines why translation failed when it did. We coded theory-practice translation failures as (i) misconceptions (incorrect or incomplete reasoning), (ii) knowledge gaps (explicitly stated uncertainty or missing knowledge), and (iii) technical skill gaps (limitations in using or interpreting developer tools). Individual segments could be coded on multiple dimensions where applicable, counts across categories are therefore not additive.

As shown in Table 4, misconceptions most frequently concerned the relationship of disclosure and consent. Participants often articulated the need for disclosure but rarely took the additional step toward consent – which is either required by Art. 5(3) of the ePrivacy Directive [11] or Art. 6(1)(a) GDPR [12]. For instance, after discovering undisclosed third-party requests in the network tab, P6 concluded: *"Everything they load, they should have told me about – but they didn't"* – P6:EP, without addressing user consent. Similarly, P5 noted: *"nowhere does it say that Twitter is involved as a third party"* – P5:EP, again stopping at disclosure. P1 stated: *"What is missing is active consent for the use of data. Or at least clear information"* – P1:EP, treating consent and information as interchangeable rather than distinct legal requirements. This pattern also appeared in V6, where participants confused the (wrong) forced agreement with the policy with consent as a lawful basis: *"The legal basis here is consent"* – P8:HP. A related misconception was the assumption that all cookies, including essential ones, require user consent.

Table 4. Most common translation failure clusters across phases. n = unique participants with at least one coded segment. EP/HP = exploration and hint phases, WP = walkthrough phase (retrospective reflection), participants may appear in both.

Category	**Subcategory**	**n**	**EP/HP**	**WP**
Misconception	Disclosure as default frame	9	9	0
	Scope/requirements of consent	6	4	2
Knowledge gap	Role/scope of functional cookies	7	7	1
	Third-party requests/IP transfer	6	3	4
	Leaky Forms	5	1	4
Technical skill gap	Network analysis	7	6	5
	Storage/cookie inspection	5	5	1
	Network analysis timing	4	4	0

Knowledge gaps clustered around (i) functional cookies, (ii) implications of third-party IP address transfers and (iii) the leaky forms [31] problem. Seven participants struggled to evaluate cookie categorization as misleading (H2) because they lacked the categorical framework to assess whether cookie consent was correctly classified. Gaps also occurred regarding third-party HTTP(S) requests. Six participants seemed unaware of the consequences of IP address transmission to external domains. For example, after enabling functional cookies and observing the third-party video domain, P3 stated: *"There's a new domain, but it doesn't set any cookies"* – P3:EP, treating absence of cookies like the absence of a privacy issue. The leaky forms problem itself constituted a knowledge gap: Five participants were unaware of it, as became apparent mostly during the walkthrough reflection *"Because I really didn't know that third-party providers are used for forms."* – P9:WP.

Technical skill gaps primarily concerned network inspection (seven participants) and its timing. Four participants who attempted network analysis did so too late or lost relevant requests by repeatedly closing and reopening developer tools. P9 and P4 realized after completing the checkout that credit card data might have been visible in network traffic, but the requests were no longer available. Beyond timing, some participants struggled to interpret observed network activity. Similar difficulties arose during cookie and storage inspection.

4.3 Perceived Value of the Privacy Range as a Training Tool

We analyzed the final post-session interviews via qualitative content analysis to capture participants' perceptions of the training environment.

Exposing the Competence Gap. A consistently reported outcome was a confrontation with gaps between perceived and actual GDPR competence. Five participants explicitly described becoming aware of how much they did not know despite recent coursework (*"That I know far, far less than I thought I did"* – P3; *"It really holds up a mirror to show you everything that's still missing"* – P4).

Complementarity with Theoretical Instruction. Participants perceived the Privacy Range as complementary to formal GDPR instruction. Theoretical knowledge was described as a prerequisite for meaningful engagement (*"I wouldn't have found a lot of things if I hadn't attended the data protection lecture beforehand."* – P0), while the practical exercise showed the limits of theory alone (*"What you do in that lecture has little to do with reality."* – P3). Four participants described the practical task as more complex and technically demanding than lecture-based learning, particularly the challenge of tracing legal rules to their technical manifestation in a running system.

Perceived Limitations and Further Development. Participants also identified concrete limitations of the current setup. The most consistent concern was the absence of structured feedback and progress indicators. Without knowing whether a discovered issue was correctly identified, participants reported feeling unable to assess their own completion (*"I don't have output like in programming where I see whether I made mistakes"* – P9). Several participants requested integrated hints that could replace the facilitator role for self-directed use (P3, P5, P8, P1) or providing "good practice" counterexamples alongside the flawed implementations (P0, P7). Less experienced participants perceived the technical guidance (e. g., on interpreting network traffic) as insufficiently detailed.

Perceived Utility and Voluntary Use. Six of ten participants expressed unconditional willingness to use the tool voluntarily; other participants expressed conditional willingness such as preparing for development work projects (P2, P5) or if the tool had added gamification elements (P8). Participants largely indicated that the tool is best suited for developers and IT practitioners with prior exposure to both GDPR and web technologies (6 participants). Six participants described the experience as engaging or enjoyable alongside its educational value, and the tool was perceived as realistic and representative of everyday web environments (5 participants).

5 Discussion

In this section, we interpret our findings and address the study's limitations.

5.1 Interpretation of Results

Our findings suggest that assuring GDPR compliance depends not only on conceptual knowledge, but also on a level of procedural competence that involves structuring the audit process (Theme 1), verifying interface claims against actual system behavior (Theme 3), and mapping observed system behavior such as network requests and cookies to legal requirements (Table 4).

The Missing Procedural Layer. Previous research has associated compliance errors with insufficient GDPR knowledge [3,16–18,33]. Our findings complicate this account. Participants who had recently completed a dedicated GDPR lecture course still lacked procedural means to activate that knowledge in an application context. This extends findings by Horstmann et al. [18], who observed similar patterns of insufficient recognition and heavy reliance on external sources among developers detecting GDPR issues in a hypothetical scenario.

The reliably investigated anchors (Theme 2) suggest a clear benefit of formal GDPR education. However, participants repeatedly failed to apply GDPR knowledge when doing so required comparing different system states, understanding when inspection must occur, or interpreting third-party requests legally. Moreover, results suggest that the interpretative nuance behind principles cannot be captured adequately by learning the principle alone. While data minimization in forms was checked by all participants, extent of user tracking (which is related to the same principle, but legally more ambiguous) was rarely investigated at all, and if so, deemed unproblematic because user consent was obtained.

The observed verification gap follows from this missing procedural layer. Without expectations about when and how system behavior should be tested, interface feedback substitutes for evidence. The technical complexity involved in implementing privacy requirements (e. g., complete deletion of user data, storage limitation) may have been underestimated in some cases – participants who did not consider what correct implementation demands saw no need to verify. Technical skill variance reinforced this gap for problems that required interpreting network traffic or storage; less-experienced participants relied more heavily on interface signals even when their intuitions were correct. Where verification required no specialized skill, however – such as re-checking data persistence in the UI after deletion – the gap was behavioral rather than a matter of capability. The five instances in which participants noticed problematic aspects we did not intend highlight both the complexity and ambiguity of GDPR application and our environment's potential to activate reasoning from different angles.

Specific Misconceptions and Gaps. Given that participants consistently framed third-party exposure as merely a transparency issue and confused policy agreement with consent, participants struggled to distinguish the respective scope of consent and disclosure requirements despite recognizing both as central GDPR concepts. Whether this pattern comes from insufficient understanding (of consent requirements or IP address transfer implications), failure to activate existing knowledge in context, or imprecise articulation due to cognitive load cannot be fully determined from our data and remains to be disentangled in future work.

The widespread unawareness of IP address transmission through third-party requests aligns with findings of limited awareness about incidental data exposure [34]. Formal GDPR education – as some participants also noted during problem reflection – likely focuses on abstract principles instead of technical examples like third-party widgets. Curricula for IT practitioners should therefore incorporate such examples.

Prior experience functioned both as heuristic guidance and as a source of problem normalization. Familiar but non-compliant design patterns like pre-enabled consent [25] were frequently accepted as standard practice, indicating that repeated exposure can override formal knowledge. This relates to findings from deceptive design research, where awareness of manipulative patterns does not protect against their influence [5]. While only a few participants explicitly stated the concern of copying common bad practices due to their prevalence, the influence of experience despite formal education likely affects implementation practices. The tendency for professional developers to orient themselves at existing implementations in order to achieve GDPR compliance was also identified in previous research [17]. Interestingly, habituated privacy-protective behavior, while desirable in practice, also prevented trainees from discovering problems (H2 and H4, as they required accepting non-essential cookies, which most participants deliberately did not do). Effective training must therefore not only impart compliance requirements but actively disrupt habituated expectations.

The Privacy Range as a Diagnostic Bridge. While GDPR principles taught in isolation provided a theoretical framework, the Privacy Range exposed the technical complexity behind them and demanded coordination of legal knowledge, technical inspection, and verification behavior. This positions the Privacy Range as a possible training instrument for the procedural competence layer that formal, legally-focused GDPR instruction might not develop on its own. Post-session interviews support this interpretation, with participants often valuing the environment for making competence boundaries visible or exposing the limits of theory alone. This aligns with the PS-I paradigm, where initial struggle with problems activates prior knowledge and thereby makes learners aware of their own knowledge gaps, increasing the effectiveness of subsequent instruction [24,32]. In our setup, participants' partially unsuccessful attempts to identify and articulate privacy-related issues revealed the specific misconceptions and procedural gaps that were then addressed and clarified by the walkthrough.

Overall, difficulties in applying GDPR knowledge appeared less related to conceptual understanding of principles than to the procedural translation into system-level verification.

5.2 Limitations and Future Work

Our study has several limitations. We used a small student sample with varying technical expertise. While our sample partially reflects the diversity found in web operation practice [34], it remains small and recruited from a single course at a single institution; this prevents generalization and demands replication with larger and professional samples, which is planned for future work.

We used the detection of privacy problems in a web application as a proxy for practical GDPR competency. However, auditing an existing system differs from eliciting or implementing privacy requirements during development. We partially addressed this by asking participants how they would handle identified issues in future work projects, but these responses remain hypothetical.

While researcher presence was necessary for the study procedure, it could have influenced both recognition outcomes and walkthrough reflections due to potential demand characteristics. Participants' explanations for missed problems may further be affected by social desirability and hindsight bias. For example, reasoning based on habituation or perceived ubiquity may partly reflect post-hoc justification for not noticing comparatively obvious issues. We mitigated social desirability effects by foregrounding the tool evaluation aspect, emphasizing that moments of friction and confusion were valuable for our research as well, and that any feedback, positive or negative, was appreciated.

Although problem difficulty and hint effectiveness were assessed in pilot sessions, we did not establish an empirical ground truth for these measures, which may confound interpretation of recognition outcomes and hint effectiveness.

Finally, it is not always clear whether participants lacked knowledge of a problem's legal background or were uncertain about the expected level of detail in their responses, which might affect problem recognition and misconception/knowledge gap classifications. In addition, the cognitively demanding task combined with concurrent think-aloud may have influenced verbalizations. Furthermore, the Privacy Range embeds a particular selection of GDPR-relevant issues, and our identified barriers are limited to these compliance requirements.

Future work will evaluate whether Privacy Range training transfers to implementation level GDPR compliance in an experimental programming study with objective outcome measures, and will compare this approach against alternative GDPR training formats. We will also extend the environment with additional scenarios and optional context-sensitive scaffolding.

6 Conclusion

We presented and preliminarily evaluated the Privacy Range, a training environment prototype that translates the interactive vulnerability detection approach from applied cyber security to the field of privacy education and specifically the GDPR. In a qualitative lab study with 10 IT students who had recently completed a dedicated GDPR lecture course, we found that barriers to applied compliance analysis arose less from absent conceptual knowledge than from difficulties in procedural application of that knowledge in context. Participants mostly possessed relevant GDPR concepts but lacked the investigative routines, technical tool fluency, and verification behavior needed to apply that knowledge in a running system. These findings suggest that formal GDPR instruction, while necessary, can be insufficient on its own – and that realistic training environments can make this gap visible and actionable. Participant feedback supports this reading, positioning the Privacy Range as complementary to theoretical instruction rather than a replacement. Future work will extend the environment and evaluate whether identifying and reflecting on privacy problems improves the ability to prevent or remediate similar issues in implementation scenarios.

Acknowledgments. This study was conducted within the research consortium ForDaySec, funded by the Bavarian State Ministry of Science and Arts (StMWK). We thank Lorenz Mrohs for his valuable contribution to the thematic analysis.

Disclosure of generative AI usage. Anthropic's *Claude Opus 4.6* was used for spell-checking and refining this text and for the curation of the supplementary material.

Disclosure of Interests. The authors have no competing interests to declare.

References

1. Alfieri, L., Brooks, P.J., Aldrich, N.J., Tenenbaum, H.R.: Does discovery-based instruction enhance learning? J. Educ. Psychol. **103**(1), 1–18 (2011)
2. Alhazmi, A., A G Arachchilage, N.: A serious game design framework for software developers to put GDPR into practice. In: Proc. ARES 2021, pp. 1–6 (2021)
3. Alhazmi, A., Arachchilage, N.A.G.: I'm all ears! Listening to software developers on putting GDPR principles into software development practice. Pers. Ubiquit. Comput. **25**(5), 879–892 (2021)
4. Berg, S.S., Moor, K.D.: Usable privacy: A study of norwegian software development practices. In: Proc. RCIS 2024 Workshops. CEUR Workshop Proceedings, vol. 3674 (2024)
5. Bongard-Blanchy, K., Rossi, A., Rivas, S., Doublet, S., Koenig, V., Lenzini, G.: "I am definitely manipulated, even when I am aware of it. it's ridiculous!" - Dark patterns from the end-user perspective. In: Proc. ACM DIS 2021, pp. 763–776 (2021)
6. Braun, V., Clarke, V.: Thematic Analysis: A Practical Guide. SAGE (2022)
7. Christensen, M., Britze, D., Vejlin, J., Sørensen, L.T., Pedersen, J.M.: The privacy universe - a game-based learning platform for data protection, privacy and ethics. In: Proc. IEEE EDUCON 2023, pp. 1–8 (2023)
8. Colesky, M., Hoepman, J.H., Hillen, C.: A critical analysis of privacy design strategies. In: Proc. IEEE SPW 2016, pp. 33–40 (2016)
9. Cruz, T., Simões, P.: Down the rabbit hole: Fostering active learning through guided exploration of a SCADA cyber range. Appl. Sci. **11**(20), 9509 (2021)
10. Ericsson, K.A., Simon, H.A.: Protocol Analysis: Verbal Reports as Data, The MIT Press (1993)
11. European Parliament and Council of the European Union: Directive 2002/58/EC on privacy and electronic communications. ePrivacy Directive (2002)
12. European Parliament and Council of the European Union: General Data Protection Regulation (Regulation (EU) 2016/679) (2016)

13. Fleiss, J.L., Levin, B., Paik, M.C.: The measurement of interrater agreement. In: Statistical Methods for Rates and Proportions, pp. 598–626. John Wiley & Sons, Ltd (2003)
14. Gale, N.K., Heath, G., Cameron, E., Rashid, S., Redwood, S.: Using the framework method for the analysis of qualitative data in multi-disciplinary health research. BMC Med. Res. Methodol. **13**, 117 (2013)
15. Gass, S.M., Mackey, A.: Stimulated Recall Methodology in Applied Linguistics and L2 Research. Routledge (2016)
16. Horstmann, S.A., et al.: "Those things are written by lawyers, and programmers are reading that." Mapping the communication gap between software developers and privacy experts. Proc. Priv. Enhancing Technol. **2024**(1), 151–170 (2024)
17. Horstmann, S.A., et al.: "Sorry for bugging you so much." Exploring developers' behavior towards privacy-compliant implementation. In: Proc. IEEE Symp. Secur. Priv. 2025, pp. 1215–1233 (2025)
18. Horstmann, S.A., Hong, S., Niazian, M., Santos, C., Naiakshina, A.: "I need to learn better searching tactics for privacy policy laws." investigating software developers' behavior when using sources on privacy issues. In: Proc. ICSE (2026), to appear
19. Huth, D., Matthes, F.: "Appropriate technical and organizational measures": identifying privacy engineering approaches to meet GDPR requirements. In: AMCIS 2019 Proceedings (2019)
20. Kimmich, B.: OWASP Juice Shop. https://owasp.org/www-project-juice-shop/ (2026). Accessed 3 Mar 2026
21. Leighton, J.P.: Think-aloud interview procedures: measuring problem-solving response processes. In: Leighton, J.P. (ed.) Using Think-Aloud Interviews and Cognitive Labs in Educational Research. Oxford University Press (2017)
22. Li, T., Agarwal, Y., Hong, J.I.: Coconut: an IDE plugin for developing privacy-friendly apps. Proc. ACM Interact. Mob. Wearable Ubiquitous Technol. **2**(4), 178:1–178:35 (2018)
23. Li, T., Neundorfer, E.B., Agarwal, Y., Hong, J.I.: Honeysuckle: Annotation-Guided code generation of in-app privacy notices. Proceedings of the ACM on Interactive, Mobile, Wearable and Ubiquitous Technologies **5**(3), 1–27 (2021)
24. Loibl, K., Roll, I., Rummel, N.: Towards a theory of when and how problem solving followed by instruction supports learning. Educ. Psychol. Rev. **29**(4), 693–715 (2017)
25. Matte, C., Bielova, N., Santos, C.: Do cookie banners respect my choice? Measuring legal compliance of banners from IAB Europe's transparency and consent framework. In: Proc. IEEE Symp. Secur. Priv. 2020, pp. 791–809 (2020)
26. Mayring, P.: Qualitative Content Analysis: A Step-by-Step Guide. SAGE (2022)
27. McDonald, N., Schoenebeck, S., Forte, A.: Reliability and inter-rater reliability in qualitative research: Norms and guidelines for CSCW and HCI practice. Proc. ACM Hum.-Comput. Interact. **3**(CSCW), 72:1–72:23 (2019)
28. Panum, T.K., Hageman, K., Pedersen, J.M., Hansen, R.R.: Haaukins: a highly accessible and automated virtualization platform for security education. In: Proc. IEEE ICALT 2019, pp. 236–238 (2019)
29. Peixoto, M., Silva, C., Lima, R., Araújo, J., Gorschek, T., Silva, J.: PCM Tool: Privacy requirements specification in agile software development. In: Proc. CBSoft 2019, pp. 108–113 (2019)
30. Senarath, A., Arachchilage, N.A.G.: Why developers cannot embed privacy into software systems? An empirical investigation. In: Proc. EASE 2018, pp. 211–216 (2018)

31. Senol, A., Acar, G., Humbert, M., Borgesius, F.Z.: Leaky forms: a study of email and password exfiltration before form submission. In: Proc. USENIX Security 2022, pp. 1813–1830 (2022)
32. Sinha, T., Kapur, M.: When problem solving followed by instruction works: Evidence for productive failure. Rev. Educ. Res. **91**(5), 761–798 (2021)
33. Stöver, A., et al.: How website owners face privacy issues: thematic analysis of responses from a covert notification study reveals diverse circumstances and challenges. Proc. Priv. Enhancing Technol. **2023**(2), 251–264 (2023)
34. Utz, C., Amft, S., Degeling, M., Holz, T., Fahl, S., Schaub, F.: Privacy rarely considered: exploring considerations in the adoption of third-party services by websites. Proc. Priv. Enhancing Technol. **2023**(1), 5–28 (2023)
35. Wijesundara, T., Warren, M., Arachchilage, N.A.G.: SoK: Enhancing privacy-preserving software development from a developers' perspective. CoRR abs/2504.20350 (2025)
36. Zimmeck, S., Goldstein, R., Baraka, D.: PrivacyFlash Pro: automating privacy policy generation for mobile apps. In: Proc. NDSS 2021 (2021)

A Quantitative Evaluation of Textual, Visual, and Interactive Explanations of a Privacy Concept in a Hospital Setting

Michael Mühlhauser(✉), Angela Fiedler, Sabine Patzl, Melissa Schütz, Marcel Soler Lopez, Simon Steuer, Dominik Herrmann, Daniela Nicklas, and Astrid Schütz

University of Bamberg, Bamberg, Germany
{mm.psi,angela.fiedler,sabine.patzl,melissa.schuetz, simon.steuer,dh.psi,daniela.nicklas,astrid.schuetz}@uni-bamberg.de, marcel.soler-lopez@stud.uni-bamberg.de

Abstract. Although the GDPR often requires informed consent, many people do not understand how their data and privacy are protected when they consent to data collection. In practical settings, however, it is still unclear how such understanding can be established. This is particularly challenging in hospitals, where patients consent to processing of sensitive data under time pressure. Related work and learning theories suggest that richer explanation formats could improve understanding of privacy-preserving approaches. We consider the use case of privacy-preserving tracking of vacuum pumps in a hospital setting. As vacuum pumps are attached to patients during wound therapy, patients would be continuously tracked without privacy protections. For our privacy concept, we created three different explanation formats: text-only, text-and-image, and text-and-interactive. In a between-subjects online survey ($N = 766$), we measured subjective and objective understanding, trust, and willingness to use a tracked vacuum pump for these formats and a control group. At least 90% of participants would use a tracked pump, without significant differences between groups. However, all explanation formats significantly improved subjective understanding and trust compared with the control group, with no differences between formats. For objective understanding, text-and-image and text-and-interactive significantly outperformed text-only, though effect sizes were small. While text-and-interactive showed a non-significant trend toward better understanding the limitations of our privacy concept, this understanding remained low. Furthermore, regardless of actual correctness, participants reported high confidence in their answers. This discrepancy questions current consent mechanisms, as no explanation format alone led to sufficient understanding for informed consent.

Keywords: Usable privacy · explanation formats · informed consent · interactive explanation · understanding

S. Nadjm-Tehrani et al. (Eds.): ARES 2026, LNCS 16898, pp. 111–133, 2027.
https://doi.org/10.1007/978-3-032-36874-4_6

1 Introduction

The General Data Protection Regulation (GDPR) often requires informed consent before personal data is collected, yet most people do not understand what they consent to [28]. This problem is particularly acute in hospitals, where patients consent to processing of sensitive health data under time pressure and in situations of dependency. When hospitals track medical assets such as vacuum pumps (VAC pumps) using Bluetooth Low Energy (BLE) technology [3,35], patients carrying those devices are effectively tracked as well. Under the GDPR, such continuous location tracking of patients constitutes processing of personal data that requires a legal basis and, depending on the implementation, may fall under the special protections for health-related data (Art. 9 GDPR). If consent is the legal basis, it is informed only if patients understand the privacy concept protecting their data. Even if tracking is based on another legal basis, hospitals must still inform patients about the tracking, and such information is only meaningful if patients can understand it.

As most patients have limited prior understanding of privacy concepts, explaining such a concept to them is a learning task within the scope of the cognitive theory of multimedia learning [20]. Its multimedia principle suggests that combining textual and visual elements in explanations leads to better understanding than text alone, as patients can then build and connect verbal and visual mental models for the privacy concept [20]. Prior work has tested this idea for differential privacy, whose mathematical guarantees are hard to convey, with inconsistent results (see Sect. 2). In practice, many systems use simpler privacy concepts [11,15]. Whether findings from the differential privacy literature transfer to privacy concepts in concrete use cases remains open, with limited research on k-anonymity [23] and privacy-preserving crowd counting [30]. No study has compared textual, visual, and interactive explanations for a non-differential privacy concept in a realistic application scenario.

We address this gap by evaluating three explanation formats (text-only, text-and-image, and text-and-interactive) for a privacy concept in a realistic hospital scenario. These explanations cover a deliberately simple threshold-based privacy concept for BLE-based VAC pump tracking in a hospital ward. As text-and-image and text-and-interactive add visual or interactive elements to the preceding format, we refer to them as richer explanation formats. Based on the cognitive theory of multimedia learning [20] and prior work [21,30,31], we compare these explanation formats with each other and a control group, and test four hypotheses: **H1)** Richer explanation formats lead to higher subjective understanding of the privacy concept. **H2)** Richer explanation formats lead to higher objective understanding of the privacy concept. **H3)** Richer explanation formats lead to higher trust in the privacy concept. **H4)** Richer explanation formats lead to higher willingness to use a tracked VAC pump.

In our between-subjects online survey ($N = 766$), both text-and-image and text-and-interactive explanations led to significantly higher objective understanding than text-only. Subjective understanding and trust did not differ across explanation formats but were significantly higher than in the control group.

Also, participants overestimated their own objective understanding, which raises doubts about consent mechanisms that rely on subjective understanding.

2 Related Work

Different techniques to effectively convey privacy information to users have been studied with privacy notices [25]. For example, Kitkowska et al. designed privacy notices with positive and negative framing communicated with text and images, and control switches for data sharing choices [16]. In the context of health wearables, Becker et al. evaluated attribute framing and argument strength regarding disclosure of data [5]. While privacy notices usually inform users about a range of data practices [25], we explain the mechanism of a privacy concept.

Other works evaluated textual [1,9], structural [1] and visual [9] explanations for different kinds of encryption [1,4,9] and private computation [13], including metaphors to convey encryption in a health-data context [18]. In most of these studies, the authors measured participants' understanding of these explanations [1,4,9,13], and their willingness to share data [1,13,18].

Most related work evaluates explanations of differential privacy and its guarantees. Although our privacy concept for VAC pump tracking does not use differential privacy, these papers offer methodological insights. Some works focused on textual explanations [7,17,23,33,34]; further research then introduced various visualisations [22,27,31] and interactive elements, e. g. buttons to click [6,31] or sliders to control the privacy budget [2,21]. To evaluate these explanations, related work uses dependent variables such as subjective [10,17,23,26,33,34] and objective understanding [10,17,23,26,31,33,34], willingness to share data [7,17,26,31,34], and sometimes trust [6,17,26,34].

However, these studies report inconsistent results regarding participants' understanding. Wen et al. evaluated textual and visual explanations of local differential privacy [31], where participants received a tailored visual illustration for their privacy concern but could switch illustrations in a menu. In a pre-post-test setting, illustrations significantly improved understanding for all three privacy concerns, while text did so only for two.

In contrast, Franzen et al. attempted to convey re-identification risks of differential privacy by designing notifications that vary in framing and conditions, e. g., percentage format or simple frequencies [10]. The authors evaluated subjective and objective understanding, the former with a composite score, the latter with an aggregated score of binary knowledge questions. For both scores, they found no significant improvements for treatment groups compared to the control condition. Interestingly, objective understanding was lower than the expected value for all notifications, and the control condition seemed to be overconfident based on their subjective understanding. Actually, Smart et al. found no significant improvement in understanding and also observed overconfidence even though they enriched textual explanations with visual components [27].

Mithila et al. created two graphical representations to make differential privacy understandable [21]. The static version contained textual explanations and illustrations for differential privacy and privacy loss depending on the privacy budget. The dynamic version had an additional slider to interactively adjust the privacy budget, updating the respective privacy loss in a bar chart. The authors evaluated these conditions against textual explanations and found no significant differences on subjective understanding. Results for objective understanding were mixed. The static group understood the definition of differential privacy best, the dynamic group the capabilities of an attacker to recover true answers from collected data.

Apart from differential privacy, there is limited related work on explaining simpler privacy concepts. Notably, Nuñez von Voigt et al. found that simpler privacy concepts such as k-anonymity are significantly easier to understand than differential privacy [23], which further motivates investigating them. Waclawek et al. created two explanations for privacy-preserving crowd counting with textual elements and illustrative images [30]. The text was framed as either functional or mechanistic. Based on insights from interviews and a field study, the authors evaluated these explanations in an online survey and found that functional explanations led to higher subjective and objective understanding. Further, the authors found a relationship between project trust and acceptance, i. e., the willingness to share their location data [30].

Similar to Mithila et al. [21] and Wen et al. [31], we evaluate textual, visual, and interactive explanation formats. Following Waclawek et al. [30], we create explanations for a privacy concept in a concrete use case without relying on differential privacy. We use the same dependent variables and measure subjective and objective understanding, trust, and willingness to use a tracked VAC pump. However, we compare text-only, text-and-image, and text-and-interactive explanations instead of functional and mechanistic explanations. Further, in contrast to Mithila et al. [21] and Wen et al. [31], we implement a full web application for the interactive condition which gives participants more room for interaction than a single slider or button.

3 Use Case: Asset Tracking in the Hospital

Hospitals have a limited number of medical assets that they have to use efficiently. However, tracking assets that are attached to patients raises privacy concerns. We collaborated with industry partners operating in the medical sector to address this problem for the specific case of VAC pump tracking. This collaboration led to the development of a privacy concept for BLE-based tracking of VAC pumps in a hospital ward, which is described in the following sections. Our methods to evaluate whether patients can understand this concept sufficiently to give informed consent will be described in Sect. 4.

3.1 Privacy-Preserving Tracking of VAC Pumps

VAC pumps are continuously attached to patients during wound therapy. This means that any BLE-based tracking application would generate fine-grained mobility data over days or weeks, which is far beyond what hospital staff observes in routine care. Such data can reveal how often and when patients leave their rooms, which may indicate sleep disturbances or other changes in health conditions. Further, this data can reveal social patterns, such as who visits whom, and disclose behaviors that patients may not want to be documented, such as visiting smoking areas or leaving the ward against medical advice. As hospital staff also move the tracked pumps, the system may also risk capturing employee movement patterns as an unintended side effect. We systematically identified these and further privacy threats in a LINDDUN GO workshop, described in Sect. 3.2. At the same time, hospital staff needs reliable information on the availability and location of VAC pumps. We address this privacy-utility tradeoff by following the data minimization principle (Art. 5(1) lit. c GDPR). Our privacy concept for the tracking application has two goals: 1) it should enable hospital staff to track unused VAC pumps while 2) protecting patients' privacy by suppressing all data from used pumps. However, our BLE infrastructure does not directly indicate if a pump is in use; pump occupancy must be inferred from mobility patterns.

To solve that problem, we propose a threshold-based privacy concept that deliberately avoids cryptographic complexity in favor of a straightforward data hiding strategy [12]. Our privacy concept uses two patterns that reliably distinguish used from unused pumps: temporal patterns (a used pump moves regularly) and spatial patterns (a pump in a restricted area is inaccessible to patients). Specifically VAC pumps are visible to hospital staff only if they have not moved for at least 24 h, or if they are located in an access-restricted area such as a storage or cleaning room. If a patient with an attached VAC pump moves at least once per day, their pump remains invisible.

However, this simplicity comes with a limitation. If patients with an attached VAC pump have not moved for at least 24 h, their VAC pumps will be visible in the tracking application. This violates the above goals of the privacy concept, as the application now tracks not only the VAC pump but also the patient it is attached to; this reveals prolonged immobility, potentially indicating a critical health condition. With our industry partners, we agreed on this privacy-utility trade-off, as it enables the hospital to also find unused pumps in patient rooms. Our survey evaluated participants' understanding of this limitation.

We implemented the privacy concept using a proxy architecture. If deployed on the hospital side between the BLE infrastructure and the tracking application backend, the proxy enforces the visibility rules on the fly and discards all data from used VAC pumps. This realizes data minimization at the architectural level, as the data does not reach the backend; no data of used pumps has to be stored.

3.2 Privacy Threat Modeling

To systematically identify privacy threats in the VAC pump tracking system, we conducted privacy threat modeling using LINDDUN GO [32]. LINDDUN GO is a lightweight, collaborative variant of LINDDUN [8] that uses privacy threat cards to guide participants through the threat elicitation process [32].

We conducted a three-hour LINDDUN GO workshop with seven participants, including researchers and industry partners operating in the medical and technology sectors. Participants assessed the relevance of the threat cards for the VAC pump tracking application based on its data flow diagram.

In total, we identified eleven privacy threats: ten in the initial workshop and one through post-processing. The threats are excessive collection of information by the tracking system (T1); lack of support for data subjects' rights (T2); risk of re-identification through additional attributes (T3); unintentional employee surveillance (T4); identification via movement patterns (T5); non-repudiation risk from a notification feature (T6); identifiable user requests (T7); insufficient transparency for data subjects (T8); unnecessary sharing of data with external parties (T9); unencrypted and detectable BLE communication (T10); and incomplete or ineffective anonymization (T11).

Insufficient transparency for data subjects (T8) is directly related to our hypotheses: we evaluate users' understanding of different explanation formats. In contrast, several of the other identified threats can be mapped to the privacy concept itself. The threshold-based visibility rules and the proxy architecture jointly mitigate the following threats: excessive data collection (T1), re-identification through additional attributes (T3), unintentional employee surveillance (T4), and identification via movement patterns (T5).

We acknowledge the limitation of ineffective anonymization (T11) for our privacy concept and evaluated participants' understanding of it in our survey. The remaining threats depend on the technical implementation of the tracking system rather than the privacy concept itself; therefore, they are out of scope.

4 Methods

Our goal is to evaluate how different explanations of the privacy concept described in Sect. 3.1 affect (H1) users' subjective and (H2) objective understanding of the concept, (H3) trust in the concept, and (H4) their willingness to use a tracked VAC pump. To ensure comparability with the related work, our choice of dependent variables follows Waclawek et al. [30], who used these four variables.

Building on the privacy concept and threat analysis described in Sect. 3, we designed one control condition and three explanations for the privacy concept: text-only, text-and-image, and text-and-interactive. As stated in Sect. 1, we choose these explanation formats based on multimedia learning theories [20] and findings from the related work [21,23,31]. To evaluate differences between explanation formats, we conducted an online survey. The explanations, survey questions, participants' response data without demographic information, and our analysis script are available online.[1]

[1] The material is on https://github.com/UBA-PSI/explanations-study.

4.1 Design of Explanations

We considered four groups in our experiment: one control group and three treatment groups. Each of the treatment groups received a different explanation: text-only, text-and-image, and text-and-interactive. These explanations were created as websites. The first author implemented the first draft of these explanations, which were then reviewed by co-authors with a background in psychology. Based on their feedback, we iteratively refined both the wording of the explanations and the user experience of the websites. As we want to measure the effect of each explanation, we kept the textual descriptions mostly identical across all groups. That is, our explanations share a common structure as illustrated in Fig. 1.

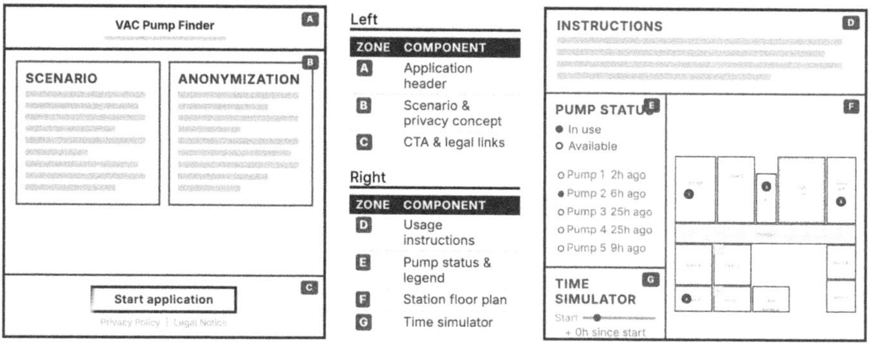

Fig. 1. Left: first page of the explanations as seen by the treatment groups. The button is not visible for the text-only group and labeled differently in the text-and-image group. Right: second page, visible in the text-and-image and text-and-interactive groups. In text-and-image, the station plan is a static image and the time simulator is absent.

Page Structure. The explanations consisted of up to two web pages. When participants opened the website, the first page was immediately visible in all explanations. Only the text-and-image and text-and-interactive explanations contained a second page, reachable by clicking on a button on the first page.

Content of the First Page. On the first page, we described the hospital scenario. That is, we briefly described the negative pressure wound therapy and explained the need for tracking of VAC pumps with a dedicated application as hospital staff otherwise has to search manually for the limited number of pumps in the clinic. For treatment groups, we additionally introduced the privacy concept, which we referred to as anonymization concept throughout the survey materials. From the perspective of patients, the core guarantee is that the tracking application cannot be used to identify who is using a specific pump, which the term anonymization captures accurately. The technical distinctions between anonymization, unlinkability, and related privacy notions in the sense of Pfitzmann and Hansen [24] are not only unfamiliar to lay users but would introduce unnecessary complexity that could distract from the concept we actually evaluate.

The explanations specified the rules as described in Sect. 3.1, namely that VAC pumps are only visible if they are in a restricted area where patients do not have access or if pumps did not move for 24 h. We also referenced our privacy policy and legal notice on the first page.

Content of the Second Page. The second page showed the tracking application either as image or as interactive web application. This page contained short instructions for participants at the top and a station plan of a hospital with adjacent UI elements.

Detailed Description of Our Explanations. The explanations for the experimental groups including the control group are detailed below.

Text-only Explanation (Text): For text-only, we used a single-page and two-column layout. The first column covers the hospital scenario outlined in the above paragraph *content of the first page*. In the second column, we described the privacy concept. We explained that only unused VAC pumps should be visible for the hospital staff in the application. Used VAC pumps, i. e., pumps attached to patients, should be invisible. We then outlined the rules of the privacy concept under which VAC pumps are visible to the staff (as presented in Sect. 3.1).

Text-and-image Explanation (Image): This explanation reused the *Text* layout and added a *view application* button revealing the second page. The second page instructed participants to try to understand how the application could support hospital staff, clarifying that the application cannot be used actively. Further, there was a screenshot of the application showing unused VAC pumps on a hospital's station plan. This screenshot included the pump status, a list of pumps with a used/unused indicator and the last movement time.

Text-and-interactive Explanation (Interactive): This explanation used the same two-column layout as *Image*, but the button was labeled *start application*. On the second page, participants saw the interactive tracking application with short usage instructions instead of the screenshot like in *Image*. We mainly explained the interactive elements of the explanation to participants: they could move VAC pumps via drag and drop, simulate global time changes with a time slider, or click on individual VAC pumps in the pump status menu. That is, pumps could be moved on the station plan to see how the pump location changes the pump's visibility. Further, participants could change when individual VAC pumps have moved the last time to see when VAC pumps appear or disappear. Participants could also use a global time slider to simulate that several hours have passed, potentially affecting the visibility of all VAC pumps. A screenshot of the tracking application is shown in Fig. 2.

Control Group: We used a single-page and single-column layout for the explanation for the control group. The explanation covered mainly the VAC-pump tracking scenario. There was only a short paragraph about the privacy concept: *To locate unused VAC pumps in the hospital without permanently showing hospital staff the location of VAC pumps, and thus patients, we employ an anonymization concept. This protects patients' privacy and their data.*

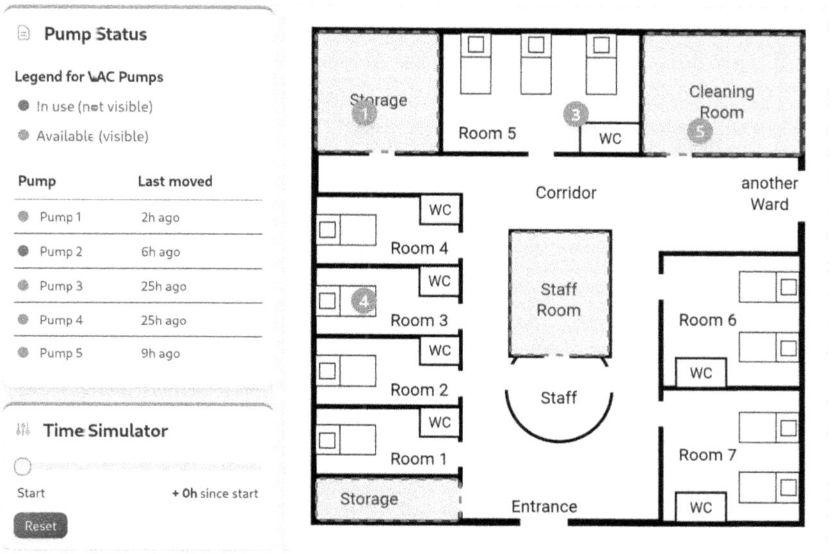

Fig. 2. Screenshot of the second page of the interactive explanation (translated).

4.2 Online Survey

We conducted an online survey as part of a larger study on privacy of location data, which was approved by the ethics committee of the university. The survey questions were implemented in SoSciSurvey [19] and participants were recruited via Prolific (www.prolific.com). In this paper, we focus on one part of the larger study, namely privacy-preserving VAC pump tracking, which was the only part comparing textual, visual, and interactive explanations. Our study participants saw all survey parts: first personality questions, then the privacy-preserving VAC pump tracking scenario followed by other scenarios.

Survey Procedure. Once participants finished the first part of the questionnaire, they were shown an introductory page describing that the following survey questions are about medical asset tracking in the hospital. As part of the online survey, participants were then instructed to visit an external website hosted by the university, i. e., the website described in Sect. 4.1. We deactivated the *Next Page* button in SoSciSurvey and enabled it only if participants clicked on the provided URL of the external website. Clicking on the URL opened the explanation website in a separate browser tab. Participants could keep it open while answering the survey questions. Afterward, participants received questions on the dependent variables in the following order: subjective understanding, trust, willingness to use a tracked VAC pump, and objective understanding. We evaluated subjective understanding and trust intentionally before willingness to use a tracked VAC pump and objective understanding so that the objective understanding questions could not influence participants' subjective ratings. After the dependent variables, we asked treatment groups about their experience with the received explanation, i. e., if explanation-specific features helped them to understand the concept or might have been confusing.

Participants. Our inclusion criteria for participants were as follows. Participants should be from the D-A-CH region, i. e., German-speaking, and we aimed to have a balanced sample regarding gender. During the time of our study, 847 participants decided to take the survey. Those participants were randomly assigned to our experimental groups. Once we removed participants who failed one of two attention checks in our questionnaire, our final sample consisted of 766 participants. The demographics of our participants are described in Table 1. While we aimed for balance between genders, we ended up with a sample dominated by males. Further, our sample is relatively young and highly educated. Participants are on average roughly thirty years old, and 45% of them have a university degree. We checked demographic differences between groups with chi-squared tests for gender and education, and a one-way Welch's ANOVA for age. Our test results indicate no significant differences between groups ($p > .05$).

Table 1. Participant demographics

	Total	Text	Image	Interactive	Control
Group Size (N)	766	190	188	185	203
Age					
Mean	30.6	30.8	30.7	30.1	30.9
Standard deviation	9.6	9.8	10.5	8.6	9.6
Gender (%)					
Female	32.8	28.9	33.0	37.8	31.5
Male	65.8	70.5	66.5	59.5	66.5
Diverse	1.4	0.5	0.5	2.7	2.0
Education (%)					
Secondary school diploma	5	6	5	6	4
Apprenticeship	9	9	7	8	13
Univ. entrance qualific.	36	38	32	37	36
Univ. degree	45	42	51	45	44
Other	4	4	6	3	3

Questions. Our dependent variables are subjective understanding, trust, willingness to use a tracked VAC pump and objective understanding. These variables and some of our questions, especially on subjective understanding, trust, and willingness to use a tracked VAC pump are based on Waclawek et al. [30]. Our survey and all other materials were in German; all items here are translated.

Subjective Understanding: To measure participants' subjective understanding, we included four statements about the tracking application and the anonymization concept in the survey. Note that we used the term anonymization concept in our survey for the reasons explained in Sect. 4.1. Participants could rate each statement on a scale from *strongly disagree (1)* to *strongly agree (10)*. The first statement (I1) was about understanding what the tracking application is used for. The second statement (I2) was about understanding the anonymization concept, the third one (I3) about being able to explain the anonymization concept to other people, and the fourth statement (I4) about understanding what the location data is used for. Example statements are: *I have understood how the anonymization concept works to protect patients*, or: *I could explain the anonymization concept to other people in my own words.*

Trust: We measured participants' trust in the anonymization concept with a single question. For that, we asked participants: *How much do you trust that the anonymization concept sufficiently protects your data?* Participants responded on a continuous slider (SoSciSurvey's default scale from 1 to 101). The endpoints of the scale were labeled *not at all* and *very much.*

Willingness to Use a Tracked VAC Pump: Regarding the willingness to use a tracked VAC pump, we first introduced participants to a short scenario: *Imagine you have to undergo a minor surgery at a hospital. During the pre-operative consultation, the doctor explains that a VAC pump will be used to support wound healing after the surgery. You have the option to receive a VAC pump without a tracking function or one with a tracking function.* Then, we asked participants one binary question: *Would you personally be willing to use a VAC pump that can be tracked within the hospital?*

Objective Understanding: For objective understanding, we asked participants several multiple-response questions. That is, participants could select multiple options for each question, where each question had four or five options including the option *none of the possible answers is correct.* The questions were of varying difficulty: restating the used technology (Q1), recalling the core mechanisms of the privacy concept (Q2), applying the visibility rules to concrete cases (Q3, Q4), and understanding the concept's limitations (Q5). Additionally, we asked for participants' confidence for each given answer on a scale from *very unsure* (1) to *very sure* (10). With these measurements, we can evaluate potential discrepancies between believed understanding and factual correctness of their answers. In the first question, we asked participants what technologies are used to track pumps in the hospital. The expected answer was *Bluetooth technology*, which was explicitly stated in the explanation. The second question was, *what measures are applied in the anonymization concept to protect the location of patients*, which was introduced to participants with the two visibility rules (Sect. 3.1). In the third and fourth question, participants had to select correct statements on whether VAC pumps would be visible or not in the tracking application under different temporal and spatial scenarios, e. g., if a VAC pump last moved 15 h ago. In the last question on objective understanding, we asked participants about the limitation of the concept. Participants should select if or what information can be deduced about patients' location data even if the anonymization concept is used.

Treatment-Specific Questions: Once participants finished answering the questions on the dependent variables, we asked them treatment-specific questions. For the *Text* group, we gave participants three statements they should rate on a scale from *strongly disagree (1)* to *strongly agree (10)*. The first statement was: *An additional explanation form would have improved understanding of the anonymization concept.* The second one was: *The textual explanation is sufficient to understand the anonymization concept.* The last one was: *I would appreciate it if anonymization concepts were not only explained in text form.*

For the *Image* group we also had three statements rated on the scale from 1 to 10. The first one was: *The visual representation of the application contributed to my understanding of the anonymization concept.* The second one was: *I would appreciate it if anonymization concepts were more frequently explained with visual representations.* The last one was: *The visual representation of the application confused me.* By framing one statement positive (contributed to understanding), and one negative (confused me), we wanted to ensure a variety of opinions.

For the *Interactive* group, we first asked participants what functionalities they used in the application: moving a VAC pump to a different room, adjusting in the pump status when a VAC pump last moved, using the time simulator to change when all VAC pumps last moved, or none of them. Afterward, the participants should rate three statements again on the scale from 1 to 10. The first statement was: *Trying out the various functions contributed to my understanding of the anonymization concept.* The second one was: *I would appreciate it if anonymization concepts were more frequently explained with interactive applications.* The last one was: *Trying out the various functions confused me.*

5 Evaluation of Explanations

In this section, we test our hypotheses H1–H4 by comparing our experimental groups on subjective understanding, objective understanding, trust, and willingness to use a tracked VAC pump. We first test our hypotheses with a significance level of $\alpha = .05$ by comparing our groups in a between-subjects design. Then, we report descriptive statistics for treatment-specific questions. All statistical analyses were implemented in *R*; for statistical tests, we used *rstatix* [14].

5.1 Hypotheses Tests

Subjective Understanding. To test if there is a difference between groups on subjective understanding, we first created a composite score. That is, we calculated the mean score from our four items on subjective understanding, where each item was measured on a scale from 1 to 10 with higher scores indicating better understanding. The composite score showed acceptable internal consistency (Cronbach's $\alpha = .79$). The mean composite scores were $M = 8.67$ ($SD = 1.38$) for *Text*, $M = 8.74$ ($SD = 1.46$) for *Image*, $M = 8.47$ ($SD = 1.55$) for *Interactive*, and $M = 6.98$ ($SD = 1.74$) for *Control*. Figure 3 shows the mean subjective understanding for each item across our groups. The three treatment groups rated these items quite similarly, while *Control* rated them lower, especially on understanding of the privacy concept (I2 in Fig. 3) and their ability to explain the concept to other people (I3 in Fig. 3).

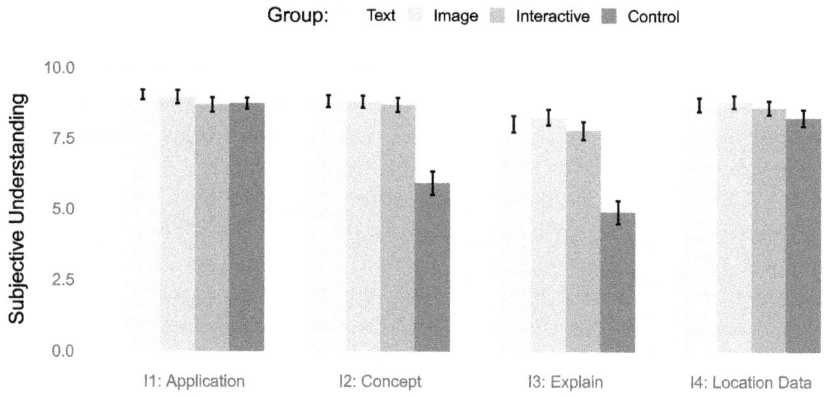

Fig. 3. Subjective Understanding for each item among the groups. Error bars visualise the 95% confidence interval. A higher score indicates a higher subjective understanding.

We use Welch's ANOVA as the omnibus test, as variances differ significantly across groups for subjective understanding ($p < .001$ for Levene's test). If the omnibus test found a significant difference on subjective understanding of our groups, we performed pairwise Games-Howell post-hoc tests, which account for multiple testing. Effect sizes are reported as Cohen's d.

We found a significant difference on subjective understanding between groups with Welch's ANOVA, $F(3, 422.58) = 49.66$, $p < .001$. The results of the pairwise post-hoc tests and effect sizes are shown in Table 2. We did not observe any significant differences between treatment groups. However, we found a significant difference in subjective understanding between the control group and all treatment groups with large effect sizes.

Given these results, H1 is not supported as richer explanation formats do not lead to higher subjective understanding. We only observe a higher subjective understanding for all explanation formats compared with the control group.

Table 2. Results for Games-Howell post-hoc tests for subjective understanding with mean difference (ΔM), confidence interval (95% CI), adjusted p-values, Cohen's d

Group 1	Group 2	ΔM	95% CI	adj. p	d
Text	Image	0.07	[−0.31, 0.44]	.968	0.05
Text	Interactive	−0.20	[−0.59, 0.19]	.552	0.14
Text	Control	−1.69	[−2.10, −1.28]	< .001	1.08
Image	Interactive	−0.27	[−0.67, 0.14]	.319	0.18
Image	Control	−1.76	[−2.17, −1.34]	< .001	1.09
Interactive	Control	−1.49	[−1.92, −1.06]	< .001	0.90

Trust. As described in Sect. 4.2, we measured trust in the privacy concept with a single question using a continuous slider with a scale from 1 to 101. The mean scores for trust were $M = 70.83$ ($SD = 20.93$) for *Text*, $M = 70.49$ ($SD = 19.98$) for *Image*, $M = 67.60$ ($SD = 22.52$) for *Interactive*, and $M = 57.78$ ($SD = 24.42$) for *Control*. Figure 4 shows the distribution of participants' ratings for trust across our groups. For trust, we used the same tests and effect size measurements as for subjective understanding, i. e., Welch's ANOVA with Games-Howell post-hoc tests ($p = .020$ for Levene's test).

Welch's ANOVA revealed a significant difference for trust in the privacy concept between our groups, $F(3, 422.67) = 13.64$, $p < .001$. The results of the pairwise post-hoc tests are shown in Table 3. We found no significant differences between our treatment groups. However, all three treatment groups had significantly higher trust in the privacy concept than *Control*. Effect sizes for *Text* ($d = 0.57$) and *Image* ($d = 0.57$) were medium, while the effect size for *Interactive* ($d = 0.42$) was small.

Given these results, H3 is not supported as richer explanation formats do not lead to higher trust in the privacy concept. We only observe a higher trust in the privacy concept for all explanation formats compared with the control group.

Table 3. Results of the Games-Howell post-hoc tests for trust with mean difference (ΔM), confidence interval (95% CI), adjusted p-values, and Cohen's d

Group 1	Group 2	ΔM	95% CI	adj. p	d
Text	Image	−0.34	[−5.77, 5.09]	.998	0.02
Text	Interactive	−3.23	[−9.03, 2.57]	.476	0.15
Text	Control	−13.05	[−18.96, −7.14]	< .001	0.57
Image	Interactive	−2.89	[−8.58, 2.80]	.557	0.14
Image	Control	−12.71	[−18.51, −6.90]	< .001	0.57
Interactive	Control	−9.82	[−15.96, −3.67]	< .001	0.42

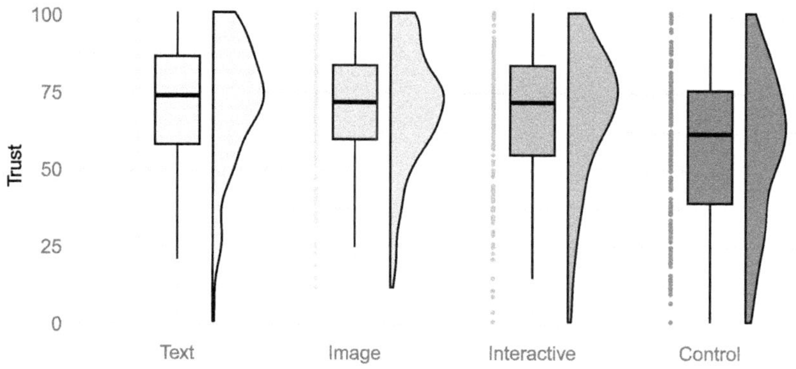

Fig. 4. Raincloud plot for trust in the privacy concept across experimental groups.

Objective Understanding. To measure participants' objective understanding, we used five multiple-response questions, and evaluated them using all-or-nothing scoring. That is, an answer for a question was correct only if all correct items and none of the distractors were selected by participants. We did not calculate any partial points, making it unlikely to answer a question correctly by guessing. This gave us a total score from 0 to 5 for each participant. Additionally, participants rated their confidence for each question they answered on a scale from 1 to 10. As participants in *Control* did not receive an explanation of the visibility rules of the privacy concept, we do not test their objective understanding. Results for Q2–Q5 would only measure random guessing, not actual understanding. Therefore, we consider only our three treatment groups ($n = 563$) for objective understanding.

The median scores of correct answers were $Mdn = 2$ ($IQR = 1$) for *Text*, and $Mdn = 3$ ($IQR = 1$) for both *Image* and *Interactive*. Figure 5 shows the proportion of correct answers per question on objective understanding across treatment groups. All groups answered Q1 mostly correctly (82.7–92.6%). We found the largest differences on Q2, where 16.3% of *Text*, 36.2% of *Image*, and 39.5% of *Interactive* answered correctly. Table 4 additionally shows the mean confidence per question for each group. In each group, participants' confidence ratings were relatively high (7.3–9.2) for all questions. Interestingly, participants' confidence for answering correctly was high regardless of the correctness of the answer. For example, fewer than 38% answered correctly on Q3 (under which conditions VAC pumps are invisible), yet confidence remained high (7.9–8.8).

We used a Kruskal-Wallis test as omnibus test instead of Welch's ANOVA since we consider the total score ranging from 0 to 5 as discrete. When the test was significant, we performed pairwise post-hoc Dunn tests with Holm correction. With our omnibus test, we found a significant difference between groups, $H(2) = 7.86$, $p = .020$, $\eta^2_H = .01$ indicating a small effect. In the group comparisons, we found that both *Image* ($p = .041$) and *Interactive* ($p = .041$) achieved significantly higher scores than *Text*. However, we could not find a significant difference between *Image* and *Interactive* ($p = .943$). Based on Fig. 5,

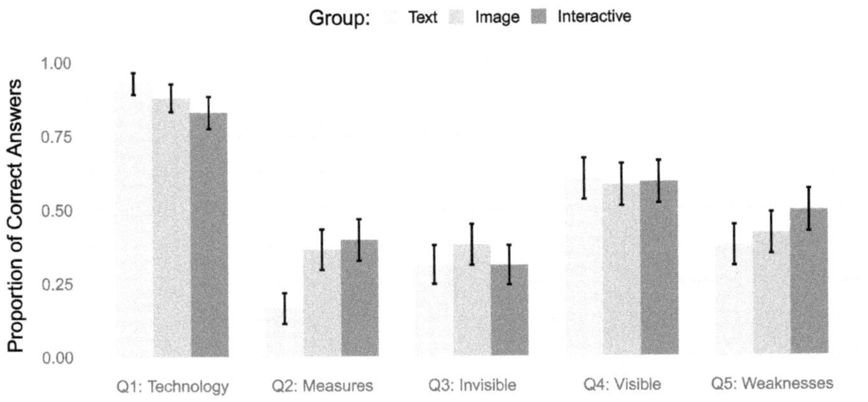

Fig. 5. Proportion of correct answers for each question on objective understanding of the privacy concept among the three treatment groups with 95% confidence intervals.

Table 4. Proportion of correct answers and mean confidence (conf. on scale 1–10) for the individual questions on objective understanding.

	Text		Image		Interactive	
	% correct	conf.	% correct	conf.	% correct	conf.
Q1	92.6	9.2	87.8	8.9	82.7	8.3
Q2	16.3	8.7	36.2	8.3	39.5	8.1
Q3	31.1	8.8	37.8	8.2	30.8	7.9
Q4	60.0	8.8	58.0	8.5	58.9	8.3
Q5	37.4	7.7	41.5	7.6	49.2	7.3

we ran exploratory chi-square tests for Q2 and Q5 as *Image* and *Interactive* performed best on these questions. The scores were significantly different for Q2, $\chi^2(2) = 27.86$, $p_{Holm} < .001$, and showed a non-significant trend for Q5, $\chi^2(2) = 5.51$, $p_{Holm} = .064$.

Given these results, H2 is only partially supported as *Image* and *Interactive* had a significantly higher objective understanding of the privacy concept compared to *Text*. However, we did not observe a higher objective understanding of the privacy concept comparing *Image* and *Interactive*.

Willingness to Use a Tracked VAC Pump. Participants answered whether they would be willing to use a tracked VAC pump on a binary scale (yes/no). The minimum expected frequency was ≈ 14, i.e., > 5. Therefore, we used a chi-square test to evaluate the willingness to use a tracked VAC pump across groups. Overall, values were high between 90.0% (*Text*) and 94.1% (*Image*). We did not find any significant difference between groups with the chi-squared test, $\chi^2(3) = 2.53$, $p = .470$, Cramer's $V = .06$.

Thus, H4 is not supported as richer explanation formats do not lead to higher willingness to use a tracked VAC pump. We observe high values for the willingness to use a tracked VAC pump across all groups regardless of the explanation.

5.2 Treatment-Specific Questions

We also asked participants several group-specific questions, i. e., only one treatment group received those questions. For *Text*, *Image*, and *Interactive* participants rated three statements on a scale from 1 to 10.

In *Text*, participants found that the textual explanation was sufficient to understand the privacy concept ($M = 7.74$, $SD = 2.04$, $Mdn = 8$). Further, the majority of participants in *Text* reported that an additional explanation form might have improved their understanding ($M = 6.71$, $SD = 2.64$, $Mdn = 7$), and that they would appreciate explanations not only in text form ($M = 6.97$, $SD = 2.45$, $Mdn = 8$).

In *Image*, participants found that the visual representation of the tracking application contributed to their understanding of the privacy concept ($M = 8.03$, $SD = 1.97$, $Mdn = 8$). Further, participants' responses indicated that privacy concepts should be explained more frequently with visual representations ($M = 8.62$, $SD = 1.48$, $Mdn = 9$), and that they did not get confused from the visual representation of the application ($M = 3.05$, $SD = 2.32$, $Mdn = 2$).

In *Interactive*, we asked participants which functionalities of the application they used. Most participants used the time simulator (88.6%) and moved a VAC pump to a different room (81.6%). 58.4% of participants used the pump status to adjust the last move time of a single VAC pump. Only 3.2% reported using none of the above functionalities of the interactive application. Further, participants reported that trying out these functions contributed to understanding the privacy concept ($M = 7.51$, $SD = 2.39$, $Mdn = 8$). Further, participants' responses indicated that privacy concepts should be explained more frequently with interactive explanations ($M = 8.20$, $SD = 2.05$, $Mdn = 9$). However, participants got slightly confused trying out the functions of the tracking application ($M = 4.39$, $SD = 2.85$, $Mdn = 4$).

6 Discussion

We evaluated how different explanations of a privacy concept for VAC pump tracking affected (1) users' subjective and objective understanding of the concept, (2) trust in the concept, and (3) their willingness to use a tracked VAC pump. For that, we used a between-subjects design with a control group and three treatment groups ($N = 766$). Each treatment group received a different explanation: text-only, text-and-image, and text-and-interactive. Our survey results show that all three explanation formats significantly improved participants' subjective understanding and trust compared with the control group. However, while visual and interactive formats significantly improved objective understanding over text-only, objective understanding was relatively low across all treatment groups. Despite this, participants' willingness to use a tracked VAC pump was high in all groups, even in the control group; we did not find any significant differences between our groups.

Subjective Understanding and Trust. Considering these results, H1 and H3 are not supported; there is no improvement in trust or subjective understanding with richer explanation formats. That is, any explanation improves participants' trust (d = 0.42–0.57) and subjective understanding (d = 0.90–1.09) of the privacy concept compared with the control group. The effect is driven by providing any explanation, not by richer explanation formats. Our results align with Mithila et al., who found no significant differences for subjective understanding comparing text, static, and interactive explanations for differential privacy [21]. However, Waclawek et al. found significantly better subjective understanding for functional explanations when comparing them to mechanistic explanations [30].

Objective Understanding. We find that H2 is partially supported. The text-and-image and text-and-interactive groups scored significantly higher than text-only on objective understanding (p = .041). These results are consistent with Wen et al. [31] and multimedia learning theories that suggest understanding of textual explanations could be improved with additional images [20]. The visual representation of the privacy-preserving tracking application might have helped participants to understand specific parts of the privacy concept better. However, the effect size was small ($\eta^2_H = .01$), and absolute scores for objective understanding were low across all groups.

Random guessing likely does not explain these low scores given the multiple-response format with all-or-nothing scoring (see Sect. 5.1). This format made guessing correctly by chance improbable; yet Q1 was answered correctly by 82.7–92.6% and Q4 by 58–60% of participants. It is more likely that the low scores reflect either misunderstanding of the privacy concept or misinterpretations of the questions by our participants, two possibilities we cannot distinguish with our data. However, as the questions were identical for the treatment groups, this uncertainty applies to the absolute scores rather than to the group differences.

The largest differences between groups were on Q2 and Q5. On Q5, 49.2% of Interactive and 41.5% of Image answered correctly, compared with 37.4% of Text. On Q2, 36.2% of Image and 39.5% of Interactive answered correctly, compared with 16.3% of Text. So, overall, our interactive elements did not lead to significantly improved understanding of the privacy concept compared to visual representations, although most participants stated they used features such as the time simulator (88.6%), or moved VAC pumps on the hospital's station plan (81.6%). The reason for that might be that these features introduced additional cognitive load [20]; participants reported more confusion from interactive elements ($M = 4.39$) than participants from the visual representation ($M = 3.05$). This low understanding is in line with related work. In the context of differential privacy, Franzen et al. found scores below chance for objective understanding [10], and Smart et al. also found low objective understanding [27]. In contrast,

Waclawek et al. found improvements in objective understanding for functional explanations when comparing them to mechanistic explanations [30].

Willingness to Use a Tracked VAC Pump. For the willingness to use a tracked VAC pump, we found that H4 is not supported. Across all groups, 90–94% of participants would use a tracked VAC pump, even without a detailed explanation or an understanding of the privacy concept. This suggests that participants' consent decisions are similar regardless of explanation formats and understanding of the privacy concept. The high willingness to use a tracked VAC pump is consistent with the high trust scores we observed, as prior work has shown that trust is associated with higher willingness to share data [30].

Overconfidence. Across all treatment groups, participants' confidence in their answers was high despite low scores on objective understanding. Depending on the question, participants rated their confidence at 7.3–9.2 on a scale from 1 to 10, even when fewer than 40% answered correctly, e. g., on Q2 or Q3. These results suggest that participants did not understand the privacy concept and only believed they understood it. This finding of overconfidence is in line with Franzen et al. [10] and Smart et al. [27], who found this discrepancy for differential privacy. This overconfidence, combined with the high willingness to use a tracked VAC pump (H4), indicates that participants do not realize their poor understanding and thus never reconsider their consent decision.

Risk Awareness. One possible explanation for the high trust, high willingness to use, and low objective understanding is that participants did not perceive the scenario as highly privacy-sensitive. They may not have grasped the concrete risks of continuous patient tracking. Our explanations described only how the privacy concept protects patient data but not the possible consequences, e. g., that movement patterns could reveal patients' health conditions. Without a sense of what is at stake, participants could have perceived the scenario as low risk, which could have led to low engagement with the explanations. This low perceived risk could explain the low absolute understanding, the overconfidence, and the near-uniform willingness to use a VAC pump across groups. It does not, however, explain why richer formats still improved objective understanding over text-only (H2), so the format mattered even where overall engagement was low. Although recent work has begun translating privacy guarantees into concrete risk scenarios [4, 7, 10, 23], explicit risk communication remains uncommon in privacy explanations. Future work should investigate whether communicating concrete tracking risks before explaining the privacy concept itself improves understanding and leads to more deliberate consent decisions.

Implications. Our results indicate that explanations might create an illusion of understanding. Participants think they understand how their data is protected, trust the privacy concept, and agree to use it. However, they do not understand how their data is protected. These findings suggest that subjective understanding of a privacy concept is not a reliable indicator of actual understanding, which poses a challenge for informed consent in practice. Further, the content of explanations is likely more important than the format, although the interactive format achieved the highest absolute scores regarding the limitations of our privacy concept. Therefore, future work should focus on explanation content and use interactive elements where they appeared most effective. Qualitative research might also clarify where and why understanding of privacy concepts is low.

Limitations. One limitation of our study is that we evaluated our explanations in an online survey rather than with real patients in a hospital setting. We could not simulate the vulnerability of patients and the time pressure they might feel when they consent to data collection. This threatens external validity, i. e., participants' answers might differ in a real hospital setting. Our participants might have scored higher on objective understanding than patients, as Tang et al. have shown that samples recruited via Prolific tend to have more privacy and security knowledge compared to the general population [29]. Further, as we used all-or-nothing scoring for objective understanding, partial scoring might capture smaller differences between explanation formats. Additionally, we did not perform any pretest, so participants might have interpreted some questions differently than intended, which, as discussed above, limits the interpretation of absolute understanding scores. Another limitation is that participants' understanding might be confounded with time spent on the explanations, as the visual and interactive explanations contained additional elements compared with the text-only explanation. As we did not collect participants' interaction time on the explanation websites, the differences between formats might be attributed partially to the interaction time rather than the format itself.

7 Conclusion

In an online survey (N = 766), we evaluated textual, visual, and interactive explanations of a threshold-based privacy concept for VAC pump tracking in a hospital setting. Richer explanation formats did not improve subjective understanding or trust beyond what any explanation achieved; for objective understanding, image and interactive formats outperformed text-only, with low absolute scores. Across all groups, participants were confident they understood the concept when they did not, and at least 90% would use a tracked pump regardless of the explanation format or understanding.

These findings suggest that explanations alone, regardless of format, are insufficient for informed consent when patients cannot assess their own understanding. Future work should prioritize explanation content over format and investigate where interactive elements appeared most effective, specifically in conveying a concept's limitations. In particular, future studies should examine whether communicating the risks of data collection explicitly is a prerequisite for informed consent. Validating these results with actual patients in a hospital, where they are vulnerable and under time pressure, remains a necessary step.

Acknowledgments. This study has been funded by the Federal Ministry of Research, Technology and Space (BMFTR) as part of the explanym (16KISA079K) project.

Explanation of AI Usage. We used Large Language Models to support the development of the explanation websites, data analysis, and writing.

Disclosure of Interests. The authors have no competing interests to declare.

References

1. Alaqra, A.S., Karegar, F., Fischer-Hübner, S.: Structural and functional explanations for informing lay and expert users: the case of functional encryption. Proc. Priv. Enhancing Technol. **2023**(4), 359–380 (2023)
2. Ashena, N., Inel, O., Persaud, B.L., Bernstein, A.: Casual users and rational choices within differential privacy. In: IEEE Symposium on Security and Privacy, SP 2024, pp. 932–950 (2024)
3. Bai, L., Ciravegna, F., Bond, R.R., Mulvenna, M.D.: A low cost indoor positioning system using bluetooth low energy. IEEE Access **8**, 136858–136871 (2020)
4. Bai, W., Pearson, M., Kelley, P.G., Mazurek, M.L.: Improving non-experts' understanding of end-to-end encryption: An exploratory study. In: IEEE European Symposium on Security and Privacy Workshops, pp. 210–219 (2020)
5. Becker, M., Matt, C., Hess, T.: It's not just about the product: how persuasive communication affects the disclosure of personal health information. Data Base **51**(1), 37–50 (2020)
6. Bullek, B., Garboski, S., Mir, D.J., Peck, E.M.: Towards understanding differential privacy: When do people trust randomized response technique? In: Proceedings of the 2017 CHI Conference on Human Factors in Computing Systems, pp. 3833–3837. ACM (2017)
7. Cummings, R., Kaptchuk, G., Redmiles, E.M.: "i need a better description": An investigation into user expectations for differential privacy. In: CCS '21: ACM SIGSAC Conference on Computer and Communications Security, pp. 3037–3052 (2021)
8. Deng, M., Wuyts, K., Scandariato, R., Preneel, B., Joosen, W.: A privacy threat analysis framework: supporting the elicitation and fulfillment of privacy requirements. Requir. Eng. **16**(1), 3–32 (2011)
9. Distler, V., Gutfleisch, T., Lallemand, C., Lenzini, G., Koenig, V.: Complex, but in a good way? How to represent encryption to non-experts through text and visuals - evidence from expert co-creation and a vignette experiment. Comput. Hum. Beh. Rep. **5**, 100161 (2022)
10. Franzen, D., von Voigt, S.N., Sörries, P., Tschorsch, F., Müller-Birn, C.: Am I private and if so, how many?: Communicating privacy guarantees of differential privacy with risk communication formats. In: Proceedings of the 2022 ACM SIGSAC Conference on Computer and Communications Security, pp. 1125–1139 (2022)
11. Garrido, G.M., Liu, X., Matthes, F., Song, D.: Lessons learned: surveying the practicality of differential privacy in the industry. Proc. Priv. Enhancing Technol. **2023**(2), 151–170 (2023)
12. Hoepman, J.-H.: Privacy design strategies. In: Cuppens-Boulahia, N., Cuppens, F., Jajodia, S., Abou El Kalam, A., Sans, T. (eds.) SEC 2014. IAICT, vol. 428, pp. 446–459. Springer, Heidelberg (2014). https://doi.org/10.1007/978-3-642-55415-5_38

13. Kacsmar, B., Duddu, V., Tilbury, K., Ur, B., Kerschbaum, F.: Comprehension from chaos: towards informed consent for private computation. In: Proceedings of the 2023 ACM SIGSAC Conference on Computer and Communications Security, pp. 210–224 (2023)
14. Kassambara, A.: rstatix: Pipe-Friendly Framework for Basic Statistical Tests (2025). https://github.com/kassambara/rstatix, r package version 0.7.3
15. Khavkin, M., Toch, E.: Differential privacy configurations in the real world: a comparative analysis. IEEE Trans. Knowl. Data Eng. **37**(11), 6334–6351 (2025)
16. Kitkowska, A., Warner, M., Shulman, Y., Wästlund, E., Martucci, L.A.: Enhancing privacy through the visual design of privacy notices: exploring the interplay of curiosity, control and affect. In: Sixteenth Symposium on Usable Privacy and Security, pp. 437–456 (2020)
17. Kühtreiber, P., Pak, V., Reinhardt, D.: Replication: the effect of differential privacy communication on German users' comprehension and data sharing attitudes. In: Eighteenth Symposium on Usable Privacy and Security, pp. 117–134 (2022)
18. Kulyk, O., Renaud, K., Costica, S.: People want reassurance when making privacy-related decisions - not technicalities. J. Syst. Softw. **200**, 111620 (2023)
19. Leiner, D.J.: SoSci Survey (version 3.7.06) (2025). https://www.soscisurvey.de
20. Mayer, R.E., Fiorella, L. (eds.): The Cambridge Handbook of Multimedia Learning. Cambridge Handbooks in Psychology, 3 edn. Cambridge University Press (2021)
21. Mithila, M.M.S., Yu, F., Martin, M.V., Wang, S.: Visualizing differential privacy: assessing infographics' impact on layperson data-sharing decisions and comprehension. In: 21st Annual International Conference on Privacy, Security and Trust, PST 2024, pp. 1–13. IEEE (2024)
22. Nanayakkara, P., Smart, M.A., Cummings, R., Kaptchuk, G., Redmiles, E.M.: What are the chances? explaining the epsilon parameter in differential privacy. In: 32nd USENIX Security Symposium, USENIX Security 2023, pp. 1613–1630 (2023)
23. Nuñez von Voigt, S., Mehner, L., Tschorsch, F.: From theory to comprehension: a comparative study of differential privacy and k-anonymity. In: Proceedings of the Fourteenth ACM Conference on Data and Application Security and Privacy, CODASPY 2024, pp. 221–232 (2024)
24. Pfitzmann, A., Hansen, M.: A terminology for talking about privacy by data minimization: anonymity, unlinkability, undetectability, unobservability, pseudonymity, and identity management (2010)
25. Schaub, F., Balebako, R., Durity, A.L., Cranor, L.F.: A design space for effective privacy notices. In: Eleventh Symposium On Usable Privacy and Security, pp. 1–17 (2015)
26. Smart, M.A., Nanayakkara, P., Cummings, R., Kaptchuk, G., Redmiles, E.M.: Models matter: setting accurate privacy expectations for local and central differential privacy. Proc. Priv. Enhancing Technol. **2025**(4), 653–678 (2025)
27. Smart, M.A., Sood, D., Vaccaro, K.: Understanding risks of privacy theater with differential privacy. Proc. ACM Hum. Comput. Interact. **6**(CSCW2), 1–24 (2022)
28. Solove, D.J.: Murky consent: an approach to the fictions of consent in privacy law. BUL Rev. **104**, 593 (2024)
29. Tang, J., Birrell, E., Lerner, A.: Replication: how well do my results generalize now? the external validity of online privacy and security surveys. In: Eighteenth Symposium on Usable Privacy and Security, pp. 367–385 (2022)
30. Waclawek, T., Fiedler, A., Schütz, M., Schütz, A.: Crowd-counting technology within the smart city context: understanding, trust, and acceptance. Frontiers in Psychology, Vol. 15 - 2024 (2024)

31. Wen, Z.A., Jia, J., Yan, H., Yao, Y., Liu, Z., Dong, C.: The influence of explanation designs on user understanding differential privacy and making data-sharing decision. Inf. Sci. **642**, 118799 (2023)
32. Wuyts, K., Sion, L., Joosen, W.: LINDDUN GO: a lightweight approach to privacy threat modeling. In: IEEE European Symposium on Security and Privacy Workshops, EuroS&P Workshops 2020, pp. 302–309 (2020)
33. Xian, L., Lee-Kan, S.M., Im, J., Schaub, F.: User-centric textual descriptions of privacy-enhancing technologies for ad tracking and analytics. Proc. Priv. Enhancing Technol. **2025**(1), 379–398 (2025)
34. Xiong, A., Wang, T., Li, N., Jha, S.: Towards effective differential privacy communication for users' data sharing decision and comprehension. In: 2020 IEEE Symposium on Security and Privacy, SP 2020, pp. 392–410 (2020)
35. Yoo, S., Kim, S., Kim, E., Jung, E., Lee, K., Hwang, H.: Real-time location system-based asset tracking in the healthcare field: lessons learned from a feasibility study. BMC Medical Informatics Decis. Mak. **18**(1), 80:1–80:10 (2018)

Network and Communication Security

Secure Wi-Fi Ranging Today: Security and Adoption of IEEE 802.11az/bk

Nikola Antonijević[1(✉)], Bernhard Etzlinger[2], Dave Singelée[3], and Bart Preneel[1]

[1] COSIC, KU Leuven, Leuven, Belgium
{nikola.antonijevic,bart.preneel}@esat.kuleuven.be
[2] Institute for Communications Engineering and RF-Systems, Johannes Kepler University Linz, Linz, Austria
bernhard.etzlinger@jku.at
[3] DistriNet (Group T), KU Leuven, Leuven, Belgium
dave.singelee@kuleuven.be

Abstract. Ranging and localisation have become critical for many applications and services. The Wi-Fi (IEEE 802.11) standard is a natural candidate for providing these functions across diverse environments, given its widespread deployment. The IEEE 802.11az amendment, finalised in 2023, introduces "Next Generation Positioning" mechanisms to secure and harden the existing insecure Wi-Fi Fine Timing Measurement (FTM) ranging solution. Moreover, the recent IEEE 802.11bk amendment increases the available bandwidth with the goal of approaching the centimetre-level ranging accuracy of ultra-wideband (UWB) systems. This paper examines to what extent these promises hold from a security and deployability perspective.

We analyse the core mechanisms of secure Wi-Fi ranging as defined in IEEE 802.11az and IEEE 802.11bk at both the logical and physical layers, combining standards analysis with simulations and measurements on commercial and development hardware. At the logical layer, we show how common deployment choices can result in unauthenticated ranging, downgrade attacks, and simple denial-of-service attacks, making it difficult to securely realise many high-stakes use cases. At the physical layer, we study the predictability of secure ranging waveforms, the security impact of symbol repetition, and how waveform design choices affect compliance with spectral masks under realistic RF behaviour.

Our results show that secure Wi-Fi ranging is highly sensitive to configuration choices and is non-trivial to implement on existing hardware. This is also evidenced by the currently limited support for secure Wi-Fi ranging in commodity devices. This paper provides practical guidelines for using secure FTM safely and recommendations to vendors and standardisation bodies to improve its robustness and deployability.

Keywords: IEEE 802.11az/bk · Fine Timing Measurement · Security

S. Nadjm-Tehrani et al. (Eds.): ARES 2026, LNCS 16898, pp. 137–159, 2027.
https://doi.org/10.1007/978-3-032-36874-4_7

1 Introduction

The family of wireless network protocols based on IEEE 802.11, commonly known as Wi-Fi, underpins connectivity for billions of devices worldwide. For an increasing number of applications, however, a device's location is as important as its ability to communicate: precise knowledge of *where* a device is can determine which services it can access and how it can be used. Since satellite-based systems such as GPS perform poorly indoors, Wi-Fi has emerged as an attractive platform for indoor ranging and localisation, leveraging infrastructure that is already widely deployed [18]. Typical examples include navigation in large buildings, asset tracking, access control and automation in smart homes and offices, and applications that depend on trustworthy proximity information [14].

The Wi-Fi Fine Timing Measurement (FTM) was first introduced in the IEEE 802.11mc amendment in 2016, enabling more precise Wi-Fi ranging by using Time of Flight (ToF) measurements to estimate the distance between two stations [12]. Prior Wi-Fi positioning systems mostly relied on received signal strength (RSS), with no standardised ToF-based ranging. FTM significantly improved the accuracy and usability of Wi-Fi-based ranging, but the original procedures did not protect the integrity or authenticity of ranging messages. Subsequent research by Schepers et al. [25] showed that legacy FTM is highly vulnerable to distance manipulation and spoofing attacks. To address these weaknesses, the IEEE 802.11az amendment was released in 2023. This Wi-Fi Next Generation Positioning (NGP) standard strengthens FTM at both the logical and physical layers, for example, through protected management frames and secure high-efficiency long training fields (HE-LTFs). Most recently, IEEE 802.11bk further extended FTM by increasing the maximum bandwidth to 320 MHz to approach the ranging accuracy of ultra-wideband (UWB), while inheriting the security mechanisms of IEEE 802.11az [13]. The resulting procedures are now consolidated in the IEEE 802.11-2024 standard [14].

Despite these developments, commercial support for secure FTM as defined in IEEE 802.11az remains limited. Only a small number of devices and development platforms publicly advertise secure FTM capabilities, and even fewer expose them in a documented, developer-accessible way. As a result, the security and deployability of secure FTM in IEEE 802.11az, and the implications for IEEE 802.11bk, have not been examined in depth. Existing security analyses focus on legacy FTM in IEEE 802.11mc and largely treat the physical layer as an idealised ranging primitive, without considering the concrete secure HE-LTF waveform or the availability of secure FTM features in deployed hardware.

This paper aims to fill this gap. We analyse the most important logical and physical-layer mechanisms of secure FTM in IEEE 802.11az and their relevance for IEEE 802.11bk. Our analysis combines a close reading of the IEEE 802.11-2024 standard with simulations in a MATLAB-based IEEE 802.11az framework and measurements on development boards that claim to support secure FTM. To the best of our knowledge, this is the first security-focused assessment of Wi-Fi Next Generation Positioning that jointly considers logical and physical mechanisms and their practical realisation.

Contributions. Our main contributions can be summarised as follows:

- **Issue-driven analysis of secure FTM.** We analyse core logical and physical-layer mechanisms of secure FTM in IEEE 802.11az and identify several classes of issues, including fragile trust assumptions in common WPA2/WPA3-Personal and PASN deployments, downgrade and denial-of-service risks, and failure modes related to secure HE-LTF counters and symbol repetition.
- **Security assessment of the secure FTM waveform.** Using a MATLAB-based model calibrated with measurements from a commercial platform, we study the predictability of secure HE-LTF waveforms under partial observation and quantify how much an attacker can bias time of arrival estimates, and thus the measured range, with advanced replicas without breaking demodulation or violating spectral constraints.
- **Deployment insights and recommendations.** We combine a snapshot of current IEEE 802.11az support in commercial and development hardware with our technical findings to explain why secure Wi-Fi ranging remains sparsely deployed. Based on this, we provide recommendations for device vendors and standardisation bodies on configuration choices and physical-layer constraints that future profiles and amendments should address.

Availability Statement. The entire source code, artefact, and a supplementary abbreviation table for reference can be accessed at https://github.com/KULeuven-COSIC/secure-wifi-ranging.

2 Background and Support for Secure FTM

This section introduces legacy Wi-Fi Fine Timing Measurement (FTM), also known as Wi-Fi Round Trip Time (RTT), and then summarises the secure FTM extensions in IEEE 802.11az/bk and their current adoption [13,14].

2.1 Fine Timing Measurement (802.11mc)

FTM, introduced in IEEE 802.11mc in 2016, enables Wi-Fi ranging by using Time of Flight (ToF) measurements instead of received signal strength (RSS), significantly improving indoor distance estimation accuracy [18]. Two parties, an *initiator* and a *responder*, engage in an FTM session that consists of negotiation, measurement exchange, and termination. Figure 1 illustrates a typical exchange between an initiator station (STA) and a responder access point (AP).

Negotiation. The initiator station (ISTA) discovers an FTM-capable responding station (RSTA) from a capability bit in the AP beacon and starts negotiation by sending an FTM Request frame (IFTMR). This request selects the measurement procedure and configures RF/PHY and protocol parameters (e.g., channel bandwidth and burst settings). Once the responder acknowledges this frame, the ISTA is ready to enter the measurement exchange phase.

Measurement Exchange. During the measurement exchange, the AP and STA send FTM message pairs to capture hardware timestamps. The AP transmits an FTM frame at time t_1 (Fig. 1), containing standard IEEE 802.11 training fields that serve both demodulation and Time of Arrival (ToA) estimation. The initiator records the receive time t_2, responds with an acknowledgement (ACK) at time t_3, and the AP receives it at time t_4. This sequence is repeated N times within the session. To deliver the captured values to the initiator, the AP embeds the t_1 and t_4 timestamps from each exchange into the payload of the subsequent FTM frame. In the first exchange of a session, these reporting fields are initialised to zero as no prior measurements exist. The final set of timestamps is delivered in a dedicated Final FTM frame.

The transmit timestamps t_1 and t_3 are scheduled transmission instants, whereas t_2 and t_4 require ToA estimation, that is, identifying the earliest detectable signal component. Various high-resolution ToA estimators have been proposed, including MUSIC-based approaches [20]. Using the four timestamps, the initiator computes the round-trip time and corresponding range $d = \frac{c}{2}\big[(t_4 - t_1) - (t_3 - t_2)\big]$, assuming propagation at the speed of light c. In practice, these individual distance estimates are averaged over the N repetitions to mitigate noise and improve the overall accuracy of the session.

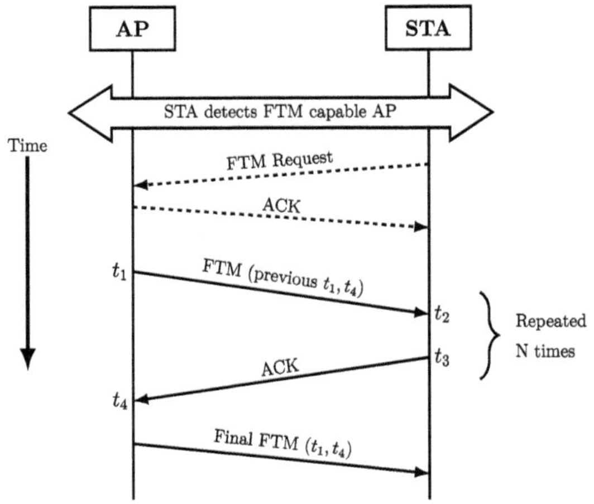

Fig. 1. Example of a typical FTM ranging session between the station (STA) and the access point (AP).

Termination. An FTM session terminates after the final burst instance, or earlier if the ISTA or RSTA transmits control values that signal termination.

2.2 Secure Fine Timing Measurement (802.11az and 802.11bk)

In 2023, the IEEE 802.11az amendment was released with the primary goal of hardening existing FTM procedures. Legacy FTM offers little integrity or authenticity protection: timestamps are sent in the clear, management frames are unencrypted, and ToA estimation training fields follow a public, deterministic structure. In multicarrier orthogonal frequency-division multiplexing (OFDM) systems like Wi-Fi, this predictability enables powerful ranging and location attacks [19]. NGP addresses these weaknesses by adding MAC and physical-layer protections. IEEE 802.11bk largely reuses these mechanisms while extending the available bandwidth and improving ranging accuracy.

Protected Management Frames. Protected Management Frames (PMF), originally introduced in IEEE 802.11w and later integrated into the main standard [14], ensure that selected management frames are cryptographically protected after key establishment. IEEE 802.11az adds FTM-related management frames to this protection set. In a secure NGP session, the FTM Request and the newly introduced Location Measurement Report (LMR) frames carrying t_1 and t_4 are protected at the MAC layer. This provides authenticity and confidentiality, preventing an active attacker from modifying timestamps or injecting forged messages without detection.

Preassociation Security Negotiation. Before IEEE 802.11az, stations authenticated and derived shared keys through mechanisms such as WPA2-Personal, 802.1X-based Enterprise authentication, and WPA3 schemes including Simultaneous Authentication of Equals (SAE). These mechanisms are coupled to association and are unsuited for lightweight ranging without a full data connection.

To decouple secure ranging from full association, NGP introduces preassociation security negotiation (PASN). PASN derives a fresh shared key for preassociation exchanges using authentication frames so that management traffic, including FTM frames, can be protected when no data-encryption keys exist.

PASN can operate in two modes [14]. When run on top of an existing authenticated Wi-Fi connection (for example a WPA3 network with established data keys), it reuses that security context to derive a separate key for preassociation exchanges, inheriting mutual authentication from the underlying protocol. When used on its own, without a prior authenticated association, PASN can still derive keys and protect management frames, but the standard explicitly does not guarantee mutual authentication. This lightweight mode reduces overhead for ranging, but it has important security implications that we analyse in Sect. 4.2.

Secure LTF Sequence. The IEEE 802.11ax PHY defines a high efficiency (HE) null data packet (NDP), a physical layer protocol data unit (PPDU) that carries no payload and consists only of preamble and training fields. In ranging mode, this HE ranging NDP is used solely for synchronisation, signalling, channel estimation, and ToA estimation. Within this preamble, the high efficiency long training fields (HE-LTFs) form the main OFDM training sequence that the receiver uses for ToA estimation.

Figure 2 focuses on this HE-LTF portion of the ranging NDP. In the legacy, non-secure format (Fig. 2a), a series of HE-LTF symbols with publicly specified deterministic patterns is transmitted back to back. This simplifies receiver design but makes channel estimates and ToA measurements susceptible to manipulation and signal-processing-based attacks [19].

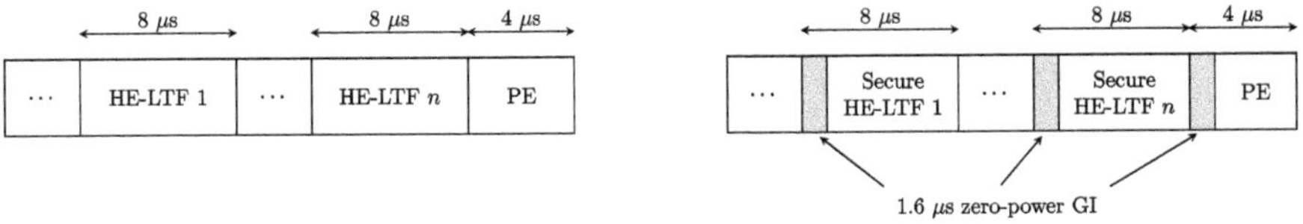

(a) Legacy HE-LTF region. (b) Secure HE-LTF region.

Fig. 2. Comparison of the HE-LTF part of an HE ranging NDP in the legacy (non-secure) and secure IEEE 802.11az formats. Earlier preamble fields and headers are omitted for clarity.

IEEE 802.11az replaces these fixed patterns with *secure HE-LTFs* (Fig. 2b), where training content is derived from secret keying material. Pairwise key material shared between initiator and responder is used to generate a pseudorandom bit stream that determines the HE-LTF symbols. Concretely, a key derivation key (KDK) embedded in the pairwise temporal key (PTK), established via PASN or conventional WPA2/WPA3 authentication, is first used to derive a long-term *secure LTF key seed* for the lifetime of the PTK. Each secure FTM measurement instance is associated with a *secure LTF counter*, initialised when the first secure session starts and incremented for every subsequent instance. A key derivation function combines the secure LTF key seed and the counter to produce per-measurement material: a Validation Sequence Authentication Code (SAC) and the keys used to generate the secure HE-LTF waveforms at the initiator and responder. The resulting bits are mapped onto 64-QAM symbols on the active subcarriers, yielding a pseudorandom training waveform. The secure LTF counter is intended to ensure that each secure HE-LTF instance is used at most once, while the Validation SAC allows the receiver to verify that the observed training waveform corresponds to the expected counter value and key.

In addition, IEEE 802.11az changes the guard interval (GI) between successive HE-LTF symbols. In the legacy format, this interval is implemented as a cyclic prefix, that is, a copy of the end of the OFDM symbol. In the secure HE-LTF format, the guard interval is forced to zero power. Removing the deterministic repetition of the cyclic prefix and using a zero-power guard interval reduces redundancy in the waveform and limits opportunities for an attacker to exploit structural correlation in FTM. We return to the implementation implications of this design choice in Sect. 5.4.

2.3 Adoption of Secure FTM

Since the release of IEEE 802.11mc in 2016, a broad range of products have added support for FTM. Google has been a major driver of this adoption: Wi-Fi RTT support is exposed to applications through the Android Wi-Fi RTT API [2], and tools such as WiFiRttScan provide convenient testing [9]. Most Google Pixel phones and several other Android devices support Wi-Fi RTT [1]. A variety of APs and development boards implement the protocol, and FTM has seen practical deployment in indoor location services, for example by IndoorAtlas [15].

In contrast, support for secure FTM as specified in IEEE 802.11az remains limited. Although the Android Wi-Fi RTT stack documents secure FTM modes, devices that actually implement these features in hardware and firmware appear to be scarce [2]. Even recent Google hardware, such as Nest Wifi Pro access points and Pixel smartphones, does not yet expose IEEE 802.11az capabilities in practice [1], and our own tests with a Google Pixel 9a and the WiFiRttLocator app did not reveal any secure FTM functionality. Public information currently mentions only a small number of enterprise-grade access points, such as the Aruba AP-734, as advertising support for secure FTM [1].

Several vendors also advertise development boards that claim IEEE 802.11az support and promise fine-grained control over PHY and MAC parameters. For this work, we relied on one such platform, which we cannot name due to a non-disclosure agreement (NDA). Despite the vendor's claim of full IEEE 802.11az compliance, we found that only a subset of secure FTM features was available in practice; the board implemented protected management frames but not secure HE-LTFs or other physical layer protections. We return to these limitations in Sect. 3.2, where we explain how they influenced our experimental design.

3 Threat Model and Methodology

Our analysis of secure FTM combines a close reading of the IEEE 802.11-2024 standard with simulations and hardware measurements to evaluate the protocol against a powerful proximal adversary.

3.1 Threat Model

In this work, we assume that the two parties who wish to determine their mutual distance are honest. Otherwise, falsifying measurements is trivial since endpoints report their own timestamps (Sect. 2.1). The adversary is a proximal third party aiming to manipulate the measured distance to bypass access controls or location restrictions. We assume a powerful active adversary in the Dolev-Yao style [6] who can arbitrarily observe and manipulate wireless traffic using high-power radios and arbitrary baseband waveforms. However, the attacker cannot compromise the honest stations' internal state, break standard cryptographic primitives, or violate physical limits like the speed of light. They possess complete knowledge of the IEEE 802.11-2024 standard and its secure FTM amendments [14].

3.2 Scope and Limitations

We focus on the secure FTM variants in IEEE 802.11az and their implications for IEEE 802.11bk, which retains the same security mechanisms over wider bandwidths. Rather than a formal proof, we perform an issue-driven analysis highlighting concrete weaknesses, limitations, and implementation pitfalls in realistic deployments using simulations and experiments. To identify these critical vulnerabilities, we systematically examined standard conformity with a dedicated 'spoofing' adversary in mind. By mapping the protocol's state machine against our attacker model, we identified structural gaps across multiple layers where security mechanisms could fail, be downgraded, or be bypassed. This approach allows us to establish a clear causal link between logical configuration choices and physical-layer exploitation.

Simulation. We use MATLAB's IEEE 802.11az examples [21,22], which implement draft IEEE P802.11az/D2.0, to parameterise and generate ranging NDP waveforms and to estimate ToA using a MUSIC super-resolution approach. We extend this baseline framework to analyse both secure and non-secure waveforms and to study ToA estimation under various channel and attacker strategies.

Experiments. Testing secure FTM in practice is challenging due to the limited availability of NGP hardware (Sect. 2.3). We relied on a development board that explicitly advertised IEEE 802.11az support; however, it only implemented protected management frames. The manufacturer (redacted via NDA) confirmed that secure HE-LTFs and physical-layer protections are not available and not planned for the current chipset due to architectural constraints (discussed further in Sect. 6.2). Despite this, we used the boards to perform FTM-based ranging, recorded the transmitted waveforms, and compared them against our simulations to establish a non-secure FTM baseline. We also cross-checked IEEE 802.11mc ranging against a commercial Google Pixel 9a. These traces and simulations form the core dataset for our physical-layer analysis (Sect. 5).

4 Logical-Layer Analysis

In this section, we analyse the logical-layer mechanisms of secure FTM in NGP and how authentication, mode selection, and configuration affect the intended security goals. We identify three main classes of issues. First, common deployment modes such as WPA2/WPA3-Personal and standalone PASN fail to bind secure FTM to a uniquely trusted infrastructure entity, limiting the security of many proposed use cases (Sect. 4.1 and Sect. 4.2). Second, several configuration and negotiation points admit downgrades from secure to legacy FTM or from secure HE-LTFs to deterministic training sequences, creating silent gaps between intended and effective security (Sect. 4.3). Third, when downgrades are prevented through strict policies, secure FTM becomes fragile from an availability perspective and is easily disrupted by simple denial-of-service attacks (Sect. 4.4).

4.1 Personal Mode Limitations

The NGP specifically aims to secure ranging across public, home, and enterprise environments [12]. However, many deployments rely on WPA2- or WPA3-Personal, which do not provide a cryptographic binding between secure FTM and a uniquely trusted infrastructure entity. In WPA2-Personal, any party with the shared passphrase can passively observe the four-way handshake, derive the pairwise temporal key (PTK), and subsequently forge protected management frames (e.g., LMR) or generate valid secure HE-LTFs for that ongoing association [14]. This allows adversaries to falsify timestamps via LMR modification or directly manipulate ranging at the physical layer (Sect. 5.3). While WPA3-Personal introduces SAE to prevent passive key recovery [29], SAE only proves knowledge of the shared password and does not authenticate a specific access point. Consequently, insiders who know the password can still deploy rogue access points ("evil twins") and establish valid secure FTM associations, a vulnerability that persists even in extensions like WPA3-PK [28]. Any secure FTM exchanges performed over these associations attest proximity to the attacker rather than to the intended anchor point. Ultimately, 'secure' ranging in Personal modes reduces to the secrecy of a widely shared password, rendering it fundamentally unsuitable for high-stakes, distance-based authorisation.

4.2 PASN

Managing shared credentials across heterogeneous devices in public or transient environments is operationally challenging, and requiring a full association for every ranging interaction is often impractical for guest navigation or *ad hoc* use cases. To reduce this overhead, NGP introduces preassociation security negotiation (PASN), which allows two stations to derive keys and protect management and FTM frames, without establishing a full data connection [11].

If PASN runs on top of an existing authenticated Wi-Fi connection, it reuses the established security context to derive fresh keys and essentially inherits the mutual authentication of the underlying WPA2 or WPA3 mechanism. The situation is different when PASN is used on its own, without a prior authenticated association: in this standalone setting, the standard explicitly does not guarantee mutual authentication between the two stations. PASN can still derive keys and protect management frames, but there is no strong binding between those keys and a long-term identifier.

As a consequence of being an unauthenticated key exchange by construction, standalone PASN is inherently vulnerable to person-in-the-middle abuse. An active adversary can first perform a PASN exchange with the access point and the station separately, establishing independent keying material with each, and then remain on the path, relaying or altering protected management frames and secure HE-LTF content between them. By crafting and forwarding frames appropriately, the attacker can steer secure FTM ranging results to attest proximity either to itself or to the honest access point. Conceptually, this mirrors the Personal mode issues in Sect. 4.1: secure FTM is not firmly bound to a specific, trusted infrastructure entity, but only to whoever can participate in the key establishment. For high-stakes NGP use cases, this again points to the need for deployments rooted in robust mutual authentication, rather than relying solely on lightweight or password-based mechanisms.

4.3 Critical Configuration Points

The security guarantees of NGP ultimately depend on how devices are configured. In practice, permissive or misaligned settings can significantly weaken the protection that secure FTM is meant to provide. Here, we highlight configuration choices that are particularly security-critical.

Ranging Mode Selection and Security Gaps. As discussed in Sect. 2.1, an FTM procedure starts when an initiator (ISTA) transmits a Fine Timing Measurement Request (FTMR) frame to the responder (RSTA). This FTMR carries crucial configuration parameters, including the ranging mode.

IEEE 802.11az introduces several modes to improve scalability and efficiency: trigger-based (TB), non-trigger-based (non-TB), enhanced distributed channel access (EDCA)-based FTM exchange, and passive TB measurement [14]. By default, stations use TB or non-TB ranging. The standard explicitly restricts EDCA-based ranging to special cases, such as 6 GHz band operation or when a station lacks TB/non-TB support, meaning EDCA acts as a legacy fallback.

This has direct security implications. Secure HE-LTFs with pseudorandom training content and zero-power guard intervals are defined only for TB and non-TB ranging. For EDCA-based ranging, secure HE-LTF mechanisms are not specified and are therefore not used. Even when MAC-level protection is in place, selecting EDCA-based ranging leaves the physical layer without the secure HE-LTF frames envisaged by NGP, creating a gap we revisit in Sect. 5.

If devices are not configured carefully, an active attacker can exploit this as a mode-level downgrade. A proximal adversary can block an FTMR in which the ISTA requests TB or non-TB ranging and instead forge an FTMR towards the RSTA that selects EDCA-based ranging. The RSTA, following the standard rules and believing that TB or non-TB ranging is unavailable, replies with parameters for an EDCA-based session. From the ISTA's perspective, this appears as a legitimate negotiation where only the legacy compatible mode is supported, so it proceeds without secure HE-LTFs. In short, EDCA-based ranging remains a legacy path that can bypass secure FTM protections at the mode-selection stage.

Negotiation-Based Downgrade from Secure to Legacy FTM. Beyond the choice of ranging mode, the FTMR also determines whether the session uses secure or legacy FTM. In IEEE 802.11az, this is reflected in whether the FTMR is sent as a protected management frame under an established PTK or as an unprotected management frame. If the ISTA has a PTK with the RSTA (a pairwise temporal key security association, or PTKSA) and sends a protected FTM Request Action frame as the initial FTMR, it signals intent to perform a secure FTM procedure. If the FTMR is sent unprotected, the ISTA initiates a non-secure, legacy FTM session.

The final mode is determined by the RSTA's policy. The standard allows an access point to require a PTKSA before accepting FTM, in which case it shall reject FTMR frames that are not protected under the PTK. In that configuration, only FTM sessions that run under a PTK are permitted. If the RSTA does not require a PTKSA, it may accept unprotected FTMR frames and proceed with a non-secure FTM procedure for compatibility with legacy devices.

Even when a PTKSA exists and the FTMR is protected, a second negotiation decides whether secure HE-LTFs are used. The ISTA indicates support, and optionally a requirement, for secure HE-LTFs by including the secure HE-LTF subelement in the Ranging Parameters element and setting the *Secure HE-LTF Required* field. If the ISTA only signals support but does not set this field to 1, or if the RSTA does not echo the secure HE-LTF subelement with *Secure HE-LTF Required* set to 1 in its response, the session proceeds with legacy, deterministic HE-LTFs even though control frames are protected at the MAC layer. From a security perspective, this is a downgrade of the ranging waveform to the non-secure baseline.

If these policies are permissive, the system is vulnerable to straightforward downgrades. An active attacker near the ISTA can block the first protected FTMR and then forge an equivalent unprotected FTMR towards the RSTA. An RSTA configured to accept both secure and non-secure FTM will respond with parameters for a non-secure session. From the ISTA's perspective, this is indistinguishable from a legitimate negotiation with a non-secure RSTA, so it proceeds with legacy FTM and predictable training sequences. Devices that support secure FTM but do not *require* both a PTK and secure HE-LTFs therefore remain exposed to silent downgrades at either the MAC or physical layer. Conversely, configuring the RSTA to require a PTK for FTM and to honour the *Secure HE-LTF Required* indication hardens the system, but reduces backward compatibility, since FTM is then only possible with peers that support protected management frames and secure HE-LTF procedures.

Error Recovery and Counter Reuse. The IEEE 802.11az standard specifies an explicit error recovery procedure for secure HE-LTF exchanges when a station detects an invalid parameter, for example when the received Validation SAC does not match the expected value. Conceptually, a failed measurement instance is marked invalid without advancing the Validation SAC or the Secure HE-LTF Counter; the next instance uses a deliberately invalid Null-SAC HE-LTF and carries the next Validation SAC and counter value in the protected R2I LMR; normal operation then resumes using these updated values.

The standard explicitly states that a station shall discard the Validation SAC used in a failed exchange and shall not use the same SAC again. Since the SAC and the secure HE-LTF keys are derived from the Secure HE-LTF Counter and the seed, this implies a strictly monotonic counter and no reuse of the associated keying material. Under normal conditions, this is straightforward to implement, but error handling, state resets, or firmware bugs can cause implementations to deviate, for example by failing to increment the counter after a recovery round or certain error conditions.

If a device improperly reuses the same counter value for multiple secure HE-LTF instances, it also reuses the Validation SAC and keying material. An attacker inferring these values can mount the physical-layer attacks on ToA estimation described in Sect. 5.3, undermining a core security goal of secure HE-LTFs. This makes correct implementation of error recovery and strict monotonicity of the Secure HE-LTF Counter a critical requirement for NGP deployments. Similar implementation flaws in counter and nonce handling have already led to practical attacks in related protocols, such as key reinstallation in WPA2 (KRACK) and nonce reuse in TLS with AES-GCM [3,27]. While hardware limitations (Sect. 2.3) prevented us from testing this specific recovery mechanism in practice, this history underlines the importance of getting these details right.

4.4 Denial-Of-Service Considerations

The configuration choices above not only introduce downgrade risks but also affect availability. If an RSTA requires both a PTK and secure HE-LTFs, an attacker can no longer silently downgrade a session. However, ranging then becomes easy to block entirely: disrupting the initial FTMR or PASN exchange prevents a secure session from being established, and a correctly configured ISTA will refuse to fall back to legacy FTM.

Even once a secure FTM session is active, the error-recovery mechanisms around the Secure HE-LTF Counter and Validation SAC offer further opportunities for disruption. Any manipulation that causes secure HE-LTF validation to fail forces a recovery round in which measurements are deliberately treated as invalid before resuming with updated counter values. By repeatedly triggering such failures under the attacker models of Sect. 4.1 and Sect. 4.2, an adversary can degrade or effectively prevent useful measurements without ever completing a single successful ranging exchange.

A strictly configured NGP deployment that correctly refuses insecure fallbacks can be robust against downgrades yet vulnerable to simple availability attacks that require only selective interference with a few protocol messages.

5 Physical-Layer Analysis

In this section, we analyse the physical-layer characteristics of secure FTM in NGP, using the simulation and measurement setup from Sect. 3.2. We first study the secure HE-LTF waveform's predictability and how much an attacker can learn from partially observed symbols. We then evaluate practical distance-reduction attacks under both deterministic and partial-observation adversary models. Finally, we examine how the zero-power guard interval interacts with realistic RF front ends and spectral-mask constraints.

5.1 Physical-Layer Signal

To ensure that our simulation setup is representative, we compared the simulated waveforms against development-board captures and confirmed agreement in the time-domain structure and overall power spectral density. Legacy FTM in IEEE 802.11mc relies on predictable HE-LTF sequences for ToA estimation. IEEE 802.11az introduces several changes: the HE-LTF content is randomised, the conventional guard interval (GI) is replaced with a zero-power GI, and a pseudorandom phase rotation is applied per stream.

In the secure format, the HE-LTF sequence is constructed from pseudorandom 64-QAM symbols and per-stream phase rotations on the active subcarriers. Depending on the bandwidth, there are 122, 242, or 498 non-zero subcarriers for 20, 40, and 80 MHz, respectively (higher bandwidths are built from the 80 MHz definition). For 20 MHz, 122 out of 256 subcarriers carry non-zero pseudorandom symbols, with the remaining subcarriers used for lower and upper guard bands, the DC subcarrier, and an alternating null pattern. To avoid repetition in the time domain, the standard uses the 2x HE-LTF type, where only half of the IFFT output is transmitted for each symbol.

5.2 HE-LTF Estimation

In the time-domain signal, an attacker aims to advance the HE-LTF so the receiver records an earlier ToA. To mount an early-detect/late-commit attack [19], in which the attacker observes the start of a symbol and immediately transmits the rest, the attacker must predict the transmitted symbol from a partial observation. This amounts to solving an underdetermined system of equations.

For an N non-zero subcarrier 64-QAM symbol with pseudorandom symbols, the entropy is $H = N \cdot \log_2 64 = 6 \cdot N$, making a brute-force search impractical even when only part of the symbol is unknown.

A more realistic approach is to infer *soft* information about the transmitted symbols from the partial observation using Bayesian inference, in particular message-passing methods [4,30]. These algorithms can incorporate structural knowledge such as the constellation diagram and channel statistics.

In a MATLAB simulation, we emulate the secure HE-LTF as an OFDM symbol with $N = 122$ non-zero subcarriers, each populated with a randomly selected 64-QAM symbol X_k, $k = 1, \ldots, N$. In addition, a common phase shift $\beta \in \{0, \pi/4\}$ is drawn at random. The corresponding time-domain signal is $\mathbf{y} = \mathbf{F}^H e^{i\beta}\mathbf{X} + \mathbf{w}$, where $\mathbf{F}$ is the unitary DFT matrix (implemented via an IFFT), $\mathbf{X}$ collects all X_k, and $\mathbf{w}$ is white Gaussian noise (AWGN channel).

From $\mathbf{y}$, the attacker observes only $M < N$ samples ($\mathbf{y}_{\text{obs}}$), and uses these to estimate the symbols and predict the unobserved part of the sequence.

The attacker seeks estimates $\hat{\mathbf{X}}$ from $\mathbf{y}_{\text{obs}}$ in order to reconstruct the full time-domain signal $\hat{\mathbf{y}} = \mathbf{F}^H\hat{\mathbf{X}}$. Following a maximum a posteriori (MAP) criterion, the optimal symbol estimate is

$$\hat{X}_k = \arg\max_{X_k} p\big(X_k \mid \mathbf{y}_{\text{obs}}\big)\,, \tag{1}$$

where the marginal posterior is $p\big(X_k \mid \mathbf{y}_{\text{obs}}\big) = \sum_\beta \sum_{X_{\sim k}} p\big(\mathbf{X}, \beta \mid \mathbf{y}_{\text{obs}}\big)$. Here, $X_{\sim k}$ denotes all X_j with $j \neq k$. By Bayes' rule, $p\big(X_k \mid \mathbf{y}_{\text{obs}}\big) \propto \sum_\beta \sum_{X_{\sim k}} p\big(\mathbf{y}_{\text{obs}} \mid \mathbf{X}, \beta\big)\, p(\mathbf{X})\, p(\beta)$. Similarly, the phase is estimated as

$$\hat{\beta} = \arg\max_{\beta} p\big(\beta \mid \mathbf{y}_{\text{obs}}\big)\,, \tag{2}$$

with $p\big(\beta \mid \mathbf{y}_{\text{obs}}\big) \propto \sum_{\mathbf{X}} p\big(\mathbf{y}_{\text{obs}} \mid \mathbf{X}, \beta\big)\, p(\mathbf{X})\, p(\beta)$. Direct marginalisation in (1) and (2) is computationally expensive, requiring on the order of $2^{6(N-1)}$ summations per $\hat{X}_k$. We therefore resort to message passing on a factor graph [30] with Monte Carlo sampling [5,7]. For the results below, we run a particle-based message-passing algorithm with 300 samples and set the noise variance such that the SNR is 7 dB.

After inference, we obtain approximate marginals for each constellation symbol and the common phase, $p\big(X_k \mid \mathbf{y}_{\text{obs}}\big)$ and $p\big(\beta \mid \mathbf{y}_{\text{obs}}\big)$. Concretely, for each X_k and for β we obtain normalised probability masses over the 64-QAM alphabet and the two phase candidates. The MAP estimates in (1) and (2) are given by the maximisers of these distributions. Figure 3 shows a time-domain symbol where 80% of the samples are observed and used for reconstruction. The reconstructed signal (green) follows the observed samples (red) closely, but the error trace (blue dotted) reveals non-negligible error outside the observation window.

To quantify both accuracy and confidence of the MAP estimate, we report for the symbols: (i) the empirical negative log-likelihood (NLL), defined as NLL $= -\log \hat{p}(x^*)$, where x^* is the ground-truth symbol and $\hat{p}(x)$ is the approximated posterior mass; and (ii) the posterior entropy $H = -\sum_x \hat{p}(x) \log \hat{p}(x)$, which decreases as the posterior concentrates around a small set of candidates.

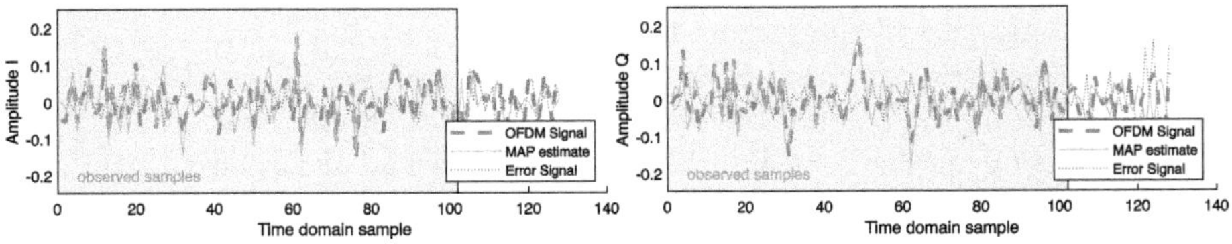

Fig. 3. Waveform reconstruction after partial observation (80%).

Figure 4 summarises the prediction limits under partial observation. In (a), the symbol-domain root mean square error (RMSE) (top) exceeds the minimum constellation distance, indicating that exact recovery of the pseudo-random sequence $\{X_k\}$ from partial samples is infeasible. Furthermore, while time-domain reconstruction (bottom) improves on the observed segment as the window increases, the error on the unobserved continuation remains largely unchanged. Figure 4b highlights that the common phase β can be estimated accurately with more observations. Although MAP symbol decisions remain unreliable, the soft posteriors over X_k sharpen with increasing observation (lower entropy and NLL). This soft information can support short-horizon forecasting or detection, but it does not enable reliable full-sequence prediction beyond the observed window.

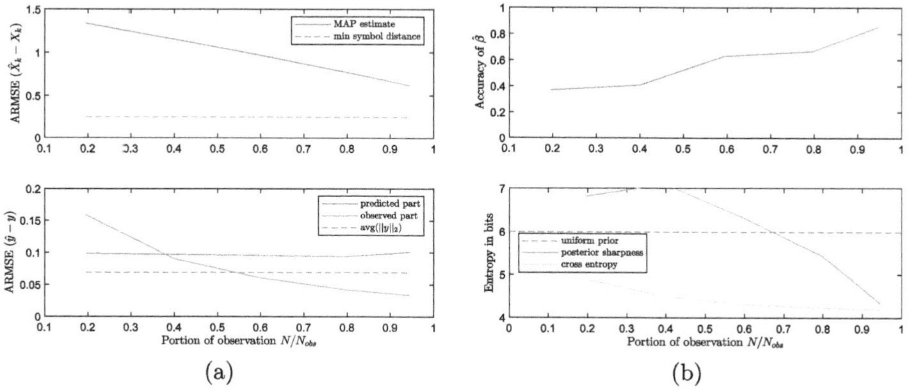

Fig. 4. Simulation results, 25 iterations. (a) Average RMSE. Top: distance between estimated and true constellation symbols, compared to minimum symbol distance. Bottom: average RMSE in time domain for the observed signal part and the predicted signal part, compared to the mean symbol energy of the HE-LTF y. (b) Top: accuracy of random phase shift estimation. Bottom: sharpness and cross entropy of the posterior function on the constellation symbols X_k.

5.3 Distance Reduction Attack

Secure HE-LTF repetitions for a given user must be unique, derived from fresh keying material and pseudorandom bits. This symbol freshness is crucial: if errors or permissive configurations (e.g., known keys, counter reuse, or disabled secure HE-LTFs in Sect. 4) make the sequence deterministic, the attacker gains full knowledge of the HE-LTF. This reduces the hard problem of predicting unseen samples to simply generating or replaying exact time-shifted replicas. Distance-reduction attacks then become considerably more practical, especially for correlation-based ToA estimators that readily lock on to the advanced replica rather than treating it as an additional multipath component.

We model an attacker that transmits an advanced waveform segment to bias the HE-LTF ToA estimate. If fully known, for instance by exploiting the vulnerabilities identified in Sect. 4, the attacker can trivially synthesise and inject the entire replica. Here, we evaluate a weaker attacker who must first observe $k\%$ of the secure HE-LTF to synthesise an advanced replica for the remainder, cancelling the legitimate component to replace it with the advanced signal. Both scenarios yield a controllable advance of the first path and a proportional distance reduction. We evaluate this bias in MATLAB using a MUSIC-based ToF estimator [17]. Figure 5a plots the distance error versus signal advance for different observation fractions k (e.g., 20% observed implies 80% advanced). Solid, dashed, and dotted curves represent SNRs of 5, 15, and 25 dB, respectively. Delaying (negative advance values) enlarges the distance, while advancing reduces it; larger advanced portions yield larger biases for the same advance. Crucially, accurately predicting a short segment already induces substantial bias, demonstrating that the weaker attacker succeeds without needing the entire sequence.

A practical limitation is that large advances increasingly distort the OFDM symbol, potentially breaking demodulation. If the sequence is already known, this symbol distortion does not occur. Under partial observation, the post-demodulation RMS EVM rises with the applied advance (Fig. 5b). Since reliable 64-QAM operation requires low error vector magnitude (EVM), extreme advances become self-defeating as demodulation fails, or become detectable through degraded PHY metrics. This aligns with IEEE 802.11az's observation that secure HE-LTF attacks introduce interference monitorable via SIR drops across repetitions [14, Annex AE]; however, practical algorithms to reliably detect such drops remain sparse.

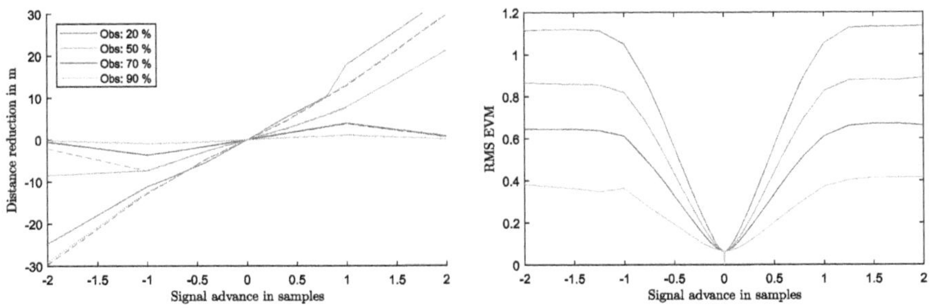

(a) (b)

Fig. 5. (a) Distance bias induced by advancing a fraction of the secure HE-LTF. The attacker observes the first $k\%$ of the secure HE-LTF to predict and transmit an advanced replica for the remaining portion. The positive x-axis denotes an advance (distance reduction), while negative values denote a delay (distance enlargement). (b) RMS error vector magnitude (EVM) after HE-LTF demodulation versus the applied signal advance.

5.4 Zero-Power GI

In this section, we examine how the zero-power guard interval interacts with the RF front end and the HE transmit spectral mask requirements [14], focusing on a 20 MHz configuration commonly used for indoor positioning.

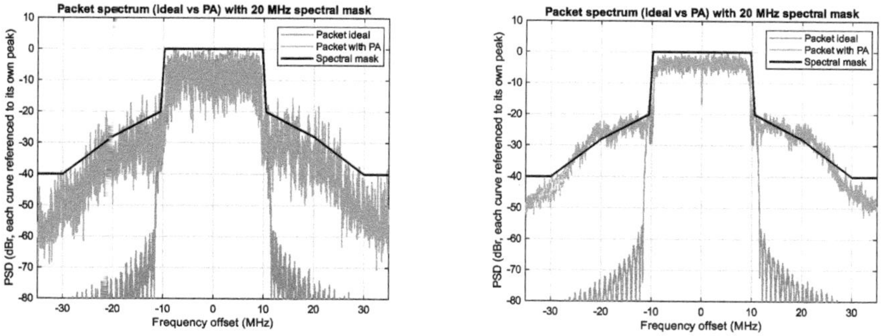

(a) Legacy HE-LTF with cyclic prefix. (b) Secure HE-LTF with zero-power GI.

Fig. 6. Simulated power spectral density of 20 MHz NDPs for the non-secure (left) and secure (right) variants, before (blue) and after (orange) the power amplifier model, compared against the standard-defined spectral mask (black). (Color figure online)

Starting from the IEEE 802.11az waveform generation example [22], we generate ranging NDP waveforms for two cases: (i) a legacy HE-LTF format with a cyclic prefix and (ii) a secure HE-LTF format with a zero-power guard interval. To approximate a practical transmitter, we pass each signal through a memoryless Rapp power-amplifier model [16] with smoothness parameter $p = 4$ and saturation level $A_{\text{sat}} = 0.7$, chosen to match the output spectrum of a legacy 20 MHz ranging waveform measured on our boards. From the resulting output signals, we compute the power spectral density (PSD) and compare it to the 20 MHz interim transmit spectral mask defined in the standard [14].

Figure 6 shows the resulting PSDs. The blue curves (ideal baseband) stay within the 20 MHz spectral mask, as expected. The orange curves (after the Rapp amplifier) exhibit spectral regrowth in both cases.

To quantify the impact of the zero-power GI, we evaluate the margin to the mask over the -30 to 30 MHz offset range. For the non-secure variant, the worst-case excess over the mask is about $+10.9$ dB, the 99th percentile margin about $+5.9$ dB, and roughly 6.7% of frequency bins exceed the mask. For the secure variant, the worst-case excess drops to about $+6.2$ dB and the 99th percentile margin to about $+4.8$ dB, but the fraction of bins above the mask rises to approximately 31.6%. In other words, the zero-power guard interval tends to spread out-of-band energy more evenly towards the mask: individual peaks are reduced, but a much larger portion of the spectrum operates close to, or above, the interim spectral limit.

6 Discussion and Recommendations

In this section, we reflect on the combined findings from our analyses and discuss their implications for secure FTM in NGP. We then relate these to the limited deployment of secure FTM and to IEEE 802.11bk.

6.1 Security Implications

NGP is intended to support applications ranging from in-store navigation and analytics to keyless entry and proximity-based access control [12]. Our logical-layer analysis indicates that, in configurations that are likely to dominate in practice, such as WPA2/WPA3-Personal networks and standalone PASN deployments (Sect. 4), secure FTM cannot reliably attest proximity to a uniquely trusted entity. Any party who knows the passphrase or can complete the PASN exchange can act as the apparent ranging peer. This makes high-stakes use cases, such as physical access control or distance-based authorisation, hard to justify when they rely directly on secure FTM in these environments. We provide a summary of these multi-layer vulnerabilities in Table 1.

Table 1. Summary of identified issues across the logical and physical layers.

Layer/Issue class	Description
Logical: Deployment modes (Personal, standalone PASN)	Secure FTM cannot be firmly bound to a uniquely trusted AP; anyone with the shared credentials can become the ranging peer.
Logical: Configuration and negotiation	Permissive settings allow downgrades from secure to legacy FTM or to deterministic HE-LTFs without breaking cryptography.
Logical: Error handling and availability	Subtle counter/SAC handling and strict policies make secure FTM fragile and easy to disable via selective interference.
Physical: Predictability and distance reduction	Attackers can exploit deterministic fallbacks or partial sequence predictability to synthesise and inject advanced replicas, reducing the measured distance.
Physical: Zero-power Guard Interval (GI)	Harsh RF switching causes out-of-band energy spread, complicating spectral mask compliance on existing hardware.

Secure FTM can still be useful in such settings for low-stakes tasks, for example, indoor navigation, coarse localisation, or non-safety-critical analytics, provided it is treated as a best-effort signal rather than a strict security boundary. In contrast, deployments that require strong guarantees about *which* device is being ranged must anchor secure FTM in robust mutual authentication, for example via 802.1X-based Enterprise networks, and must enforce strict policies that require both a PTK and secure HE-LTFs and disallow fallback to legacy modes. As Sect. 4.4 shows, this hardening improves integrity but also makes secure FTM more susceptible to simple denial-of-service.

The physical-layer results sharpen these conclusions. When secure HE-LTFs are implemented as specified, with fresh keying material, monotonic counters, and pseudorandom symbols, partial observations yield only soft information. If secure HE-LTFs are disabled, counters are reused, or the same training symbols reappear across instances (Sect. 4.3), the problem collapses to recording one symbol and replaying time-shifted replicas, enabling correlation-based distance reduction. Overall, the intended security of NGP only materialises when authentication, configuration, and physical-layer behaviour all satisfy relatively strong assumptions; otherwise, the effective guarantees are significantly weaker than the design suggests. The same observations apply to IEEE 802.11bk, which reuses NGP's security mechanisms.

6.2 Limited Support and Deployment Challenges

In Sect. 2.3, we observed that secure FTM support in commercial devices and development platforms is scarce. Our analysis suggests technical and economic reasons for this slow adoption.

Physical-Layer Constraints and Spectral Masks. With realistic power-amplifier nonlinearities, the secure HE-LTF with a zero-power GI operates closer to, and in parts above, the transmit spectral mask than the legacy cyclic-prefix waveform (Sect. 5.4). Staying within both the standard mask and regulatory limits may require additional linearity margin, lower transmit power, or stronger filtering, which increases RF complexity compared to legacy FTM.

Zero-Power GI Implementation Cost. A true zero-power GI requires fast, well-controlled switching of the transmit chain so that the output power drops and recovers within a single OFDM symbol without spectral splatter or timing distortion. Analogue front ends that were designed around a conventional cyclic prefix are unlikely to meet these constraints with firmware changes alone, so full zero-power GI support tends to require non-trivial hardware adaptations.

Baseband Life Cycles and Business Incentives. If secure HE-LTFs and zero-power GIs cannot be added purely in software, vendors need new or updated baseband silicon, with multi-year design and qualification cycles. Our logical-layer results indicate that the strongest security benefits arise only in tightly managed Enterprise-style deployments, while common Personal-mode networks cannot safely support the most ambitious use cases. This combination of hardware cost and comparatively narrow high-assurance use cases reduces the incentive to prioritise secure FTM over existing legacy FTM support.

Taken together, these factors suggest that the limited availability of secure FTM is not merely a delay in adoption, but reflects genuine RF, hardware, and deployment hurdles that must be addressed before NGP can deliver its intended security properties at scale.

6.3 Recommendations

In its current form, secure FTM is better suited to low- and medium-stakes applications than to high-assurance access control. In common WPA2/WPA3-Personal and standalone PASN deployments (Sect. 4), secure FTM cannot reliably attest proximity to a uniquely trusted entity. We therefore advise against using it as the primary security anchor for keyless entry or distance-based authorisation. Instead, secure FTM is appropriate for indoor navigation or non-safety-critical analytics, where ranging is treated as a best-effort signal rather than a strict security boundary.

Where stronger guarantees are required, secure FTM must be rooted in mutual authentication (e.g., 802.1X-based Enterprise networks) alongside strict configuration policies. Devices supporting secure FTM should default to requiring a PTK, avoid EDCA-based legacy fallbacks when trigger-based modes are available, and honour secure HE-LTF requirements. Furthermore, error recovery mechanisms must maintain strictly monotonic counters and prevent keying material reuse (Sect. 4.3) to avoid undermining physical-layer protections.

For standardisation and certification, we recommend explicitly mapping deployment models to supported use cases, distinguishing environments that tolerate Personal mode from those requiring Enterprise-grade mutual authentication. Finally, given the demanding RF requirements of the zero-power GI (Sect. 5.4), future amendments should explore hybrid designs such as a reduced-power pseudorandom sequence. This avoids both deterministic cyclic prefixes and harsh RF switching, easing spectral-mask compliance and lowering barriers to adoption.

7 Related Work

Security of Wi-Fi FTM and Multicarrier Ranging. Early security analyses focus on the original, non-secure IEEE 802.11mc FTM procedures. Schepers et al. provide an end-to-end analysis demonstrating practical distance manipulation and spoofing attacks, and discuss protocol-level mitigations [25], while Henry et al. show how attackers bias location estimates in GPS-like settings [10]. Subsequent work benchmarks FTM accuracy on IoT devices [26], explores privacy risks and parameter exposures [24], and proposes crowd-wisdom defences for 802.11mc and early 802.11az deployments [11]. Complementing this, physical-layer studies demonstrate how deterministic OFDM training and cyclic prefixes enable precise distance-reduction and extension attacks [19], prompting the use of super-resolution estimators like frequency-domain MUSIC [20]. While these works highlight critical vulnerabilities and multicarrier exploitation strategies, they largely predate the finalised NGP mechanisms and treat the physical layer as an abstract ranging primitive.

Positioning Performance and Deployments of Secure FTM. With the standardisation of NGP, recent literature has shifted towards positioning performance. Works evaluate 802.11az-based ranging at millimetre-wave frequencies [23], explore parameter choices and communication capabilities [8], and survey indoor positioning across the 802.11mc/az/bk amendments [18]. Concurrently, industry documentation illustrates growing FTM adoption: Android exposes Wi-Fi RTT support via its APIs [2], Google documents 802.11mc-compatible devices [1], and providers like IndoorAtlas advertise FTM-backed solutions [15]. However, these academic and industrial efforts focus primarily on legacy FTM or performance metrics, offering limited analysis of protocol robustness against active adversaries. To the best of our knowledge, no peer-reviewed work provides a combined protocol- and waveform-level security analysis of the finalised secure FTM procedures in IEEE 802.11az/bk, nor quantifies how these features are exposed in deployed commercial and development hardware.

8 Conclusion

In this paper, we examined the security and adoption of secure Wi-Fi ranging as defined in IEEE 802.11az, combining standards analysis with simulations and measurements on commercial and development hardware.

At the logical layer, we showed that common WPA2/WPA3-Personal and standalone PASN deployments cannot reliably attest proximity to a uniquely trusted entity, remaining vulnerable to unauthenticated ranging, downgrades, and denial-of-service. At the physical layer, we analysed secure waveform predictability, the impact of symbol repetition, and how the zero-power guard interval interacts with spectral masks under realistic RF nonlinearity.

Our results indicate that secure Wi-Fi ranging is highly sensitive to configuration choices and difficult to integrate under current RF and deployment constraints, which helps to explain its limited support in existing devices. We outlined where secure FTM can reasonably be used today and provided recommendations for vendors and standardisation bodies to clarify security guarantees and reduce implementation barriers in future profiles and revisions.

Acknowledgments. This work was supported by the Flemish Government through the Cybersecurity Research Program (VOEWICS02), by COST Action CA22168 – Physical Layer Security for Trustworthy and Resilient 6G Systems, by the "University SAL Labs" initiative of Silicon Austria Labs and its Austrian partner universities for applied fundamental research for electronic-based systems, and by the Linz Center of Mechatronics in the framework of the Austrian COMET-K2 programme.

Disclosure of Interests. The authors have no competing interests to declare that are relevant to the content of this article.

References

1. Android: Wi-Fi location: Ranging with RTT. https://developer.android.com/develop/connectivity/wifi/wifi-rtt#supported-devices. Accessed 7 Jan 2026
2. Android Open Source Project: Wi-Fi RTT (2026). https://source.android.com/docs/core/connect/wifi-rtt. Accessed 7 Jan 2026

3. Böck, H., Zauner, A., Devlin, S., Somorovsky, J., Jovanovic, P.: Nonce-disrespecting adversaries: Practical forgery attacks on GCM in TLS. In: 10th USENIX Workshop on Offensive Technologies (WOOT 16) (2016)
4. Dauwels, J.: On variational message passing on factor graphs. In: IEEE international symposium on information theory, pp. 2546–2550. IEEE (2007)
5. Dauwels, J., Korl, S., Loeliger, H.A.: Particle methods as message passing. In: IEEE International Symposium on Information Theory. IEEE (2006)
6. Dolev, D., Yao, A.: On the security of public key protocols. IEEE Trans. Inf. Theory **29**(2), 198–208 (1983)
7. Etzlinger, B., Haselmayr, W., Springer, A.: Message passing methods for factor graph based MIMO detection. Wireless Advanced. IEEE (2011)
8. Famili, A., Atalay, T., Stavrou, A.: Unlocking the potential of IEEE 802.11az: a deep dive into ranging capabilities. In: 2025 International Conference on Computing, Networking and Communications (ICNC), pp. 763–769. IEEE (2025)
9. Google LLC: WifiRttLocator App. https://play.google.com/store/apps/details?id=com.google.android.apps.location.rtt.wifirttlocator. Accessed 7 Jan 2026
10. Henry, J., Busnel, Y., Ludinard, R., Montavont, N.: Ranging and Location attacks on 802.11 FTM. In: 2021 IEEE 32nd Annual International Symposium on Personal, Indoor and Mobile Radio Communications (PIMRC), pp. 1481–1486. IEEE (2021)
11. Henry, J., Busnel, Y., Ludinard, R., Montavont, N.: Reducing FTM ranging and location attack exposure with crowd-wisdom. In: IPIN 2021: 9th International Conference on Indoor Positioning and Indoor Navigation, pp. 1–16 (2021)
12. IEEE Standards Association: Newly Released IEEE 802.11az Standard Improving Wi-Fi Location Accuracy is Set to Unleash a New Wave of Innovation (2026). https://standards.ieee.org/beyond-standards/newly-released-ieee-802-11az-standard-improving-wi-fi-location-accuracy-is-set-to-unleash-a-new-wave-of-innovation/. Accessed 26 Jan 2026
13. IEEE Standards Association et al.: IEEE Standard for Local and Metropolitan Area Networks–Part 11: Wireless LAN MAC and PHY Specifications Amendment 3: 320MHz Positioning. IEEE Std 802.11bk-2025 (2025)
14. IEEE Standards Association et al.: IEEE Standard for Local and Metropolitan Area Networks–Part 11: Wireless LAN Medium Access Control (MAC) and Physical Layer (PHY) Specifications. IEEE Std 802.11-2024 (2025)
15. IndoorAtlas: Unlock Smart Spaces with IndoorAtlas (2026). https://www.indooratlas.com/. Accessed 7 Jan 2026
16. Jayati, A.E., Sipan, M.: Impact of nonlinear distortion with the rapp model on the GFDM system. In: 2020 Third International Conference on Vocational Education and Electrical Engineering (ICVEE) (2020)
17. Jiokeng, K., Jakllari, G., Tchana, A., Beylot, A.L.: When FTM discovered MUSIC: accurate WiFi-based ranging in the presence of multipath. In: IEEE INFOCOM 2020-IEEE Conference on Computer Communications, pp. 1857–1866. IEEE (2020)
18. Kosek-Szott, K., Szott, S., Ciezobka, W., Wojnar, M., Rusek, K., Segev, J.: Indoor positioning with Wi-Fi location: a survey of IEEE 802.11 mc/az/bk fine timing measurement research. Comput. Commun. (2025)
19. Leu, P., Kotuliak, M., Roeschlin, M., Capkun, S.: Security of multicarrier time-of-flight ranging. In: Proceedings of the 37th Annual Computer Security Applications Conference, pp. 887–899 (2021)
20. Li, X., Pahlavan, K.: Super-resolution TOA estimation with diversity for indoor geolocation. IEEE Trans. Wireless Commun. **3**(1), 224–234 (2004)

21. MathWorks: 802.11az Positioning Using Super-Resolution Time of Arrival Estimation. https://www.mathworks.com/help/wlan/ug/802-11az-indoor-positioning-using-super-resolution-time-of-arrival-estimation.html. Accessed 13 Jan 2026
22. MathWorks: 802.11az Waveform Generation (2026). https://www.mathworks.com/help/wlan/ug/802-11az-waveform-generation.html. Accessed 13 Jan 2026
23. Picazo-Martínez, P., Barroso-Fernández, C., Martín-Pérez, J., Groshev, M., de la Oliva, A.: IEEE 802.11az Indoor Positioning with mmWave. IEEE Commun. Mag. **62**(10), 126–131 (2023)
24. Schepers, D., Ranganathan, A.: Privacy-preserving positioning in Wi-Fi fine timing measurement. In: Proceedings on Privacy Enhancing Technologies (2022)
25. Schepers, D., Singh, M., Ranganathan, A.: Here, there, and everywhere: security analysis of Wi-Fi fine timing measurement. In: Proceedings of the 14th ACM Conference on Security and Privacy in Wireless and Mobile Networks (2021)
26. Singh, G., Pandey, A., Prakash, M., Andreoni, M., Baddeley, M.: Benchmarking and security considerations of Wi-Fi FTM for ranging in IoT devices. In: Proceedings of Cyber-Physical Systems and Internet of Things Week, p. 2023 (2023)
27. Vanhoef, M., Piessens, F.: Key reinstallation attacks: forcing nonce reuse in WPA2. In: Proceedings of the 2017 ACM SIGSAC Conference on Computer and Communications Security, pp. 1313–1328 (2017)
28. Vanhoef, M., Robben, J.: A security analysis of WPA3-PK: implementation and precomputation attacks. In: Pöpper, C., Batina, L. (eds.) ACNS 2024. LNCS, vol. 14584, pp. 217–240. Springer, Cham (2024). https://doi.org/10.1007/978-3-031-54773-7_9
29. Vanhoef, M., Ronen, E.: Dragonblood: analyzing the dragonfly handshake of WPA3 and EAP-PWD. In: 2020 IEEE Symposium on Security and Privacy (SP), pp. 517–533. IEEE (2020)
30. Wymeersch, H.: Iterative Receiver Design. Cambridge University Press, Cambridge (2007)

LNTest: A Testbed for Evaluating Bitcoin Lightning Network-Based Botnets

Thomas Bakaysa[1], Ahmet Kurt[1(✉)], Abdul-Salem Beibitkhan[2], Jesus Maria Romo Diaz de Leon[1], Tag Kalat[1], Joshua Kramer[1], Estela Rodriguez[1], Abraham Watkins[1], and Abdullah Aydeger[3]

[1] East Texas A&M University, RELLIS Campus, Bryan, TX 77807, USA
{tbakaysa,jromodiazde,tkalat,jkramer2,erodriguez80, awatkins12}@leomail.tamuc.edu, ahmet.kurt@etamu.edu
[2] North American University, Stafford, TX 77477, USA
abyeibitkhan@na.edu
[3] Florida Institute of Technology, Melbourne, FL 32901, USA
aaydeger@fit.edu

Abstract. Bitcoin's Lightning Network (LN) can be exploited as a covert, low-cost command-and-control (C&C) channel for botnets, as demonstrated by the LNBot and D-LNBot designs. However, both remain proof-of-concept prototypes evaluated only through simulation, leaving key questions about real-world topology formation, propagation complexity, and resilience to takedowns unanswered. We present LNTest, the first reusable testbed for LN-based botnets, built from Core Lightning nodes containerized with Docker over a shared Bitcoin Core *regtest* chain. LNTest supports three overlay topology modes (a deterministic chain, autonomous peer discovery, and user-supplied graphs), enabling controlled experiments across different botnet structures. Using LNTest, we report three main findings. First, D-LNBot's autonomous formation protocol does not produce the uniform chain from its design; instead, it creates a *clustered chain* in which cliques are linked by bridge nodes whose removal fragments the network. Second, command propagation scales linearly with botnet size ($\Theta(n)$), not the $O(m \log n)$ previously claimed, and gains nothing from higher neighbor connectivity. Third, the overlay topology determines the effectiveness of takedown strategies: uniform-degree chains resist targeted removal but fragment under random failure, scale-free topologies show the opposite pattern, and the autonomous clustered chain is fragile under both, making it the most vulnerable of the three. LNTest is released as open source, with a script that reproduces all our experiments, to support reproducible research on LN-based botnet defenses.

Keywords: Lightning Network · botnet · command and control · testbed · payment channel networks

T. Bakaysa and A. Kurt—These authors contributed equally to this work.

S. Nadjm-Tehrani et al. (Eds.): ARES 2026, LNCS 16898, pp. 160–182, 2027.
https://doi.org/10.1007/978-3-032-36874-4_8

1 Introduction

Botnets remain a persistent and versatile threat on today's Internet. Modern botnets power large-scale distributed denial-of-service (DDoS) attacks, credential stuffing, spam, ransomware, and crypto-mining campaigns. Recent surveys show that botnets are becoming harder to detect and dismantle, partly because their command-and-control (C&C) infrastructures are shifting from simple centralized servers to distributed overlays with no single point of failure [36]. As a result, law enforcement and defenders often struggle to keep up, even when individual infections are well understood [16].

One emerging trend is to use public blockchains as C&C channels that are difficult to censor or take down. Researchers have proposed schemes that hide commands inside Bitcoin [28] transactions or Ethereum smart contracts, including ZombieCoin [3], ChainChannels [12], BlockchainBot [13], and SCBot [24]. Real-world malware has followed suit: the Pony malware hid its C&C server addresses inside the Bitcoin blockchain [35], and Tsundere stored its C&C server address in an Ethereum contract [37]. These examples show that blockchain-based C&C is no longer hypothetical.

What makes blockchains attractive for this purpose is that they offer pseudonymous accounts, are replicated across thousands of nodes worldwide, and are extremely hard to tamper with [7,17]. Prior work has analyzed these threats and proposed countermeasures [7,13], but most efforts stay at the level of analysis or small prototypes and do not give defenders a reusable environment to test and stress botnet designs under controlled conditions.

Bitcoin's Lightning Network (LN), a payment-channel network (PCN) built on top of Bitcoin, makes the problem worse. LN enables near-instant, low-cost payments that can carry hidden data, so an attacker can send botnet commands disguised as ordinary payments, cheaply, quickly, and almost invisibly. Two recent works, LNBot [21] and D-LNBot [20], have shown that this is feasible. However, both are proof-of-concept prototypes that leave important questions open. D-LNBot claims that commands propagate in $O(m \log n)$ time but tests this only in simulation, never on real Lightning nodes. Its peer discovery protocol is presented as producing a uniform chain topology, but its actual behavior under realistic conditions has not been tested. Most importantly, neither work studies how the choice of overlay topology affects resilience to partial takedowns, the question that matters most from a defender's perspective.

These gaps cannot be filled by simulations alone; they require running real Lightning software in a setting where the overlay topology, botnet size, neighbor connectivity, injection point, and takedown strategy are all controlled variables. Existing botnet testbeds such as DDoSim [29] and DDoShield-IoT [10] focus on traditional IoT and DDoS botnets and do not support blockchain- or payment-channel-based C&C. To the best of our knowledge, no testbed exists that (i) runs on unmodified, production-grade Bitcoin and Lightning software, (ii) scales to hundreds of C&C servers, and (iii) lets researchers compare different overlay topologies and takedown strategies on real nodes. To fill this gap, we introduce LNTest.

LNTest is a self-contained LN-based botnet testbed built from Bitcoin Core and Core Lightning (CLN) nodes running on Bitcoin *regtest* (a private, local blockchain) and containerized with Docker. It supports three overlay topology modes: a deterministic chain matching the D-LNBot design, autonomous peer discovery following D-LNBot's formation protocol [20] under realistic deployment conditions, and user-supplied graphs that let researchers test any topology they choose (e.g., scale-free networks modeled after the real Lightning Network). Using LNTest, we conduct the first experimental study of LN-based botnet topologies on real Lightning nodes. Our **contributions** are:

❶ We design and implement LNTest, the first testbed for LN-based botnets. Its three topology modes let researchers directly compare how overlay structure affects command speed and resistance to takedowns.

❷ We run D-LNBot's peer discovery protocol on real Lightning nodes for the first time using LNTest's autonomous mode. We find that it does *not* produce the uniform chain shown in the original paper [20]. Instead, it creates a *clustered chain*: groups of tightly connected nodes linked by a small number of bridge nodes. This topology delivers commands just as fast as the ideal chain, but it is far more fragile: removing the bridge nodes splits the botnet into disconnected pieces.

❸ We measure command propagation delay across up to 500 C&C nodes and show that propagation time grows linearly with botnet size ($\Theta(n)$), not the $O(m \log n)$ that D-LNBot claimed [20], and is independent of the neighbor count m. We also run takedown experiments (both random and targeted) across three topologies (D-LNBot chain, Barabási–Albert (BA) scale-free, and autonomous clustered chain) and show that it is the topology, not just the size of the botnet, that determines whether a takedown fragments the network or leaves it intact.

❹ We release LNTest's source code and documentation at https://github.com/ThomasBakaysaJr/LNTest to support reproducible research and future work on detecting and defending against Lightning-based botnets.

The rest of this paper is organized as follows. Section 2 provides background on LN and its use as a C&C channel. Section 3 reviews related work. Section 4 describes the design of LNTest. Section 5 presents our experimental results. Section 6 discusses implications, ethical considerations, and limitations, and Sect. 7 concludes.

2 Background

This section provides the background on Bitcoin's Lightning Network needed to understand LNTest's design and experiments.

2.1 Payment Channels and the Lightning Network

A payment channel lets two parties send money back and forth without writing every transaction to the blockchain. The two parties lock funds into a shared on-chain output and then exchange signed updates off-chain; only the final balance is settled on-chain when the channel is closed. This makes individual payments fast (seconds instead of minutes) and cheap (no mining fees per payment).

The Lightning Network (LN) [31] connects many such channels into a network. If Alice has a channel with Bob and Bob has a channel with Carol, Alice can pay Carol by routing the payment through Bob. The payment is secured at each hop by a hashed time-locked contract (HTLC), which ensures that either the full payment goes through or nobody loses funds. To protect privacy, LN wraps each payment in layers of encryption (onion routing) so that intermediate nodes only know their immediate predecessor and successor, not the full path.

Two LN mechanisms are especially relevant to this work. First, *gossip*: LN nodes announce their channels to the network, and other nodes store these announcements in a local channel graph. This is how nodes learn about the network's topology and discover potential peers. In LNTest, the autonomous formation mode relies on gossip to let C&C servers find each other (Sect. 4.3). Second, *keysend*: a way to send a payment to a node without first requesting an invoice from it.[1] Keysend payments can carry custom data in type-length-value (TLV) fields that are visible only to the final recipient, not to intermediate routing nodes. All three botnet designs we discuss use keysend to deliver commands (Sect. 2.3).

2.2 LN-Based Botnet Designs

Two prior works have proposed using LN as a botnet C&C channel.

LNBot [21] uses a centralized one-to-many model: the botmaster sends each command to every C&C server individually as a series of LN keysend payments, one per character, whose amounts encode the character via ASCII or Huffman coding. This design is simple but creates a single point of failure at the botmaster.

D-LNBot [20] addresses this with a distributed design. Instead of the botmaster reaching each C&C server individually, C&C servers form a chain-like overlay among themselves. Each node CC_i connects to its m nearest predecessors (CC_{i-1} through CC_{i-m}), creating overlapping neighborhoods. To build this chain without a central coordinator, D-LNBot introduces a formation protocol: newly infected machines connect to an *innocent node* (a publicly-reachable LN node) and discover other C&C servers by scanning the Lightning Network for channels whose capacity matches a pre-agreed rule. A node closes its innocent-node channel after m newer C&C servers have joined the network, so it is no longer discoverable. D-LNBot claims that commands propagate through this chain in $O(m \log n)$ time, based on the assumption that the topology resembles an m-ary tree. However, both the topology and the propagation time have only been evaluated in simulation, not on real Lightning nodes.

[1] Keysend specification: https://github.com/lightning/blips/blob/master/blip-0003.md.

2.3 Command Embedding via Keysend

LNBot, D-LNBot, and LNTest all send commands as Lightning keysend payments, but they carry the command differently.

LNBot encodes one character per payment using the payment amount itself, requiring multiple payments per command. D-LNBot attaches a full command as a data blob to a single keysend payment using a Core Lightning plugin.

LNTest takes a simpler approach: it places the command text and a sequence counter directly into a custom TLV field attached to a standard keysend payment. The sequence counter allows receiving nodes to detect duplicates (since flooding causes the same command to arrive from multiple neighbors) and to track which commands they have already processed and forwarded. Because TLV fields are encrypted end-to-end by LN's onion routing, intermediate nodes along the payment path cannot read the command; only the intended C&C server can.

3 Related Work

We review prior work on botnet testbeds, LN-based botnets, other blockchain-based botnets, and network resilience analysis.

Botnet Testbeds: Existing botnet testbeds target traditional IoT and DDoS botnets. DDoSim [29] emulates large-scale IoT botnets in an ns-3/Docker environment; DDoShield-IoT [10] extends it with Mirai-style binaries for IDS evaluation; Gotham Testbed [9] provides a reproducible IoT security platform; Calvet et al. [8] created and took down a 3000-node in-the-lab botnet; the testbed of Kumar and Lim [19] analyzes IoT botnets in a securely contained environment; and Parthipan et al. [30] review peer-to-peer botnet emulation testbeds and propose a conceptual model for them. None considers blockchains or payment-channel networks as the C&C substrate. LNTest fills this gap.

LN-Based Botnets: LNBot [21] and D-LNBot [20], the two LN-based botnets introduced in Sect. 2, were both evaluated only in simulation. LNTest is the first to run them on production-grade CLN nodes, revealing the clustered chain that D-LNBot's autonomous protocol actually forms, with $\Theta(n)$ propagation rather than the claimed $O(m \log n)$ (Sects. 5.1 and 5.2).

Blockchain-Based Botnets: Beyond LN, a range of blockchain-based C&C designs have been proposed: on Bitcoin, the Testnet botnet [11], ZombieCoin and its successor [3,4], CoinBot [38], ChainChannels [12], DUSTBot [41], and Kamenski et al.'s resilient scheme [17]; on Ethereum, Botract [5], Unblockable Chains [42], Sweeny's private-chain design [34], and SCBot [24]; on IOTA, BlockchainBot [13], OICL [14], and ZombieCoin 3.0 [15]; and on Monero [26]. All confirm the appeal of blockchain C&C but provide individual prototypes rather than a reusable testbed for systematic topology and resilience experiments.

Network Resilience and LN Topology: Our takedown experiments connect to classical results in network science. Albert et al. [2] showed that scale-free networks are robust to random failure but fragile under targeted hub removal, precisely the asymmetry we observe on BA topologies in Sect. 5.3. Empirical studies of the real Lightning Network underscore its exposure to such targeted attacks: Zabka et al. [39] found it highly and increasingly centralized, with the top 5% of nodes carrying the vast majority of payment routes, and Rohrer et al. [32] demonstrated that centrality-based removal strategies can disconnect the LN with only a small fraction of nodes removed. Our contribution is to reproduce and extend these findings in a controlled botnet testbed where topology, takedown strategy, and C&C parameters are all independent variables.

4 LNTest Design

LNTest is designed around three goals motivated by the limitations of existing LN-based botnet prototypes [20,21]: (i) *topology flexibility*, so that researchers can study how overlay structure affects propagation and resilience; (ii) *reproducibility*, so that experiments can be repeated exactly across machines and over time; and (iii) *low-overhead monitoring*, so that the orchestrator can track every node's state in real time without perturbing the system under test.

4.1 Overview

LNTest runs entirely on a single host machine. It uses Docker containers to isolate each Lightning node and Bitcoin *regtest* to provide a private, deterministic blockchain that never touches the public Bitcoin network. Built on unmodified Bitcoin Core and Core Lightning, the system consists of four logical components, each chosen to mirror a specific role in LN-based botnet architectures:

Bitcoin Core runs directly on the host and provides the shared on-chain layer. All channel funding, confirmations, and closures go through this single node, giving the orchestrator full control over block production and transaction timing.

C&C servers are CLN instances, each in its own Docker container, that form the botnet's overlay by opening payment channels to one another. In D-LNBot and custom modes the orchestrator opens these channels directly; in autonomous mode each container discovers peers via the innocent node and opens its own channels. Commands propagate through this overlay by flooding. The overlay topology is not fixed: LNTest supports three modes (a deterministic D-LNBot chain, autonomous peer discovery, and user-supplied graphs), letting researchers study how structure affects propagation speed and takedown resilience (Sect. 4.3).

Botmaster is a separate CLN node that opens a channel to one or more C&C servers to inject commands into the overlay. Because this channel can be opened to any node, the botmaster's injection point is an experimental variable: researchers can measure how entry position affects propagation delay.

Innocent node is a CLN node that acts as a rendezvous point during overlay formation. In autonomous mode, C&C servers discover each other by scanning

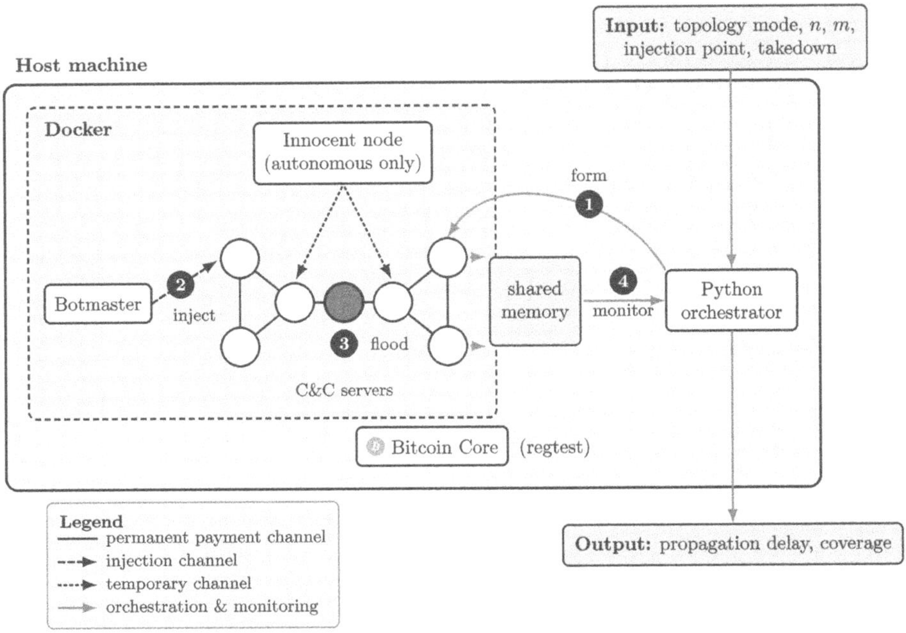

Fig. 1. Overview of LNTest's architecture. The botmaster, innocent node, and C&C servers are Core Lightning containers in Docker, while Bitcoin Core, the shared memory, and the orchestrator run on the host. On-chain links to the single *regtest* Bitcoin Core are omitted for clarity. The example overlay is an autonomous clustered chain (Sect. 5.2): cliques joined by a bridge node (red) whose removal splits it. (Color figure online)

the innocent node's channel list for peers that match a shared capacity-based rule. In the other two modes, the innocent node is present but not used for discovery. Once formation is complete, the innocent node plays no further role, and the overlay operates independently.

A Python orchestrator on the host coordinates these four components and drives each experiment through the two phases described in Sects. 4.3 and 4.5. Figure 1 shows how they interact: the C&C servers form the overlay through permanent payment channels, the botmaster reaches it through an injection channel, and in autonomous mode each node opens a temporary channel to the innocent node for peer discovery; the numbered badges trace the workflow from formation to monitoring. The orchestrator tracks every node's state through shared memory, and all nodes rely on Bitcoin Core for on-chain operations.

We run LNTest on Bitcoin *regtest*, not Mainnet or public Testnet, because controlled, reproducible experiments need a chain we fully control. Mining blocks on demand and funding nodes locally makes timing, funding, and confirmations deterministic across runs and lets us fund the hundreds of nodes our largest tests need. Public Testnet gives none of this: even Testnet4 suffers miner-gamed block timing, frequent reorgs, and depleted faucets; Mainnet is excluded on ethical and cost grounds [2]

4.2 Networking

Every Lightning node (the botmaster, the innocent node, and all C&C servers) runs as a Core Lightning instance inside its own Docker container. All containers share the host's network namespace (*--network host*), and each CLN process binds to 127.0.0.1 on a unique port, so no traffic leaves the machine. Deterministic port assignment (base port plus node index) allows the orchestrator to address any node by its index without maintaining a registry. C&C containers additionally share the host's inter-process communication (IPC) namespace (*--ipc = host*), which gives them write access to the shared memory buffers used for real-time status reporting (Sect. 4.4).

Bitcoin Core runs directly on the host in *regtest* mode and serves as the shared on-chain layer. Each CLN instance connects to it via JSON-RPC on localhost and polls it for new blocks. As a result, all on-chain activity, peer-to-peer Lightning traffic, and orchestration commands stay entirely within the host, and LNTest never contacts the public Bitcoin network.

4.3 Overlay Formation

We now describe how LNTest forms the C&C overlay; Sect. 4.5 then covers how it evaluates resilience. To build the overlay, the orchestrator initializes the regtest chain (reused across sweep iterations), launches all containers, and either wires the channels itself or waits for the nodes to form them (Algorithm 1).

LNTest offers three ways to create the overlay, each targeting a different research question.

D-LNBot Mode: The orchestrator builds the sequential chain described in the D-LNBot paper [20]: each node CC_i opens channels to its m immediate predecessors ($CC_{\max(1, i-m)}$ through CC_{i-1}); together with the m successors that later open channels to it, each interior node ends up with $2m$ channels. Because the orchestrator controls every channel, the result is deterministic and reproducible across runs.

Custom Mode: The orchestrator reads an arbitrary graph from a JSON file and wires exactly those channels. This lets researchers test any topology they choose (scale-free graphs, small-world networks, real LN snapshots, or hand-crafted structures) on real Lightning nodes.

Autonomous Mode: This mode simulates a realistic D-LNBot deployment: rather than wiring the topology from outside, each node discovers its own peers (Algorithm 1). Containers launch one at a time with random delays (log-normal,

[2] Testnet4 keeps a 20-minute minimum-difficulty rule that miners still exploit to mine empty blocks on demand; a fix remains unmerged as of June 2026 (https://github.com/bitcoin/bitcoin/pull/35081).

median 30 s, clamped to [10, 90] s), reflecting the variability of D-LNBot's malware pipeline, where a newly infected machine must download a Lightning client, sync, obtain funding, and wait for channel confirmations before it can participate. Each node advertises itself and finds peers through a shared capacity-based rule (a pre-agreed funding amount that distinguishes C&C channels from ordinary ones); a small Core Lightning plugin caps each node at $2m$ inbound C&C channels; this keeps a node that is briefly flooded with connection requests from ballooning into an oversized hub, and it has no other effect on the topology. Because multiple nodes scan at the same time, they discover each other mutually, so the topology that emerges is *not* the clean chain from D-LNBot's paper; we characterize it experimentally in Sect. 5.2.

Algorithm 1. Overlay Formation

Require: n C&C nodes; active neighbors per node m; mode
    $M \in \{\text{DLNBOT}, \text{CUSTOM}, \text{AUTONOMOUS}\}$; edge set F (if M=CUSTOM)
Ensure: overlay $G = (V, E)$
initialize regtest; launch Innocent, Botmaster; $V \leftarrow \{CC_1, \dots, CC_n\}$
if M = AUTONOMOUS **then**
    for $i = 1 \dots n$: launch and fund CC_i; wait δ_i ▷ $\delta_i \sim$ lognormal, med. 30 s
    each CC_i runs DISCOVER(i) once online; $E \leftarrow$ formed channels
else
    if M=DLNBOT **then** $E \leftarrow \{(i, j) : \max(1, i-m) \le j < i\}$ **else** $E \leftarrow F$
    launch and fund V; open all channels in E
end if
return G
procedure DISCOVER(i) ▷ runs on CC_i
    advertise: open a discovery-rule channel to Innocent
    plugin: reject inbound opens once $\deg_{\text{in}}(CC_i) = 2m$
    while $\deg_{\text{in}}(CC_i) < m$: open $\le m$ channels to new advertisers in Innocent's channels
    close Innocent channel
end procedure

In D-LNBot and custom modes the per-node channel manager is disabled, so the orchestrator keeps full control and opens exactly the prescribed channels; in autonomous mode each node instead runs the discovery loop of Algorithm 1 concurrently with the others. This concurrency is the crux of our formation finding: D-LNBot's formation protocol [20] is an idealized, effectively sequential procedure meant to build a uniform chain (which its complexity analysis then models as an m-ary tree), whereas Algorithm 1 reflects how formation actually executes, with many nodes discovering peers at once. The result is the clustered chain of Sect. 5.2, not the uniform chain D-LNBot intends.

4.4 Command Dissemination and Monitoring

Once the topology is established, commands spread through the overlay by flooding. The botmaster injects a command at one or more C&C servers (the injection points) as a Lightning *keysend* payment, with the command text embedded in a custom TLV (type-length-value) field. When a C&C node receives a new command, it immediately forwards the same payment to every neighbor it has a channel with. These forwards are dispatched in parallel, one thread per neighbor, rather than sequentially. Every command carries a sequence counter, and each node tracks which counters it has already processed. If a node receives the same command from a second neighbor, it simply ignores the duplicate. This ensures that every reachable node receives each command and forwards it only once, despite the redundant copies that flooding delivers.

Reception is event-driven: a node reacts the moment a keysend arrives rather than polling on a fixed interval, so it forwards immediately. Each keysend arrives as a paid invoice, from which the command is extracted.

Propagation Complexity: The chain's structure explains why delay is linear. With mid-chain injection, the farthest node is about $n/2$ positions away, and each flooding hop advances the command about m positions, so coverage takes $H \approx n/(2m)$ hops. The per-hop time τ is proportional to m: the relaying node settles a keysend to each of its up to $2m$ neighbors, which a single Core Lightning daemon does largely one at a time. The two factors cancel, $T = H\tau \approx (n/(2m)) \cdot m = \Theta(n)$: a wider neighborhood shortens the path but makes each hop proportionally heavier. The bound is tight, not just an upper limit: the wavefront must cross all H hops, each costing $\propto m$, so linear growth is a lower bound as well, giving $\Theta(n)$ rather than merely $O(n)$. Delay is therefore linear in n and flat in m, not the logarithmic $O(m \log n)$ of D-LNBot's m-ary-tree model.

Algorithm 2. Resilience Evaluation

Require: overlay $G = (V, E)$; k commands per level; removal levels P ($\{0\%\}$ if none); strategy $S \in \{\text{RANDOM}, \text{TARGETED}\}$
Ensure: delay $t_{p,j}$ and coverage $c_{p,j}$ for every level p, command j

$R \leftarrow$ rank V on intact G ▷ by degree (TARGETED) or fixed-seed shuffle (RANDOM)
for $p \in P$ **do**
  remove $R[1 \dots \lfloor pn \rfloor]$ from G ▷ cumulative
  $v \leftarrow$ highest-degree node in G's largest surviving component
  for $j = 1 \dots k$ **do**
    Botmaster keysends command j at v; each node floods it onward
    record $t_{p,j}, c_{p,j}$ ▷ 60 s stall before full coverage $\Rightarrow$ partition
  end for
end for
return $\{(t_{p,j}, c_{p,j})\}$

To give the orchestrator a real-time view of the network without the overhead of reading log files, LNTest uses POSIX shared memory (SHM). Before launching the containers, the orchestrator allocates a small status buffer for each C&C node. As a node creates channels, joins the overlay, and forwards commands, it writes its current state into this buffer. The orchestrator simply reads the buffers to track how far each command has propagated, which nodes are online, and when coverage has stalled, all with minimal latency.

4.5 Resilience Evaluation

LNTest measures resilience by simulating a takedown, which Algorithm 2 formalizes. It shuts down some of the C&C nodes and checks whether commands still reach the rest. Nodes are removed either at random or in a targeted way that takes the highest-degree nodes first. The takedown grows step by step, and each step adds to the nodes already removed. This makes it one steadily worsening attack rather than a fresh cut each time. A takedown can split the overlay into several disconnected components, so after each step the botmaster injects from the highest-degree node in the largest surviving component to maximize its reach. A command whose coverage stalls for 60 s before reaching every survivor counts as a partition.

5 Experiment Results

We now present our experimental results. Our primary metric is *propagation delay*: the time from when the botmaster sends a command until the last surviving C&C node receives it. For every data point we issue the command 10 times and report the mean propagation delay; the repeated sends average out per-command jitter. If the network partitions, the orchestrator detects the stall and stops early. We also report *coverage*: the fraction of surviving nodes that received the command, which matters in takedown experiments where the network may be partitioned.

All experiments ran on a single workstation: a Supermicro tower with a 16-core AMD Ryzen Threadripper PRO 3955WX CPU and 64 GB DDR4 3200 MT/s RAM, running Ubuntu 26.04 on a 1 TB Toshiba KXG60ZNV1T02 NVMe SSD (PCIe Gen3 ×4). Fast storage proved essential: an initial install on the machine's 2 TB 7200 RPM SATA hard drive was unusably slow because the many co-located Lightning nodes generate heavy concurrent disk I/O, so we moved the system to the NVMe SSD. The software stack is Bitcoin Core[3] version 31.0, Core Lightning [6] version 26.06rc2, and Docker 29.5.2.

[3] https://github.com/bitcoin/bitcoin.

5.1 Scalability

We first ask how propagation delay grows with botnet size. Using D-LNBot mode with $m = 4$ active neighbors and injecting each command from the middle of the chain, we varied the number of C&C servers from 10 to 100 in steps of 10, and then from 100 to 500 in steps of 100 to probe behavior well beyond proof-of-concept scale. Figure 2 shows the results.

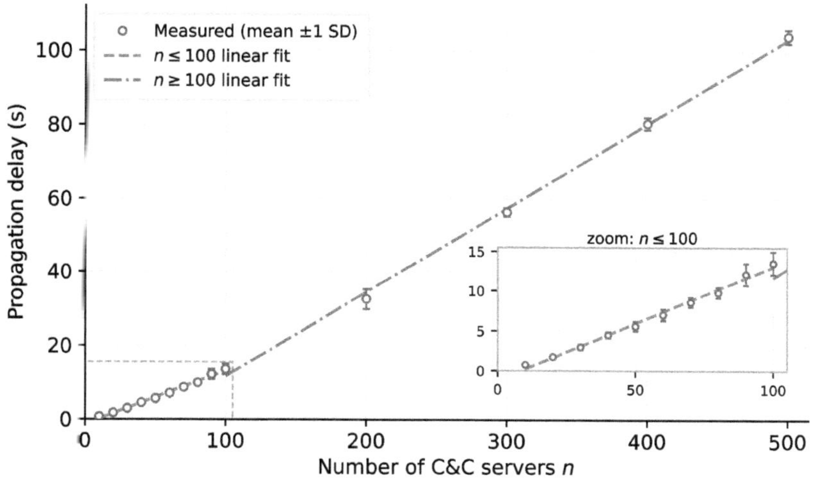

Fig. 2. Propagation delay vs. number of C&C servers ($m = 4$, D-LNBot chain, mid-chain injection). Markers show the mean of 10 commands with ± 1 standard deviation error bars; coverage is 100% at every size. The two regimes are fit separately: $t = 0.143n - 1.20$ ($R^2 = 0.993$) for $n \leq 100$ and $t = 0.229n - 11.28$ ($R^2 = 0.998$) for $n \geq 100$. The inset zooms into the $n \leq 100$ regime.

Through $n = 100$, propagation delay grows linearly with the number of nodes: a fit gives $t = 0.143n - 1.20$ ($R^2 = 0.993$), so each additional C&C server adds about 0.14 s. At $n = 100$ the mean delay is 13.5 s, and coverage is 100% in every run, with no command ever lost. The trend continues well past proof-of-concept scale. At $n = 500$ commands still reach every node in 104 s on average, again at 100% coverage.

This linear scaling confirms the $\Theta(n)$ analysis of Sect. 4.4 and contradicts the $O(m \log n)$ that D-LNBot [20] predicted by treating the chain as an m-ary tree. The real overlay is a chain of overlapping neighborhoods, not a tree, so the command wavefront advances only a bounded number of positions per hop and the delay grows linearly with n, governed by botnet size rather than neighbor count, far slower than the logarithmic growth D-LNBot predicted.

The linear fit is near-perfect through $n = 100$, the range relevant to existing proof-of-concept designs; beyond it a second, steeper linear regime appears, with the per-node cost rising from 0.14 s to 0.23 s (Fig. 2). This drift is not a path-length effect, since the number of hops from the injection point to the farthest node stays at exactly $\lceil n/(2m) \rceil$ (we verified this on the reconstructed overlays), nor a host-resource limit, since even at $n = 500$ the workstation uses only about half of its 16 CPU cores on average (Sect. 5.6). Instead, each forwarding hop settles more slowly as the overlay grows. The cost is not route computation, which stays negligible (a few milliseconds), but the per-keysend HTLC settlement, which lengthens as each node services a larger, busier channel graph. The conclusion is unchanged: propagation is linear in n, so a larger botnet is strictly slower, never faster.

5.2 Autonomous Formation Topology

A key question is what topology D-LNBot's formation protocol actually produces when run on real Lightning nodes under realistic conditions. As described in Sect. 4.3, the autonomous mode launches containers with staggered delays (log-normal, median 30 s) and lets each node discover peers by scanning the innocent node's channels. We ran this mode at two scales: $n = 20$ and $n = 50$, both with $m = 4$. Each command was injected from $CC_{\lceil n/2 \rceil}$, as in the scalability runs.

Results: At both scales the formation protocol produced a connected overlay that delivered every command to all nodes (100% coverage; mean delay 2.0 s at $n = 20$, 5.45 s at $n = 50$, averaged over five formations). But the topology was not the uniform chain of D-LNBot's paper. Instead we observed a *clustered chain* (Fig. 3): a sequence of cliques of roughly m nodes at degree $2m$, each ringed by peripheral nodes at degree m and joined to its neighbors by bridge nodes whose removal would split the overlay. The degree distribution is roughly bimodal, peaking at the clique-core degree ($2m = 8$) and the peripheral degree ($m = 4$). Because the overlay forms nondeterministically, its structure varies across runs at $n = 50$ (two to four bridge nodes in our five formations); at $n = 20$, by contrast, all five formations produced the *identical* clustered chain with two bridges (CC9 and CC17), so this run-to-run variation emerged only at $n = 50$.

Why Cliques Form Instead of a Chain: The key insight is that D-LNBot's formation protocol includes continuous peer monitoring: each node keeps scanning for new peers as long as it is active. When multiple nodes have overlapping active periods (inevitable with staggered arrivals), they discover each other mutually and all open channels to one another, forming a clique. Because each node keeps accepting peers until m have connected to it, and a new node arrives roughly every 30 s (the median inter-arrival), about m nodes are forming at the same time, so they interconnect into a clique of size $\approx m$. Once its members reach m inbound connections they disconnect from the innocent node, and the next arrival starts a fresh cluster. This process repeats, producing the observed chain of cliques.

Comparison with the Ideal D-LNBot Chain: Table 1 compares the two topologies at $n = 50$.

The two topologies have comparable diameter and propagation speed. But they differ fundamentally in vulnerability: the ideal chain has no bridge nodes

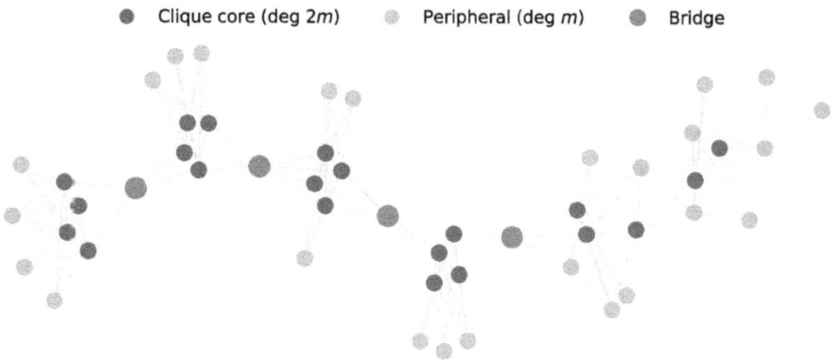

Fig. 3. A representative overlay produced by D-LNBot's autonomous formation protocol at $n = 50$, $m = 4$: a clustered chain of cliques (cores at degree $2m = 8$, dark blue; peripheral nodes at degree $m = 4$, light blue) joined by bridge nodes (red) whose removal splits the overlay; intermediate-degree nodes are gray. Because formation is nondeterministic, the bridge count varies across runs. (Color figure online)

Table 1. Ideal D-LNBot chain vs. the autonomous clustered chain ($n = 50$, $m = 4$), both injected from $CC_{\lceil n/2 \rceil}$ (CC25). Clustered-chain values are means over five formations (Fig. 3 shows a representative one); its bridge count varies across runs.

Property	D-LNBot chain	Clustered chain
Avg. degree	7.6	6.2
Diameter	13	12
Bridge nodes	0	2–4
Mean delay (10 msgs)	5.58 s	5.45 s
Coverage	100%	100%

(every interior node has $2m$ connections, giving many redundant paths), whereas the clustered chain always contains bridge nodes, each a single point of failure whose removal fragments the overlay (in the representative run of Fig. 3, removing the four bridges splits it into five components). We evaluate this vulnerability quantitatively in the takedown experiments below.

5.3 Resilience to Takedowns

We now ask the central question for defenders: how much of the botnet must be taken down to stop commands from reaching all nodes, and does the answer depend on topology? We test three topologies (the D-LNBot chain, a BA scale-free graph, and the autonomous clustered chain from Sect. 5.2) under two strategies, random removal and targeted removal of the highest-degree nodes, at five removal percentages (10%–50%). All runs use $n = 50$ and $m = 4$ with cumulative removal. After each removal step the botmaster re-injects from the highest-degree node in the largest surviving component (Sect. 4.5), so its reach is never wasted on a fragment it cannot leave. The D-LNBot chain and the BA graph are fixed, and the random removal order is seeded, so a takedown on them is fully reproducible and we run each once. Only the autonomous topology is nondeterministic, since a fresh graph forms on every run, so we repeat it five times and plot the mean coverage with shaded min–max bands (Fig. 4). The specific graph varies across the five runs, but the structural patterns hold.

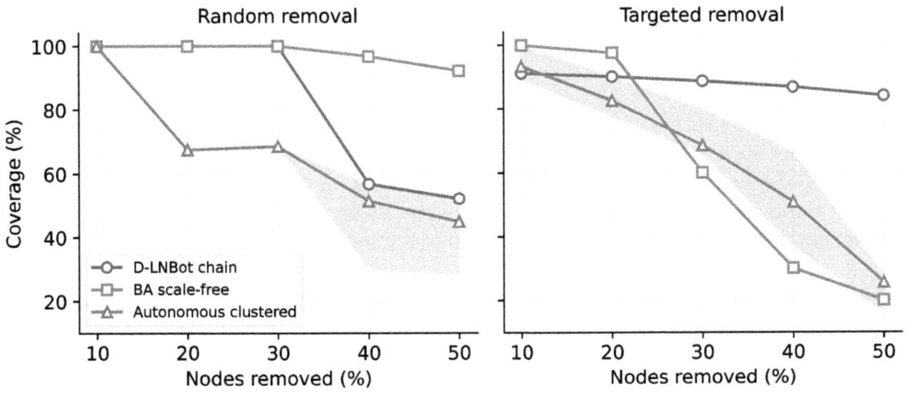

Fig. 4. Coverage vs. fraction of nodes removed for three topologies under random and targeted takedown ($n = 50$, $m = 4$), with each command injected from the highest-degree node in the largest surviving component. A drop below 100% means the network has partitioned. For the autonomous topology, the only nondeterministic one, the line is the mean over five runs and the shaded band their min–max range.

D-LNBot Chain: Under random removal, the chain stays intact through 30% (100% coverage, delays around 5 s) and partitions at 40%, where coverage falls to 57%. Random removal scatters the missing nodes along the chain, creating several disconnected fragments, and the botmaster reaches only the nodes in its own fragment.

Targeted removal partitions the chain at the very first level (10%), yet the resulting coverage (91%) is *higher* than random removal at 40% (57%), and it stays high as more nodes fall (84% even at 50%). This counterintuitive result has a structural explanation. In the D-LNBot chain, 42 of the 50 nodes share the same degree ($2m = 8$); only the four nodes at each end have lower degrees. Because these interior nodes are all tied at degree 8, the targeted strategy takes them in index order, always removing a consecutive block (CC5–CC9 at 10%, CC5–CC14 at 20%, and so on) that makes a single clean cut and orphans only the four lowest-indexed nodes (CC1–CC4). The botmaster sits in the larger fragment and reaches almost every surviving node there. Degree-based targeting thus provides *no useful signal* on the chain, where almost every node has the same degree: ranking C&C nodes by degree reveals nothing about which removals would actually fragment the overlay.

BA Scale-Free: The BA graph tells the opposite story. Random removal barely dents it: coverage holds at 100% through 30% and slips only to 97% at 40% and 92% at 50%, when a few low-degree nodes lose all their links. This is because random removal is unlikely to hit the small number of high-degree hubs that hold the graph together.

Targeted removal, by contrast, is devastating. Coverage is still 100% at 10%, but then collapses as the hubs fall: 98% at 20%, 60% at 30%, 30% at 40%, and just 20% at 50%. The most-connected hubs are removed first; the graph absorbs the loss of the first few, but once enough are gone the periphery they held together loses its links and splinters off, so the giant component shrinks with every further removal.

Autonomous Clustered Chain: The autonomous topology is the only one fragile under *both* strategies; the values here are the mean of five fresh formations. Random removal partitions it almost immediately, coverage falling from 100% at 10% to about 68% at 20% and drifting down to roughly 45% at 50%, because the clustered chain has far fewer redundant paths than the D-LNBot chain or the BA graph, so even scattered removals tend to hit a bridge. Targeted removal bites early too (93% at 10%) and then declines steadily, from 83% at 20% to 26% at 50%: removing the highest-degree nodes strips out the dense clique cores and, as it proceeds, the high-degree bridges that join the clusters (Sect. 5.2), progressively splitting the overlay. Either way the overlay fragments well before half its nodes are gone, making it the most vulnerable of the three: every other topology withstands at least one strategy, whereas the clustered chain fragments under both.

Key Insight: topology determines resilience, not just size. All three topologies have the same size and the same m, yet they respond to takedowns in completely different ways: the uniform-degree chain resists targeted removal but fragments under heavy random failure, the BA graph shows the mirror image, and the clustered chain is fragile to both.

5.4 Effect of Active Neighbor Count

In D-LNBot's chain topology, each C&C server opens channels to its m nearest predecessors. We vary m from 2 to 6 at three scales ($n = 50$, $n = 100$, and $n = 200$) to measure how the neighbor count affects propagation delay. Table 2 summarizes the results.

At all three scales, a larger m never reduces propagation delay. It is essentially flat across m at $n = 50$ (within 0.4 s, about 7% of the mean) and rises gently with m at larger scales: from 11.8 to 13.7 s at $n = 100$, and from 26.2 to 35.1 s at $n = 200$. This contradicts the intuition that more neighbors should make propagation faster. The reason is the same trade-off derived in Sect. 4.4: a wider neighborhood carries each command farther per hop, shortening the path (its length scales as n/m), but makes each node settle proportionally more keysends at every hop. The two effects cancel, so delay stays $\Theta(n)$ rather than dropping as $\Theta(n/m)$ or compounding as $\Theta(nm)$. The mild residual rise with m reflects

Table 2. Mean propagation delay (seconds) vs. active neighbor count m, with each command injected from the middle of the chain ($CC_{\lceil n/2 \rceil}$).

m	$n = 50$	$n = 100$	$n = 200$
2	5.60	11.79	26.20
3	5.45	12.67	29.74
4	5.74	13.46	32.41
5	5.38	13.50	33.84
6	5.63	13.67	35.05

the heavier per-keysend settlement that more channels per node add (Sect. 5.1). Botnet size n, not neighbor count m, governs propagation delay.

5.5 Effect of Injection Point

We vary the botmaster's injection position on a fixed D-LNBot chain ($n = 50$, $m = 4$) across five settings: a uniformly random node, the bottom (oldest) end, the middle, the top (youngest) end, and multi-source injection from all three fixed positions simultaneously. Table 3 shows the results.

Table 3. Propagation delay for different botmaster injection positions ($n = 50$, $m = 4$, D-LNBot chain).

Injection Position	Delay (s)	Coverage
Random	7.45	100%
Bottom (oldest node)	8.47	100%
Middle	5.68	100%
Top (youngest node)	8.48	100%
Multi-source (bottom+middle+top)	4.18	100%

Among single injection points the middle is fastest (5.7 s), roughly 1.5× faster than either end (about 8.5 s), because it halves the longest distance a command must travel along the chain. A uniformly random node, averaged over five runs, falls in between (7.5 s). Multi-source injection from all three positions at once is faster still (4.2 s): the three simultaneous sources further shorten the longest path, and because forwarding is event-driven, this shorter path outweighs the extra work of handling the duplicate commands. These results are specific to the chain's symmetric structure; other topologies may behave differently.

5.6 Hardware Resources Consumed by LNTest

We measured LNTest's resource consumption by monitoring all Docker containers throughout a run. At $n = 100$ ($m = 4$, D-LNBot topology), the 102 containers (100 C&C servers, one botmaster, one innocent node) use roughly 8–9 GB of RAM and average about 4 of the host's 16 CPU cores in steady state, with brief peaks during the channel-opening phase. At $n = 500$, the 502 containers use about 47 GB of RAM and average roughly 8 cores. Per-node memory grows only slowly with scale (from about 89 MB to 97 MB per node), so memory is the binding constraint: a 64 GB workstation can host on the order of 650–700 nodes, and a 16 GB laptop around 150. Even at $n = 500$ the CPU stays well below saturation, so these experiments are bounded by propagation delay (Sect. 5.1) rather than by host resources.

6 Discussion

6.1 Findings and Implications for Defense

Our first main finding is that the topology a botnet *actually* forms can differ substantially from the topology its protocol *prescribes*. D-LNBot's formation protocol is designed to produce a uniform chain, but concurrent peer discovery instead yields a *clustered chain* whose bridge nodes are single points of failure (Sect. 5.2). This structural weakness does not appear in the published design [20] and would be invisible to a defender who reasons only from the protocol specification. The implication is that defenders should profile the *deployed* overlay (for instance, by monitoring channel-open patterns on the blockchain [33]) rather than assuming the published topology holds.

Second, our takedown experiments reveal that the *type* of overlay topology largely determines which disruption strategy is effective (Sect. 5.3). The D-LNBot chain and the BA scale-free graph are each vulnerable to only one strategy, whereas the autonomous clustered chain fragments under *both*: its bridge nodes are structurally critical and, unlike the D-LNBot chain, distinguishable by degree. The practical takeaway for defenders is clear: a takedown strategy must be matched to the observed topology.

Third, command propagation scales linearly with botnet size ($\Theta(n)$) and is independent of the neighbor count m, not $O(m \log n)$ as D-LNBot claimed [20], because the overlay behaves like a chain rather than a tree (Sect. 5.1). Even at 500 nodes commands still reach every node without partitioning, so LN-based C&C is practical well beyond proof-of-concept scale. This underscores the urgency of developing detection mechanisms and evaluating them under controlled conditions, which is exactly what LNTest provides. Existing detectors target on-chain Bitcoin botnets [40], whereas LN-based C&C hides commands in off-chain, encrypted payments.

6.2 Ethical Considerations

LNTest is a dual-use tool: the same features that make it valuable for defensive research could be misused to refine real-world LN-based botnets. Similar concerns have long been raised for traditional botnet testbeds and are discussed in dual-use research guidelines for cybersecurity [18,25]. To reduce risk, we deliberately restrict LNTest to Bitcoin *regtest*, bind all Lightning nodes to the host's loopback interface, and focus exclusively on C&C behavior rather than malware payloads. We recommend that users maintain these constraints, avoid connecting LNTest to public networks, and follow institutional ethics processes before running large-scale experiments.

6.3 Limitations

LNTest models only the C&C layer of an LN-based botnet. We assume that C&C servers are already compromised machines capable of running full Lightning nodes. In practice, many large botnets rely on compromised IoT devices and home routers with limited resources, as recent campaigns against outdated D-Link devices illustrate[4]. Porting our design to such constrained hardware, or combining LNTest with existing IoT botnet testbeds, is left for future work.

Our experiments use a regtest-based deployment on a single machine, with overlays of up to 500 C&C nodes. The real Lightning Network has thousands of public nodes, dynamic channel balances, background payment traffic, and non-trivial fee dynamics [33,39]. We also use a single LN implementation (Core Lightning); heterogeneous deployments mixing CLN [6], LND [23], Eclair [1], and Rust Lightning [22] may exhibit different routing behavior or failure modes. Furthermore, we assume all C&C channels have sufficient liquidity and do not model long-lived jamming attacks that could lock HTLC slots and delay command propagation [27]. Because LNTest also runs entirely on localhost with no real network latency, the propagation delays we report are dominated by Core Lightning's per-hop payment-processing time rather than by network transport, and should be viewed as optimistic lower bounds under idealized conditions.

Finally, our degree-based targeted takedown strategy is deliberately simple: it ranks nodes by degree and removes them in descending order. On the uniform-degree D-LNBot chain this provides no useful signal, which is itself a finding (Sect. 5.3). More sophisticated strategies, such as betweenness-centrality removal [32] or bridge-targeted disruption, may prove more effective. The main value of LNTest lies in comparing *relative* trends across topologies, takedown strategies, and injection points, and in providing a common, reproducible baseline for future work on LN-based botnet defenses.

7 Conclusion

We presented LNTest, a self-contained Bitcoin *regtest* testbed for experimentally studying Lightning Network-based botnets. Built from production-grade Bitcoin Core and Core Lightning nodes containerized with Docker, LNTest supports three overlay topology modes (deterministic chain, autonomous peer discovery,

[4] https://www.bleepingcomputer.com/news/security/malware-botnets-exploit-outdated-d-link-routers-in-recent-attacks/.

and user-supplied graphs) and lets researchers control botnet size, neighbor connectivity, injection point, and takedown strategy as independent variables.

Our experiments produced three main findings. First, D-LNBot's autonomous formation protocol does not produce the uniform chain described in its design: instead, concurrent peer discovery creates a clustered chain with bridge nodes that are single points of failure. Second, command propagation scales linearly with botnet size ($\Theta(n)$) and is unaffected by the neighbor count, not $O(m \log n)$ as previously claimed, because the overlay behaves like a chain rather than a tree. Third, the overlay topology determines which takedown strategy is effective: degree-based targeting devastates scale-free topologies but is useless against uniform-degree chains, random removal shows the opposite pattern, and the autonomous clustered chain, the topology D-LNBot actually produces, is fragile under both strategies. These results demonstrate that defenders must profile the deployed overlay before choosing a disruption strategy.

By releasing LNTest, we provide a reproducible platform for future work on LN-based botnet defenses. Natural extensions include betweenness-centrality-based takedown strategies, heterogeneous Lightning implementations, and integration with IoT botnet testbeds to model resource-constrained deployments.

Disclosure of Interests. The authors have no competing interests to declare that are relevant to the content of this article.

References

1. ACINQ: A scala implementation of the Lightning Network (2015). https://github.com/ACINQ/eclair
2. Albert, R., Jeong, H., Barabási, A.L.: Error and attack tolerance of complex networks. Nature **406**(6794), 378–382 (2000)
3. Ali, S.T., McCorry, P., Lee, P.H.-J., Hao, F.: ZombieCoin: powering next-generation botnets with bitcoin. In: Brenner, M., Christin, N., Johnson, B., Rohloff, K. (eds.) FC 2015. LNCS, vol. 8976, pp. 34–48. Springer, Heidelberg (2015). https://doi.org/10.1007/978-3-662-48051-9_3
4. Ali, S.T., McCorry, P., Lee, P.H.J., Hao, F.: ZombieCoin 2.0: managing next-generation botnets using Bitcoin. Int. J. Inf. Secur. **17**(4), 411–422 (2018)
5. Alibrahim, O., Malaika, M.: Botract: abusing smart contracts and blockchain for botnet command and control. Int. J. Inf. Comput. Secur. **17**(1–2), 147–163 (2022)
6. Blockstream: Core Lightning: Lightning Network implementation focusing on spec compliance and performance (2015). https://github.com/ElementsProject/lightning
7. Böck, L., Alexopoulos, N., Saracoglu, E., Mühlhäuser, M., Vasilomanolakis, E.: Assessing the threat of blockchain-based botnets. In: 2019 APWG Symposium on Electronic Crime Research (eCrime), pp. 1–11 (2019)
8. Calvet, J., et al.: The case for in-the-lab botnet experimentation: creating and taking down a 3000-node botnet. In: Proceedings of the 26th Annual Computer Security Applications Conference, pp. 141–150. Association for Computing Machinery (2010)

9. Sáez-de Cámara, X., Flores, J.L., Arellano, C., Urbieta, A., Zurutuza, U.: Gotham testbed: a reproducible IoT testbed for security experiments and dataset generation. IEEE Trans. Dependable Secure Comput. **21**(1), 186–203 (2024)
10. De Vivo, S., Obaidat, I., Dai, D., Liguori, P.: DDoShield-IoT: a testbed for simulating and lightweight detection of IoT botnet DDoS attacks. In: 2024 54th Annual IEEE/IFIP International Conference on Dependable Systems and Networks Workshops (DSN-W), pp. 1–8 (2024)
11. Franzoni, F., Abellan, I., Daza, V.: Leveraging bitcoin Testnet for bidirectional botnet command and control systems. In: Bonneau, J., Heninger, N. (eds.) FC 2020. LNCS, vol. 12059, pp. 3–19. Springer, Cham (2020). https://doi.org/10.1007/978-3-030-51280-4_1
12. Frkat, D., Annessi, R., Zseby, T.: ChainChannels: private botnet communication over public blockchains. In: IEEE International Conference on Internet of Things (iThings) and IEEE Green Computing and Communications (GreenCom) and IEEE Cyber, Physical and Social Computing (CPSCom) and IEEE Smart Data (SmartData), pp. 1244–1252. (2018)
13. Gao, H., Li, L., Chang, X., Wan, J., Li, J., Du, J., Zhang, X.: BlockchainBot: A novel botnet infrastructure enhanced by blockchain technology and IoT. Electronics **11**(7) (2022)
14. Gao, H., Li, L., Lei, H., Tian, N., Lin, H., Wan, J.: One IOTA of countless legions: a next-generation botnet premises design substrated on blockchain and internet of things. IEEE Internet Things J. **11**(5), 9107–9126 (2024)
15. Gao, H., Li, L., Lin, H., Chang, X., Wan, J., Li, J., Zhu, F.: ZombieCoin3.0: on the looming of a novel botnet fortified by distributed ledger technology and internet of things. In: 2021 IEEE 23rd Int Conf on High Performance Computing & Communications; 7th Int Conf on Data Science & Systems; 19th Int Conf on Smart City; 7th Int Conf on Dependability in Sensor, Cloud & Big Data Systems & Application (HPCC/DSS/SmartCity/DependSys), pp. 1625–1634 (2021)
16. Georgoulias, D., Pedersen, J.M., Falch, M., Vasilomanolakis, E.: Botnet business models, takedown attempts, and the Darkweb market: a survey. ACM Comput. Surv. **55**(11), 219:1–219:39 (2023)
17. Kamenski, D., Shaghaghi, A., Warren, M., Kanhere, S.S.: Attacking with Bitcoin: using bitcoin to build resilient botnet armies. In: Herrero, Á., Cambra, C., Urda, D., Sedano, J., Quintián, H., Corchado, E. (eds.) CISIS 2020. AISC, vol. 1267, pp. 3–12. Springer, Cham (2021). https://doi.org/10.1007/978-3-030-57805-3_1
18. Kolstoe, S.E.: A framework for reviewing dual use research. In: Iphofen, R., O'Mathúna, D. (eds.) Ethical Issues in Covert, Security and Surveillance Research, Emerald Publishing Limited (2021)
19. Kumar, A., Lim, T.J.: A secure contained testbed for analyzing IoT botnets. In: Gao, H., Yin, Y., Yang, X., Miao, H. (eds.) TridentCom 2018. LNICST, vol. 270, pp. 124–137. Springer, Cham (2019). https://doi.org/10.1007/978-3-030-12971-2_8
20. Kurt, A., Erdin, E., Akkaya, K., Uluagac, S., Cebe, M.: D-LNBot: a scalable, cost-free and covert hybrid botnet on Bitcoin's Lightning network. IEEE Trans. Dependable Secure Comput. **21**(4), 2162–2180 (2024)
21. Kurt, A., Erdin, E., Cebe, M., Akkaya, K., Uluagac, A.S.: LNBot: A covert hybrid botnet on Bitcoin Lightning network for fun and profit. In: Computer Security - ESORICS 2020, pp. 734–755. Springer International Publishing (2020)
22. Lightning Dev Kit: A highly modular Bitcoin Lightning library written in Rust. It's rust-lightning, not Rusty's Lightning! (2018). https://github.com/lightningdevkit/rust-lightning

23. Lightning Labs: Lightning Network Daemon. https://github.com/lightningnetwork/lnd (2016)
24. Liu, C., et al.: SCBot: building lightweight and flexible C&C based on smart contract. In: ICASSP 2025 - 2025 IEEE International Conference on Acoustics, Speech and Signal Processing (ICASSP), pp. 1–5 (2025)
25. Macnish, K., van der Ham, J.: Ethics in cybersecurity research and practice. Technol. Soc. **63**, 101382 (2020)
26. Mengidis, A.: Blockchain-based command and control for next generation botnets. Master's thesis, International Hellenic University (2019). https://repository.ihu.gr/handle/11544/29362
27. Mizrahi, A., Zohar, A.: Congestion attacks in payment channel networks. In: Borisov, N., Diaz, C. (eds.) FC 2021. LNCS, vol. 12675, pp. 170–188. Springer, Heidelberg (2021). https://doi.org/10.1007/978-3-662-64331-0_9
28. Nakamoto, S.: Bitcoin: a peer-to-peer electronic cash system (2008). https://bitcoin.org/bitcoin.pdf
29. Obaidat, I., Kahn, B., Tavakoli, F., Sridhar, M.: Creating a large-scale memory error IoT botnet using NS3DockerEmulator. In: 2023 53rd Annual IEEE/IFIP International Conference on Dependable Systems and Networks (DSN), pp. 470–479 (2023)
30. Parthipan, M., Laghari, S.U.A., Jaisan, A., Baig, A., Ali, M.A., Karuppayah, S.: Insights into peer-to-peer botnet dynamics: reviewing emulation testbeds and proposing a conceptual model. Bull. Electr. Eng. Inform. **14**(3), 2077–2096 (2025)
31. Poon, J., Dryja, T.: The Bitcoin Lightning network: Scalable off-chain instant payments. Technical report, Lightning Network (2016). https://lightning.network/lightning-network-paper.pdf
32. Rohrer, E., Malliaris, J., Tschorsch, F.: Discharged payment channels: quantifying the Lightning network's resilience to topology-based attacks. In: 2019 IEEE European Symposium on Security and Privacy Workshops (EuroS&PW), pp. 347–356. IEEE (2019)
33. Seres, I.A., Gulyás, L., Nagy, D.A., Burcsi, P.: Topological analysis of Bitcoin's lightning network. In: Pardalos, P., Kotsireas, I., Guo, Y., Knottenbelt, W. (eds.) Mathematical Research for Blockchain Economy. SPBE, pp. 1–12. Springer, Cham (2020). https://doi.org/10.1007/978-3-030-37110-4_1
34. Sweeny, J.: Botnet resiliency via private blockchains. Technical report, SANS Institute (2017). https://www.sans.org/white-papers/38050
35. Taniguchi, T., Griffioen, H., Doerr, C.: Analysis and takeover of the Bitcoin-coordinated Pony malware. In: Proceedings of the 2021 ACM Asia Conference on Computer and Communications Security, pp. 916–930. Association for Computing Machinery (2021)
36. Thanh Vu S.N., Stege, M., El-Habr, P.I., Bang, J., Dragoni, N.: A survey on botnets: incentives, evolution, detection and current trends. Future Internet **13**(8) (2021)
37. Ubiedo, L.: Blockchain and node.js abused by Tsundere: an emerging botnet. *Securelist* (Kaspersky) technical blog (2025). https://securelist.com/tsundere-node-js-botnet-uses-ethereum-blockchain/117979/
38. Yin, J., Cui, X., Liu, C., Liu, Q., Cui, T., Wang, Z.: CoinBot: a covert botnet in the cryptocurrency network. In: Meng, W., Gollmann, D., Jensen, C.D., Zhou, J. (eds.) ICICS 2020. LNCS, vol. 12282, pp. 107–125. Springer, Cham (2020). https://doi.org/10.1007/978-3-030-61078-4_7
39. Zabka, P., Foerster, K.T., Decker, C., Schmid, S.: A centrality analysis of the Lightning network. Telecommun. Pol. **48**(2), 102696 (2024)

40. Zarpelão, B.B., Miani, R.S., Rajarajan, M.: Detection of bitcoin-based botnets using a one-class classifier. In: Blazy, O., Yeun, C.Y. (eds.) WISTP 2018. LNCS, vol. 11469, pp. 174–189. Springer, Cham (2019). https://doi.org/10.1007/978-3-030-20074-9_13
41. Zhong, Y., Zhou, A., Zhang, L., Jing, F., Zuo, Z.: DUSTBot: a duplex and stealthy p2p-based botnet in the Bitcoin network. PLoS ONE **14**(12), e0226594 (2019)
42. Zohar, O.: Unblockable Chains - a POC on using blockchain as infrastructure for malware operations (2018). https://github.com/platdrag/UnblockableChains

A Communication Channel Redundancy Extension for Data Distribution Service

Lóránt Meszlényi(✉), Florian Hartl, and Stefan Katzenbeisser

University of Passau, Passau, Germany
meszlenyi.lorant@uni-passau.de

Abstract. The Data Distribution Service (DDS) middleware standard has gained widespread adoption in safety-critical systems, including automotive, aerospace, and industrial automation, where communication reliability is a foundational requirement. However, deployments operating under high safety integrity levels, like railway systems, mandate the presence of multiple redundant communication channels. While DDS supports component redundancy with Quality of Service (QoS) attributes, it lacks a standardized way for communication redundancy mechanisms. In this paper, we propose a communication channel-redundancy extension to DDS. We evaluate our extension under diverse simulated network conditions, including packet loss, link degradation, and full channel failure, comparing it against standard DDS protocol. Our results demonstrate that the proposed extension achieves highly available communication with no measurable performance degradation under nominal conditions, positioning DDS as a modern solution for high safety requirements.

Keywords: DDS · safety-critical systems · communication redundancy · distributed systems · high availability · network simulation

1 Introduction

Modern cyber-physical systems (autonomous vehicles, robots, industrial control systems, avionics and medical devices) increasingly depend on distributed software components that must coordinate over shared communication infrastructure. Control algorithms are distributed over a number of nodes and hence safe and secure communication is mandatory to achieve fault-free operation. Especially in high-risk domains, like railway systems, power distribution, standards and regulations mandate a multichannel communication system [10]. From a security perspective, a single-channel architecture can be easily attacked by adversaries by executing denial-of-service attacks, link-layer jamming or targeted hardware interference. The absence of communication redundancy simultaneously undermines availability under faults *and* resilience under adversarial conditions (Fig. 1).

One of the emerging and widely accepted communication protocols is the Data Distribution Service (DDS) standard. As an open standard with multiple

S. Nadjm-Tehrani et al. (Eds.): ARES 2026, LNCS 16898, pp. 183–200, 2027.
https://doi.org/10.1007/978-3-032-36874-4_9

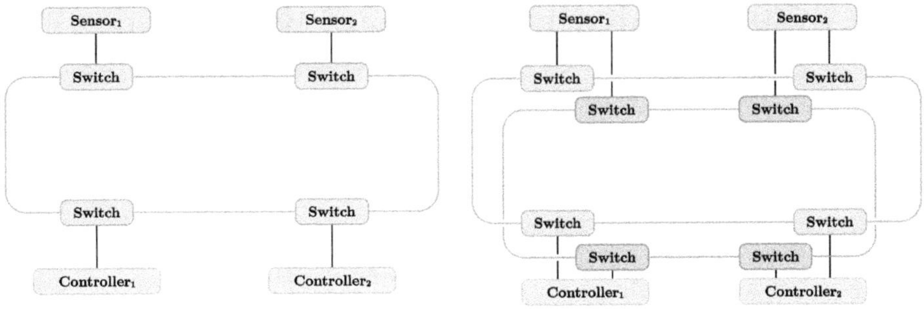

(a) DDS on conventional Ethernet.

(b) DDS redundancy extension enabling dual-ring redundancy.

Fig. 1. Comparison of the traditional DDS network and the new DDS network using our proposal.

independent implementations and publish-subscribe architecture, it was already investigated as communication protocol for high-safety cloud in railway systems [27]. Practically it is used not only in large-scale, geographically distributed control systems [14,28], but also in unmanned [29] and manned vehicle-scale control systems [19].

DDS allows the developer to describe the properties of the communication using Quality of Service (QoS) properties. Moreover it allows redundancy at the *component* level by deploying multiple publishers or subscribers. But it offers no native abstraction for transmitting the same data stream over multiple independent physical or logical network paths. Existing deployments can therefore either accept a single point of failure, or adopt proprietary, vendor-specific extensions that fragment interoperability and complicate safety certification.

In this paper, we address this gap by proposing a communication channel-redundancy extension to the DDS standard. Our extension introduces a transparent multipath transmission layer that operates beneath the DDS application interface, requiring no modifications to existing application logic. We define a wire-format specification to ensure interoperability across implementations, and we evaluate the extension under simulated adverse network conditions. Our contributions are threefold:

- We describe the Data Distribution Standard (DDS) and its current capabilities for highly available communication requirements.
- We propose a novel redundancy extension for establishing redundant communication channels for DDS including a wire format specification.
- We evaluate the extension through systematic performance testing, demonstrating high availability under fault conditions with negligible overhead under normal operation.

The remainder of this paper is structured as follows. Section 2 examines the DDS standard and its existing mechanisms for dependable communication. Section 3 surveys related work on protocol-level redundancy in DDS and in safety-critical communication systems more broadly. Section 4 presents our proposed extension and its implementation. Section 5 reports experimental results, and Sect. 6 concludes the paper.

2 Background

2.1 Redundant Communication in Safety-Critical Systems

Modern safety-critical systems adhere the Safety Integrity Level (SIL) classification, as defined in the IEC 61508 standard for functional safety of electrical, electronic, and programmable electronic systems [18]. At the highest level, SIL 4, the probability of a dangerous failure per hour is bounded in the range of 10^{-9} to 10^{-8}. This constraint requires a systematic redundancy approach at every layer of the system architecture including the communication layer.

For example in railway applications, standards such as EN50159 mandate that safety-related transmission systems provide adequate protection against failure modes including message loss, corruption, duplication, and channel-level failure [5]. Similarly, in the aerospace domain, DO-178C and the ARINC 664 (AFDX) specification prescribe deterministic, redundant dat networks to meet the requirements [4]. Automotive functional safety, described by ISO 26262, likewise requires that safety-relevant communication paths be designed with sufficient redundancy to meet the Automotive Safety Integrity Level (ASIL) targets derived from hazard analysis [7]. Similar requirements are demanded by the DIN EN 61850-5 in the design of power generation and distribution systems [8]. Across all these domains, redundant communication paths are required to satisfy the requirements for highest integrity level.

The underlying rationale is grounded in probabilistic risk assessment. Even highly reliable physical communication media exhibit non-zero failure ranges due to hardware degradation, electromagnetic interference, connector faults, or transient disturbances. A single-channel architecture exposes the system to these failure modes without mitigation. A possible and widely employed solution is to use multiple parallel communication paths to increase the probability of the message arriving at least once at the destination.

2.2 The Data Distribution Service (DDS)

The Data Distribution Service (DDS) is a data-centric publish-subscribe middleware standard published by the Object Management Group (OMG) [24]. It is designed to facilitate scalable, real-time, and decoupled communication in distributed systems. It has seen broad adoption in safety-critical domains including aerospace applications [2], autonomous vehicles [1,11], industrial control systems, robotic platforms [30], and defense applications [3].

DDS employs a brokerless, dynamic peer-to-peer communication model according to Fig. 2, where *DataWriters* and *DataReaders* are decoupled and communicate using topics. The middleware handles discovery and matching of

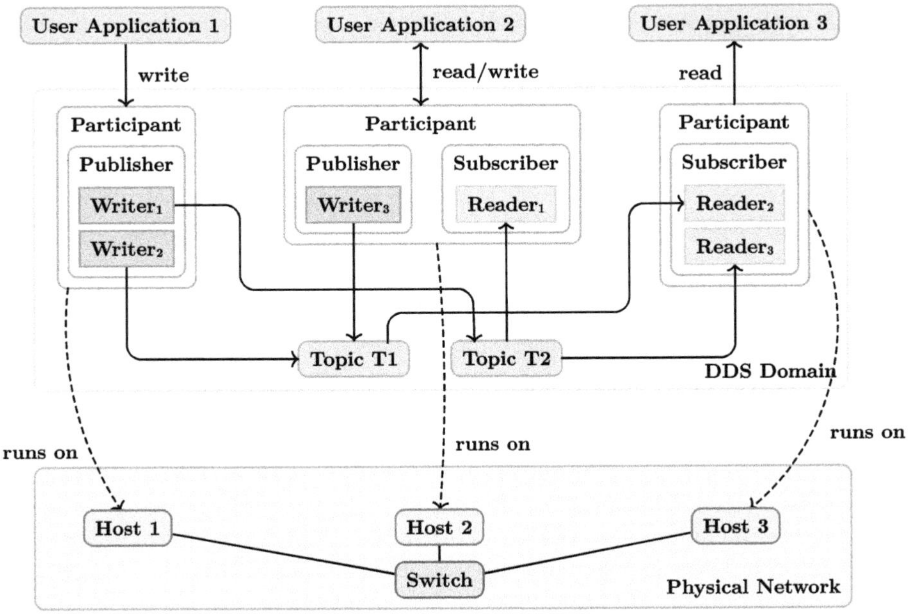

Fig. 2. Exemplary communication network with DDS with component based redundancy. Both Writer_1 and Writer_3 are publishing to the same topic T1 to increase its availability.

participants depending on topics and also the transport layer. A central mechanism that allows the matching of participants are *Quality of Service* (QoS) attributes, that steer the communication between participants. They allow the developer to express non-functional requirements of the communication including reliability, durability, deadline, liveliness and ownership. DDS offers a variety of QoS properties to express communication properties, as described in Table 1. The middleware enforces these policies at the transport level.

2.3 Component-Based Redundancy in DDS

DDS offers also the OWNERSHIP QoS property, that can be used for component-level redundancy. In this model, multiple *DataWriter* instances publish to the same topic, but with different "strength" attributes. When data arrives at the *DataReader*, it selects the packets with the highest strength value and drops the others. When this policy is set to EXCLUSIVE, a data-object can only be modified by the DataWriter with the highest strength value, while updates from other DataWriters are ignored. DataWriters that do not currently own a data-object are not explicitly notified and therefore continue publishing. As depicted in Fig. 3, multiple writers publish data to the same topic with different strength. In case of a failure one of the writers, the reader still receives updates from the functioning writer ensuring a seamless takeover. The LIVELINESS QoS policy

Table 1. Quality of Service properties and their purpose described in the OMG-DDS specification including our proposed extension for redundancy.

Name	Scope	Purpose
Time Based Filter	▲	Limits incoming data traffic rate to reduce bandwidth consumption.
Resource Limits	▲	Blocks a writer when the outgoing queue exceeds a configured threshold.
Reader and Writer Data Lifecycle	▲	Controls deletion of data associated with stale writers and readers.
Durability	•	Enables late-joining subscribers to receive previously published data samples.
History	•	Configures retention of historical data for retransmission or late-joining subscribers.
Reliability	•	Governs retransmission of data and acknowledgement of receipt.
Deadline	♦	Defines the maximum permitted inter-arrival period for data samples.
Lifespan	♦	Defines an expiration time after which data samples are considered invalid.
Latency Budget	♦	Indicates the urgency of data delivery to the middleware.
Transport Priority	♦	Sets the priority of the underlying transport mechanism, if supported.
Ownership and Ownership Strength	■	Restricts write access to a topic to a single owner under EXCLUSIVE access, with precedence determined by ownership strength.
Liveliness	★	Requires either the middleware or the application to periodically assert its liveliness to remote participants.
Destination Order	▽	Defines the ordering of topic changes by source or destination timestamp.
Redundancy	■	Allows to use multiple communication channels to increase availability.

▲ Resource Sensitivity • Data Availability ♦ Data Timeliness ■ Redundancy ★ Liveliness ▽ Determinism

controls the timing of the takeover procedure, since it determines up until what time a writer can be considered alive. If the current owner of a data-object is no longer "alive" the DataWriter with the next highest strength value becomes the new owner and can now modify the data-object.

2.4 Limitations of Component-Based Redundancy

The described behavior in Sect. 2.3 allows the implementation of redundancy concept, it faces several drawbacks:

Resource intensity Even DataWriters that do not own the corresponding data-object still need to publish updates to the topic. Therefore, they require the same amount of memory and computing power as the currently active writer. Because of this, the amount of redundant DataWriters also directly affects the performance of the entire system.

Random message ordering in case of takeover When a new writer becomes owner, sequence numbers and timestamps originate from a different source. Depending on the DESTINATION_ORDER policy, this may introduce discontinuities or temporary reordering at subscribers.

Certification challenges Certification challenges arise in high-integrity domains. Safety cases for SIL 4 systems typically require independence arguments between redundant channels. Logical writer redundancy within a single

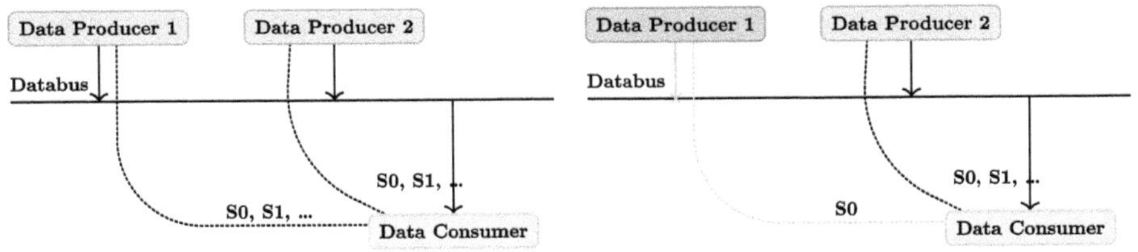

(a) Fault-free case. Both producers are sending samples to the consumer.

(b) Producer 1 has a fault an no longer produces samples.

Fig. 3. Multiple data producers are writing to the same consumer. The consumer filter the data based on the OWNERSHIP QoS policy in the fault-free case and relies on from producer 2 when producer 1 has a fault.

middleware stack does not provide sufficient architectural separation to satisfy such independence criteria.

Non-Deterministic Failover The failover mechanism depends on the LIVELINESS QoS policy detecting the fault of the current owner. This detection involves a configurable lease timeout. This inherently causes a timegap between a failure and the backup writer taking ownership. In safety-critical systems with hard real-time requirements, this non-deterministic recovery window may violate timing guarantees.

Missing network path redundancy All redundant DataWriters may still share the same physical network interface, switch, or transport channel. A link failure, network misconfiguration, or targeted denial-of-service attack can therefore simultaneously affect all writers. The redundancy is logical, not infrastructural, and thus insufficient for SIL 3/4 communication requirements.

3 Related Work

Research related to our proposed extension are distributed in three areas: extensions to the DDS standard itself mainly focusing on time-sensitive networking described in Sect. 3.1, communication redundancy mechanisms in other safety-critical protocols described in Sect. 3.2, and network-level frame replication techniques described in Sect. 3.3.

3.1 Extensions to the Data Distribution Service

Several recent contributions address deterministic communication behavior in DDS by integrating Time-Sensitive Networking (TSN). TSN is a set of IEEE 802.1 standards that provides bounded latency and deterministic delivery over Ethernet. The work of Li et al. [20], Agarwal et al. [9], Lu et al. [21] demonstrate that combining TSN scheduling mechanisms with DDS QoS policies can satisfy hard real-time requirements in industrial and automotive contexts. However, these contributions focus on latency determinism and bandwidth reservation, and do not address channel-level redundancy.

Bandwidth-aware extensions to DDS have also been proposed. Park et al. [25] introduces mechanisms to adapt DDS communication to available network bandwidth, improving resilience under congestion. While such approaches improve robustness under degraded or saturated network conditions, they remain confined to a single communication channel and therefore do not protect against channel-level failures.

Modern DDS implementations, including CycloneDDS [13], RTI Connext DDS [26], and Fast DDS [15], support binding to multiple network interfaces and can therefore receive data on several interfaces simultaneously. However, none of these implementations provide a standardized mechanism to transmit data redundantly across multiple channels in parallel. As a result, the sending path remains a single point of failure, and interoperability of any vendor-specific workaround across implementations is not guaranteed.

3.2 Redundancy in Safety-Critical Communication Protocols

Protocols specifically designed for high safety integrity levels commonly incorporate communication redundancy as a first-class feature. The RaSTA protocol [32], standardized for use in railway control applications, provides redundant transmission over multiple parallel channels to meet the requirements of EN 50159. Similarly, Bertieri et al. [12] propose a safety communication layer with redundant channel support targeted at railway and industrial automation systems. In general, all protocols follow the layered architectural principle to fulfill the requirements of EN 50159:

Redundancy Layer The lower layer focuses on providing highly available communication by utilizing multiple parallel transport channels. If one communication path fails or becomes unreliable, the system can continue operating through alternative channels, ensuring continuous service availability.

Reliability Layer The upper layer implements the core safety mechanisms required for critical railway applications. It monitors the communication latency of the communication channel and ensures reliable message exchange.

However, both approaches are point-to-point communication protocols and therefore lack the scalable, brokerless publish-subscribe architecture that makes DDS attractive for large distributed systems. Porting their redundancy concepts to a DDS environment is non-trivial and has not been addressed in the literature. While Meszlényi et al. [22] already investigated the use of the DDS protocol in railway systems as replacement for the RaSTA protocol, in their work they bypass the challenge of multipath redundancy by introducing the replication layer above the DDS middleware layer. In their solution, multiple DDS instances in multiple subnets send the packets independently. While this solution achieves redundancy without altering the DDS protocol, it requires fundamental changes in the network and software infrastructure.

A further concern with especially the RaSTA protocol is the use of outdated cryptographic standards. A security analysis of the RaSTA protocol [17] reveals reliance on outdated cryptographic primitives, raising questions about their suitability in adversarial environments. This motivates the adoption of modern middleware standards such as DDS, which can leverage contemporary security extensions, as the foundation for safety-critical communication.

3.3 Network-Level Frame Replication

At the network layer, IEEE 802.1CB defines a standard for Frame Replication and Elimination for Reliability (FRER), which replicates Ethernet frames across multiple paths and eliminates duplicates at the receiver to achieve seamless redundancy [6]. Fejes et al. [16] propose a lightweight implementation of this mechanism using the eXpress Data Path (XDP) framework, enabling high-performance frame replication directly in the Linux kernel without dedicated hardware.

While IEEE 802.1CB and its implementations provide robust link-layer redundancy, they operate below the middleware layer and require network infrastructure that supports the standard. In contrast, our proposed extension implements redundancy within the DDS middleware itself, making it deployable on commodity IP networks without modifications to the underlying network infrastructure, and exposing redundancy configuration through the familiar DDS QoS interface.

4 DDS Redundancy Extension

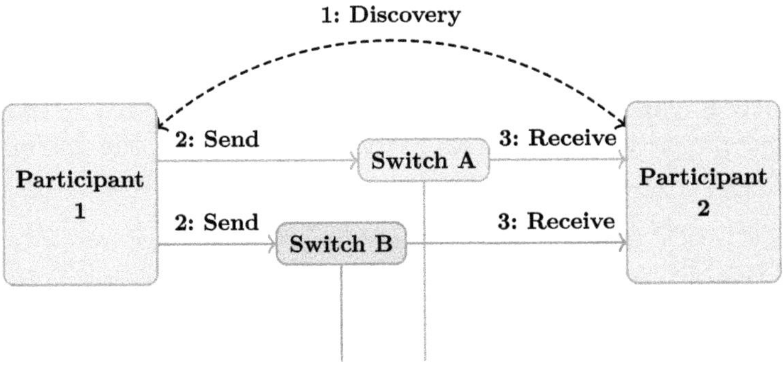

Fig. 4. Protocol changes addressed by introducing multipath redundancy for DDS.

In order to add the use of redundant communication channels to DDS, we identify three key challenges also depicted in Fig. 4:

1. Discovery of redundant locators

2. Multiplication of messages at the publisher
3. De-duplication of messages at receiver side

In the following, we describe each key challenge and our proposed solution under the assumption that multiple communication links between hosts are available and should be used. We further require compatibility of our extension with existing DDS implementations. In its core design, our proposal is similar to the RaSTA protocol described in Sect. 3.2 and relies on sequence numbers (SN) for message deduplication. For our experimental verification, we used a prototypical DDS implementation based on embeddedRTPS [23].

For our design, we assume the use of the DDS Security extension. It provides authentication, integrity protection and replay protection for all messages. Under this model, an attacker may delay, drop, or reorder packets on individual communication paths but cannot forge, modify, or inject valid protocol messages. The redundancy extension therefore operates on authenticated traffic only and treats all received copies as cryptographically valid instances of the same DDS message. Its fault model is limited to omission faults and independent path failures across redundant channels, while Byzantine message manipulation is assumed to be mitigated by the DDS Security layer.

4.1 Redundant Discovery Extension

Before participants can communicate directly, they need to identify each other during the discovery phase. The DDS standard offers the subprotocols Simple Participant Discovery Protocol (SPDP) and Simple Endpoint Discovery Protocol (SEDP). In order for our extension to remain transparent to the other DDS processes, our implementation uses only one interface for discovery messages. We extend the SEDP protocol with the announcement of the redundant interface locators. The DDS discovery process uses standardized frames for discovery. Our extension extends the default frames SEDP message frames with additional `Locator_t` fields to announce the presence of redundant locators. The new proposed structure of the SEDP messages is depicted in Table 3. Implementations without our extension ignore the additional field can are able to communicate in a fallback manner (Table 2).

4.2 Data Writing

Whenever a message is sent redundantly, it passes two stages:

- SN number assignment and
- replication according to the number of interfaces.

This SN is shared by all copies of a single message, and will be used to identify duplicates on the receiving side. The redundancy SN is assigned by the thread-safe *MessageFactory* component in our implementation, which ensures that each new message receives a unique SN. In order to improve the efficiency of the deduplication of messages, our implementation adds the additional redundancy SN as

Table 2. Descriptions of the data-fields contained in SEDP messages extended with redundant unicast locators.

Attribute	Type	Description
Unicast Locator	FullLengthLocator	Locator used for sending non-redundant data-messages
Additional Redundant Unicast Locators	FullLengthLocator[*]	List of locators available for use for redundant communication
Multicast Locator	FullLengthLocator	Locator used for sending messages using multicast
Topic	char[*]	Name of the topic used to communicate
Data Type	char[*]	Name of the data type contained in data-messages
Entity Key Hash	EntityId_t	Hash used to identify the modified data-object
GUID Prefix	GuiId_t	Unique identifier of this participant
Optional QoS Settings	N/A	The QoS policies set/requested by this participant
Security	bool	The security settings used by this participant

part of the main message header. Once the header of an incoming message has been processed, copies of a previously seen message can be immediately identified without the need to handle any attached submessages. When a message is published by a *DataWriter*, it is duplicated for each combination of the available local and remote interfaces and sent over the corresponding channels.

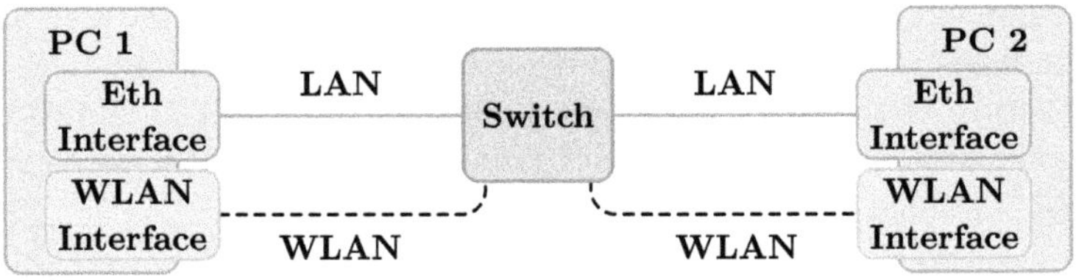

Fig. 5. Experiment topology for enabling multipath redundancy.

4.3 Data Reading

Our extension uses the redundancy sequence numbers to identify and subsequently ignore duplicated messages. Each participant stores the last received redundancy SN of other participants. When a message is received, the attached redundancy SN is compared to the last stored SN of the sending participant. If the redundancy SN of an incoming message has been seen before, that message is ignored. Therefore, a message will only be processed if it is the first of the redundant copies to arrive, making duplication of messages transparent for the following message processing steps. However, in order to avoid conflicts with the identification of missing messages, defined as part of the Reliability QoS, our extension does not react to messages arriving out of order and instead only removes copies of previously seen messages.

5 Evaluation

We evaluate the presented extension in a series of experiments. In Sect. 5.1 we describe the experimental setup, including the network topology and other software components used in the experiment. In Sect. 5.2 we describe the experiments regarding reliability and compare our solution based on metrics (a) message loss and (b) number of retransmissions. Further in Sect. 5.3 we examine the performance of our results using round-trip-time (RTT) measurements and show the memory implications of our extension in Sect. 5.4.

5.1 Setup

Our experimental setup contains two computers (PC_1, PC_2) that are connected over an Ethernet switch as depicted in Fig. 5. In our experiments we test our extension in a heterogeneous network. Both computers communicate using wired Ethernet connection with a transfer speed of 1 Gbit s−1. Additionally when the redundancy extension is enabled, each computer uses a wireless Ethernet connection transporting data at a rate of up to 135 Mbit s−1 with a frequency of 2.4 GHz PC_1 always acts as the publisher and runs on Windows 10 Operating System with an Intel Core i7-10700F processor and a total of 16 GB of RAM. PC_2 uses the Windows 11 Home as its operating system and is equipped with an Intel Core i5-12400 processor and 16 GB RAM. Both PCs use Windows Subsystem for Linux Version 1 in order to execute the experiments. The Publisher sends data messages with a total size of 60 bytes as well as heartbeat messages with a size of 52 bytes with a frequency of 2 Hz representing a safety-critical control function. Both the publisher and the subscriber communicated using the "HelloWorld" topic, publishing and receiving messages respectively. The same topic was also used by the subscriber to acknowledge incoming data messages.

5.2 Experiment Reliability

In this experiment we aim to measure the communication reliability. Therefore we evaluate our solution empirically using chaos testing. In this method, random but controlled faults are injected into the transport channels.

Experiment Setting. To simulate an unstable network, the chaos testing tool Clumsy [31] was used that is able to inject controlled faults into the network communication. Incoming messages on both communication channels were dropped at a random probability. Therefore, both the wired and wireless Ethernet links of our setup were equally affected. For our tests only messages sent by the publisher were dropped before reaching the subscriber. In all experiments the RELIABILITY QoS property was enabled. This QoS property is responsible for a reliable communication by retransmitting not arrived messages and should be always enabled for safety-relevant communication. We measure the reliability with a message drop rate of 10%, 20%, 30%, 40% and 50%. Our preliminary experiments showed that a drop rate above 50% without redundancy extension results in a complete collapse of the communication between the participants. Protocol relevant messages (heartbeat, SEDP and SPDP) were not transmitted and hence the participants were unable to connect.

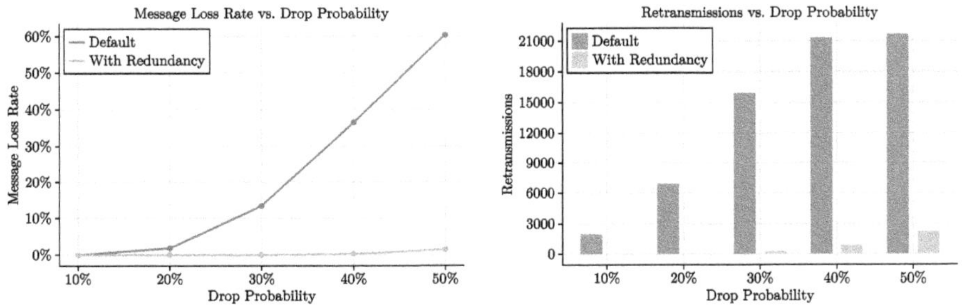

(a) Message loss ratio in dependence of the message drop probability.

(b) Number of retransmissions depending on the message drop probability.

Fig. 6. Experiment results comparing the default DDS behavior and our redundancy extension.

Table 3. Comparison of communication reliability between the default DDS and our redundancy extension.

	Default		**Extension**	
Drop rate	**Retrans.**	**Loss Rate**	**Retrans.**	**Loss Rate**
10%	1969	0.0%	3	0.0%
20%	6884	1.9%	52	0.0%
30%	15943	13.4%	252	0.0%
40%	21321	36.55%	854	0.29%
50%	21659	60.34%	2239	1.5%

Results. Figure 6 depicts the result of our experiment and the detailed results are shown in Table 3. The table shows the number of retransmissions for every 10 000 messages and the loss rate relative to the total amount of messages in dependence of the message drop rate. The required amount of retransmissions is significantly lower when using our redundancy extension: Our extension improved the communication reliability by lowering the number of retransmissions issued by the reliable communication setting of the middleware:

- In the worst case scenario with a drop probability of 50%, our extension required 89.66% less retransmissions than the default case.
- For lower drop probabilities, our extension is consistently able to reduce the retransmission count by approximately 96%.

Similarly, the rate at which a message could not be recovered at all was also lowered when the redundancy extension was enabled. Our extension achieved to avoid completely losing any messages for drop rates of up to 30%. In comparison 13.40% of messages were unrecoverable when only relying on the default DDS Reliability QoS feature.

5.3 Experiment Latency

In order to measure the impact our extension on efficiency, we measure the round-trip-time (RTT) of messages.

Experiment Setting. The setup for the tests includes a single publisher sending data messages to one subscriber. Once a data message was received by the subscriber, an acknowledgment message is sent back to the publisher and the time difference is recorded (Fig. 7 and Table 4).

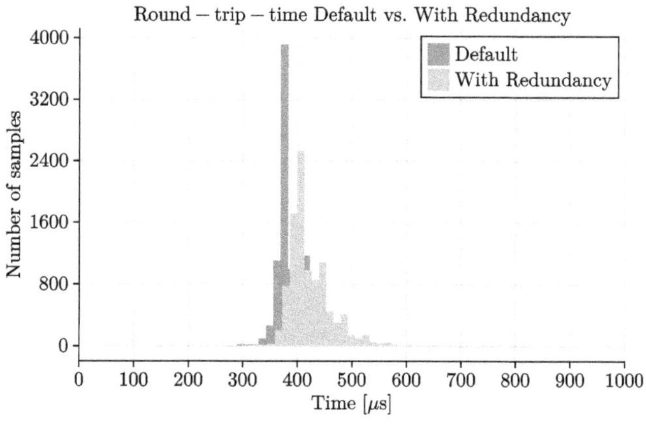

Fig. 7. Comparison of the RTT without (Default) and with our redundancy extension.

Table 4. Round-trip-time statistics comparing default DDS to our redundancy extension.

Property	Default RTT [μs]	With Redundancy RTT [μs]
Mean	397.05	423.25
Std. Dev.	185.60	48.19
Min	143.20	279.81
Max	13449.98	1610.24
95th Pctl.	460.03	499.97
99th Pctl.	520.19	570.11

Results. When measuring the time between sending a data message and receiving the corresponding acknowledgment, our extension caused an increase in the average RTT of approximately 6.60%. When examining the 95th and 99th percentile of measured RTT values, our extension caused an increase of approximately 8.68% and 9.58% respectively.

5.4 RAM Requirements

The final metric that was used to evaluate our implementation was static and dynamic memory consumption.

Experiment Setting. For the measurement of the dynamic memory, the tool "Valgrind" was used to find the peak memory consumption during runtime. We used up to five publishers, that all write to the same topic. At the same time, up to five subscribers listened to incoming updates for that same topic. The publisher sends 10 000 messages.

Experiment Results. The baseline memory consumed without redundancy extension was 28.73 MB for both publishers and subscribers. The memory consumption did not increase when adding other participants, since the implementation aims to be constant-memory. Corresponding data is stored in fixed-size arrays and allocated statically, as depicted in Fig. 8. When using the redundancy extension, the baseline memory consumption was 28.81 MB. For each participant present in the network, an additional 112 bytes were allocated in order to store the redundant connection data. This additional data included the redundant locators and the redundancy SNs stored for each other participant. While two subscribers or two publishers would not communicate with one another, additional space was still reserved upon first contacting each other during the discovery phase. In total, our extension increased the baseline memory consumption by approximately 1.00% with an additional 112 bytes per participant, showing only a negligible impact.

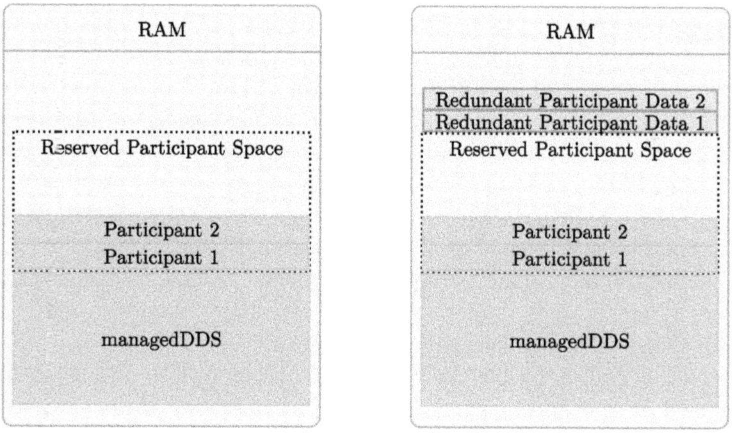

Fig. 8. Memory layout in a network with 2 participants for default (left) and redundant (right) configurations.

5.5 Discussion

The results of Experiment 1 show a significant improvement when operating over an instable network. Even when using only one additional redundant interface per participant, the amount of retransmissions required for sending data remains comparatively low even when 50% of messages were dropped. This also results in less messages being lost overall and therefore ensuring more available communication.

When measuring the RTT of messages we found that our extension increases the time needed for processing messages. This increase can be explained as a result of the added steps for duplicating and deduplicating messages. While our extension does increase the RTT of messages, the measured impact on average was still below 7%, showing no significant loss in efficiency. Finally, our analysis of the RAM consumption of our extension revealed that each new participant in the network increases the memory needed by all other participants. Since our extension can be implemented with constant memory, it is possible to calculate the largest amount of needed RAM depending on the maximum amount of participants in the network.

6 Conclusion

In this paper, we proposed a communication channel-redundancy extension to DDS that addresses this gap at the middleware level. Our extension introduces an augmented endpoint discovery protocol that announces redundant locators to remote participants, a message replication layer that assigns shared sequence numbers and transmits copies over all available interfaces and the belonging deduplication mechanism at the receiver that ensures transparency to the application layer. The extension requires no to existing DDS application logic and the proposed changes aim to keep interoperability with unextended implementations.

Our experimental evaluation demonstrates that the extension substantially improves communication availability under adverse network conditions. At a packet drop rate of 50%, the extension reduced retransmissions by 89.66% and cut the message loss rate from 60.34% to 1.5%. At drop rates up to 30%, message loss was eliminated entirely. The overhead introduced under nominal conditions is modest: the median round-trip time increased by approximately 7.88%, with the 99th percentile increasing by 9.58%. Memory overhead is constant per additional participant (112 bytes), making the resource footprint predictable and suitable for constrained embedded deployments.

These results indicate that communication channel redundancy can be effectively realized at the middleware level without requiring changes to the underlying network infrastructure or the application layer. This approach offers clear advantages for high-integrity deployments: redundancy behavior is expressed through a standardized QoS interface, making it auditable and amenable to safety certification.

Several directions remain open for future work. First, formalizing our extension as a proposed addendum to the OMG DDS specification would enable standardized, cross-vendor adoption and strengthen its role in safety certification arguments. Second, the frame replication and de-duplication logic can be extended with operating-system specific improvements, like acceleration using kernel-bypass techniques such as AF_XDP, which could reduce per-message processing overhead further for high-frequency control loops. Third, future work should propose and evaluate a backward-compatible fault-tolerant discovery mechanism that is able to announce all locators on multiple interfaces.

Declaration of competing interests. The authors have no competing interests to declare that are relevant to the content of this article.

References

1. Adlink DDS vortex opensplice. https://www.adlinktech.com/en/vortex-opensplice-data-distribution-service. Accessed 18 Sept 2024
2. Kongsberg defence and aerospace intercom DDS. https://www.kongsberg.com/kda/what-we-do/defence-and-security/c4isr/intercom-dds/. Accessed 18 Sept 2024
3. Rti connext professional. https://www.rti.com/products/connext-professional. Accessed 18 Sept 2024
4. Aircraft data network, part 7: Avionics full-duplex switched ethernet (afdx) network (2005)
5. Railway applications - communication, signalling and processing systems - safety-related communication in transmission systems (2010)
6. Ieee standard for local and metropolitan area networks–frame replication and elimination for reliability (2017). https://standards.ieee.org/ieee/802.1CB/5703/
7. Road vehicles - functional safety (2018)

8. DIN EN 61850-5:2025-01, kommunikationsnetze und -systeme für die automatisierung in der elektrischen energieversorgung - teil 5: Kommunikationsanforderungen für funktionen und gerätemodelle (IEC 61850-5:2013 + AMD1:2022); deutsche fassung EN 61850-5:2013 + a1:2022. Tech. rep., DIN Media GmbH, Berlin (2024)
9. Agarwal, T., Niknejad, P., Barzegaran, M.R., Vanfretti, L.: Multi-level time-sensitive networking (TSN) using the data distribution services (DDS) for synchronized three-phase measurement data transfer. IEEE Access **7**, 131407–131417 (2019). https://doi.org/10.1109/ACCESS.2019.2939497
10. Antonova, G., Frisk, L., Tournier, J.C.: Communication redundancy for substation automation. In: 64th Annual Conference for Protective Relay Engineers, pp. 344–355. (2011). https://doi.org/10.1109/CPRE.2011.6035636
11. AUTOSAR: Specification of data distribution service for classic platform - autosar cp r24-11 (2024). https://www.autosar.org/fileadmin/standards/R24-11/CP/AUTOSAR_CP_SWS_DataDistributionService.pdf, aUTOSAR_CP_SWS_DataDistributionService, Document ID 1069
12. Bertieri, D., Ceccarelli, A., Zoppi, T., Mungiello, I., Barbareschi, M., Bondavalli, A.: Development and validation of a safe communication protocol compliant to railway standards. J. Braz. Comput. Soc. **27**(1) (2021)
13. Eclipse Cyclone DDS Contributors: Eclipse cyclone dds. GitHub repository; open-source implementation of the OMG DDS specification (2026). https://github.com/eclipse-cyclonedds/cyclonedds. Accessed 27 Feb 2026
14. Endeley, R., Fleming, T., Jin, N., Fehringer, G., Cammish, S.: A smart gateway enabling OPC UA and DDS interoperability. In: 2019 IEEE SmartWorld, Ubiquitous Intelligence & Computing, Advanced & Trusted Computing, Scalable Computing & Communications, Cloud & Big Data Computing, Internet of People and Smart City Innovation (SmartWorld/SCALCOM/UIC/ATC/CBDCom/IOP/SCI), pp. 88–93 (2019). https://doi.org/10.1109/SmartWorld-UIC-ATC-SCALCOM-IOP-SCI.2019.00058
15. eProsima: eprosima fast dds. GitHub repository for a C++ implementation of the OMG DDS standard (2026). https://github.com/eProsima/Fast-DDS. Accessed 27 Feb 2026
16. Fejes, F., Orosi, F., Varga, B., Farkas, J.: Lightweight implementation of per-packet service protection in ebpf/xdp (2023). https://netdevconf.info/0x17/25
17. Heinrich, M., Vieten, J., Arul, T., Katzenbeisser, S.: Security analysis of the Rasta safety protocol. In: 2018 IEEE International Conference on Intelligence and Security Informatics (ISI), pp. 199–204 (2018). https://doi.org/10.1109/ISI.2018.8587371
18. International Electrotechnical Commission: Functional safety of electrical/electronic/programmable electronic safety-related systems (2010)
19. Kugele S., Hettler, D., Peter, J.: Data-centric communication and containerization for future automotive software architectures. In: 2018 IEEE International Conference on Software Architecture (ICSA), pp. 65–6509. IEEE (2018)
20. Li, B., Zhu, Y., Yao, X., Jiang, C., Lu, K., Sun, Z.: Enabling deterministic transmission for dds by leveraging ieee 802.1qbv time-sensitive networking. Computer Networks **261**, 111128 (2025). https://doi.org/10.1016/j.comnet.2025.111128, https://www.sciencedirect.com/science/article/pii/S1389128625000969
21. Lu, J., Zhu, H., Huang, T., Zhang, H., Han, G.: TS-DDS: data distribution service (DDS) over in-vehicle time-sensitive networking (tsn) mechanism research. In: 2023 15th International Conference on Communication Software and Networks (ICCSN), pp. 30–36 (2023). https://doi.org/10.1109/ICCSN57992.2023.10297343

22. Meszlényi, L., Christl, M., Püllen, D., Katzenbeisser, S.: Academic paper secure railway communication: Adapting dds for safety-critical signaling applications. Tagungsband p. 35 (2025)
23. Meszlényi, L., Kahle, J., Püllen, D., Kowalewski, S., Katzenbeisser, S., Kampmann, A.: Towards timing isolation for mixed-criticality communication in software-defined vehicles. In: 2025 IEEE International Automated Vehicle Validation Conference (IAVVC), pp. 1–8 (2025). https://doi.org/10.1109/IAVVC61942.2025.11219644
24. Object Management Group (OMG): OMG Data Distribution Service (DDS) Standard, Version 1.4 (2015). http://www.omg.org/spec/DDS/1.4, oMG Document Number formal/15-04-10
25. Park, H.S., Jang, J.H., Kim, J.D., Jung, H.I., Lee, S.H.: Bandwidth-aware DDS communication in wlan. In: 2012 International Conference on Systems and Informatics (ICSAI2012), pp. 1542–1546 (2012). https://doi.org/10.1109/ICSAI.2012.6223332
26. Real-Time Innovations, Inc.: DDS standard — data distribution service for real-time systems. Product page describing the Data Distribution Service (DDS) connectivity standard (2026). https://www.rti.com/products/dds-standard. Accessed 27 Feb 2026
27. Rother, B., et al.: Analysis of safety-critical communication protocols for on-premise sil4 cloud in railways. In: Collart-Dutilleul, S., Haxthausen, A.E., Lecomte, T. (eds.) RSSRail 2022. LNCS, vol. 13294, pp. 211–220. Springer, Cham (2022). https://doi.org/10.1007/978-3-031-05814-1_15
28. Schmidt, D.C., van't Hag, H.: Addressing the challenges of mission-critical information management in next-generation net-centric pub/sub systems with opensplice DDS. In: 2008 IEEE International Symposium on Parallel and Distributed Processing, pp. 1–8 (2008). https://doi.org/10.1109/IPDPS.2008.4536567
29. Schneider, S., Farabaugh, B.: Is DDS for you? A Whitepaper by Real-Time Innovations, pp. 1–5 (2009)
30. Stanford Artificial Intelligence Laboratory et al.: Robotic operating system. https://www.ros.org
31. Tao, C.: Clumsy 0.3 (2022). https://jagt.github.io/clumsy/. Accessed 03 Mar 2026
32. in DIN und VDE, D.K.E.E.I.: Din vde v 0831-200 vde v 0831-200:2015-06 electric signalling systems for railways (2015). https://www.vde-verlag.de/standards/0800234/din-vde-v-0831-200-vde-v-0831-200-2015-06.html

Traffic Analysis and Intrusion Detection

WardenMind: Flow-Driven Bayesian Detection of Storage Covert Channels

Baptiste Bazin[1], Alexis Bonnecaze[1], Mehdi Chourib[1], and Kevin Thiry-Atighehchi[2(✉)]

[1] Aix Marseille Univ, CNRS, I2M, Marseille, France
{baptiste.bazin,alexis.bonnecaze,mehdi.chourib}@univ-amu.fr
[2] CREA, École de l'Air et de l'Espace, Base aérienne 701, Salon-de-Provence, France
kevin.thiry@ecole-air.fr

Abstract. Covert channels enable stealthy data exfiltration inside otherwise legitimate traffic. In practice, a warden cannot block all covert exfiltration without harming legitimate traffic. The realistic goal is therefore to reduce leakage while preserving acceptable Quality of Service. We present WardenMind, a *software* warden designed to be deployable by resource-constrained operators. It relies only on standard IPFIX records and commodity software, without programmable hardware or network-stack changes. Only a small fraction of high-risk flows triggers costly interventions. For each flow, WardenMind computes a calibrated covert-risk estimate. It then selects among progressively stronger actions with a Bayesian cost model that balances residual leakage against QoS impact. The policy is updated online so that fixed thresholds do not have to be retuned every time traffic conditions change. On a controlled flow-level dataset built from MAWI traffic and CIC-Bell DNS exfiltration traces, WardenMind achieves strong detection performance, reaching 92.4% TPR with 0.47% FPR with two actions, and 81.2% TPR with 0.33% FPR with three actions, while capturing only 0.85% of legitimate traffic.

Keywords: Network covert channels · Flow-based detection · Network warden · Bayesian decision theory

1 Introduction

A network covert channel (NCC) enables information transfer in a way that is not intended or permitted by the system design, typically by exploiting hidden or unexpected network behavior. In practice, such channels can conceal command-and-control exchanges or data exfiltration within otherwise legitimate traffic. Detection alone is not enough. The defense must also make covert communication harder without penalizing benign traffic too much [26].

NCCs are commonly divided into two main forms. *Storage channels* encode information in protocol-visible fields, whereas *timing channels* encode information in packet timing [15,26]. In this paper, we focus on *storage covert channels*

S. Nadjm-Tehrani et al. (Eds.): ARES 2026, LNCS 16898, pp. 203–224, 2027.
https://doi.org/10.1007/978-3-032-36874-4_10

because their effects are more naturally reflected in deployable flow telemetry than fine-grained timing behavior.

A *warden* is a network element whose objective is to prevent, detect, or disrupt covert communication. Whether it only observes traffic or actively modifies it, a deployable warden must preserve *quality of service (QoS)*, including *latency*, *jitter*, *throughput*, and *packet loss*. It must therefore balance mitigation benefit against operational cost [26]. Classic active-warden approaches based on traffic normalization can eliminate many opportunities for covert storage [8], but always-on packet-level intervention is costly and difficult to generalize in production environments.

At the same time, prior work suggests that purely local reasoning is often insufficient. Cabaj *et al.* [3] show that distributed network covert channels can spread hidden communication across flows, protocols, hosts, or hiding methods to improve stealth and evade detection. Wendzel *et al.* [23] show in parallel that many published covert-channel techniques reduce to recurring patterns, motivating countermeasures beyond ad hoc channel-by-channel defenses. Adaptive-warden work further shows that fixed rules become brittle as traffic and covert behavior evolve [5,14]. Thus, single-flow reasoning is often insufficient, yet the defense must remain lightweight.

NetWarden [24] is a useful reference point. It shows that covert-channel mitigation can preserve QoS through an inline fast-path/slow-path design, but relies on programmable datapaths and direct packet-level intervention. We study a complementary operating point: a software-only warden built on *Internet Protocol Flow Information eXport (IPFIX)* [2]. IPFIX and related flow-monitoring frameworks are widely used for scalable network observation and security analysis [10,22]. This makes them attractive for deployable covert-channel defense, but it also changes the control problem. Flow records are the natural units of observation, whereas mitigation is better expressed over recurring traffic contexts such as services, protected source scopes, or destination ranges. We treat these contexts as broader *traffic classes*. Our design therefore uses flows as units of evidence and traffic classes as units of control. It does not replace stronger packet-level defenses. Instead, flow records indicate where stronger mitigation is worth applying, so intrusive normalization can remain selective and limited to classes whose recent behavior justifies intervention. This passive-warden perspective is consistent with prior analytics-based work [11].

Our Approach. How can a deployable warden driven by flow records turn observations at flow level into mitigation decisions that remain both affordable and effective against covert storage behavior? WardenMind addresses this question with a pipeline that separates *flow-level observation* from *traffic-class-level control*. Rather than attaching mitigation directly to individual completed flow records, it extracts evidence at flow granularity, aggregates that evidence over traffic classes, and then selects the least costly mitigation action for the corresponding class.

WardenMind has four stages. It first collects IPFIX records and derives flow-level features designed to capture indicators of storage-channel manipulation. It then aggregates these features into a suspicion score and calibrates that score into an interpretable risk estimate. This matters because downstream action selection is based on expected cost. Raw scores are useful for ranking, whereas calibrated risk estimates are better suited to cost-sensitive decisions [16,25]. WardenMind then aggregates recent flow-level evidence at the level of a traffic class, since IPFIX provides evidence at flow granularity while mitigation is more naturally expressed over broader control units. Finally, it chooses one action from {ALLOW, CAPTURE, NORMALIZE} using Bayesian cost-sensitive decision-making. Following Elkan's minimum-risk framework [7], the selected action minimizes expected loss under explicit covert-loss and benign-impact costs, which can be updated online as traffic conditions and operator priorities change.

The design has three useful properties. Evidence extraction remains lightweight and driven by flow records, while stronger interventions are reserved for traffic classes whose recent evidence indicates elevated risk. Decisions are *graded and interpretable* rather than based on brittle thresholds. The system also accounts for QoS by design. It prefers the lightest effective action and limits user visible performance regressions.

Contributions. We make four main contributions. First, we introduce an IPFIX-driven architecture for storage covert channel mitigation that cleanly separates flow-level observation from traffic-class-level control, making the design both deployable and operationally meaningful. Second, we design a feature extraction and calibration pipeline that converts flow observations into calibrated risk estimates suitable for decision-making rather than mere ranking. Third, we cast mitigation as a Bayesian cost-sensitive action-selection problem over traffic classes, so that the trade-off between leakage reduction and QoS impact is explicit in the policy itself. Fourth, through experiments on a controlled flow-level dataset built from MAWI benign traffic [9,13] and CIC-Bell DNS exfiltration traces [20], we show that the proposed adaptive Bayesian warden achieves up to 92.4% TPR with 0.47% FPR, and 81.2% TPR with 0.33% FPR while capturing only 0.85% of legitimate traffic, significantly improving the operational trade-off between detection effectiveness and intervention cost compared with naive and static Bayesian baselines.

Outline. Section 2 reviews prior work on covert channels, wardens, and flow-based monitoring. Section 3 presents the WardenMind pipeline, including feature extraction, calibration, traffic-class aggregation, Bayesian action selection, and online adaptation. Section 4 evaluates the approach. Section 5 concludes the paper.

2 Related Work

The warden model is classically introduced through Simmons' prisoners' problem [21]. Zander *et al.* [26] already emphasize a constraint that remains central today. A useful defense must reduce covert capacity while remaining deployable and limiting collateral impact on legitimate traffic. Caviglione [4] shows that many countermeasures remain tied to specific channel constructions, which limits their generality and scalability in operational settings.

A classic line of defense is traffic normalization. Fisk *et al.* [8] introduced the active-warden model and showed that rewriting protocol fields to stricter canonical forms can eliminate many opportunities for covert storage. This remains a relevant approach, but it also has a practical limitation: always-on per-packet intervention is costly, intrusive, and difficult to generalize in production environments.

This limitation becomes more apparent when the threat itself is no longer strictly local. Cabaj *et al.* [3] show that covert channels can be distributed across multiple flows, protocols, or hosts, thereby reducing visibility and weakening purely local detection strategies. A related lesson comes from the pattern-based literature. Wendzel *et al.* [23] show that many covert channel techniques can be reduced to a smaller set of recurring patterns, which suggests that defenses should not be developed only channel by channel, but also around broader traffic families and reusable mitigation policies. These works show why reasoning above the level of an individual flow is necessary. When covert behavior is distributed across multiple flows or only becomes visible through recurring traffic patterns, a deployable defense benefits from operating on aggregated traffic scopes rather than on isolated records.

Recent work also suggests that wardens benefit from being adaptive rather than purely static. Chourib, Wendzel, and Mazurczyk [5] argue that fixed rule sets are insufficient against adaptive covert peers and propose a warden strategy that adjusts its behavior to observed traffic. Repetto *et al.* [19] also illustrate the value of structured observation and statistical indicators for covert channel analysis.

Our work also builds on the practical literature on flow telemetry. IPFIX is standardized as a protocol for exporting flow information from an exporting process to a collecting process [2]. More broadly, Hofstede *et al.* [10] show that NetFlow/IPFIX provides a scalable and widely deployed observability pipeline, while Sperotto *et al.* [22] explain why flow records can preserve enough information for security monitoring without incurring the full cost of packet-level inspection. These references support the idea that an IPFIX based warden can be realistic even if it does not operate inline on every packet. They also help motivate the distinction between units of observation and units of control. In an IPFIX setting, the exported flow record is naturally the elementary unit of observation, whereas mitigation is more naturally expressed over recurring traffic contexts such as services, destinations, or broader traffic classes. In practice, deployable network controls are typically applied to such recurring contexts rather than to a single completed record. In the same spirit, Iglesias *et al.* [11] study covert channel detection in what they explicitly describe as a passive-warden scenario, showing that useful detection can be performed without directly modifying the traffic.

NetWarden [24] shows that selective disruption can reduce covert capacity while preserving TCP performance through a fast-path/slow-path architecture.

At the same time, NetWarden occupies a different design point from ours: its mitigation logic is inline and tied to programmable datapath support. Rather than assuming a programmable fast path, we consider a software-only setting based on exported flow records and decisions taken over traffic classes. A broader systems view also appears in recent work on warden network functions. Litzinger *et al.* [12] study how such functions can be deployed and optimized at network scale, a direction that is consistent with transforming flow-level observations into decisions taken over more aggregated traffic scopes.

Beyond the covert channel and warden literature, our framework also relates to work on cost-sensitive decision-making. Elkan [7] formalizes the Bayes minimum-risk perspective, in which an estimate of event likelihood is combined with an explicit cost model to minimize expected loss. Complementarily, the literature on probabilistic calibration highlights the value of well calibrated estimates when they are later used in decision rules [16,25].

Overall, our work lies at the intersection of these lines of research. Compared with packet-centric active wardens [8], it avoids deep packet intervention for most traffic by relying on IPFIX telemetry as the primary observation substrate. Compared with NetWarden [24], it trades inline packet-level control for a software-only, flow-driven design. Compared with prior flow-based monitoring and security-analysis pipelines [10,22], it does not stop at per-flow scoring, but explicitly aggregates flow-level evidence into traffic classes and links that evidence to cost-aware action selection. This positions the design for environments where deployability, scalability, and operational transparency matter alongside mitigation capability.

3 System Design

This section describes the assumptions and architecture of WardenMind.

Threat Model. We consider an attacker exfiltrating data through storage covert channels embedded in legitimate-looking traffic. The warden observes IPFIX records only and is not given the exact embedding rule or any channel-specific signature. It therefore acts as an uninformed warden, relying on IPFIX-visible deviations within traffic classes. Timing channels and statistically indistinguishable modifications are outside our scope.

Architecture Overview. Our adaptive warden targets covert storage channels and is designed for scalable deployment under limited operational resources. The architecture operates solely on flow-level summaries exported via IPFIX, avoiding deep packet inspection while remaining practical on high-speed links. The system follows a four-stage pipeline: IPFIX collection and preprocessing, feature extraction and suspicion scoring, probabilistic risk estimation, and Bayesian cost-aware decision-making with online adaptation. Each stage refines flow evidence to enable selective interventions under QoS constraints.

3.1 IPFIX Collection and Preprocessing

The first stage ingests IPFIX flow records. These records compress packet-level activity into compact flow summaries. This is the main reason IPFIX is attractive operationally. Instead of inspecting every packet, the warden reasons over a much smaller stream of structured records.

IPFIX is template-based: exporters advertise which Information Elements appear in each flow record. We use standard IPFIX as specified in RFC 7011, with Information Elements drawn from the IPFIX information model and the IANA IPFIX Information Elements registry [2,6]. In practice, the fields available to the warden depend on the template deployed by the exporter, so two networks can both use IPFIX while exporting different information. Most exporters nevertheless provide a common core. This core includes flow start and end timestamps, the 5-tuple, the transport protocol, packet and byte counters, and TCP control information that summarizes flags such as SYN, FIN, and RST, often encoded as a compact bitmask. A bitmask indicates whether a flag appeared at least once, but it does not provide per-flag packet counts. Ratios and entropy features therefore require exporters that provide per-flag counters via richer templates. Other fields can be present but are less uniform across deployments. A common example is a TTL value that summarizes packets in the flow, such as the initial TTL or an average TTL. Richer summaries, such as a TTL distribution within the flow, are typically not part of default templates and may require exporter-specific extensions or custom templates. Entropy-style features for TTL or IPID require distributional summaries (e.g., histograms) that are not part of typical IPFIX deployments and are enabled only when supported by the exporter/template.

Preprocessing improves robustness and reduces noise before analysis. We normalize timestamps to a consistent reference, discard records with missing or inconsistent fields, and filter flows that are too small to provide meaningful evidence. Examples include extremely short-lived flows and flows with negligible volume. This keeps downstream processing focused on informative traffic and reduces sensitivity to exporter artifacts.

3.2 Feature Extraction and Suspicion Scoring

Once preprocessed, each flow is mapped to a feature vector designed to capture indicators of storage-channel manipulation. In a storage covert channel, the sender encodes data by manipulating protocol-visible fields or header values, rather than by modulating fine-grained inter-packet timing. This makes flow summaries a good fit, since many useful signals survive aggregation at the flow level. We organize features into three families, each with a clear role.

Flow-Shape Features. Flow-shape features provide context and help control false positives under workload shifts. They include flow duration, packet and byte rates, average packet size, and a packet-to-byte ratio sanity check. These signals are not uniquely characteristic of covert storage channels, but they reduce false positives and help interpret other anomalies.

Protocol-Semantics Features. Protocol-semantics features capture violations of expected TCP control behavior. Storage channels often require unusual control behavior, or they may disturb control patterns when fields are manipulated. Using TCP control summaries commonly exported in IPFIX, we compute ratios of key flags, including SYN, FIN, and RST. We also compute a session coherence indicator that captures whether control flags reflect a plausible TCP lifecycle. When per-flag counters are available, we additionally compute a TCP flag entropy feature as a compact measure of how concentrated or irregular the control signaling is within the flow. When only an aggregated bitmask is exported, we omit this feature and rely on ratios and coherence instead. The intent is not to fully reconstruct TCP state, but to detect clear inconsistencies with typical connection behavior in the given environment.

Header-Manipulation Features. Header-manipulation features target header fields that remain syntactically valid but become statistically unusual when manipulated. A practical example is TTL. Some exporters support richer header summaries through custom templates or extensions. When such distributional summaries are available, we can enable entropy-style features for TTL or IPID as optional refinements. However, most IPFIX deployments export only a single representative TTL value rather than a per-flow distribution. To keep the design deployable, our core header feature therefore uses the TTL information commonly provided by exporters, such as an initial TTL or an average TTL value.

When TTL is exported, we score how atypical the observed TTL is relative to benign baselines for comparable flows. We define comparability through a lightweight traffic class built from IPFIX fields. A typical class uses source and destination prefixes, transport protocol, and destination port. For example, DNS over UDP on port 53 is scored against DNS-like traffic, while VoIP over UDP is scored against its own baseline. We learn an admissible TTL set or a robust TTL range for each class from benign traffic. If a flow's TTL falls outside the admissible region, the anomaly score increases with the distance from that region. This range-violation and rarity framing matches how many storage channels behave in practice. They push values outside what is normally observed for the same path and service context.

Some deployments provide richer TTL summaries through custom templates or exporter extensions. When such summaries are available, we can optionally incorporate a TTL variability signal as a refinement. The core system does not depend on these extensions. Similarly, IPID-based entropy is enabled only when the exporter provides the required distributional summaries.

Feature Summary. Table 1 summarizes the feature families and their anomaly mappings. Optional features are enabled only when the deployed IPFIX templates export the required Information Elements, such as per-flag counters or distributional header summaries.

Let f denote a flow. Each raw feature $x_i(f)$ is mapped to an anomaly score $a_i(f) \in [0, 1]$ using statistics estimated from benign traffic and refreshed peri-

Table 1. Feature families and anomaly mappings for IPFIX-based storage-channel detection.

Family	Feature	Mapping to anomaly score $a_i(f) \in [0, 1]$
Flow-shape	Flow duration; packet rate; byte rate; average packet size; packet-to-byte ratio	Robust deviation from benign percentiles, computed per traffic class.
Protocol semantics	TCP SYN ratio; TCP FIN ratio; TCP RST ratio; session coherence; TCP flag entropy (optional)	Deviation from benign ranges learned per traffic class. Session coherence is a rule-based violation score derived from exported control summaries. TCP flag entropy is used only when per-flag counters or richer flag summaries are exported.
Header manipulation	TTL deviation and rarity; TTL variability (optional); TTL entropy (optional); IPID entropy (optional)	Distance to an admissible region learned per traffic class. Variability and entropy signals are enabled only when the exporter provides the required distributional summaries, and are robustly scaled.
Optional context features	Protocol–port consistency; source IP/port reuse	Low-weight contextual and rarity signals over sliding windows, used for triage and prioritization.

odically. We use robust, percentile-based normalization so that extreme values do not dominate the score. Distributional features use quantile- or IQR-based scaling. Rule-based and range-based features map deviations from admissible behavior to higher anomaly values proportional to how far the observation lies outside the expected region.

Intuitively, the anomaly score measures how far a value deviates from what is typical for similar traffic, using robust statistics that are less sensitive to outliers.

For a distributional feature value x observed in traffic class c, we compute a robust location and scale from benign traffic, denoted by median_c and IQR_c. We then map x to an anomaly score with IQR normalization and truncation:

$$a(x) = \max\left(0, \min\left(1, \frac{|x - \mathrm{median}_c|}{\mathrm{IQR}_c}\right)\right).$$

For features where only one tail is meaningful (*e.g.*, unusually high rates), we use a one-sided variant that scores deviations beyond the relevant tail of the benign distribution, rather than symmetric deviation around the median. In practice, we apply the same scaling but clamp negative deviations to zero for one-sided features.

For range-based signals such as TTL, we learn a class-specific admissible region $\mathcal{R}_c$ from benign traffic and score the distance outside this region: $a_{\text{range}}(x) = \max\left(0, \min\left(1, \frac{d(x,\mathcal{R}_c)}{\tau_c}\right)\right)$, where $d(x, \mathcal{R}_c) = 0$ for $x \in \mathcal{R}_c$ and otherwise equals the distance to the nearest boundary of $\mathcal{R}_c$. In our implementation, $\mathcal{R}_c$ is a robust interval derived from benign percentiles, and τ_c is a scaling factor derived from benign quantiles.

Methodology for Application-Robust Anomaly Scoring. To remain reliable across very different services, anomaly scoring must avoid global thresholds. What is normal depends strongly on the service, and a single threshold would either trigger many false positives or miss attacks. Our approach therefore defines each anomaly relative to expected behavior in a comparable context and measures deviations using robust statistics.

We maintain benign baselines for lightweight traffic classes derived from IPFIX fields. Each class is defined by transport protocol and destination port, and can be further refined with source and destination prefixes when path effects matter. This class definition is intentionally simple and separates broad service families without requiring application inspection. More generally, our approach relies on observed traffic characteristics to detect covert behavior, which is consistent with prior work on covert channel detection from traffic features [17]. For distributional features such as rates, sizes, and ratios, we map values to $a_i(f) \in [0, 1]$ using quantile-based or IQR-based scoring within the class. In this view, suspicious means being in the tails of what is normal for the class, regardless of absolute scale. For protocol-semantics and header-manipulation features, we rely on conformance tests and distance to an admissible region learned from the same class. This directly captures storage-channel behavior as range violations or rare values. When a class has insufficient history, which can happen for rare or new applications, we avoid over-interpreting sparse baselines. We back off to coarser classes and reduce reliance on the most sensitive signals until the reference stabilizes. This keeps scores comparable and fair across applications while remaining compatible with large-scale IPFIX deployments.

Normalization and Scoring. Suspicion scoring aggregates per-feature anomalies into a composite signal. For a given flow f, we compute

$$s(f) = \sum_i w_i \, a_i(f),$$

which provides a lightweight ranking score that is subsequently calibrated into a probability for risk-aware decision-making in Sect. 3.3.

Storage covert channels typically work by manipulating fields that should be relatively stable for a given path or protocol state, such as TTL patterns or TCP control behavior. For this reason, we treat header- and protocol-semantics features as primary evidence, since they are the most directly tied to the attacker's writeable surface. In contrast, flow-shape features are less specific to covert storage, but they are useful in practice to avoid flagging benign workload shifts and to contextualize unusual header values. In our implementation, weights can be learned on a small calibration set when labels are available. When labels are not available, we use uniform weights and rely on ablation studies to verify that performance is not the result of a single hand-tuned parameter.

Implementation Scope and Deployability. Because this paper focuses on storage channels, we deliberately avoid per-packet timing features. Standard IPFIX flow records do not provide the fine-grained packet timing needed to characterize timing channels reliably, and including such features would either require non-standard exporter support or undermine the deployability claim. Optional fields such as richer TTL summaries are treated as refinements that can improve sensitivity when available, but the core pipeline relies only on commonly exported IPFIX fields.

3.3 Probability Calibration

Our feature pipeline outputs a suspicion score $s(f) \in [0, 1]$ for each flow f (Sect. 3.2). The score is best viewed as a relative measure of suspiciousness. Larger values indicate that, according to the IPFIX-based features, the flow looks more compatible with storage-channel manipulation. This makes the score useful for triage and ranking, but it is not yet a probability.

Calibration is needed because probabilities have a specific meaning that a raw score usually does not. When the system outputs $p = 0.8$, the intended interpretation is that among many similar flows, roughly 80% should actually be covert. By contrast, the numerical scale of $s(f)$ is shaped by feature normalization, weight choices, and the traffic mix. Even though $s(f)$ lies in $[0, 1]$, $s(f) = 0.7$ does not generally mean a 70% chance of covert activity. This distinction matters because our next stage performs cost-sensitive Bayesian action selection (Sect. 3.5). That decision stage computes expected losses and therefore requires a quantity that behaves like a probability. If the risk estimate is systematically mis-scaled, the system can become consistently too aggressive or too permissive even when the ranking of flows is correct.

We address this by learning a calibration function $g(\cdot)$ that maps suspicion scores to calibrated risk estimates, $p(f) = g(s(f)) \in [0, 1]$. After calibration, the output is intended to be reliable. Among flows assigned $p \approx 0.2$, roughly 20% should truly be covert, and among flows assigned $p \approx 0.8$, roughly 80% should be covert. Probability calibration and reliability assessment are well-studied in the ML literature, and our approach follows standard practice for transforming classifier scores into accurate probability estimates [16, 25].

To keep evaluation unbiased, all reported results use a fixed 70/30 split. We reserve 30% of the dataset as a held-out test set and never use it to tune weights, fit the calibrator, or choose thresholds. The remaining 70% is used for model development. Within the 70% development portion, we keep calibration separate from score construction by using disjoint subsets. We first build the suspicion score on one subset, including choosing normalization baselines and any score parameters. We then fit the calibration mapping $g(\cdot)$ on a separate subset that the scoring stage never sees. This prevents the calibrator from simply learning the quirks of the data used to construct the score.

When labeled examples are available, we fit $g(\cdot)$ with Platt scaling [18], which learns a one-dimensional logistic mapping from score to probability $g(s) = \sigma(\beta_0 + \beta_1 s) = 1/(1+\exp(-(\beta_0+\beta_1 s)))$. The parameter β_0 shifts the curve to reflect how rare covert flows are in the calibration environment, while β_1 controls how quickly probability rises as the score increases. We then use the calibrated probability estimate in the downstream decision stage.

A final practical issue is class imbalance. In real deployments, covert flows are rare, but experimental datasets are often enriched with injected attacks to enable evaluation. Because calibration is sensitive to the class prior $\pi = \Pr(Y = 1)$, a calibrator trained directly on enriched data tends to output probabilities that are too high for deployment. We therefore correct for prior mismatch by applying a prior adjustment to the calibrated odds, which is equivalent to shifting the intercept of the logistic mapping, so that predicted probabilities reflect the expected prevalence in the target environment. This prevents the decision stage from being overly pessimistic.

We report both ranking quality and calibration quality. Ranking quality is measured with ROC-AUC and PR-AUC to show how well the score separates covert from benign flows. Calibration quality is assessed with reliability diagrams and summary metrics such as Expected Calibration Error (ECE) and the Brier score to show whether predicted probabilities match observed frequencies. For completeness, we also report an uncalibrated baseline that directly uses $p(f) = s(f)$. This preserves ranking but typically yields unreliable probabilities, and it quantifies how much calibration improves downstream cost-sensitive decisions.

3.4 From Flow-Level Risk to Traffic-Class Risk

The previous stage outputs a calibrated risk estimate $p(f) \in [0, 1]$ for each observed flow f. In WardenMind, flows are the basic units of evidence, while decisions are taken at the level of *traffic classes*, i.e., short-lived control units grouping flows that share a common operational context.

Formally, each observed flow f is mapped to a class $E = \phi(f)$, where ϕ is derived from IPFIX fields. A traffic class is defined so that its member flows are similar enough to share both a statistical baseline and a common mitigation policy. In practice, class definitions combine service-related fields, such as transport protocol and destination port, with optional source- or destination-side scopes when exfiltration control or path sensitivity must be captured explicitly.

For each traffic class E, WardenMind maintains an aggregate risk estimate $p(E) \in [0, 1]$ over a short time horizon. This quantity is not the exact probability that the entire class is covert. Rather, it is an operational risk signal summarizing how strongly recent evidence in that class supports mitigation.

Let $\mathcal{F}_W(E)$ denote the set of recent flows assigned to traffic class E within a sliding window W. We first aggregate the calibrated per-flow risks $\{p(f) : f \in \mathcal{F}_W(E)\}$ into a window-level evidence term

$$\bar{p}_W(E) = A\big(\{p(f) : f \in \mathcal{F}_W(E)\}\big),$$

where $A(\cdot)$ is an aggregation operator. In practice, we use either the mean, which captures the overall risk level in the class, or a high quantile, which remains sensitive to a small number of highly suspicious flows.

To stabilize the signal under bursty traffic, we smooth this evidence over time with an exponential moving average $p_t(E) = \lambda\, \bar{p}_W(E) + (1 - \lambda)\, p_{t-1}(E)$, where $\lambda \in (0, 1]$ controls the trade-off between responsiveness and stability. When a traffic class has insufficient support, WardenMind backs off to a coarser class definition and correspondingly reduces the influence of the estimate until sufficient history accumulates.

This stage bridges evidence and control in WardenMind: flows are the smallest units of observation, while traffic classes are the smallest units of control.

3.5 Bayesian Decision-Making

WardenMind uses the traffic-class risk $p(E)$ from Sect. 3.4 to select how strongly to intervene. In our default instantiation, the traffic class is defined as $E =$ (source scope, transport protocol, destination port, destination prefix), where source scope may denote a source host, source prefix, or protected source zone depending on deployment granularity. This definition captures service context, source-side exfiltration scope, and coarse path effects while remaining directly derivable from IPFIX.

The warden selects one action per traffic class over a short policy window. We use three actions. ALLOW leaves the class unchanged. CAPTURE increases visibility through targeted logging or selective packet capture. NORMALIZE enables an active sanitization policy when enforcement is available, for example by rewriting selected header fields to canonical values or constraining admissible values for fields that should remain stable. These actions provide a graded response compatible with a deployable flow-driven control loop.

Choosing among actions requires trading off security benefit and operational impact. For each action a, $C_{\text{covert}}(a)$ denotes the residual loss if covert activity is present and a is applied, while $C_{\text{legit}}(a)$ denotes the cost paid when the traffic class is benign. The latter captures QoS degradation and operational overhead; the former captures remaining covert capacity or exposure. Costs are relative, and only their ratios matter.

Given a class-level risk estimate $p(E)$, the expected loss of applying action a to traffic class E is $\ell_a(p(E)) = p(E)\, C_{\text{covert}}(a) + (1 - p(E))\, C_{\text{legit}}(a)$. The warden selects the action that minimizes expected loss,

$$a^*(E) \in \arg \min_{a \in \{\text{ALLOW}, \text{CAPTURE}, \text{NORMALIZE}\}} \ell_a(p(E)).$$

This rule is easy to interpret: low risk favors low-impact actions, whereas higher risk justifies paying greater operational cost to reduce residual leakage. A natural escalation policy is obtained when $C_{\text{legit}}(\text{ALLOW}) < C_{\text{legit}}(\text{CAPTURE}) < C_{\text{legit}}(\text{NORMALIZE})$ and $C_{\text{covert}}(\text{ALLOW}) > C_{\text{covert}}(\text{CAPTURE}) > C_{\text{covert}}(\text{NORMALIZE})$. Under this structure, the policy escalates from ALLOW to CAPTURE to NORMALIZE as risk increases.

Because $\ell_a(p)$ is affine in p, transitions occur only at indifference points where two actions have the same expected loss. For actions a and b, the indifference point $p^*_{a,b}$ solves $\ell_a(p) = \ell_b(p)$, giving

$$p^*_{a,b} = \frac{C_{\text{legit}}(b) - C_{\text{legit}}(a)}{\left(C_{\text{legit}}(b) - C_{\text{legit}}(a)\right) + \left(C_{\text{covert}}(a) - C_{\text{covert}}(b)\right)}.$$

Thus, with three actions, the decision rule behaves like two risk thresholds induced by explicit costs rather than by hand-tuned heuristics. As an example initialization, we use the illustrative costs $(C_{\text{covert}}, C_{\text{legit}}) = (10, 0)$, $(4, 2)$, and $(2, 4)$ for ALLOW, CAPTURE, and NORMALIZE, respectively. This yields $\ell_{\text{ALLOW}}(p) = 10p$, $\ell_{\text{CAPTURE}}(p) = 2 + 2p$, and $\ell_{\text{NORMALIZE}}(p) = 4 - 2p$. The corresponding thresholds are $p^*_{\text{ALLOW,CAPTURE}} = 0.25$ and $p^*_{\text{CAPTURE,NORMALIZE}} = 0.5$. The induced policy is therefore transparent: ALLOW for $p(E) < 0.25$, CAPTURE for $0.25 \leq p(E) < 0.5$, and NORMALIZE for $p(E) \geq 0.5$. Note that only the relative scale of the costs matters. Multiplying all costs by the same positive constant leaves the expected-loss ordering unchanged, and therefore induces the same thresholds and policy.

In implementation, we discard any action that is dominated on both covert and benign outcomes, and we resolve boundary ties by preferring the least intrusive action. The cost table above is only an initialization: Sect. 3.7 explains how WardenMind updates these costs over time from observed feedback.

3.6 Cost Construction

The decision rule in Sect. 3.5 requires, for each action a, a benign cost $C_{\text{legit}}(a)$ and a covert cost $C_{\text{covert}}(a)$. The benign cost measures how intrusive the action is when applied to legitimate traffic, whereas the covert cost measures the residual loss that remains when covert activity is present despite applying that action. In a live deployment, these quantities could incorporate detailed QoS and system measurements. In our dataset-driven evaluation, however, we use a simpler construction that is directly observable from labeled traces and remains faithful to the semantics of the action set.

We associate each action a with two base severity parameters: a benign severity $b_{\text{legit}}(a)$ and a covert residual-loss severity $b_{\text{covert}}(a)$. The benign severity increases with action intrusiveness, so that $b_{\text{legit}}(\text{ALLOW}) < b_{\text{legit}}(\text{CAPTURE}) < b_{\text{legit}}(\text{NORMALIZE})$, while the covert residual-loss severity decreases with mitigation strength, so that $b_{\text{covert}}(\text{ALLOW}) > b_{\text{covert}}(\text{CAPTURE}) > b_{\text{covert}}(\text{NORMALIZE})$. This ordering matches the intended semantics of the action space: ALLOW has the smallest benign impact but leaves the largest covert risk unresolved, while NORMALIZE is more intrusive but leaves the smallest residual covert loss.

In the dataset-based experiments, we instantiate these base severities on a normalized scale. Unless stated otherwise, we use $b_{\text{legit}}(\text{ALLOW}) = 0.0$, $b_{\text{legit}}(\text{CAPTURE}) = 0.2$, $b_{\text{legit}}(\text{NORMALIZE}) = 0.4$, and $b_{\text{covert}}(\text{ALLOW}) = 1.0$, $b_{\text{covert}}(\text{CAPTURE}) = 0.4$, $b_{\text{covert}}(\text{NORMALIZE}) = 0.2$. These values serve as semantic anchors rather than universal constants. Since the Bayesian decision rule depends on relative costs rather than absolute scale, equivalent rescaled versions would induce the same qualitative policy structure.

Let $\pi_t(E) \in [0, 1]$ denote the fraction of covert flows in traffic class E during window t, as determined from the labels in the evaluation dataset. We define the instantaneous observed cost of applying action a to class E in window t as

$$\widehat{c}_t(a, E) = (1 - \pi_t(E))\, b_{\text{legit}}(a) + \pi_t(E)\, b_{\text{covert}}(a).$$

If a class is entirely benign in a given window, the observed cost reduces to the benign severity of the action. If it is entirely covert, the observed cost reduces to the corresponding covert residual-loss severity. For mixed windows, the observed cost reflects the composition of the class.

This formulation is intentionally simple. Offline traces do not provide reliable deployment-level measurements such as true enforcement latency, CPU contention, or storage pressure under live operating conditions. We therefore instantiate costs from quantities that are fully observable and reproducible in the dataset: the composition of each traffic class and the relative severity of the actions. This yields a transparent basis for evaluating Bayesian action selection before introducing online adaptation.

The base severities above also define the initial action costs used at the start of the adaptation process:

$$C^{(0)}_{\text{legit}}(a) = b_{\text{legit}}(a), \qquad C^{(0)}_{\text{covert}}(a) = b_{\text{covert}}(a).$$

3.7 Online Cost Adaptation

The construction in Sect. 3.6 provides an initial and fully observable instantiation of action costs for offline evaluation. In practice, however, the relative burden and benefit of actions may evolve over time as traffic composition or attacker behavior changes. WardenMind therefore treats the initial costs as semantic anchors and updates them online from successive class-level observations.

For each action a, WardenMind maintains two running estimates: $C^{(t)}_{\text{legit}}(a)$, the benign cost of applying a, and $C^{(t)}_{\text{covert}}(a)$, the residual covert loss associated with a. These estimates are initialized from the base severities in Sect. 3.6:

$$C^{(0)}_{\text{legit}}(a) = b_{\text{legit}}(a), \qquad C^{(0)}_{\text{covert}}(a) = b_{\text{covert}}(a).$$

At time t, each traffic class E yields an instantaneous observed cost $\widehat{c}_t(a, E) = (1 - \pi_t(E))\, b_{\text{legit}}(a) + \pi_t(E)\, b_{\text{covert}}(a)$, where $\pi_t(E)$ is the fraction of covert flows in class E during window t. To update the benign and covert components separately, WardenMind forms the class-conditional observations

$$\widehat{c}_{\text{legit},t}(a, E) = \big(1 - \pi_t(E)\big)\, b_{\text{legit}}(a), \qquad \widehat{c}_{\text{covert},t}(a, E) = \pi_t(E)\, b_{\text{covert}}(a).$$

Let $\mathcal{E}_t(a)$ denote the set of traffic classes that received action a during window t. When $|\mathcal{E}_t(a)| > 0$, the benign and covert feedback signals for action a are computed as

$$\widetilde{c}_{\text{legit},t}(a) = \frac{1}{|\mathcal{E}_t(a)|} \sum_{E \in \mathcal{E}_t(a)} \widehat{c}_{\text{legit},t}(a, E),$$

$$\widetilde{c}_{\text{covert},t}(a) = \frac{1}{|\mathcal{E}_t(a)|} \sum_{E \in \mathcal{E}_t(a)} \widehat{c}_{\text{covert},t}(a, E).$$

These quantities summarize how costly action a was on benign and covert traffic over the current update window.

The running action costs are then updated by exponential smoothing:

$$C_{\text{legit}}^{(t+1)}(a) = (1 - \alpha_{\text{legit}})\, C_{\text{legit}}^{(t)}(a) + \alpha_{\text{legit}}\, \widetilde{c}_{\text{legit},t}(a),$$

$$C_{\text{covert}}^{(t+1)}(a) = (1 - \alpha_{\text{covert}})\, C_{\text{covert}}^{(t)}(a) + \alpha_{\text{covert}}\, \widetilde{c}_{\text{covert},t}(a),$$

where $\alpha_{\text{legit}}, \alpha_{\text{covert}} \in (0, 1]$ control the adaptation rate. Small values emphasize stability, whereas larger values allow faster adaptation to changes in traffic composition or adversarial strategy.

To prevent unstable updates, WardenMind applies three safeguards. First, costs are clipped to the bounded interval $[0, 1]$ to ensure numerical stability and direct interpretability. Second, if an action is applied too rarely in a given window, that window does not trigger an update for that action, which avoids over-correcting costs from insufficient support. Third, after each update, the cost table is adjusted to satisfy the ordering constraints required by the Bayesian policy:

$$C_{\text{legit}}(\text{ALLOW}) < C_{\text{legit}}(\text{CAPTURE}) < C_{\text{legit}}(\text{NORMALIZE}),$$

$$C_{\text{covert}}(\text{ALLOW}) > C_{\text{covert}}(\text{CAPTURE}) > C_{\text{covert}}(\text{NORMALIZE}).$$

This ensures that temporary fluctuations do not reverse the intended ordering of actions.

In the experiments, this adaptation loop is fully observable because the dataset provides the labels needed to compute $\pi_t(E)$ for each class and each window. This makes it possible to evaluate directly whether the running costs track changes in traffic composition and covert channel prevalence, without confounding the adaptation mechanism with uncertainty in the feedback source.

Overall, online cost adaptation allows WardenMind to retain the interpretability of an explicit Bayesian cost model while avoiding a brittle, permanently fixed cost table. The policy remains transparent and cost-driven, but its thresholds evolve with the data observed over time rather than remaining hand-tuned once and for all.

4 Experimental Evaluation

The experimental evaluation relies on a controlled dataset constructed from publicly available network traces and labeled covert-channel traffic sources. The benign baseline traffic was obtained from the MAWI Working Group Traffic Archive, a long-running backbone traffic repository widely used in network measurement research [9,13,20]. A representative capture from the MAWI Samplepoint-F trace was extracted and preprocessed by filtering IP, TCP, and UDP traffic while preserving original timestamps and packet ordering. The trace contains approximately 9.7 million packets captured over an 86-second interval and serves as the primary benign reference distribution for feature calibration. As with any real-world trace, MAWI cannot be guaranteed to be covert-free; we therefore treat it as benign background traffic for controlled evaluation rather than as verified clean traffic.

To generate covert storage-channel samples, DNS exfiltration flows were extracted from the CIC-Bell-DNS-EXF-2021 dataset released by the Canadian Institute for Cybersecurity. This dataset originates from the intrusion-detection dataset generation framework introduced by Sharafaldin et al. [20], which provides labeled network traffic traces specifically designed for evaluating security detection systems. The malicious DNS flows were extracted directly from the original PCAP files without modification, ensuring label integrity and experimental reproducibility.

The final evaluation dataset was constructed at the flow level by combining benign traffic from the MAWI archive with covert flows from the CIC-Bell dataset. Flow identities were defined using the canonical 5-tuple (source IP, destination IP, source port, destination port, protocol), and forward and reverse packets were merged into unified flows. Several prevalence-controlled scenarios were generated to evaluate the robustness of the detection framework under different covert traffic ratios, including realistic (0.5%), hard (5%), medium (10%), and easy (15%) covert-flow prevalence levels.

To ensure experimental rigor, the dataset was split at the flow level into disjoint training, validation, and test sets using a 70%/15%/15% split. The splitting process enforced strict flow-ID separation across partitions to prevent information leakage between training and evaluation stages. All preprocessing steps, including flow indexing, feature extraction, and dataset construction, were implemented in Python 3.11 with reproducible scripts and deterministic random seeds, and the corresponding Python software is publicly available in the accompanying repository [1].

All experiments were conducted on a Linux environment (Ubuntu 22.04 LTS). Packet processing and trace inspection relied on standard network analysis tools such as tcpdump, capinfos, and Wireshark-compatible PCAP utilities, while flow extraction and statistical analysis were implemented using Python libraries including NumPy, Pandas, and Scikit-learn.

4.1 Evaluation Metrics

To evaluate the effectiveness of the proposed warden architecture, we employ several complementary metrics focusing on both detection capability and operational decision quality.

First, we assess the discrimination power of the suspicion score through the Receiver Operating Characteristic (ROC) curve. The ROC curve illustrates the trade-off between the true positive rate (TPR) and the false positive rate (FPR) for different score thresholds, demonstrating the score's effectiveness in distinguishing legitimate flows from covert flows.

Beyond the effectiveness of the score, the main evaluation criterion in our framework is the decision cost. Using the predefined cost matrices described in Sect. 3.6, we calculate the cumulative cost of actions taken on each flow. This metric captures the operational impact of the warden by jointly accounting for missed detections and unnecessary interventions.

For adaptive wardens, we further monitor the evolution of the learned parameters over time. In particular, we track the temporal evolution of the estimated action costs and the corresponding decision thresholds. These measurements illustrate how the system adapts to the observed traffic composition and adjusts its intervention strategy.

These metrics collectively provide a comprehensive view of the system's performance, balancing detection capabilities with operational pragmatism.

4.2 Baseline Comparison

To evaluate the proposed adaptive warden, we compare it against several baseline strategies with increasing decision sophistication. The first baseline is a *Naive Warden*, which selects defensive actions randomly according to the estimated probability of covert traffic (*i.e.* $\Pr(action = \text{NORMALIZE}|p) = p$ for a calibrated probability p). Although simplistic, this strategy provides a lower bound on performance. The second baseline is a *Static Bayesian Warden.* Actions are selected using Bayesian decision theory with a fixed cost matrix, resulting in static decision thresholds derived from the cost model. Finally, we evaluate the *Adaptive Per-Class Bayesian Warden.* In this configuration, action costs are continuously updated based on the observed traffic composition, leading to dynamically evolving decision thresholds. All strategies are evaluated on the same datasets using identical scoring models and cost definitions to ensure a fair comparison.

4.3 Results and Analysis

We now analyze the performance of the proposed warden architecture using the metrics defined in the previous section.

Score Discrimination. Figure 1 presents the ROC curve obtained on the evaluation dataset. The results show that covert flows generally receive higher suspicion scores than legitimate ones, resulting in a clear separation between the two distributions However, the remaining overlap indicates that perfect discrimination is not achievable, which motivates the need for cost-aware decision strategies rather than simple thresholding.

In practice, meaningful operating points correspond to very low false-positive regimes, which reflect realistic deployment constraints for network wardens.

To better characterize the operational performance of the score, we report representative operating points on the ROC curve. When the false-positive rate is constrained to 10%, we correctly identify approximately 90.6% of covert flows. Under a stricter constraint of 1% false positives, the detection rate remains 54.7%, meaning that more than half of covert communications can still be detected while maintaining a very low false-alarm level.

Decision Cost Comparison. We then evaluate the operational impact of the different warden strategies by measuring the cumulative decision cost over the sequence of processed flows. Table 2 reports the detection performance of the different warden strategies. For each strategy, we report the True Positive Rate (TPR), the False Positive Rate (FPR), and the proportion of legitimate and covert flows that are captured.

Overall, Bayesian decision strategies significantly outperform the naive warden by reducing the false positive rate while maintaining higher detection rates. In particular, strategies based on quantile aggregation tend to achieve higher TPR values than those relying on mean aggregation. Adaptive wardens further improve performance by adjusting their decision costs to the observed traffic distribution. This behavior can be explained by the asymmetry of the score distributions: legitimate flows are often concentrated near low suspicion values, while covert flows are less concentrated near the highest scores. As a result, a single legitimate flow can significantly reduce the mean score of a class, potentially hiding covert activity, whereas quantile-based aggregation gives more weight to suspicious flows.

We also observe that allowing three actions generally leads in lower TPR but better FPR than restricting the warden to only two actions. The additional intermediate action enables the warden to react more flexibly to uncertain situations by separating normalization and capture decisions.

These trends are further reflected in the operational performance shown in Fig. 2, which presents the evolution of the cumulative decision cost for each strategy. As expected, the naive warden incurs the highest cost due to the absence of structured decision-making. In contrast, Bayesian decision strategies significantly reduce the total cost by selecting actions that minimize the expected loss given the estimated probability of covert traffic. We observe that adaptive wardens approach the optimal cumulative cost, achieving an average cost per flow of approximately 0.015.

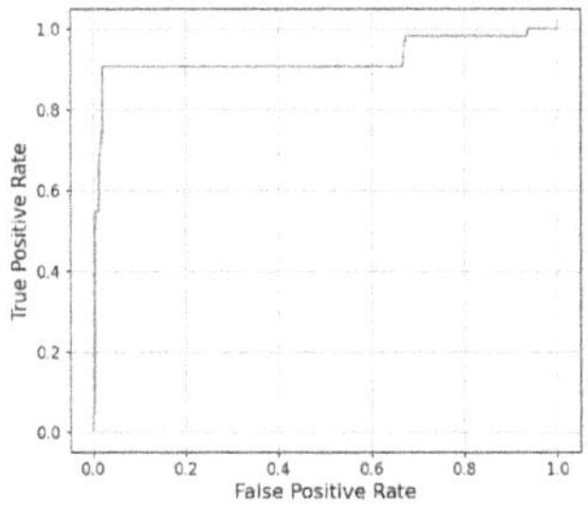

Fig. 1. ROC curve of the flow-level suspicion score on the evaluation dataset.

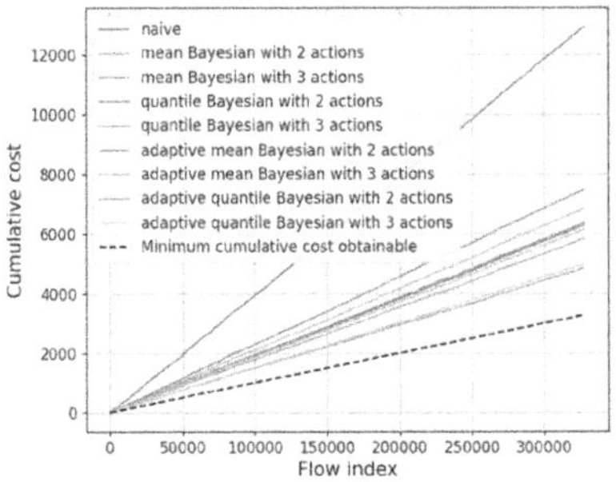

Fig. 2. Cumulative cost comparison for different warden strategies.

Table 2. TPR, FPR and capture ratios for different warden strategies.

Warden type	TPR	FPR	$\mathbf{Capture}_{\text{legit}}$	$\mathbf{Capture}_{\text{covert}}$
Naive warden	0.438	0.0183	—	—
Mean Bayesian (2 actions)	0.759	0.00326	—	—
Mean Bayesian (3 actions)	0.428	0.00387	0.00387	0.360
Quantile Bayesian (2 actions)	0.812	0.00432	—	—
Quantile Bayesian (3 actions)	0.788	0.00470	0.00470	0.0528
Adaptive mean Bayesian (2 actions)	0.812	0.00495	—	—
Adaptive mean Bayesian (3 actions)	0.727	0.00171	0.00833	0.147
Adaptive quantile Bayesian (2 actions)	0.924	0.00472	—	—
Adaptive quantile Bayesian (3 actions)	0.812	0.00326	0.00207	0.131

Adaptive Behavior. To better understand the dynamics of the adaptive warden, we analyze the evolution of the learned cost and thresholds over time.

Figure 3 and Fig. 4 show how respectively the estimated costs and estimated thresholds associated with different actions evolve as the system processes new flows. The costs gradually stabilize as more observations are incorporated, leading to increasingly consistent decisions.

This confirms that adaptive cost learning maintains efficient decision policies as traffic evolves.

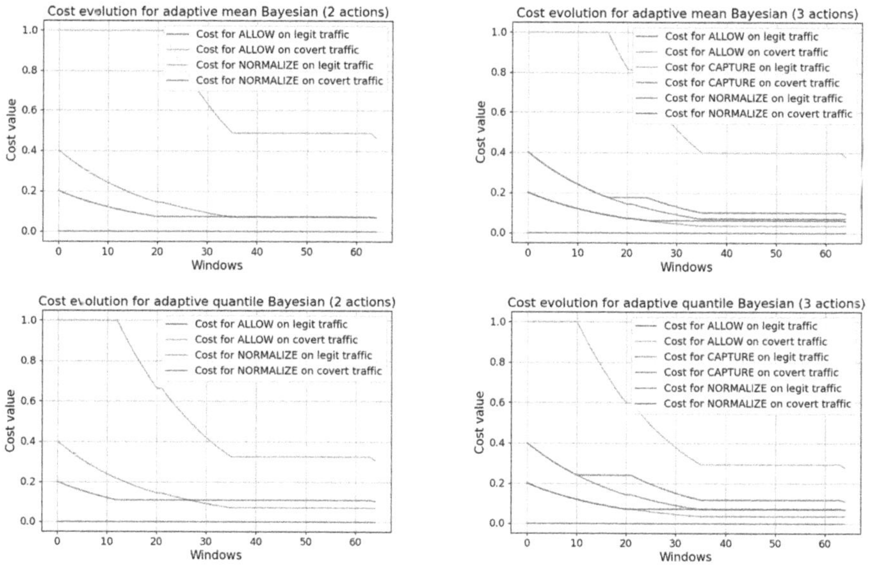

Fig. 3. Cost evolution for adaptative wardens over time windows.

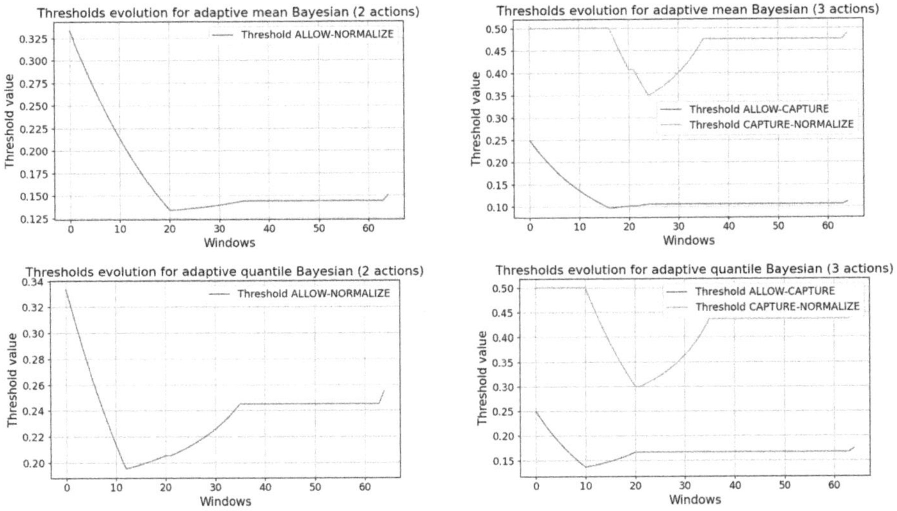

Fig. 4. Thresholds evolution for adaptative wardens over time windows.

5 Concluding Remarks

We presented WardenMind, a software warden for covert storage channels based on IPFIX telemetry, calibrated risk estimation, and Bayesian cost-aware action selection. Results show strong detection with low operational impact, while online cost adaptation avoids fixed-threshold rigidity under evolving traffic, priorities, and adversarial behavior.

Several limitations remain. Our experiments combine MAWI background traffic with one DNS exfiltration family from CIC-Bell-DNS-EXF-2021; they therefore do not prove equal accuracy for all storage covert channels. Channels that preserve class-specific header and flow statistics, deliberately mimic benign baselines, or slowly shift them may be harder to detect. Thus, our contribution is the flow-driven calibrated decision framework, not a universal detector for every hiding method.

The approach also requires enough flow volume to calibrate probabilities and learn stable cost estimates. Performance may degrade in very low-traffic environments or when telemetry is sparse or heavily aggregated. The 86-s MAWI Samplepoint-F trace supports controlled flow-level evaluation but not long-term operational claims, and real deployments are still needed to measure live enforcement cost and QoS impact.

Finally, this paper focuses on storage channels, for which relevant signals remain visible at IPFIX flow granularity. Timing channels require fine-grained packet timing and fast-path enforcement, as illustrated by NetWarden [24]. In that setting, WardenMind would mainly contribute the decision layer: calibrated risks and learned costs could be compiled into compact lookup tables mapping risk bins and traffic classes to escalation levels.

Acknowledgments. The authors thank the anonymous reviewers for their constructive comments and suggestions.

Disclosure of Interests. The authors have no competing interests to declare that are relevant to the content of this article.

References

1. Python Experiments for WardenMind. https://github.com/WardenMind/Flow-Driven-Bayesian-Detection-of-Storage-Covert-Channels (2026)
2. Aitken, P., Claise, B., Trammell, B.: Specification of the IP Flow Information Export (IPFIX) Protocol for the Exchange of Flow Information. RFC 7011 (2013). https://doi.org/10.17487/RFC7011
3. Cabaj, K., Zórawski, P., Nowakowski, P., Purski, M., Mazurczyk, W.: Efficient distributed network covert channels for internet of things environments. J. Cybersecur. **6**(1) (2020). https://doi.org/10.1093/cybsec/tyaa018
4. Caviglione, L.: Trends and challenges in network covert channels countermeasures. Appl. Sci. **11**(4), 1641 (2021). https://doi.org/10.3390/app11041641
5. Chourib M., Wendzel, S., Mazurczyk, W.: Adaptive warden strategy for countering network covert storage channels. In: 2021 IEEE 46th Conference on Local Computer Networks (LCN), pp. 148–153. IEEE (2021). https://doi.org/10.1109/LCN52139.2021.9524939
6. Claise, B., Trammell, B.: Information Model for IP Flow Information Export (IPFIX). RFC 7012 (2013). https://doi.org/10.17487/RFC7012
7. Elkan, C.: The foundations of cost-sensitive learning. In: Proceedings of the Seventeenth International Joint Conference on Artificial Intelligence (IJCAI) (2001). https://doi.org/10.5555/1642194.1642224
8. Fisk, G., Fisk, M., Papadopoulos, C., Neil, J.: Eliminating steganography in internet traffic with active wardens. In: Petitcolas, F.A.P. (ed.) IH 2002. LNCS, vol. 2578, pp. 18–35. Springer, Heidelberg (2002). https://doi.org/10.1007/3-540-36415-3_2
9. Fontugne, R., Borgnat, P., Abry, P., Fukuda, K.: Mawilab: Combining diverse anomaly detectors for automated anomaly labeling and performance benchmarking. In: Proceedings of the 6th International Conference on Emerging Networking Experiments and Technologies (CoNEXT), pp. 1–12. ACM (2010). https://doi.org/10 1145/1921168.1921179
10. Hofstede, R., Celeda, P., Trammell, B., Drago, I.: Flow monitoring explained: from packet capture to data analysis with NETFLOW and IPFIX. IEEE Commun. Surv. Tutor. **16**(4), 2037–2064 (2014). https://doi.org/10.1109/COMST.2014.2321898
11. Iglesias, F., Annessi, R., Zseby, T.: Dat detectors: uncovering TCP/IP covert channels by descriptive analytics. Secur. Commun. Networks **9**(15), 3011–3029 (2016). https://doi.org/10.1002/sec.1531
12. Litzinger, S., Keller, J., Caviglione, L.: Optimization of warden network functions for mitigating network covert channels. J. Netw. Syst. Manage. **34**(1), 23 (2026). https://doi.org/10.1007/s10922-025-10000-x
13. MAWI Working Group: Mawi working group traffic archive (2024). http://mawi.wide.ad.jp/mawi/
14. Mazurczyk, W., Wendzel, S., Chourib, M., Keller, J.: Countering adaptive network covert communication with dynamic wardens. Futur. Gener. Comput. Syst. **94**, 712–725 (2019). https://doi.org/10.1016/j.future.2018.12.047

15. Mazurczyk, W., Wendzel, S., Zander, S., Houmansadr, A., Szczypiorski, K.: Information hiding in communication networks: fundamentals, mechanisms, applications, and countermeasures. Wiley-IEEE Press (2016). https://doi.org/10.1002/9781119081715
16. Niculescu-Mizil, A., Caruana, R.: Predicting good probabilities with supervised learning. In: Proceedings of the 22nd International Conference on Machine Learning (ICML '05), pp. 625–632. ACM (2005). https://doi.org/10.1145/1102351.1102430
17. Nowakowski, P., Zórawski, P., Cabaj, K., Mazurczyk, W.: Network covert channels detection using data mining and hierarchical organisation of frequent sets: an initial study. In: Proceedings of the 15th International Conference on Availability, Reliability and Security, pp. 69:1–69:10. ACM (2020). https://doi.org/10.1145/3407023.3409217
18. Platt, J.C.: Probabilistic outputs for support vector machines and comparisons to regularized likelihood methods. In: Smola, A.J., Bartlett, P., Schölkopf, B., Schuurmans, D. (eds.) Advances in Large Margin Classifiers, pp. 61–74. MIT Press (1999)
19. Repetto, M., Caviglione, L., Zuppelli, M.: BCCSTEGO: a framework for investigating network covert channels. In: Proceedings of the 16th International Conference on Availability, Reliability and Security (ARES '21), pp. 68:1–68:7. ACM (2021). https://doi.org/10.1145/3465481.3470028
20. Sharafaldin, I., Lashkari, A.H., Ghorbani, A.A.: Toward generating a new intrusion detection dataset and intrusion traffic characterization. In: Proceedings of the 4th International Conference on Information Systems Security and Privacy (ICISSP), pp. 108–116. SciTePress (2018). https://doi.org/10.5220/0006639801080116
21. Simmons, G.J.: The prisoners' problem and the subliminal channel. In: Chaum, D. (ed.) Advances in Cryptology: Proceedings of CRYPTO '83, pp. 51–67. Springer, Boston (1984). https://doi.org/10.1007/978-1-4684-4730-9_5
22. Sperotto, A., Schaffrath, G., Sadre, R., Morariu, C., Pras, A., Stiller, B.: An overview of IP flow-based intrusion detection. IEEE Commun. Surv. Tutor. **12**(3), 343–356 (2010). https://doi.org/10.1109/SURV.2010.032210.00054
23. Wendzel, S., Zander, S., Fechner, B., Herdin, C.: Pattern-based survey and categorization of network covert channel techniques. ACM Comput. Surv. **47**(3), 50:1–50:26 (2015). https://doi.org/10.1145/2684195
24. Xing, J., Kang, Q., Chen, A.: NetWarden: Mitigating network covert channels while preserving performance. In: 29th USENIX Security Symposium (USENIX Security 20), pp. 2039–2056. USENIX Association (2020). https://doi.org/10.5555/3489212.3489327
25. Zadrozny, B., Elkan, C.: Transforming classifier scores into accurate multiclass probability estimates. In: Proceedings of the Eighth ACM SIGKDD International Conference on Knowledge Discovery and Data Mining, pp. 694–699. ACM (2002). https://doi.org/10.1145/775047.775151
26. Zander, S., Armitage, G., Branch, P.: A survey of covert channels and countermeasures in computer network protocols. IEEE Commun. Surv. Tutor. **9**(3), 44–57 (2007). https://doi.org/10.1109/COMST.2007.4317620

Encrypted but Detectable: Malware Detection in TLS Traffic Using JA4/JA4S Fingerprints and Machine Learning

Faisal Alsubaiei, Hamed Alhusseini, and Tassos Dimitriou(✉)

Computer Engineering Department, Kuwait University, Shadadiya, Kuwait
{faisal.alsubaiei,hamid.husseini}@ku.edu.kw, tassos.dimitriou@ieee.org

Abstract. The widespread adoption of encryption has greatly enhanced user privacy but also complicated network security monitoring. Traditional intrusion detection systems (IDS) that rely on payload inspection have become ineffective as most communications are now secured using Transport Layer Security (TLS). This work proposes a privacy-preserving framework for detecting malware in TLS-encrypted traffic by combining JA4 and JA4S fingerprinting techniques with supervised machine learning algorithms on a large-scale dataset of 72,816 TLS flows spanning 19 malware families.

The proposed approach extracts unique TLS handshake fingerprints and leverages classifiers such as Random Forest, XGBoost, and Logistic Regression to classify encrypted traffic. By analyzing metadata rather than payloads, the system maintains data confidentiality and regulatory compliance. A rigorous fingerprint-level splitting protocol ensures zero overlap between training and test fingerprint combinations, with all 20,815 test flows corresponding to entirely unseen fingerprints. To validate that ML classifiers contribute genuine generalization beyond fingerprint memorization, we introduce a non-ML majority-label baseline, which achieves only 26.09% accuracy when forced to generalize to unseen fingerprints. XGBoost outperforms this baseline by +72.71%, achieving 98.80% accuracy and 97.69% F1-score, while Random Forest achieves 96.79% accuracy. Prior statistical analysis demonstrated 87% fingerprint uniqueness for malware family discrimination; our work shows that these distinctive fingerprints enable highly accurate machine learning-based classification, offering an effective privacy-preserving approach for malware detection in encrypted traffic.

Keywords: Malware detection · TLS fingerprinting · JA4/JA4S · Machine learning · Encrypted traffic · Network security

1 Introduction

The rapid growth of encrypted network traffic has reshaped cybersecurity practices. Nearly 90% of internet communications now use TLS encryption [12],

S. Nadjm-Tehrani et al. (Eds.): ARES 2026, LNCS 16898, pp. 225–247, 2027.
https://doi.org/10.1007/978-3-032-36874-4_11

which protects users from eavesdropping but simultaneously conceals malicious activities. Traditional intrusion detection systems (IDS) and firewalls [6,17] that rely on payload inspection have become ineffective in this environment, as they cannot analyze encrypted content without compromising privacy and incurring significant computational overhead. This creates a critical security gap: attackers exploit encryption to hide command-and-control (C2) communications, malware distribution, and data exfiltration within encrypted tunnels, making encrypted malware detection one of today's most pressing cybersecurity challenges [26].

Conventional approaches to detecting malware rely on deep packet inspection (DPI), which requires decrypting traffic to examine payload content. However, this approach has three major limitations. Decryption violates user privacy expectations and regulatory requirements such as GDPR [32] and CCPA [1]. Additionally, decryption at scale demands substantial processing resources [21], limiting real-time applicability in large networks. Furthermore, attackers use certificate pinning [10] and advanced encryption to prevent monitoring altogether. Researchers have therefore investigated metadata-based and fingerprint-based approaches that identify malware patterns without decryption. TLS fingerprinting, the process of extracting unique characteristics from the TLS handshake and hashing them to identify applications, has emerged as a promising privacy-preserving alternative. Early fingerprinting methods such as JA3 and JA3S [2] showed promise but suffered from hash collisions and limited adaptability. The newer JA4+ suite [3] addresses these limitations, but systematic evaluation of its effectiveness when combined with machine learning for malware detection remains limited.

This work proposes a comprehensive framework that combines JA4 and JA4S fingerprinting with supervised machine learning to detect malware in encrypted traffic while preserving privacy.

Contributions. We make several key contributions:

- We propose a hybrid approach that systematically combines client-side (JA4) and server-side (JA4S) fingerprints with machine learning for malware classification.
- We assemble and describe a large-scale dataset of 72,816 TLS flows combining 36,957 malicious flows from 19 malware families obtained from malware-traffic-analysis.net [9] and the CTU-13 dataset [11], and 39,436 benign flows from Wireshark captures [33], public PCAP repositories, and benign background traffic from CTU-13.
- We develop a fingerprint-level splitting methodology that guarantees zero overlap between training and test fingerprints, ensuring all 20,815 test flows correspond to entirely unseen fingerprint combinations.
- We introduce a non-ML majority-label baseline to empirically validate that ML classifiers learn genuine structural patterns rather than memorizing fingerprint-to-label mappings, demonstrating a +72.71% accuracy improvement over the baseline.
- We define a clear experimental methodology using Random Forest, XGBoost, and Logistic Regression classifiers across three feature configurations, vali-

dated through cross-validation, overfitting analysis, label permutation testing, and cross-fingerprint generalization analysis.
- Finally, we demonstrate that the system achieves detection without decrypting traffic, maintaining data confidentiality and regulatory compliance.

Organization. The remainder of this paper is organized as follows. Section 2 defines the problem statement and relevant research questions. Section 3 reviews related work on TLS fingerprinting, machine learning for encrypted traffic classification, and existing malware detection approaches. Section 4 presents preliminaries including notation, definitions, and our threat model. Section 5 describes the methodology, dataset details, and experimental setup. Section 6 presents experimental results and statistical analysis. Finally, Sect. 7 summarizes our findings and outlines directions for future research.

2 Problem Statement

The proliferation of encrypted malware communications presents a fundamental challenge to network security monitoring: how can organizations detect malicious activities within TLS-encrypted traffic without violating user privacy or regulatory compliance requirements? Traditional deep packet inspection techniques require decryption, which contradicts privacy regulations such as GDPR [32] and CCPA [1], imposes substantial computational overhead [21], and may be technically infeasible when attackers employ certificate pinning [10]. This work addresses the following research problem: *Given a stream of TLS-encrypted network flows, can we accurately classify traffic as malicious or benign by analyzing only metadata extracted from TLS handshakes, specifically JA4 and JA4S fingerprints, combined with supervised machine learning, while maintaining privacy and real-time detection capabilities?*

This work addresses several key research questions:

- What is the discriminative power of JA4 and JA4S fingerprints for distinguishing malicious from benign TLS traffic?
- Which supervised machine learning algorithms (Random Forest, XGBoost, or Logistic Regression) achieve the best performance for this classification task?
- How does the combination of JA4 and JA4S fingerprints compare to using either fingerprint alone?

By answering these questions, this work aims to provide empirical evidence on the effectiveness of JA4 and JA4S fingerprinting combined with machine learning for privacy-preserving malware detection in encrypted traffic.

Formally, we define the problem as follows. Let $\mathcal{F} = \{f_1, f_2, \ldots, f_n\}$ represent a collection of TLS network flows, where each flow f_i consists of a sequence of encrypted packets. For each flow f_i, we extract a feature vector $\mathbf{x}_i = (ja4_i, ja4s_i)$ consisting of the JA4 client fingerprint and JA4S server fingerprint obtained from the TLS handshake. The classification task is to learn a function $h : \mathbf{x}_i \rightarrow \{0, 1\}$ that maps each feature vector to a binary label, where 0 indicates benign traffic and 1 indicates malicious traffic. The objective is to maximize classification accuracy while maintaining the following constraints:

- *Privacy preservation*: no decryption of payload content is required.
- *Computational efficiency*: detection must be feasible in real-time for large-scale networks.
- *Generalization*: the classifier must perform well on previously unseen malware families and benign applications.

3 Related Work

Research into malware detection in encrypted traffic has evolved significantly over the past decade, transitioning from statistical flow analysis to advanced fingerprint-based and machine learning approaches. This section reviews key developments and positions our work within the existing research landscape.

3.1 Early Flow-Based Approaches

Anderson and McGrew [4] were among the first researchers to demonstrate that machine learning could classify encrypted traffic by analyzing flow-level metadata such as packet lengths, inter-arrival times, and flow duration, rather than payload content. Their seminal work showed that statistical features alone could achieve reasonable classification accuracy. Garcia et al. [11] advanced this area by comparing multiple botnet detection techniques and confirming that non-payload metadata features can effectively distinguish malicious network connections from benign traffic.

These foundational approaches continued to evolve, with researchers refining flow-based feature sets for encrypted traffic analysis. Prasse et al. [24] demonstrated that network flow features combined with LSTM networks can detect malware in encrypted HTTPS traffic, achieving 64% recall at 70% precision on real network data. Komarek and Somol [15] showed that timing patterns and byte transfer statistics derived from web proxy logs provide robust indicators for identifying infected endpoints communicating via HTTPS. Kohout [14] further validated that flow-level features including bytes sent/received, duration, and inter-arrival time enable scalable malware detection in corporate networks without payload inspection, establishing flow-based analysis as a foundation for privacy-preserving encrypted traffic classification.

3.2 TLS Fingerprinting Methods

A major breakthrough in encrypted traffic analysis came with the development of TLS fingerprinting techniques. Early approaches, specifically JA3 and its server-side counterpart JA3S [2], proposed methods which encode handshake properties including cipher suites, extensions, and supported versions into hash strings that uniquely identify client and server implementations. This approach revolutionized encrypted traffic analysis by enabling application identification without decryption [31]. However, early fingerprinting methods suffered from significant limitations. The MD5-based hashing was prone to collisions, and the method lacked standardization across different implementations [16].

To overcome these limitations, the JA4+ suite [3] was proposed, which provides structured and collision-resistant encoding for TLS fingerprints. JA4+ improves upon earlier methods by incorporating additional TLS parameters, using a human-readable format, and ensuring standardization across sessions. Recent analysis by Matoušek et al. [20] analyzed JA4+ effectiveness on real-world datasets, examining its advantages in distinguishing between different malware families and benign applications compared to earlier fingerprinting methods. Their comprehensive study demonstrated that combining JA4, JA4S, and SNI fingerprints achieves 87% uniqueness with 79% malware family coverage.

3.3 Machine Learning for Encrypted Traffic Classification

Machine learning has become increasingly central to modern encrypted traffic classification. López-Martín et al. [18] demonstrated that convolutional neural networks (CNNs) can detect patterns in encrypted data streams. Rezaei and Liu [26] conducted a comprehensive survey of deep learning methods for encrypted traffic classification, emphasizing their potential while noting challenges in computational cost and model explainability.

Building on these foundations, Lotfollahi et al. [19] proposed their Deep Packet approach, which uses deep learning for encrypted traffic classification without requiring manual feature extraction. Their work demonstrated that CNNs and stacked autoencoders can effectively learn representations directly from raw encrypted traffic, achieving high accuracy on both application identification and traffic categorization tasks.

Shekhawat et al. [28] conducted a comprehensive feature analysis of encrypted malicious traffic, comparing statistical features and their discriminative power for malware detection. Their work demonstrated that XGBoost and Random Forest achieve nearly 99% accuracy when using properly selected features from encrypted traffic, validating the effectiveness of ensemble methods. This study emphasized feature analysis based on machine learning models rather than relying solely on human expertise to identify relevant features. While [28] focused on extracting and analyzing 38 statistical features through comprehensive feature engineering, our work takes a complementary approach by evaluating the recently introduced JA4+ fingerprints [3] as a minimal feature set (only JA4 and JA4S) for malware detection. Additionally, we employ rigorous fingerprint-level splitting to prevent data leakage, whereas traditional approaches use flow-level splitting that may overestimate performance when the same fingerprints appear in both training and testing sets.

Calderon [8] conducted behavior testing to identify HTTP and HTTPS network packets using machine learning methods to detect malware characteristics. Their experimental results showed precision and recall exceeding 96% on average, demonstrating that behavioral features extracted from encrypted traffic provide strong discriminative power for malware detection.

Komarek and Somol [15] addressed the challenge of detecting end-nodes infected with malware that communicates via HTTPS by modeling communication patterns based on timing and transferred bytes. Their approach focused on web proxy logs to analyze traffic generated by end nodes in monitored networks, achieving 90% precision and 100% recall on real network data.

Kohout [14] proposed a statistical descriptor approach to identify HTTPS communication patterns using a map-reduce framework for efficient feature extraction from large-scale web traffic logs. Their framework extracted features including bytes sent and received, duration, and inter-arrival time, achieving 90% precision and 60% recall while providing a scalable solution for encrypted traffic analysis in corporate networks.

Barut et al. [7] conducted a comprehensive performance study comparing various machine learning and deep learning algorithms for malware detection on encrypted traffic. They evaluated models including Random Forest, SVM, and deep neural networks on two datasets, analyzing not only classification accuracy but also computational requirements and resource utilization. Their findings revealed that simpler machine learning models like Random Forest can achieve comparable or superior accuracy to complex deep learning models while requiring significantly fewer computational resources.

Prasse et al. [24] proposed one of the first methods to apply neural networks to encrypted HTTPS traffic by modeling flow-level characteristics without payload inspection. Their approach demonstrated that temporal patterns in encrypted traffic can be exploited for malware detection, reporting moderate precision and recall under realistic experimental settings. While effective, their results also highlighted challenges related to generalization and performance degradation when evaluated on future traffic traces.

3.4 Hybrid Approaches

Recent work has explored combining fingerprinting with behavioral analysis and machine learning. Anderson et al. [5] investigated methods for deciphering malware's use of TLS without requiring decryption, demonstrating that TLS metadata combined with contextual flow data can effectively identify malware.

Shen et al. [29] proposed a method that combines TLS fingerprinting using second-order Markov chains with application attribute bigrams for encrypted traffic classification. Their approach showed that incorporating both temporal patterns from Markov chains and structural TLS handshake features significantly improves classification accuracy compared to using either method independently.

Polo-Peyres et al. [22] compared a MalDIST-inspired statistical model with a JA4+-based fingerprint classifier, achieving up to 98.28% accuracy on a dataset containing four malware families. Their work also introduced JA4TS, a TCP-layer fingerprint designed to remain effective when Server Name Indication (SNI) information is encrypted. However, their evaluation employed flow-level splitting, allowing identical fingerprint combinations to appear in both training and testing sets. In contrast, our work adopts fingerprint-level splitting to eliminate train/test fingerprint overlap and evaluates performance across a broader dataset comprising 19 malware families.

These findings further validate the potential of hybrid approaches that leverage both structural information from fingerprints and behavioral patterns from machine learning features.

3.5 Research Gap and Motivation for This Work

While prior research has investigated TLS fingerprinting methods such as JA3, JA3S, and JA4+, as well as machine learning-based approaches for encrypted traffic classification, these directions have largely evolved independently. As a result, there is limited systematic research that integrates modern JA4+ fingerprints with supervised machine learning classifiers and evaluates their effectiveness on real-world malware datasets.

JA4+ was officially released in September 2023 [3], making it a recent development in network fingerprinting. Early studies on encrypted traffic classification have primarily relied on flow-level statistical features or legacy fingerprinting techniques. In contrast, Matoušek et al. [20] provided the first large-scale empirical analysis of JA4+ fingerprints, demonstrating that combined JA4, JA4S, and SNI fingerprints achieve 87% uniqueness with 79% malware family coverage on real-world datasets. Their work established the statistical discriminative power of JA4+ fingerprints but focused on characterization metrics such as uniqueness and coverage rather than integrating these fingerprints into supervised machine learning classifiers for malware detection.

This limitation becomes more evident when contrasted with earlier hybrid approaches. For example, Shen et al. [29] combined TLS fingerprinting with machine learning using Markov chain-based representations, but their methodology predates the standardized JA4+ framework. Similarly, Barut et al. [7] conducted a comprehensive evaluation of machine learning algorithms for encrypted traffic malware detection, yet relied on flow-based statistical features rather than structured TLS fingerprinting.

Overall, existing studies tend to emphasize either:

- fingerprinting methods evaluated through statistical analysis without machine learning classification,
- machine learning approaches based on flow-level features without structured fingerprinting, or
- academic datasets that may not capture realistic malware diversity and evasion behavior.

Consequently, it remains unclear whether the statistical distinctiveness observed in JA4+ fingerprints translates into robust, generalizable malware detection performance when used as features in supervised learning models.

Our work addresses this gap by proposing a comprehensive framework that systematically integrates JA4 and JA4S fingerprints with supervised machine learning algorithms, evaluated on a large-scale dataset of 72,816 TLS flows combining real malware traffic from malware-traffic-analysis.net [9], botnet traffic from the CTU-13 dataset [11], and realistic benign traffic from Wireshark captures [33] and public PCAP repositories. By comparing Random Forest, XGBoost, and Logistic Regression under a rigorous fingerprint-level splitting protocol that prevents data leakage, and validating against a non-ML majority-label baseline, we provide empirical evidence that JA4+ fingerprints enable genuine generalization rather than fingerprint memorization, establishing them as effective features for privacy-preserving malware detection.

Table 1 summarizes the key differences between our proposed approach and related work in this domain.

4 Preliminaries

This section establishes the foundational concepts, notation, and assumptions underlying our proposed framework for malware detection in encrypted traffic.

4.1 TLS and JA4/JA4S Fingerprint Structure

During the TLS handshake [25], client and server exchange ClientHello (H_c) and ServerHello (H_s) plaintext messages that expose cipher suites, extensions, and protocol versions. A fingerprinting function ϕ encodes these parameters into a compact string that identifies applications or malware families without payload decryption [2].

JA4 [3] structures this as a_b_c, where component a encodes protocol, TLS version, SNI presence, and extension/cipher counts; component b is a 12-character hash of sorted cipher suites (sorting resists randomization evasion); and component c is a 12-character hash of sorted extensions excluding GREASE values. For example, `t13d190900_9dc949149365_97f8aa674fd9` denotes TCP, TLS 1.3, SNI present, 19 cipher suites, 9 extensions. JA4S mirrors this structure for the ServerHello, encoding the server's chosen cipher suite and extensions, providing complementary server-side signal [3].

4.2 Feature Vector Representation

For each TLS flow $f_i \in \mathcal{F}$, we construct a feature vector $\mathbf{x}_i$ by extracting both JA4 and JA4S fingerprints during the handshake. Formally, let $\phi_{JA4}(H_c)$ denote the JA4 fingerprinting function applied to the ClientHello message, and $\phi_{JA4S}(H_s)$ denote the JA4S fingerprinting function applied to the ServerHello message. The feature vector is then

$$\mathbf{x}_i = (\phi_{JA4}(H_{c,i}), \phi_{JA4S}(H_{s,i})). \tag{1}$$

Table 1. Comparison of related work on TLS fingerprinting and machine learning for malware detection.

Study	Fingerprinting	ML Classifier	Dataset	Accuracy/Performance
Anderson & McGrew [4]	Flow metadata	DT, RF	Custom	~95% accuracy
Shen et al. [29]	Markov chains	Bigram analysis	Academic	~92% accuracy
Althouse [2]	JA3, JA3S	Statistical	Real traffic	Fingerprint-based
Komarek & Somol [15]	Web proxy logs	Fingerprint-based	Real network	P: 90%, R: 100%
Prasse et al. [24]	Network flow	LSTM	Real HTTPS	P: 70–90%, R: 41–64%
Calderon [8]	HTTPS packets	Weka framework	Real traffic	P: 96%, R: 96%
Shekhawat et al. [28]	Statistical features	XGBoost, RF, SVM	CTU-13	XGB: 99%, RF: 98%
Barut et al. [7]	Flow features	RF, SVM, DNN	Benchmark	RF: 96%, DNN: 95%
Matoušek et al. [20]	JA4 + JA4S + SNI	Statistical	Real malware	87% uniqueness
Polo-Peyres et al. [22]	JA4+, JA4S, JA4TS, SNI	RF	4 malware families	98.28% (flow-level)
This work	**JA4 + JA4S**	**RF, XGBoost, LR**	**Real malware/Benign (72,816 flows)**	**RF: 96.79%*, XGB: 98.80%***

"P" denotes Precision and "R" denotes Recall.
*Classification accuracy with fingerprint-level splitting on entirely unseen fingerprint combinations (zero train/test overlap).
Note: Matoušek et al. [20] report fingerprint uniqueness metrics (87% unique fingerprints) rather than classification accuracy, as they used statistical analysis without machine learning classifiers.
Polo-Peyres et al. [22] report 98.28% accuracy using flow-level splitting, whereas our work employs fingerprint-level splitting with zero train/test fingerprint overlap

Each component of the fingerprint (the three parts a, b, and c for both JA4 and JA4S) are treated as separate features, resulting in a six-dimensional categorical feature space. These categorical features are then encoded using `OrdinalEncoder` [27] for input to machine learning classifiers. The resulting encoded values do not imply any semantic or numerical ordering between fingerprints, they are used solely to provide a compact numerical representation suitable for machine learning models.

4.3 Classification Task

Given a labeled dataset $\mathcal{D} = \{(\mathbf{x}_1, y_1), (\mathbf{x}_2, y_2), \ldots, (\mathbf{x}_n, y_n)\}$, where $\mathbf{x}_i$ is the feature vector and $y_i \in \{0, 1\}$ is the binary label (0 for benign, 1 for malicious), the goal is to learn a classifier $h : \mathcal{X} \rightarrow \{0, 1\}$ that minimizes the classification error. We evaluate three supervised learning algorithms: Random Forest, XGBoost, and Logistic Regression. The performance of each classifier is assessed using standard metrics including accuracy, precision, recall, F1-score, and area under the ROC curve (AUC).

4.4 Algorithm Selection Rationale

We selected Random Forest, XGBoost, and Logistic Regression based on the following considerations informed by prior research.

Random Forest was chosen due to its demonstrated effectiveness in prior work on encrypted traffic classification [7]. Barut et al. [7] showed that Random Forest achieves comparable or superior accuracy to deep learning models while requiring significantly fewer computational resources, making it suitable for real-time detection in large-scale networks. Additionally, Random Forest provides feature importance metrics and is robust to overfitting through ensemble learning.

XGBoost represents the state-of-the-art in gradient boosting algorithms and has achieved exceptional performance on numerous classification benchmarks. We include XGBoost to evaluate whether its advanced regularization techniques and optimized implementation can further improve detection accuracy compared to Random Forest. XGBoost's ability to handle categorical features efficiently makes it particularly suitable for fingerprint-based classification.

Logistic Regression serves as a linear baseline classifier to establish the inherent separability of malicious and benign fingerprints in the feature space. If Logistic Regression achieves competitive performance, it would indicate that fingerprint patterns are linearly separable, enabling deployment of lightweight detection systems. Conversely, superior performance by Random Forest or XGBoost (as confirmed by our results) demonstrates the value of capturing non-linear relationships in fingerprint data.

4.5 Threat Model and Assumptions

We consider an adversarial setting where attackers deploy malware that communicates over TLS-encrypted channels to evade detection. Our threat model makes the following assumptions about adversary capabilities and defender constraints.
Adversary Capabilities. The adversary uses TLS encryption to conceal C2 communications, malware updates, and data exfiltration, and may select any cipher suites, TLS versions, and extensions supported by their implementation. They may also randomize TLS parameters or employ evasion techniques such as cipher stunting [3].
Defender Constraints. The defender cannot decrypt TLS traffic due to privacy regulations (GDPR, CCPA), but has access to a network monitoring point where TLS handshakes are visible in cleartext, along with labeled training data of known malicious and benign flows. Detection must operate in real-time to enable timely response.
Algorithmic Dependencies. Our proposed framework relies on the following properties of TLS implementations and network behavior:

- *Fingerprint Consistency:* Malware families exhibit relatively consistent TLS fingerprint patterns due to their underlying TLS library implementations. While individual parameters may vary across connections, the combination of JA4 and JA4S provides sufficient discriminative power to identify malware families. This property has been empirically validated by our results showing 98.80% accuracy with fingerprint-level splitting on 72,816 TLS flows.
- *Dataset Representativeness:* The training dataset is representative of real-world traffic distributions for the malware families and benign applications included. However, we acknowledge that adversaries may develop new evasion techniques over time, requiring periodic model retraining with updated

samples to maintain detection effectiveness. Families such as HTBOT and Zeus, which exhibit TLS configurations resembling benign traffic, illustrate this limitation and motivate future work on adversarial robustness.

Under this threat model, our proposed framework aims to detect malware by identifying anomalous or known-malicious fingerprint patterns while preserving user privacy and maintaining computational efficiency.

5 Methodology

This section describes our experimental methodology, including dataset collection, feature extraction, and the machine learning pipeline used to evaluate the effectiveness of JA4 and JA4S fingerprints for malware detection.

5.1 Data Collection

We assembled a dataset consisting of both malicious and benign TLS traffic from multiple sources to train and evaluate our classifiers.

Malicious Traffic. Malicious TLS flows were collected from two sources. The primary source is malware-traffic-analysis.net [9], which provided labeled PCAP files covering a diverse range of malware families. The secondary source is the CTU-13 dataset [11], a publicly available benchmark dataset of botnet traffic captured at the Czech Technical University, which provided additional malicious flows representing botnet command-and-control communications. Together, these sources contributed 36,957 malicious TLS flows spanning 19 malware families: AgentTesla (756 flows), BazarLoader (702 flows), Bumblebee (749 flows), Bunitu (7,661 flows), Dridex (200 flows), Emotet (919 flows), HTBOT (5,882 flows), IceID (640 flows), KoiLoader (152 flows), LummaStealer (146 flows), NetSupport RAT (477 flows), PikaBot (602 flows), QakBot (812 flows), Remcos RAT (208 flows), TrickBot (8,294 flows), XLoader (222 flows), Zeus (236 flows), and additional mixed-label samples. This diversity ensures our classifiers are exposed to a wide range of malware behaviors and TLS implementation patterns.

Benign Traffic. Benign TLS flows were collected from two sources, contributing a combined total of 39,436 flows. The first source consists of flows captured using tcpdump and Wireshark during normal browsing activities including Google, YouTube, Gmail, GitHub, LinkedIn, and X, representing typical user web activity. The second source is the CTU-13 dataset [11], which contributed additional benign background traffic captured in a real university network environment, further diversifying the benign class beyond controlled browsing sessions.

Dataset Summary. The raw dataset contains 76,393 TLS flows. After removing 3,577 flows associated with 32 mixed-label fingerprint combinations (fingerprints appearing with both benign and malicious labels), the final dataset comprises 72,816 flows across 1,784 unique JA4+JA4S fingerprint combinations.

5.2 Fingerprint Extraction and Dataset Construction

All packet captures were processed using the JA4+ reference implementation (ja4.py) [3], extracting client-side JA4 and server-side JA4S fingerprints from each PCAP via `ja4.py -J --ja4 --ja4s input.pcap -f output.json`. All metadata (IP addresses, ports, SNI, packet lengths) was discarded to avoid data leakage, ensuring the classifier learns exclusively from TLS handshake characteristics. Malicious and benign fingerprints were then merged and encoded using scikit-learn's OrdinalEncoder with `handle_unknown="use_encoded_value"` to handle unseen categories at test time. Three feature configurations were evaluated: JA4 only, JA4S only, and combined JA4+JA4S.

5.3 Fingerprint-Level Train/Test Split

A critical methodological consideration in TLS fingerprint-based classification is the proper separation of training and testing data. In our dataset of 72,816 TLS flows, many flows share identical JA4+JA4S fingerprint combinations due to the nature of TLS implementations: malware from the same family typically relies on the same TLS library configuration, while benign applications maintain stable handshake parameters across connections. Our analysis identified 1,784 unique JA4+JA4S fingerprint combinations, with an average repetition rate of approximately 41 flows per fingerprint.

If a standard flow-level split were applied, randomly dividing the 72,816 flows into training and testing sets, the same fingerprint combinations would appear in both subsets. This would introduce a data leakage issue, allowing the model to memorize fingerprint-to-label associations instead of learning discriminative patterns, leading to artificially inflated test accuracy.

To ensure a rigorous and leakage-free evaluation, we adopt *fingerprint-level splitting*. First, all 1,784 unique JA4+JA4S fingerprint combinations are identified. We then perform a stratified split on these unique fingerprints (70% for training, 30% for testing) to preserve class balance. All flows associated with training fingerprints are assigned to the training set (52,001 flows), while all flows associated with testing fingerprints are assigned to the testing set (20,815 flows). We verify that there is zero fingerprint overlap between the training and testing partitions.

A direct consequence of this strict splitting protocol is that *all* 20,815 test flows correspond to fingerprint combinations entirely unseen during training. This enforces a genuine generalization setting rather than a trivial memorization-based one, and motivates our inclusion of a non-ML majority-label baseline (Sect. 6.2) to confirm that ML classifiers learn structural patterns rather than fingerprint-level lookup rules.

5.4 Model Training

Three classifiers were evaluated with the following configurations.

Random Forest was employed as an ensemble-based classifier to capture non-linear relationships in JA4 and JA4S fingerprint features. The model was configured with 300 decision trees using bootstrap aggregation, which improves robustness and reduces overfitting by averaging multiple randomized trees.

Logistic Regression was used as a linear baseline classifier to assess the inherent separability of the extracted fingerprint features. The model was trained using default hyperparameters with L2 regularization, providing an interpretable reference point for comparison against more complex ensemble methods.

XGBoost was utilized as a gradient-boosted decision tree model to achieve high predictive performance on structured fingerprint data. The classifier was trained with 300 estimators and a maximum tree depth of 6, balancing model complexity and generalization performance.

Each model was trained using each feature configuration. Performance was measured using accuracy, precision, recall, F1-score, ROC-AUC, and confusion matrices as defined in Sect. 5.5.

Cross-Validation. To verify robustness and generalization capability, 5-fold stratified cross-validation was applied. Tree-based models (Random Forest and XGBoost) demonstrated consistent performance across folds with variance less than 0 3%, indicating strong stability and generalization to unseen data.

Overfitting Detection. Training and testing accuracy were compared to detect overfitting. Models achieved near-perfect training accuracy with test accuracy above 96%, confirming limited overfitting and good generalization.

Leakage Testing. To validate that results originate from genuine fingerprint patterns rather than data leakage or memorization, we conducted three validation experiments: a label permutation test, a feature importance analysis, and a cross-fingerprint generalization test under a stricter JA4-level split. Full results are reported in Sect. 6.6.

5.5 Evaluation Metrics

Performance is assessed using standard binary classification metrics [23,30]: accuracy, precision, recall, F1-score, ROC-AUC, and confusion matrices (True positives-TP, True Negatives-TN, False Positives-FP, False Negatives-FN). Model stability is evaluated using 5-fold stratified cross-validation [13].

6 Results

This section presents our experimental results comparing classifier performance across different feature configurations. All results are based on 72,816 TLS flows (after removing 3,577 flows associated with 32 mixed-label fingerprints), comprising 1,784 unique JA4+JA4S fingerprint combinations split at the fingerprint level into 52,001 training flows and 20,815 test flows.

6.1 Overall Performance

Table 2 presents the classification results using combined JA4 and JA4S fingerprints under fingerprint-level splitting, including a non-ML majority-label baseline.

Table 2. Classification Results with JA4 + JA4S Combined Features (Fingerprint-Level Split), including Non-ML Baseline

Classifier	Accuracy	Precision	Recall	F1
Majority-Label Baseline	26.09%	26.09%	100.00%	41.38%
Logistic Regression	20.47%	19.32%	64.53%	29.74%
Random Forest	96.79%	98.79%	88.77%	93.51%
XGBoost	98.80%	98.54%	96.85%	97.69%

XGBoost achieved the highest overall performance with 98.80% accuracy, 96.85% recall, and 99.85% ROC-AUC. Random Forest performed comparably with 96.79% accuracy and 98.88% ROC-AUC. More importantly, both ensemble methods maintain excellent performance even under rigorous fingerprint-level evaluation. Logistic Regression underperformed significantly with only 20.47% accuracy and 29.74% F1-score, confirming that the relationship between fingerprint features and traffic labels is non-linear and cannot be captured by a linear classifier.

These results provide empirical validation that machine learning classifiers can effectively leverage JA4+ fingerprints for malware detection. Matoušek et al. [20] demonstrated through statistical analysis that JA4+JA4S+SNI fingerprints achieve 87% uniqueness in distinguishing malware families. Our work builds upon this foundation by showing that these distinctive fingerprints enable highly accurate machine learning-based classification, achieving 96.79–98.80% accuracy in identifying malicious versus benign encrypted traffic.

6.2 Comparison with Non-ML Majority-Label Baseline

To directly address whether the ML classifier contributes beyond a simple fingerprint lookup table, we evaluate a non-ML majority-label baseline. For each fingerprint observed during training, the baseline assigns the majority label of all flows sharing that fingerprint. For fingerprints absent from the training set, it falls back to the global majority class.

A critical result of our fingerprint-level splitting protocol is that *all* 20,815 test flows correspond to fingerprints entirely unseen during training (zero overlap between training and test fingerprint sets). Consequently, the baseline is forced to fall back to the global majority class (malicious) for every test flow, yielding only 26.09% accuracy and an F1-score of 41.38%, while producing 15,385 false positives and zero true negatives.

In contrast, XGBoost achieves 98.80% accuracy on the same set of entirely unseen fingerprints, representing an absolute improvement of +72.71% over the baseline. SImilarly, Random Forest improves by +70.70%. Furthermore, XGBoost correctly classifies 15,307 benign flows that the baseline misclassifies entirely, while producing only 78 false positives and 171 false negatives out of 20,815 flows.

These results demonstrate that ML classifiers do not merely memorize fingerprint-to-label mappings. Instead, they learn generalizable structural patterns from JA4 and JA4S fingerprint encodings, such as TLS version fields, cipher suite counts, and extension hashes, enabling accurate classification of previously unseen fingerprint combinations. This finding directly validates the contribution of supervised machine learning over non-ML alternatives for privacy-preserving malware detection in encrypted traffic.

Table 3. Random Forest Performance by Feature Configuration (Fingerprint-Level Split)

Features	Accuracy	F1-Score	ROC-AUC
JA4 Only	99.27%	98.61%	99.07%
JA4S Only	59.99%	44.24%	73.37%
JA4 + JA4S	96.79%	93.51%	98.88%

6.3 Feature Configuration Comparison

Table 3 compares Random Forest performance across different feature configurations. These results reveal several important findings. JA4 fingerprints alone achieve the highest accuracy (99.27%) and F1-score (98.61%), demonstrating that client-side TLS characteristics are the primary discriminative signal for malware detection in our dataset.

In contrast, JA4S fingerprints alone perform poorly (59.99% accuracy, 44.24% F1-score), only marginally above random classification. This suggests that server-side TLS parameters exhibit high overlap between malicious and benign traffic, likely because both categories frequently communicate with servers using similar TLS configurations (e.g., common CDNs or hosting providers).

Counterintuitively, combining JA4 and JA4S yields *lower* accuracy (96.79%) than JA4 alone (99.27%). This result indicates that the weak discriminative power of JA4S introduces noise into the feature space, degrading the overall classification performance when combined with JA4. This finding has a practical implication: in resource-constrained environments, deploying JA4 fingerprints alone is not only simpler but also more accurate than using the combined JA4+JA4S representation.

These results extend and refine prior findings by Matoušek et al. [20], who reported that combined JA4, JA4S, and SNI fingerprints achieve 87% uniqueness for malware family discrimination. Our classification experiments show that this uniqueness is driven primarily by the client-side JA4 component, with JA4S contributing limited additional discriminative value for supervised classification on our dataset.

6.4 Confusion Matrix Analysis

Table 4 presents the confusion matrices for Random Forest and XGBoost using combined JA4 + JA4S features under fingerprint-level splitting.

Table 4. Confusion Matrices for Ensemble Classifiers (JA4 + JA4S, Fingerprint-Level Split)

Classifier	TN	FP	FN	TP
Random Forest	15,326	59	610	4,820
XGBoost	15,307	78	171	5,259

XGBoost achieves a false negative rate of 3.15% (171 out of 5,430 malicious flows), while Random Forest produces a higher false negative count of 610 (11.23%), reflecting its lower recall compared to XGBoost. In terms of false positives, Random Forest generates fewer false alarms (59 vs. 78), indicating a slightly more conservative classification boundary.

These results highlight a trade-off between the two ensemble methods: XGBoost offers superior recall (96.85% vs. 88.77%), making it more suitable for security-critical deployments where failing to identify malware is more costly than generating false alarms. Random Forest, on the other hand, produces fewer false positives, which may be preferable in environments where alert fatigue is a primary concern.

Overall, both classifiers demonstrate strong performance on 20,815 entirely unseen test flows, confirming that the proposed framework generalizes effectively to new TLS fingerprint combinations not observed during training.

6.5 Computational Performance Measurements

In addition to classification accuracy, we evaluated the computational efficiency of each classifier to inform deployment decisions. All timing measurements were

Table 5. Computational Performance on Standard Hardware (52,001 training/20,815 test samples)

Classifier	TrainingTime (s)	TestingTime (s)	Time perSample (ms)	Throughput(samples/s)
Random Forest	1.312	0.118	0.00568	176,113
Logistic Regression	0.078	0.0001	0.00001	182,030,449
XGBoost	0.360	0.019	0.00091	1,095,515

conducted on a standard workstation equipped with an Intel Core i7 processor and 16 GB RAM, using Python 3.11 with scikit-learn 1.3.0 and XGBoost 2.0.0.
Training Phase: Table 5 presents the training time for each classifier on 52,001 samples. Random Forest training completed in 1.312 s, XGBoost in 0.360 s, and Logistic Regression in 0.078 s. These training times are acceptable for operational deployment, as model training can be performed offline during scheduled maintenance windows. Training time scales linearly with dataset size, and even for datasets exceeding 500,000 samples, training would complete within minutes on commodity hardware.
Inference Phase: Classification of the 20,815 test samples completed in 0.118 s for Random Forest, corresponding to approximately 0.006 milliseconds per sample and a throughput of 176,113 samples per second. XGBoost achieved higher throughput at 1,095,515 samples per second (0.019 s total, 0.001 ms per sample), while Logistic Regression demonstrated exceptional inference speed at over 182 million samples per second. These performance characteristics confirm that all three classifiers far exceed typical enterprise network traffic volumes and are suitable for real-time network monitoring.
Deployment Feasibility: The computational analysis reveals that inference latency is well below the typical requirements for real-time network security monitoring (<10 ms per flow). Even Random Forest, the slowest of the three classifiers, processes over 176,000 flows per second, which is sufficient for enterprise networks handling thousands of concurrent TLS connections. XGBoost's superior throughput (approximately 6× faster than Random Forest) makes it particularly suitable for high-volume environments, while maintaining higher accuracy than Random Forest (98.80% vs. 96.79%).

These results confirm that the proposed framework is computationally feasible for production deployment in real-time network monitoring systems, with all classifiers demonstrating acceptable training times and inference latencies suitable for operational use.

6.6 Validation of Genuine Generalization

To confirm that the reported results reflect genuine learning of discriminative TLS patterns rather than fingerprint memorization or data leakage, we conducted three independent validation experiments.

Label Permutation Test. In each of ten independent trials, training labels were randomly shuffled to break the correspondence between fingerprint features and class labels, and XGBoost was retrained from scratch on the permuted data. Table 6 summarizes the results.

Table 6. Label Permutation Test Results (XGBoost, 10 Trials)

Condition	Accuracy
Real labels	98.80%
Permuted labels (avg)	36.54%
Permuted labels (max)	67.32%
Permuted labels (min)	21.20%
Gap (real – permuted avg)	**+62.26%**

The collapse to near-random performance under label permutation confirms that the model's discriminative power originates from genuine structural patterns in JA4 and JA4S fingerprints rather than from data leakage or label memorization. The +62.26% gap between real and permuted accuracy provides strong statistical evidence that the learned decision boundaries reflect true signal in the data.

Feature Importance Analysis. To understand which fingerprint component drives classification, we analyzed feature importance for both Random Forest and XGBoost. Table 7 presents the results.

Table 7. Feature Importance: JA4 vs JA4S

Feature	Random Forest	XGBoost
JA4 (client-side)	69.44%	70.57%
JA4S (server-side)	30.56%	29.43%

Both models consistently assign higher importance to JA4 client-side fingerprints, with JA4 accounting for approximately 70% of the classification signal. This result is directly consistent with the feature configuration comparison (Sect. 6.3), where JA4 alone achieves 99.27% accuracy, higher than the combined JA4+JA4S representation (96.79%). The dominance of JA4 importance confirms that client-side TLS characteristics are the primary discriminative signal, and that JA4S introduces noise that slightly degrades performance when combined with JA4.

Cross-Fingerprint Generalization Test. To evaluate generalization under an even stricter condition than our primary fingerprint-level split, we performed an additional evaluation splitting at the JA4 level rather than the JA4+JA4S tuple level. This prevents any JA4 fingerprint seen during training from appearing in the test set, regardless of its paired JA4S value. Table 8 presents the results under this stricter protocol (28,323 training flows, 10,685 test flows, zero JA4 overlap).

Table 8. Cross-fingerprint Generalization: JA4-Level Split vs JA4+JA4S-Level Split

Split Protocol	Classifier	Accuracy	ROC-AUC
JA4+JA4S-level (primary)	Random Forest	96.79%	98.88%
JA4+JA4S-level (primary)	XGBoost	98.80%	99.85%
JA4-level (stricter)	Random Forest	67.48%	68.21%
JA4-level (stricter)	XGBoost	66.55%	77.37%

The performance reduction under the JA4-level split is expected and informative. It reveals that the model's generalization relies on the combination of JA4 and JA4S patterns: when JA4 is entirely unseen, the remaining signal from JA4S alone is insufficient for high accuracy. This is consistent with the feature importance results showing JA4S contributing approximately 30% of the classification signal. An interesting note is that 155 JA4S fingerprints are shared between training and test sets in this stricter split, reflecting the fact that malicious and benign flows frequently share server-side TLS configurations (e.g., both connecting to Microsoft or Google infrastructure), which limits the discriminative power of JA4S in isolation.

Validation Summary. Table 9 summarizes the three validation experiments and their implications.

Table 9. Summary of Validation Experiments

Test	Key Result	Conclusion
Label Permutation	Permuted avg: 36.54%	No data leakage
Feature Importance	JA4: ∼70%	Client-side drives signal
Strict Split (JA4)	Accuracy: ∼67%	JA4+JA4S jointly needed

Together, these three validation tests provide strong evidence that the reported classification results reflect genuine learning of discriminative TLS behavioral patterns. The label permutation test rules out data leakage, the feature importance analysis identifies the client-side JA4 fingerprint as the primary signal, and the cross-fingerprint generalization test confirms that both JA4 and JA4S contribute to the model's generalization capability.

6.7 Discussion

Our results demonstrate that JA4 and JA4S fingerprinting combined with ensemble machine learning achieves strong malware detection under rigorous fingerprint-level evaluation. XGBoost achieves 98.80% accuracy and Random Forest 96.79%, validating that these fingerprints enable effective machine learning-based malware detection on a large-scale dataset of 72,816 TLS flows across 1,784 unique fingerprint combinations. The baseline comparison directly addresses whether the ML classifier contributes beyond a simple fingerprint lookup table. Since fingerprint-level splitting guarantees zero overlap between training and test fingerprints, a majority-label lookup baseline achieves only 26.09% accuracy, as it cannot generalize to unseen fingerprint combinations. The substantial gap between the baseline and ensemble classifiers (+72.71% for XGBoost, +70.70% for Random Forest) provides strong empirical evidence that the ML models capture structural regularities in JA4 and JA4S encodings rather than relying on fingerprint memorization. This is further confirmed by the label permutation test, where XGBoost trained on shuffled labels achieves only 36.54% average accuracy across ten trials, compared to 98.80% with real labels.

Contextualizing within the JA4+ landscape, Matoušek et al. [20] reported 87% fingerprint uniqueness through statistical analysis alone; our work shows this translates into 96.79–98.80% classification accuracy on entirely unseen fingerprint combinations.

The finding that JA4 alone (99.27%) outperforms JA4+JA4S (96.79%) has a clear practical implication: server-side configurations are frequently shared between malicious and benign traffic (e.g., both communicating with Microsoft or Google infrastructure), so JA4S introduces noise rather than signal in our dataset, making JA4 alone the preferred choice for resource-constrained deployments.

The poor performance of Logistic Regression (20.47% accuracy) confirms that fingerprint–label relationships are non-linear, requiring ensemble methods to capture complex decision boundaries.

7 Conclusions

This work presented a privacy-preserving framework for malware detection in TLS-encrypted traffic using JA4 and JA4S fingerprints with supervised machine learning. On 72,816 TLS flows spanning 19 malware families, XGBoost achieved 98.80% accuracy and 97.69% F1-score under fingerprint-level splitting, where all 20,815 test flows corresponded to unseen fingerprint combinations. The +72.71% improvement over a majority-label baseline, validated through label permutation testing, demonstrates that the models learn meaningful patterns rather than memorizing fingerprint-label associations.

A key finding is that JA4 alone (99.27%) outperforms JA4+JA4S (96.79%), suggesting that shared server-side TLS configurations can introduce noise. Furthermore, all evaluated classifiers satisfy real-time deployment requirements.

Future work should evaluate the framework on larger and more diverse datasets, investigate robustness against fingerprint mimicry and evasion techniques, and extend the approach to multi-class malware family classification. Deployment in operational environments and integration with IDS/IPS platforms such as Snort, Suricata, and Zeek would further validate practical applicability. Combining JA4/JA4S fingerprints with additional network metadata, including flow statistics, DNS behavior, and certificate attributes, may further improve robustness and generalization.

As encrypted traffic continues to dominate network communications, metadata-based approaches will remain important for maintaining security while preserving user privacy.

Acknowledgments. The authors would like to thank the reviewers for their constructive and helpful comments.

Disclosure of Interests. The authors have no competing interests to declare that are relevant to the content of this article.

References

1. California Consumer Privacy Act (CCPA) (2018). cal. Civ. Code §§1798.100-1798.199
2. Althouse, J.: TLS fingerprinting with JA3 and JA3S (2019). https://medium.com/salesforce-engineering/tls-fingerprinting-with-ja3-and-ja3s-247362855967, salesforce Engineering via Medium. Accessed 06 Mar 2026
3. Althouse, J.: JA4+ network fingerprinting. FoxIO Blog (2023). https://blog.foxio.io/ja4-network-fingerprinting. Accessed 06 Mar 2026
4. Anderson, B., McGrew, D.: Identifying encrypted malware traffic with contextual flow data. In: Proceedings of the ACM Workshop on Artificial Intelligence and Security (AISec '16). https://doi.org/10.1145/2996758.2996768
5. Anderson, B., Paul, S., McGrew, D.: Deciphering malware's use of TLS (without decryption). J. Comput. Virol. Hacking Techniques **14** (2018). https://doi.org/10.1007/s11416-017-0306-6
6. Axelsson, S.: Intrusion detection systems: a survey and taxonomy. Technical Report 99-15, Dept. of Computer Engineering, Chalmers Univ. of Technology (April 2000)
7. Barut, O., Grohotolski, M., DiLeo, C., Luo, Y., Li, P., Zhang, T.: Machine learning based malware detection on encrypted traffic: A comprehensive performance study. In: Proceedings of the 7th International Conference on Networking, Systems and Security, pp. 45–55. NSysS '20 (2020). https://doi.org/10.1145/3428363.3428365
8. Calderon, P., Hasegawa, H., Yamaguchi, Y., Shimada, H.: Malware detection based on HTTPS characteristic via machine learning. In: Proceedings of the 4th International Conference on Information Systems Security and Privacy - Volume 1: ICISSP, pp. 410–417. INSTICC, SciTePress (2018). https://doi.org/10.5220/0006654604100417

9. Duncan, B.: Malware traffic analysis. Online malware traffic repository (nd). https://malware-traffic-analysis.net. Accessed 06 Mar 2026
10. Fahl, S., Harbach, M., Muders, T., Baumgärtner, L., Freisleben, B., Smith, M.: Why Eve and Mallory love Android: an analysis of Android SSL (in)security. In: Proceedings of the 2012 ACM Conference on Computer and Communications Security. CCS '12, New York, NY, USA, pp. 50–61. Association for Computing Machinery (2012). https://doi.org/10.1145/2382196.2382205
11. García, S., Grill, M., Stiborek, J., Zunino, A.: An empirical comparison of botnet detection methods. Comput. Secur. **45**, 100–123 (2014). https://doi.org/10.1016/j.cose.2014.05.011
12. Google: Https encryption on the web. Google Transparency Report (2024). https://transparencyreport.google.com/https/overview. Accessed 06 Mar 2026
13. Kohavi, R.: A study of cross-validation and bootstrap for accuracy estimation and model selection. In: Proceedings of the 14th International Joint Conference on Artificial Intelligence - Volume 2. IJCAI'95, San Francisco, CA, USA, pp. 1137–1143. Morgan Kaufmann Publishers Inc. (1995)
14. Kohout, J., Komárek, T., Čech, P., Bodnár, J., Lokoč, J.: Learning communication patterns for malware discovery in HTTPS data. Expert Syst. Appl. **101**, 129–142 (2018). https://doi.org/10.1016/j.eswa.2018.02.010
15. Komárek, T., Somol, P.: End-node fingerprinting for malware detection on HTTPS data. In: Proceedings of the 12th International Conference on Availability, Reliability and Security. ARES '17, New York, NY, USA. Association for Computing Machinery (2017). https://doi.org/10.1145/3098954.3107007
16. Korczynski, M., Duda, A.: Markov chain fingerprinting to classify encrypted traffic, pp. 781–789 (2014). https://doi.org/10.1109/INFOCOM.2014.6848005
17. Liao, H.J., Richard Lin, C.H., Lin, Y.C., Tung, K.Y.: Intrusion detection system: a comprehensive review. J. Netw. Comput. Appl. **36**(1), 16–24 (2013). https://doi.org/10.1016/j.jnca.2012.09.004
18. Lopez-Martin, M., Carro, B., Sanchez-Esguevillas, A., Lloret, J.: Network traffic classifier with convolutional and recurrent neural networks for internet of things. IEEE Access **PP**, 1–1 (2017). https://doi.org/10.1109/ACCESS.2017.2747560
19. Lotfollahi, M., Shirali Hossein Zade, R., Jafari Siavoshani, M., Saberian, M.: Deep packet: a novel approach for encrypted traffic classification using deep learning. Soft Comput. **24** (2020). https://doi.org/10.1007/s00500-019-04030-2
20. Matoušek, P., Ryšavý, O., Burgetová, I.: Experience report: using JA4+ fingerprints for malware detection in encrypted traffic. In: Proceedings of 20th International Conference on Network and Service Management, pp. 1–5. Institute of Electrical and Electronics Engineers, Prague (2024). https://doi.org/10.23919/CNSM62983.2024.10814358, https://www.fit.vut.cz/research/publication/13252/
21. Naylor, D., et al.: The cost of the "s" in HTTPS. In: Proceedings of the 10th ACM International on Conference on Emerging Networking Experiments and Technologies, pp. 133–140. CoNEXT '14, New York, NY, USA. Association for Computing Machinery (2014). https://doi.org/10.1145/2674005.2674991
22. Polo-Peyres, E., López de Vergara, J.E., Sutter, G., González, I., de Pedro, L.: Detecting malware in encrypted network traffic using machine learning and TLS fingerprints. In: Proceedings of the 17h International Conference on Ubiquitous Computing and Ambient Intelligence (UCAmI 2025) (2025). https://doi.org/10.1007/978-3-032-16995-2_29
23. Powers, D.M.W.: Evaluation: from precision, recall and F-measure to ROC, informedness, markedness and correlation (2020). https://arxiv.org/abs/2010.16061

24. Prasse, P., Machlica, L., Pevný, T., Havelka, J., Scheffer, T.: Malware detection by analysing network traffic with neural networks. In: 2017 IEEE Symposium on Security and Privacy Workshops (SPW), pp. 205–210 (2017). https://doi.org/10.1109/SPW.2017.8
25. Rescorla, E.: The transport layer security (TLS) protocol version 1.3. RFC 8446, Internet Engineering Task Force (IETF) (2018). https://www.rfc-editor.org/rfc/rfc8446
26. Rezaei, S., Liu, X.: Deep learning for encrypted traffic classification: an overview (2018). https://doi.org/10.48550/arXiv.1810.07906
27. scikit-learn: Machine Learning in Python. scikit-learn (2024). https://scikit-learn.org/stable/modules/generated/sklearn.preprocessing.OrdinalEncoder.html
28. Shekhawat, A.S., Troia, F.D., Stamp, M.: Feature analysis of encrypted malicious traffic. Expert Syst. Appl. **125**(C), 130–141 (2019). https://doi.org/10.1016/j.eswa.2019.01.064
29. Shen, M., Wei, M., Zhu, L., Wang, M.: Classification of encrypted traffic with second-order Markov chains and application attribute bigrams. Trans. Info. For. Sec. **12**(8), 1830–1843 (2017). https://doi.org/10.1109/TIFS.2017.2692682
30. Sokolova, M., Lapalme, G.: A systematic analysis of performance measures for classification tasks. Inf. Process. Manage. **45**(4), 427–437 (2009). https://doi.org/10.1016/j.ipm.2009.03.002
31. Velan, P., Čermák, M., Čeleda, P., Drašar, M.: A survey of methods for encrypted traffic classification and analysis. Int. J. Network Manage **25**(5), 355–374 (2015). https://doi.org/10.1002/nem.1901
32. Voigt, P., dem Bussche, A.V.: The EU General Data Protection Regulation (GDPR). Springer (2017). https://doi.org/10.1007/978-3-319-57959-7
33. Wireshark Foundation: Wireshark sample captures. Public packet capture repository (2024). https://wiki.wireshark.org/SampleCaptures. Accessed 06 Mar 2026

NetFlowMeter: High-Performance Network Flow Feature Extraction

Ettore Ermes Pennucci[1(✉)], Gregorio Dalia[1], Andrea Di Sorbo[1], and Corrado Aaron Visaggio[2]

[1] University of Sannio, Benevento, Italy
{e.pennucci,g.dalia}@studenti.unisannio.it, disorbo@unisannio.it
[2] University of Foggia, Foggia, Italy
corrado.visaggio@unifg.it

Abstract. Network flow feature extraction is a critical component of machine learning-based network IPS/IDS systems. In this context, many promising approaches and benchmark databases have been proposed in the literature. However, when they rely on offline processing of packet captures (pcap files), the real-world applicability of these approaches is limited due to performance overhead. To bridge this gap, this short paper presents NetFlowMeter, a tool aimed at significantly enhancing the practicality of large-scale network flow feature extraction, enabling the processing of multi-gigabyte pcap files on commodity hardware. Since NetFlowMeter's design is based on the specifications of CICFlowMeter, the tool behind widely used datasets such as CICIDS2017, it represents a seamless drop-in replacement for current machine learning pipelines. We validate performance and accuracy by comparing the two tools; experimental results show an order of magnitude improvement in processing speed while maintaining the same flow features. Besides, we identify and report a number of bugs in CICFlowMeter that led to incorrect feature extraction in published datasets.

Keywords: Network Security · Network Intrusion Detection · Machine Learning · Performance

1 Introduction

In recent years, unauthorized access and malicious activities targeting networked systems have attracted increasing attention due to their significant operational, economic, and strategic impact [16]. This context has motivated substantial research efforts on techniques for protecting network infrastructures. Among these, Network Intrusion Detection Systems (NIDS) represent one of the major research directions [7], as they aim to detect malicious activity in network traffic. Over time, this effort has led to the development of widely adopted signature-based tools, such as Snort[1] and Suricata[2]. In parallel, machine learning-based

[1] https://www.snort.org/.
[2] https://suricata.io/.

S. Nadjm-Tehrani et al. (Eds.): ARES 2026, LNCS 16898, pp. 248–259, 2027.
https://doi.org/10.1007/978-3-032-36874-4_12

approaches have emerged as an increasingly active research topic [2], with the aim of detecting threats without relying on pre-defined signatures.

One of the most common techniques for applying machine learning to network traffic is flow analysis [3]: individual packets that compose traffic are grouped into flows, which are then aggregated into discrete feature vectors that can be used with tabular machine learning algorithms; the piece of software that performs this operation is called a flow extractor. Finally, a machine learning model is trained and evaluated on the resulting dataset. Applying such systems in practice requires the ability to process the features and evaluate the model in almost real-time with limited impact on the rest of the system.

CICFlowMeter[3] is a widely adopted feature extractor in the research community and numerous published datasets were produced with it [12] [1] [13].

In this paper, we present NetFlowMeter, a tool designed to improve the runtime efficiency of CICFlowMeter. Unlike previous efforts mainly focused on fixing functional issues in the original tool, our work is centered on the analysis of the CICFlowMeter codebase to identify performance bottlenecks and mitigate them through targeted optimizations. Our evaluation shows that NetFlowMeter generates the same output as CICFlowMeter from the same input PCAP files, while achieving faster execution and lower memory usage.

Our work is motivated by both our empirical observations of CICFlowMeter when processing large PCAP files and prior reports highlighting the difficulty of using the tool on large datasets [6]. Previous studies have also shown that CICFlowMeter suffers from functional bugs that may lead to incorrect feature extraction [5]. However, to the best of our knowledge, no prior work has provided a comprehensive analysis of its performance bottlenecks. Such an evaluation is essential to determine whether research-oriented flow extraction tools are suitable for deployment in realistic operational settings [14].

More specifically, the main contributions of our work are as follows:

(i) We perform a comprehensive analysis of the CICFlowMeter source code, identifying a number of issues that lead to performance bottlenecks. In addition, we identify previously undocumented feature extraction bugs, such as min/max aggregations reporting incorrect values due to logic bugs, an edge case in TCP flow termination handling, non-compliant TCP retransmission tracking, and improper decoding of ICMP flows. These issues affect published datasets generated with CICFlowMeter.

(ii) We design and implement NetFlowMeter, a high-performance network flow feature extractor written from the ground up in C#, with a focus on performance and correctness. NetFlowMeter implements the same feature set as CICFlowMeter, allowing it to serve as a drop-in replacement in existing machine learning pipelines. NetFlowMeter is released as open source under the MIT license[4] and is compatible with all major desktop operating systems.

[3] https://www.unb.ca/cic/research/applications.html.

[4] https://github.com/DefenceTechSecurity/NetFlowMeter.

(iii) We validate NetFlowMeter against CICFlowMeter in terms of processing time, memory usage, and correctness, demonstrating superior performance, with up to twenty times faster processing while retaining equivalent output. This allows processing multi-gigabyte PCAP files on a normal workstation in a considerably shorter time frame.

2 Related Work

CICFlowMeter is an open-source network flow feature extractor developed by the Canadian Institute for Cybersecurity (CIC) and used to generate a number of public datasets for network intrusion detection research, including CICIDS2017 [12], CICIDS2018 [1], and CICDDoS2019 [13].

Datasets produced with CICFlowMeter are usually distributed in two forms: raw packet captures (PCAP files) and pre-processed features (e.g., CSV and parquet). PCAP files contain the original network traffic as it passed through the wire; they are relevant whenever researchers want to develop custom analysis passes or perform deep analysis of flow contents. CSV files contain the fixed-length feature vectors extracted from the original traffic, they are used for training and evaluating machine learning models.

CICFlowMeter was previously analyzed by Engelen et al. [5]; the authors identified several correctness issues around TCP flag processing and flow termination logic. They propose a fixed version of CICFlowMeter which results in higher machine learning accuracy on the CICIDS2017 dataset. Limitations of the CICFlowMeter data model are also well documented in the literature [4]. Rosay et al. [10] identified a number of issues within the original CICFlowMeter, including the presence of "NaN" values in the output due to divide-by-zero bugs and the negative flow duration in certain cases; however, a small number of these issues still persist in the latest versions of CICFlowMeter. The authors propose LycoSTand as an alternative feature extractor with a different set of features.

The authors of the original CICFlowMeter tool also published a successor called NTLFlowLyzer [11] which extends CICFlowMeter with additional statistical features for a total of 348. However, feature importance analysis from the literature [8] indicates that, in CICIDS2017, only the top 4 features contribute to over 90% of the performance across various types of machine learning models. While this is a limitation of the dataset rather than the tool, it suggests that additional features provide diminishing returns, for this reason and also due to the widespread adoption of datasets produced with it in the research community, we decided to focus on CICFlowMeter. Indeed, it is worth noting that some of the datasets generated with CICFlowMeter themselves have been critiqued in literature as well due to the high class imbalance [9], leaving models trained on these datasets prone to overfitting. However, these issues are orthogonal to the feature extraction process and are not discussed further in this paper.

Similar to previous work, we build upon Engelen et al. [5] efforts of improving CICFlowMeter and identify issues that lead to incorrect feature extraction.

In addition, we focus on performance bottlenecks. We propose NetFlowMeter, which achieves processing speeds up to twenty times faster than CICFlowMeter while keeping output compatibility.

3 NetFlowMeter Design

NetFlowMeter's goal is to be a seamless drop-in replacement for CICFlowMeter in existing machine learning workflows, all while improving the processing time and resource usage of the feature extraction process. We also design NetFlowMeter to be flexible and extensible, allowing for easy addition of new features and integration of the extraction logic as a library into third-party projects. Here, we describe the design of NetFlowMeter and the rationale behind our choices.

We started by observing the behavior of CICFlowMeter when processing large pcap files. Its inability to scale to larger datasets has been previously discussed [6] and we could confirm this in our experiments. Indeed, we observed that, as the input pcap size increases, the processing time grows significantly. In particular, we noted CPU usage spikes across all cores, even though CICFlowMeter is a single-threaded application. In our experience, a machine with 16 GB of RAM is not able to process files larger than 3GB without failing due to out-of-memory errors. Moving the processing to a more powerful cluster allowed us to work with larger files, but we could still observe the abnormal CPU usage behavior and seemingly random pauses to the process.

During testing, we occasionally obtained the error message ``java.lang.OutOfMemoryError: GC overhead limit exceeded`` which indicates that the Java Virtual Machine is spending too much time performing garbage collection and not enough time executing the program, usually due to excessive memory usage[5]. This explains the CPU spikes and the way processing time scales non-linearly with the input size, most importantly it hints at the root cause of performance issues: excessive reliance on in-memory data structures. With this insight, we performed an analysis of CICFlowMeter's source code on GitHub[6]; the code is divided into the Java main application and a fork of the C++ library jNetPcap[7] used for parsing network protocols. We observed that the Java side stores all active flows, including the individual packets that compose them, until the processing of the entire PCAP file is complete, confirming the garbage collection bottleneck hypothesis.

We evaluated all the features implemented in CICFlowMeter and noticed that all of them are calculated by aggregating packets using statistics that can be computed on-the-fly as packets are observed. The aggregation functions used are average, minimum, maximum and standard deviation; of these the only non-trivial to implement for a stream of data is the standard deviation but in literature this is a solved problem using Welford's online algorithm [15]. This became

[5] https://stackoverflow.com/questions/1393486/error-java-lang-outofmemoryerror-gc-overhead-limit-exceeded.

[6] https://github.com/GintsEngelen/CICFlowMeter.

[7] https://github.com/GintsEngelen/CICFlowMeter/blob/master/jnetpcap/readme.txt.md.

a core design principle for NetFlowMeter: we want to minimize the amount of past data that needs to be stored in memory, compute features incrementally as packets are processed and flush completed flows to the output file as soon as they are terminated.

The NetFlowMeter project is composed of two main components: a class library `NetFlowMeter` which implements the bulk of the logic, and a command line interface `NetFlowMeter.Cli` which provides a user-friendly no-code way to produce CSV files from PCAP inputs. The set of supported features is identical to CICFlowMeter and, with the exception of some of the bugs highlighted in the following section, the results produced by NetFlowMeter are numerically equivalent to CICFlowMeter.

All the components of NetFlowMeter use carefully selected data structures and algorithms to minimize overhead. Packet ingestion uses a custom PCAP parser backed by a memory pool to reduce allocations and garbage collection pressure. Additionally, this enables abstracting the data source, allowing reading compressed packets via a `GzipStream`[8], streaming them from a network location with a `NetworkStream`[9] or capturing real-time data with libpcap[10].

We extensively profiled the hot paths of execution in order to identify potential bottlenecks. For example, looking up a flow by its identifier via a hash table is one of the most common operations in the processing pipeline, NetFlowMeter encodes a flow ID as a GUID (128-bit integer) which can be stored inline and hashed via a fixed complexity function. By comparison, CICFlowMeter stores flow identifiers as strings, these have to be individually allocated for every packet via serialization and, since they do not have a fixed length, they also require a more expensive hashing process.

Another example is TCP flag counting: CICFlowMeter uses a `HashMap` storing the count of each TCP flag as a key-value pair. This requires 8 string hash operations and a dictionary lookup for each packet, one for each flag. NetFlowMeter instead defines an integer field for each TCP flag and increments it directly.

This first version of NetFlowMeter strives to maximize output compatibility with CICFlowMeter and as such it inherits some of its shortcomings. In particular, there is a major design flaw concerning how the timeout of alive flows is checked. A flow is closed and evicted from memory only when the TCP connection cleanly terminates or when it reaches a timeout. However, the timeout is evaluated only when a packet belonging to that flow is observed. This means that a flow that is not cleanly closed will be kept in memory indefinitely[11]. This design makes CICFlowMeter poorly suited for real-time network processing without periodically cutting PCAP files or restarting it, since memory would grow without limits otherwise. To mitigate this issue, we implement a feature that periodically flushes expired in-memory flows to free up memory. However,

---

[8] https://learn.microsoft.com/en-us/dotnet/api/system.io.compression.gzipstream.

[9] https://learn.microsoft.com/en-us/dotnet/api/system.net.sockets.networkstream.

[10] https://github.com/the-tcpdump-group/libpcap.

[11] java/cic/cs/unb/ca/jnetpcap/FlowGenerator.java#L110.

this affects how flows are grouped and feature computation in a way that is not compatible with CICFlowMeter. For this reason, in the current version of NetFlowMeter, this feature is disabled by default and requires explicit opt-in via the command line argument `-- flush`. In future work, we aim to better evaluate its impact, with the objective of enabling this memory optimization by default.

Finally, in CICFlowMeter, TCP retransmissions are tracked through the `TcpRetransmissionDTO` class[12]. This class contains metadata about each TCP packet, such as the sender address, the SEQ and ACK numbers, and the window value from the TCP header. These are stored in a `Set`[13] for each flow, which grows unbounded as packets are added, exacerbating the garbage collection issues. Retransmissions are counted when a packet produces the same `TcpRetransmissionDTO` as one that has been seen before. Although this method can detect physical retransmissions of packets, it does not fully align with the TCP definition of retransmitted data[14]. The TCP protocol retransmits data when the acknowledgment (ACK) number received from a peer does not match the expected number. Therefore, tracking retransmissions necessitates accurately counting the bytes transmitted and acknowledged by each peer, instead of merely searching for repeated packets on the network. This difference can also be observed using Wireshark, the leading open source network analysis software, even for simple flows the number of retransmissions reported by CICFlowMeter does not match the one computed by Wireshark. An example of this issue can be seen in Fig 1, where a packet with `SEQ = 43` and `Length = 696` is retransmitted; however, between the original packet and the retransmission the sender has received more data by the other peer and as such the new packet has a higher ACK number, this will cause CICFlowMeter not to count it as retransmitted data.

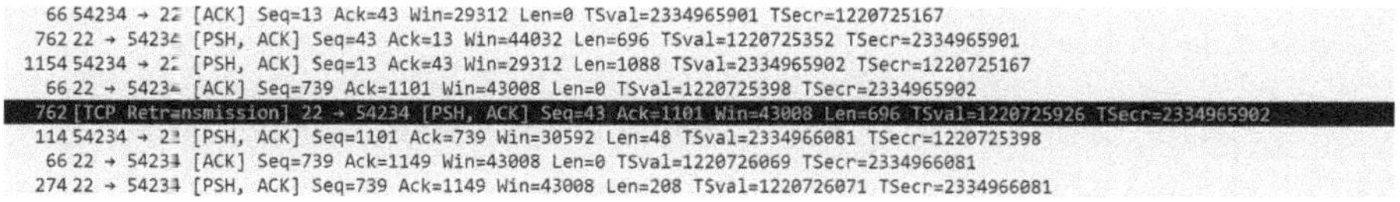

Fig. 1. A case of TCP retransmission in Wireshark. The retransmitted packet has a different ACK number which causes it not to be counted by CICFlowMeter

NetFlowMeter currently implements the same algorithm, but only storing the last 300 packets observed rather than the complete history of a flow. This number was chosen empirically, in the CICIDS2017 dataset it is enough to achieve output compatibility and it is believed to be accurate enough for general use. We consider this a compromise to align with CICFlowMeter output, the current implementation suffers from the same core flaw outlined above; in future work,

[12] java/cic/cs/unb/ca/jnetpcap/TcpRetransmissionDTO.java#L9-L16.
[13] java/cic/cs/unb/ca/jnetpcap/BasicFlow.java#L87.
[14] https://www.ietf.org/rfc/rfc793.txt.

we plan to introduce an algorithm closer to the TCP specification to match the results observed in Wireshark.

4 Validation and Benchmarking

The performance gains of NetFlowMeter are evaluated by processing the CICIDS2017 raw PCAP files with both CICFlowMeter and NetFlowMeter. For each test, we measure the total processing time and peak memory usage. All tests are performed on a Linux virtual machine with 80GB of RAM and 32 vCPUs. Each file is processed with a standalone invocation of the tool, as we observed inconsistent performance in CICFlowMeter when processing multiple files in the same run due to the aforementioned garbage collection issues.

Tables 1 and 2 show respectively how long it takes and how much memory is needed to process each file averaged on three runs of each file, the deviation between runs is below 10% and was not reported. We observe a **20x** speedup in wall-clock time and a **6x** reduction in memory usage. In particular, profiling shows that NetFlowMeter's biggest bottleneck is I/O speed; we confirmed this by observing only a slight degradation in processing times even on a consumer laptop with 16GB of RAM and an Intel i7 11th Gen CPU. Instead, CICFlowMeter suffers from the Java garbage collector taking over most of its CPU time; with the same laptop, none of the tested files could be processed successfully. Note that NetFlowMeter is also implemented using a garbage-collected language, the implication here is not that the Java garbage collector is the root cause of performance issues but rather that the programming issues outlined in the previous section cause it to misbehave.

Table 1. Comparison of wall-clock time needed to process CICIDS2017 with NetFlowMeter and CICFlowMeter.

File	Size	CICFlowMeter	NetFlowMeter
Monday-WorkingHours.pcap	11GB	397.3 s	16.1 s
Tuesday-WorkingHours.pcap	11GB	438.7 s	15.7 s
Wednesday-workingHours.pcap	13GB	518.8 s	20.7 s
Thursday-WorkingHours.pcap	7.8GB	360.2 s	14.8 s
Friday-WorkingHours.pcap	8.3GB	430.1 s	18.8 s

Furthermore, NetFlowMeter supports the -- `flush` command-line flag which enables a garbage collection-like behavior that flushes closed flows to the output as soon as their timeout elapses; memory usage is greatly reduced at the slight expense of some processing time, as seen in Table 3

By profiling the program it was possible to clearly isolate the bottleneck caused by the flush option, Fig. 2 shows that serializing the output data structures in the function `FlushTimedOutFlows` takes as much CPU time as the core

Table 2. Comparison of memory usage when processing CICIDS2017.

File	Size	CICFlowMeter	NetFlowMeter
Monday-WorkingHours.pcap	11GB	5363.3 MB	884.7 MB
Tuesday-WorkingHours.pcap	11GB	5115.0 MB	784.0 MB
Wednesday-workingHours.pcap	13GB	4577.7 MB	775.7 MB
Thursday-WorkingHours.pcap	7.8GB	5141.7 MB	804.3 MB
Friday-WorkingHours.pcap	8.3GB	5756.0 MB	1097.3 MB

Table 3. Wall-clock and memory usage of NetFlowMeter when processing CICIDS2017 with the -- `flush` option. This produces a different ordering and aggregation of flows when compared to CICFlowMeter.

File	Memory usage	Wall-clock time
Monday-WorkingHours.pcap	183.0 MB	18.0 s
Tuesday-WorkingHours.pcap	190.7 MB	16.9 s
Wednesday-workingHours.pcap	217.7 MB	23.7 s
Thursday-WorkingHours.pcap	242.6 MB	15.7 s
Friday-WorkingHours.pcap	536.3 MB	20.9 s

packet analysis logic performed in `AddPacket`. In future work, we plan to experiment with asynchronous I/O as it is expected to yield additional performance gains.

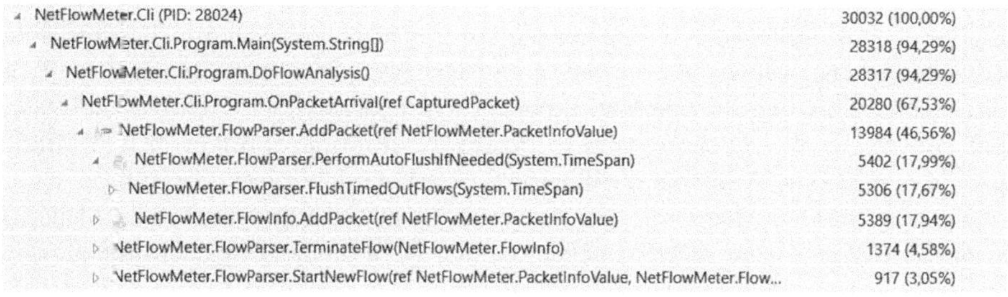

Fig. 2. CPU profiling of NetFlowMeter, on the left side the function name is displayed, the right side shows the cumulative % of CPU time used by all invocations of the function. Hot paths are indicated with an icon before the name.

Our benchmarks indicate that with NetFlowMeter, even the largest pcap files from CIC-IDS2017 can be processed in less than a minute on a commodity laptop instead of requiring a powerful server or cluster.

The second phase of validation is correctness. To this aim, we implemented a CSV comparison tool within `NetFlowMeter.Cli` which compares NetFlowMeter output with a reference CSV file generated by CICFlowMeter. The tool compares each flow, feature by feature, using its flow ID, reporting any missing flows or different features. This enabled thorough debugging of NetFlowMeter until it achieved the desired degree of accuracy. Furthermore, this process enabled the identification of previously-unknown bugs in CICFlowMeter that cause incorrect feature extraction. Since these issues have been partly mitigated in NetFlowMeter, the output comparison tool includes a configurable ignore list to skip features that are known not to match. In particular, we identified four features that are incorrectly computed:

- `Fwd Seg Size Min` and `Bwd Seg Size Min` are computed as the minimum value of the segment size between the packet that is being analyzed and the current stored minimum[15]. However, the two variables that store the minimum for the forward and backward directions are initialized in a mutually exclusive way[16] in the first packet handler, which can only be called once per flow. This means that the minimum segment size for one of the two directions is never initialized properly and remains zero in the final output.
- `FWD Init Win Bytes` and `Bwd Init Win Bytes` suffer from the same issue; only one of these can ever be initialized for each flow, depending on which peer sent the first packet[17]. The other variable remains zero for the entire flow duration.

Another bug we identified is related to the RST flag handling in TCP connections. In CICFlowMeter, when a connection duration exceeds the alive timeout[18] (hardcoded to 120 s[19]), the flow is forcibly split, likely as an attempt to avoid aggregating too much data. However, if this flow cut occurs just before a RST packet is seen, the RST flag is not counted in either of the two flows. This is because handling TCP flags is done in a branch that can only be reached when the flow is not timed out[20]. The consequence of this bug is that CICFlowMeter occasionally keeps flows alive after one of the two peers has already closed the connection. This bug interacts with packet aggregation logic and it is the reason that causes the `-- flush` option to produce a different number of flows under specific conditions. Additional differences are documented on GitHub[21].

Finally, we also observed a major oversight in the implementation of ICMP flows. Firstly, the way ICMP packet parsing is implemented does not account for payload size. This means that all of the metrics related to the content of a packet are always zero[22] and do not contribute to machine learning in any way. Furthermore, the logic that decides whether two ICMP packets should be part

[15] java/cic/cs/unb/ca/jnetpcap/BasicFlow.java#L328-L329.
[16] java/cic/cs/unb/ca/jnetpcap/BasicFlow.java#L201-L224.
[17] java/cic/cs/unb/ca/jnetpcap/BasicFlow.java#L202-L203.
[18] java/cic/cs/unb/ca/jnetpcap/FlowGenerator.java#L94.
[19] java/cic/cs/unb/ca/ifm/CICFlowMeter.java#L67.
[20] java/cic/cs/unb/ca/jnetpcap/FlowGenerator.java#L177.
[21] NetFlowMeter.Cli/Testing/CICComparison.cs L7.
[22] java/cic/cs/unb/ca/jnetpcap/PacketReader.java#L138-L142.

of the same flow is potentially wrong. ICMP packets start with the `type` field, which identifies the kind of information present in the packet; `type` is followed by the `code` field, which can specify additional context for this message type[23]. The comments in CICFlowMeter imply that the intended behavior is that flows with the same values for `type` and `code` should be part of the same flow[24]. However, the implementation has a bug; it uses the operator `&&` instead of `||` in a negated condition, causing it to accept packets even when only one of the two fields matches[25]. ICMP support being incomplete is a major oversight, as ICMP tunneling is a known exfiltration technique since the early 2000 s[26] and as such should be in scope for a tool like CICFlowMeter. NetFlowMeter implements ICMP support by properly populating size fields and merging all packets between two peers in a single flow. This was chosen to logically aggregate ICMP echo requests and responses (i.e., "ping" packets) as they have different `type` numbers. Analyzing the impact of such changes and evaluating better aggregation strategies is planned for future work.

5 Conclusion and Future Work

This short paper introduced NetFlowMeter, a high-performance network flow feature extractor capable of processing multi-gigabyte pcap files on commodity laptops. NetFlowMeter matches the feature set produced by CICFlowMeter while greatly reducing the processing time. This allows researchers and practitioners willing to (i) reproduce published experiments from the original pcap files, (ii) collect original datasets, or (iii) tweak and extend the feature extraction process to do so with considerably shorter iteration times and lower hardware requirements. NetFlowMeter's performance and low hardware requirements lower the barrier to entry for network traffic research, enabling even smaller labs and individual researchers to work with large pcap datasets. Shorter iteration cycles allow for faster development, feature engineering, and reproducibility of prior studies that used CICFlowMeter. Overall, it has the potential to broaden participation, improve research rigor, and support scalable network security studies.

The paper also highlighted several bugs in CICFlowMeter affecting the quality of published datasets. Some were already documented in the literature, while others were newly discovered during the development process. NetFlowMeter addresses some of these bugs while maintaining overall compatibility with CICFlowMeter output. Future work includes extending NetFlowMeter with additional features and fixing the open issues noted in the previous sections, while evaluating the impact of these changes on machine learning performance.

---

[23] https //www.rfc-editor.org/rfc/rfc792.html.
[24] java/cic/cs/unb/ca/jnetpcap/FlowGenerator.java#L192.
[25] java/cic/cs/unb/ca/jnetpcap/FlowGenerator.java#L193-L194.
[26] https://www.cs.uit.no/daniels/PingTunnel/.

Disclosure of Interests. Ettore Ermes Pennucci is an employee at Defence Tech Holding spa, which sponsored the development of NetFlowMeter. The remaining authors have no competing interests to declare.

References

1. A realistic cyber defense dataset (cse-cic-ids2018). https://registry.opendata.aws/cse-cic-ids2018
2. Abdulganiyu, O.H., Tchakoucht, T.A., Saheed, Y.K.: A systematic literature review for network intrusion detection system (ids). Int. J. Inf. Secur. **22** (2023). https://doi.org/10.1007/s10207-023-00682-2
3. Boutaba, R., et al.: A comprehensive survey on machine learning for networking: evolution, applications and research opportunities. J. Internet Serv. Appl. **9**(1), 16 (2018). https://doi.org/10.1186/s13174-018-0087-2
4. Catillo, M., Pecchia, A., Villano, U.: Multicids: anomaly-based collective intrusion detection by deep learning on iot/cps multivariate time series. Internet Things **30**, 101519 (2025). https://doi.org/10.1016/j.iot.2025.101519
5. Engelen, G., Rimmer, V., Joosen, W.: Troubleshooting an intrusion detection dataset: the cicids2017 case study. In: 2021 IEEE Security and Privacy Workshops (SPW), pp. 7–12. IEEE (2021). https://doi.org/10.1109/SPW53761.2021.00009
6. Flood, R., Aspinall, D.: Measuring the complexity of benchmark nids datasets via spectral analysis. In: 2024 IEEE European Symposium on Security and Privacy Workshops (EuroS&PW), pp. 335–341 (2024). https://doi.org/10.1109/EuroSPW61312.2024.00043
7. Goldschmidt, P., Chudá, D.: Network intrusion datasets: a survey, limitations, and recommendations. Comput. Secur. **156**, 104510 (2025)
8. Kurniabudi, S., Darmawijoyo, D., Idris, B., Bamhdi, M.Y., Budiarto, A.M., R.: Cicids-2017 dataset feature analysis with information gain for anomaly detection. IEEE Access **8**, 132911–132921 (2020). https://doi.org/10.1109/ACCESS.2020.3009843
9. Leevy, J.L., Khoshgoftaar, T.M.: A survey and analysis of intrusion detection models based on cse-cic-ids2018 big data. Journal of Big Data **7**(1) (2020). https://doi.org/10.1186/s40537-020-00382-x
10. Rosay, A., Carlier, F., Cheval, E., Leroux, P.: From CIC-IDS2017 to LYCOS-IDS2017: a corrected dataset for better performance. In: WI-IAT '21: IEEE/WIC/ACM International Conference on Web Intelligence, Melbourne VIC Australia, 14–17 December 2021, pp. 570–575 (2021). https://doi.org/10.1145/3486622.3493973
11. Shafi, M., Lashkari, A.H., Roudsari, A.H.: Ntlflowlyzer: towards generating an intrusion detection dataset and intruders behavior profiling through network and transport layers traffic analysis and pattern extraction. Comput. Secur. **148**, 104160 (2025). https://doi.org/10.1016/j.cose.2024.104160
12. Sharafaldin, I., Lashkari, A.H., Ghorbani, A.A.: Toward generating a new intrusion detection dataset and intrusion traffic characterization. In: International Conference on Information Systems Security and Privacy (2018). https://api.semanticscholar.org/CorpusID:4707749
13. Sharafaldin, I., Lashkari, A.H., Hakak, S., Ghorbani, A.A.: Developing realistic distributed denial of service (ddos) attack dataset and taxonomy. In: 2019 International Carnahan Conference on Security Technology (ICCST), pp. 1–8 (2019). https://doi.org/10.1109/CCST.2019.8888419

14. Verkerken M., Callewaert, M., D'hooge, L., Wauters, T., Volckaert, B., De Turck, F.: Rustiflow: bridging the gap between security research and practice using ebpf-based network flow extraction. In: 2025 IEEE European Symposium on Security and Privacy Workshops (EuroS&PW), pp. 203–216 (2025). https://doi.org/10.1109/EuroSPW67616.2025.00030
15. Welford, B.P.: Note on a method for calculating corrected sums of squares and products. Technometrics **4**(3), 419–420 (1962). https://doi.org/10.1080/00401706.1962.10490022
16. Yang, Z., et al.: A systematic literature review of methods and datasets for anomaly-based network intrusion detection. Comput. Secur. **116**, 102675 (2022)

Network-Based Detection of Mobile Fake Base Stations

Sanish Gurung[1(✉)], Tuomo Lehtilä[2], Amy Sokhna Sidibé[1], Gizem Akman[1], and Valtteri Niemi[1]

[1] Department of Computer Science, University of Helsinki, Helsinki, Finland
sanish.gurung@helsinki.fi
[2] Department of Mathematics and Statistics, University of Turku, Turku, Finland

Abstract. Fake Base Station (FBS) impersonates a legitimate base station (BS) to deceive mobile devices, facilitating attacks such as man-in-the-middle, denial-of-service, call eavesdropping, message interception, and location tracking. We propose a robust FBS detection method using 3GPP-standardized measurement reports that BSs receive from UEs. Before evaluating detection performance, the ns-3 derived datasets are compared with data from a real test network. We show that the method provides high detection accuracy, and an alarm is raised reasonably fast.

Keywords: fake base station · FBS detection · ns-3 · z-score

1 Introduction

Base stations (BSs) play a critical role in mobile networks by connecting mobile devices to the core network and the Internet. Fake Base Stations (FBS), also known as IMSI Catchers, try to impersonate legitimate base stations and deceive User Equipment (UE) into establishing connections [21]. These rogue entities cause security and privacy issues, e.g., intercepting sensitive data, disrupting network operations, and tracking users' location [2,21].

Various methods have been proposed for detecting FBS: application-based, sensor-based, and network-based approaches. Although lightweight and easily deployable, the effectiveness of application-based solutions is limited due to device-level data constraints. Sensor-based methods provide richer data but require investments in additional infrastructure. Network-based methods overcome these challenges by analyzing already collected data within the mobile network, such as measurement reports, system logs, or base station configurations [12,20]. A Measurement Report (MR), standardized by 3GPP [3,5], is generated by the UE based on the signal strength and quality observed from neighboring BSs. The configuration of MRs is controlled by network operators to balance accuracy, overhead, and responsiveness. This control makes them helpful in detecting irregularities caused by FBS.

We propose a network-level FBS detection mechanism. First, we use the ns-3 simulator to generate experimental data on Reference Signal Received Power

S. Nadjm-Tehrani et al. (Eds.): ARES 2026, LNCS 16898, pp. 260–271, 2027.
https://doi.org/10.1007/978-3-032-36874-4_13

(RSRP) values reported by UEs to base stations. We introduce FBS as an additional entity into the simulator architecture. It emulates a legitimate base station, thereby creating a network comprising two base stations that share the same Physical Cell Identity (PCI): one authentic and one counterfeit.

The additional FBS in the simulation network is mobile, but otherwise imitates a legitimate base station. Using data gathered from the simulations, we perform a statistical analysis to decide whether there is an FBS in the network. It turns out that the statistical method works at least as well as machine learning techniques, which have been widely explored in the literature, e.g., in Nakarmi et al. [19]. Our proposed method detects FBS in each of our 445 cases within the first 60 s and produces zero false positives for our validation data.

2 Background and Related Work

Fake Base Stations (FBSs) are specialized devices that emulate legitimate base stations, but can emit higher-powered signals to attract mobile devices [2,20]. These devices are typically small and portable, and can be carried around while hidden in a car [8,21]. Structurally, FBS comprises two functional components: a radio front-end for transmitting and receiving radio waves, and a network back-end that simulates a fake cellular core network. FBSs facilitate various forms of passive and active attacks. Active attacks can expose permanent subscriber identities (IMSI), device-specific hardware capabilities (UE capabilities), and fine-grained location data through forced measurement reports [21,22]. Furthermore, FBSs can downgrade cellular connections to less secure networks, e.g., to 2G, to facilitate continued exploitation [20,24].

The Measurement Report (MR) provides information on the surrounding network environment, including signal measurements of serving and neighboring cells, which are collected by UEs in *Idle* or *Connected* state [3]. The received signal strength is reported in the form of Reference Signal Received Power (RSRP), which is a positive integer value, and a higher *RSRP* indicates a stronger signal. MRs are generated at regular intervals or when specific events occur, e.g., a significant change in signal strength [3,12]. Karaçay et al. [13] detect FBS using MRs by comparing signal strengths received in a cellular network.

The Physical Cell Identifier (PCI) is a 9-bit value assigned to each cell in the physical layer of LTE [25], used to identify and synchronize with a specific cell, detect its broadcast signals, send MR to the serving cell, and perform handovers. The limited number of unique PCI values in LTE can be reused across different regions, causing [14]: (1) PCI collision: two neighboring cells are assigned the same PCI, and (2) PCI confusion: two non-neighboring cells share the same PCI but are both visible to the UE. In both cases, the UE struggles to correctly identify the cells, leading to handover failures, dropped calls, or degraded service. We consider an active attacker operating an FBS configured to broadcast the PCI of a legitimate BS. By transmitting a signal at a higher power, the FBS forces the UE to measure a stronger RSRP of the spoofed PCI [17,21]. When the UE detects multiple signals indicating the same PCI, it typically selects the one with the strongest RSRP.

The FBS detection mechanisms can be broadly categorized into app-based, sensor-based, and network-based [2,12,20]. *App-based detection* typically involves applications that could be installable or integrated on the user device without requiring additional infrastructure [12,20]. These applications access the cellular network through the user device, gather and analyze the data, detect anomalies suggesting FBS activity, and display the results with real-time notifications [10,15,16,20]. However, this technique is prone to errors due to the limited amount of information that a single user device can gather [12]. *Sensor-based detection* operates on dedicated hardware systems that continuously monitor broadcast signals from nearby base stations [12,20]. This approach is preferred in terms of geographic coverage and persistence of data collection, but requires additional infrastructure [20]. *Network-based detection* leverages the extensive data collection inherent in networks. Collected data, such as precise locations, update requests, and operator logs can be used for FBS detection [7,9,20]. Hence, additional data collection for FBS detection is not required; instead, MRs can be used, as recommended by 3GPP [2,6]. This enables advanced analysis without the overhead associated with other detection methods [18–20].

Our work builds on top of that of Nakarmi et al. [19]. They applied Machine Learning (ML) methods on MRs gathered from ns-3 simulations. In particular, they simulated a setup with an FBS following a preselected trajectory, 12 BSs arranged in a grid, and between 100 and 200 UEs. The authors applied eight ML methods on this data. We observed two limitations in their work: (1) the network has data from multiple BSs, but they only utilized data from a single BS at a time (they mentioned this as a possible future improvement) and (2) their system was designed for a false positive rate of 0.5% under normal conditions. As a BS obtains thousands of MRs per minute, there would be many false positives even under standard conditions.

3 Data Collection and Processing

The real-world deployment of an FBS is not publicly allowed due to privacy risks towards users and security concerns in mobile networks. Thus, we run our experiments in the ns-3 simulator. We also collected measurements from an indoor test network to compare their distribution with the simulated ns-3 data. The experiments were carried out in a real 5G test network, with two 5G TeleWell UEs and two stationary BSs, using the n77 frequency band. In ns-3, we configured two UEs and two stationary BSs with the same transmission power as the real base stations. We configured the simulator with 'ThreeGppIndoorOffice-PropagationLossModel' to mimic the indoor test network [1]. The key statistical metrics of *RSRP* distributions from BSs in the real test network and ns-3 simulations were as follows. The two real BSs obtained mean *RSRP* as 73.8 and 67.9, while the two simulated BSs obtained 73.7 and 69.0. The medians from real BSs were 77 and 67, while simulated BSs obtained 74 and 71. A bigger difference was with standard deviations: real BSs observed 17.3 and 15.3, while simulated BSs observed 4.3 and 6.6. It is not surprising that the simulation has less variance than the real-world case, as it does not include all environmental factors. However, experiments showed that an ns-3 simulation can provide fairly realistic data.

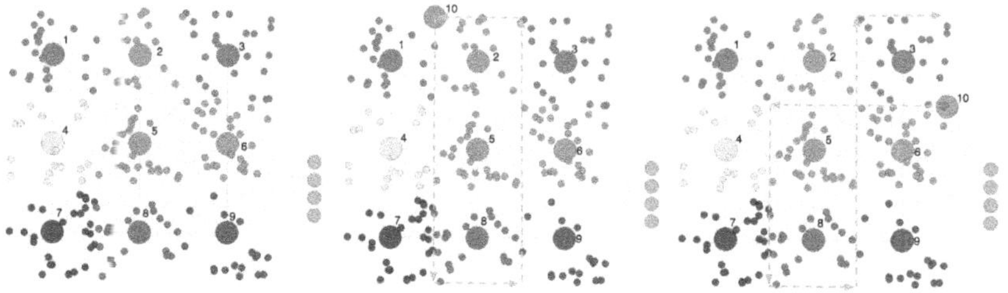

(a) Normal Case (b) FBS's Box Route (c) FBS's Random Route

Fig. 1. Three Cases of Simulation Topology.

We defined a network topology of nine BSs with unique PCIs (1–9), shown in nine colors in Fig. 1a. As the simulator lacks a built-in method to set up an FBS, we added a tenth BS (PCI 10, in tan color) to emulate an FBS. The UEs (smaller circles) are attached to their serving cells and share the same color. The cyan circles in Fig. 1 represent the 4G LTE core network functions. Figures 1b and c present two FBS mobility patterns, in orange dashed lines. In both scenarios, the FBS moves through the area while masquerading as a legitimate BS. This reflects a scenario where an adversary moves strategically through the network to maximize intercepted UEs while evading detection and localization.

Table 1. Simulation Parameters.

Parameter	Value	Parameter	Value
Grid size	1500 m × 1500 m	Propagation loss model	Friis propagation loss
Number of UEs	200		
Number of eNBs	9	Carrier Frequency	1800 MHz
BS heights	25 m	eNB Power	50 dBm
FBS height	2 m	FBS Power	56 dBm
UE heights	1.5 – 2.5 m	Training simulation time	500 s & 1000 s
UE Speed	2 m/s	Validation simulation time	500 s
FBS Speed	20 m/s	Testing simulation time	200 s & 225 s

We deployed 200 UEs in all simulations, each following a random walk with a speed of 2 m/s and changing direction every 10 s. The UEs' boundary area spans from -250 m to 1250 m in both x and y directions. Table 1 summarizes the simulation parameters of our experiments. We configured the base stations symmetrically to validate our hypothesis that geographically similar deployments yield comparable detection performance. The propagation loss model is *Friis free-space*, whereas Nakarmi et al. [19] use *Okumura-Hata* model, which requires transmitter–receiver distances greater than 1 km. The ns-3 code and datasets from the simulations are available in Github [11].

Training and Validation Datasets consist of measurement reports obtained without an FBS. The main purpose of training datasets is to analyze and understand the normal behavior of the network for each serving cell. We generated 20 training datasets with each lasting 500 s, and five validation datasets under the same conditions. Both datasets follow the same data processing scheme. First, we extracted the following features: *Time*, *ServingCellId*, $RSRP_i$. Then we partitioned the data according to *ServingCellId*. For each resulting sub-dataset, the data points are aggregated in 2-second intervals for each $RSRP_i$ column, and the mean of the nonzero values is computed.

Testing Dataset contains measurement reports collected in the presence of the FBS. The transmission power of the FBS was higher, and it moved in a defined trajectory with a speed of 20 m/s. Each UE was manually attached to the nearest legitimate BS at the start of the simulation. The simulation is run for 200 s for the box route (Fig. 1b), and 225 s for the random route (Fig. 1c). These durations allow the FBS to fully traverse each trajectory at a fixed speed. We conducted 25 simulations for the box route and 24 for the random route. UEs report signals only from the BSs they listen to; otherwise, the BS is reported as 0. The UE reporting interval varies between 0.12 s and 0.2 s. A range mapping of real values of measured RSRP is done as defined in 3GPP [4].

We partition the data points according to *ServingCellId*, while excluding the data points whose *ServingCellId* is 10, because FBS is not part of the real network. Nine variants of the partitioned data are created. In all variants, the column of $RSRP_{10}$ is discarded, while a masquerading technique is applied for the FBS to impersonate cell number $i \in \{1, \ldots, 9\}$. For masquerading as cell i, we replace the value of $RSRP_i$ with $max(RSRP_i, RSRP_{10})$ for each MR, reflecting typical UE behavior. Similarly, as in the training, we aggregate the MRs in 2-second intervals for each feature and compute the mean value.

Figure 2 compares RSRP_5 from the perspectives of serving cells 2, 6, and 8 between the cases where we have no FBS (left) and when an FBS is moving along the box route impersonating as BS 5 (right). We notice clear differences, highlighted by red, between the two cases.

4 Detection Technique

We ran ML algorithms similar to the ones used in Nakarmi et al. [19]. However, in our simulation set-up, the results were not as favorable as reported in [19] regarding false positives and false negatives, perhaps due to the lack of a sufficiently detailed technical description that would allow perfect replication.

Our setup includes an additional base station, which probably makes detection more difficult than in the set-up of Nakarmi et al. In our configuration, FBS

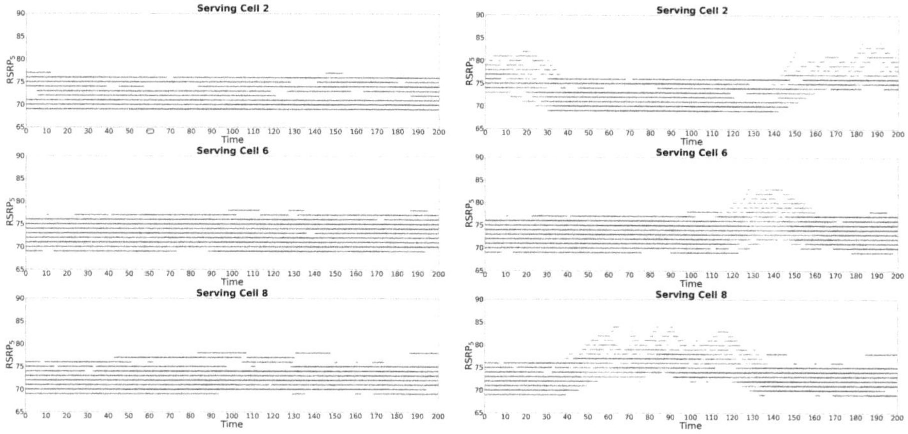

Fig. 2. Comparison of $RSRP_5$ values received by serving cells 2, 6, and 8 with FBS (right) and without FBS (left).

masquerades using a legitimate PCI. This means a forest-based classifier often misclassifies an anomalous data point as non-anomalous because both classes now represent similar RSRP values. Compared to our case, Nakarmi et al. [19] were able to perform well with the Anomaly Detection Forest [23]. Another difficulty is with the generation of benign data during the training phase. As obtaining fully labeled training data is infeasible in the real world, supervised machine learning fails due to a lack of labeled data points for distinguishing anomalies and benign cases. Semi-supervised learning also did not perform well in our setup. Due to the poor performance by the ML approach, we employed statistical methods to detect the presence of FBSs on the network level instead of one-to-one data point classification.

Our FBS detection method considers every $2s$ using a 30-second sliding window. Training a separate ML model for each serving cell is not required, saving computational resources, and eliminating the need to store additional parameters. We utilize the concept of the *z-score*, which helps observe the relative position of each data point within the distribution and identify outliers. Let x denote the individual data point, μ denote the mean of the data points, and σ denote the standard deviation of the data points. Then we get the z-score as $z = \frac{x-\mu}{\sigma}$. A z-score can be positive or negative, and both may predict anomalous behavior. Hence, when we sum multiple z-scores, we need to avoid the positive and negative values from canceling each other out. We avoid this by squaring the z-scores, which also highlights the exceptionally anomalous cases.

We initiate detection with the processed training data, which contains the mean RSRP values for $2s$ intervals. We denote by $RSRP_j^k(SC_t)$ as the average RSRP value of neighbor cell j ($RSRP_j$) obtained by serving cell t (SC_t) during the k-th time interval. We first use the processed data from each of the 20 training runs to calculate the means (μ_j^t) and standard deviations of (σ_j^t) for every possible serving cell-neighbor cell pair (t, j). In our 3×3 grid of 9 legitimate base stations, this results in 72 unique serving-neighbor pairs (9×9), as each of the 9 cells acts as a serving cell t that monitors the other 8 cells. In addition, each of the 9 serving cells receives RSRP measurements for its own signal ($j = t$). Sometimes the value $RSRP_j^k(SC_t)$ is missing, especially when j and t refer to opposite corners in the simulation topology, e.g., $j = 1$ and $t = 9$. The missing values are excluded from the mean and standard deviation calculations.

After computing the means and standard deviations for each pair $RSRP_j$-SC_t, we determine the Global Anomaly Score Threshold (GAST) from the training data. The idea is to constantly monitor anomaly scores ($AS(j, k, t)$) for $RSRP_j$-SC_t pairs, and when $AS(j, k, t)$ exceeds the GAST, the corresponding serving cell alarms. By masquerading as a legitimate station and transmitting high-power signals, the FBS forces the UE to report values that deviate significantly from the legitimate historical baselines (μ_j^t, σ_j^t), thus triggering a statistical anomaly. Note that FBS has to use a high-power signal, since otherwise it cannot attract UEs. If an alarm is received from two serving cells within a short time interval, a network-wide alarm for a FBS is raised. To compute GAST, we use anomaly scores $AS(j, k, t)$ obtained from the following formula:

$$\mathrm{AS}(j, k, t) = \sum_{i=k-14}^{k} \left(z(RSRP_j^i(SC_t))\right)^2 \tag{1}$$

where $z(RSRP_j^i(SC_t))$ refers to the *z-score*, $z(RSRP_j^i(SC_t)) = \frac{RSRP_j^i(SC_t) - \mu_j^t}{\sigma_j^t}$. We compute the anomaly score $AS(j, k, t)$ as the sum of squared z-scores for 15 consecutive $2s$ intervals. We compute the AS over the 15 time intervals to avoid false positives caused by a small number of erroneous MRs. On the other hand, we limit the number of intervals to 15 to capture fast-moving FBSs that may briefly appear in the vicinity of the serving cell. If this system is applied to a particular environment, one may adjust the number of intervals used for the AS depending on the likelihood of false positives, the presence of fast-moving FBSs, or the need to reduce response time.

Sometimes, the value $RSRP_j^i(SC_t)$ is missing. Then, set $z(RSRP_j^i(SC_t)) = 0$, so that it does not affect the anomaly score. In practice, this is done by setting $RSRP_j^i(SC_t) = \mu_j^t$. Once we have computed ASs for all 30-second intervals in our training data, we can compute GAST according to the following formula:

$$GAST = \frac{3}{2} \cdot \max_{j,k,t}(\mathrm{AS}(j, k, t)) + \frac{1}{2}\mu_{j,k,t}(\mathrm{AS}(j, k, t)). \tag{2}$$

Next, we explain how serving cells give a *local alarm*, and how the network triggers a *network-wide alarm*. Each serving cell t updates its anomaly score for each neighbor cell j in its vicinity (in our case, we have considered for each SC_t each of the nine $RSRP_j$ values) after every interval, that is, it updates value $AS(j, k, t)$ every 2 s. If the value $AS(j, k, t)$ exceeds GAST, serving cell SC_t gives a local alarm. Then, if there is also an alarm from another serving cell in the vicinity of SC_t within the last minute, a network-wide alarm is raised. We require at least two serving cells observing an anomaly to avoid false positives due to local problems. Parameter GAST takes into account both the maximum and the mean value of AS. This parameter should be small enough to allow detection of an FBS, but large enough to avoid false positives. As we observed no false positives, our GAST is more likely to be too large than too small.

5 Results

The minimum mean RSRP value μ_j^t was 65, and the maximum was 81. The value μ_j^t is large when neighbor cell j and serving cell t are close to each other, and μ_j^t obtains its maximum value of 81 when $j = t$. The minimum values are only obtained by the serving cells in the opposite corners. Furthermore, $|\mu_j^t - \mu_t^j| \leq 1$ holds for all pairs of j and t, hence RSRP values are quite symmetric, as expected. Also, serving cells in symmetric positions, such as SC_1 and SC_9, have symmetric mean values. In this case, we even have $\mu_1^t = \mu_9^{10-t}$ for all values of t.

The standard deviation σ_j^t differ more than the mean. However, standard deviation values are between 0.3 and 0.8 except for pairs SC_1, SC_9 and SC_3, SC_7. These exceptions are probably due to the large distance between BSs, which implies many missing $RSRP_j^i(SC_t)$ values. A large standard deviation value leads to a small z-score and therefore to a smaller anomaly score (AS) according to Eq. (1). However, our detection algorithm can handle these exceptional cases, as the mean values for these pairs are small (65). This means, e.g., that when FBS masquerades as SC_9 and comes close to SC_1, we observe a large increase in μ_9^1 and therefore a large z-score leading to a large AS. After computing the mean and standard deviation values, we computed anomaly scores for every 30-second interval in the training datasets. The maximum AS is 232, while the mean AS is 14.5. Based on the values, we obtain the global anomaly score threshold (GAST) using Eq. (2): $GAST = 356.0$. We compared the ASs from the validation data to GAST, based on 5 simulations. All ASs were smaller than GAST, hence no false positives were found: the maximum AS in validation data was 197.6, obtained by serving cell 5 for $RSRP_8$. Next, we will discuss the cases where an FBS exists.

In Fig. 3, we present how the AS changes over time for serving cell 5 and $RSRP_4$ when the FBS moves along the box route. The AS crosses the GAST twice; first when FBS passes serving cell 5 from the left side and later when it passes the same cell from the right side.

In Table 2 (left), we have analyzed all 25 simulations with FBS masquerading as one of the nine BSs, that is, 225 cases. The table shows how many times a BS does *not* raise an alarm. We see that our method does not allow a serving cell to detect an FBS masquerading as the serving cell itself. It is also harder for serving cells to detect an FBS, when the FBS masquerades as one of its closest neighbors. However, unless FBS is masquerading as number 2, 4, or 5, it can be detected by at least seven BSs, and when masquerading as numbers 2 or 5, it can still be detected by at least six BSs. Because a network-wide alarm is triggered whenever at least two serving cells cross the anomaly threshold within 1 minute,

Table 2. The number of runs a serving cell X (SCX) does not raise an alarm (false negatives) when FBS masquerades as BS Y (FY) over 25 simulation runs using box movement (left) and 24 simulation runs using a random route (right).

	F1	F2	F3	F4	F5	F6	F7	F8	F9		F1	F2	F3	F4	F5	F6	F7	F8	F9
SC1	25	10	0	11	0	0	0	0	0	SC1	24	24	1	24	1	1	1	1	5
SC2	0	25	0	0	0	0	0	0	0	SC2	0	24	0	0	1	0	0	0	0
SC3	0	3	25	0	0	0	0	0	0	SC3	0	0	24	0	0	0	0	0	0
SC4	2	0	0	25	9	0	2	0	0	SC4	1	0	0	24	8	0	2	0	0
SC5	0	0	0	0	25	0	0	0	0	SC5	0	0	0	0	24	0	0	0	0
SC6	0	0	6	0	12	25	0	0	8	SC6	0	0	3	0	11	24	0	0	0
SC7	0	0	0	3	0	0	25	19	0	SC7	0	0	0	4	0	0	24	20	0
SC8	0	0	0	0	0	0	0	25	0	SC8	0	0	0	0	0	0	0	23	0
SC9	0	0	0	0	0	3	0	0	25	SC9	0	0	0	0	0	3	0	2	24

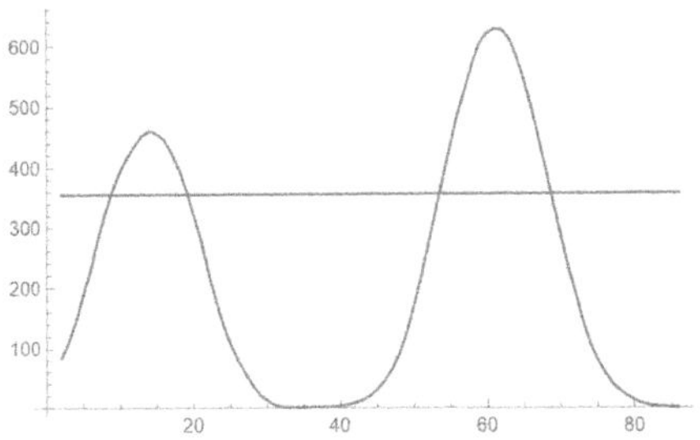

Fig. 3. Anomaly scores for serving cell 5, $RSRP_4$. The x-axis presents the time moment i, and the y-axis presents the anomaly score. The plotted line corresponds to values $AS(RSRP_4^i(SC_5))$, and the horizontal line represents GAST.

it follows from the pigeonhole principle that a network-wide alarm is raised in all simulations using the box route, regardless of which BS the FBS is posing as.

Unless FBS masquerades as number 2 or 5, our method gives an alarm at the earliest possible moment. If FBS masquerades as 2 or 5, the network-wide alarm is triggered at the earliest possible moment in 19 out of 25 (19 out of 25, resp.) cases, and always by moment 4 (moment 10, resp.).

We also conducted 24 simulations along a randomly chosen route, see Fig. 1c. In Table 2 (right), we show which BSs trigger alarms. The random route is slightly harder to detect than the box route. A notable difference occurs with serving cell 1. This is expected as FBS never comes close to BS 1 or passing serving cell 1. Considering the columns of Table 2 (right), we see that, regardless of the base station FBS is posing as, it is detected by at least four BSs, hence an alarm is triggered in every case. When FBS masquerades as BS 5, the alarm comes at moment 13. Otherwise, we detect it at latest at moment 3.

6 Discussion and Conclusion

Real-life adversaries might try to evade detection by adopting strategic routes of travel. Our evaluation against both box and random routes demonstrates that movement through the vicinity of UEs creates detectable RSRP deviations. We did not cover the case where the FBS does not move at all. But we anticipate that our system should also work in these situations, as the stationary FBS would still affect the RSRP values, movement itself does not affect the RSRP values, and AS of each moment is not affected by earlier ASs.

Since UEs report the strongest signal, FBS faces a trade-off: lowering its transmission power reduces its effectiveness in intercepting UEs, but maintaining high power causes it to be statistically visible. Albeit the grid-based ns-3 simulation gives a controlled environment, detection logic is deployment-agnostic. The statistical baseline (μ_j^t, σ_j^t) is unique to every pair regardless of the topology. This implies that our approach is applicable to real-world cellular deployment.

Our detection method is inherently scalable because it is based on local continuous monitoring of ASs (See Eq. (1)) over a 30-second sliding window at 2-second intervals. The coverage of a network-wide alarm should not be too large, as then the alarm would not be helpful in localizing the FBS. For example, the network-wide alarm could cover one tracking area. Applying multiple FBSs is not likely to prevent detection because then RSRP values only increase, which leads to increasing z-scores and also increasing ASs. With multiple FBSs deployed, the system generates localized alerts that aggregate into a network-wide alarm.

The integrity of the training data is paramount. If an adversary were present during the benign data collection phase, they could poison the statistical baseline. To mitigate this risk, we recommend that network operators establish datasets within controlled test networks or during verified maintenance windows to ensure the integrity of the model against adversarial manipulation. Future work could find out how well the method performs when the UEs move according to some pattern, e.g., via roads or in large groups such as bus passengers. Conducting experiments in a real test network is a possible future direction.

Acknowledgments. The research was supported by Business Finland projects 10769/31/2022 and 2123/31/2025. Tuomo Lehtilä's research was also supported by Research Council of Finland grants 338797 and 358718.

Disclosure of Interests. The authors have no competing interests to declare that are relevant to the content of this article.

References

1. Propagation — model library (ns-3 version 3.46). https://www.nsnam.org/docs/release/3.46/models/html/propagation.html (2025). Accessed 03 Oct 2025
2. 3GPP: Study on 5G Security Enhancements Against False Base Stations (FBS), 33.809 Tech. Rep (2023)
3. 3GPP: E-UTRA Radio Resource Control, Tech. Spec. 36.331 (2025)

4. 3GPP: E-UTRA Requirements for Support of Radio Resource Management. Tech. Spec **36**, 133 (2025)
5. 3GPP: NR Radio Resource Control. Tech. Spec **38**, 331 (2025)
6. 3GPP: Security Architecture and Procedures for 5G System. TS **33**, 501 (2025)
7. Alrashede, H., Shaikh, R.A.: IMSI Catcher Detection Method for Cellular Networks. In: Proceedings of the 2nd ICCAIS, pp. 1–6. IEEE (2019)
8. Cichonski, J., Franklin, J.M., Bartock, M.: Guide to LTE security. Special Publication NIST SP 800-187, Gaithersburg, MD, USA (2017)
9. Dabrowski, A., Petzl, G., Weippl, E.R.: The Messenger Shoots Back: network Operator Based IMSI Catcher Detection. In: Research in Attacks, Intrusions, and Defenses, vol. 9854, pp. 279–302. Springer International Publishing (2016)
10. Dabrowski, A., Pianta, N., Klepp, T., Mulazzani, M., Weippl, E.: IMSI-catch me if you can: IMSI-catcher-catchers. In: Proceedings 30th ACSAC, pp. 246–255. ACM (2014)
11. Gurung, S., Lehtilä, T., Sidibé, A.S., Akman, G., Niemi, V.: Experiments for Detection of FBS (2026). https://github.com/Sanish32/FBS-Detection
12. Heijligenberg, T., Rupprecht, D., Kohls, K.: The attacks aren't alright: large-Scale simulation of fake base station attacks and detections. In: Proceedings of the 17th CSET, pp. 54–64. ACM (2024)
13. Karaçay, L., et al.: A Network-Based Positioning Method to Locate False Base Stations. IEEE Access **9**, 111368–111382 (2021)
14. Li, P., Yang, H., Kim, I., Liu, Z., Li, S.: Cluster-based hybrid approach for configuration and optimization in 5G EN-DC heterogeneous networks. J. Netw. Syst. Manage. **32**, 24 (2024)
15. Li, Y., Peng, C., Yuan, Z., Li, J., Deng, H., Wang, T.: Mobileinsight: extracting and analyzing cellular network information on smartphones. In: Proceedings of the 22nd Mobile Computing and Networking, pp. 202–215. ACM (2016)
16. Li, Z., et al.: FBS-Radar: uncovering Fake Base Stations at Scale in the Wild. In: Proceedings of the 24th NDSS. Internet Society (2017)
17. Mubasshir, K.S., Karim, I., Bertino, E.: Gotta Detect 'Em All: fake base station and multi-step attack detection in cellular networks. In: Proceedings of the 34th USENIX Conference on Security Symposium, No. 276 (2025)
18. Nakarmi, P.K., Ersoy, M.A., Soykan, E.U., Norrman, K.: Murat: multi-RAT False Base Station Detector (2021)
19. Nakarmi, P.K., Sternby, J., Ullah, I.: Applying machine learning on RSRP-based features for false base station detection. In: Proceedings of the 17th ARES. ACM (2022)
20. Park, S., Shaik, A., Borgaonkar, R., Seifert, J.P.: Anatomy of commercial IMSI catchers and detectors. In: Proceedings of the 18th ACM Workshop on Privacy in the Electronic Society, pp. 74–86. ACM (2019)
21. Shaik, A., Borgaonkar, R., Asokan, N., Niemi, V., Seifert, J.P.: Practical attacks against privacy and availability in 4G/LTE mobile communication systems. In: Proceedings of the 23rd NDSS. Internet Society, CA, USA (2016)
22. Shaik, A., Borgaonkar, R., Park, S., Seifert, J.P.: New vulnerabilities in 4G and 5G cellular access network protocols: exposing device capabilities. In: WiSec, pp. 221–231. ACM (2019)
23. Sternby, J., Thormarker, E., Liljenstam, M.: Anomaly Detection Forest. In: ECAI **325**, 1507–1514 (2020)

24. Sun, S., Abualhaol, I., Poitau, G., Esswie, A., Repeta, M.: An ensemble approach for fake base station detection using temporal graph analysis and anomaly detection. In: Wireless Telecommunications Symposium, pp. 1–6. IEEE (2024)
25. Telcoma Global: What is in LTE and 5G? (2025). https://telcomaglobal.com/p/what-is-pci-in-lte-and-5g. Accessed 24 Dec 2026

Bots, Malware, Phishing

Detecting Bot Detection: Prevalence, Techniques, and Implications for Web Measurement Research

Ralf Gundelach(✉), Michael Mühlhauser, and Dominik Herrmann

University of Bamberg, Bamberg, Germany
{rg.psi,mm.psi,dh.psi}@uni-bamberg.de

Abstract. Browser automation frameworks are essential tools for security and privacy research on the web, yet bot detection scripts increasingly probe their artifacts, threatening measurement validity as automated browsers may be blocked or served different content. Prior work measures detection deployment, while we measure blocking-induced sample loss. Through a literature survey of top-tier security, privacy, and web measurement venues, we find that 83% of papers omit any discussion of bot detection blocking. To address this gap, we conduct a measurement study of 10,000 websites across four browser configurations (40K page visits in total) to quantify detection prevalence and employed techniques. Using custom instrumentation to detect when sites probe for automation, we develop a taxonomy of bot detection techniques and measure how often they appear in practice. Chromium headless encounters a 15% soft block rate compared to 7% for other configurations. Across all conditions, 82% of blocks are attributable to bot detection (59% vendor-confirmed, 23% inferred from condition-dependent blocking), predominantly by providers with integrated bot detection such as Cloudflare (37% block rate) and Akamai (26%). A header spoofing experiment establishes that 75% of Chromium-headless-only blocks are caused by header-level signals alone, yet JavaScript-based environment probing is more extensive than current blocking rates suggest. These findings demonstrate that bot detection creates systematic, provider-correlated sample loss that the web measurement community neither measures nor reports. The downstream effect on specific measurement outcomes remains future work.

Keywords: Bot Detection · Browser Fingerprinting · Browser Automation · Web Crawling · Reproducibility

1 Introduction

Browser automation frameworks have been crucial for web security and privacy research. They enable large-scale measurements of tracking [7] and vulnerability scanning [14]. However, the validity of these measurements is endangered by bot

S. Nadjm-Tehrani et al. (Eds.): ARES 2026, LNCS 16898, pp. 275–296, 2027.
https://doi.org/10.1007/978-3-032-36874-4_14

detection, a factor whose implications for measurement validity are not yet well characterized.

Website providers deploy anti-bot defenses for legitimate purposes, such as credential stuffing mitigation and scraping protection [2]. These defenses, either in the form of community-driven projects or commercial anti-bot services offered by companies like Cloudflare, Akamai, and PerimeterX/HUMAN[1], have become ubiquitous across the web. This dynamic is compounded by the rise of large language models (LLMs): bot detection vendors now explicitly market capabilities to block AI scrapers[2], tightening defenses that also affect researchers using the same tools. The deployment of bot detection measures creates a fundamental threat to measurement validity: automated browsers may be blocked, rate-limited, or served different content than human users, causing previous measurement studies to silently reflect only the subset of sites that did *not* block automation.

Prior work has examined bot detection from specific angles, like reverse engineering individual detectors [10], measuring framework detectability [15], and analyzing cloaking in adversarial settings [22]. However, no study has systematically measured how bot detection affects web measurement research at scale with respect to blocking outcomes.

We address this gap through three contributions:

1. We establish a measurement blind spot through a literature survey of 81 papers at top-tier venues, finding that 83% omit any discussion of bot detection blocking.
2. We map the domains of the Tranco Top 1M [18], a toplist used in many measurement studies, to their autonomous systems. We show that a majority of websites are served through CDNs with bot detection capabilities, unavoidably exposing crawling experiments to detection infrastructure.
3. We scan the top 10,000 sites of the Tranco Top 1M across four browser conditions and find that blocking is provider-driven: Cloudflare and Akamai block at the highest rates (37% and 26%), while providers without default-on bot detection range from 0–16%. A header spoofing experiment (Sect. 5.3) shows that 75% of Chromium-headless blocks are caused by header-level signals alone, yet browser environment probing is more extensive than current blocking rates suggest, with 46% of sites checking JavaScript properties that are only present in automated browsers.

---

[1] Cloudflare, "Bot Solutions," https://developers.cloudflare.com/bots/; Akamai, "Bot Manager," https://akamai.com/products/bot-manager; HUMAN Security, "Bot Protection," https://humansecurity.com/platform/solutions/bot-detection-mitigation.

[2] Cloudflare, "Declare your AIndependence," https://blog.cloudflare.com/declaring-your-aindependence-block-ai-bots-scrapers-and-crawlers-with-a-single-click/; HUMAN Security, "Controlling AI-driven Content Scraping," https://www.humansecurity.com/learn/blog/controlling-ai-driven-content-scraping-with-human/.

Our findings demonstrate that bot detection creates systematic sample loss correlated with CDN infrastructure that the community neither measures nor reports, with direct consequences for the validity of published results. Our crawler, dataset, analysis notebooks, and per-paper literature survey codings are publicly available.[3] Per-site screenshots are excluded from the released dataset for copyright reasons.

The rest of this paper is structured as follows: Sect. 2 discusses background and related work. Section 3 presents our literature survey. Section 4 quantifies CDN prevalence through DNS resolution of the Tranco Top 1M. Section 5 describes our measurement methodology and results. Section 6 discusses implications, recommendations, and limitations. Section 7 concludes this work.

2 Background and Related Work

Research on detecting web measurement frameworks is limited. Demir et al. [6] surveyed 117 measurement studies and found that undocumented bot evasion strategies and varying crawler setups severely impact results. We draw on related work in browser fingerprinting measurement, which shares our methodology of intercepting API accesses at scale, and on web bot detection research, where prior studies have identified detection scripts through string matching, examined the fingerprinting surface of OpenWPM, and evaluated anti-bot services from a defender's perspective.

2.1 Browser Fingerprinting

Englehardt and Narayanan developed OpenWPM, an open-source web measurement framework, which they used to conduct a large-scale measurement of tracking on 1M websites [7]. By instrumenting JavaScript APIs (Canvas, WebRTC, AudioContext, and Battery API), they were able to measure fingerprinting by third parties. Iqbal et al. [9] extended OpenWPM to track access to the Performance API and WebGL, as they found that these APIs were also used by popular fingerprinting scripts. They applied a syntactic-semantic based approach and found that browser fingerprinting is present on over a quarter of the Alexa Top 10K and over 10% of the Top 100K. Vastel et al. [19] introduced FP-Scanner, a fingerprint scanner that can detect inconsistencies in browser fingerprints and whether the presented fingerprint is genuine or not. Bahrami et al. employed a graph-based approach on historical snapshots of the Alexa Top 100K to discover previously unknown fingerprinting APIs through clustering [3]. Boussaha et al. used dynamic taint tracking to measure fingerprinting severity across the Tranco Top 100K, finding that 8% of domains perform high-severity fingerprinting [4]. However, these automated measurements likely underestimate the prevalence of fingerprinting. Annamalai et al. [1] demonstrated that automated crawls miss up to 45% of the fingerprinting websites encountered by real users, largely due to bot detection mechanisms and consent banners blocking crawler access.

[3] https://doi.org/10.5281/zenodo.20334022.

2.2 Web Bot Detection

Jonker et al. reverse-engineered a commercial client-side web bot detector [10]. They identified behavior-based detection using event handlers, code injection routines for script-website communication, and detection based on DOM properties. By extending the open-source library fingerprint2.js, they determined the fingerprinting surface of 14 web bots. Using derived keyword patterns, they scanned the Alexa Top 1M and found 127,799 sites with matching scripts. Detection prevalence was higher in the top 100K (15.7K sites) compared to lower ranks (averaging 12.7K per 100K). Jueckstock et al. developed VisibleV8, which instruments the V8 JavaScript engine at the browser level to log all native API accesses [11]. During a crawl of the Alexa Top 50K, they discovered that 29% of websites loaded scripts that were probing for 46 JavaScript namespace artifacts associated with automated browser platforms. Krumnow et al. analyzed the detectability of OpenWPM, the resilience of its data recording, and the prevalence of OpenWPM detection [15]. They scanned the Tranco Top 100K and determined that 14% of the front pages detected OpenWPM, rising to 19% when sub-pages were visited. Vastel et al. [20] provided the first systematic analysis of fingerprinting-based crawler detection: they crawled the Alexa Top 10K with Chromium headless and identified 291 sites (2.9%) that block crawlers, of which 93 use browser fingerprinting, and further evaluated evasion resilience by incrementally spoofing crawler attributes.

Other work takes an adversarial perspective. Azad et al. [2] evaluated commercial anti-bot services and found that while basic bots (Python, PhantomJS) are blocked on over 75% of protected sites, less common browsers (Safari, mobile Chrome) bypass up to 82%. Venugopalan et al. [21] solicited traffic from 20 bot services against a honey site and found evasion rates of 45–53%; they proposed FP-Inconsistent, which detects bots through fingerprint inconsistencies, reducing evasion by 45–48%.

Prior work has established that bot detection scripts are widely deployed [10, 11, 15], but these studies measure detection *presence*, e. g., whether a site loads with capabilities for detecting automated browsers, not detection *impact*: whether the site actually blocks automated browsers, serves altered content, or behaves differently across browser configurations as a consequence of the detection. The distinction matters, as deploying a detection script does not imply blocking: Krumnow et al. found that many sites probe for automation signals without necessarily acting on the result. However, when active mitigation is encountered, the impact on measurement validity can be significant. Jueckstock et al. [12] found that crawler configurations and anti-bot defenses introduce significant measurement bias, altering the advertising and tracking domains encountered by up to 19%. Vastel et al. take a step further by measuring actual blocking, but their resilience evaluation covers 40 selected sites with a single browser engine. Our study shifts the focus from evasion resilience to infrastructure-level prevalence: we measure blocking outcomes across 10,000 sites and four browser conditions, identifying which providers drive blocking and establishing through a causal experiment which signals cause it.

3 Bot Detection Reporting in Web Measurement Studies

This section addresses our first contribution by establishing a measurement blind spot in web measurement research. To motivate the need for better bot detection transparency, we conducted a systematic literature review of bot detection reporting practices in recent crawling studies. We describe our methodology in Sect. 3.1 and present the results in Sect. 3.2.

3.1 Methods

We surveyed papers published between 2020 and 2025 at top-tier security, privacy, and web measurement venues: USENIX Security, IEEE S&P, CCS, NDSS, WWW, IMC, and PETS. For each paper, we read the title and abstract to determine whether it involved automated web crawling of multiple websites. More specifically, we included papers that performed automated web crawling on multiple websites using automated browsers and excluded papers that relied on command line tools or existing datasets without novel data collection. We decided to exclude command line tools, as most security and privacy web measurement studies use real browsers, prominently the OpenWPM framework[4]. Furthermore, none of our browser-based detection vectors (C8–C12) would apply, diluting our results.

We evaluated papers on twelve criteria organized in two dimensions: General reproducibility (C1–C6) and bot detection awareness (C7–C12). Our framework builds on the reproducibility criteria established by Demir et al. [6], who surveyed 117 crawling papers (2016–2021) and identified 18 documentation criteria. Notably, their criterion C8 ("State bot detection evasion approach") exhibited the highest omission rate at 88%, suggesting that detection-related methodology is systematically under-documented. We retained six core reproducibility criteria adapted from Demir et al. and expanded their single bot detection criterion into six sub-criteria that separately assess detection outcomes and mitigation methods. This decomposition enables finer-grained analysis of which detection-related aspects researchers document versus omit. We employed a categorical coding scheme summarized in Table 1.

All papers were independently coded by the first author. To assess coding reliability, a stratified subset of 20 papers (25%) was independently double-coded by the second author, yielding a Cohen's κ of 0.90 (almost perfect agreement) across 260 rating pairs. We attribute the high agreement to the predominantly objective nature of our criteria (e.g., whether a tool is named or a URL is provided), which leaves limited room for subjective interpretation. The 16 disagreements (6.2%) were resolved through discussion.

Reproducibility Criteria (C1–C6). Criteria C1–C3 and C6 are self-explanatory from Table 2. We clarify two criteria with non-obvious thresholds:

[4] OpenWPM, "Studies," https://github.com/openwpm/studies/blob/main/studies.md.

Table 1. Rating scale for criterion evaluation.

Rating	Description
Satisfies	The paper provides sufficient detail to replicate the methodology (e. g., exact tool names, version numbers, parameter values, or links to artifacts)
Partial	The paper acknowledges the aspect but lacks actionable detail (e. g., "used a custom WebDriver" without implementation details, "added delays" without timing values)
Omit	The paper does not address this aspect

C4: Browser Documented. A paper satisfies this criterion if browser and version number are named (e. g., "Firefox 140"). Papers only mentioning the browser or browser family receive partial credit.

C5: Dataset Documented. A paper satisfies this criterion if it names the site list source (e. g., Tranco, Alexa, CrUX), quantifies the scope (N sites or pages), and provides a version or snapshot date for the list (e. g., Tranco list ID, Alexa retrieval date). Papers that name the source and scope but omit the list version receive partial credit.

Bot Detection Awareness Criteria (C7–C12). These criteria assess transparency regarding bot detection risks and countermeasures. They are grounded in known detection vectors documented in evasion frameworks [15][5] and community resources[6] that enumerate automation-specific artifacts, browser fingerprinting surfaces, and behavioral signals. Criterion C7 captures detection outcomes, while C8–C12 capture mitigation methods.

C7: Failure Rate Reported. Whether the paper reports failures or detection incidents. This criterion has two components:

1. *C7a: Error Rate Reported.* General scan failures (e. g., "X% of scans failed", "N timeouts"). Qualitative mentions receive partial credit.
2. *C7b: Blocking Rate Reported.* Explicit discussion of bot detection or blocking (e. g., "X% of sites blocked our crawler", "N CAPTCHAs encountered"). Qualitative mentions receive partial credit. We note that omission is ambiguous: it may indicate no failures occurred, that failures were unreported, or that failed sites were silently excluded.

[5] berstend, "puppeteer-extra-plugin-stealth," https://github.com/berstend/puppeteer-extra; DuckDuckGo, "tracker-radar-collector," https://github.com/duckduckgo/tracker-radar-collector.

[6] AbrahamJuliot, "CreepJS," https://github.com/AbrahamJuliot/creepjs; Vastel, "Detecting Selenium Chrome," https://datadome.co/bot-management-protection/detecting-selenium-chrome/.

C8: Display Mode Documented. Whether the paper specifies headless versus headed browser execution. A paper satisfies this criterion by explicitly stating the display mode. Implied references ("ran without display", "Chrome extension", or tools that default to headless mode such as Puppeteer) receive partial credit. Note that we also treat "crawling with a Chrome extension" as ambiguous and therefore award only partial credit: Historically, Chrome could run extensions only in headed mode, but extension support in headless mode was introduced in 2023.[7] Without an explicit statement, or a reproducible configuration description, it is not possible to determine whether the crawl was performed with a visible display or in headless mode.

C12: Stealth Measures Documented. Criteria C9–C11 are self-explanatory from Table 2. For C12, rate limiting, user agent configuration, and display mode are excluded as they are captured separately in C8–C10.

Table 2. Criteria for evaluating Web measurement studies.

	ID	Criterion	Description
Reproducibility	C1	Crawler Available	Crawling implementation is publicly accessible (e. g., GitHub, Zenodo)
	C2	Data Available	Collected data is publicly accessible
	C3	Tool Documented	Crawling technology is named (e. g., Selenium, Puppeteer, OpenWPM)
	C4	Browser Documented	Browser is specified for browser-based crawlers
	C5	Dataset Documented	Site list source, scope, and version are specified (e. g., Tranco ID N7QVW, top 10k)
	C6	Crawl Date Reported	Temporal information is provided
Bot Detection	C7a	Error Rate Reported	General scan failures are quantified
	C7b	Blocking Rate Reported	Bot detection or blocking incidents are discussed
	C8	Display Mode Documented	Headless vs. headed execution is specified
	C9	User Agent Documented	HTTP User-Agent configuration is specified
	C10	Rate Limiting Documented	Request timing and throttling are specified
	C11	IP Infrastructure Documented	Network infrastructure is named (e. g., AWS, university network)
	C12	Stealth Measures Documented	Active evasion techniques are specified (e. g., stealth plugins)

3.2 Results

Having screened the titles and abstracts of 132 papers across seven venues, we identified 81 that match our inclusion criteria (PETS: 21, WWW: 17, IMC: 14, S&P: 10, CCS: 9, USENIX: 8, NDSS: 2), published between 2020 and 2025. Table 3 summarizes the results.

Reproducibility (C1–C6). Tool choice (C3) is nearly universally documented (99%), with OpenWPM being the most common framework (25 papers), followed by Selenium (16), Puppeteer (14), and custom implementations (12). Dataset documentation (C5) reaches 58% when requiring a versioned or dated site list, with Tranco (40 papers) having largely replaced Alexa (24) as the preferred

7 https://github.com/puppeteer/puppeteer/issues/659; https://developer.chrome.com/blog/removing-headless-old-from-chrome.

Table 3. Criterion evaluation results across 81 papers.

	Criterion	Satisfies		Partial		Omit	
		n	%	*n*	%	*n*	%
Reprod.	C1: Crawler Available	41	51	4	5	36	44
	C2: Data Available	23	28	7	9	51	63
	C3: Tool Documented	80	99	1	1	0	0
	C4: Browser Documented	37	46	42	52	2	2
	C5: Dataset Documented	47	58	34	42	0	0
	C6: Crawl Date Reported	42	52	11	14	28	35
Bot Det.	C7a: Error Rate Reported	37	46	9	11	35	43
	C7b: Blocking Rate Reported	4	5	10	12	67	83
	C8: Display Mode Documented	25	31	18	22	38	47
	C9: User Agent Documented	11	14	5	6	65	80
	C10: Rate Limiting Documented	6	7	2	2	73	90
	C11: IP Infrastructure Doc.	29	36	16	20	36	44
	C12: Stealth Measures Doc.	19	23	7	9	55	68

toplist. Browser choice (C4) is named in 98% of papers, though only 46% specify the version number.

Code and data availability remain limited: while a slight majority of papers release their crawling code (C1: 51%), only 28% share their collected data (C2). Crawl dates (C6) are reported by 52%, with another 14% providing only vague temporal references.

Bot Detection Awareness (C7–C12). The bot detection criteria reveal a systematic documentation gap. The most striking finding is C7b: only 5% of papers explicitly quantify bot detection or blocking rates, and 83% omit any discussion of blocking entirely. This is notable because, as our measurement study demonstrates (Sect. 5), bot detection is deployed on a substantial fraction of popular websites and can silently affect crawl results.

General error rates (C7a) fare better, with 46% providing quantified failure counts, though 43% still omit error reporting entirely. Display mode (C8) is omitted by 47% of papers, despite headless execution being a primary bot detection signal. User-Agent configuration (C9) is documented in only 20% of papers. Rate limiting (C10) has the highest omission rate at 90%. IP infrastructure (C11) is documented in 56% of papers, often because studies use cloud vantage points as part of their methodology. Active stealth measures (C12) are documented in 32% of papers, with the remainder neither employing nor discussing evasion techniques.

Across the seven bot detection criteria (C7a–C12), papers address an average of only 2.4 out of 7 criteria. Eight papers (10%) do not address any bot detection criterion at all. Only a single paper addresses six criteria; none addresses all seven.

4 Prevalence of Content Distribution Networks

To quantify the potential impact of bot detection on web measurements, we performed DNS resolution on the Tranco Top 1 Million domains and mapped them to infrastructure providers. Major CDNs such as Cloudflare and Akamai also offer bot detection services, making CDN prevalence a proxy for bot detection exposure.

4.1 Data Collection

As a data source, we used the Tranco Top 1 Million list [18] from February 25, 2026 (ID: GVL9K), as it is one of the most widely used top lists in web measurement research that we encountered during our literature survey. We resolved all A records for all domains using a parallelized Python program with dnspython, configured with three public DNS resolvers from Google (8.8.8.8), Cloudflare (1.1.1.1), and Quad9 (9.9.9.9) for redundancy.

Of the 1 million domains, 893,411 (89.3%) resolved to at least one A record, yielding 1,472,477 A records in total. The remaining 106,589 domains returned NXDOMAIN or timed out, consistent with parked, expired, or misconfigured entries commonly found in aggregated toplists [18].

4.2 Analysis Method

We mapped the resolved IP addresses to their owning autonomous system (AS) using the IPinfo Lite dataset (CSV snapshot 2026-01-29). Of 1,472,477 A records, 1,380,865 (93.8%) were successfully matched to an AS owner. Where multiple AS names refer to the same organization (e. g., "Cloudflare London, LLC" and "Cloudflare, Inc."), we consolidated them into a single entity. Note that we count A records rather than unique domains, so our percentages reflect infrastructure footprint: providers whose domains resolve to multiple A records (e. g., for load balancing) are weighted proportionally higher.

4.3 Results

Our analysis reveals a significant concentration of web infrastructure among a small number of providers, which is in line with previous work [13]. Cloudflare alone accounts for 40.0% of AS-matched A records, followed by Amazon at 16.9%. The top 3 providers cover 59.2% and the top 5 cover 63.5%. Note that Fig. 1 uses all resolved A records as the denominator (including the 6.2% not matched to an AS), yielding slightly lower percentages.

As shown in Fig. 1, this concentration shifts across popularity tiers. Amazon dominates among the top 1k at 32.0% of resolved A records, but its share decreases to 15.9% across the full million. Cloudflare shows the inverse trend, growing from 14.5% in the top 1k to 37.6% in the top 1M. This suggests that the most popular websites rely more heavily on enterprise-grade CDN and cloud providers, while lower-ranked sites increasingly adopt Cloudflare, likely due to its accessible free and low-cost tiers which include bot detection by default.

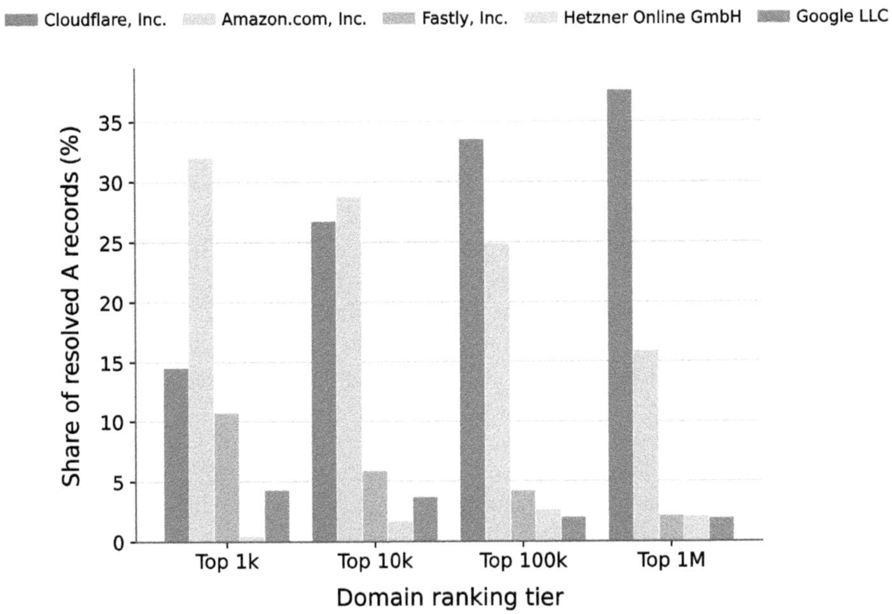

Fig. 1. AS ownership share across Tranco domain ranking tiers (top 5 providers).

Table 4 combines infrastructure prevalence with blocking outcomes from our measurement study (Sect. 5). Several of these providers offer bot detection services, notably Cloudflare (Bot Management, enabled by default on free plans), Akamai (Bot Manager), and Fastly (Signal Sciences); however, hosting on a capable provider does not guarantee active detection, as services like AWS WAF are opt-in and paid. The blocking rates confirm that infrastructure provider is the primary correlate of bot detection: Cloudflare (37.0%) and Akamai (26.4%) block at rates far above the overall average, while providers without default-on bot detection range from 0–16%. Notably, Akamai's high block rate is almost entirely unclassified by vendor signatures in the HTTP responses (103 of 110 blocked sites), consistent with Akamai serving generic error pages without vendor branding. This means that researchers receiving these responses have no straightforward way to distinguish bot detection blocks from legitimate server errors, making silent sample loss particularly difficult to detect.

Table 4. Top 10 Autonomous Systems by A record count (Tranco Top 1M) with blocking rates from our Top 10K scan. Block rate: percentage of sites in the Top 10K hosted on this AS that received HTTP 403/429/503 in at least one browser condition (prevalence is computed on Tranco Top 1M, blocking rates on the Top 10K sample). Rates shown only for providers with ≥100 sites in the Top 10K.

AS Name	A records	%	Sites (10K)	Blocked	Block rate
Cloudflare, Inc.	553,014	40.0	2,128	788	37.0
Amazon.com, Inc.	233,600	16.9	1,720	280	16.3
Fastly, Inc.	31,470	2.3	321	50	15.6
Hetzner Online GmbH	30,746	2.2	91	4	—
Google LLC	28,140	2.0	531	27	5.1
Akamai Connected Cloud	23,802	1.7	417	110	26.4
OVH SAS	21,825	1.6	81	3	—
Microsoft Corporation	18,874	1.4	162	24	14.8
Hostinger International Ltd	13,799	1.0	1	0	—
DigitalOcean, LLC	11,071	0.8	22	4	—

5 Prevalence of Bot Detection and Impact on Web Measurement Studies

Having established that bot detection reporting is systematically absent from web measurement research (Sect. 3) and that a majority of popular websites are served through CDN infrastructure with bot detection capabilities (Sect. 4), we now address our third contribution. We quantify how often bot detection actually blocks automated browsers and characterize the detection techniques and services involved.

5.1 Methods

Instrumentation Approach. While previous works instrumented individual APIs, we take a different approach. Before page scripts execute, we inject JavaScript that dynamically configures proxies for *all* property accesses and function calls. A proxy is a JavaScript metaprogramming feature that allows us to intercept and log all property accesses on an object. This maximizes API coverage without relying on a predefined list of instrumentation targets. We additionally flag APIs associated with browser fingerprinting and automation detection, derived from the following sources:

1. **WPM$_{\textbf{hide}}$** [15], an evasion module developed for OpenWPM
2. **puppeteer-extra-plugin-stealth**[8], an evasion library that has been used in past research [5]

[8] berstend, "puppeteer-extra-plugin-stealth," https://github.com/berstend/puppeteer-extra/tree/master/packages/puppeteer-extra-plugin-stealth.

3. **Tracker Radar Collector**[9], a puppeteer-based crawler featuring evasion methods that collects third party request data, also used in previous research [16]
4. **Documented Detection Techniques**: Properties identified in research [11] and community resources[10]

From these four sources, we compiled 132 JavaScript properties. Accesses to one or more of these properties signal that a site may be attempting to detect automated browsers. We categorize the properties into three confidence tiers based on their specificity to automation detection, as many also serve legitimate fingerprinting purposes:

1. **Tier 1**: No legitimate use case except for automation detection. These are browser properties that are injected by automation frameworks (e.g., `navigator.webdriver`, `window._selenium`).
2. **Tier 2**: Strong automation detection indicators that also serve other use cases. For instance, `chrome.runtime` and `navigator.plugins` can be used to fingerprint a browser or to detect discrepancies in its fingerprint, which would indicate an automated browser.
3. **Tier 3**: APIs that are generally used for fingerprinting browsers, but could also be used to detect browser automation (e.g., `navigator.userAgent`).

Tier 1 accesses represent unambiguous detection attempts, while Tier 3 accesses could also stem from regular fingerprinting and must be interpreted in context.

Instrumentation Architecture. Our instrumentation operates at three levels:

- **Property interception.** We install a recursive `Proxy` on the `window` object whose `get` trap intercepts property accesses, logs them, and returns nested proxies that track the full property path (e.g., `navigator.permissions.query`).
- **Prototype patching.** For non-configurable properties on built-in prototypes (e.g., `Document.prototype`, `Navigator.prototype`, `RTCPeerConnection.prototype`), we replace prototype getters and methods with instrumented versions that log accesses before delegating to the original implementation.
- **Honeypot properties.** Bot detection scripts often check for properties that automation frameworks inject (e.g., `window._selenium`). These properties do not exist in our browser, but by planting them as invisible traps that log any access attempt and return `undefined`, we can detect when a site is probing for automation without revealing our browser as automated.

[9] DuckDuckGo, "tracker-radar-collector", https://github.com/duckduckgo/tracker-radar-collector.

[10] Abraham Juliot, "CreepJS", https://github.com/abrahamjuliot/creepjs; https://stackoverflow.com/a/41220267.

While signal tiers and instrumentation methods are related, they are not equivalent. Tiers reflect semantic confidence (what an API access implies about detection intent), whereas instrumentation methods reflect technical constraints (how we capture the access). For instance, Tier 1 includes both honeypot properties that do not exist in real browsers (e. g., `window._selenium`) and real automation artifacts that require property interception (e. g., `navigator.webdriver`). Each logged access records: the full property path (symbol), operation type (`GET`/`HAS`/`SET`/`CALL`), caller script location, timestamp, and assigned confidence tier. When an API is accessed more than 500 times, we record a `LIMIT_REACHED` event, a threshold used in prior work to detect Canvas and performance-based fingerprinting [9][11]. Additionally, all scripts are stored with their URL and script content for *bot detection vendor* attribution.

Experimental Conditions. We examine two factors: browser engine (Firefox and Chromium) and display mode (headless and headed). Previous work and industry practice suggest that headless browsers exhibit detectable properties, and that browser engines differ in their exposed API sets. For instance, Firefox removed the Battery API in version 52 to reduce fingerprinting by trackers [17], and such browser engine differences can themselves be used as fingerprinting signals [9]. This 2×2 design yields four conditions, each applied to every site in our sample. All conditions use Playwright for consistent automation semantics across browser engines. While Playwright itself is detectable, our instrumentation executes before page scripts and all four conditions share the same automation framework, so any Playwright-specific bias affects all conditions equally. As we discuss below, scanning from a datacenter IP rather than a residential network affects absolute blocking rates, but our paired design still allows us to observe meaningful differences between the 2×2 conditions. To minimize confounds, all scans are run from a single Hetzner datacenter in Nuremberg, ensuring a uniform region and ASN type, with IP rotation between batches and randomized scan order to avoid repeated same-site requests from the same IP in quick succession. Table 5 summarizes our crawler configuration.

Site Selection and Sampling. We draw the first 10,000 sites of the Tranco Top 1 Million list [18]. As in Sect. 4, we use the Toplist from February 25, 2026. Sites are shuffled deterministically with a documented seed value for reproducibility purposes and partitioned into 10 batches of 1,000 sites each. Within each batch, we generate 4,000 scans (1,000 sites × 4 conditions), again shuffled with a documented per-batch seed to distribute same-site scans temporally.

Execution Protocol. Scans proceed in batches with IP rotation between them. After each batch, we delete the virtual machine along with its public IP address

[11] https://github.com/UmarIqbal/OpenWPM/blob/9e6234ef7a542c5d4bf56493eb3b39840c7dfecb/automation/Extension/firefox/data/content.js.

Table 5. Crawler configuration summary.

Parameter	Value
Automation framework	Playwright 1.57.0
Browser engines	Chromium 143.0.7499.4, Firefox 144.0.2
Display modes	Headless, headed
Site list	Tranco Top 10K (ID: GVL9K, 2026-02-25)
Scan date	2026-02-27 to 2026-03-02 (spoofing: 2026-03-03)
User-Agent	Playwright defaults (unmodified)
Rate limiting	IP rotation between batches of 1,000 sites
IP infrastructure	Hetzner Cloud, Nuremberg, DE (datacenter)
Stealth measures	None (default Playwright configuration)

and restore it from a snapshot, thus receiving a different IP address. Each scan is executed as follows:

1. **Navigation**: Load the page with a 30-second timeout
2. **Idle Detection**: Wait until no new API accesses have been recorded for 2 s, or 30 s have passed in total. Meanwhile, all properties are logged as described previously
3. **Terminate Scan**: Finally the browser saves a screenshot to the file system and marks the scan as successful. Screenshots serve as ground truth for manual verification of blocking responses (Sect. 5.3)

Our study minimizes harm and impact by only visiting publicly accessible homepages and not performing interactions beyond the front page load. We do not collect personal data.

This design ensures all four conditions for a given site execute under the same IP address and within a narrow time window, enabling paired comparisons that control for IP reputation and site content variability. We specifically rotate IPs to mitigate known measurement artifacts, as previous research demonstrates that web scanners frequently encounter "refusenik" websites that systematically drop connections or alter content based on the degraded reputation of the scanner's network vantage point [2,8,12].

Methodological Caveats. Three aspects of our instrumentation affect interpretation. First, our JavaScript proxies create detectable artifacts; sophisticated detection scripts can identify proxied objects via `Function.prototype.toString()` inspection or timing side-channels. However, this primarily affects our API access counts (Sect. 5.4), not our blocking measurements: HTTP-level blocking decisions (403/429/503) are made by CDN infrastructure independently of client-side JavaScript. The observed headless-vs-headed blocking asymmetry (Sect. 5.3) and header spoofing results (Sect. 5.3) are based on HTTP-level outcomes, not API counts, and are therefore not affected by instrumentation detectability. Second, we capture only client-side JavaScript detection; server-side mechanisms

(IP reputation, TLS fingerprinting, behavioral analysis) are outside our observational scope, making our prevalence estimates a lower bound. Third, observing an API access does not establish that a site acted on the result: a site may probe `navigator.webdriver` for telemetry without blocking. We correlate signal access with scan outcomes but cannot establish definitive causal links; only Tier 1 signals are unambiguously detection-related. We discuss further limitations in Sect. 6.

5.2 Results

We present our findings across two research questions: detection prevalence and cross-condition differences (RQ1), and the detection landscape including techniques and services (RQ2). Because not every site completed all four conditions (due to DNS failures, timeouts, or SSL errors), denominators vary by analysis. RQ1 reports per-condition totals out of 10,000 sites each, with paired comparisons on the 6,936 Chromium and 7,063 Firefox sites where both headless and headed conditions returned an HTTP response. API prevalence in RQ2 uses the 7,944 sites with at least one successful scan that produced property-access data.

5.3 Detection Prevalence (RQ1)

Table 6 shows the detection classification across all four browser conditions. We classify each scan based on its HTTP status code and scan outcome into *success* (any 2xx response), *soft block* (HTTP 403 Forbidden, 429 Too Many Requests, or 503 Service Unavailable), and *timeout* (page did not respond within 30 s). Not all soft blocks necessarily represent bot detection, so we validate this classification below by analyzing response bodies and cross-condition blocking patterns.

Table 6. Detection classification by browser condition (n=10,000 sites per condition). Not shown: ~2,100–2,450 infrastructure failures (DNS, SSL, connection errors) per condition, screenshot timeouts (~440 Chromium, ~150 Firefox), and ~170–220 other HTTP status codes (3xx, 500, etc.).

Condition	Success (2xx)		Soft block		Nav. timeout	
	n	%	n	%	n	%
Chromium headless	5,550	55.5	1,521	15.2	117	1.2
Chromium headed	6,435	64.4	721	7.2	109	1.1
Firefox headless	6,462	64.6	678	6.8	92	0.9
Firefox headed	6,457	64.6	677	6.8	98	1.0

Chromium headless is a clear outlier at 15.2%, while the remaining three conditions cluster between 6.8–7.2%. This gap is driven by the interaction of browser engine and display mode, not by either factor alone: among the 6,936

Chromium sites where both headless and headed conditions completed, 772 sites are blocked exclusively in headless mode compared to only 14 blocked exclusively in headed mode. Among the 7,063 paired Firefox sites, the headless/headed difference is negligible (15 vs. 12 sites).

A key contributing factor is the `sec-ch-ua` Client Hints header, which exposes `HeadlessChrome` as a brand value in Chromium's headless mode. Firefox does not implement Client Hints, eliminating this detection vector entirely. Additionally, Playwright's Chromium headless User-Agent string includes "Headless-Chrome" and exposes the full build number (`143.0.7499.4`) rather than the reduced form used in headed mode (`143.0.0.0`).

Header Spoofing Experiment. To establish causality, we re-crawled the 798 sites that received HTTP 403 exclusively in Chromium headless with spoofed HTTP headers: we replaced `HeadlessChrome` with `Chrome` in the User-Agent string and removed the `HeadlessChrome` brand from the `sec-ch-ua` header, matching headed Chromium's headers exactly. Of 784 sites that returned a response, 590 (75%) returned HTTP 2xx, while 194 (25%) remained blocked, indicating deeper detection layers (e. g., JavaScript fingerprinting, behavioral analysis, or TLS fingerprinting). Consistent with this, our instrumentation shows that `navigator.userAgentData` (the Client Hints JavaScript API) is probed on 730 of the originally blocked sites, and `navigator.userAgent` on 489, suggesting that both detection signals are widely deployed.

Same Infrastructure, Escalated Response for Headless. Of the 1,554 sites soft-blocked in at least one condition, 1,521 (97.9%) are blocked in *Chromium headless*, while the three other conditions each see 677–721 blocks. Of the 750 sites blocked in at least one non-*Chromium headless* condition, 717 (95.6%) are also blocked in *Chromium headless*, confirming that the same infrastructure drives blocking across conditions but escalates its response for headless Chromium.

82% of Blocks are Attributable to Bot Detection. To validate that soft blocks represent active bot detection, we classify response bodies by matching their content against known patterns of bot detection vendors (e. g., Cloudflare challenge pages, DataDome block pages). Table 7 shows the results by unique site. Of the 1,554 sites with at least one soft block, we identify a known vendor on 919 (59.1%). The remaining 635 sites lack vendor signatures. To distinguish bot detection from infrastructure-level errors, we examine cross-condition behavior: 282 sites (18.1%) are blocked uniformly across every condition in which they responded, potentially resulting from geographic restrictions, ASN-based blocks, or server misconfigurations. The remaining 353 sites (22.7%) show condition-dependent blocking, with 334 (94.6%) blocked in Chromium headless, consistent with the header-level detection mechanism established above. We manually verified all vendor-confirmed classifications by inspecting their screenshots and response bodies. Combining vendor-confirmed and condition-dependent blocks, we attribute 1,272 sites (81.9%) to bot detection, with 282 (18.1%) representing infrastructure-level access denial.

Table 7. Bot detection vendor signatures in HTTP 403/429/503 response bodies, by unique site. Each site is assigned to the highest-priority vendor match across all four conditions.

Category	Sites	%
Cloudflare (challenge)	792	51.0
DataDome	65	4.2
PerimeterX/HUMAN	26	1.7
CAPTCHA	23	1.5
Incapsula/Imperva	13	0.8
Subtotal (vendor-confirmed)	**919**	**59.1**
Unclassified (condition-dependent)	353	22.7
Unclassified (uniform)	282	18.1
Total	**1,554**	**100.0**

Blocking is Provider-Driven, Not Rank-Driven. Blocking does not correlate with site popularity (Mann-Whitney U, $p < 0.001$, $r = -0.07$) but with infrastructure provider: as shown in Table 4, Cloudflare (37%) and Akamai (26%) block at the highest rates, while providers without default-on bot detection range from 0–16%.

5.4 Detection Landscape (RQ2)

While 75% of current blocks rely on header-level signals, the JavaScript-based detection infrastructure already deployed is more extensive than current blocking rates reflect. Our proxy-based instrumentation (Sect. 5.1) captures not only which APIs are probed, but also which scripts perform the probing, enabling caller-level attribution of detection activity. The most common Tier 3 APIs (e. g., `navigator.userAgent`, `localStorage`) are each accessed on over 75% of sites but reflect standard web development practice. We focus first on Tier 1 signals, which have no legitimate use case except automation detection, then examine how vendors combine signals across tiers into integrated detection pipelines.

34% of Sites Probe for Automation Artifacts. The most prevalent Tier 1 signal is `navigator.webdriver`, accessed on 2,730 (34%) of 7,944 successfully scanned sites. This property returns `true` in all Playwright-controlled browsers regardless of display mode, making it the single most common bot detection check in our dataset. We group the 28 individual Tier 1 signals into eight automation framework families, reporting the percentage of 7,944 sites that probe at least one signal in each family: WebDriver API (43%), PhantomJS (32%), NightmareJS (31%), WebDriver Protocol (29%), Selenium (28%), Chrome DevTools (21%), Awesomium (20%), and ChromeDriver (8%). Across all eight families, 3,649 sites (46%) probe at least one Tier 1 signal, indicating that automation detection is deployed on nearly half of the successfully scanned sites. Notably, sites still probe for discontinued frameworks such as PhantomJS and NightmareJS, suggesting that detection scripts accumulate checks without removing obsolete ones.

Bot Detection Scripts Rank Among the Most Common Third-Party Scripts. Cross-referencing our response body classification (Table 7) with script URLs reveals two distinct delivery models. *Visible* vendors serve detection scripts from identifiable domains: Cloudflare from `challenges.cloudflare.com` (705 sites), DataDome from `ct.captcha-delivery.com` (61 sites), and PerimeterX/HUMAN from `client.px-cloud.net` (25 sites). In contrast, *invisible* vendors such as Incapsula/Imperva proxy detection logic through first-party domains or operate server-side, so script domain analysis alone undercounts detection deployment. We can therefore only provide a lower bound of bot detection script prevalence by counting scripts from visible vendors. To do so, we group minified script variants by their lexical structure[12]. Cloudflare Turnstile ranks as the 6th most deployed third-party script on the Tranco Top 10K (794 sites), ahead of major analytics libraries, with Google reCAPTCHA at rank 17 (398 sites). Bot detection scripts are thus among the most common third-party scripts on the web.

Vendors Combine Honeypot Probing with Browser Fingerprinting. Cross-referencing script callers with both signal tiers and blocking outcomes reveals that major bot detection vendors deploy integrated detection pipelines that combine window-level honeypot probing with multi-category browser fingerprinting within a single script execution (Table 8). We restrict this analysis to sites that block even headed browsers, representing the most aggressive detection, and report only scripts that probe at least three window-level honeypots. Note that site counts here reflect script-level attribution and may exceed the response-body counts in Table 7, where sites are assigned to a single highest-priority vendor. Cloudflare's detection scripts probe an average of 13 honeypots and cover all eight fingerprinting categories we track (Canvas, Audio, WebGL, Speech, Fonts, Dimensions, Permissions, Plugins) across 303 headed-blocked sites where our scanner recorded property-access data. Prior work reverse-engineered a single commercial detector and found it combines fingerprinting with detection [10]. Our instrumentation confirms this pattern at scale: across hundreds of sites, all three vendors combine honeypot probing and multi-category fingerprinting within a single script execution.

Summary. Bot detection blocking is widespread, affecting 7–15% of the Tranco Top 10K depending on browser configuration, with over 80% attributable to bot detection rather than infrastructure errors. The blocking gap is driven by header-level signals that identify Chromium headless, as confirmed by a spoofing experiment that unblocks 75% of affected sites. The detection landscape is

[12] We tokenize scripts with esprima (https://pypi.org/project/esprima/) and hash the token sequences.

Table 8. Bot detection vendor pipelines on headed-blocked sites. Honeypots: number of automation artifacts probed. FP categories: fingerprinting categories exercised (of 8).

Vendor	Blocked sites	Honeypots	FP categories
Cloudflare	303	13	8/8
DataDome	41	4	6/8
PerimeterX/HUMAN	13	7	8/8

dominated by a small number of vendors, most prominently Cloudflare, whose scripts combine automation probing with comprehensive browser fingerprinting.

6 Discussion and Implications

Why CDN-Correlated Bias Differs From Other Sampling Biases. Unlike rank-based or geographic biases, which can be addressed through stratified sampling, CDN-correlated attrition is invisible to the sampling process: researchers cannot determine which CDN a target site uses before crawling, and therefore cannot compensate for differential blocking rates. Because providers with default-on bot detection block at 26–37% while others range from 0–16% (Table 4), the resulting sample loss correlates with infrastructure features such as security posture and bot management defaults, not with the content properties that measurement studies aim to capture.

Implications for Published Results. When a crawler receives a challenge page or HTTP 403, the tracking scripts, third-party requests, and advertising infrastructure on the actual page go unobserved. To illustrate: Iqbal et al. [9] report fingerprinting on over a quarter of the Alexa Top 10K. Our data shows that even Firefox-based crawlers are blocked on 7% of sites, predominantly by Cloudflare, which itself deploys fingerprinting scripts on its challenge pages. Whether blocked sites exhibit higher or lower fingerprinting prevalence cannot be determined without a human-browsing baseline, but the bias is systematic and CDN-correlated rather than random. A replication of such a study today would systematically miss all Cloudflare-blocked sites, potentially undercounting fingerprinting on sites that deploy both bot detection and tracking, or overcounting it if challenge pages are mistakenly analyzed as regular content.

Detection Infrastructure Exceeds Current Blocking. The detection infrastructure already deployed is more extensive than blocking rates suggest: `navigator.webdriver` is probed on 34% of sites, and Tier 1 automation honeypots are checked on 46%. The AI scraping boom accelerates this trend: agentic AI traffic grew 6,900% year-over-year in 2025[13], prompting CDN vendors to

[13] HUMAN Security, "Agentic Commerce Traffic," https://www.humansecurity.com/learn/blog/agentic-commerce-traffic-black-friday-cyber-monday/.

deploy default-on blocking of AI crawlers[14] and introduce pay-per-crawl monetization models[15]. Academic web measurement relies on the same automation toolchain (Playwright, Puppeteer, OpenWPM), meaning that researchers face increasingly aggressive blocking as a side effect of these vendor countermeasures.

Limitations. Beyond the instrumentation caveats discussed in Sect. 5.1, our study has several scope limitations. All scans originate from a single vantage point (a European datacenter) at a single point in time; multi-vantage-point measurements would reveal whether blocking varies by geography or IP reputation. Our sample is limited to the Tranco Top 10K; we visit only homepages. Our methodology captures only explicit HTTP error responses (403/429/503); content degradation within HTTP 200 responses is outside our observational scope. Finally, we lack a true human-browsing baseline; our headed conditions approximate but do not fully replicate manual browsing. Despite these limitations, our core findings hold: the paired 2×2 design controls for site-level and temporal variation, the header spoofing experiment establishes causality for the dominant blocking mechanism, and the CDN-correlation finding is independent of vantage point or sample size.

7 Conclusion

Our measurement of 10,000 websites across four browser configurations shows that bot detection creates systematic sample loss: soft block rates range from 7–15% depending on configuration, with 82% attributable to bot detection. Because blocking is provider-driven, not rank-driven, the resulting attrition is CDN-correlated and cannot be addressed through stratified sampling, yet 83% of measurement papers we surveyed do not report it. As header-level signals are patched and AI-driven scraping intensifies vendor countermeasures, blocking rates will likely increase, making this an urgent methodological concern.

We recommend that future measurement studies at minimum: (1) report the browser engine, version, and display mode used; (2) quantify the blocking or failure rate observed during crawling; (3) document the CDN composition of their sample, as infrastructure provider is a confound for blocking; (4) describe any stealth measures employed or deliberately omitted. Longitudinal replication and a human-browsing baseline to determine the direction of the resulting bias are natural next steps.

Acknowledgments. IP address data is powered by IPinfo (https://ipinfo.io). We used Claude (Anthropic) during the development of our scanning infrastructure for debugging, code review, and drafting SQL analysis queries. All technical decisions,

[14] Namecheap, "Could Cloudflare's Bot Blocker Impact Your Brand's Discoverability?" https://www.namecheap.com/blog/could-cloudflares-bot-blocker-impact-your-brands-discoverability/.

[15] Cloudflare, "Introducing Pay Per Crawl," https://blog.cloudflare.com/introducing-pay-per-crawl/.

experimental design, and interpretation of results were made by the authors. The final manuscript was proofread with LLM assistance.

Disclosure of Interests. The authors have no competing interests to declare that are relevant to the content of this article.

References

1. Annamalai, M.S.M.S., De Cristofaro, E., Bilogrevic, I.: Beyond the crawl: Unmasking browser fingerprinting in real user interactions. In: WWW, pp. 3896–3907. ACM (2025). https://doi.org/10.1145/3696410.3714871
2. Azad, B.A., Starov, O., Laperdrix, P., Nikiforakis, N.: Web runner 2049: Evaluating third-party anti-bot services. In: DIMVA. LNCS, vol. 12223, pp. 135–159. Springer (2020). https://doi.org/10.1007/978-3-030-52683-2_7
3. Bahrami, P.N., Iqbal, U., Shafiq, Z.: FP-Radar: Longitudinal measurement and early detection of browser fingerprinting. Proc. Priv. Enhancing Technol. **2022**(2), 557–577 (2022). https://doi.org/10.2478/POPETS-2022-0056
4. Boussaha, S., Hock, L., Bermejo, M., et al.: FP-tracer: Fine-grained browser fingerprinting detection via taint-tracking and entropy-based thresholds. Proc. Priv. Enhancing Technol. **2024**(3), 540–560 (2024). https://doi.org/10.56553/POPETS-2024-0092
5. Bui, D., Tang, B., Shin, K.G.: Do opt-outs really opt me out? In: CCS, pp. 425–439. ACM (2022). https://doi.org/10.1145/3548606.3560574
6. Demir, N., Große-Kampmann, M., Urban, T., Wressnegger, C., Holz, T., Pohlmann, N.: Reproducibility and replicability of web measurement studies. In: WWW, pp. 533–544. ACM (2022). https://doi.org/10.1145/3485447.3512214
7. Englehardt, S., Narayanan, A.: Online tracking: A 1-million-site measurement and analysis. In: CCS, pp. 1388–1401. ACM (2016). https://doi.org/10.1145/2976749.2978313
8. Gundelach, R., Herrmann, D.: Cookiescanner: An automated tool for detecting and evaluating GDPR consent notices on websites. In: ARES, pp. 148:1–148:8. ACM (2023). https://doi.org/10.1145/3600160.3605000
9. Iqbal, U., Englehardt, S., Shafiq, Z.: Fingerprinting the fingerprinters: Learning to detect browser fingerprinting behaviors. In: SP, pp. 1143–1161. IEEE (2021). https://doi.org/10.1109/SP40001.2021.00017
10. Jonker, H., Krumnow, B., Vlot, G.: Fingerprint surface-based detection of web bot detectors. In: ESORICS (2). Lecture Notes in Computer Science, vol. 11736, pp. 586–605. Springer (2019). https://doi.org/10.1007/978-3-030-29962-0_28
11. Jueckstock, J., Kapravelos, A.: VisibleV8: In-browser monitoring of JavaScript in the wild. In: IMC, pp. 393–405. ACM (2019). https://doi.org/10.1145/3355369.3355599
12. Jueckstock, J., Sarker, S., Snyder, P., et al.: Towards realistic and reproducible web crawl measurements. In: WWW, pp. 80–91. ACM / IW3C2 (2021). https://doi.org/10.1145/3442381.3450050
13. Kashaf, A., Sekar, V., Agarwal, Y.: Analyzing third party service dependencies in modern web services: Have we learned from the Mirai-Dyn incident? In: IMC, pp. 634–647. ACM (2020). https://doi.org/10.1145/3419394.3423664
14. Klein, D., Musch, M., Barber, T., Kopmann, M., Johns, M.: Accept all exploits: Exploring the security impact of cookie banners. In: ACSAC, pp. 911–922. ACM (2022). https://doi.org/10.1145/3564625.3564647

15. Krumnow, B., Jonker, H., Karsch, S.: How gullible are web measurement tools?: a case study analysing and strengthening openwpm's reliability. In: CoNEXT, pp. 171–186. ACM (2022). https://doi.org/10.1145/3555050.3569131
16. Moti, Z., Senol, A., Bostani, H., Zuiderveen Borgesius, F.J., Moonsamy, V., Mathur, A., Acar, G.: Targeted and troublesome: Tracking and advertising on children's websites. In: SP, pp. 1517–1535. IEEE (2024). https://doi.org/10.1109/SP54263.2024.00118
17. Olejnik, L., Acar, G., Castelluccia, C., Díaz, C.: The leaking battery - A privacy analysis of the HTML5 battery status API. In: DPM/QASA@ESORICS. LNCS, vol. 9481, pp. 254–263. Springer (2015). https://doi.org/10.1007/978-3-319-29883-2_18
18. Le Pochat, V., Van Goethem, T., Tajalizadehkhoob, S., Korczynski, M., Joosen, W.: Tranco: A research-oriented top sites ranking hardened against manipulation. In: NDSS. The Internet Society (2019). https://doi.org/10.14722/ndss.2019.23386
19. Vastel, A., Laperdrix, P., Rudametkin, W., Rouvoy, R.: Fp-Scanner: The privacy implications of browser fingerprint inconsistencies. In: USENIX Security Symposium, pp. 135–150. USENIX Association (2018). https://doi.org/10.5555/3361338.3361453
20. Vastel, A., Rudametkin, W., Rouvoy, R., Blanc, X.: FP-Crawlers: Studying the resilience of browser fingerprinting to block crawlers. In: Workshop on Measurements, Attacks, and Defenses for the Web (MADWeb), co-located with NDSS. San Diego, CA, USA (2020). https://doi.org/10.14722/madweb.2020.23010
21. Venugopalan, H., Munir, S., Ahmed, S., Wang, T., King, S.T., Shafiq, Z.: FP-Inconsistent: Measurement and analysis of fingerprint inconsistencies in evasive bot traffic. In: IMC, pp. 134–149. ACM (2025). https://doi.org/10.1145/3730567.3732919
22. Zhang, P., Oest, A., Cho, H., Sun, Z., Johnson, R., Wardman, B., Sarker, S., Kapravelos, A., Bao, T., Wang, R., Shoshitaishvili, Y., Doupé, A., Ahn, G.: CrawlPhish: Large-scale analysis of client-side cloaking techniques in phishing. IEEE Secur. Priv. **20**(2), 10–21 (2022). https://doi.org/10.1109/MSEC.2021.3129992

Detecting Phishing on Shared-Domain Hosting Services Using LLM-Based Contextual Mismatch Reasoning

Sho Inuzuka[1](✉), Takaaki Toda[1,2], Daiki Chiba[3], and Tatsuya Mori[1,2,4]

[1] Waseda University, Tokyo, Japan
{inuzuka,todatakaaki,mori}@nsl.cs.waseda.ac.jp
[2] RIKEN AIP, Tokyo, Japan
[3] Tokyo Metropolitan University, Tokyo, Japan
daiki.chiba@ieee.org
[4] NICT, Tokyo, Japan

Abstract. Phishing attacks that exploit shared-domain hosting services (SHSs) are increasing. On these services, many independent user sites coexist under the same provider-managed domain, making conventional URL- and domain-based detection features ineffective. To address this challenge, we leverage large language models (LLMs) and propose an LLM-workflow-based detection method consisting of three components: Brand Analyzer, Content Analyzer, and Judge. The proposed method classifies pages based on the contextual mismatch arising from the combination of brand popularity and prompts for sensitive actions, while also outputting the rationale behind its verdict to improve explainability. We implemented the proposed method using two LLM configurations, GPT-4.1-mini and Qwen3-8B, and conducted a comparative evaluation against a machine learning (ML)-based baseline and two LLM-based baselines on two test datasets: the Impersonation dataset, which contains brand-impersonation phishing sites, and the Non-impersonation dataset, which contains malicious sites that do not impersonate well-known brands. On the Impersonation dataset, the proposed method achieved service-agnostic detection with very high recall. On the Non-impersonation dataset, the proposed method also detected malicious sites that the baselines missed, showing that its detection capability extends beyond brand-impersonation phishing. A case study further confirmed that the method can present its decision-making process based on contextual mismatch in an explainable manner.

Keywords: Phishing Detection · Shared-domain Hosting Services · Large Language Models · Explainability

1 Introduction

Phishing remains a serious cybercrime and a major means of stealing credentials and money. The Anti-Phishing Working Group reported observing 1,130,393

S. Nadjm-Tehrani et al. (Eds.): ARES 2026, LNCS 16898, pp. 297–320, 2027.
https://doi.org/10.1007/978-3-032-36874-4_15

phishing attacks in the second quarter of 2025 alone [2]. In recent years, a growing number of these attacks have exploited shared-domain hosting services, namely platforms that allow anyone to publish web content on the Internet for free or at low cost under a provider-managed domain. Representative examples include Cloudflare's developer-oriented domains `pages.dev` and `workers.dev`, where phishing abuse grew approximately two- to three-fold between 2023 and 2024 [5].

The defining characteristic of these services, and the root cause of their detection difficulty, is that they operate as *shared-domain hosting services* (hereafter SHSs): many independent user sites, both benign and malicious, coexist under the same provider-managed domain. Prior work such as FreePhish studied phishing abuse of free website builder services (FWBs) [22], which represent a subset of SHSs. Conventional phishing-detection techniques have relied on heuristic URL- and domain-based features, such as the presence of a TLS certificate, the reputation of the top-level domain (TLD), and domain age. However, on SHSs, TLS certificates are provisioned automatically when a page is published, and pages operate under a domain controlled by the service provider. Consequently, these features are identical for both benign and malicious pages hosted on the same service, rendering them ineffective for discrimination.

To address this issue, FreePhish [22,25], a machine learning (ML)-based detection method targeting specific SHSs, has been proposed. Nevertheless, ML-based phishing detection on SHSs faces two key challenges. First, it is difficult to detect phishing in a service-agnostic manner. ML models trained on specific services tend to generalize poorly to unseen ones. Second, such methods struggle to capture contextual mismatch. For example, a page on an SHS that prominently indicates a well-known brand while prompting sensitive actions exhibits such a mismatch. Such higher-level patterns cannot be captured by the fixed feature representations that ML methods rely on.

Given these challenges, conventional ML-based approaches are insufficient for service-agnostic detection of phishing sites on SHSs. Therefore, we propose a new detection method based on a large language model (LLM) workflow. An LLM workflow is a structured pipeline that sequentially connects prompting, context acquisition, and inference steps, and outputs both the final decision and the rationale. Rather than relying on service-specific features, our method uses contextual signals derived from page content for detection.

While prior work has explored LLM-based phishing detection, no method has been designed specifically for detecting phishing sites on SHSs. Our study fills this gap by designing and evaluating an LLM-workflow-based detection method that explicitly accounts for the shared-domain environment. The proposed method is implemented as an LLM workflow consisting of three components: Brand Analyzer, Content Analyzer, and Judge. The Brand Analyzer estimates the brand indicated by a given page and its popularity, while the Content Analyzer summarizes the page, analyzes its structure, and identifies prompts for sensitive actions. The Judge integrates these analyses and produces the final verdict primarily based on the contextual mismatch arising from the combination of brand popularity and prompts for sensitive actions.

To evaluate the proposed method, we collected URLs of benign and malicious sites across multiple SHSs and constructed test data by saving the corresponding screenshots and DOM snapshots. We evaluated the proposed method on two test datasets: the Impersonation dataset and the Non-impersonation dataset. The Impersonation dataset contains malicious sites that impersonate well-known brands. For this dataset, we selected 10 SHSs and collected 5 benign and 5 malicious samples from each service, yielding 100 samples in total. The 10 SHSs comprise 5 services included in FreePhish's training data (Seen services) and 5 services not included (Unseen services). The Non-impersonation dataset contains malicious sites that do not impersonate well-known brands. It consists of 14 samples (5 benign and 9 malicious) collected from a single Seen service.

We evaluated the proposed method against one ML-based baseline (FreePhish) and two LLM-based baselines (KnowPhish and PhishVLM). On the Impersonation dataset, FreePhish degraded substantially on Unseen services (F1: 0.66 → 0.42), indicating that it is prone to missing phishing sites hosted on services not included in its training data. KnowPhish performed strongly under both conditions (F1: 0.89 / 0.97), whereas PhishVLM had high precision but low recall (F1: 0.67 / 0.52). In contrast, the proposed method, evaluated under two LLM configurations (`GPT-4.1-mini` and `Qwen3-8B`), achieved a recall close to 1.00 under both conditions, confirming service-agnostic detection with few misses. With `GPT-4.1-mini`, it achieved F1 scores of 0.97 (Seen) and 0.96 (Unseen), demonstrating strong detection performance.

Moreover, in the evaluation on the Non-impersonation dataset, none of FreePhish, KnowPhish, and PhishVLM detected any malicious samples (true positive count, TP = 0). In contrast, the proposed method exhibited detection capability under both LLM configurations. In particular, it detected all nine malicious samples when using `Qwen3-8B` (TP=9). A case study further confirmed that the method can capture contextual mismatch based on the combination of brand popularity and prompts for sensitive actions, and can output an interpretable rationale for its decisions.

The main contributions of this study are as follows.

- We propose a new detection method for phishing sites hosted on SHSs that leverages the contextual understanding capability of LLMs, and demonstrate its effectiveness.
- By using brand popularity and prompts for sensitive actions as central signals and providing the rationale leading to the verdict, we improve explainability.
- To facilitate reproducibility and encourage future replication studies, we publicly release the implementation of the proposed method at: https://github.com/INU-SHO/shared-domain-phish-detector.

2 Background and Related Work

2.1 Free Website Building and Shared-Domain Hosting Services

A wide variety of platforms allow anyone to publish web content for free or at low cost. Following prior work [22], we collectively refer to such platforms as Free Website Building services (FWBs). From the perspective of phishing detection, the defining property of these services is that they operate as SHSs: many independent user sites, both benign and malicious, coexist under the same provider-managed apex domain (e.g., as subdomains or subpaths). Here, the apex domain refers to the registrable domain without any subdomain; for example, the apex domain of `www.example.com` is `example.com`. This shared-domain structure is the root cause of the detection difficulty discussed throughout this paper. Table 1 lists representative examples of SHSs, organized into three broad categories based on their primary use cases; note that real-world services often span multiple categories.

The first category, **CMS / Site builders**, includes services such as Blogger and Google Sites that allow general users to build and publish web pages via GUI-based editors or content management interfaces. The second category, **Developer-oriented hosting**, targets developers and encompasses static hosting (e.g., GitHub Pages), developer platforms that combine static delivery with serverless execution environments (e.g., Netlify, Vercel, and Azure Static Web Apps), and edge/serverless platforms (e.g., Cloudflare Workers). The third category, **Forms / marketing / enterprise publishing**, covers purpose-specific services such as form builders (e.g., Google Forms, Zoho Forms), marketing landing-page builders (e.g., Mailchimp), enterprise publishing platforms (e.g., Microsoft SharePoint Online), and e-commerce page builders (e.g., Square Online Store).

As shown in Table 1, SHSs have continued to emerge from the late 1990s to the present, diversifying from traditional CMS and site-builder services into static hosting, serverless-integrated platforms, and specialized publishing tools. Their scale of adoption has also grown substantially: for example, Wix reported 282.4 million registered users at the end of 2024, a 7% year-over-year increase [27], and Netlify, which introduced a free plan in 2024, announced that the number of developers on its platform had exceeded 5 million [20]. Table 1 and these figures together indicate that SHSs are used at large scale and continue to expand in both diversity and adoption.

Table 1. A broad landscape of Shared-domain Hosting Services (SHSs). The rightmost column indicates whether the service was selected as a detection target in FreePhish.

Category	Services	Since	FreePhish [22]
CMS / Site builders			
CMS	Blogger	1999	✓
CMS	WordPress	2005	✓
Site builder	Wix	2006	✓
Site builder	Jimdo	2007	–
Site builder	Weebly	2007	✓
Site builder	Yola	2007	✓
Site builder	hPage	2007	✓
Site builder	Google Sites	2008	✓
Site builder	Strikingly	2012	–
Site builder	Webflow	2013	–
Site builder	Carrd	2016	–
Site builder	GoDaddy Sites	2017	✓
Developer-oriented hosting			
Hosting	000webhost	2007	✓
Static hosting	GitHub Pages	2008	✓
Hosting	Firebase Hosting	2014	✓
Dev platform	Netlify	2014	–
Static hosting	GitLab Pages	2015	–
Sandbox hosting	Glitch	2017	✓
Edge/serverless	Cloudflare Workers	2018	–
Dev platform	Vercel	2020	–
Dev platform	Cloudflare Pages	2021	–
Dev platform	Azure Static Web Apps	2021	–
Forms / marketing / enterprise publishing			
Forms	Google Forms	2008	✓
Enterprise publishing	SharePoint Online	2011	✓
Forms	Zoho Forms	2015	✓
E-commerce pages	Square Online Store	2019	✓
Email/landing	Mailchimp	2019	✓

Notes. "Since" denotes the year of general availability (GA) when an official GA announcement exists. ✓indicates that the service is selected as a detection target in FreePhish; "–" otherwise

2.2 Challenges in Detecting Phishing on SHSs

Conventional phishing detection techniques have relied on URL- and domain-specific features such as the presence of a TLS certificate, the reputation of the top-level domain (TLD), and domain age. These features are designed under the assumption that attackers tend to avoid configuring HTTPS [9] and to use newly registered domains (i.e., domains with short age) [18]. However, on SHSs, TLS is often provisioned automatically when a page is published, and pages are operated under the service provider's public domain as subdomains or subpaths. Consequently, on SHSs, these features do not help distinguish benign from malicious pages.

For example, as illustrated in Fig. 1, consider a setting where the public domain of an SHS provider is `example.com`, and a benign site (`https://benign.example.com/`) and a malicious site (`https://malicious.example.com/`) are operated as subdomains under `example.com`. In this setting, (1) because TLS certificates are automatically issued by the service, pages are served over HTTPS regardless of maliciousness. (2) Likewise, the TLD is always `.com` because it is determined solely by the provider's public domain (`example.com`). (3) Furthermore, WHOIS information is provided for the registrable domain (here, `example.com`) rather than for each subdomain. That is, it does not directly provide page-level registration dates or domain-age information for individual pages created as subdomains. Consequently, features such as TLS certificate presence, TLD, and domain age are identical for both benign and malicious sites, making it difficult to distinguish phishing sites on SHSs using conventional URL- and domain-based features alone.

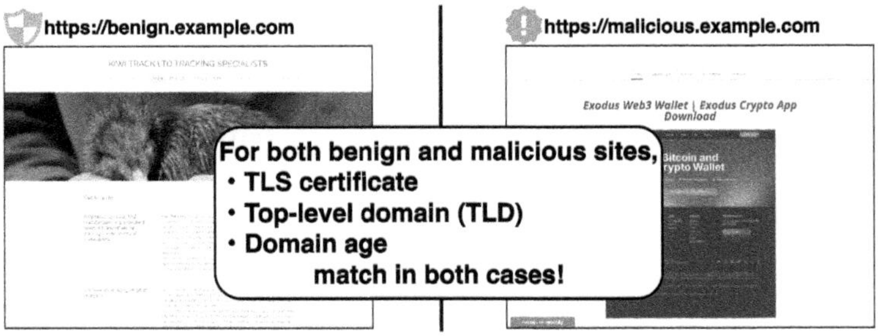

Fig. 1. Motivating example on a shared-domain hosting service (SHS). A benign site (left) and a malicious site (right) are hosted under the same apex domain `example.com`. Therefore, both share (1) TLS certificates, (2) the same TLD (`.com`), and (3) domain age (age of `example.com`).

2.3 Phishing Detection Targeting SHSs

Saha Roy et al. [22] proposed FreePhish, a detection framework for phishing sites that abuse Free Website Building services (FWBs). A key contribution of their work is that, through large-scale measurements across multiple FWBs, they characterized phishing abuse on FWBs and evaluated the limitations of existing anti-phishing countermeasures against FWB phishing. FreePhish targets the 17 services marked with check symbols in Table 1 and determines maliciousness based on features extracted from a web page's URL and HTML.

However, ML-based approaches such as FreePhish have two key limitations when applied to the broader class of SHSs. First, service-agnostic detection is challenging. Because URL and HTML structures vary across SHS providers, models trained on a specific set of services are prone to distribution shift on unseen services, limiting their ability to generalize across diverse SHSs.

Second, these approaches fail to capture contextual anomalies that arise from the shared-domain hosting structure. In general, phishing sites impersonate well-known brands to deceive users and then prompt sensitive actions such as credential entry [1,15,21]. In contrast, well-known legitimate brands typically host pages that prompt such sensitive actions on infrastructure under their own administrative control [16], and thus are unlikely to host them on SHSs. A page on an SHS that strongly indicates a specific brand while prompting sensitive actions is contextually anomalous. Such an anomaly can serve as a detection cue. However, ML-based methods, which operate on correlations among individual features, struggle to capture this kind of higher-level contextual signal.

2.4 LLM-Based Phishing Detection

Several recent studies have leveraged LLMs for phishing detection. Representative examples include ChatPhishDetector [10], KnowPhish [13], PhishLLM [16] and DEMO [12]. Table 2 compares these conventional LLM-based methods and our proposed method from the perspectives of workflow structure, training requirements, explainability, target environment, and runtime. All of these methods share the common characteristic of using a combination of URL, screenshot, and HTML (or DOM) as input features. In the following, we organize each method along the multiple perspectives shown in Table 2. Note that the runtime values are those reported in each original paper.

Table 2. Comparison of representative LLM-based phishing detection methods.

Method	Workflow	Training-Free	Explainable Output	Designed for SHSs	Runtime (s)
ChatPhishDetector [10]	Single LLM call	●	●	○	14.4[a]
PhishLLM [16]	Multi-step LLM + web search	◐	○	○	3.2[a]
KnowPhish [13]	Single LLM call + KG* lookup	◐	○	○	2.0[b]
DEMO [12]	Multi-step LLM + rule injection	●	○	○	1.3[c]
Proposed	Multi-step LLM + web search	●	●	●	6.4[d]

Legend: ● = Yes, ◐ = Partially Yes, ○ = No
* KG: knowledge graph
LLM models used in each row's runtime measurement: [a] GPT-3.5
[b] GPT-3.5-turbo-instruct
[c] Llama-3.3-70B
[d] GPT-4 1-mini

Workflow structure. ChatPhishDetector adopts the simplest design, reasoning over the entire page context with a single LLM call. KnowPhish combines LLM-based page summarization with a knowledge graph. PhishLLM and our proposed method combine multi-step LLM reasoning with web search. DEMO is designed to inject rule-based decision criteria into multi-step LLM reasoning.

Training requirements. ChatPhishDetector, DEMO, and our proposed method require no additional training. In contrast, PhishLLM and KnowPhish require supervised training for credential-requiring page (CRP) analysis components in their pipelines.

Explainable output. The Explainable Output column in Table 2 indicates whether the final output of each method enhances explainability. Only ChatPhishDetector and our proposed method include natural-language rationales in their final outputs. For PhishLLM, KnowPhish, and DEMO, explainability is supported by intermediate representations (e.g., estimated brand names or computed scores) rather than by the final output itself.

Designed for phishing detection on SHSs. Conventional LLM-based methods aim at general-purpose phishing detection and are not designed specifically for SHSs. Our proposed method differs fundamentally in that it primarily targets phishing detection on SHSs.

2.5 Subdomain-Abuse Detection

Liu et al. [14] studied domain shadowing attacks, in which a legitimate apex domain is compromised and a large number of malicious subdomains are generated. They proposed Woodpecker, a method that automatically detects such shadowed domains using passive DNS (PDNS), and revealed that domain shadowing is abused not only for exploit kits but also for phishing. Although domain shadowing abuses compromised domains rather than legitimate hosting platforms, it shares a structural property with SHSs: many independent sites coexist under a single apex domain, making per-site discrimination through domain-level features difficult.

3 LLM-Workflow-Based Phishing Detection on SHSs

3.1 Overall Design

Figure 2 illustrates the overall design of the proposed method, which is organized into two stages: data preprocessing and an LLM workflow. The method takes as input a URL, its corresponding screenshot, and a DOM snapshot, and outputs a verdict on the target's maliciousness along with the rationale leading to that decision.

In the data preprocessing stage, the raw inputs are transformed into a set of structured representations suitable for LLM-based analysis. Specifically, the stage produces four elements: the Apex Domain extracted from the URL to identify the SHS provider, a Screenshot Wordlist obtained by applying optical character recognition (OCR) to the screenshot, the DOM Title extracted from the <title> element, and a Parsed DOM in which non-content elements have been removed to retain only structural and textual information. These outputs serve as inputs to the LLM workflow. The details of each preprocessing step are described in Sect. 3.2.

The LLM workflow consists of three components that operate in a structured pipeline (Sect. 3.3). The Brand Analyzer estimates the brand indicated by a given page and quantifies its popularity using both the LLM's internal knowledge and a web search API. The Content Analyzer summarizes the page content, describes its structure, and identifies elements that prompt users toward sensitive actions. Finally, the Judge integrates the outputs of both analyzers in the context that the page is hosted on an SHS, evaluates the contextual mismatch arising from the combination of brand popularity and prompts for sensitive actions, and produces the final verdict with its rationale.

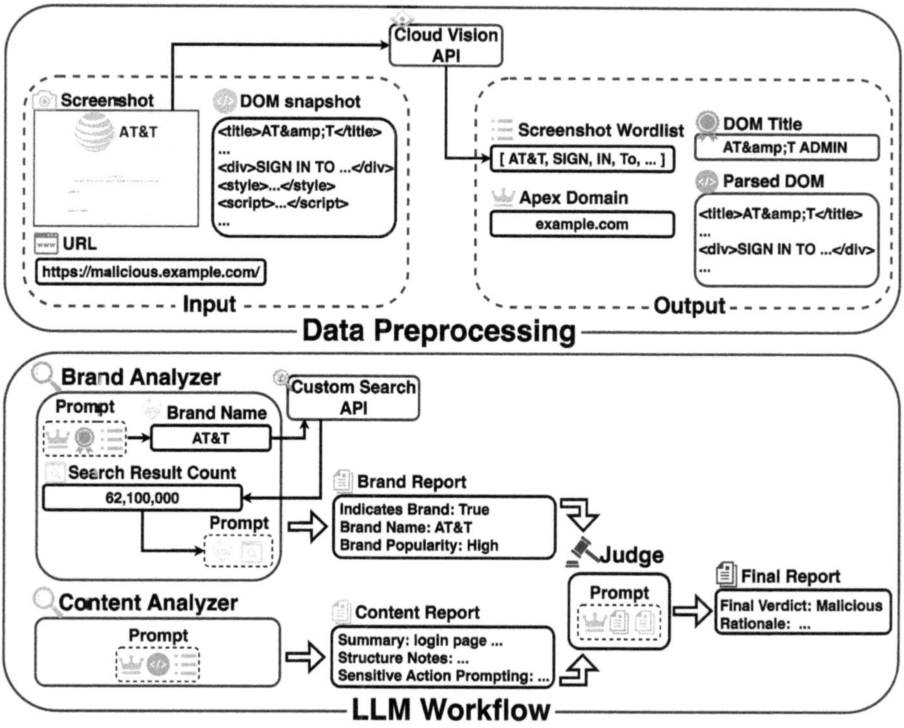

Fig. 2. Overall workflow of the proposed method.

3.2 Data Preprocessing

During data preprocessing, the method takes as input a URL, its corresponding screenshot, and a DOM snapshot. It then produces four elements required to construct prompts for the downstream LLM workflow: Apex Domain, Screenshot Wordlist, DOM Title, and Parsed DOM. Specifically, from the URL, it extracts the apex domain as Apex Domain. It then extracts visible text from the screenshot as Screenshot Wordlist. From the DOM snapshot, it further extracts the page title as DOM Title. In addition, it removes elements unnecessary for analysis from the DOM body and generates Parsed DOM, a formatted text representation used for analysis.

3.3 LLM Workflow

Design of the LLM Workflow. LLM-based systems can be categorized into workflows and agents [11]. Workflows have predefined execution paths and are designed to operate in a fixed order. In contrast, agents are dynamic: they can decide their own procedures and tool usage at runtime. The key difference lies in whether the execution path is fixed in advance or determined dynamically during execution.

In this study, we implement the proposed method as an LLM workflow to make the processing steps explicit and to ensure reproducibility and controllability in our evaluation. The workflow comprises three components: the Brand Analyzer, the Content Analyzer, and the Judge. This three-component design reflects the structure of the contextual mismatch we aim to detect: the Judge produces its final verdict based on the combination of brand popularity and prompts for sensitive actions, while the two upstream analyzers handle these two distinct types of evidence separately. We note that this three-component design is one reasonable choice rather than the only optimal one. The Brand Analyzer and the Content Analyzer operate independently to analyze brand-related information (e.g., brand name and brand popularity) and content-related information (e.g., page summary, page structure, and prompts for sensitive actions), respectively, and output their results as a Brand Report and a Content Report. The Judge integrates both reports and outputs the final verdict and its rationale as a Final Report, in the context that the page is hosted on an SHS.

Brand Analyzer. The Brand Analyzer determines whether the page under analysis indicates a brand and, if so, infers the brand name and its popularity, outputting the results as a Brand Report.

First, it constructs a prompt using Apex Domain, Screenshot Wordlist, and DOM Title, and provides it to the LLM to decide whether the page indicates a brand. If the page is judged not to indicate a brand, it outputs `Indicates Brand` as `False` and the brand name as `Uncertain`.

Next, only when `Indicates Brand` is `True`, it determines brand popularity (`Brand Popularity`) based on the web search hit counts for the inferred brand name. `Brand Popularity` takes one of two values: `High` or `Low`. When

`Indicates Brand` is `False`, `Brand Popularity` is set to `Uncertain`. Finally, the Brand Analyzer outputs whether the page indicates a brand (`Indicates Brand`), the inferred brand name (`Brand Name`), and the estimated popularity (`Brand Popularity`) as the Brand Report.

Content Analyzer. The Content Analyzer summarizes the page under analysis, describes its structure, and extracts candidates for prompting users to perform sensitive actions, outputting the results as a Content Report.

It constructs a prompt using Apex Domain, Screenshot Wordlist, and Parsed DOM, and summarizes what the page appears to be used for (e.g., login or a blog) as `Summary`. The `Summary` provides the Judge with overall page-level context that supports both its final verdict and the rationale it outputs. Next, it describes whether the layout and navigation of the page are consistent with common structures as `Structure Notes`, and additionally reports any structural irregularities, such as a large number of hidden elements or the presence of many links unrelated to the purported topic; this structural element was added based on the empirical observation that some non-phishing malicious sites on SHSs exhibit structural anomalies. Finally, if the page contains elements that prompt users to perform sensitive actions (e.g., credential entry, software downloads, or cryptocurrency wallet connection), it reports them as `Sensitive Action Prompting`. The Content Analyzer ultimately outputs `Summary`, `Structure Notes`, and `Sensitive Action Prompting` as the Content Report.

Judge. The Judge integrates the Brand Report and the Content Report and outputs the final verdict and its rationale. Specifically, it constructs a prompt using Apex Domain, the Brand Report, and the Content Report, and outputs the final maliciousness verdict (`Final Verdict`) together with the rationale (`Rationale`). The final verdict takes one of three labels: `Malicious`, `Suspicious`, or `Benign`. The label `Suspicious` represents cases where the evidence is insufficient to conclusively declare maliciousness, but anomalies remain.

For decision making, the Judge applies the following logic, depending on the Brand Report and the Content Report.

Branch 1: Well-Known Brand Indicated (High-Popularity Brand). A page indicating a well-known brand that is hosted on an SHS is treated as contextually anomalous by itself; a clean page structure is not interpreted as evidence of benignness. If any prompts for sensitive actions (e.g., a login flow) are observed, the Judge outputs `Malicious`; otherwise it outputs `Suspicious`.

Branch 2: Personal-Blog-Like Page (No Brand, or Low-Popularity Brand). The Judge places greater weight on the Content Report. If prompts for sensitive actions are observed, it outputs `Malicious`. If structural anomalies are reported, it outputs `Suspicious`, and `Malicious` when the anomalies are strong. When neither prompts for sensitive actions nor structural anomalies are reported, it outputs `Benign`.

The rationale (`Rationale`) is output as short natural-language bullet points grounded only in the observed facts contained in the Brand Report and the Content Report, and it avoids definitive claims based on speculation.

3.4 Implementation Details

LLM Configuration. In the proposed method, we prepared two LLM configurations for inference in the three components (Brand Analyzer, Content Analyzer, and Judge). Specifically, the configurations use: (1) `GPT-4.1-mini` (model version `2025-04-14`) via API [17], and (2) `Qwen3-8B`, an open-source model that can be executed in a local environment. In both configurations, the workflow structure and the prompts for all components are identical; only the LLM differs.

Generating Screenshot Wordlist via OCR. To provide the LLM with important cues about brand identity and prompts for sensitive actions even when text cannot be obtained from the DOM (e.g., when text is embedded in images), we extract visible text from screenshots. For screenshot text extraction, we use the OCR functionality provided by Google Cloud Vision API [6]. We split the OCR output by line breaks and generate Screenshot Wordlist as a line-by-line list.

Extracting the Apex Domain. To provide the LLM with hosting-environment context, we extract the service provider's public domain (the apex domain) from the URL under analysis. Specifically, we obtain the hostname from the URL and derive the apex domain by parsing the hostname based on the Public Suffix List [19]. The Public Suffix List enumerates registrable suffixes such as `com` and `co.uk`, enabling the apex domain to be determined uniquely.

Generating Parsed DOM and Controlling Input Length. When generating Parsed DOM from a DOM snapshot, we retain only structural elements useful for understanding the page's purpose and requested user actions while keeping the input length manageable. To this end, we perform progressive simplification inspired by the HTML reduction strategy (Algorithm 1 in their paper) in ChatPhishDetector [10].

We simplify the DOM in a staged manner. We remove non-rendered or low-value elements (comments, `<script>`, `<style>`, and `<br>`) and keep only structure-informative tags (e.g., `head/title/meta/body`, headings, paragraphs, links/images, tables, lists, and form labels), unwrapping all others to flatten the hierarchy. We drop textless elements and truncate `data:` URIs and overly long `href/src` values to avoid input bloat. If the result still exceeds the limit, we iteratively downsample elements under `<body>` by removing portions from the middle until it fits.

We reduced the input to fit within 500,000 characters when using GPT-4.1-mini and within 15,000 characters when using Qwen3-8B. These character limits were empirically chosen by the authors to avoid exceeding the maximum context window of each model.

Determining Brand Popularity. To determine brand popularity, we combine quantitative evidence with the LLM's internal knowledge of well-known brands. We query the Google Custom Search JSON API [7] with `"<Brand Name>" official site` and pass the returned total hit count to the Brand Analyzer. To stabilize the judgment, we also include in the prompt reference hit counts obtained by issuing the same query for three major global telecommunications providers. The Brand Analyzer then reasons over three complementary signals to produce a popularity label: the model's internal recognition of the brand, the queried hit count, and the reference hit counts. The prompt explicitly notes that hit counts can be inflated for short or common-word brand names due to homonym collisions. This allows the model to cross-check the quantitative signal against its internal recognition of the brand.

4 Evaluation

4.1 Experimental Settings

Evaluation Methodology. We evaluated the proposed method using an ML-based baseline, FreePhish [22,25], and two LLM-based baselines, KnowPhish [13] and PhishVLM [3,16].

The FreePhish implementation and dataset are publicly available in the GitHub repository [25]. However, the released code partially differed from the feature extraction and training procedures described in the paper. In addition, the published dataset was incomplete and did not contain all data required for reproduction. Therefore, in this study, we re-implemented FreePhish based on both the original paper and the released code, and re-collected the datasets used for training and evaluation. Our re-implementation achieved an accuracy of 0.92, compared with the 0.97 reported in the original paper, with a slight tendency toward false positives. For KnowPhish, since no official implementation is publicly available, we re-implemented it based on the original paper. When evaluated on the dataset provided in the GitHub repository [8], our re-implementation achieved an accuracy of 0.89, compared with the 0.92 reported in the original paper, with a slight tendency toward false negatives. For PhishVLM, we used the vision-language model (VLM) variant released in the PhishLLM GitHub repository [3].

As described in Sect. 3.3, the proposed method was evaluated under two LLM configurations. In particular, inference with `Qwen3-8B` was conducted on a compute environment equipped with an NVIDIA H100 NVL GPU (24 GB VRAM), with 4 CPU cores and 64 GB of main memory allocated. For KnowPhish and PhishVLM, we executed the entire pipeline on the same GPU environment, and used `GPT-4.1-mini (2025-04-14)` via API [17] for both baselines to align with the commercial-model configuration of the proposed method.

We evaluated the proposed method against the baselines on both the Impersonation and Non-impersonation datasets. When computing evaluation metrics, we treated `Malicious` and `Suspicious` outputs from the proposed method as malicious, and `Benign` as benign. For experiments on the Impersonation dataset, we also measured the average runtime per sample for all methods. For the LLM-based methods, we further estimated the average API cost per sample, which includes all API usage (e.g., OCR, LLM inference, and web search) required to analyze a single sample.

Datasets. We collected data from urlscan.io [24] and obtained screenshots and DOM snapshots corresponding to previously analyzed URLs. Because FreePhish requires training, we separately collected a training dataset for FreePhish. We also collected two test datasets, the Impersonation dataset and the Non-impersonation dataset, for evaluating the proposed method and each baseline.

For the FreePhish training data, we retrieved samples from the 17 services selected as detection targets in the FreePhish paper (the services marked with check symbols in Table 1 in Sect. 2.1). We queried urlscan for pages that were successfully retrieved, collecting malicious candidates using urlscan's brand flag (a unique identifier for each detected brand) and benign candidates using the absence of any malicious verdict and the absence of a brand flag. Because manual verification at this scale was infeasible, we relied on urlscan's automated verdicts as labels, yielding 2,983 samples analyzed by December 31, 2023 (1,800 benign and 1,183 malicious). Since this training dataset is required only for FreePhish, residual label noise in the training set does not directly affect the evaluation of any method other than FreePhish.

For the Impersonation dataset, we collected samples analyzed between January 1, 2024 and January 12, 2026 using the same urlscan filters as for the training data. Each candidate was then manually inspected and labeled by one of the authors; for benign samples we additionally required zero malicious detections on VirusTotal [26] to provide an objective check on benign labeling. As shown in Table 3 (a), the dataset consists of two conditions: five services included in FreePhish training (Seen services) and five services not included in FreePhish training (Unseen services). For each service, we collected five benign and five malicious samples, resulting in 100 samples in total (Table 3 (b)). This dataset includes only impersonation-based phishing sites as malicious samples.

For the Non-impersonation dataset, we collected samples during the same collection period as the Impersonation dataset. Through manual inspection of urlscan's benign candidate pool on one of the Seen services, we identified nine pages that, despite not being flagged as malicious by urlscan, were actually malicious. Rather than impersonating brands, these pages appear to be ordinary benign content unrelated to the malicious content they distribute (e.g., yoga or photography pages). They function as link-based doorways that lead visitors to multiple malicious external resources, typically through lists of outbound links or embedded PDF documents containing such links. We labeled them as malicious based on manual inspection together with VirusTotal evidence: every page contained multiple outbound links whose destinations were each flagged as malicious by multiple VirusTotal engines, and eight of the nine pages themselves had at least one VirusTotal detection. We constructed the Non-impersonation dataset by combining these nine malicious pages with five benign pages from the Impersonation dataset that are hosted on the same Seen service, yielding 14 samples in total (Table 3 (b)).

4.2 Accuracy Evaluation Results

Accuracy Results on the Impersonation Dataset. Table 4 reports the accuracy evaluation results on the Impersonation dataset. To account for variance in the evaluation, we ran FreePhish with 10 different random seeds (seeds 1–10) for training and ran each LLM-based method 10 times, and report the mean and standard deviation across these runs. Proposed (GPT-4.1-mini) achieved a recall of 1.00 under both the Seen services and Unseen services conditions, while Proposed (Qwen3-8B) also maintained a high recall (1.00 for Seen and 0.98 for Unseen), demonstrating that misses are minimized regardless of the LLM model used. In particular, Proposed (GPT-4.1-mini) achieved an accuracy of 0.97, a precision of 0.94, a recall of 1.00, and an F1 score of 0.97 under the Seen services condition, and an accuracy of 0.95, a precision of 0.92, a recall of 1.00, and an F1 score of 0.96 under the Unseen services condition, demonstrating strong detection performance. Proposed (Qwen3-8B) achieved an accuracy of 0.82, a precision of 0.74, a recall of 1.00, and an F1 score of 0.85 under the Seen services condition, and an accuracy of 0.75, a precision of 0.67, a recall of 0.98, and an F1 score of 0.80 under the Unseen services condition. Compared with the GPT-4.1-mini configuration, its precision was lower; however, it maintained recall while achieving a reasonable level of detection performance.

FreePhish achieved an F1 score of 0.66 under the Seen services condition, whereas its F1 score dropped to 0.42 under the Unseen services condition. This degradation was primarily attributable to a decline in recall (0.51 $\rightarrow$ 0.29), indicating that it is prone to missing phishing sites hosted on services not included in its training data. KnowPhish achieved the highest accuracy and F1 score (0.97 and 0.97, respectively) under the Unseen services condition, comparable to Proposed (GPT-4.1-mini), while its performance under the Seen services condition (accuracy and F1 of 0.89) remained below that of Proposed (GPT-4.1-mini). This indicates that KnowPhish is also competitive at detecting phishing on SHSs. However, unlike the proposed method, KnowPhish relies on supervised training of an XLM-RoBERTa-based CRP classifier and on an offline-constructed brand knowledge base. PhishVLM exhibited relatively high precision but low recall (0.50 for Seen services and 0.35 for Unseen services), resulting in F1 scores of 0.67 and 0.52, respectively.

Regarding the non-determinism of LLM-based methods, KnowPhish and PhishVLM exhibited standard deviations of at most 0.02 across all accuracy metrics, while the proposed method showed larger variation, with maximum standard deviations of 0.05 for Qwen3-8B and 0.03 for GPT-4.1-mini.

From the perspective of average runtime, the ML-based method FreePhish was the fastest at 0.002 s per sample. In contrast, LLM-based methods incurred substantially higher overhead than the ML-based approach. When comparing only the LLM-based methods, KnowPhish was the fastest at 2.59 s on average, followed by Proposed (GPT-4.1-mini) at 6.43 s, PhishVLM at 7.09 s, and Proposed (Qwen3-8B) at 15.6 s. Regarding the average API cost per sample, KnowPhish was the lowest at $0.0017, followed by PhishVLM at $0.0047, Proposed (Qwen3-8B) at $0.0050, and Proposed (GPT-4.1-mini) at $0.0127. The proposed method (GPT-4.1-mini) therefore incurs a higher per-sample cost than the LLM-based baselines, while the proposed method (Qwen3-8B) is comparable to the LLM-based baselines in cost.

Overall, the proposed method maintained high recall independent of the service condition and, in particular when using a commercial model, achieved strong detection performance across both Seen and Unseen conditions. Although KnowPhish was competitive on the Unseen condition, the proposed method does not require any supervised training or an offline-constructed knowledge resource.

Table 3. Composition of the Impersonation and Non-impersonation datasets.

(a) Services in each condition

Seen	Unseen
Weebly	Vercel
Blogger	Webflow
Wix	Netlify
Google Sites	Strikingly
GitHub Pages	Azure Static Web Apps

(b) Sample counts per condition

	Seen		Unseen	
Dataset	Benign	Malicious	Benign	Malicious
Impersonation	25	25	25	25
Non-impersonation†	5	9	–	–

† All Non-impersonation samples were collected from a single service among the Seen services.

Table 4. Accuracy evaluation results on the Impersonation dataset.

	Seen services				Unseen services				Overhead
Method	Acc.	Prec.	Rec.	F1	Acc.	Prec.	Rec.	F1	Time (s)
FreePhish [22, 25]	0.74±0.04	0.95±0.04	0.51±0.08	0.66±0.07	0.60±0.02	0.77±0.11	0.29±0.04	0.42±0.04	**0.002***
KnowPhish [13]	0.89±0.01	0.94±0.02	0.84±0.01	0.89±0.01	**0.97**±0.01	0.99±0.02	0.96±0.00	**0.97**±0.01	2.59±0.25
PhishVLM [3, 16]	0.75±0.01	**1.00**±0.00	0.50±0.02	0.67±0.02	0.67±0.01	**1.00**±0.00	0.35±0.02	0.52±0.02	7.09±1.44
Proposed[a]	0.82±0.04	0.74±0.05	**1.00**±0.00	0.85±0.03	0.75±0.03	0.67±0.03	0.98±0.02	0.80±0.02	15.6±5.93
Proposed[b]	**0.97**±0.01	0.94±0.02	**1.00**±0.00	**0.97**±0.01	0.95±0.02	0.92±0.03	**1.00**±0.00	0.96±0.02	6.43±0.74

[a] Qwen3-8B; [b] GPT-4.1-mini; * FreePhish's full Overhead value is 0.00202 ± 0.00014 s
Notes. FreePhish is the ML-based baseline; the other methods are LLM-based. Seen/Unseen indicates whether the hosting service is included in the FreePhish training data

Accuracy Results on the Non-Impersonation Dataset. Table 5 reports the confusion matrix counts, namely true positives (TP), false positives (FP), true negatives (TN), and false negatives (FN), on the Non-impersonation dataset, based on a single run of each method. None of FreePhish, KnowPhish, and PhishVLM detected any malicious samples (TP=0). This indicates that all baseline methods struggle to detect malicious sites that do not indicate well-known brands.

In contrast, the proposed method exhibited detection capability on the Non-impersonation dataset under both LLM configurations. In particular, Proposed (Qwen3-8B) achieved strong performance with TP=9, FP=1, TN=4, and FN=0, confirming that it can detect non-impersonation malicious sites without misses. Proposed (GPT-4.1-mini) also achieved reasonable performance with TP=7, FP=0, TN=5, and FN=2.

However, in terms of false positives, FreePhish, KnowPhish, PhishVLM, and Proposed (GPT-4.1-mini) produced zero FPs, whereas Proposed (Qwen3-8B) produced one FP. This suggests a relatively higher false-positive tendency under the Qwen3-8B configuration. Overall, these results demonstrate that the proposed method can detect malicious sites beyond brand-impersonation phishing.

Table 5. Confusion matrix results on the Non-impersonation dataset (5 benign and 9 malicious; total 14).

Method	TP	FP	TN	FN
FreePhish [22,25]	0	0	5	9
KnowPhish [13]	0	0	5	9
PhishVLM [3,16]	0	0	5	9
Proposed (Qwen3-8B)	9	1	4	0
Proposed (GPT-4.1-mini)	7	0	5	2

4.3 Case Study

In this section, we take a closer look at a case in which the proposed method (GPT-4.1-mini) correctly classified a phishing site hosted on an SHS as `Malicious`. Specifically, we analyze a phishing site impersonating the login page of AT&T, a major U.S. telecommunications provider. We describe the evidence on which the proposed method made the correct `Malicious` decision. The following discussion is organized according to the outputs of the Brand Analyzer, the Content Analyzer, and the Judge.

Behavior of the Brand Analyzer. The Brand Analyzer determined, based on information derived from the screenshot and the DOM snapshot, that the page indicates a brand (`Indicates Brand: True`) and that the brand name is

AT&T (`Brand Name: AT&T`). It also judged the brand to have high popularity (`Brand Popularity: High`) by combining web search hit counts for the inferred brand and reference brands with the LLM's internal knowledge. These results confirm that the Brand Analyzer correctly recognized the brand indicated by the target page and assessed its popularity appropriately.

Behavior of the Content Analyzer. The Content Analyzer summarized the page as "a login page asking users to enter their User ID and Password" (see `Summary` in Fig. 3). Regarding the page structure, it reported that the page exhibits a typical login-page layout in which a form is placed at the center of a multi-column layout, and that no notable structural anomalies were observed (see `Structure Notes` in Fig. 3). In addition, as a candidate signal of prompting sensitive actions, it reported a request for credential entry based on the User ID/Password input form and the `Continue` button (see `Sensitive Action Prompting` in Fig. 3). Overall, these results confirm that the Content Analyzer appropriately reported the page summary, structural characteristics, and candidates for prompting sensitive actions.

Behavior of the Judge. The Judge output `Malicious` as the final verdict (see `Final Verdict` in Fig. 4). As its rationale, it stated that (1) the page indicates the well-known brand AT&T despite being hosted on an SHS, which is contextually anomalous. It further reported that (2) the page explicitly requests credential input (User ID and Password) via a login form, indicating prompting toward a sensitive action (see `Rationale` in Fig. 4). Overall, these results confirm that, under the context that the page is hosted on an SHS, the Judge correctly captured contextual mismatch by combining the content signals of the presence of a well-known brand and prompts for a sensitive action (credential entry), and thus correctly classified the page as `Malicious`. We also confirmed that it was able to concisely justify its decision based on observable facts contained in the Brand Report and the Content Report.

4.4 Analysis of Failed Cases

In this section, we describe the cases in which the proposed method produced incorrect predictions, separately for each LLM configuration.

Under the GPT-4.1-mini Configuration. On the Impersonation dataset, we observed four false positives on average across 10 runs, which fell into three patterns. First, the method judged a page as malicious solely because a brand-indicating page was hosted on SHSs, even though the brand was not well known. Second, although the page content itself did not appear suspicious, the method still flagged it as suspicious because a page indicating a well-known brand was hosted on SHSs. Third, links to external login sites were mistakenly overemphasized as evidence of maliciousness.

Summary:
This appears to be a login page asking users to enter their User ID and Password to sign in, likely for accessing an AT&T Mail service, based on visible prompts and labels.

Structure Notes:
The page structure is typical for a login form with input fields and a submit button within a centered layout. There are no large menus, excessive hidden items, or multiple download links noted in the provided DOM snippet. The layout uses a three-column grid with the login form in the center column. The DOM and screenshot show consistent labeling and no structural anomalies.

Sensitive Action Prompting:
Prompted action: authentication/credential entry. Mechanism: on-page form with text inputs for 'User ID' and 'Password', and a prominent button labeled 'Continue'. Evidence: parsed DOM contains inputs named for User ID and Password with a 'Continue' button; screenshot_wordlist includes 'User ID', 'Password', and 'Continue', and indicates 'Sign in' prompting.

Fig. 3. Details of the Content Report.

Final Verdict: Malicious

Rationale:

- The website impersonates a well-known brand, AT&T, hosted on a free hosting domain (weebly.com), which is a contextual anomaly and inherently suspicious given the brand and hosting context rules.
- The page prompts a sensitive action, specifically authentication credential entry requesting User ID and Password for sign-in, which combined with the well-known brand indication on free hosting, is a strong indicator of malicious intent as phishing.

Fig. 4. Details of the Final Report.

On the Non-impersonation dataset, we observed two false negatives. In one case, the Content Analyzer failed to sufficiently capture structural irregularities of the page. In the other case, the Content Analyzer reported an unusually large number of download links in the Content Report, but the Judge did not adequately interpret this irregularity, leading to a misclassification.

Under the Qwen3-8B Configuration. On the Impersonation dataset, we observed 21 false positives and one false negative on average across 10 runs. Approximately half of these false positives were cases in which the model overreacted to page-structure cues. Specifically, many misclassifications occurred when the Content Analyzer noted in the Content Report that parts of the `Parsed DOM` were unclear due to reductions introduced during parsing, and the Judge excessively treated this statement itself as a maliciousness signal. We also observed cases where the Judge overemphasized the presence of contact forms as evidence of maliciousness, as well as misclassifications stemming from incorrect brand-name extraction. Regarding the false negative, the brand name was not correctly identified.

On the Non-impersonation dataset, we observed one false positive caused by an incorrect brand-name inference.

A likely contributing factor to the higher false-positive rate under Qwen3-8B is its much smaller context window. As described in Sect. 3.4, the Parsed DOM input is truncated to 15,000 characters for Qwen3-8B, compared with 500,000 characters for GPT-4.1-mini. With this more aggressive truncation, portions of the DOM that would support a benign interpretation may be lost, causing the Content Analyzer to report uncertainty about the truncated Parsed DOM. The Judge then overreacts to this uncertainty and treats it as evidence of maliciousness, consistent with the observation above.

5 Discussion

5.1 Limitations

This section summarizes practical limitations of the current implementation that are largely orthogonal to the method's core design.

Non-Determinism of LLM Outputs. We use the default values for LLM inference parameters such as `temperature` and `top_p`. Because LLM outputs are stochastic, the verdict and its rationale may vary across runs even for identical inputs. In our experiments, all LLM-based methods showed variation in accuracy metrics across runs. The proposed method exhibited somewhat larger variation than the baselines.

Inference Cost. The proposed method incurs a higher inference cost per sample than conventional ML-based methods, which can become a bottleneck when processing large volumes of URLs at scale. On the other hand, LLM inference prices have been declining rapidly: for models with performance comparable to GPT-3.5, the cost dropped to approximately 1/280 of its previous level over 18 months [23].

No Support for Real-Time Detection. In our evaluation, we used screenshots and DOM snapshots captured at a past point in time via urlscan.io [24]. The proposed method therefore does not directly provide real-time detection at present. Transitioning to real-time operation would require on-the-fly page retrieval, introducing challenges such as CAPTCHA circumvention [4] and inference latency management.

Lack of Objectivity in Popularity Estimation. For popularity estimation, we provided search hit counts of three major telecommunications providers as reference values in the prompt. However, these references were chosen based on empirical judgment, and the sensitivity of detection performance to changes in these reference values has not been systematically evaluated. A more reproducible approach could combine multiple indicators, such as web traffic rankings, social media presence, and brand-registry databases, and systematically evaluate threshold validity across diverse brand categories.

5.2 Scope and Generalizability

The proposed method targets pages hosted on SHSs, where conventional URL- and domain-based features become uninformative, making detection particularly challenging. For pages hosted on custom domains outside SHSs, existing detection techniques that leverage domain age, WHOIS information, and TLS certificate characteristics remain effective.

That said, broadening the method's scope is a promising direction. Extending it to pages on arbitrary custom domains could be enabled by adding a component that obtains hosting-environment information (e.g., DNS records, WHOIS data, hosting provider identification) and providing that context to the prompts. We also anticipate that the approach may be applicable to other types of threats that exploit shared-domain structures, such as domain shadowing [14], where adversaries inject malicious content under subdomains of legitimate domains.

5.3 Input Modality and Adversarial Robustness

The proposed method uses both screenshots and DOM content as inputs, but the relative contribution of each modality has not been analyzed. An ablation study comparing screenshot-only, DOM-only, and combined configurations would clarify each modality's role and inform future design choices.

This question is closely tied to adversarial robustness. The current evaluation does not consider attackers who deliberately attempt to evade the proposed method, for example by rendering brand information as images, injecting misleading text into the DOM, or using client-side rendering. Because the method takes both visual inputs and DOM, evasion targeting one modality could potentially be compensated by the other. However, evaluating this complementary resilience first requires understanding each modality's contribution under non-adversarial conditions.

5.4 Decision Logic Refinement

Under the current method, we observed false positives in which elements that can appear on legitimate sites (e.g., contact forms or login links) were overemphasized as high-risk evidence. Future work should validate the legitimacy of such elements by examining where user-submitted data or navigation is directed (e.g., an official domain, a known authentication provider, or a suspicious domain hosted on an SHS), rather than treating them as binary signals.

Structural patterns also caused errors: some false negatives stemmed from insufficient extraction of structural irregularities (e.g., long lists of unrelated links), while some false positives resulted from the Judge interpreting limited information in the truncated `Parsed DOM` as a maliciousness signal. Defining explicit extraction criteria for structural anomalies, and preventing missing inputs from being directly interpreted as malicious, are necessary improvements.

5.5 Workflow Optimization and Agentic Extensions

The current fixed three-component workflow ensures reproducibility and ease of evaluation, but it does not adapt to the characteristics of individual pages. One direction is to explore whether a simpler two-stage configuration (e.g., merging the two analyzers) can achieve comparable accuracy at lower cost. A more fundamental extension is to introduce agentic capabilities, allowing the system to dynamically decide which analysis steps to execute based on intermediate results. Such an adaptive design could improve both detection accuracy and efficiency by allocating computational resources according to the difficulty of each case.

5.6 Operational Deployment

In operational deployment, the same attacker often generates multiple similar phishing pages on a single SHS. Incorporating a feedback mechanism that accumulates past detection results and uses them to inform future judgments, for example by flagging clusters of structurally similar pages under the same apex domain, could improve both detection efficiency and coverage. Furthermore, the proposed method's ability to output natural-language rationales for its decisions could facilitate integration with SHS providers' abuse-reporting workflows, potentially accelerating the takedown of detected phishing pages.

6 Conclusion

In this study, we proposed an LLM-workflow-based method for detecting phishing sites hosted on shared-domain hosting services (SHSs), where conventional URL- and domain-based features are ineffective due to the shared-domain structure. The proposed method consists of three components: Brand Analyzer, Content Analyzer, and Judge. By combining brand popularity with prompts for sensitive actions, the Judge evaluates contextual mismatch and outputs both a verdict and an interpretable rationale.

Our evaluation against ML- and LLM-based baselines on the Impersonation and Non-impersonation datasets yielded three key findings. First, the proposed method achieves service-agnostic detection: it maintained high recall (1.00 with `GPT-4.1-mini` and at least 0.98 with `Qwen3-8B`) under both Seen and Unseen service conditions, whereas FreePhish suffered a sharp performance drop on unseen services (F1: 0.66 → 0.42). Second, with `GPT-4.1-mini`, the method achieved F1 scores of 0.97 (Seen) and 0.96 (Unseen), demonstrating strong detection performance. Third, on the Non-impersonation dataset, the proposed method detected malicious samples that none of the baselines could identify (TP=0 for all baselines), showing that it can also detect non-impersonation malicious sites.

Several directions for future research emerge from this work. On the methodological side, analyzing the contribution of each input modality (DOM vs. screenshot) and investigating adversarial robustness against deliberate evasion are important next steps. Extending the fixed workflow toward an agentic architecture that adaptively selects analysis steps based on intermediate results could improve both accuracy and efficiency. On the practical side, enabling real-time detection through on-the-fly page retrieval, broadening the scope beyond SHSs to custom-domain environments, and incorporating detection history for operational deployment represent promising avenues for making the approach deployable at scale.

Acknowledgment. This paper is based on results obtained from a project, JPNP24003, commissioned by the New Energy and Industrial Technology Development Organization (NEDO).

Disclosure of Interests. The authors have no competing interests to declare that are relevant to the content of this article.

References

1. Abdelnabi, S., et al.: VisualPhishNet: zero-day phishing website detection by visual similarity. In: Proceedings ACM CCS (2020)
2. APWG: Phishing activity trends report 2nd quarter 2025 (2025). https://docs.apwg.org/reports/apwg_trends_report_q2_2025.pdf
3. code-philia: PhishVLM (2025). https://github.com/code-philia/PhishVLM
4. Deniz, F., et al.: MANTIS: Detection of zero-day malicious domains leveraging low reputed hosting infrastructure. In: Proceedings IEEE S&P (2025)
5. Fortra: Cloudflare's pages.dev and workers.dev domains increasingly abused for phishing (2024). https://www.fortra.com/blog/cloudflare-pages-workers-domains-increasingly-abused-for-phishing
6. Google: Cloud Vision API. https://docs.cloud.google.com/vision/docs. Accessed: 20 May 2026
7. Google: Custom Search JSON API. https://developers.google.com/custom-search/v1/overview. Accessed: 20 May 2026
8. imethanlee: KnowPhish (2024). https://github.com/imethanlee/KnowPhish
9. Kim, D., et al.: Security analysis on practices of certificate authorities in the HTTPS phishing ecosystem. In: Proceedings ACM ASIA CCS (2021)
10. Koide, T., et al.: ChatPhishDetector: detecting phishing sites using large language models. IEEE Access **12**, 154381–154400 (2024)
11. LangChain: Workflows and agents. https://docs.langchain.com/oss/python/langgraph/workflows-agents. Accessed: 20 May 2026
12. Li, Y., et al.: When semantic plausibility becomes a liability: LLM-based phishing detection from an adversarial asymmetry perspective. Cyber Secur. Appl. **4**, 100126 (2026)
13. Li, Y., et al.: KnowPhish: large language models meet multimodal knowledge graphs for enhancing reference-based phishing detection. In: Proceedings USENIX Security (2024)
14. Liu, D., et al.: Don't let one rotten apple spoil the whole barrel: towards automated detection of shadowed domains. In: Proceedings ACM CCS (2017)
15. Liu, R., et al.: Inferring phishing intention via webpage appearance and dynamics: a deep vision based approach. In: Proceedings USENIX Security (2022)
16. Liu, R., et al.: Less defined knowledge and more true alarms: reference-based phishing detection without a pre-defined reference list. In: Proceedings USENIX Security (2024)

17. Microsoft Azure: Azure OpenAI in Foundry Models. https://azure.microsoft.com/en-US/products/ai-foundry/models/openai/. Accessed: 20 May 2026
18. Moura, G.C.M., et al.: Characterizing and mitigating phishing attacks at ccTLD scale. In: Proceedings ACM CCS (2024)
19. Mozilla Foundation: Public suffix list. https://publicsuffix.org/. Accessed: 20 May 2026
20. Netlify: Introducing Netlify's Free plan (2024). https://www.netlify.com/blog/introducing-netlify-free-plan/
21. Oest, A., et al.: Sunrise to sunset: Analyzing the end-to-end life cycle and effectiveness of phishing attacks at scale. In: Proceedings USENIX Security (2020)
22. Saha Roy, S., et al.: Phishing in the free waters: A study of phishing attacks created using free website building services. In: Proceedings ACM IMC (2023)
23. Stanford HAI: AI Index 2025: State of AI in 10 Charts (2025). https://hai.stanford.edu/news/ai-index-2025-state-of-ai-in-10-charts
24. urlscan.io: Url and website scanner. https://urlscan.io/. Accessed: 20 May 2026
25. UTA-SPRLab: freephish (2023). https://github.com/UTA-SPRLab/freephish
26. VirusTotal: VirusTotal. https://www.virustotal.com/. Accessed: 20 May 2026
27. Wix.com Ltd.: Form 20-F for the Fiscal Year Ended December 31, 2024. https://www.sec.gov/Archives/edgar/data/1576789/000162828025014212/wix-20241231.htm. Accessed: 20 May 2026

DomainBERT: Transformer-Based Domain Generation Algorithm Detection

Arthur Drichel[1(✉)], Yannick Sautter[2], and Ulrike Meyer[1]

[1] RWTH Aachen University, Aachen, Germany
{drichel,meyer}@itsec.rwth-aachen.de
[2] step3IT GmbH, Neumünster, Germany
y.sautter@groupios.com

Abstract. Modern botnets use Domain Generation Algorithms (DGAs) to create resilient Command and Control (C2) channels to the botnet master. Although Machine Learning (ML) classifiers have been demonstrated to achieve high detection rates, recent studies reveal intrinsic biases that adversaries can exploit to evade detection. To mitigate these biases, a bias-reduced classification framework has been proposed, which limits bias in the detection process, albeit at the expense of detection performance. This trade-off presents opportunities for additional improvements in DGA detection. In this context, we propose DomainBERT, a novel model that outperforms the current state of the art, particularly in the practically relevant low-FPR regime. These results are achieved in a temporal and spatial bias-free setting, demonstrating the classifier's ability to generalize well across time and across different networks.

Keywords: Network security · DNS security · Intrusion detection · Domain Generation Algorithm (DGA) · Botnet · Machine Learning (ML)

1 Introduction

Domain Generation Algorithms (DGAs) are pseudorandom algorithms that generate a large number of Algorithmically-Generated Domains (AGDs) to bypass traditional blocklists and maintain robust communication channels that are resilient against disruptions, such as domain seizures or Command and Control (C2) server takedowns. DGAs ultimately enable compromised devices (bots) to receive commands from the botnet master for carrying out malicious actions such as DDoS attacks or spam campaigns. Thereby, DGAs create an asymmetric dynamic: defenders must block every AGD, while the botmaster needs only a single domain that resolves successfully to maintain control of the botnet.

Context-free deep learning (DL) classifiers have consistently delivered state-of- the-art (SOTA) performance for detecting DGA domains (e.g., [8,9,11]). By relying solely on the domain name for classification, they provide a lightweight, non-intrusive approach that also outperforms feature-based methods, achieving

S. Nadjm-Tehrani et al. (Eds.): ARES 2026, LNCS 16898, pp. 321–332, 2027.
https://doi.org/10.1007/978-3-032-36874-4_16

accuracies up to 99.92%, TPRs of 99.98%, and FPRs as low as 0.15%. As bots query all AGDs, most of which are unregistered/non-existent domains (NXDs), until they hit a domain registered by the botnet master, many approaches focus on classifying non-resolving DNS traffic (NX-traffic) (e.g., [8–11]).

However, recent work [7] has exposed biases in such classifiers that attackers can exploit, for instance, by swapping the TLD used or simply prepending "www." to evade detection. To counter this, the authors propose a bias-reduced setting that confines classification to the effective Second-Level Domain (e2LD), thus focusing on the registrable portion of the domain and eliminating arbitrary domain name signals that the botnet master can freely choose. While, the proposed bias-reduced setting [7] effectively mitigates classification bias, it incurs a significant performance degradation, with the SOTA classification performance dropping to a TPR of 89% at a fixed FPR of 0.8%.

In addition, DL classifiers are known to be vulnerable to adversarial attacks that exploit gaps in training data to evade detection. This vulnerability was comprehensively analyzed and addressed in the context of DGA detection by [12].

The current SOTA DGA model for bias-reduced classification, E2LD-ResNet [8], is built upon the architecture of residual neural networks (ResNets). However, since the development of ResNets, significant advancements have been made in the field of ML, resulting in the emergence of various innovative architectures. Notably, Transformers [29] stand out among these advances, which have influenced a wide range of applications. Although Transformers and the attention mechanism have been explored for DGA classification in previous works, such as [11,25], the development of these models has been undertaken with relatively minimal effort, particularly with regard to pre-training, which is a crucial aspect of achieving optimal performance in many Natural Language Processing (NLP) tasks. Specifically, pre-training Transformers on a large corpus of natural language has been shown to improve their feature extraction capabilities, leading to improved performance on a variety of downstream tasks, which could also be leveraged to improve the effectiveness of DGA classifiers.

In this work, we conduct a comprehensive study on the application of pre-trained Transformers for DGA detection and examine their potential to enhance SOTA classification performance. Our primary contributions are as follows:

1. **Transformer-based Models**: We explore the application of various novel Transformer-based architectures to DGA classification and investigate the impact of different fine-tuning approaches on their performance.
2. **Domain Name Pre-Training**: We investigate the domain-specific pre-training of top-performing Transformer-based models for DGA detection and develop a framework for creating pre-trained models that exhibit robust generalization across time and across different networks. This leads to the proposal of a novel model, DomainBERT, which surpasses the SOTA performance by achieving an 11.23% increase in ROC AUC within the FPR interval of $[0, 0.01]$, and a 13.98% higher TPR at a fixed FPR of 0.0014.

We release the source code for our DomainBERT model, including the domain-specific training approach that substantially improves classification performance. In addition, we release our evaluation scripts to facilitate reproducibility and encourage further research.[1]

2 Related Work

Our emphasis on utilizing pre-trained Transformers is primarily driven by their proven effectiveness in the closely related domain of phishing URL detection in which DL models are trained to distinguish between benign and phishing URLs. Notably, Maneriker et al. [18] pioneered the investigation of fine-tuning Bidirectional Encoder Representations from Transformers (BERT) [5] models for phishing URL detection, laying the groundwork for subsequent research. Building upon this foundation, Wang et al. [30] demonstrated that domain-specific pre-training can further enhance classification performance, surpassing Maneriker et al.'s approach. More recently, Li et al. [15] introduced the pre-trained URLBERT model, which not only leverages domain-specific pre-training but also incorporates concepts from adversarial training to improve the model's robustness in extracting semantic features. Ultimately, domain-specific pre-training appears to be a promising approach for enhancing the detection performance of Transformer-based models in the context of DGA detection.

3 Evaluation Overview

This section provides an overview of the remainder of this paper, outlines the experiments detailed in Sect. 4, and describes the data sources used.

Outline: Sect. 4.1 describes our proposed domain-specific pre-training. Section 4.2 presents a pre-selection of the most promising Transformer models, which we comparatively evaluate in Sect. 4.3. In Sect. 4.4, we conduct a real-world study designed to mirror an actual deployment, avoiding both temporal and spatial experimental biases. In Sect. 4.5, we analyze the inference speed of the models and assess their ability to handle the traffic volume of NXDs typically seen in large real-world networks. Finally, Sect. 4.6 provides a brief outlook on the potential of utilizing Transformer models for DGA multiclass classification, which involves attributing AGDs to the DGAs that generated them.

3.1 Data Sources

In total, we utilize six data sources for our evaluations. Two of these sources provide NXDs captured from real-world networks at different points in time, allowing us to evaluate the temporal robustness and cross-network generalizability of the classifiers. Three additional sources supply further domain names that are used during the pre-training phase of the Transformer models. Finally, we obtained AGDs produced by reverse-engineered DGAs from the Open Source Threat Intelligence (OSINT) feed of DGArchive [23], which are used for pre-training, fine-tuning, and evaluation.

[1] https://gitlab.com/rwth-itsec/domainbert.

- **University Network:** Our first source for real-world NXDs comes from the central DNS resolvers of RWTH Aachen University. The served networks include academic, administrative, student-residence, and hospital subnets. From a one-month record (mid-October 2017 to mid-November 2017) we extract more than 35 million unique NXDs.
- **Company Network:** Our second source for real-world NXDs consists of multiple DNS resolvers geographically distributed across Asia, Europe, and the US, serving the networks of Siemens AG. From this source, we obtain approximately 373 million unfiltered NXDs that were captured in April 2019.
- **Day in the Life of the Internet:** The DNS Operations, Analysis, and Research Center's data collection program, known as the Day in the Life of the Internet (DITL), collects DNS traffic from DNS root servers. We obtained access to the B-Root name server traffic from two 48-hour windows: 2023-04-11 to 2023-04-13, and 2017-04-11 to 2017-04-13 [21].
- **Centralized Zone Data Service:** Through the Centralized Zone Data Service (CZDS) of the Internet Corporation for Assigned Names and Num- bers (ICANN) [14], we obtained access to 1068 zone files. The zone files, downloaded in late March 2024, contain approximately 217 million domains.
- **Public Domain Lists:** Additionally, we gather domains from multiple publicly available top-site ranking lists: Cisco Umbrella [28], Majestic Million [3], Tranco [24], BuiltWith [2], Cloudflare Radar [4], and DomCop [6]. We also make use of the CIC-Bell-DNS-2021 dataset [17], which contains frequently accessed benign domains.
- **DGArchive:** We obtain AGDs from the OSINT feed of DGArchive, a continuously updated repository of domains produced by reverse-engineered DGAs. At the time of writing it contains roughly 199 million unique domains generated by 115 different DGA families.

4 BERT for DGA Classification

Transformer networks, initially designed for sequence-to-sequence tasks such as translation, comprise an encoder-decoder architecture that is not directly suited for classification tasks. However, Devlin et al. [5] introduced the BERT architecture, a widely adopted approach for general text classification. Building on this, we analyze the suitability of different BERT-based models for DGA classification, given their proven effectiveness in various classification tasks. Thereby, we specifically investigate the efficacy of utilizing pre-trained Transformer models and fine-tuning them for the downstream task of DGA detection.

4.1 Domain-Specific Pre-Training

We leverage the fact that pre-training does not require labeled data and primarily focuses on general features of the data domain. Our pre-training dataset consists of 3 476 538 valid and unique NXDs extracted from the 2017 and 2023 DITL datasets, which are paired with approximately the same number of 3 099 584 resolvable domains stratified across the 1068 gTLD zone files obtained from the CZDS. Additionally, we incorporate 2 793 959 AGDs from DGArchive, where the number of samples from each DGA is capped at a maximum of 50 000. To prevent the models from retaining knowledge of specific domains from the pre-training phase, which could potentially influence its performance during subsequent evaluations, we employ a sampling strategy that excludes any e2LD present in the fine-tuning and testing datasets from the pre-training dataset. However, this approach results in only 78 DGAs being represented in the pre-training dataset, as some DGAs have all their available AGDs included in the datasets used subsequently for evaluation.

Pre-training is performed using the AdamW optimizer with a batch size of 256, a learning rate of 3e-5, $\beta_1 = 0.9$, $\beta_2 = 0.999$, and an L2 weight decay of 0.01, while employing a warmup ratio of 0.1 to mitigate training instabilities.

4.2 Pre-Selecting Models

Given the computational expense of pre-training, we conduct a pre-selection of the most promising approaches by conducting a 5-fold cross-validation (CV). To construct a dataset, we follow the approach proposed by Drichel and Meyer [7] for a bias-reduced classification setting, utilizing a combination of university network data and malicious AGDs from DGArchive. To this end, we filter the university data against DGArchive to remove any overlapping malicious domains, eliminate invalid domains, and then reduce the remaining domains to their e2LDs. We pair these samples with malicious AGDs by sampling at most 1550 effective Second-Level Domains (e2LDs) from all 115 DGAs. If fewer AGDs are available for a DGA, all of its e2LDs are included. This results in a balanced dataset containing approximately 263k e2LDs.

We evaluate BERT [5], as well as its successors, including RoBERTa [16], DistilBERT [27], and DeBERTaV3 [13] in its xsmall configuration, denoted as DeBERTaV3-xsmall. Additionally, we include URLBERT [15] in our evaluation, as it has been pre-trained on a domain-specific corpus that is more closely related to our task. In this context, we investigate the impact of initializing the model weights using pre-training on large NLP corpora, as opposed to random initialization, and compare it to our domain-specific pre-training approach using the custom-created pre-training dataset. Finally, we also examine the optimal sequence of pre-training, specifically whether domain-specific pre-training should be performed sequentially after NLP pre-training or from scratch, to determine the most effective strategy for initializing the model weights. We follow the recommendations of BERT [5] by introducing a single fully-connected classification layer after the last BERT layer, where the input dimension of this layer depends on the specific BERT model architecture. Additionally, we explore an alternative strategy as proposed by Safaya et al. [26], which applies a CNN architecture to the last four layers of BERT to improve classification performance.

Training is performed using the AdamW optimizer, with a cross-entropy loss function, a batch size of 256, and an initial learning rate of 1e-5. The models are trained for 20 epochs, utilizing early stopping with a patience of five epochs to prevent overfitting. To stabilize the training process, we employ the techniques proposed by Mosbach et al. [19], which involve linearly increasing the learning rate from a near-zero value to the target learning rate over the first 20% of training steps, followed by a linear decrease towards zero for the remaining steps.

Table 1. Statistical analysis of TPRs at three different fixed FPRs.

Model	FPR = 0.001			FPR = 0.01			FPR = 0.1		
	TPR	p	P	TPR	p	P	TPR	p	P
E2LD-ResNet	0.33821	-	-	0.57917	-	-	0.89762	-	-
B-DeBERTaV3-xsmall	0.27271	0.99804	0.00024	0.54128	1.00000	0.00000	0.91430	**0.00000**	0.18303
B-DomainBERT	0.52442	**0.00000**	**1.00000**	**0.71867**	**0.00000**	**1.00000**	0.97198	**0.00000**	**1.00000**
B-DomainBERT+CNN	**0.53235**	**0.00000**	**1.00000**	0.71794	**0.00000**	**1.00000**	**0.97204**	**0.00000**	**1.00000**

Results: The preliminary study yields the following key findings: DeBERTaV3-xsmall emerges as the top-performing model among all the NLP pre-trained models. In contrast, URLBERT exhibits subpar performance, with its ROC curve consistently positioned below that of the E2LD-ResNet model. Notably, fine-tuning NLP pre-trained models achieves superior results compared to training models with randomly initialized weights from scratch. Furthermore, fine-tuning domain-specific pre-trained models yields even better performance than fine-tuning NLP pre-trained models, highlighting the benefits of tailored pre-training for DGA detection. Additionally, our results show that domain-specific pre-training is most effective when performed sequentially after NLP pre-training.

Consequently, we select the top-performing model, the NLP pre-trained De-BERTaV3-xsmall, combined with domain-specific pre-training for our subsequent evaluations. In the following, we refer to this novel, domain-specific pre-trained model as B-DomainBERT. Additionally, we evaluate the NLP pre-trained DeBERTaV3-xsmall without our domain-specific pre-training, referred to as B-DeBERTaV3-xsmall, to assess the impact of the domain-specific pre-training on the model's performance. Employing a CNN architecture for the last layers, as proposed by Safaya et al. [26], yields slight improvements in classification performance. We denote models that use this modification with a +CNN suffix.

4.3 Comparative Evaluation

We create 10 new datasets, in the same way as for pre-selecting promising models, to facilitate a comparative study with the SOTA approach E2LD-ResNet. We perform a 5-fold CV on each of the 10 datasets, resulting in 50 evaluation runs, which enables a statistical comparison of the classifiers.

To this end, we perform a frequentist correlated t-test [20], which takes into account the correlation due to the overlapping training sets within the CV.

The results of the frequentist correlated t-test are p-values which reflect the degree of data compatibility with the null hypothesis. Here, an extremely small p-value indicates a significantly better classifier compared to the SOTA classifier E2LD-ResNet. Furthermore, we perform a Bayesian correlated t-test [1] to mitigate the well-known problems of null hypothesis significance testing for comparing ML classifiers. For this test, we employ a Region Of Practical Equivalence (ROPE) of 1%, meaning that we consider two classifiers to be statistically equivalent if the difference in their performance is less than the specified ROPE threshold. In Table 1, we display averaged TPRs at the three FPRs of 0.001, 0.01, and 0.1 for E2LD-ResNet, B-DeBERTaV3-xsmall, B-DomainBERT, and B-DomainBERT+CNN.

B-DeBERTaV3-xsmall performs worse than E2LD-ResNet at FPRs of 0.001 and 0.01, but surpasses it at an FPR of 0.1, although this result is not statistically significant according to the Bayesian correlated t-test. In contrast, B-DomainBERT significantly outperforms E2LD-ResNet at all evaluated FPRs, achieving a notable improvement of over 18.6% in TPR at an FPR of 0.001. Using a CNN architecture for the last layers yields a slight improvement in performance at an FPR of 0.001, but has a negligible effect at higher thresholds.

These results are intriguing, as they highlight the significant impact of domain-specific pre-training on the performance of BERT-based DGA classifiers. Although B-DeBERTaV3-xsmall and B-DomainBERT share the same underlying model architecture and were fine-tuned on the same training datasets, they produce significantly different results. The key difference between them lies in the domain-specific pre-training, which is only applied to B-DomainBERT.

4.4 Real-World Study

Now, we conduct a real-world study in which we aim to reflect a real-world deployment as closely as possible by avoiding temporal as well as experimental spatial biases [22]. Temporal bias is introduced by temporally inconsistent evaluations which integrate future knowledge about testing samples into the training phase. Using stratified k-fold CV can introduce temporal bias in two ways: First, k-fold CV does not ensure that all training samples are strictly temporally precedent to the testing ones. Second, the benign and malicious samples in the datasets do not necessarily have to come from the same time window (e.g., one-month real-world benign data compared to several years of DGArchive data). Spatial bias arises from using an unrealistic ratio of benign to malicious samples in the test data. For the DGA detection use case, most queried domains within a network are benign. Using balanced test datasets can provide a false sense of security as a significant class imbalance can lead to base-rate fallacy where evaluation metrics such as TPR and FPR are misleading.

To address these experimental biases, we train classifiers using the real-world benign e2LDs from the university network recorded from mid-October 2017 to mid-November 2017, as well as DGArchive data that was available until the end of the recording period. In detail, DGArchive contains approximately 53 million unique e2LDs generated by 85 different DGAs up to this point in time. Training a classifier using this data mitigates one of the two experimental temporal biases as the malicious samples are from the same time window as the benign samples. To mitigate the second experimental temporal bias, that requires that all training samples are strictly temporally precedent to the testing ones, we evaluate the classifiers on approximately 373 million benign NXDs captured in the company networks in April 2019 and AGDs from DGArchive that were generated by DGAs in April 2019. Within April 2019, 46 DGAs (four of which are not included in the training data and are thus unknown to the classifier) generated approximately 1.2 million domains. In this way, we eliminate the experimental temporal biases, and can guarantee that the benign samples come from different networks and that the time interval between the occurrence of the training and the test samples is about 17 months. Thus, by employing this methodology, we gain the additional benefit of being able to evaluate not only the real-world performance of DGA classifiers but also their ability to generalize across different networks and maintain their effectiveness over time.

To eliminate the experimental spatial bias, it is required to approximate the true ratio of benign to malicious samples in the test data. As it is unclear, how many DGAs are present in a real-world network, we conduct an experiment to estimate the worst-case classification performance. To this end, for each DGA in the test data, we evaluate the classifier using all AGDs generated in April 2019 of that particular DGA and all 373 million benign NXDs. In total, we thus evaluate a model using 46 test sets, since there are 46 DGAs that generate at least one domain in April 2019.

For this study, we additionally adapt the domain-specific pre-training dataset to mitigate any potential temporal bias in our domain-specific pre-training process. To this end, we combine the top one million domains reported by Cisco for 2017-11-01 [28] with 1 808 885 AGDs sampled from DGArchive data that was available until 2017-11-01, where the number of AGDs per DGA is limited to at most 50 000.

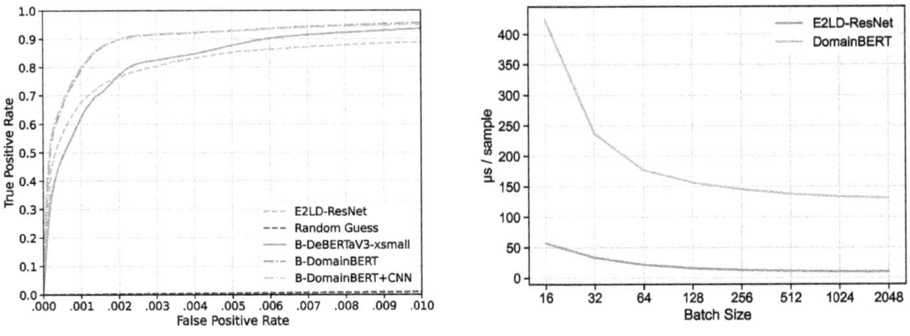

(a) Real-world study.

(b) Inference times.

Fig. 1. (a) ROC curves averaged over five repetitions and 46 evaluation runs. (b) Inference times as a function of batch size.

In Fig. 1a, we show the averaged ROC curves across five repetitions for E2LD-ResNet, B-DeBERTaV3-xsmall, B-DomainBERT, and B-DomainBERT+CNN. The results we obtain in the real-world study reflect the results from the statistical analysis. In terms of the average ROC AUC scores, restricted to the FPR range of [0,0.01], the classifiers yield the following results: 0.80496 for E2LD-ResNet, 0.82246 for B-DeBERTaV3-xsmall, 0.89428 for B-DomainBERT, and 0.89537 for B-DomainBERT+CNN. Once again, DomainBERT significantly outperforms E2LD-ResNet, and these results reaffirm the importance of domain-specific pre-training in achieving optimal performance with BERT-based DGA classifiers. The top-performing model, B-DomainBERT+CNN, outperforms the SOTA model E2LD-ResNet by 13.98% at an FPR of 0.0014, and achieves a relative improvement of 11.23% in partial AUC within the practically relevant FPR range of [0,0.01]. On average, the performance difference is 8.78% in the FPR interval between 0 and 0.01.

However, it is essential to note that the NLP pre-trained models may still introduce a degree of temporal bias, as they were trained on large corpora of text data that may post-date the training data interval, potentially influencing the results. Nevertheless, we consider any potential bias introduced by the NLP pre-training to be negligible in real-world DGA classification, as DeBERTaV3-xsmall's relatively poor performance suggests that the benefits of temporally consistent domain-specific pre-training, as seen in B-DomainBERT, outweigh any potential temporal bias.

Finally, the real-world study suggests that the BERT-based models, similar to E2LD-ResNet, exhibit remarkable robustness over time and demonstrate good generalizability across different networks.

4.5 Inference Times

In the following, we compare the inference speed of B-DomainBERT with E2LD-ResNet. To this end, we measured the inference times of the classifiers in the experiments outlined in Sect. 4.3. Since B-DomainBERT shares its architecture with B-DeBERTaV3-xsmall, their inference times are identical, and therefore, B-DeBERTaV3-xsmall is omitted from the comparison. All models were executed on an NVIDIA Tesla H100 GPU. In Fig. 1b, we illustrate the inference times for E2LD-ResNet and B-DomainBERT as a function of batch size. Within the company network (see Sect. 3.1), there are on average 148 NXDs queried per second, with a maximum of 2471 NXDs per second. Thus a model has at most 405us to process a single domain. Although B-DomainBERT is slower than E2LD-ResNet, the inference time of B-DomainBERT improves with larger batch sizes of 32 and above to such an extent that it meets the latency requirement of 405μs required for the classification of all NXDs in large real-world networks, such as those employed by the company. Ultimately, we argue that the extra latency is outweighed by B-DomainBERT's superior detection performance.

4.6 Multiclass Classification

Now, we briefly examine the potential of leveraging DomainBERT for DGA multiclass classification, where AGDs are attributed to the DGAs that generated them, to enable targeted remediation measures. To this end, we create a new balanced dataset D_M. As Drichel and Meyer [7] noted, reducing to e2LDs is not suitable for multiclass classification, since the TLD plays a significant role in attributing DGAs. Therefore, we train the multiclass classifiers on Fully Qualified Domain Names (FQDNs), sampling a maximum of 10 000 domains per class. The multiclass dataset D_M comprises 703 344 samples in total. As a benchmark, we use the SOTA M-ResNet model [7], optimized for multiclass classification. To adjust our models to the multiclass setting, we configure the classification output layer to have a dimension of $n = 116$ to accommodate all 116 classes. In the following, we denote multiclass classifiers with a leading "M". In Table 2, we present the results of this experiment. All BERT-based models achieve a higher F1-score than the M-ResNet model, with M-DomainBERT surpassing M-DeBERTaV3-xsmall, and M-DomainBERT+CNN achieving the highest scores.

Table 2. Multiclass classification: averaged F1-score, precision, and recall.

Model	F1-Score	Precision	Recall
M-ResNet	0.78617	0.81828	0.78570
M-DeBERTaV3-xsmall	0.79409	0.81291	0.79302
M-DomainBERT	0.79449	0.81720	0.79312
M-DomainBERT+CNN	**0.79907**	**0.81847**	**0.79759**

5 Conclusion

In this work, we investigated the usage of NLP pre-trained BERT models for DGA classification. In combination with an analysis of different fine-tuning methodologies, we proposed a novel model, DomainBERT, which outperforms the state of the art, particularly in the practically relevant low-FPR regime. These results were achieved in a temporal and spatial bias-free setting, demonstrating the classifier's ability to generalize well across time and across networks.

We release the source code for DomainBERT, including the domain-specific pre-training approach that substantially improves classification performance.[1]

Ethical Data Handling. No Personal Identifiable Information (PII) is present in our datasets. The real-world NXDs we received consist solely of domain names extracted from recorded queries, without any additional references, such as IP addresses. All other domain names are publicly available or actively shared with us for our research.

Disclosure of Interests. The authors have no competing interests to declare that are relevant to the content of this article.

References

1. Benavoli, A.: Time for a Change: a tutorial for comparing multiple classifiers through bayesian analysis. Machine Learning Research 18(77) (2017)
2. BuiltWith® Pty Ltd: Top 1m Rank (2024), Accessed on 02 May 2024
3. Chudnovsky, A., Pitchford, S.: Majestic Million (2024), Accessed on 02 May 2024
4. Cloudflare: domain rankings (2024), Accessed on 02 May 2024
5. Devlin, J., et al.: BERT: Pre-training of Deep Bidirectional Transformers for Language Understanding. In: Human Language Technologies, Volume **1** (2019)
6. DomCop: top 10 million websites based on Open data from Common Crawl & Common Search (2024), Accessed on 02 May 2024
7. Drichel, A., Meyer, U.: alse sense of security: Leveraging XAI to analyze the reasoning and true performance of context-less DGA classifiers. In: RAID. ACM (2023)
8. Drichel, A., Meyer, U.: A Comprehensive Study on Multi-Task Learning for Domain Generation Algorithm (DGA) Detection, p. PST. (2024)
9. Drichel, A.: Analyzing the Real-World Applicability of DGA Classifiers, ARES (2020)
10. Drichel, A.: Making use of nxt to nothing: the effect of class imbalances on dga detection classifiers. ACM, ARES (2020)
11. Drichel A.: Extended Abstract: A transfer learning-based training approach for DGA classification. In: DIMVA. Springer, Cham (2024). https://doi.org/10.1007/978-3-031-64171-8_20
12. Drichel, A., et al.: Towards Robust Domain Generation Algorithm Classification. In: ASIA CCS. ACM (2024)
13. He, P.: DeBERTaV3: improving DeBERTa using ELECTRA-Style Pre-Training with Gradient-Disentangled Embedding Sharing. In: ICLR (2023)
14. Internet Corporation for Assigned Names and Numbers: Zone Requests — Centralized Zone Data Service (2024) Accessed on 26 Mar 2024
15. Li, Y.: URLBERT: a contrastive and adversarial Pre-trained model for URL classification (2024). arXiv:2402.11495
16. Liu, Y.: RoBERTa: a robustly optimized BERT pretraining approach (2019). arXiv:1907.11692
17. Mahdavifar, S., et al.: Classifying malicious domains using DNS traffic analysis. In: DASC. IEEE (2021)
18. Maneriker, P., et al.: URLTran: improving phishing URL detection using transformers. In: MILCOM. IEEE (2021)
19. Mosbach, M.: On the Stability of Fine-tuning BERT: misconceptions, Explanations, and Strong Baselines. In: ICLR (2021)
20. Nadeau, C., Bengio, Y.: Inference for the Generalization Error. In: Advances in Neural Information Processing Systems, vol. 12, MIT Press (1999)
21. Operations, U.R., project, U.: Day in the life of the internet (DITL) april, 2017 and april, 2023 dataset
22. Pendlebury, F.: TESSERACT: eliminating experimental bias in malware classification across space and time. In: USENIX Security. USENIX (2019)
23. Plohmann, D., et al.: A Comprehensive Measurement Study of Domain Generating Malware. In: USENIX Security. USENIX (2016)

24. Pochat, V.L.: Tranco: a research-oriented top sites ranking hardened against manipulation. In: NDSS (2019)
25. Ren, F., et al.: Integrating an Attention Mechanism and Deep Neural Network for Detection of DGA Domain Names. In: ICTAI. IEEE (2019)
26. Safaya, A.: KUISAIL at SemEval-2020 Task 12: bERT-CNN for offensive speech identification in social media. In: Semantic Evaluation (2020)
27. Sanh, V., et al.: DistilBERT, a distilled version of BERT: smaller, faster, cheaper and lighter. In: EMC2 (2020)
28. Umbrella, C.: Umbrella Popularity List (2016), Accessed on 02 May 2024
29. Vaswani, A.: Attention Is All You Need. In: Advances in Neural Information Processing Systems, vol. **30**, Curran Associates, Inc (2017)
30. Wang, Y., et al.: A Large-Scale Pretrained Deep Model for Phishing URL Detection. In: ICASSP. IEEE (2023)

Operationalizing Zero-Day Malware: A Detection-Space Framework with Time-Split Experimental Validation

Nasser Al-Hadhrami(✉)

University of Technology and Applied Sciences, Muscat, Oman
nasser.almur@utas.edu.om

Abstract. The term zero-day malware is frequently used in cybersecurity discourse, yet it lacks a consistent operational definition suitable for experimental evaluation. While zero-day vulnerabilities are formally defined as previously unknown software flaws, the notion of zero-day malware is often conflated with newly discovered variants, polymorphic samples, or malware exploiting zero-day vulnerabilities. This ambiguity complicates benchmarking and obscures evaluation of detection systems under realistic unseen-threat conditions. In this paper, we introduce a detection-space-based operational definition of Zero-Day Malware (ZDM) as malicious code that lies outside the decision boundary of deployed detection models at time t_0, remaining undetected until model update at time t_1. We formalize the Zero-Day Window $\Delta t = t_1 - t_0$ as a measurable performance metric. To validate this framework, we conduct time-split experiments using a real-world malware dataset and compare signature-based detection, closed-set machine learning, and open-set recognition models. Results demonstrate that traditional closed-set classifiers significantly overestimate zero-day performance when temporal separation is ignored, while open-set methods provide uncertainty-aware handling of previously unseen samples and support earlier identification of emerging threats. Our findings provide a reproducible methodology for evaluating zero-day malware detection and establish a measurable bridge between conceptual definition and experimental validation.

Keywords: Zero-Day Malware · Malware Detection · Open-Set Recognition · Machine Learning Security · Temporal Evaluation · Cyber Threat Detection

1 Introduction

The cybersecurity community has long recognized the challenge posed by previously unseen threats. While the concept of a "zero-day vulnerability" is well established and generally refers to a software flaw that is unknown to vendors and defenders, the term "zero-day malware" remains considerably less precise. In practice, the term is often used to describe newly observed malware, polymorphic variants, previously unseen samples, or malware that exploits undisclosed

S. Nadjm-Tehrani et al. (Eds.): ARES 2026, LNCS 16898, pp. 333–343, 2027.
https://doi.org/10.1007/978-3-032-36874-4_17

vulnerabilities. As a result, the same term may refer to different phenomena depending on the context.

This ambiguity creates difficulties for both researchers and practitioners. Without a clear operational definition, it becomes challenging to compare detection systems, interpret reported results, or determine whether a particular malware sample should be considered zero-day. The problem is further compounded by the fact that many malware detection studies evaluate their methods using random train-test splits, which allow information from future samples to influence the learned model. Although such evaluations often produce impressive performance metrics, they do not accurately reflect the conditions under which defenders encounter emerging threats in practice.

Recent studies have highlighted the importance of temporally realistic evaluation for malware detection and have shown that random splits can substantially overestimate real-world performance [2,3]. At the same time, research on open-set recognition has emphasized the need for detection systems to explicitly account for previously unseen samples rather than assuming that all future observations belong to known classes [7,8]. Despite these advances, there is still no widely accepted framework that defines zero-day malware in relation to detection capability and time.

In this paper, we address this gap by introducing a detection-space-based operational definition of Zero-Day Malware (ZDM). Rather than linking zero-day status exclusively to vulnerability novelty, we define a malware instance as zero-day when it falls outside the detection capability available at the time of first encounter. Under this view, zero-day status is not an intrinsic property of the malware itself, but a state that depends on the relationship between the malware and the deployed detection system. This perspective allows the concept to be formalized and evaluated experimentally.

Building upon this definition, we introduce the notion of a *the Zero-Day Window* (Δt), representing the period during which a malware sample remains undetected. We then validate the proposed framework using a time-split experimental design based on the EMBER dataset, comparing signature-based, closed-set, and open-set detection approaches under realistic temporal conditions.

The main contributions of this paper are as follows:

1. We propose a detection-space-based operational definition of Zero-Day Malware.
2. We formalize the concept of the Zero-Day Window (Δt) as a measurable indicator of detection latency.
3. We present a reproducible time-split evaluation methodology aligned with the proposed definition.
4. We experimentally compare signature-based, closed-set, and open-set detection paradigms under realistic temporal conditions.
5. We demonstrate how evaluation methodology influences the perceived capability of malware detection systems to handle previously unseen threats.

The primary contribution of this work is the operational formalization of Zero-Day Malware and the associated evaluation framework; the experimental study serves as an illustrative validation of the proposed formulation.

The remainder of this paper is organized as follows. Section 2 reviews the most relevant literature on zero-day threats, malware detection, and temporally realistic evaluation. Section 3 introduces the proposed operational definition and formal framework. Section 4 describes the experimental methodology, while Sect. 5 presents the results. Finally, Sects. 6 and 7 discuss the implications and limitations of the work and Sect. 8 concludes the paper.

2 Related Work

The notion of a zero-day has traditionally been associated with previously unknown software vulnerabilities. Studies of real-world zero-day attacks have shown that attackers often exploit undisclosed vulnerabilities long before vendors become aware of them, creating a significant window of exposure for defenders [1,15]. Subsequent research has examined the lifecycle, disclosure process, and economics of zero-day vulnerabilities, further establishing the concept within vulnerability management and cyber defense [11,12]. While these works provide a clear understanding of what constitutes a zero-day vulnerability, they do not formally define when a malware instance itself should be considered zero-day.

A related body of research has focused on malware evolution and evasion techniques. Polymorphic and metamorphic malware continuously alter their code structure to evade traditional signature-based detection, while modern threats increasingly employ packing, obfuscation, sandbox evasion, and fileless execution techniques [5,6,9,10]. These studies explain how malware adapts to bypass defensive mechanisms, but they generally characterize novelty as an evasion strategy rather than a measurable detection state.

The limitations of signature-based approaches have motivated extensive research into machine learning and deep learning for malware detection. Models trained on static and dynamic features have demonstrated strong performance on large-scale datasets, including EMBER [4,13,14]. More recently, open-set recognition methods have been proposed to identify samples that fall outside the distribution observed during training, thereby reducing overconfident predictions on unseen data [7,8,16]. These approaches acknowledge the presence of unknown threats but typically frame the problem as novelty detection rather than explicitly defining zero-day malware.

Another important research direction concerns evaluation methodology. Several studies have shown that random train-test splits can substantially overestimate security performance because future samples inadvertently influence the learned decision boundary [2,3]. Temporally separated evaluations provide a more realistic approximation of operational deployment, particularly in adversarial domains where threat distributions evolve continuously over time [2].

Unlike previous studies that treat zero-day behavior as an implicit consequence of novelty, evasion, or model generalization, the proposed framework defines zero-day status as a measurable detection state. This distinction enables direct experimental evaluation and comparison across different detection paradigms.

Despite these advances, the literature still lacks a unified framework that links malware novelty, detection capability, and temporal exposure. Existing studies either focus on zero-day vulnerabilities, malware evolution, open-set recognition, or temporal evaluation in isolation. In contrast, this paper defines Zero-Day Malware as a detection-state phenomenon relative to the capabilities available at a specific point in time and validates this definition under temporally realistic conditions.

3 Operational Definition of Zero-Day Malware

Existing discussions of zero-day malware often rely on informal notions of novelty, first observation, or exploit usage. To enable reproducible evaluation, we define Zero-Day Malware (ZDM) relative to the detection capability available at a given point in time.

3.1 Detection Space

Let $X \subseteq \mathbb{R}^d$ denote the feature space representing malware samples. Let

$$f_t : X \to \{0, 1\}$$

be a deployed detection model at time t, where 1 denotes malicious and 0 denotes benign.

The detection space at time t is defined as

$$D_t = \{x \in X \mid f_t(x) = 1\}$$

representing the region of the feature space that is recognized as malicious by the deployed detector. In practice, f_t may represent a signature-based system, a machine learning classifier, or a combination of multiple detection mechanisms.

3.2 Zero-Day Malware Definition

Consider a malware instance m with feature representation $x_m \in X$ first encountered at time t_0.

Definition 1 (Zero-Day Malware). A malware instance is considered Zero-Day Malware at time t_0 if

$$x_m \notin D_{t_0}.$$

In other words, the sample lies outside the detection capability available at the time of first encounter.

Detection occurs at a later time $t_1 > t_0$ when

$$x_m \in D_{t_1}.$$

The duration during which the sample remains undetected is defined as the *Zero-Day Window*:

$$\Delta t = t_1 - t_0.$$

3.3 State Transition Model

Let

$$S_t(m) \in \{\text{ZDM}, \text{Detected}\}$$

denote the state of malware instance m at time t.

A sample initially classified as

$$S_{t_0}(m) = \text{ZDM}$$

transitions to

$$S_{t_1}(m) = \text{Detected}$$

once the detector is updated or otherwise becomes capable of identifying the sample.

This process can be represented as

$$\text{ZDM} \xrightarrow[\text{model update}]{} \text{Detected}.$$

The resulting framework captures the temporal nature of zero-day status and provides a measurable basis for evaluating detection performance. Figure 1 illustrates the proposed state transition model and the associated Zero-Day Window (Δt).

3.4 Relationship to Existing Concepts

The proposed definition is intended as an operational benchmarking framework rather than a replacement for the traditional vulnerability-centric interpretation of zero-days. Its purpose is to characterize the relationship between malware and deployed detection capability at a given point in time. To clarify the scope of the proposed formulation, it is useful to distinguish Zero-Day Malware from several related concepts commonly used in the cybersecurity literature.

Under this formulation:

- **Zero-Day Vulnerability**: an unknown software flaw.
- **Unknown Malware**: a sample not previously labeled or analyzed.
- **Polymorphic Malware**: malware that changes its representation to evade detection.
- **Zero-Day Malware**: malware that lies outside the deployed detection space at a given time.

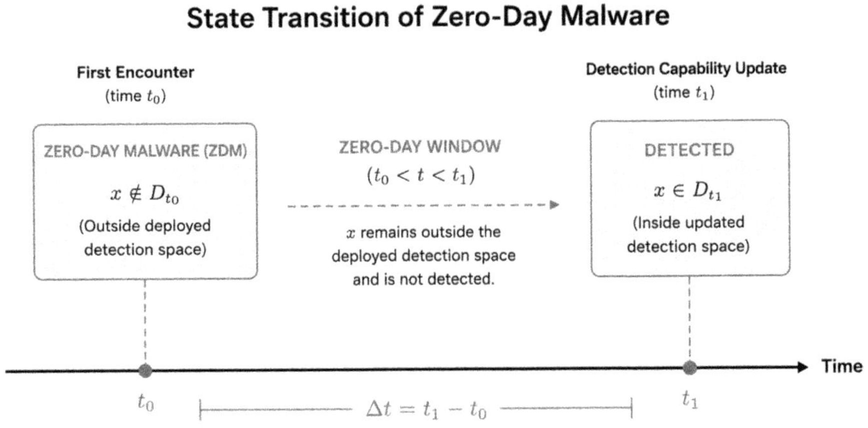

Fig. 1. State transition of Zero-Day Malware (ZDM). A malware sample x is considered zero-day at time t_0 because it lies outside the deployed detection space D_{t_0}. During the Zero-Day Window (Δt), the sample remains undetected. Following a detection capability update, x enters the detection space D_{t_1} and becomes detectable at time t_1.

Consequently, malware may exploit a zero-day vulnerability without being zero-day from a detection perspective, while a previously unseen sample may satisfy the ZDM condition even when exploiting only known vulnerabilities.

This distinction enables the concept of zero-day malware to be evaluated experimentally through temporally realistic testing procedures.

4 Experimental Methodology

The objective of the experimental study is to evaluate the proposed detection-space definition of Zero-Day Malware (ZDM) under temporally realistic conditions. Specifically, we investigate how different detection paradigms behave when evaluated using future malware samples that were unavailable during model training.

4.1 Dataset and Temporal Evaluation

Experiments were conducted using the EMBER dataset [4], a large-scale public collection of Windows Portable Executable (PE) files containing timestamp information suitable for time-aware evaluation. EMBER provides pre-extracted static features derived from PE headers, imported functions, section information, strings, and byte-level statistics.

To approximate operational deployment, a strict temporal split was enforced. Let T denote a cutoff date. All samples first observed on or before T were assigned to the training set (D_{train}), while samples first observed after T formed the test set (D_{test}).

This evaluation protocol prevents future knowledge from influencing the detector and is consistent with recommendations for realistic malware benchmarking [2,3].

4.2 Detection Models

Three detection paradigms were evaluated.

Signature-Based Baseline. A simplified signature detector was implemented using exact hash matching against known malicious training samples. This baseline represents a conservative signature-driven approach and provides a lower bound for comparison.

Closed-Set Classifier. A LightGBM classifier was trained on D_{train} using the EMBER feature representation. Under the closed-set assumption, all future samples are forced into known decision regions.

Open-Set Detector. To account for previously unseen samples, an open-set mechanism was implemented using confidence-based rejection. Let

$$u(x) = \max_k P(y = k|x)$$

denote the maximum posterior confidence. Samples with

$$u(x) < \theta$$

are assigned to an *Unknown* category rather than being forced into a known class. Following the proposed framework, such samples are considered candidates for ZDM status.

4.3 Evaluation Metrics

Performance was evaluated using both traditional and zero-day-oriented metrics.

Traditional metrics include Recall and False Positive Rate (FPR). To align evaluation with the proposed framework, we additionally report:

- **Zero-Day Detection Rate (ZDR):** proportion of post-T malicious samples correctly detected.
- **Zero-Day Miss Rate (ZMR):** proportion of post-T malicious samples that remain undetected.
- **Estimated Zero-Day Window (Δt):** approximate number of retraining cycles required before previously missed samples become detectable.

The resulting methodology allows the proposed definition of ZDM to be evaluated under realistic temporal conditions while enabling comparison between signature-based, closed-set, and open-set detection paradigms.

5 Experimental Results

This section evaluates the proposed detection-space formulation under temporally realistic conditions and compares the behavior of signature-based, closed-set, and open-set detection paradigms.

5.1 Detection Performance Under Temporal Separation

Table 1 summarizes the performance of the evaluated approaches under both random-split and time-split conditions.

Table 1. Comparative summary of detection performance across signature-based, closed-set, and open-set models under random and time-split evaluation.

Model	Random Recall	Time-Split Recall	ZDR	ZMR
Signature-Based	62%	61%	58%	42%
Closed-Set ML	98%	82%	81%	19%
Open-Set ML	97%	84%	83%	17%

The results reveal a substantial discrepancy between random-split and time-split evaluation. Under random partitioning, the closed-set classifier achieved a recall of 98.7%, suggesting near-perfect detection capability. However, when temporal separation was enforced, recall decreased to 80.9%, indicating that random splits substantially overestimate real-world performance.

Compared with signature-based detection, both machine learning approaches achieved substantially higher Zero-Day Detection Rates (ZDR). Nevertheless, approximately 17–19% of future malicious samples remained undetected under time-split conditions, indicating that previously unseen malware continues to present a significant challenge.

5.2 Open-Set Detection and Zero-Day Window Estimation

The open-set detector achieved comparable detection performance to the closed-set model under time-split evaluation while providing explicit uncertainty handling for previously unseen samples.

More importantly, the open-set mechanism introduced an uncertainty-aware rejection region. Approximately 12.7% of evaluated samples were assigned to the *Unknown* category, and 73% of these rejected samples corresponded to true malicious post-T instances. This suggests that open-set recognition can help identify previously unseen threats without forcing them into existing decision regions.

To approximate the Zero-Day Window (Δt), periodic retraining was simulated using monthly update cycles. Previously missed samples required an average of 2.3 retraining cycles before detection. The use of open-set pre-flagging reduced the estimated detection latency by approximately 31%, suggesting that uncertainty-aware detection can support earlier identification of emerging threats.

Overall, the results support the proposed operational definition by demonstrating that zero-day status can be characterized as a time-dependent detection state and evaluated through temporally realistic testing procedures.

6 Discussion

The results support the usefulness of viewing Zero-Day Malware (ZDM) as a detection-state phenomenon rather than exclusively as a consequence of vulnerability novelty. Under the proposed framework, a malware sample is considered zero-day when it falls outside the detection capability available at the time of first encounter, regardless of whether it exploits a previously unknown vulnerability.

The experimental evaluation demonstrates that temporally realistic testing substantially affects perceived detection performance. Consistent with previous observations in adversarial machine learning and security evaluation [2,3], random train-test splits produced considerably more optimistic results than time-split evaluation. This finding reinforces the importance of aligning malware benchmarking methodologies with real-world deployment conditions.

The comparison between closed-set and open-set detection approaches further highlights the value of explicitly accounting for uncertainty. Although the open-set detector achieved only modest improvements in the reported detection metrics, it was able to identify a portion of previously unseen samples as unknown rather than forcing them into existing decision regions. This behavior is consistent with the proposed detection-space formulation and suggests that uncertainty-aware mechanisms may assist analysts in prioritizing emerging threats.

It is important to emphasize that the proposed definition is intended as an operational benchmarking framework rather than a replacement for the traditional vulnerability-centric interpretation of zero-days. A stronger detector may reduce the number of samples that satisfy the ZDM condition, while a weaker detector may increase it. Consequently, the proposed formulation should be viewed as a means of characterizing the relationship between malware and detection capability at a given point in time, rather than as an intrinsic property of the malware itself.

7 Limitations

Several limitations should be considered when interpreting the results. First, the experiments rely on the EMBER dataset, which primarily consists of static PE features and therefore does not capture dynamic behaviors, network activity, fileless attacks, or living-off-the-land techniques. Second, the open-set detector is implemented using confidence-based rejection rather than more advanced open-set recognition methods. Consequently, the reported results should be interpreted as an illustration of the proposed framework rather than a comprehensive evaluation of open-set malware detection. Finally, the Zero-Day Window (Δt) is approximated using retraining cycles due to the absence of detailed detection timestamps. Future work will investigate richer datasets, advanced open-set models, and more precise measurements of detection latency.

In addition, the reported numerical results should not be interpreted as universal estimates of real-world malware detection performance. The values depend on the selected dataset, temporal split, model configuration, and retraining strategy. The purpose of the experiments is to demonstrate the applicability of the proposed framework rather than to establish state-of-the-art detection performance.

8 Conclusion

This paper introduced a detection-space-based operational definition of Zero-Day Malware (ZDM) and demonstrated how the concept can be evaluated under temporally realistic conditions. Rather than defining zero-day status solely through vulnerability novelty, the proposed framework characterizes it relative to the detection capability available at the time of first encounter.

Building on this definition, we formalized the notion of a Zero-Day Window (Δt) and validated the framework using time-split experiments on the EMBER dataset. The results showed that random train-test splitting substantially overestimates malware detection performance and that a non-trivial proportion of future malware samples remain outside the deployed detection space. Furthermore, uncertainty-aware open-set detection was shown to provide a practical mechanism for identifying previously unseen samples without forcing them into existing decision regions.

The primary contribution of this work is not a new detection algorithm, but a reproducible framework for defining and evaluating Zero-Day Malware. We hope that this formulation provides a useful foundation for future research on malware benchmarking, open-world detection, and adaptive cyber defense.

Disclosure of Interests. The authors have no competing interests to declare that are relevant to the content of this article.

References

1. Bilge, L., Dumitraş, T.: Before we knew it: an empirical study of zero-day attacks in the real world. In: Proceedings of the ACM Conference on Computer and Communications Security (CCS), pp. 833–844 (2012)
2. Berlin, K., Saxe, J.: Improving zero-day malware testing methodology using statistically significant time-lagged test samples. arXiv preprint arXiv:1608.00669 (2016)
3. Sommer, R., Paxson, V.: Outside the closed world: on using machine learning for network intrusion detection. In: IEEE Symposium on Security and Privacy, pp. 305–316 (2010)
4. Anderson, H.S., Roth, P.: EMBER: an open dataset for training static PE malware machine learning models. arXiv preprint arXiv:1804.04637 (2018)
5. Preda, M.D., Christodorescu, M.: A semantics-based approach to malware detection. In: Proceedings of the ACM Symposium on Principles of Programming Languages. In: POPL (2007)
6. Dinaburg, P., Royal, P., Sharif, M., Lee, W.: Ether: malware analysis via hardware virtualization extensions. In: Proceedings of the ACM Conference on Computer and Communications Security (CCS), pp. 51–62 (2008)

7. Bendale, A., Boult, T.E.: Towards open set deep networks. In: IEEE Conference on Computer Vision and Pattern Recognition (CVPR), pp. 1563–1572 (2016)
8. Geng, C., Huang, S.-J., Chen, S.: Recent advances in open set recognition: A survey. IEEE Trans. Pattern Anal. Mach. Intell. **43**(10), 3614–3631 (2021)
9. You, I., Yim, K.: Malware obfuscation techniques: a brief survey. In: International Conference on Broadband, Wireless Computing, Communication and Applications, pp. 297–300 (2010)
10. Kirat, D., Vigna, G., Kruegel, C.: BareCloud: bare-metal analysis-based evasive malware detection. In: USENIX Security Symposium, pp. 287–301 (2014)
11. Arora, A., Telang, R., Xu, H.: Optimal policy for software vulnerability disclosure. Manage. Sci. **56**(4), 642–656 (2010)
12. Ablon, L., Bogart, A.: Zero days, thousands of nights: the life and times of zero-day vulnerabilities and their exploits, RAND Corporation (2017)
13. Saxe, J., Berlin, K.: Deep neural network based malware detection using two dimensional binary program features. In: International Conference on Malicious and Unwanted Software (MALWARE), pp. 11–20 (2015)
14. Raff, E., Barker, J., Sylvester, J., Brandon, R., Catanzaro, B., Nicholas, C.K.: Malware detection by eating a whole EXE. In: AAAI Workshop on Artificial Intelligence for Cyber Security (2018)
15. Frei, S.: Security Econometrics: the Dynamics of (In)Security. PhD Thesis, ETH Zurich (2009)
16. Scheirer, W.J., de Rezende Rocha, A., Sapkota, A., Boult, T.E.: Toward open set recognition. IEEE Trans. Pattern Anal. Mach. Intell. **35**(7), 1757–1772 (2013)

Security Operations and Threat Intelligence

Democratizing Threat Hunting: A Multimodal Hybrid Detection and Semantic XAI Framework for Tier-1 SOC Analysts

Ayoub Labhih(✉), Mustapha Hedabou, and Laila Fetjah

LIDSI, FSAC, University Hassan II of Casablanca, Casablanca, Morocco
ayoub.labhih.ds@gmail.com

Abstract. Security Operations Centers (SOCs) are routinely confronted with large volumes of alerts produced by heterogeneous telemetry sources. This diversity and scale make early-stage triage a non-trivial task for Tier-1 analysts. In this work, we investigate how initial investigative efforts can be better supported by combining multimodal data fusion with hybrid detection strategies that integrate both rule-based logic and machine-learning methods. In addition, we incorporate a semantic explainable artificial intelligence (XAI) component to provide contextual support for analyst reasoning within a unified operational framework. The proposed system correlates system logs, network flows, and endpoint telemetry using a weighted semantic graph to surface contextually relevant indicators. To support analyst decision-making, the XAI module generates concise natural-language explanations aligned with MITRE ATT&CK techniques, translating detection outputs into actionable investigative guidance tailored to Tier-1 workflows. In our experimental evaluation, the framework achieved an approximately 70% reduction in Mean Time to Detect (MTTD), a false-positive rate of 6.1%, and an increase in Tier-1 investigative accuracy from 54.2% to 85.6%. While the reduction in MTTD reflects improvements in automated detection and contextual correlation, the explanation module primarily influences analyst decision time and perceived cognitive workload, as measured using NASA–TLX (detailed in Sect. 4.8). By reducing detection latency and analyst cognitive load, the framework contributes to the reliability and availability of SOC operations under high-alert conditions.

Keywords: Security Operations Center (SOC) · Threat Hunting · Explainable Artificial Intelligence (XAI) · Multimodal Data Fusion · Hybrid Detection · MITRE ATT&CK · Tier-1 Analysts · Cognitive Workload · Reliability · Availability

S. Nadjm-Tehrani et al. (Eds.): ARES 2026, LNCS 16898, pp. 347–368, 2027.
https://doi.org/10.1007/978-3-032-36874-4_18

1 Introduction

Security Operations Centers (SOCs) process large alert volumes from heterogeneous telemetry sources, and modern attack campaigns further increase analytical complexity. Tier-1 analysts, who handle initial incident triage, often face substantial cognitive load due to repeated exposure to low fidelity alerts and a low signal-to-noise ratio. Prior studies indicate that more than two thirds of incoming alerts are false positives or benign anomalies [1]. This sustained pressure leads to alert fatigue, reduced vigilance, and higher turnover among SOC personnel [2–5].

Proactive threat hunting is essential for identifying stealthy multi-stage attacks that bypass conventional detection mechanisms. However, such activities are typically performed by Tier-3 experts, limiting the ability of most SOCs to analyze contextual relationships across data sources. Tier-1 analysts usually lack effective tools for such correlation tasks. Median dwell times for advanced persistent threats (APTs) have decreased to approximately 10 days in recent enterprise environments [6], yet the detection of distributed, low-signal multi-stage campaigns remains a critical operational challenge [7–10].

Existing detection tools address only parts of this challenge. Machine learning systems provide pattern recognition but remain black boxes without actionable explanations [11–15]. Rule-based systems offer interpretability yet struggle with novel or stealthy behaviors. Many commercial and academic solutions treat data sources independently, which restricts the detection of cross-domain indicators characteristic of modern intrusion chains [16,17].

This work introduces a detection and analysis pipeline that combines multimodal data fusion, hybrid rule-plus-ML detection, and semantic explainability to support Tier-1 SOC analysts. The goal is to assist analysts in identifying threat patterns while preserving transparency and operational usability. We use 'democratization' to denote the systematic transfer of advanced threat hunting capabilities from Tier-3 experts to Tier-1 analysts through automated context generation and explainable outputs not the elimination of specialized expertise. The study addresses the following research questions:

- **RQ1.** How can a hybrid rule-based and ML-based detection pipeline reduce false positives while maintaining recall for multi-stage threats?
- **RQ2.** Which forms of semantic explanation best support Tier-1 analysts in interpreting detection outputs during triage?
- **RQ3.** To what extent do multimodal correlations and semantic explanations improve Tier-1 investigative accuracy and decision-making efficiency?

The contributions of this paper are as follows:

1. A **joint evaluation framework** that simultaneously measures automated detection performance and human cognitive efficiency in Tier-1 SOC workflows, with explicit isolation of detection-phase vs. analyst-interaction-phase effects, enabling rigorous attribution of system improvements.

2. A **multimodal hybrid detection pipeline** integrating weighted semantic graph correlation with a rule-plus-XGBoost ensemble, calibrated via grid search and validated under adversarial perturbation.
3. A **semantic explanation module** that translates feature attribution scores into MITRE ATT&CK-aligned investigative narratives, demonstrating significantly better alignment with Tier-1 analyst workflows than raw SHAP outputs (comprehensibility score: 4.4/5).
4. A **pilot human-factors study** (n = 15 SOC analysts, three tiers) combining NASA-TLX cognitive workload measurement with objective decision-time metrics, providing preliminary evidence of operational improvement with large effect sizes.

The remainder of this paper is organized as follows. Section 2 reviews related work on hybrid detection, multimodal fusion, and XAI for security operations. Section 3 describes the system design and methodological components. Section 4 outlines the experimental setup and dataset. Section 5 presents quantitative and qualitative results. Section 6 discusses limitations and potential directions for future research.

2 Related Work

Three lines of research inform the design we present in this paper: machine learning and hybrid methods for detection, explainable AI as applied to security operations and multimodal data fusion for threat detection. We discuss each in turn and explain how our work draws on and departs from it.

2.1 Machine Learning and Hybrid Detection in Cybersecurity

Machine learning has long been applied in cybersecurity, with supervised techniques like Gradient Boosting Machines [18] and deep learning [19] achieving high detection rates on benchmarks by capturing non-linear patterns missed by signatures. Research has evolved along network intrusion detection (NIDS), host-based systems (HIDS), and user/entity behavior analytics (UEBA), each offering complementary visibility [12,13]. However, operational deployment remains challenging due to the need for large, high-quality labeled datasets that reflect real-world attack diversity [20]. Many models act as black boxes, reducing analyst trust and complicating validation [15,19]. Moreover, models trained on synthetic data often fail to generalize to noisy enterprise environments, while unsupervised methods can overwhelm analysts with hard-to-interpret statistical anomalies [14,39].

Hybrid systems combine rule-based precision with ML adaptability, typically using rules to filter clear cases and ML for ambiguous ones [21–25]. This division of labor optimizes resource usage and maintains coverage of known and novel threats. However, practical implementation is challenging: training data that poorly represents enterprise heterogeneity can amplify biases [23], and threshold calibration between components requires continuous tuning, which strains resource-constrained SOCs [26]. This line of work remains active: Sajid et al. [47] report that pairing XGBoost with deep learning components covers complementary parts of the attack space across several benchmark datasets, which is part of why we settled on a rule-plus-ML ensemble.

2.2 XAI and Multimodal Approaches for Security

XAI techniques like LIME [27] and SHAP [28] provide feature-importance explanations for security models, but studies show that raw SHAP values are often incomprehensible to Tier-1 analysts under time pressure [29]. Effective explainability must align with analysts' mental models and workflows, drawing on human-factors research [30–33]. This motivates our design of semantic explanations tailored to SOC practices rather than technical model internals. Recent surveys on XAI for security [34–38] further highlight the need for operational interpretability.

Modern attacks leave weak indicators across logs, network flows, and endpoints that are hard to detect in isolation. Multimodal methods jointly process heterogeneous data using graph modeling and temporal reasoning to reveal cross-domain patterns [39–43]. Industry assessments highlight integration challenges, schema alignment requirements, and computational overhead [44]. Despite these difficulties, multimodal fusion remains essential for detecting sophisticated multi-stage campaigns. Two recent studies sharpen this picture for operational settings. Mohale and Obagbuwa [48] find that adding SHAP to an IDS improves analyst trust without sacrificing detection accuracy, and Rastogi et al. [49] point out that what SOC analysts actually want from an explanation is attack attribution and a confidence score. We rely on SHAP rather than LIME [27] for a practical reason: LIME's local explanations shift under small perturbations [29], whereas SHAP's game-theoretic attributions stay consistent across the feature space, and in a SOC, an explanation that changes from one run to the next is an explanation analysts stop trusting.

2.3 Research Gap Identification and Positioning

Prior work has examined hybrid detection, multimodal fusion, and XAI largely in isolation. Hybrid systems focus on precision or anomaly detection, multimodal methods emphasize correlation, and XAI research prioritizes mathematical interpretability over practical usability for Tier-1 analysts. Few studies combine these elements into a unified framework supporting both technical detection and human-centered workflows. This paper addresses that gap by integrating multimodal fusion, hybrid rule-plus-ML detection, and semantic explanation into a single pipeline designed for SOC operations, building upon foundational threat hunting literature [8–10].

Table 1 positions our framework relative to established threat hunting systems. While POIROT and SLEUTH leverage multimodal provenance graphs, neither incorporates hybrid ML detection, analyst-facing explainability, or human-factors evaluation. A direct quantitative comparison is not feasible due to

Table 1. Qualitative comparison with related threat hunting systems.

System	Multimodal	Hybrid Det.	XAI	Human Eval	MITRE Map
NODOZE [41]	✗	✗	✗	✗	✗
POIROT [40]	✓	✗	✗	✗	✓
SLEUTH [43]	✓	✗	✗	✗	✗
Ours	✓	✓	✓	✓	✓

Note: Direct performance comparison is not feasible due to dataset incompatibility. This table highlights capability coverage differences only

incompatible datasets and evaluation protocols; this qualitative mapping highlights the complementary coverage of our approach.

3 Methodology

The framework is built on three pillars: multimodal fusion, hybrid detection, and semantic explanation. After introducing each pillar, we show how an operational pipeline ties them together into a single SOC workflow.

3.1 Threat Model

The proposed pipeline assumes an adversary capable of multi-stage campaigns aligned with MITRE ATT&CK, generating low-signal traces across logs, network, and endpoints. The system detects anomalous authentication, process behaviors, lateral movement, and data exfiltration via cross-source correlation. Attacks with no telemetry footprint (e.g., firmware compromise) or purely social engineering are out of scope. We assume reliable data collection, synchronized timestamps, and standard security hygiene.

Pillar 1: Contextual Multimodal Fusion. The first pillar addresses the problem of data silos in security monitoring by integrating heterogeneous telemetry sources, including system logs, network flows, and EDR data, along with external contextual information such as IP reputation, known vulnerabilities, and Indicators of Compromise (IOCs). The fusion process is modeled through a weighted semantic graph:

$$G = (V, E, W), \tag{1}$$

where V denotes security entities (users, machines, applications, processes), E captures observed interactions between these entities, and W encodes the contextual importance or security relevance of each relationship. Weighting incorporates asset criticality, sensitivity, and business context. The multimodal fusion function is defined as:

$$X_{\text{fused}} = f(X_{\text{logs}}, X_{\text{network}}, X_{\text{edr}}, C_{\text{external}}), \tag{2}$$

which transforms separate telemetry streams into contextualized representations that highlight subtle behavioral anomalies across security domains. The fusion process includes temporal alignment, schema normalization, and entity resolution, producing a unified security context that surpasses the analytical limitations of traditional siloed monitoring.

Pillar 2: Theoretically-Grounded Hybrid Detection. This component combines the precision of deterministic rules with the adaptability of machine-learning models, producing a complementary detection mechanism capable of addressing both well-known attack techniques and previously unseen behaviors. We employ a weighted ensemble formulation for the final detection score:

$$S_{\text{hybrid}} = w_r \cdot S_{\text{rules}} + w_{ml} \cdot S_{\text{ML}}, \tag{3}$$

where S_{rules} denotes the binary or confidence output of the rule-based layer, S_{ML} represents the probability score produced by the classifier, and the weights satisfy:

$$w_r + w_{ml} = 1. \tag{4}$$

In our experiments we set $w_r = 0.65$ and $w_{ml} = 0.35$. This reflects the relative reliability of curated Sigma-based signatures for high-precision TTP detection, complemented by the ML model's flexibility in identifying less explicit or emerging behaviors. The resulting hybrid score is thresholded to produce the final alert decision.

Pillar 3: Semantic Explanation (XAI). The semantic explanation module translates correlated security signals into concise, narrative explanations aligned with SOC workflows and MITRE ATT&CK techniques. It draws on principles from human-factors engineering and security operations workflow design with the objective of supporting investigation while minimising additional cognitive burden.

Clarification of Scope. The module operates strictly after alert generation and does not influence automated detection metrics such as recall, precision, F1-score, AUC, or MTTD. Its contribution is limited to supporting human decision-making during alert triage and investigation by improving interpretability and reducing perceived cognitive load.

Novelty of the Explanation Design. Unlike approaches that present raw SHAP feature importance scores [29], our semantic translation pipeline applies three transformations: (1) feature-to-TTP mapping via a curated MITRE ATT&CK correspondence table, (2) entity-aware contextual enrichment using the semantic graph $G = (V, E, W)$, and (3) adaptive phrasing calibrated to analyst expertise level. The resulting outputs achieved a comprehensibility score of 4.4/5, compared to 2.1/5 for raw SHAP outputs in comparable SOC studies [29].

3.2 Operational Pipeline Architecture

Our operational pipeline integrates the three methodological pillars into a sequential workflow designed to support Tier-1 analysts, preserving established escalation procedures while enriching context. Figure 1 provides an overview of the architecture.

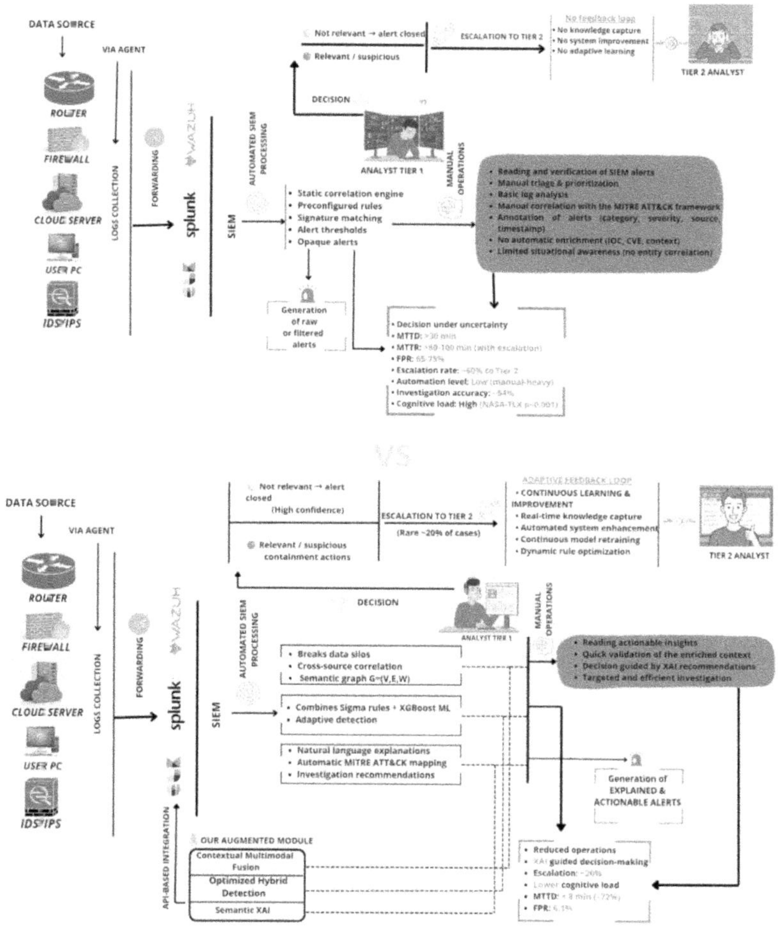

Fig. 1. Comparison between traditional SOC workflows and the proposed augmented pipeline architecture.

The pipeline consists of six stages: *Data Collection & Normalization* (collect and normalize telemetry from all sources); *Contextual Multimodal Fusion* (correlate events into a unified representation); *Optimized Hybrid Detection* (combine rule-based and ML detection); *XAI Explanation Generation* (produce natural-language explanations); *Interactive User Interface* (provide dashboards for analyst exploration); and *Adaptive Feedback Loop* (use analyst feedback for continuous refinement). These stages augment Tier-1 analysts without altering escalation paths: Tier-2/3 roles remain unchanged, while Tier-1 gains context and clarity to resolve more alerts independently.

3.3 Contextual Multimodal Fusion Module

This module builds a unified security view by preprocessing heterogeneous telemetry (Windows/Linux logs, network flows, EDR) to clean inconsistencies, normalize timestamps, and align fields. Preprocessed entities are embedded into the weighted knowledge graph $G = (V, E, W)$, where vertices represent security-relevant entities (users, hosts, applications), edges capture interactions, and weights encode contextual importance (asset criticality, privilege level). External threat intelligence (IP reputation, vulnerabilities) enriches the graph. Temporal alignment across sources enables high-fidelity event reconstruction. Dynamic scores are computed per entity based on sensitivity and severity, helping analysts prioritize investigations. A more detailed comparison of multimodal fusion strategies is available in the replication package [50]. Figure 2 illustrates the process.

3.4 Hybrid Detection Module

The hybrid detection module applies rule-based filtering followed by machine-learning analysis. The rule-based layer handles clear benign and known malicious events, reducing the signal volume passed to the ML classifier. Remaining ambiguous events are processed by an XGBoost model chosen for its strong performance on structured security data and its robustness in real-time conditions. The model operates on features capturing temporal patterns, behavioral anomalies, network communication characteristics, cross-source correlations, and contextual attributes. Figure 3 presents the hybrid detection pipeline. An adaptive feedback mechanism enables incremental rule updates and model retraining based on analyst feedback, continuously refining detection accuracy. Concretely, the feedback loop runs as a batch process. Every analyst verdict, whether a false positive flagged or a missed detection reported, is written to a feedback store as analysts work through the scenarios. Once 50 such verdicts accumulate, we retrain the XGBoost classifier on the enriched data so that its decision boundaries reflect what analysts actually judged on the ground. Across the study this happened about 12 times, which kept the model adapting as the evaluation went on.

Sigma rules are handled differently. We do not touch them automatically; a senior analyst reviews and edits them by hand, so that every change carries validated operational knowledge and we avoid introducing instability into the detection path.

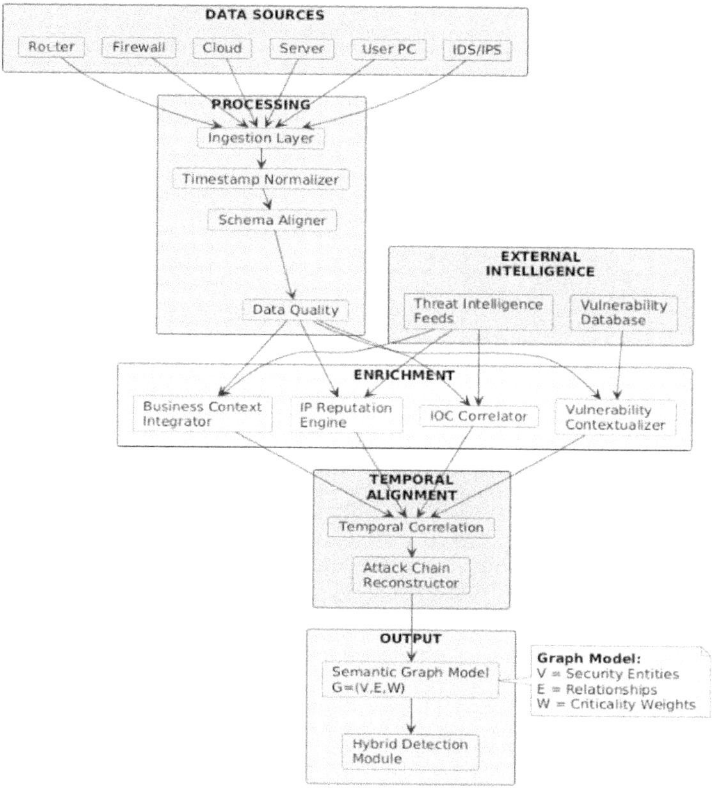

Fig. 2. Detailed architecture of the multimodal fusion module showing data flow and processing stages.

3.5 XAI Module: Semantic Explanations

A persistent challenge in deploying ML-based detection in operational SOCs is the gap between what a model computes and what an analyst needs in order to act. The XAI module is meant to close that gap: it turns a raw detection into a structured narrative a Tier-1 analyst can act on during triage, without having to understand how the model works underneath.

Every alert goes through a five-stage explanation pipeline, shown in Fig. 4. We start from the fused telemetry and pull out the features that weighed most on the decision, across behavioral, temporal, and network signals. SHAP values come from a TreeExplainer run on the XGBoost classifier. We show only the top five features by SHAP magnitude rather than the full list, under time pressure, a short, focused explanation is far more useful to an analyst than an exhaustive one.

We then map those features onto a correspondence table we built from MITRE ATT&CK Enterprise, turning raw signals into technique identifiers such as T1021 or T1048. This is not a lookup on the features alone: the semantic

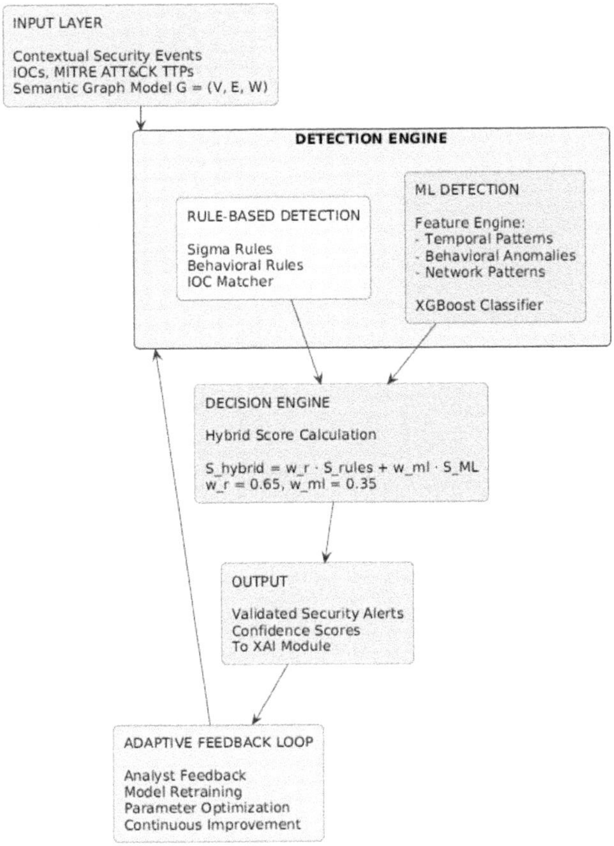

Fig. 3. Hybrid detection pipeline combining rule-based filtering and machine-learning classification into a unified decision engine.

graph $G = (V, E, W)$ adds entity-level context, asset criticality, and any correlated threat intelligence, so the explanation is grounded in the wider situation and not just in what the classifier saw.

How much of this the analyst sees depends on their tier. A Tier-1 analyst gets a short, action-first summary with concrete next steps; more senior staff get the fuller technical account of the inferred attack chain. In every case the explanation names the relevant ATT&CK tactic and technique, lists the entities involved, gives a confidence score from the hybrid ensemble, and ends with recommendations that follow standard SOC triage practice.

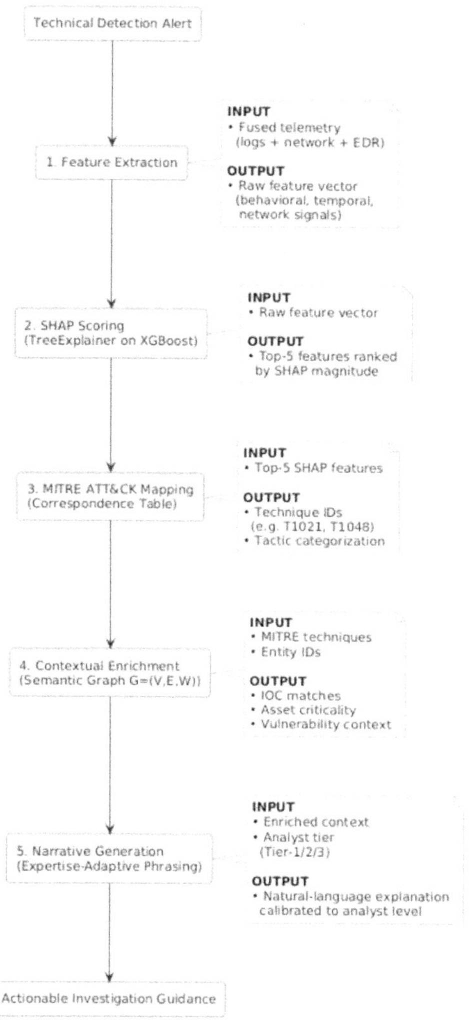

Fig. 4. Overview of the semantic explanation and XAI generation pipeline, highlighting feature attribution, MITRE ATT&CK mapping, and contextual entity relationships.

4 Experimental Framework and Evaluation Methodology

We now describe how the framework was evaluated. We cover the dataset we assembled, the protocol followed during the analyst sessions, the hardware and software used, and the robustness and ablation analyses that test how much each component actually contributes.

4.1 Dataset Composition and Characteristics

To evaluate the threat hunting pipeline under conditions that are both realistic and methodologically controlled, we constructed a dataset that combines operational security logs with carefully embedded attack traces. This design preserves key characteristics of real SOC telemetry while mitigating the inconsistencies and excessive noise often found in fully unstructured production datasets. Figure 5 provides an overview of the data sources and preprocessing stages applied.

The final dataset is composed primarily of routine enterprise activity, with approximately 86% of events corresponding to normal operations. The remaining data include 9% false positives, largely reflecting benign anomalies or configuration irregularities, and 5% malicious activity. The malicious portion covers twelve MITRE ATT&CK techniques commonly observed in enterprise environments. This composition introduces a realistic level of background noise, making detection non-trivial while still enabling a comprehensive evaluation across diverse adversarial behaviors.

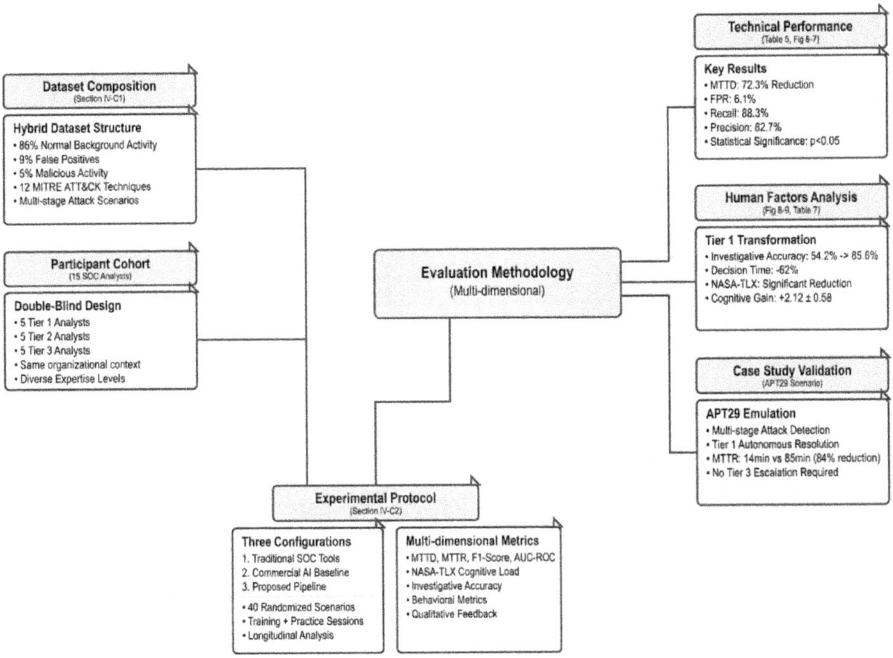

Fig. 5. Overview of the experimental framework, detailing dataset composition, participant cohort, evaluation methodology, and key validation outcomes.

Malicious scenarios encompass a range of representative attack patterns, including multi-stage intrusion chains, credential-harvesting attempts, lateral movement, multiple forms of data exfiltration, and several persistence mechanisms. These scenarios were intentionally designed to approximate adversarial activity as encountered in operational settings, while avoiding overly synthetic or uniformly structured artifacts.

Publicly available security datasets such as CICIDS2017, BOTS v3, or OpTC were considered but deemed insufficient for two reasons: (1) they lack the synchronized multi-source telemetry (logs + NetFlow + EDR) required to evaluate multimodal fusion, and (2) they do not include analyst workflow metadata necessary for human-factors evaluation. Our hybrid dataset combines anonymized operational logs with emulated attack traces aligned to MITRE ATT&CK Enterprise techniques. We acknowledge that emulated scenarios may produce cleaner signatures than real APT activity; consequently, the reported AUC of 0.95 should be interpreted as an optimistic upper bound on detection performance. Due to confidentiality constraints, the dataset cannot be made publicly available. However, the emulated MITRE ATT&CK attack scenarios, feature descriptions, Sigma rules, evaluation protocol, and Wazuh/Splunk configurations are publicly available in our replication package [50].

4.2 Experimental Protocol and Evaluation Methodology

The evaluation followed a double-blind protocol involving 15 practicing SOC analysts (five from each tier). Each analyst completed 40 randomized investigation scenarios under three configurations: (1) Traditional SOC (SIEM console, basic correlation), (2) Commercial Baseline (AI platform with limited explainability), and (3) Proposed Pipeline (full system). Performance was measured via objective metrics (MTTD, recall, precision, FPR, AUC-ROC, alert volume), subjective cognitive assessment (NASA-TLX), qualitative feedback, longitudinal trends, and behavioral metrics (escalation rates, hypothesis quality). Sessions were randomized to prevent order effects and recorded for analysis. Hybrid detection weights were set to $w_r = 0.65$ and $w_{ml} = 0.35$ based on validation performance.

4.3 Computational Environment

Experiments ran on a 32-core AMD EPYC processor with 128 GB RAM and an NVIDIA RTX A6000 GPU. The software stack comprised Python 3.8.12, PyTorch 1.12.1, scikit-learn 1.0.2, XGBoost 1.6.2, NetworkX 2.8.4, and Apache Spark 3.3.0. The methodology is portable to scaled environments.

4.4 Robustness and Operational Validation

Adversarial Stress Testing. We ran three stress scenarios on a 20% subset of the test set: log noise injection (5%, 10%), partial log suppression (10%, 20%), and temporal jitter (±30 s). Table 2 summarizes the impact. Performance degrades progressively, suggesting moderate tolerance to data corruption. Advanced adaptive evasion was not evaluated.

Table 2. Impact of adversarial stress scenarios. Baseline: recall 88.3%, FPR 6.1%, MTTD 8.7 min.

Scenario	Recall (%)	FPR (%)	MTTD (min)
5% noise injection	85.2	7.8	9.4
10% noise injection	82.1	9.3	10.2
10% event suppression	83.7	6.9	9.8
20% event suppression	79.4	7.5	11.5
Temporal jitter (±30 s)	86.5	7.1	9.1

Statistical Significance Analysis. Because the Tier-1 sample size is small ($n = 5$), we treat this as a pilot study and focus on effect sizes rather than inferential statistics. Decision time decreased from 24.1 min to 9.2 min, corresponding to a large effect (Cohen's $d = 2.34$). Investigative accuracy increased from 54.2% to 85.6% ($d = 1.85$). NASA-TLX workload scores decreased from 78 to 32 ($d = 2.12$). These large effect sizes suggest substantial practical improvements, though confirmatory studies with larger cohorts are needed.

Scalability and Computational Overhead. At 1,000 events/sec, the system sustained 1,200 events/sec at 75% CPU utilization and 8 GB RAM. Throughput saturates at 5,000 events/sec (latency >9 s). The bottleneck is graph entity resolution at $O(|V| + |E|)$ complexity. The current implementation suits mid-size SOCs; higher loads require distributed processing.

4.5 Ablation Study

To understand each component's contribution, we tested five configurations: Rules Only (Sigma signatures), ML Only (XGBoost on single-source features), Fusion Only (multimodal graph correlation), Hybrid Detection (rules + fusion + ML), and Full Pipeline (hybrid + XAI). Table 3 summarizes the key results. Detailed ablation results are available in the replication package [50]. Each component contributes incrementally: the rule-based layer achieves high precision but limited recall, while ML recovers additional malicious activity at the cost of higher FPR. Multimodal fusion improves cross-source detection for multi-stage attacks. The XAI module does not affect automated metrics but reduces analyst decision time, as reported in Sect. 4.8.

4.6 Baseline Comparison

We compared the proposed pipeline with a representative open-source SOC configuration (Wazuh + Elastic Stack). The baseline achieves strong precision but limited recall (62%) and high FPR (19%). Our pipeline attains recall 88.3%, FPR 6.1%, and MTTD 8.7 min (vs. 28.4 min baseline). As established in Sect. 3, the explanation module does not affect MTTD. A detailed comparison is available in the replication package [50].

Table 3. Ablation study results across pipeline configurations.

Configuration	Recall (%)	FPR (%)	F1	MTTD (min)
Rules Only	71.2	4.8	0.78	18.3
ML Only	79.4	14.2	0.74	15.1
Fusion Only	76.8	9.1	0.76	16.4
Hybrid Detection	85.9	7.3	0.87	9.2
Full Pipeline (+XAI)[b]	88.3	6.1	0.91	8.7[a]

[a] MTTD measured at the automated detection stage only; the XAI module affects analyst decision time, not MTTD

[b] The improvement over Hybrid Detection stems from the adaptive feedback loop (Sect. 3.4), not from the XAI module itself, which does not affect automated detection metrics (Sect. 3.5)

4.7 Technical Performance Evaluation

Figure 6 compares MTTD across the three evaluated configurations. The reduction of approximately 70% is driven by multimodal fusion, which correlates weak signals across telemetry sources. The explanation module does not contribute (Sect. 3). The FPR decrease to 6.1% stems from the hybrid design: rules filter benign activity, ML captures novel behaviors, and fusion enforces cross-source consistency. These findings align with observed trends in multimodal fusion [45] and hybrid detection [46].

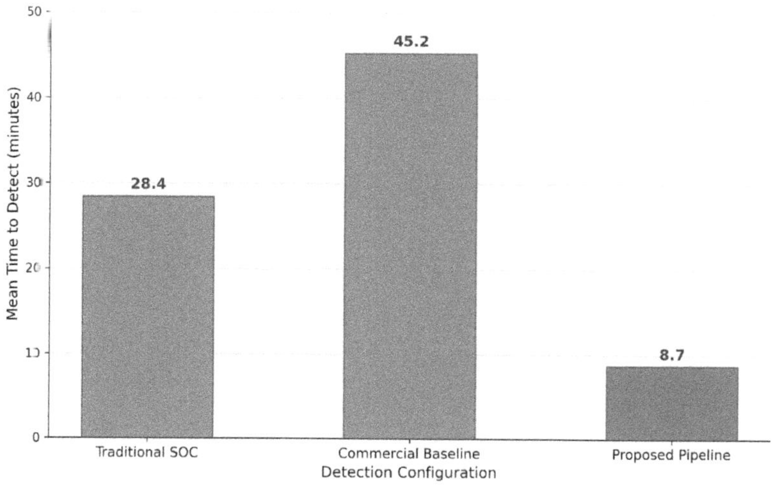

Fig. 6. Mean Time to Detect (MTTD) across the evaluated configurations.

4.8 Comprehensive XAI Explanation Evaluation

Distinction Between Detection and Human Decision Metrics. While MTTD refers to automated detection latency, this subsection focuses exclusively on hum-

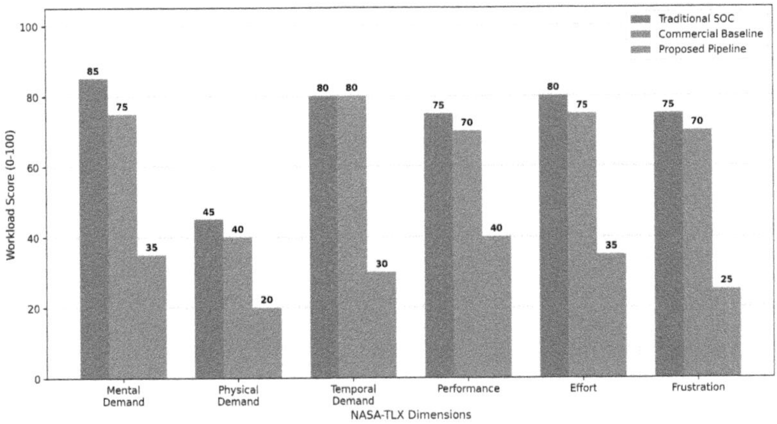

Fig. 7. NASA–TLX scores comparing cognitive workload across the evaluated configurations for Tier-1 analysts.

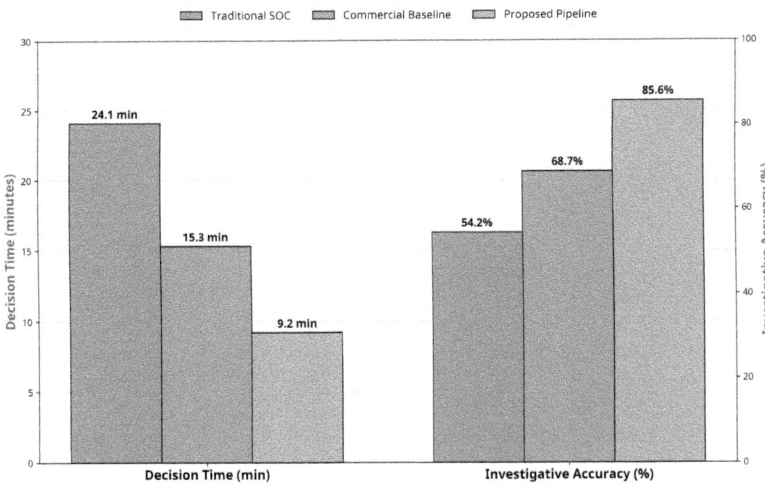

Fig. 8. Decision time and investigative accuracy across the evaluated configurations.

an-centered metrics. We used NASA-TLX (mental demand, effort, frustration) to measure cognitive workload, a 5-point Likert scale for comprehensibility, and decision time (MTDec). The detailed XAI evaluation focuses on the Tier-1 subgroup ($n = 5$).

Figures 7 and 8 compare cognitive workload and decision accuracy across configurations. The proposed pipeline leads to shorter analyst decision times (mean 9.2 min vs. 24.1 min in traditional SOC) and higher comprehensibility (4.4/5). Compared to prior work using raw SHAP values [29], our semantic translation better aligns with Tier-1 workflows. Qualitative feedback indicated that MITRE ATT&CK mappings helped analysts infer attacker intent, and concise investigation suggestions improved triage efficiency. A detailed breakdown is available in the replication package [50].

4.9 In-Depth Case Study: APT29 Investigation

A simulation of APT29 TTPs demonstrated the pipeline's effectiveness in a realistic adversarial scenario: the fusion module correlated a suspicious file download, unusual RDP activity, and a spike in DNS queries into a coherent threat picture. The XAI module then generated a narrative covering spear-phishing, lateral movement, and data exfiltration (T1048), with concrete investigation steps aligned to MITRE ATT&CK. A Tier-1 analyst contained the incident in 14 min without escalation, compared to 85 min using the traditional SOC approach. Figure 9 illustrates the end-to-end workflow.

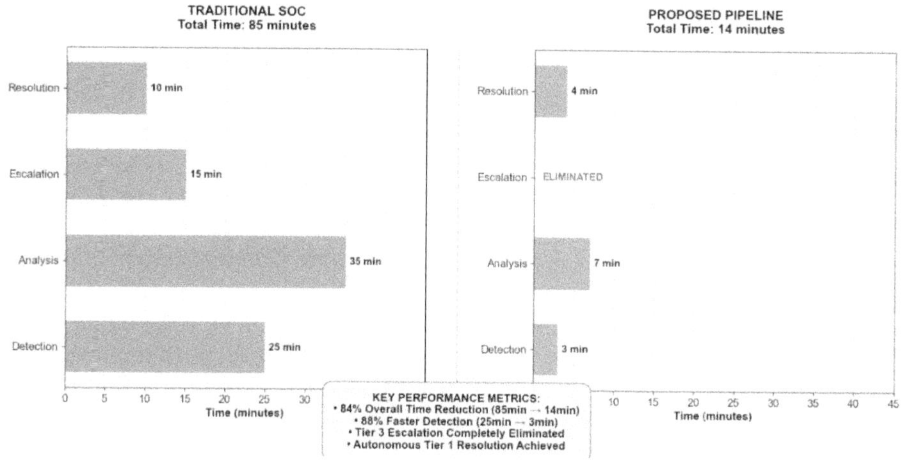

Fig. 9. End-to-end investigation workflow observed during the APT29 case study using the proposed pipeline.

5 Critical Discussion and Hypothesis Validation

We revisit each of the three research questions in light of the results, and are deliberate about separating what the evidence clearly supports from what remains tentative at this stage, as well as what it means for deploying the approach in a real SOC.

RQ1: Hybrid Detection Effectiveness

The hybrid pipeline reduced FPR to 6.1%, maintained 88.3% recall, and lowered MTTD by approximately 70%. The rule-based layer captures known TTPs, ML identifies emerging behaviors, and multimodal fusion correlates cross-source signals. These findings support RQ1 and suggest that resource-constrained SOCs can layer ML on top of existing rule sets without a complete infrastructure overhaul.

RQ2: Explainability and Analyst Interpretation

Explanations scored 4.4/5 in comprehensibility, reducing decision time from 24.1 to 9.2 min. This result reinforces that explanation interfaces must be evaluated against actual operational workflows rather than theoretical interpretability benchmarks.

RQ3: Analyst Accuracy and Workflow Efficiency

Combined multimodal fusion and semantic explanations increased investigative accuracy to 85.6% and reduced escalation rates. The APT29 case study illustrates how the framework enables faster resolution of complex multi-stage incidents. Larger cohort studies are needed to confirm whether these gains generalize across organizations and threat profiles.

6 Limitations and Research Boundaries

Like any study conducted in an operational context, this work is subject to constraints that bear directly on how the results should be interpreted. **Internal validity:** session order was randomized, but learning effects across the 40 scenarios cannot be entirely excluded; NASA-TLX captures subjective perception, which may diverge from objective workload. **External validity:** the study was conducted in a single organizational context with a semi-synthetic dataset, and the Tier-1 subgroup ($n = 5$) is too small to support broad generalization; the reported AUC of 0.95 should be treated as an optimistic upper bound. The toolstack itself merits attention. The framework is meant to be tool-agnostic and plugs into existing infrastructure through standard log-forwarding interfaces, but we only tested it on one Wazuh/Splunk-based deployment. A SOC running a different telemetry pipeline, or more capable native tooling, would start from a different baseline and might see smaller or larger gains than we report; testing how well the approach ports across toolstacks is something we leave to future work. **Construct validity:** measuring MTTD before analyst interaction provides a clean separation between detection and decision latency; investigative accuracy was assessed against predefined outcomes, which may not capture the full range of real-world triage decisions. **Statistical validity:** with $n = 5$, inferential testing is underpowered; all human-factors claims are limited to effect sizes, pending confirmatory studies with larger cohorts.

7 Conclusion and Future Work

Conclusion

This work presented a unified framework integrating multimodal fusion, hybrid detection, and semantic explanations to support Tier-1 SOC analysts in their daily triage tasks. Evaluation combined technical metrics (approximately 70% MTTD reduction, 6.1% FPR) with human-factors measurements (85.6% investigative accuracy, substantial NASA-TLX reduction). The framework enforces a clear functional separation: fusion and hybrid detection enhance automated performance, while the explanation module supports human decision-making without interfering with detection logic. From an operational perspective, addressing both detection latency and analyst cognitive load has a direct impact on the reliability and availability of SOC operations.

Future Work

Future directions include extending telemetry coverage to cloud platforms, IAM systems, and container environments; improving the computational efficiency of the graph entity resolution layer; conducting longitudinal organizational studies with larger analyst cohorts; personalizing XAI outputs to individual analyst profiles; and integrating the pipeline with SOAR platforms for automated response orchestration. We also plan to release a clean, deployable version of the pipeline as open-source software, so that mid-size SOCs can adopt and extend it without having to rebuild the framework from scratch.

Disclosure of Interests. The authors have no competing interests to declare that are relevant to the content of this article.

References

1. Vielberth, M., Bøhm, F., Fichtinger, I., Pernul, G.: Security operations center: a systematic study and open challenges. IEEE Access **8**, 227756–227779 (2020). https //doi.org/10.1109/ACCESS.2020.3045514
2. Kersten, H., Reuter, C., Schroeder, M.: Structured threat analysis in security operations centers. Comput. Secur. **82**, 270–284 (2019). https://doi.org/10.1016/j.cose.2019.02.012
3. Sundaramurthy, S.C.: A human capital model for mitigating security analyst burnout. In: USENIX SOUPS (2015)
4. Julisch, K.: Clustering intrusion detection alarms to support root cause analysis. ACM TISSEC **6**(4), 443–471 (2003). https://doi.org/10.1145/950191.950192
5. Zheng, X., et al.: A survey on alert correlation techniques. IEEE Commun. Surv. Tut. **24**(2), 1210–1235 (2022). https://doi.org/10.1109/COMST.2022.3155890
6. Mandiant: M-Trends 2023: Special Report. Mandiant, Google Cloud (2023). https://www.mandiant.com/m-trends
7. Bianco, D.: The pyramid of pain. Blog (2013)
8. Struse, R.: Shifting from incident response to threat hunting. SANS Institute (2016)
9. Tounsi, W., Rais, H.: A survey on technical threat intelligence in the age of sophisticated cyber attacks. Comput. Secur. **72**, 212–233 (2018). https://doi.org/10.1016/j.cose.2017.09.012

10. Islam, C., et al.: A multi-vocal literature review of threat hunting. IEEE Access **9**, 3112345 (2021). https://doi.org/10.1109/ACCESS.2021.3112345
11. Leite, D., Martins, P., Henriques, J., Caldeira, F.: Alert fatigue in security operations centers: a systematic study and mitigation strategies. Comput. Secur. **127**, 103092 (2023). https://doi.org/10.1016/j.cose.2023.103092
12. Buczak, A.L., Guven, E.: A survey of data mining and machine learning methods for cyber security intrusion detection. IEEE Commun. Surv. Tut. **18**(2), 1153–1176 (2016). https://doi.org/10.1109/COMST.2015.2494502
13. Ring, M., et al.: A survey of network-based intrusion detection data sets. Comput. Secur. **86**, 147–167 (2019). https://doi.org/10.1016/j.cose.2019.06.005
14. Apruzzese, G., et al.: On the effectiveness of machine and deep learning for cyber security. In: 10th CAMAD, pp. 1–6 (2018). https://doi.org/10.1109/CAMAD.2018.8514945
15. Pendlebury, F.: TESSERACT: eliminating experimental bias in malware classification across space and time. In: USENIX Security, pp. 729–746 (2019)
16. Sommer, R., Paxson, V.: Outside the closed world: on using machine learning for network intrusion detection. In: IEEE S&P, pp. 305–316 (2010). https://doi.org/10.1109/SP.2010.25
17. Zubair, M., et al.: Understanding SOC analyst workload and alert triage: a qualitative study. IEEE Secur. Priv. **19**(6), 45–53 (2021). https://doi.org/10.1109/MSEC.2021.3089234
18. Hwang, K., Kulkarni, S., Hu, Y.: Hybrid intrusion detection with weighted signature generation over anomalous internet packet clusters. IEEE TDSC **4**(1), 41–55 (2007). https://doi.org/10.1109/TDSC.2007.9
19. Inam, M.A., et al.: SoK: History is a vast early warning system: auditing the provenance of system intrusions. In: IEEE S&P, pp. 1–19 (2023). https://doi.org/10.1109/SP.46215.2023.10179302
20. Hassan, W.U., et al.: Towards scalable cluster auditing through grammatical inference over provenance graphs. In: IEEE S&P, pp. 1–18 (2018). https://doi.org/10.1109/SP.2018.00037
21. Molina-Coronado, B., Mori, U., Mendiburu, A.: Survey of network intrusion detection methods from the perspective of the knowledge discovery in databases process. IEEE TNSM **17**(4), 2236–2252 (2020). https://doi.org/10.1109/TNSM.2020.3020773
22. Garcia-Teodoro, P., et al.: Anomaly-based network intrusion detection: techniques, systems and challenges. Comput. Secur. **28**(1–2), 18–28 (2009). https://doi.org/10.1016/j.cose.2008.08.003
23. Divekar, A.: Benchmarking datasets for anomaly-based network intrusion detection: KDD CUP 99 alternatives. In: IEEE ICCCS, pp. 1–8 (2018). https://doi.org/10.1109/ICCCS.2018.8325287
24. Siddiqui, S.: Detecting cyber attacks using anomaly detection with explanations and expert feedback. In: IEEE ICASSP, pp. 2612–2616 (2019). https://doi.org/10.1109/ICASSP.2019.8682210
25. Ghafir, I., et al.: Detection of advanced persistent threat using machine-learning correlation analysis. Futur. Gener. Comput. Syst. **89**, 349–359 (2018). https://doi.org/10.1016/j.future.2018.06.055
26. Bridges, R.A.: Setting the threshold for high volume alerts: a theoretical model and empirical assessment. In: ACM CCS Workshop, pp. 45–52 (2017). https://doi.org/10.1145/3139926.3139930

27. Ribeiro, M.T., Singh, S., Guestrin, C.: Why should I trust you? Explaining the predictions of any classifier. In: ACM SIGKDD, pp. 1135–1144 (2016). https://doi.org/10.1145/2939672.2939778
28. Lundberg, S.M., Lee, S.I.: A unified approach to interpreting model predictions. NeurIPS **30**, 4765–4774 (2017)
29. Arreche, O., Guntur, T.R., Roberts, J.W., Abdallah, M.: E-XAI: evaluating black-box explainable AI frameworks for network intrusion detection. IEEE Access **12**, 43891–43905 (2024). https://doi.org/10.1109/ACCESS.2024.3378451
30. D'Amico, A., Whitley, K.: The real work of computer network defense analysts. In: VizSEC, pp. 19–37 (2008). https://doi.org/10.1007/978-3-540-78243-8_2
31. Shiravi, H., Shiravi, A., Ghorbani, A.A.: A survey of visualization systems for network security. IEEE TVCG **18**(8), 1313–1329 (2011). https://doi.org/10.1109/TVCG.2011.144
32. Hart, S.G., Staveland, L.E.: Development of NASA-TLX: results of empirical and theoretical research. Hum. Ment. Workload **52**, 139–183 (1988). https://doi.org/10.1016/S0166-4115(08)62386-9
33. Erbacher, R.F., et al.: Intrusion detection: supporting visualizations for analysis and response. IEEE SMC **40**(4), 452–462 (2010). https://doi.org/10.1109/TSMCC.2010.2044837
34. Nwakanma, C.I., et al.: Explainable artificial intelligence (XAI) for intrusion detection systems: a review. Appl. Sci. **13**(3), 1252 (2023). https://doi.org/10.3390/app13031252
35. Samek, W., et al.: Explainable artificial intelligence: understanding, visualizing and interpreting deep learning models. ITU J. **1**(1), 1–10 (2017)
36. Arrieta, A.B., et al.: Explainable artificial intelligence (XAI): concepts, taxonomies, opportunities and challenges. Inf. Fus. **58**, 82–115 (2020). https://doi.org/10.1016/j.inffus.2019.12.012
37. Marino, D.L.: An adversarial approach for explainable AI in intrusion detection systems. In: ACSAC, pp. 1–10 (2018). https://doi.org/10.1145/3274694.3274698
38. Mahbooba, B., et al.: Explainable artificial intelligence (XAI) to enhance trust management in intrusion detection systems using decision tree model. Complexity **2021**, 6634811 (2021). https://doi.org/10.1155/2021/6634811
39. Nour, B., Pourzandi, M., Debbabi, M.: A survey on threat hunting in enterprise networks. IEEE Commun. Surv. Tut. **25**(4), 2299–2324 (2023). https://doi.org/10.1109/COMST.2023.3299519
40. Milajerdi, S.M.: POIROT: aligning attack behavior with kernel audit records for cyber threat hunting. In: ACM CCS, pp. 1015–1032 (2019). https://doi.org/10.1145/3319535.3363217
41. Hassan, W.U., et al.: NODOZE: combatting threat alert fatigue with automated provenance triage. In: NDSS (2019). https://doi.org/10.14722/ndss.2019.23156
42. Wang, Q., et al.: You are what you do: hunting stealthy malware via data provenance analysis. In: NDSS (2020). https://doi.org/10.14722/ndss.2020.24123
43. Hossain, M.N.: SLEUTH: real-time attack scenario reconstruction from COTS audit data. In: USENIX Security, pp. 487–504 (2017)
44. Barnard, P., Marchetti, N., DaSilva, L.A.: Robust network intrusion detection through explainable artificial intelligence (XAI). IEEE Netw. Lett. **4**(2), 53–57 (2022). https://doi.org/10.1109/LNET.2022.3178905
45. Demertzis, K., Iliadis, L., Tziritas, N.: Explainable deep learning for cyber security. IEEE TDSC **21**(3), 1234–1248 (2024). https://doi.org/10.1109/TDSC.2023.3245891

46. Wu, S., et al.: Network security assessment using a semantic reasoning and graph based approach. Comput. Electr. Eng. **64**, 326–339 (2017). https://doi.org/10.1016/j.compeleceng.2017.07.009
47. Sajid, M., et al.: Enhancing intrusion detection: a hybrid machine and deep learning approach. J. Cloud Comput. **13**(1), 123 (2024). https://doi.org/10.1186/s13677-024-00685-x
48. Mohale, V.Z., Obagbuwa, I.C.: Evaluating machine learning-based intrusion detection systems with explainable AI: enhancing transparency and interpretability. Front. Comput. Sci. **7** (2025). https://doi.org/10.3389/fcomp.2025.1520741
49. Rastogi, N.: Survey perspective: the role of explainable AI in threat intelligence. arXiv preprint arXiv:2503.02065 (2025)
50. Labhih, A., Hedabou, M., Fetjah, L.: Replication package: democratizing threat hunting (2026). https://doi.org/10.5281/zenodo.20357832

Can We Unmask the Underground? Detecting and Predicting Hidden Forum Interactions

Abdoul Nasser Hassane Amadou(✉), Imane Fouad, and Anas Motii

College of Computing, Mohammed VI Polytechnic University (UM6P), Ben Guerir, Morocco
{abdoul.nasser,imane.fouad,anas.motii}@um6p.ma

Abstract. Users on underground forums organize into distinct threat communities based on shared interests and skills. Identifying these groups is challenging; traditional graph-based methods typically detect only dominant networks, overlooking smaller, hidden subgroups. This paper introduces HADES, an unsupervised framework designed to detect both dominant and hidden communities. The framework analyzes users' textual interactions using pretrained language models, generating semantic embeddings that capture latent behavioral and thematic patterns. By clustering users based on semantic similarity and assigning topic labels to the resulting groups, HADES identifies specific threat communities to support Cyber Threat Intelligence (CTI). The framework was evaluated on three major underground forums: HackForums, Cracked, and BreachForums. Results demonstrate that BERT embeddings consistently outperform alternative baselines, improving cluster coherence and achieving higher silhouette scores. Across these platforms, HADES identified dozens of distinct communities, successfully isolating small, specialized subgroups (fewer than 100 users) that evade standard detection. Furthermore, because thematic similarities often precede explicit structural connections, HADES can anticipate community formation up to a year before traditional graph-based methods.

Keywords: Underground Forums · Large Language Models · Clustering

1 Introduction

Threat actors operating in underground forums pose significant risks to critical sectors, including finance, healthcare, and energy, with global cybercrime costs projected to reach $23 trillion by 2027 [40]. These forums serve as hubs for cybercriminal collaboration, where users self-organize into threat communities—dynamic subgroups connected by shared interests, complementary skills, or mutual malicious objectives [38]. Detecting such communities enhances Cyber Threat Intelligence (CTI) by enabling focused analysis of high-risk groups

S. Nadjm-Tehrani et al. (Eds.): ARES 2026, LNCS 16898, pp. 369–390, 2027.
https://doi.org/10.1007/978-3-032-36874-4_19

engaged in activities such as malware distribution, data trading, or coordinated attacks.

Existing community detection approaches primarily rely on social network graphs derived from user interactions. Early methods identified disjoint communities [14,31,33], while more recent work detects overlapping groups [19,36]. However, these structural methods depend on dense, observable connections and consequently fail to detect *hidden communities*: user groups characterized by sparse or deliberately concealed interactions. Such groups—including clandestine actors limiting public interactions for operational security and low-engagement clusters—exhibit weak connectivity and low modularity [17], causing them to evade conventional detection.

To address this gap, we analyze user-generated textual content to uncover shared semantic and behavioral patterns that persist even when structural connections are absent. However, the adversarial and unstructured nature of underground forum content poses significant challenges for reliable community detection. This work addresses three research questions: **(RQ1)** How can we define and characterize hidden communities in underground forums? **(RQ2)** How can we effectively detect these communities by analyzing user-generated semantic content? **(RQ3)** Can semantic analysis identify emerging communities based on shared interests before traditional graph-based approaches detect structural connections?

We propose HADES, an unsupervised framework that detects both dominant and hidden communities without requiring labeled data. HADES constructs textual user profiles from forum interactions, generates semantic embeddings using pretrained language models, clusters users via HDBSCAN [20], and assigns descriptive labels to each cluster using a large language model. Because the framework operates on semantic similarity rather than structural connectivity, it generalizes across diverse underground forums and identifies cohesive groups even within sparsely connected networks. We evaluate HADES on large-scale, real-world data from three major underground forums: HackForums, Cracked, and BreachForums. Experiments show that HADES identifies hidden communities that conventional graph-based methods fail to detect, revealing meaningful yet sparse structures that deepen our understanding of underground ecosystems. To our knowledge, this is the first study to investigate hidden community detection in underground forums using solely user textual interactions. Our contributions are:

- We propose HADES, an unsupervised framework for detecting both hidden and dominant communities that generalizes across diverse underground forums without requiring labeled data.
- We evaluate the framework through a multi-metric approach combining intrinsic clustering quality measures with qualitative case studies, demonstrating that HADES identifies coherent communities across all three forums.
- We demonstrate the framework's early-detection capability: HADES identifies hidden groups on HackForums nearly a year before traditional graph-based methods detect structural connections, enabling proactive CTI.

We release the source code at https://github.com/osteoner/HADES to facilitate reproducibility and enable the application of our methodology to other datasets.

2 Related Works

Understanding how threat actors organize within underground forums has attracted growing research attention, driven by the need to support proactive CTI. Early studies focused on finding influential or central actor groups within social networks. Pete et al. [31] applied centrality-based social network analysis to identify key members, such as vendors and moderator groups. Huang et al. [13] used topic modeling and graph analysis to filter for high-ranking users. More recently, Amadou et al. [1,2] advanced key hacker identification by first integrating centrality measures with topic modeling and subsequently combining large language models with graph neural networks to jointly model user features and interaction structure. Recent approaches apply community detection algorithms directly to forum network graphs, representing users as nodes and interactions as edges. These methods include using a surprise function on multigraphs to find unexpected community structures [33] and applying modularity-based algorithms to identify overlapping or influential groups [36]. To systematically evaluate these approaches, Manatova et al. [19] compared 18 algorithms across five prominent underground forums. However, a key limitation of these structural methods is their bias toward highly active users and their dependence on dense, observable network connections. Consequently, they often fail to detect communities whose interactions are deliberately sparse, fragmented, or designed to evade detection.

To address this gap, we propose HADES, a semantics-driven framework that detects both dominant and hidden communities. Rather than relying on interaction graph topology, HADES clusters users based on the thematic content of their discussions and profile attributes, enabling the detection of cohesive groups even when structural connections are sparse or absent.

3 System Design

This section presents the HADES framework, which consists of three stages: (i) modeling users through their textual interactions to generate comprehensive semantic embeddings using pretrained language models; (ii) clustering users into structurally and semantically cohesive communities; and (iii) identifying high-threat actor groups to prioritize investigations for CTI analysts.

3.1 Problem Formulation

Let $G = (V, E)$ denote an underground forum network, where V is a set of n users and E is a set of m interaction edges. A community structure $\mathcal{C} = \{c_1, c_2, \ldots, c_K\}$ partitions users into subgroups, where each $c_k = (V_k, E_k)$ forms a comparatively dense subgraph of G. Standard quality functions such as modularity [25] and conductance [41] quantify community structure by measuring intra-group cohesion and inter-group separation, respectively. However, these measures assume sufficient edge density and fail in sparse networks such as underground forums, where interactions are irregular and many accounts exhibit minimal activity.

As illustrated in Fig. 1, dominant communities are large, densely connected groups of users who interact frequently and openly share resources. Their visible connections and high activity levels make them easily identifiable via standard graph-based analysis. In contrast, hidden communities are challenging to detect. Members of these groups may interact infrequently or maintain a low profile, yet they remain united by shared interests, behavioral patterns, or discussion topics. Their sparse connections allow them to blend into the broader forum or overlap with dominant groups, successfully evading traditional detection methods. For example, Fig. 1 shows a phishing community that appears as two disconnected groups under standard analysis due to limited direct interactions. In reality, these users form a single, cohesive community united by shared phishing activities.

The objective of HADES is to detect these hidden communities by leveraging shared interests, semantic topics, and profile attributes rather than relying solely on structural edges.

Formally, given a set of n forum users $\mathcal{U} = \{u_1, u_2, \ldots, u_n\}$, the framework achieves four objectives. First, it **models user profiles** $\mathcal{S} = \{s_1, s_2, \ldots, s_n\}$, where each s_i aggregates the metadata, actions, and content of user u_i. Second, it **embeds users** into $\mathcal{E} = \{e_1, e_2, \ldots, e_n\}$, where each $e_i \in \mathbb{R}^d$ captures semantic and behavioral features. Third, it **clusters users** into $\mathcal{C} = \{c_1, c_2, \ldots, c_K\}$, grouping those who discuss similar threats, tools, or illicit services. Finally, it **labels clusters** by computing $\mathcal{R} = \text{label}(\{(c_1, S_1), \ldots, (c_K, S_K)\})$, producing descriptive tags to guide CTI analysts.

This pipeline is expressed as:

$$\mathcal{S} = f_{\text{model}}(\mathcal{U}), \ \mathcal{E} = f_{\text{embed}}(\mathcal{S}), \ \mathcal{C} = f_{\text{cluster}}(\mathcal{E}), \ \mathcal{R} = f_{\text{label}}(\mathcal{C})$$

where f_{model} constructs user profiles, f_{embed} generates vector representations, f_{cluster} discovers communities, and f_{label} assigns interpretable semantic tags.

3.2 System Overview

This section details the architecture of HADES, illustrated in Fig. 2. The system pipeline comprises four main components: (1) a data selection and preprocessing module (Sect. 3.3) that extracts data from prominent underground forums to capture a broad spectrum of cybercriminal activity (e.g., hacking, malware, and marketplaces) and removes noise such as HTML tags and URLs; (2) a user representation module (Sect. 3.4) that models forum members as comprehensive textual profiles by aggregating metadata and historical content to capture latent behavioral patterns; (3) an embedding and clustering module (Sect. 3.6) that applies a pretrained language model and HDBSCAN [20] to discover both dominant and hidden communities; and (4) a cluster labeling module (Sect. 3.7) that prompts an LLM to extract representative content and categorize each identified community. Finally, Sect. 3.8 details the intrinsic metrics used to evaluate system performance.

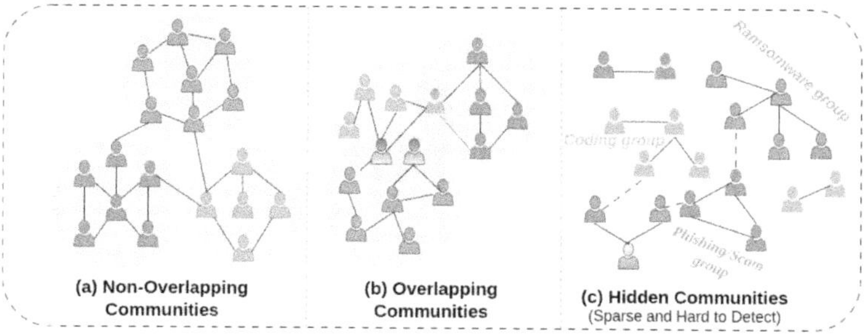

Fig. 1. Conceptual comparison of community structures in underground forum networks. Traditional graph-based methods detect dominant communities via dense interactions, while hidden communities lack such structural density but remain unified by shared semantic interests.

3.3 Dataset and Preprocessing

Data Source. We used the CrimeBB dataset [28], an established archive of cybercriminal forum activity [6,12,27,30]. The corpus contains approximately 110 million posts authored by 6 million members across 36 forums, providing a comprehensive empirical basis for analyzing global cybercriminal communities.

Underground Forum Selection. From this corpus, we selected three English-language forums based on their diverse user behaviors, varying levels of technical sophistication, and roles as hubs for sharing exploits, source code, and illicit tools: *HackForums*[1] focuses on malware, social engineering, and fraud techniques; *Cracked*[2] operates as a marketplace for cracked software and stolen credentials, emphasizing account cracking and fraud; and *BreachForums*[3], the successor to RaidForums, serves as a primary platform for distributing leaked databases and exploits. Table 1 summarizes the key characteristics of these forums. By hosting interactions ranging from technical knowledge sharing to explicit transactions involving illicit services, these platforms provide robust environments for studying group structures within cybercriminal networks.

[1] `https://hackforums.net/`.
[2] `https://cracked.net/`.
[3] `https://breachforums.st/`.

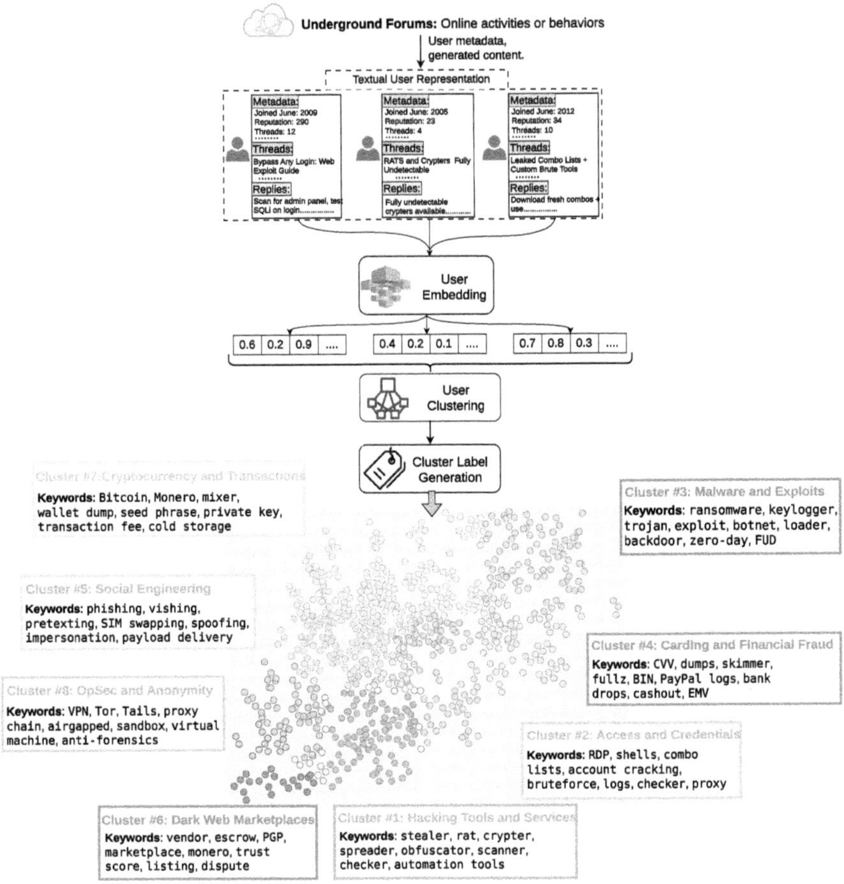

Fig. 2. Architecture of the HADES framework.

Data Preprocessing. Raw forum data is inherently noisy and unstructured. We applied a standardized preprocessing pipeline [18] to reduce noise and normalize the text before embedding and clustering. Specifically, we (1) removed HTML markup and other non-informative text; (2) replaced URLs, cited posts, quotations, and source code with canonical tokens (`URL`, `CITE`, `QUOTE`, `CODE`); and (3) filtered out non-Latin characters. This pipeline reduces the dimensionality of the feature space, improving both computational efficiency and clustering interpretability [32].

3.4 Textual User Representation

To uncover latent behavioral patterns and characterize members within underground forums, we represent each individual as a cohesive textual sequence. As illustrated in Fig. 3, user profiles contain metadata and records of various

Table 1. **Characteristics of the selected underground forum datasets.**

Forum	Posts	Threads	Members	Time Span
HackForums	42,474,325	4,148,196	716,058	Jan 2007 – Sep 2024
Cracked	2,977,800	419,517	897,760	Apr 2018 – Jun 2023
BreachForums	737,922	34,412	119,260	Mar 2022 – Sep 2024

activities, such as initiating threads, replying to posts, and sending direct messages. We define each user through two primary components: **Metadata** and **Content**. Metadata includes *usernames* (identifiers that often indicate specialization or experience, e.g., *CardMaster2024*, *MalwareExpert*); *reputation scores* (forum-specific trust indicators derived from peer feedback, resource-quality ratings, moderator endorsements, and transaction histories); and *activity metrics* (such as the number of contributed posts and initiated threads). Content comprises *threads* (complete discussions, including tutorials, tool sharing, marketplace advertisements, and operational planning) and *posts* (message-level contributions reflecting technical expertise and communication patterns).

We construct each user profile by concatenating these components into a single textual sequence. This sequence-based approach captures complex user attributes more effectively than traditional feature representations, aligning with findings in recent studies [1,7]. We encode the metadata as follows:

$$\texttt{[M]}\ \textit{username}\ \texttt{[SEP]}\ \textit{reputation}\ \texttt{[SEP]}\ \textit{thread\_count}\ \ldots$$

where [M] marks the start of the metadata segment and [SEP] separates individual attributes. We apply this same schema to threads and replies, introducing each with specific segment tokens. To explicitly distinguish these segments during encoding, we add the special tokens [M] (metadata), [T] (threads), and [R] (replies) to the embedding model's vocabulary. Figure 4 illustrates an example of the resulting user sequence.

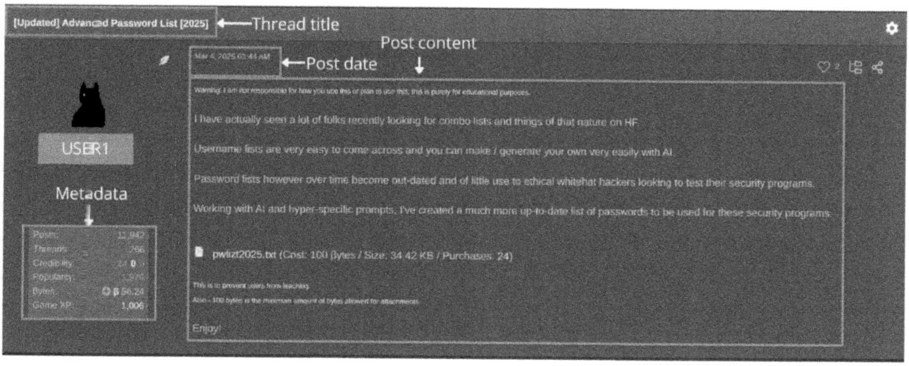

Fig. 3. Anonymized example of user interactions on HackForums.

3.5 User Embedding

The embedding process transforms variable-length textual content into fixed-length vectors, with dimensionality typically ranging from 256 to 1,536 depending on the model. Approaches range from term-based models, such as Term Frequency-Inverse Document Frequency (TF-IDF) [42], which measure word importance through frequency statistics but lack semantic depth [35], to advanced contextual embeddings generated by LLMs. Early word embeddings, such as Word2Vec [22] and GloVe [29], captured semantic relationships through co-occurrence patterns but assigned static vectors to words independent of their context. Contextual models such as BERT (Bidirectional Encoder Representations from Transformers) resolved this limitation by producing dynamic embeddings that reflect the surrounding text, thereby significantly improving semantic accuracy [9]. Subsequent LLMs, such as OpenAI's GPT, generate general-purpose embeddings [5] that capture complex linguistic patterns across a diverse range of applications.

The HADES framework embeds each user sequence into a dense vector using a transformer-based encoder suited for clustering. These embeddings capture both contextual semantics and structural information to represent comprehensive user activity profiles.

Let $S_u = \{M_u, T_u, R_u\}$ denote the textual sequence for user u, where M_u is metadata, T_u is thread content, and R_u is reply content. The sequence is tokenized into a sequence of tokens $\{t_1, t_2, \ldots, t_n\}$, which includes any required special tokens. The embedding model f_θ, parameterized by θ, maps the tokenized sequence to a dense vector:

$$\mathbf{z}_u = f_\theta(S_u) = \text{Pool}\big(\text{Transformer}_\theta(\{t_1, t_2, \ldots, t_n\})\big) \in \mathbb{R}^d$$

The $\text{Transformer}_\theta$ applies self-attention and feed-forward layers to generate contextualized token representations. These representations are then aggregated via a mean-pooling operation (Pool) into a fixed-length vector. This ensures the resulting embedding $\mathbf{z}_u$ captures both the semantic content and the structural relationships within the user's sequence.

To generate these embeddings, we selected three transformer models that span distinct architectural paradigms and representational trade-offs, enabling a systematic comparison of embedding strategies for underground forum user clustering. Specifically, we evaluate: (1) BERT [9], which provides robust bidirectional representations of user sequences; (2) T5 [34], a sequence-to-sequence model capable of broad semantic understanding; and (3) All-MiniLM-L6 [39], a distilled model optimized for efficient text representation, making it particularly suited for clustering due to its optimal balance of accuracy and computational speed.

3.6 User Clustering

The user embedding vectors $\mathbf{z}_u \in \mathbb{R}^d$, derived from structured user sequences using transformer-based encoders, serve as the input for clustering. These vectors

[M] USER01 [SEP]23[SEP]0[SEP]408[T] tut make your private keylogger etc serial protected source code[SEP]somebody pls crack hashes for me[SEP]biohazard keylogger v1 0 100 fud public made by vipermakd[SEP]solo scantime crypter 100 fud made by vipermakd public[SEP]simple msn freezer by vipermakd[SEP]best hacking tools 2010[SEP] tut basic keylogger tutorial for n00bs by vipermakd.....[R]can somebody crack this hash for me when i try to do it it says inval d hash ...[SEP]this is a rare steam cd key stealer source code i found after a long search....[SEP]i have have two premium accounts for sale 2 premium accounts 100 working sold.....

Fig. 4. Segmented textual user representation.

encapsulate behavioral patterns, facilitating the discovery of community structures comprising semantically similar users within underground forums. Given the high-dimensional, noisy, and potentially non-linearly separable nature of the embedding space, we examined a diverse set of clustering algorithms. Traditional algorithms like k-means [16] are computationally efficient but require predefined cluster counts and assume spherical distributions. Hierarchical Agglomerative Clustering (AHC) [24] identifies diverse cluster structures without preset parameters but comes with substantial computational costs. Spectral clustering [26] uses eigenvalue decomposition to identify non-convex clusters, and Fuzzy C-means [3] supports soft clustering through partial membership. Finally, Hierarchical Density-Based Spatial Clustering of Applications with Noise (HDBSCAN) [20] constructs a cluster hierarchy and extracts stable clusters without a predefined count.

Discovering communities within underground forums requires an approach tailored to the unique properties of these embedding spaces. The transformer-derived vectors ($\mathbf{z}_u$) capture high-dimensional behavioral patterns that necessitate an algorithm with three core capabilities: **(1)** discovering clusters without a predefined count, reflecting the unknown number of underlying communities; **(2)** identifying communities of arbitrary shape and density to accommodate diverse social structures (e.g., small, dense expert groups versus large, diffuse novice communities); and **(3)** handling noise to isolate anomalous actors. While the previously mentioned algorithms offer partial solutions, none simultaneously meet all three criteria. For instance, k-means [16] imposes rigid spherical assumptions and requires a pre-specified cluster count; spectral clustering [26] is computationally prohibitive for large user bases; and agglomerative methods [24] lack robustness to the noise and outliers common in this domain.

Therefore, we selected HDBSCAN [20], which directly aligns with these requirements. HDBSCAN operates without a predefined number of clusters, enabling data-driven exploration of community structures. Its density-based formulation identifies non-spherical clusters of varying densities. Critically, it explicitly models the data distribution to isolate noise, treating anomalous users as outliers rather than forcing them into ill-fitting clusters. HDBSCAN provides a robust method for extracting reliable communities from the complex and noisy ecosystems of underground forums.

3.7 Cluster Label Generation

HADES generates interpretable labels for each cluster using an open-source LLM. Recent work has demonstrated the effectiveness of LLMs for labeling cybercrime and security-related content at scale. Valeros et al. [45] applied fine-tuned LLMs to translate and annotate underground forum data across languages, while Mischinger et al. [23] explored LLM-based classification of non-English cybercrime forums. Building on these methodological foundations, our labeling pipeline follows a structured sampling, generation, and validation protocol designed for the noisy, adversarial language characteristic of underground forums.

For each cluster, we randomly sample the textual content of 20 users and prompt the LLM to identify an appropriate thematic category. Text exceeding the model's context window is truncated to the maximum supported length. To assess label consistency, we repeated this sampling process five times per cluster, evaluating 100 distinct users per cluster in total. The prompt used for this task is provided in Fig. 5. To verify the quality and reliability of the generated labels, we conducted a manual validation. One evaluator assessed whether the generated label accurately captured the dominant theme of the sampled content.

3.8 Evaluation Metrics

We assess cluster quality along two dimensions: structural integrity and semantic coherence. Structural integrity measures geometric separation and compactness in the embedding space, while semantic coherence evaluates whether clusters represent topically consistent groups—a defining trait of underground forum communities.

For structural integrity, we use three standard metrics. The **Silhouette Score (SS)** [37] quantifies how well each embedding fits its assigned cluster relative to neighboring clusters, ranging from −1 (poor) to 1 (well-separated). The **Calinski-Harabasz Index (CH)** [8] compares between-cluster dispersion to within-cluster dispersion, with higher values indicating denser, more distinct clusters. The **Dunn Index (DI)** [10] measures the ratio of minimum inter-cluster distance to maximum intra-cluster diameter, with higher values indicating compact, well-separated communities.

For semantic coherence, we define a metric that measures topical alignment between clusters and forum themes. For a cluster C_i with centroid $\boldsymbol{\mu}_i$ and a set of M topic embeddings $\{\mathbf{t}_j\}_{j=1}^{M}$, the **Semantic Coherence (SC)** score is:

$$SC_i = \max_j \frac{\boldsymbol{\mu}_i \cdot \mathbf{t}_j}{\|\boldsymbol{\mu}_i\|_2 \|\mathbf{t}_j\|_2}$$

The overall score is the average SC_i across all clusters, with values closer to 1 indicating strong topical alignment. Together, the structural metrics confirm geometric separation of user behaviors, while semantic coherence verifies that these boundaries align with meaningful forum themes.

Prompt – Label Generation

```
[Role] You are an expert in underground forums and community
analysis. Your task is to analyze examples of user posts from a
single cluster and suggest a concise label that best describes the
overall topic or theme of the cluster.
[Input Samples] Below are twenty examples of user posts from a
single cluster:

  – "Anyone selling fresh logs? PM rates."
  – "Looking for botnet access, serious buyers only."
  – "Guide: Building your own stealer for private use."
  – "Selling PayPal verified accounts, BTC accepted."
  – "Tutorial: How to cash out stolen credentials."
  – .........

[Constraints] 1. The label must be concise (one to four words). 2.
Avoid overly generic terms and ensure the name reflects the main
activity or theme. 3. OUTPUT FORMAT: Return ONLY the name. Do not
include explanations, punctuation, or additional text.
[Example Output] Credential Theft & Account Fraud
```

Fig. 5. Structured prompt template for automated cluster labeling.

4 Results and Discussions

4.1 Experimental Setup

Experiments were conducted on a high-performance computing cluster running RedHat Linux, equipped with an NVIDIA A100 GPU (80 GB VRAM). All implementations were developed in Python 3.8.5. The evaluated pretrained language models embeddings include BERT[4], T5[5], and All-MiniLM-L6[6], all of which were accessed via the Hugging Face `transformers` library [15].

We generated labels using Qwen2.5 [43], a 7.62-billion-parameter decoder-only LLM. This model supports input sequences of up to 128,000 tokens and outputs of up to 8,000 tokens, accommodating long, information-rich contexts. To mitigate high-dimensionality effects, all embeddings were reduced to 50 dimensions using UMAP [21] before clustering. We then applied HDBSCAN for clustering, setting `min_cluster_size` to 5, `min_samples` to 1, and using the Euclidean distance metric.

[4] https://huggingface.co/google-bert/bert-base-uncased.
[5] https://huggingface.co/google/flan-t5-base.
[6] https://huggingface.co/sentence-transformers/all-MiniLM-L6-v2.

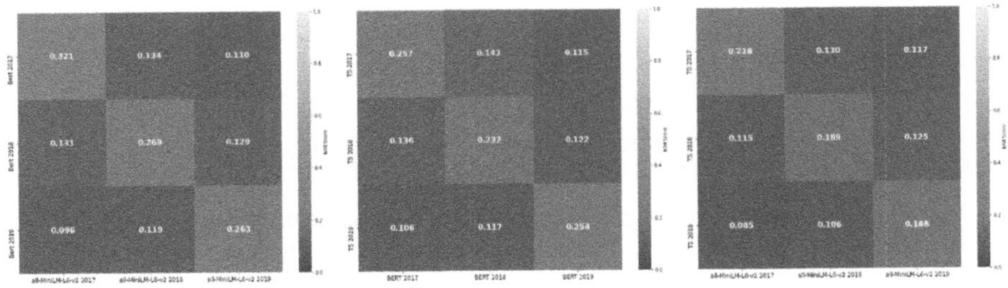

(a) BERT vs All-MiniLM (b) BERT vs T5 (c) T5 vs All-MiniLM

Fig. 6. Structural similarity of community partitions across embedding models. NMI heatmaps compare the communities generated using BERT, All-MiniLM-L6, and T5 embeddings on HackForums (2017–2019).

4.2 General Clustering Overview

Table 2 presents the clustering results for various combinations of forums, embeddings, and the HDBSCAN algorithm. These results reveal a clear hierarchy in embedding performance, demonstrating that model choice significantly affects both clustering quality and the nature of the detected communities. BERT embeddings outperform the alternatives across most metrics. For example, BERT achieves the highest Silhouette Score of 0.423 on Cracked and HackForums, indicating well-separated and cohesive clusters. Additionally, BERT achieves the highest Calinski-Harabasz Index (CHI), which measures the ratio of between-cluster to within-cluster dispersion, peaking at 2,502.45 on BreachForums. This strong performance reflects BERT's pre-training on large, diverse text corpora, which enables it to capture nuanced semantics and subtle distinctions in user language and behavior. Consequently, BERT produces context-aware vector representations that facilitate the identification of coherent user groups. Although All-MiniLM-L6 achieves a notable Silhouette Score of 0.476 on BreachForums, its performance on other forums, similar to that of T5, is moderate, producing clusters that are less geometrically distinct than those of BERT. Nevertheless, both All-MiniLM-L6 and T5 produce clusters with strong semantic coherence and thematically consistent topics. This indicates that while BERT excels at forming mathematically distinct groups, All-MiniLM-L6 and T5 remain effective for thematic grouping despite less separation in the vector space. However, All-MiniLM-L6 exhibits dataset-dependent variability in semantic coherence, a sensitivity potentially linked to its training characteristics.

We quantitatively compare the community partitions generated by different pretrained language model embeddings using the Normalized Mutual Information (NMI) score. NMI is a standard information-theoretic metric that measures the similarity between two sets of communities on a scale from 0 to 1, where a high score indicates similar community structures. Figure 6 shows pairwise NMI comparisons of communities detected using BERT, All-MiniLM-L6, and T5 over three years (2017–2019) on HackForums. We observe consistently high NMI scores between communities detected with BERT and All-MiniLM-L6 during this period, particularly in 2017, which aligns with their similar architectures. In contrast, T5 achieves lower NMI scores when compared to BERT and All-MiniLM-L6, indicating that T5 captures different semantic features and produces distinct user groupings.

Table 2. Quantitative evaluation of clustering performance across different pretrained embedding models.

Dataset	Embedding	SS	CHI	Dunn	SC	# Communities
HackForums	BERT	**0.423**	**351.34**	0.209	**0.992**	56
	All-MiniLM-L6	0.318	90.59	**0.286**	0.875	42
	T5	0.155	86.69	0.270	0.792	39
Cracked	BERT	**0.423**	**336.79**	0.196	**0.994**	86
	All-MiniLM-L6	0.320	83.71	0.232	0.894	76
	T5	0.304	157.31	**0.277**	0.710	65
BreachForums	BERT	**0.476**	219.53	0.074	**0.965**	52
	All-MiniLM-L6	0.442	**2502.45**	0.177	0.894	48
	T5	0.315	1222.92	**0.235**	0.882	31

The choice of embedding model significantly shapes the structure of the detected communities. For instance, applying BERT embeddings to HackForums identified 56 distinct communities, compared to 39 with T5. This difference highlights the varying representational capacities of the embeddings; BERT's ability to capture fine-grained distinctions facilitates the detection of more specialized subgroups. Consequently, the choice of embedding model is a crucial methodological decision that shapes the scale, characteristics, and interpretation of the identified communities, as well as their underlying social structures.

Lessons learned. Our analysis demonstrates that the architecture and training paradigms of pretrained language model embeddings significantly influence community detection. Models sharing the same architecture and training data, such as BERT and All-MiniLM-L6, tend to produce similar community structures, though BERT consistently performs best. Across forums, BERT achieves the highest Silhouette Score (0.423) and Calinski-Harabasz Index (2,502.45), achieving well-separated, semantically coherent clusters that capture subtle user differences. While All-MiniLM-L6 and T5 also form meaningful communities, their clusters are less distinct, and their performance is less consistent. Notably, BERT identifies more fine-grained communities, such as 56 in HackForums, compared to 42 with T5, highlighting its capacity to capture nuanced user subgroups. Furthermore, the similarity between communities detected by BERT and All-MiniLM-L6 declines over time as the forum evolves, reflecting the impact of a changing user base and content diversity.

4.3 Community Evolution Analysis

To evaluate community evolution in underground forums, we compared HADES, which utilizes BERT embeddings, with the Louvain algorithm [4] used in prior studies [19]. We conducted this comparison using data from HackForums over three years (2017–2020), tracking 16,111 active users. Our analysis indicates that while both methods detect broad community structures, HADES more effectively identifies hidden communities and assigns descriptive labels.

We constructed annual social graphs by linking users who contributed to threads initiated by others, modeling implicit social connections consistent with previous research [13,19,31]. Users posting in the same thread were considered socially connected, enabling us to capture interaction dynamics and information flow. For HADES, we represented each user's annual activity as a sequence and generated corresponding embeddings. Both the Louvain algorithm and HADES were applied separately to the user data for each year, allowing for a direct temporal comparison between the two approaches. As shown in Fig. 7a and c, the Louvain algorithm primarily identified large, dominant communities and did not assign descriptive labels. Furthermore, in 2017, the Louvain algorithm classified 36.1% of users (6,366 out of 16,111) into 6,335 single-user communities. This fragmentation reflects the sparsity of the underlying interaction graph [44]. In contrast, HADES produced no single-user communities (0%) during the same period, demonstrating its capability to resolve hidden group affiliations and apply informative labels despite sparse network interactions.

By 2019, user interactions had evolved significantly:

- **Integration of Isolated Users:** Of the 5,829 users isolated in 2017 (Fig. 7a), 4,365 (74.88%) joined multi-user communities by 2019 (Fig. 7c), with over 13% of previously isolated users integrating into the largest community. HADES had already grouped these users into communities such as the "General Discussion Hub" in 2017 (Fig. 7d), demonstrating its capacity to detect latent ties before they manifest structurally.
- **Community Transitions:** Among the 10,326 users located in multi-user communities in 2017, 7,391 (71.58%) transitioned into the primary community by 2019, often migrating between groups with overlapping interests.
- **Emergence of Community C2:** A notable community, labeled C2 by the Louvain algorithm in 2019 (Fig. 7f), consisted of 3,966 users. Of these, 3,416 (86.13%) had been isolated in 2017 (Fig. 7a). HADES identified the foundation of this community as early as 2017 (Fig. 7d), grouping 52.94% of these users into a "Hacking & Security" community. This early detection underscores HADES's consistency in tracking community evolution over time.

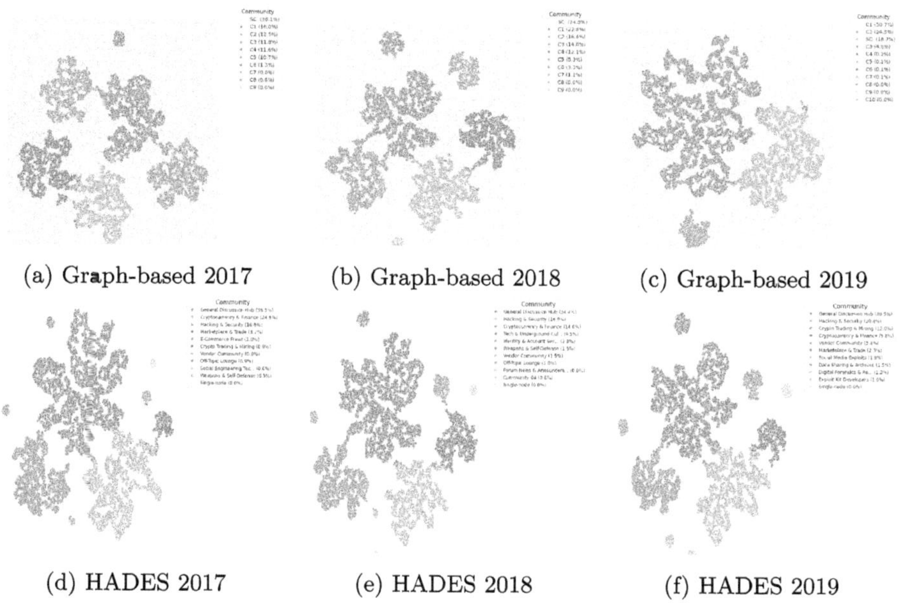

(a) Graph-based 2017 (b) Graph-based 2018 (c) Graph-based 2019

(d) HADES 2017 (e) HADES 2018 (f) HADES 2019

Fig. 7. Longitudinal t-SNE visualization of community evolution on HackForums (2017–2019). The graph-based approach initially isolates a large number of users into single-node communities (gray points).

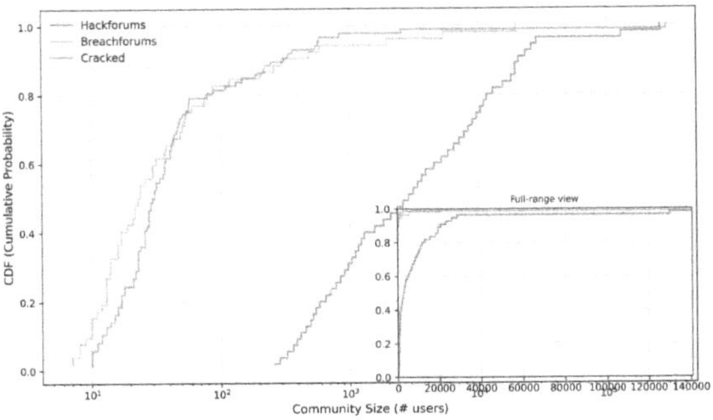

Fig. 8. Cumulative Distribution Function (CDF) of community sizes across three underground forums.

> **Lessons learned.** While the Louvain algorithm effectively detects dominant communities, it is limited by sparse interaction graphs, often resulting in numerous single-node communities. In contrast, HADES identifies both prominent and hidden communities, detecting latent group affiliations up to a year before they manifest in graph-based structural analyses. Furthermore, the model generates consistent, descriptive labels that capture the thematic evolution of user discussions over time. This capacity for early detection enables the proactive tracking of community evolution, providing a robust approach for analyzing and anticipating dynamic shifts within online communities.

4.4 Dataset-Specific Insights

Using HADES with BERT embeddings, we qualitatively analyzed communities across three underground forums. This analysis identified distinct thematic hubs focused on General Discussion, Hacking, Gaming, Coding, Technology, Markets, and Finance. Table 3 lists the 10 largest and 10 smallest communities. A clear pattern emerged: the largest communities on each forum are broad, general-interest hubs with the highest membership. Examples include the "General Discussion Hub" on HackForums (260,470 members), "Lounge" on Cracked (289,820 members), and "General Discussion" on BreachForums (19,995 members). Other major communities center on high-engagement topics such as trading, hacking, and cryptocurrency. In contrast, the smallest communities are highly specialized and often dedicated to illicit activities. As shown in Fig. 8, more than 80% of communities on Cracked and BreachForums have fewer than 100 users. For example, the "Ransomware Groups" community on BreachForums and the "Dark Market" community on Cracked consist of only 7 to 16 members each. These micro-communities facilitate collaboration on niche underground services, such as phishing kit development or unauthorized data trading. HackForums, by comparison, exhibits a substantially higher level of activity, containing 11 times more posts and 9 times more threads than the other two forums combined (Table 1). Consequently, even its smallest communities comprise approximately 260 members. Figure 8 shows that 80% of HackForums communities fall within the range of 260 to 1,000 users. Such communities are difficult to detect using traditional graph-based methods that rely solely on user interactions, because their formation is typically driven by shared interests, may take years to develop, and often requires a high-profile member to attract others. By leveraging user interests, our framework can not only detect these communities but also predict their emergence up to a year in advance. Examining the "Exploit Kit Developers" community on HackForums, we found that although members share similar interests, they often possess varying levels of expertise. For example, an advanced user might post a detailed tutorial on building a Python remote access trojan (RAT), providing the full source code and techniques for evading detection, while offering advanced features via private message. Conversely, a novice user (e.g., "CrypterNoob") might seek advice on applying crypters to obfuscate RATs and avoid antivirus detection. Although both users participate in the same community and engage with similar topics, the disparity in their technical proficiency is significant. This contrast demonstrates that community membership reflects shared interests rather than uniform technical skill or experience.

Lessons learned. Our qualitative analysis shows that underground communities exhibit both broad and highly specialized structures. Large, general-interest hubs attract the majority of users, while numerous smaller micro-communities often focus on specific illicit activities. This distinction highlights the limitations of traditional graph-based community detection methods, which rely primarily on user interactions. Such methods often fail to identify emerging communities, particularly those built around shared interests, for years after their formation, or until a high-profile member triggers broader growth. In contrast, HADES can detect and anticipate the emergence of these communities up to a year in advance. Furthermore, we observe that community membership is driven by shared interests rather than uniform expertise, with members ranging from novices seeking guidance to experts sharing advanced techniques.

4.5 Practical Implications

HADES offers several practical advantages for CTI operations. First, it detects communities engaged in high-risk activities, such as exploit kit development and Malware-as-a-Service—without requiring a pre-constructed interaction graph. Unlike graph-based methods, which depend on long observation windows to establish reliable interaction networks, our framework identifies emerging communities earlier by leveraging semantic similarity alone. This enables analysts to monitor illicit groups, anticipate evolving threats, and develop countermeasures before attacks mature.

Second, the communities identified by HADES can be enriched through integration with complementary frameworks. Event-level detection systems such as EventHunter [12] could link detected communities to specific threat incidents (e.g., zero-day disclosures, malware releases), providing analysts with both the *who* (community membership) and the *what* (specific events). Similarly, cybersecurity named entity recognition models such as CyberNER [11] could extract structured indicators of compromise from community content, enabling a direct path from community detection to actionable intelligence.

Table 3. Size and thematic diversity of the top-10 largest and smallest detected communities.

Rank	HackForums	Size	BreachForums	Size	Cracked	Size
			Largest Communities			
1	General Discussion Hub	260,470	General Discussion	19,995	Lounge	289,820
2	Marketplace & Trade	130,235	Exchange Forum	5,495	Hacktivism	2,561
3	Crypto Trading & Mining	28,652	Leeching & Piracy	1,967	Fiesta Exploit	844
4	Cryptocurrency & Finance	26,047	Dark Web Pharmacies & Med.	593	Thanks Humor	587
5	Fraud & Scam Reports	23,442	Leaked Data & CC Dumps	495	Graphic Design	580
6	Data Sharing & Archives	20,838	Android RAT & Exploits	303	Hack Discussion	554
7	Vendor Community	19,535	Anime Recommendations	206	Bitcoin Leeches	369
8	Tech & Underground Culture	19,535	Business Data Marketplace	119	Underground Hacks	316
9	Off-Topic Lounge	18,233	Electronic Music Forum	61	Leak Community	340
10	Hacking & Security	15,628	Movie Sharing & Streaming	54	Internet Humor	250
			Smallest Communities			
1	Credential Stuffing Groups	547	Ransomware Groups	16	Dork Quality	16
2	Darknet Escrow Services	521	Child Exploitation & Porn	16	Bitcoin Forum	16
3	Exploit Kit Developers	495	Hacked IoT Devices	10	Xbox Sharing	12
4	Blackhat SEO Networks	456	Social Dynamics & Ethics	10	Crypto Passerby	11
5	Spam-as-a-Service Crews	417	Hacking & Credential Trading	10	Underground Deals	11
6	Cashout Services	391	Twitter Data Leak	9	Crypto Forums	13
7	Bulletproof Hosting	365	Markets & Sales	8	AI Discourse	10
8	Initial Access Brokers	326	Tools & Hacking Techniques	8	Dark Market	10
9	Malware-as-a-Service	287	Unauthorized Access Systems	7	Bitcoin Forum	10
10	Phishing Kit Developers	260	Underground Markets & Deals	7	Dark Market	10

5 Limitations and Future Work

A primary limitation of this study is the computational overhead of large-scale experiments. Specifically, generating dense vector embeddings with models like BERT for millions of users before clustering is resource-intensive. These constraints restricted our evaluation to smaller models, hindering a comprehensive analysis of state-of-the-art LLMs. Future work should explore efficiency improvements to enable the evaluation of larger models. Second, evaluating our approach is constrained by the lack of ground-truth data. Because baseline labels are unavailable, we relied on manual qualitative verification to assess community boundaries and mitigate the risk of LLM hallucinations during label generation. Developing annotated benchmark datasets would facilitate rigorous quantitative evaluation. Third, our evaluation is limited to English-language forums. Underground forums operate in many languages, including Russian, Chinese, Arabic, and Portuguese, and the preprocessing pipeline currently filters out non-Latin characters, which would remove potentially informative content in multilingual contexts. Extending HADES to non-English forums is a natural direction for future work. Finally, expanding our limited search for HDBSCAN parameters could refine community boundaries and improve the framework's effectiveness.

6 Ethical Considerations

Our research uses the CrimeBB academic dataset [28], which consists of historical, publicly available text collected from underground forums. We accessed these data under a formal Data Use Agreement (DUA) with the Cambridge Cybercrime Centre, which prohibits the redistribution of raw data. Given the sensitive nature of this domain, we adhered to strict ethical standards. Because our study is entirely non-interventional and relies exclusively on public posts, it involved no interaction with forum users.

7 Conclusion

This paper introduces HADES, an unsupervised framework designed to detect both dominant and hidden threat communities within cybercriminal underground forums. By using pretrained language models to generate semantic embeddings from user textual representations, our approach captures shared interests and latent behavioral patterns that traditional graph-based methods often overlook. By clustering users based on this semantic similarity and assigning topic labels to the resulting clusters, HADES identifies specific threat communities to support CTI. Our evaluation across HackForums, Cracked, and BreachForums demonstrates that BERT-based embeddings consistently achieve high cluster coherence. This allows the framework to successfully isolate small, highly specialized micro-communities, often comprising fewer than 100 users, that typically evade conventional detection. Furthermore, because users engage with specific topics before establishing explicit structural connections, tracking these semantic patterns enables HADES to identify emerging communities up to a year earlier than graph-based methods. This framework provides a scalable, proactive tool for CTI, allowing security analysts to monitor and anticipate evolving threats.

Acknowledgements. The authors gratefully acknowledge the Cambridge Cybercrime Centre, UK, for providing access to the CrimeBB dataset, which made this research possible.

Disclosure of Interests. The authors have no competing interests to declare that are relevant to the content of this article.

References

1. Amadou, A.N.H., Motii, A., Elouardi, S., Bergou, E.H.: EUREKHA: enhancing user representation for key hackers identification in underground forums. In: 2024 IEEE 23rd International Conference on Trust, Security and Privacy in Computing and Communications (TrustCom), pp. 387–398 (2024). https://doi.org/10.1109/TrustCom63139.2024.00073
2. Amadou, A.N.H., Motii, A., Jouhari, M.: HC-HackerRank: identifying key hackers in cybercrime social network forums. In: 2024 7th International Conference on Advanced Communication Technologies and Networking (CommNet), pp. 1–8 (2024). https://doi.org/10.1109/CommNet63022.2024.10793292
3. Bezdek, J.C., Ehrlich, R., Full, W.: FCM: the fuzzy c-means clustering algorithm. Comput. Geosci. **10**(2–3), 191–203 (1984). https://doi.org/10.1016/0098-3004(84)90020-7
4. Blondel, V.D., Guillaume, J.L., Lambiotte, R., Lefebvre, E.: Fast unfolding of communities in large networks. J. Stat. Mech.: Theory Exp. (10), P10008 (2008). https://doi.org/10.1088/1742-5468/2008/10/P10008
5. Brown, T., et al.: Language models are few-shot learners. Adv. Neural Inf. Process. Syst. **33**, 1877–1901 (2020). https://dl.acm.org/doi/abs/10.5555/3495724.3495883
6. Cabrero-Holgueras, J., Pastrana, S.: A methodology for large-scale identification of related accounts in underground forums. Comput. Secur. **111**, 102489 (2021). https://doi.org/10.1016/j.cose.2021.102489
7. Cai, Z., et al.: LMBot: distilling Graph Knowledge into Language Model for Graph-Less Deployment in Twitter Bot Detection. In: Proceedings of the 17th ACM International Conference on Web Search and Data Mining, pp. 57–66 (2024). https://doi.org/10.1145/3616855.3635843
8. Caliński, T., Harabasz, J.: A dendrite method for cluster analysis. Commun. Stat. - Theory Methods **3**(1), 1–27 (1974). https://doi.org/10.1080/03610927408827101
9. Devlin, J., Chang, M.W., Lee, K., Toutanova, K.: BERT: pre-training of deep bidirectional transformers for language understanding. In: Proceedings of the 2019 Conference of the North American Chapter of the Association for Computational Linguistics: Human Language Technologies, vol. 1, pp. 4171–4186 (2019). https://doi.org/10.18653/v1/N19-1423
10. Dunn, J.C.: Well-separated clusters and optimal fuzzy partitions. J. Cybern. **4**(1), 95–104 (1974). https://doi.org/10.1080/01969727408546059
11. Ech-Chammakhy, Y., Motii, A., Rabii, A., Azrara, O., Chbili, J.: CyberNER: a Harmonized STIX Corpus for Cybersecurity Named Entity Recognition. In: 2025 IEEE 24th International Conference on Trust, Security and Privacy in Computing and Communications (TrustCom), pp. 2190–2197 (2025). https://doi.org/10.1109/Trustcom66490.2025.00255
12. Ech-Chammakhy, Y., Motii, A., Rabii, A., Chbili, J.: EventHunter: dynamic clustering and ranking of security events from hacker forum discussions. In: Proceedings of the 28th International Symposium on Research in Attacks, Intrusions and Defenses, pp. 552–565 (2025). https://doi.org/10.1109/RAID67961.2025.00044
13. Huang, C., Guo, Y., Guo, W., Li, Y.: HackerRank: identifying key hackers in underground forums. Int. J. Distrib. Sens. Netw. **17**(5) (2021). https://doi.org/10.1177/15501477211015145

14. Huang, S.Y., Ban, T.: A Topic-Based Unsupervised Learning Approach for Online Underground Market Exploration. In: Proceedings of 18th IEEE International Conference on Trust, Security and Privacy in Computing and communications/13th IEEE International Conference on Big Data Science and Engineering (TrustCom/BigDataSE), pp. 208–215 (2019). https://doi.org/10.1109/TrustCom/BigDataSE.2019.00036
15. Hugging Face: Hugging Face – The AI community building the future (2024). https://huggingface.co/. Accessed 27 May 2025
16. Jin, X., Han, J.: K-means clustering. In: Encyclopedia of Machine Learning, pp. 563–564 (2010). https://doi.org/10.1007/978-0-387-30164-8_425
17. Li, J., et al.: A comprehensive review of community detection in graphs. Neurocomputing **600**, 128169 (2024). https://doi.org/10.1016/j.neucom.2024.128169
18. Maharana, K., Mondal, S., Nemade, B.: A review: data pre-processing and data augmentation techniques. Global Transitions Proc. **3**(1), 91–99 (2022). https://doi.org/10.1016/j.gltp.2022.04.020
19. Manatova, D., DeVries, C., Samtani, S.: Understand your shady neighborhood: an approach for detecting and investigating hacker communities. Decis. Support Syst. **184**, 114271 (2024). https://doi.org/10.1016/j.dss.2024.114271
20. McInnes, L., Healy, J., Astels, S., et al.: HDBSCAN: hierarchical density based clustering. J. Open Sour. Softw. **2**(11), 205 (2017). https://doi.org/10.21105/joss.00205
21. McInnes, L., Healy, J., Saul, N., Großberger, L.: UMAP: uniform manifold approximation and projection. J. Open Sour. Softw. **3**(29), 861 (2018). https://doi.org/10.21105/joss.00861
22. Mikolov, T., Chen, K., Corrado, G., Dean, J.: Efficient estimation of word representations in vector space. arXiv preprint arXiv:1301.3781 (2013). https://doi.org/10.48550/arXiv.1301.3781
23. Mischinger, M., Hughes, J., Vitiugin, F., Pastrana, S., Hutchings, A., Suarez-Tangil, G.: Lost in translation: analyzing non-english cybercrime forums. In: 2025 APWG Symposium on Electronic Crime Research, pp. 1–16 (2025). https://doi.org/10.1109/eCrime66972.2025.11327989
24. Müllner, D.: Modern hierarchical, agglomerative clustering algorithms. arXiv preprint arXiv:1109.2378 (2011). https://doi.org/10.48550/arXiv.1109.2378
25. Newman, M.E., Girvan, M.: Finding and evaluating community structure in networks. Phys. Rev. E **69**(2), 026113 (2004). https://doi.org/10.1103/PhysRevE.69.026113
26. Ng, A., Jordan, M., Weiss, Y.: On spectral clustering: analysis and an algorithm. Adv. Neural Inf. Process. Syst. **14** (2001). https://dl.acm.org/doi/10.5555/2980539.2980649
27. Paracha, A.A., Arshad, J., Khan, M.M.: SUS You're SUS!–Identifying influencer hackers on dark web social networks. Comput. Electr. Eng. **107**, 108627 (2023). https://doi.org/10.1016/j.compeleceng.2023.108627
28. Pastrana, S., Thomas, D.R., Hutchings, A., Clayton, R.: CrimeBB: enabling cybercrime research on underground forums at scale. In: Proceedings of the 2018 World Wide Web Conference, pp. 1845–1854 (2018). https://doi.org/10.1145/3178876.3186178
29. Pennington, J., Socher, R., Manning, C.D.: GloVe: global vectors for word representation. In: Proceedings of the 2014 Conference on Empirical Methods in Natural Language Processing, pp. 1532–1543 (2014). https://doi.org/10.3115/v1/D14-1162

30. Pete, I., et al.: PostCog: a tool for interdisciplinary research into underground forums at scale. In: 2022 IEEE European Symposium on Security and Privacy Workshops, pp. 93–104 (2022). https://doi.org/10.1109/EuroSPW55150.2022.00016
31. Pete, I., Hughes, J., Chua, Y.T., Bada, M.: A social network analysis and comparison of six dark web forums. In: 2020 IEEE European Symposium on Security and Privacy Workshops, pp. 484–493 (2020). https://doi.org/10.1109/EuroSPW51379.2020.00071
32. Petukhova, A., Fachada, N.: TextCL: a Python package for NLP preprocessing tasks. SoftwareX **19**, 101122 (2022). https://doi.org/10.1016/j.softx.2022.101122
33. Pourhabibi, T., Ong, K.L., Kam, B.H., Boo, Y.L.: DarkNetExplorer (DNE): exploring dark multi-layer networks beyond the resolution limit. Decis. Support Syst. **146**, 113537 (2021). https://doi.org/10.1016/j.dss.2021.113537
34. Raffel, C., et al.: Exploring the limits of transfer learning with a unified text-to-text transformer. J. Mach. Learn. Res. **21**(140), 1–67 (2020). https://dl.acm.org/doi/abs/10.5555/3455716.3455856
35. Ramos, J., et al.: Using TF-IDF to Determine Word Relevance in Document Queries. In: Proceedings of the First Instructional Conference on Machine Learning, vol. 242, pp. 29–48 (2003). https://api.semanticscholar.org/CorpusID:14638345
36. Ríos, S.A., Muñoz, R.: Dark Web portal overlapping community detection based on topic models. In: Proceedings of the ACM SIGKDD Workshop on Intelligence and Security Informatics (2012). https://doi.org/10.1145/2331791.2331793
37. Rousseeuw, P.J.: Silhouettes: a graphical aid to the interpretation and validation of cluster analysis. J. Comput. Appl. Math. **20**, 53–65 (1987). https://doi.org/10.1016/0377-0427(87)90125-7
38. Samtani, S., Chinn, R., Chen, H.: Exploring hacker assets in underground forums. In: IEEE International Conference on Intelligence and Security Informatics, pp. 31–36 (2015). https://doi.org/10.1109/ISI.2015.7165935
39. Sentence-Transformers: all-MiniLM-L6-v2 (2024). https://huggingface.co/sentence-transformers/all-MiniLM-L6-v2
40. SentinelOne: Key Cybersecurity Statistics for 2026 (2026). https://www.sentinelone.com/cybersecurity-101/cybersecurity/cyber-security-statistics/
41. Shi, J., Malik, J.: Normalized cuts and image segmentation. IEEE Trans. Pattern Anal. Mach. Intell. **22**(8), 888–905 (2000). https://doi.org/10.1109/34.868688
42. Sparck Jones, K.: A statistical interpretation of term specificity and its application in retrieval. In: Document Retrieval Systems, pp. 132–142 (1988). https://dl.acm.org/doi/10.5555/106765.106782
43. Team, Q.: Qwen2.5: a party of foundation models (2024). https://qwenlm.github.io/blog/qwen2.5/
44. Traag, V.A., Waltman, L., van Eck, N.J.: From Louvain to Leiden: guaranteeing well-connected communities. Sci. Rep. **9** (2019). https://api.semanticscholar.org/CorpusID:53041707
45. Valeros, V., Sirokova, A., Catania, C., Garcia, S.: Towards Better Understanding of Cybercrime: the Role of Fine-Tuned LLMs in Translation. In: 2024 IEEE European Symposium on Security and Privacy Workshops, pp. 91–99 (2024). https://doi.org/10.1109/EuroSPW61312.2024.00017

It's a Match! Transitioning from Manual Search to Deterministic Expert Routing

Mathis Müller[1(✉)], Raphael Neudert[2], and Günther Pernul[1]

[1] University of Regensburg, Regensburg, Germany
{mathis.mueller,guenther.pernul}@ur.de
[2] Nexis GmbH, Regensburg, Germany
raphael.neudert@nexis-secure.com

Abstract. The number of incidents in modern SOCs creates high workload for the security experts involved especially due to overhead in the routing layer: once an incident is deemed relevant, it must be assigned to a domain expert responsible for the affected system. As enterprise system landscapes and ownership structures grow, manual ownership identification and ticket handoffs become a dominant source of delay, variance, and misrouting. We present a generalized process model that automatically connects SOCs to security systems. We apply this process to the connection between SOCs and IAM systems, arguing that IAM systems serve as the latest and most reliable source of truth for knowledge of people and their responsibilities. Our contributions include a formalized queuing and process model as well as a technical implementation that utilizes CTI data to identify a responsible domain expert via IAM, thereby enabling automated assignment. This approach reduces both workload and the mean time to resolve incidents. We evaluate the approach with model-level extraction accuracy and a discrete-event simulation of the routing stage, embedding the model in a real-world-data SOC use case.

Keywords: SOC · IAM · CTI · Automation in security

1 Introduction

Security Operations Centers (SOCs) have been established as the nervous system of cybersecurity in modern enterprises. Yet, despite the sophistication of contemporary detection pipelines, they still face a challenge. While proficient at detecting malicious activity, they often struggle to translate this recognition into tangible, system-level action [2,11]. The discrepancy between detection and response, between awareness and action, has been identified as the pivotal impediment to enterprise defense [2,34]. Although high alert volume and "alert fatigue" are well-documented challenges [13,28], recent findings indicate that even with optimal triage and filtering, a non-trivial volume of security incidents inevitably accumulates at the remediation stage [2].

This final stage, often termed the "last mile" of incident handling, is where the operational momentum frequently stalls, impacting Mean Time To Resolve

S. Nadjm-Tehrani et al. (Eds.): ARES 2026, LNCS 16898, pp. 391–412, 2027.
https://doi.org/10.1007/978-3-032-36874-4_20

(MTTR) [34]. The pivotal impediment is not technical detection, but operational friction: asset ownership data is often incomplete [2,32], and delegation processes to responsible service teams stagnate in manual ticket queues [10,29]. In practice, the lack of accurate organizational context, specifically the identification of Domain Experts, can substantially contribute to downstream handling latency [34]. Inaccurate or missing asset ownership information inevitably facilitates initial misrouting, which triggers a cycle of reassignment. Empirical evidence from incident triage [5] indicates that reassignment is both frequent and costly, with reassigned incidents experiencing substantial time inflation.

To resolve this, the structural interdependence between Security Operations Center (SOC) and Identity and Access Management (IAM) must be formalized. Current Security Operations Centers (SOCs) research highlights the lack of a holistic view and the challenge of integrating those diverse context data sources into the incident resolution process [32]. Here, IAM serves as the critical connective tissue: it dynamically links the static technical layer, represented by asset databases, to the fluctuating organizational layer, embodied in HR systems. Thereby, it maintains the most current truth regarding responsibilities and ownership [16]. When this identity intelligence remains siloed, the SOC lacks the contextual accuracy needed for automated routing on identity information retrieval. Consequently, we argue that the systematic integration of IAM-derived context is not merely a tooling decision, but a structural requirement to bridge the gap between detection and remediation, reducing MTTR.

To formally analyze the impact of this integration, we model the SOC not merely as a detection tool, but as a stochastic routing system subject to rigid queuing constraints. This perspective explains why response times do not increase linearly but instead exponentially, specifically when identifying Domain Experts relies on manual, unstructured investigation [19]. While the industry often cites the "shortage of professionals" as the root cause [32], recent studies suggest that variance is the true adversary [34]. Adding more analysts increases capacity (μ) but does not address the high variability (c_s^2) inherent in manual expert discovery. By framing the SOC-to-IAM connection as a queuing network, we can mathematically estimate how transitioning from stochastic search to deterministic lookup stabilizes the incident backlog even under realistic, high-load conditions. Therefore, we identified the following research questions:

- **RQ1: How can the identification of Domain Experts be automated to reduce stochastic delays introduced by manual workflows?**
- **RQ2: How can the high time variance from manual workflows be reduced to stabilize routing-layer time and thereby reduce MTTR?**

Taken together, RQ1 and RQ2 define a joint systems problem: the routing step must strive to be both automated and stabilizing for the overall process. We therefore address them with a combined artifact-and-analysis design: The Threat Intelligence and Identity Resolution (TIIR) process model. It provides deterministic Domain Expert identification from free-text incident information, while the formal process model and simulation quantify the impact of removing manual routing variance and discuss its implications for MTTR. To answer the research questions, this paper makes three contributions:

1. A variance-aware process model of the routing layer, using Little's Law and Kingman to explain why manual expert identification dominates tail latency.
2. A technical pipeline that transforms free-text CTI into a grounded vendor-product/CPE representation and links it to IAM-based ownership for deterministic Domain Expert identification.
3. A two-level evaluation: (i) component accuracy for CPE extraction and (ii) a discrete-event simulation quantifying TIIR under varying load and misrouting rates.

The remainder of the paper is structured as follows: In Sect. 2, we provide context on queuing systems and IAM, as well as related work and the methodology used. Section 3 presents the formalization of the SOC-to-IAM process model as a queuing system. In Sect. 4, we detail the structure of our process model and examine the components necessary for the TIIR process. Section 5 contains the formalization, technical implementation, and technical validation. Section 6 evaluates TIIR in a real-world data simulation scenario. In Sect. 7, we discuss our work and limitations. Finally, Sect. 8 concludes the paper.

2 Background, Related Work and Methodology

To contextualize our proposed TIIR model, we first outline the operational friction in current SOC workflows, the untapped potential of IAM data, and the theoretical underpinnings of queuing networks.

2.1 Incident Timing Metrics and Process-Level Components

Standardized incident timing metrics are required to compare operational performance across teams and tools. FIRST's Security Incident Timing Metrics provides cross-industry definitions for key timing records and metrics (e.g., time-to-respond, contain, or remediate) [7]. In industry practice, MTTR remains one of the most widely used top-level indicators for SOC efficiency and incident handling, but operational performance cannot be reduced to speed alone. Instead, SOCs must balance response speed, decision quality, and available analyst capacity, and therefore commonly track timing measures such as time to triage, time to decision, and related workload indicators alongside MTTR. This process perspective is particularly relevant for manual routing and assignment sub-processes because delays arise not only from average handling time but also from variability and variance introduced by waiting, hand-offs, and reassignment loops. We therefore isolate the routing and assignment step and model it via Mean Time to Correct Assignment (MTTCA), as a process-level metric that captures the elapsed time from ticket creation to correct assignment to the responsible Domain Expert. MTTCA is not a replacement for MTTR, as reducing MTTCA reduces the routing contribution to MTTR.

2.2 SOC, CTI and Incident Handling

The SOC is often described as the nervous system of modern cybersecurity operations, functioning as the primary ingestion point for events, alerts, and Cyber Threat Intelligence (CTI) [32]. For this paper, we use the term SOC as an abstract umbrella concept rather than referring to any specific organizational unit, tooling, or architecture. While some organizations separate the SOC intake from specialized incident handling [1,2], these terminological details do not affect our proposed TIIR process model. The SOC's core mandate is to ingest heterogeneous data streams, ranging from internal telemetry to external intelligence feeds, and translate them into actionable defense measures.

A major challenge in this workflow is the structural variance of input data. CTI is defined as the ensemble of evidence-based actionable knowledge about adversaries [30] and is critical for proactive defense. However, external CTI often arrives in unstructured or semi-structured formats that do not align with internal asset databases [4,25]. Before an incident can be resolved, SOC Analysts must manually normalize the data, identify affected vendors and products, and determine the threat's scope. This manual normalization acts as a significant latency driver, directly increasing the MTTR [4].

In particular, extracting valid CPE 2.3 identifiers from free-text is a prerequisite for deterministic asset and ownership mapping, because CPE provides a standardized vendor/product identity that can be joined with enterprise inventories and IAM ownership data.

Modern incident handling is rarely a solitary task performed solely within the SOC. While Security Experts in the SOC are responsible for detection, triage, and initial containment, the ultimate remediation often requires privileges and context held by decentralized Domain Experts [34]. These experts manage the specific applications, identities, or infrastructure segments referenced in a threat report. Consequently, the SOC functions effectively as a dispatcher in a queuing system: it must route enriched incident data to the correct Domain Expert to execute authorized changes, e.g., patch a vulnerability or reset a compromised account [34]. The efficiency of the entire incident lifecycle, therefore, hinges not only on technical detection but also on the speed and accuracy of this organizational routing. This is precisely the gap our TIIR process model aims to automate.

2.3 Identity and Access Management

IAM systems manage digital identities, authorizations, and access to resources in enterprise systems [12,18]. They therefore maintain mappings between subjects, permissions, roles, and organizational responsibilities, including policy owners and Domain Experts with specific knowledge about the governed permissions or resources [18]. In enterprise settings, these identities can represent individual Domain Experts as well as roles or groups that assume collective responsibility; depending on the access-control model, permissions may also be delegated or derived from role and attribute assignments [12]. Since IAM systems can map organizational structure and manage employees' permissions and roles, they provide a relevant organizational context layer for identifying accountable personnel [12]. This makes IAM an under-leveraged knowledge base for incident routing: if the affected technical object can be linked to an IAM-governed resource, the SOC can identify responsible, already authorized personnel rather than relying on manual ownership search. Similar to our use of SOC as an umbrella term, we use IAM broadly to refer to the identity, role, authorization, and ownership infrastructure that links personnel data to governed technical resources. Where no single IAM system provides this view, TIIR can instead operate over an equivalent authoritative data provider that links personnel, role, ownership, and asset-management data. An ongoing challenge in IAM systems is achieving satisfactory data quality, especially regarding the correct labeling of authorizations and their corresponding software. Kern et al. [18] investigated metrics for measuring data quality. Signs of low data quality are mostly outdated or missing identity data. Examples include administration accounts that still carry the name or email address of the person responsible prior to a reassignment. The current SOC infrastructure is also prone to similar quality problems [32], since changes in responsibilities and assignments must be tracked separately by the SOC team.

2.4 SOC as a Queuing System

From an abstract perspective, the process of handling security-related events within the SOC is comparable to an industrial production process. Similar to the organization of raw materials [15], incident data is collected, enriched, and routed along a value chain to the appropriate decision-makers. The efficiency of the entire SOC relies fundamentally on the seamless handover between these steps. Thus, the SOC acts as a flow production system with asynchronous material flow. Because incident arrival times and the time required to identify and reach Domain Experts vary stochastically, queues inevitably form. These queues prevent an immediate blocking of downstream remediation actions, but they introduce latency [15]. Consequently, this value chain behaves as a stochastic queuing system. While Little's Law ($L = \lambda W$) [20] governs the macroscopic relationship between backlog (L), arrival rate (λ), and residence time (W), it is the variability in processing these steps that drives the waiting times [15,19].

2.5 Related Work

Modern SOCs are increasingly transitioning from reactive incident handling to proactive, automated response paradigms. Xi et al. [33] show that Agentic AI can dynamically construct responses such as host isolation. However, these systems still struggle with decisions requiring organizational knowledge. Thus, human coordination remains a persistent bottleneck in incident handling. Although Empl et al. [8] demonstrate that SOAR can reduce response latency, Vielberth et al. [32] note that human-in-the-loop steps are still orchestrated manually, typically via ticketing systems. This results in substantial delays in the incident handling.

In adjacent domains, expert recommendation and automated assignment have been studied more extensively: bug triage recommends developers from historical bug reports and expertise traces [3], online-service incident triage predicts responsible teams from incident text, prior assignments, discussions, and reassignment traces while showing that reassignment is frequent and costly [5,6], and customer-support or ITSM work routes support requests or measures assignment delay from historical support archives [23], workflow artifacts, knowledge bases [31], and operational KPIs [9]. In contrast, incident assignment in SOCs commonly relies on manually maintained data structures that are less accurate and timely [21]. Current literature also focuses on protecting identities from compromise [24,27] rather than on leveraging IAM data as an operational directory.

To the best of our knowledge, no prior work integrates SOC automation, CTI/Common Platform Enumeration (CPE)-based incident grounding, IAM-based organizational modeling, and Domain Expert identification. Our work addresses this gap by treating IAM as a real-time representation of organizational structure and by enabling automated, principled mapping from incidents to accountable Domain Experts, effectively operationalizing the final step of incident handling.

2.6 Methodology

Our work is grounded in the principles of Design Science Research (DSR) Methodology, as outlined by Hevner et al. [14] and Peffers et al. [22]. DSR is primarily used to create and evaluate innovative artifacts, such as models, processes, or implementations that address significant real-world problems. In our research, we aim to develop a formal process model and its corresponding prototype to effectively bridge the gap in identification from the SOC to relevant Domain Experts. Evaluation is crucial for determining the artifact's utility and efficacy in solving the identified problem, thereby aligning with DSR principles. To rigorously evaluate, we applied a quantitative validation focused on the TIIR process model, which consists of three steps. Initially, a proof-of-concept confirms the basic functionality and consistency of the entire process model data pipeline, showing the correct derivation of dependency information from IAM data. Secondly, performance testing assesses the key technical criteria of accuracy and efficiency. As a final step, a simulation is used to quantify improvement in MTTCA and to discuss its implications for the routing contribution to MTTR.

3 Formal Process Modeling

Having introduced the core concepts, a formal model is presented to quantify the operational friction in manual SOCs. We validate and parameterize the model using empirical findings from recent field studies [2,19,34]. A quantitative validation and evaluation of those operational implications will be done in Sects. 5 and 6.

To strictly quantify the necessity of automation beyond simple speed improvements, we derive a model based on queuing theory. We abstract the SOC as a stochastic processing system in which stability is determined not only by capacity but also by variance.

3.1 Deterministic Baseline: Capacity and Structure

In an ideal scenario, the system capacity is governed by the *Cycle Time* (C) [15]. If the SOC must handle a target volume of incidents (X) within a planning period (T), e.g., one shift, the maximum allowable time per alert is defined as:

$$C = \frac{T}{X} \tag{1}$$

This theoretical value C represents the upper limit for the service time per incident. If the actual processing time exceeds this limit, the system enters an unstable state in the form of backlog accumulation.

The incident handling process is rarely a monolithic task but rather a sequence of dependent operations. Formally, we model this as a Directed Acyclic Graph (DAG) $G = (V, E)$, where nodes V represent tasks (e.g., "Context Enrichment", "Expert Identification") and edges E represent strict precedence constraints. Following the classic formulation of the *Simple Assembly Line Balancing Problem* (SALBP) [26], the incident response process consists of a set of distinct tasks ($i = 1, \ldots, N$) into workstations (m) such that the sum of task times (t_i) at any station does not exceed the cycle time (C).

$$\sum_{i \in S_m} t_i \leq C \tag{2}$$

where S_m is the set of tasks assigned to station m. In a manual SOC, this condition is frequently violated because the task times t_i are not static but fluctuate heavily with incident complexity. This violation necessitates a shift from deterministic observations to the stochastic queuing perspective.

3.2 Stochastic Reality: Kendall, Little's Law and Kingman

Unlike rigid manufacturing lines, SOC operations exhibit high variability in both arrival and service times. The system is formally characterized using the standard Kendall notation [17] as a ($G/G/m$) queue. In this nomenclature, the first symbol denotes the inter-arrival time distribution, the second the service time distribution, and m the number of parallel working Security Analysts.

Despite this distributional complexity, the system's macroscopic state remains subject to fundamental conservation laws. The primary relationship governing the long-term stability is Little's Law [20]:

$$E[L] = \lambda \cdot E[W] \tag{3}$$

which states that the average backlog ($E[L]$) is directly proportional to the arrival rate (λ) and the mean time to resolve ($E[W]$).

We view end-to-end MTTR as the sum of multiple lifecycle components. This paper isolates the routing and assignment components and models them as MTTCA. Accordingly, $\mathbb{E}[W]$ in the following queueing model refers to routing-layer time in the system, not to the full end-to-end incident-resolution time.

While Little's Law describes the system's state, it does not explain the cause of delays. To understand why manual SOCs struggle even when theoretically staffed correctly ($\rho < 1$), we must look at the impact of variability using Kingman's Approximation [15]:

$$E[W] \approx \underbrace{\left(\frac{\rho}{1-\rho}\right)}_{\text{Utilization}} \cdot \underbrace{\left(\frac{c_a^2 + c_s^2}{2}\right)}_{\text{Variability}} \cdot \tau + \tau \tag{4}$$

Here, τ is the mean service time, ρ is the utilization factor, c_a^2 represents the squared coefficient of variation for inter-arrival times, and c_s^2 is the squared coefficient of variation for service times. This equation reveals that high variance (c_s^2) in manual processing acts as a multiplier for wait times.

3.3 The Expert Identification Bottleneck

We apply this model specifically to the identification and routing phase, which is the process of finding the correct Domain Expert for an affected asset. Recent empirical research [19] highlights this specific phase as a critical source of both operational latency (τ) and process variance (c_s^2). This empirical evidence illustrates the severe cost of this friction. In a large-scale analysis of 115 million alerts, Yang et al. [34] found that 65% of true attacks necessitate multi-analyst collaboration. This structural dependence on external experts correlates with a drastic increase in investigation time. We argue that within a queuing framework, this dependency manifests as a massive inflation of the mean service time τ, including the idle wait times in MTTCA inherent in asynchronous communication steps. We use this as a qualitative motivation that coordination-heavy incidents can inflate downstream handling time.

Qualitative field studies by Kersten et al. [19] provide insight into the root cause of this instability. Their observations reveal that Tier-1 analysts frequently lack explicit data of domain expertise, forcing them to rely on implicit knowledge to route tickets. This reliance fundamentally alters the nature of the process: it transforms what should be a deterministic routing step into a stochastic search with high error rates. From a mathematical perspective, this introduces significant variance ($c_s^2 \gg 0$) into the service distribution, which, according to Kingman's approximation, acts as a multiplier for the overall queue latency.

Propagation of Variability. Finally, considering the SOC as a sequential workflow, variability is not contained but propagates. According to the linking equation derived by Hopp and Spearman [15], the output variability of one stage (c_d^2) is determined by its utilization (ρ), the arrival variability (c_a^2), and the service variability (c_s^2):

$$c_d^2 \approx \rho^2 c_s^2 + (1 - \rho^2) \cdot c_a^2 \quad (5)$$

This relationship implies that a highly variable expert identification process phase ($c_s^2 \gg 0$) acts as a noise generator. Particularly under high load ($\rho \to 1$), the output variability becomes dominated by the service process ($c_d^2 \approx c_s^2$), which injects stochastic volatility into the subsequent remediation queue, destabilizing downstream operations regardless of their own efficiency. By automating this identification phase ($c_s^2 \to 0$), we effectively install a low-pass filter that stabilizes the entire downstream chain.

Empirical Validation of Model Parameters. Recent field studies visually confirm the friction points modeled by our queuing parameters:

Kersten et al. [19] map the investigation steps of Tier-1 analysts (cf. Fig. 2 in [19]). Their data reveal a non-linear, oscillating search pattern in which analysts repeatedly switch contexts to gather information. This chaotic search path provides empirical evidence of a high coefficient of variation ($c_s^2 \gg 0$).

Alahmadi et al. [2] show qualitatively that analysts distinguish between false positives and "benign triggers", i.e., alarms that technically match a rule but are operationally non-actionable in the local environment. Their key contribution is therefore not a quantitative benign-trigger rate, but the observation that incident validation depends on organization-specific context. In a manual setup, retrieving this context increases the effective service time (τ) and introduces analyst-dependent variation. Together, Alahmadi et al. and Kersten et al. support our central modeling assumption: missing context and implicit knowledge turn routing into a high-variance search process, whereas TIIR aims to replace that search with structured context retrieval and deterministic resolution.

3.4 Implications for Automation

This derivation highlights that automation serves two distinct, quantifiable functions in the SOC context:

1. Capacity Effect: Reducing the routing and assignment variability directly improves MTTCA and therefore reduces the routing-layer contribution to MTTR ($E[W]$) and the mean service time (τ) while increasing effective throughput under fixed staffing.
2. Stability Effect: Driving c_s^2 downward reduces downstream variability propagation and lowers the risk that waiting times escalate (under high load) as utilization approaches one, as shown by Kingman's approximation.

4 TIIR Process Model

Based on the formal necessity to minimize service time variance ($c_s^2 \rightarrow 0$) derived in Sect. 3, we propose the Threat Intelligence and Identity Resolution (TIIR) process model. The high-level architecture, depicted in Fig. 1, will be enhanced by the description of three components: the Transformer in Sect. 4.1, the Loader in Sect. 4.2 and the IAM System in Sect. 4.3.

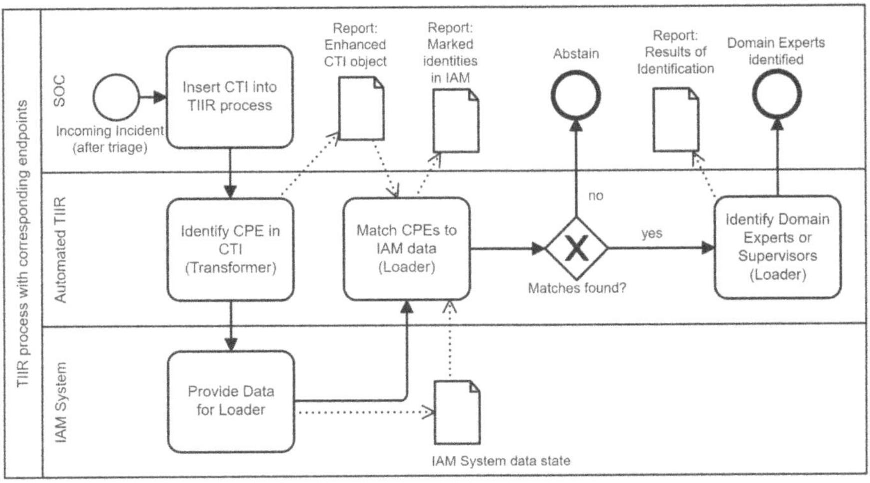

Fig. 1. The TIIR process model encompasses a three-layer structure which connects the IAM system and the SOC. The information gathered during an execution may be used to start sub- and follow-up processes.

4.1 Transformer: Input Normalization

The primary function of the Transformer is to act as a variance-reduction filter for incoming CTI data. Raw incidents from a SOC often vary in granularity, as they may be presented in plain text or structured formats, e.g., JSON. Incomplete input data creates "noise" that hinders automated processing.

As detailed in Fig. 2, the Transformer parses these disparate inputs to construct an enhanced CTI object. It targets the logic required for downstream automation by harmonizing data into standard taxonomies. As highlighted by Serzantov et al. [27], threats specifically target distinct asset types and their life cycle stages. To address this, the Transformer enriches the incident with the Common Platform Enumeration (CPE)[1] to uniquely identify the affected technical asset. By enforcing this structure, the Transformer reduces downstream routing variability caused by analyst-dependent normalization.

[1] https://nvd.nist.gov/products/cpe.

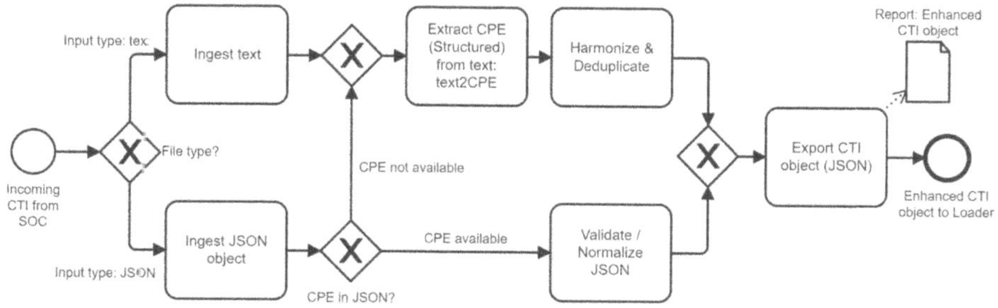

Fig. 2. The Transformer standardizes heterogeneous incident descriptions into a structured CTI object with CPE-based identifiers for downstream routing.

4.2 Loader: Deterministic Rule Application

The Loader serves as the decision engine that implements the bounded low-variance $\mathcal{O}(1)$ lookup logic proposed in our formal process model. In contrast to the Transformer, it uses only deterministic methods and operates on a predefined set of rules. Its process steps are detailed in Fig. 3. The Loader's first task is to match the enhanced CTI object received from the Transformer with IAM data. If matches to the IAM data exist, the associated Domain Experts are identified and the second report is generated. The task "Apply Rule set to induce changes" will then determine which rules predefined by the SOC and Domain Experts should be triggered and executed. The actions prescribed by the rules may temporarily modify the extracted IAM data, which may subsequently be reimported into the IAM system.

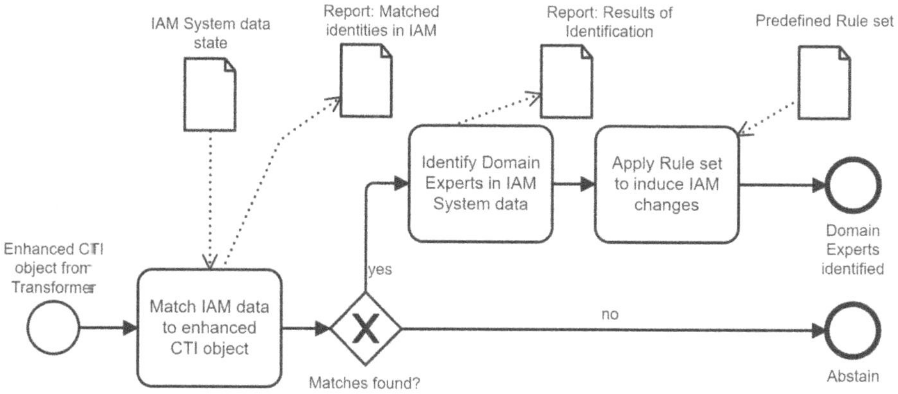

Fig. 3. The Loader replaces human investigation with a deterministic lookup based on predefined rules, ensuring a bounded, low-variance lookup time, reducing the service time (τ).

4.3 IAM System: Domain Expert Resolution

To maintain system integrity, the modified IAM data file provided by the Loader must be imported with security and regulatory requirements in mind. Data changes should be imported only into attribute fields designed to store the temporal modifications necessary to identify and possibly notify the Domain Experts. This provides two benefits: First, the IAM system can cleanly revert to its baseline state once the threat is mitigated. Second, the IAM System would be able to enforce the notifications on its own terms. Since the information has now reached the affected identities in the IAM system, there are several ways to return identified Domain Expert to the SOC. As a first step, automated tasks or processes within the IAM are required, which react to data changes and follow the chain of ownership present for the identities. This may lead to a direct owner which is set as an attribute on the affected identities. Alternatively, there is a group or a role configured as owner, in which case the IAM system can deduce the personnel assigned to it. If the deduced personnel is not present or marked as absent, this chain may either lead to the substitute owners or an attribute similar in function at the affected identities themselves or to the supervisors of the absent personnel. As the entire organizations hierarchy is contained in the IAM system due to its connection to HR systems, a Domain Expert or a supervisor who can delegate to an appropriate expert is reached eventually. Starting from here, there are at least two possible paths. Either the identified personnel is notified by the IAM system, e.g. via E-Mail, and asked to report to the SOC, or the SOC receives a list of candidates which they may contact.

For example, consider an incident description that indicates a vulnerability in SAP. The Transformer would normalize the free-text report to the CPE

$$cpe : 2.3 : a : sap : netweaver : 7.50 : * : * : * : * : * : * : *$$

and the Loader matches it to the governed IAM object `SAP-NW-750-PROD`. The owner attribute of this object points to the role `sap-basis-admins`. The IAM System resolves this role to a set of personnel accounts with supervisors attached. The SOC therefore receives either a directly notifiable available Domain Expert or a ranked fallback contact who can delegate to the correct expert.

5 Formalization, Implementation and Validation

In this chapter, we formalize the TIIR reference implementation and specify how its model-level outputs are transformed into routing decisions for the system-level evaluation. Unlike the architectural view in Sect. 4, this chapter focuses on the data objects, transformation functions, and the confidence-gated decision logic. We subsequently demonstrate the implementation and validity of TIIR.

5.1 Formalization of the TIIR Process Model

To ensure deterministic downstream behavior, we first formalize the data flow and the transformation logic. In plain terms, TIIR first converts an incident into a normalized technical object and then resolves this object against routable ownership records. Let $S = \langle id, \dots \rangle$ denote a raw input object (e.g., a ticket, STIX object, or CVE-derived text fragment). We define the following sets:

- $\mathbb{UUID}$: the set of globally unique identifiers,
- $\mathbb{CPE}$: the set of valid Common Platform Enumeration (CPE 2.3) identifiers,
- $\mathbb{CTX}$: the set of contextual attributes relevant for routing (e.g., criticality, asset metadata),
- $\mathbb{OBJ}$: the set of routable IAM target objects (e.g., identities, permissions),
- $\mathbb{VER}$: the set of version identifiers.

Definition 1 (Enhanced CTI Object). The intermediate object produced by semantic normalization is the typed tuple C:

$$C = \langle id \in \mathbb{UUID},\ cpe \subseteq (\mathbb{CPE} \cup \bot), ctx \in (\mathbb{CTX} \cup \bot)\rangle. \tag{6}$$

It is derived from the raw object S by the extraction functions:

- $C.id := S.id$
- $C.cpe$ can be extracted from the infrastructure, malware, note, observed data, opinion, and report STIX Domain Objects of S, if present.
- $C.ctx$ can be extracted from the infrastructure, malware, note, observed data, opinion, and report STIX Domain Objects of S, if present.
- $\bot$ is a fallback marker if a mapping is not possible.

where each C denotes a deterministic or confidence-gated extraction step.
Definition 2 (Loader Function). The **Loader** δ consumes an Enhanced CTI Object C and applies a subset R of the predefined static rules $\mathbb{R}$ to the imported IAM state Σ_{IAM}.

$$\delta : R \times \Sigma_{IAM} \rightarrow \Sigma'_{IAM} \tag{7}$$

The resulting assignment decision is determined by a rule set $R(C) \subseteq \mathbb{R}$ derived from C. Each rule $r \in \mathbb{R}$ has the form

$$r = \langle target \in \mathbb{OBJ},\ version \in \mathbb{VER} \cup \{\bot\},\ ctx \in \mathbb{CTX} \cup \{\bot\}\rangle \mapsto action, \tag{8}$$

where *action* denotes a deterministic routing or IAM-linked resolution action. The Loader function ϕ executes the following mapping steps:

1. identify $target \in \mathbb{OBJ}$ from *cpe* and *ctx* of C if possible;
2. derive a relevant $version \in \mathbb{VER}$ from *cpe* if possible;
3. apply matching rules $r \in \mathbb{R}$;
4. if no valid mapping exists, emit $\bot$ and trigger fallback handling.

All rules that are identified by the Loader in matching their $target, version, cxt$ are added to the rule set R. The resulting state Σ'_{IAM} is the modified IAM configuration, which is then reimported by the IAM system. This formal separation ensures that the complex ML-based inference by the Transformer yields only deterministic, pre-expected results via (ϕ) by applying R during (δ).

After formalizing the TIIR process model, a proof-of-concept implementation is created. It consists of a Transformer based on a Mistral model, a Loader written in Python, and a pseudonymous IAM dataset. The code and test artifacts are available in our repository: https://github.com/soctoiam/soc_to_iam.

5.2 The Transformer

The Transformer accepts two input modalities: free text and JSON. JSON input may contain structured fields such as CVE or STIX attributes. If a valid CPE is present, the pipeline skips extraction and continues directly with deterministic routing. Otherwise, the process mirrors the behavior of free-text input and performs semantic normalization (cf. Fig. 2). The technical challenge is to realize the mapping $S \rightarrow C$ when explicit identifiers are missing from the source. For this, a specialized LLM was integrated. If the required information is unavailable, the threat description is sent to the retrained model. The LLM is used to normalize unstructured input into a structured intermediate object that can be checked, grounded, and, if necessary, rejected by a confidence-gated fallback rule. We recognize that, on a high level, LLMs appear to provide non-deterministic outputs. However, the LLM component is necessary to obtain structured mappings from free text and to facilitate SOC Analysts' work. In addition, the Loader was designed to generate a deterministic fallback solution in the event of unclear statements or special cases. The reliability of the derived rules (R) depends entirely on the quality of the upstream normalization in C. If the Transformer fails to populate *cpe* correctly, the derived rules will be flawed. Additionally, we do not claim novelty in LLM extraction or rule-based lookup in isolation. The contribution is the deterministic integration of CTI normalization, grounded technical identifiers, and IAM-linked responsibility resolution for SOC routing. *text2CPE (populating cpe)* Populating the set $cpe \subseteq \mathbb{CPE}$ requires the generative extraction of vendor, product, additional targets, and version strings into a JSON schema compatible with the NIST CPE 2.3 standard. While discriminative models struggle with the task's generative nature, LLMs require constraints to ensure strict syntactic precision. Yet two properties make this task non-trivial: (i) high precision requirements for vendor/product identity and (ii) structured output constraints, including multiple affected components and version ranges. Our initial approach was to extract relevant information using regex, keyword matching, or supervised multi-label classification. In addition to not handling multiple CPEs well, whether from a single vendor or from different vendors, regex struggles to accurately extract version(s). Constraints like "affects versions between 2.4 and 3.1, excluding 2.4.7", and similar terms make exact matching nearly impossible. We argue that LLMs are the best choice here. Our two-stage design resolves this tension: the Mistral model performs semantic extraction (maximizing recall of relevant vendor/product/version signals), while the Hybrid Match step enforces deterministic grounding against the official CPE dictionary, thereby maximizing precision. This separation of concerns ensures that the Loader never receives a CPE identifier that does not match the standard.

Generative Extraction. Using QLoRA, we fine-tuned `Mistral7B-Instructv0.3` to the schema requirements of CPE identifiers without full-parameter retraining. The model is instructed to output a JSON object containing part, vendor, product, target software, and version-boundary fields.

Dataset Construction Pipeline. Training on the raw NVD corpus is inefficient and prone to severe vendor bias. To ensure robust generalization, we constructed a high-quality, stratified dataset of 59,000 records derived from NVD data. The construction pipeline enforces a rigorous balance: Raw NVD records are parsed to create a "Gold Standard" mapping of natural language descriptions to structured CPE components. We applied dynamic capping to prevent bias and overfitting toward dominant vendors such as Microsoft or Adobe, resulting in a low Herfindahl-Hirschman Index (HHI ≈ 0.0034) for vendor diversity. The End-to-End training pipeline is shown in Fig. 4.

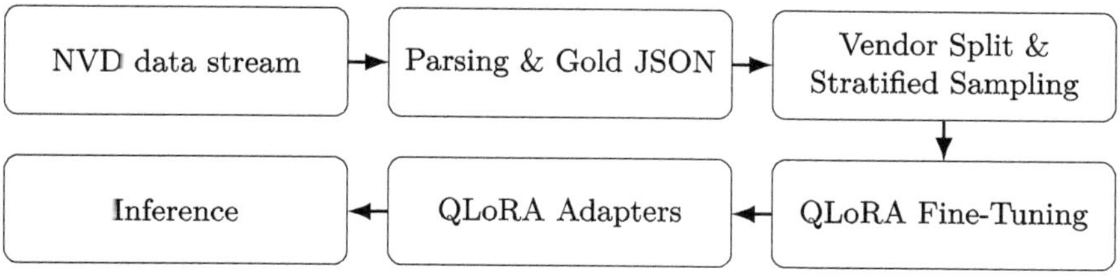

Fig. 4. End-to-end training pipeline: From raw CVEs to a stratified 59,000 CPE subset and QLoRA adapters.

A fundamental limitation of generative models in this context is nondeterministic output, including hallucinated vendor and product combinations. To constrain this behavior, we implemented a deterministic post-processing step for Retrieval-Augmented Generation (RAG) called *Hybrid Match*. The raw output of the Mistral model is not accepted at face value. Instead, it serves as a semantic query against a TF-IDF indexed CPE knowledge base. If the best score falls below a fixed threshold, the candidate is rejected. Otherwise, it is grounded to the matched CPE entry. This step bridges the gap between semantic extraction and the formal rigidity required for downstream routing.

Evaluation of CPE Extraction. We evaluated the system on $N = 300$ samples derived from the NVD stream. Table 1 reports the results for the baseline LLM and the final grounded variant used for the DES (cf. Sect. 6) calibration. The final grounded model is the pragmatic calibration point for the MTTCA simulation because it is the deployed first-hop decision mechanism. Its primary improvement over the baseline is a substantial increase in precision, which is crucial because false routing decisions are costlier than abstentions. This component evaluation is not intended as an exhaustive benchmark of CPE extraction methods. The reported $N = 300$ evaluation, therefore, serves as a feasibility and calibration point for the TIIR routing model.

5.3 The Loader

The Loader δ constitutes the execution phase of the TIIR process model, operationalizing the formal function ϕ. It is triggered immediately by the Transformer

Table 1. Impact of grounding and validation on free-text to CPE extraction. Precision and recall are computed on vendor-product identity matches (set-match on (`part`, `vendor`, `product`)). The baseline itself shows solid performance (F1 0.52). The RAG layer's primary contribution is a significant boost in precision to 0.81, effectively filtering out hallucinations and raising overall F1 to 0.57.

Metric	Baseline (LLM)	RAG (Hybrid Match)	Improvement (%)
Precision	0.7262	**0.8155**	+12.30%
Recall	0.4058	**0.4412**	+8.72%
F1-Score	0.5207	**0.5726**	**+9.97%**

upon successful generation of an enhanced CTI object. The Loader operates on a static rule set and a pseudonymous IAM state. The Loader's primary objective is to determine the rules that will be activated. The proposed changes are then evaluated against the IAM data while ensuring data integrity and reversibility. Its purpose is to resolve a normalized (cpe, ctx) tuple to a bounded, deterministic routing or IAM-linked resolution decision. The first step iterates through the imported IAM data and tries to match each entry to a *target* of the enhanced CTI object. This matching relies on a deterministic matching logic, ensuring $\mathcal{O}(1)$ execution complexity per IAM data object. Once the targets are resolved, the script constructs the required data modification payload and creates a modified version of the imported data file. Then an API call to the IAM system could trigger a data import on these modified files. The design implication is important for the evaluation: stochasticity is confined to the Transformer stage and to the empirical arrival and service processes. The Loader itself is deterministic and therefore contributes negligible variance compared with manual routing and reassignment loops. The formalization supports incidents affecting multiple assets ($C.\text{cpe} > 1$). The Loader iterates over multiple grounded CPE candidates and aggregates all resulting permission and account matches into a single report.

6 Evaluation

The TIIR process is evaluated at two levels: (i) component-level free-text to CPE extraction quality (cf. Table 1) and (ii) system-level routing performance using a discrete-event simulation (DES) of MTTCA, the time from ticket creation until assignment to the correct domain expert. MTTCA is not the same as end-to-end MTTR; rather, it isolates the routing-layer component of MTTR, which is the process segment targeted by TIIR. Domain Expert routing has two paths: manual routing or automatic processing by TIIR. Therefore, using TIIR, three outcomes are possible: successful automatic recognition p_{correct}, incorrect automatic recognition and though misroute $p_{\text{auto-misroute}}$, and no automatic recognition p_{abstain}. In cases of $p_{\text{auto-misroute}}$ and p_{abstain}, the incident is routed manually afterwards. To parameterize the DES, we treat precision P

and recall R (cf. Table 1) as deployment proxies for the first routing decision under two simplifying assumptions: at most one confidence-accepted TIIR decision per ticket, and successful IAM resolution once a correctly grounded identifier is available. The first-hop TIIR outcomes become $p_{\text{correct}} = R = 0.4412$, $p_{\text{auto-misroute}} = R(1/P - 1) = 0.0998$, and $p_{\text{abstain}} = 1 - R/P = 0.4590$. The end-to-end first-time routing probability is therefore $p_{\text{route-ok}} = p_{\text{correct}} \cdot p_{\text{IAM}}$. In the present DES, we set $p_{\text{IAM}} = 1$ to isolate routing-layer effects on MTTCA. Accordingly, the DES should be read as a scenario analysis and optimistic upper bound for routing-layer gains, not as a field measurement of end-to-end MTTR.

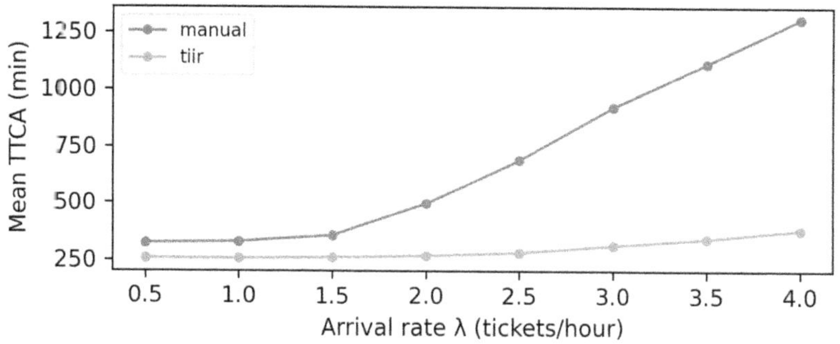

Fig. 5. Mean TTCA as a function of arrival rate λ. Manual routing increases from 323.9 min at $\lambda = 0.5$ to 1308.9 min at $\lambda = 4.0$, whereas TIIR increases only from 257.2 to 378.6 min. The hockey-stick effect from about $\lambda = 2.0$ onward indicates queueing amplification in the manual routing stage.

We use Trinkenreich et al. as the primary source for absolute manual assignment times because it directly reports the "Open" → "Assigned" bottleneck with mean 109.3 min, median 51.5 min, and maximum 26.3 h [31]. For *relative* reassignment dynamics, we use Chen et al., who report reassignment rates between 4.11% and 91.58% and an average 10.16× inflation of incident-triage time when reassignment occurs [6]. We treat Powell et al. and the Freshservice Benchmark as contextual sensitivity anchors, not as primary MTTCA calibration sources, because they measure different assignment workflows [9,23]. Figure 5 reports the resulting DES outcomes over increasing arrival rates. Based on these academic and practical parameters, the MTTCA for the TIIR and the manual assignment process can be calculated. A full documentation on the calculation process is available in the repository. The results presented in Fig. 5 show that the TIIR process is faster in general and is also better able to keep a stable mean time if presented with high ticket loads. This is consistent with our queueing argument from Sect. 3.

7 Discussion and Limitations

While the TIIR process technically enables the automated detection of Domain Experts, its effectiveness relies on factors beyond pure algorithmic performance. In this section, we discuss the dependencies on data quality and justify our validation and evaluation approach against the backdrop of recent empirical findings in SOC operations.

Compared with the related work discussed in Sect. 2.5, TIIR addresses a different mechanism. Prior SOC automation and SOAR approaches automate response actions but leave the resolution of organizational responsibilities largely manual. Expert-recommendation and ticket-routing approaches learn assignees or categories from historical tickets, labels, discussions, reassignment traces, and knowledge bases. Whereas TIIR resolves incidents from standardized CTI/CPE identifiers to accountable Domain Experts through authoritative IAM ownership and delegation data.

The proposed automation pipeline is subject to the "Garbage In, Garbage Out" principle. Although the Transformer is designed to reduce variance, it cannot reconstruct missing information. As noted in our implementation, the Transformer relies on extracting explicit signals from incidents. If the initial incident report lacks sufficient detail about the affected system, the enhanced CTI object C remains sparse, resulting in a fallback in the Loader. The Loader's determinism is bound by its rule set $\mathbb{R}$. As identified by Kersten et al. [19], analysts often rely on implicit knowledge because explicit documentation is missing. If this implicit knowledge is not formalized into the Loader's rules, the automation will default to generic reactions, potentially missing nuance. This mirrors the "context gap" identified by Alahmadi et al. [2], in which missing contextual information leads to misclassifying benign triggers. The routing logic assumes that assets are correctly mapped to Domain Experts in the IAM system. If the IAM data itself is stale, the automated routing will function technically but fail operationally. However, unlike a manual process, in which such issues lead to indefinite wait times, our process generates an immediate exception report. This shifts the failure mode from a silent stalling to an explicit error (cf. Fig. 3, "Matches exist?; No", allowing the SOC to address data quality issues systematically.

We explicitly chose a technical validation and evaluation, as shown in Sects. 5 and 6, over a field study. Following the Design Science Research (DSR) methodologies of Hevner et al., we argue that a comprehensive, generalizable real-world assessment of SOC-specific MTTR improvements is inherently complex due to the high heterogeneity of SOC environments. Each organization employs a unique security stack and operational maturity level. As Yang et al. [34] demonstrated, organizational-specific factors, such as collaboration structures, strongly influence incident handling times. Deriving generalized statistics from a single-case deployment of our TIIR process would therefore lack external validity. Additionally, instead of measuring a real-time MTTR reduction in a single environment, our work validates the mechanism of the reduction. We proved that our Transformer reduces the infinite set of natural-language variances to a finite set of identifiers ($\mathbb{CPE}$). We also proved that the Loader replaces the stochastic search process, identified by Kersten et al. [19] as a root cause of delay, with a deterministic $\mathcal{O}(1)$ lookup. We acknowledge that the reported MTTCA gains are scenario-based estimates under stated assumptions, not direct field measurements of end-to-end incident resolution. The DES further assumes successful IAM resolution once a correctly grounded identifier is available ($p_{\text{IAM}} = 1$), which isolates routing effects but likely overestimates performance where IAM data are stale or incomplete. The DES assumption of successful IAM resolution after correct grounding should be interpreted as an optimistic routing-layer upper bound. To address this issue, we added an extra simulation file in the repository. In this simulation, different p_{IAM} sensitivity sweeps influence the results. But, crucially, every verifiable reduction in manual effort or service time variance constitutes a tangible operational gain. By formalizing the TIIR process model and providing a technically valid implementation, we lay a foundation that enables organizations to measure and realize these immediate operational benefits within their specific context. Finally, we note that every system incurs implementation and maintenance costs. These are not in the scope of this academic research. The prototypical implementation of TIIR is open source and can be used accordingly. The simulation can be utilized in cost and benefit calculations.

8 Conclusion

As a first contribution, this paper analyzes production workflows to compare them to Domain Expert identification. For the second contribution, it identifies the stochastic variance inherent in these manual expert discoveries as the primary bottleneck for scalability. Therefore, it introduces the TIIR process model.

TIIR reduces routing-layer delay by automating Domain Expert identification and assignment, thereby lowering MTTCA and the routing contribution to MTTR. This answers RQ1 and RQ2. A key enabler is the transformation of free-text descriptions into CPE 2.3 identifiers, which allows deterministic joins and IAM ownership data. It thereby shows that the automated connection between the SOC and the IAM system increases the SOC's capacity for incident handling. Together with the quantification and evaluation of TIIR, this provides the third contribution.

As the process model addresses the reduction of information silos in general, its use can enable other researchers to further reduce the workload for SOC operators. An interesting opportunity for future work is to abstract the TIIR process model to connect other security systems, such as network infrastructure and firewall systems, in a similar fashion to the SOC. As interconnectivity continues to grow, reducing knowledge silos may provide comparable benefits as the connection of SOC to IAM systems. Moreover, this process could be adapted outside of the information systems world. Security specialists from other disciplines (e.g., electricity, chemical processing, etc.) also work based on SOC incidents and could benefit from the TIIR process model. The automated communication with such systems provides direct access to first-hand information. It circumvents the time-consuming communication with system administrators about log data or manual evaluation in monitoring software for specific attack patterns arising from a newly detected incident.

Given the inherent trade-off between a SOC team's available resources and the volume of incidents requiring attention, we contend that implementing the TIIR process model benefits organizational security.

9 Ethical Considerations

Before initiating our research, we evaluated our methodology on potential ethical concerns. This work is exempt from human-subjects ethics review, since it did not involve human subjects, personal data, or user-generated content. However, we recognize the importance of considering ethical implications beyond data collection and the responsible use of the proposed technology.

Disclosure of Interests. The authors have no competing interests to declare that are relevant to the content of this article.

References

1. Agyepong, E., Cherdantseva, Y., Reinecke, P., Burnap, P.: A systematic method for measuring the performance of a cyber security operations centre analyst. Comput. Secur. **124**, 102959 (2023). https://doi.org/10.1016/j.cose.2022.102959
2. Alahmadi, B.A., Axon, L., Martinovic, I.: 99% false positives: a qualitative study of SOC analysts' perspectives on security alarms. In: 31st USENIX Security Symposium (USENIX Security 22), pp. 2783–2800. USENIX Association, Boston, MA, August 2022. https://www.usenix.org/conference/usenixsecurity22/presentation/alahmadi
3. Anvik, J., Hiew, L., Murphy, G.C.: Who should fix this bug? In: Proceedings of the 28th International Conference on Software Engineering, ICSE '06, pp. 361–370. Association for Computing Machinery, New York, NY, USA (2006). https://doi.org/10.1145/1134285.1134336
4. Bratsas, C., Anastasiadis, E.K., Angelidis, A.K., Ioannidis, L., Kotsakis, R., Ougiaroglou, S.: Knowledge graphs and semantic web tools in cyber threat intelligence: a systematic literature review. J. Cybersecur. Priv. **4**(3), 518–545 (2024). https://doi.org/10.3390/jcp4030025
5. Chen, J., He, X., et al.: An empirical investigation of incident triage for online service systems. In: Proceedings of the 2019 IEEE/ACM 41st International Conference on Software Engineering: Software Engineering in Practice (ICSE-SEIP), pp. 111–120. IEEE (2019). https://doi.org/10.1109/ICSE-SEIP.2019.00020
6. Chen, J., et al.: Continuous incident triage for large-scale online service systems. In: Proceedings of the 2019 34th IEEE/ACM International Conference on Automated Software Engineering (ASE), pp. 364–375. IEEE (2019). https://doi.org/10.1109/ASE.2019.00042

7. Chiarini, F., Sacher-Boldewin, D., Wilkins, L., Zajicek, M.: Security Incident Timing Metrics version 1.0: Specification Document. FIRST.Org, Inc., May 2023. https://www.first.org/global/sigs/metrics/Security-Incident-Timing-Metrics_v1.0.pdf, version 1.0
8. Empl, F., Schlette, D., Pernul, G.: SOAR4IoT: securing IoT assets with digital twins. In: 17th International Conference on Availability, Reliability and Security, ARES 2022. ACM, New York, NY, USA (2022). https://doi.org/10.1145/3538969.3544464
9. Freshworks: Freshservice benchmark report 2025: Faster, smarter it support. Technical report, Freshworks (2025). https://www.freshworks.com/freshservice/benchmark-report-2025/
10. Fuchs, S., Drieschner, C., Wittges, H.: Improving support ticket systems using machine learning: a literature review, January 2022. https://doi.org/10.24251/HICSS.2022.238
11. Ghadermazi, J., Shah, A., Jajodia, S.: A machine learning and optimization framework for efficient alert management in a cybersecurity operations center. Digit. Threat. **5**(2) (2024). https://doi.org/10.1145/3644393
12. Glöckler, J., Sedlmeir, J., Frank, M., Fridgen, G.: A systematic review of identity and access management requirements in enterprises and potential contributions of self-sovereign identity: J. glöckler. Bus. Inf. Syst. Eng. **66**(4), 421–440 (2024)
13. Hassan, W.U., Milajerdi, S.M., Eshete, B., Gjomemo, R., Sekar, R., Venkatakrishnan, V.N.: NoDoze: combatting threat alert fatigue with automated provenance triage. In: Network and Distributed System Security Symposium (NDSS) (2019). https://doi.org/10.14722/ndss.2019.23349
14. Hevner, A.R., March, S.T., Park, J., Ram, S.: Design science in information systems research. MIS Q. **28**(1), 75–105 (2004)
15. Hopp, W.J., Spearman, M.L.: Factory Physics, 3rd edn. Waveland Press, Long Grove, IL (2011)
16. Hummer, M., Groll, S., Kunz, M., Fuchs, L., Pernul, G.: Measuring identity and access management performance-an expert survey on possible performance indicators. In: ICISSP, pp. 233–240 (2018). https://doi.org/10.5220/0006557702330240
17. Kendall, D.G.: Stochastic processes occurring in the theory of queues and their analysis by the method of the imbedded Markov chain. Ann. Math. Stat. **24**(3), 338–354 (1953). http://www.jstor.org/stable/2236285
18. Kern, S., Baumer, T., Fuchs, L., Pernul, G.: Maintain high-quality access control policies: an academic and practice-driven approach. In: Atluri, V., Ferrara, A.L. (eds.) Data and Applications Security and Privacy XXXVII, pp. 223–242. Springer, Cham (2023). https://doi.org/10.1007/978-3-031-37586-6_14
19. Kersten, L., Beelen, K., Zambon, E., Snijders, C., Allodi, L.: A field study to uncover and a tool to support the alert investigation process of tier-1 analysts. In: Network and Distributed System Security Symposium (NDSS). The Internet Society, San Diego, CA (2025)
20. Kleinrock, L.: Queueing Systems. Volume I: Theory. Wiley (1975)
21. Onwubiko, C., Ouazzane, K.: Challenges towards building an effective cyber security operations centre. Int. J. Cyber Situational Awareness (IJCSA) **4**(1), 11–39 (2019)
22. Peffers, K., Tuunanen, T., Rothenberger, M.A., Chatterjee, S.: A design science research methodology for information systems research. J. Manage. Inf. Syst. (JMIS) **24**(3), 45–77 (2007)

23. Powell, M., Rotz, J.A., O'Malley, K.D.: How machine learning is improving U.S. Navy customer support. Proc. AAAI Conf. Artif. Intell. **34**(08), 13188–13195 (2020). https://doi.org/10.1609/aaai.v34i08.7023
24. Puchta, A., Baumer, T., Müller, M., Pernul, G.: IAM Meets CTI: make identity and access management ready for cyber threat intelligence. In:: Ferrara, A.L., Krishnan, R. (eds.) IFIP Annual Conference on Data and Applications Security and Privacy, pp. 44–52. Springer, Cham (2024). https://doi.org/10.1007/978-3-031-65172-4_3
25. Saeed, S., Suayyid, S.A., Al-Ghamdi, M.S., Al-Muhaisen, H., Almuhaideb, A.M.: A systematic literature review on cyber threat intelligence for organizational cybersecurity resilience. Sensors **23**(16), 7273 (2023). https://doi.org/10.3390/s23167273
26. Salveson, M.E.: The assembly-line balancing problem. Trans. Am. Soc. Mech. Eng. **77**(6), 939–947 (2022). https://doi.org/10.1115/1.4014559
27. Serzantov, V., Kupris, E., Schreck, T.: Identity threats and where to find them: mapping ITDR and MITRE ATT&CK. In: 2025 IEEE European Symposium on Security and Privacy Workshops (EuroS&PW). IEEE (2025). https://doi.org/10.1109/EUROSPW67616.2025.00062
28. Sundaramurthy, S.C., et al.: A human capital model for mitigating security analyst burnout. In: Eleventh Symposium On Usable Privacy and Security, SOUPS 2015, pp. 347–359. USENIX Association, Ottawa, July 2015. https://www.usenix.org/conference/soups2015/proceedings/presentation/sundaramurthy
29. Sundaramurthy, S.C., Wesch, M., Ou, X., McHugh, J., Rajagopalan, S.R., Bardas, A.: Humans are dynamic. Our tools should be too. innovations from the anthropological study of security operations centers. IEEE Internet Comput., 1 (2017). https://doi.org/10.1109/MIC.2017.265103212
30. Tounsi, W., Rais, H.: A survey on technical threat intelligence in the age of artificial intelligence. Comput. Secur. **72**, 212–227 (2018). Discusses CTI definitions and data heterogeneity challenges. https://doi.org/10.1016/j.cose.2017.11.008
31. Trinkenreich, B., Confort, V.T.F., Santos, G., Santoro, F.M.: Toward using business process intelligence to support incident management metrics selection and service improvement. In: Proceedings of the 27th International Conference on Software Engineering and Knowledge Engineering, SEKE 2015, pp. 522–527 (2015). https://doi.org/10.18293/SEKE2015-110
32. Vielberth, M., Böhm, F., Fichtinger, I., Pernul, G.: Security operations center: a systematic study and open challenges. IEEE Access **8**, 227756–227779 (2020). https://doi.org/10.1109/ACCESS.2020.3045514
33. Xi, Z., Chen, W., Guo, X., He, W., Ding, Y., Hong, B., Zhang, M., Wang, J., Jin, S., Zhou, E., et al.: The rise and potential of large language model based agents: a survey. Sci. China Inf. Sci. **68**(2), 121101 (2025). https://doi.org/10.1007/s11432-024-4222-0
34. Yang, L., et al.: True attacks, attack attempts, or benign triggers? An empirical measurement of network alerts in a security operations center. In: 33rd USENIX Security Symposium (USENIX Security 24), pp. 1525–1542. USENIX Association, Philadelphia, PA, August 2024. https://www.usenix.org/conference/usenixsecurity24/presentation/yang-limin

Smart Contracts and Cryptocurrency

Beyond Theft: How Underestimated Smart Contract Vulnerabilities Enable Extortionware

Riccardo Preatoni[1(✉)], Christian Scholz[2], Jens-Rene Giesen[2], Alessandro Brighente[1], Lucas Davi[2], and Mauro Conti[1,3]

[1] University of Padova, Padova, Italy
riccardo.preatoni@phd.unipd.it
{alessandro.brighente,mauro.conti}@unipd.it
[2] University of Duisburg-Essen, Essen, Germany
{christian.scholz,jens-rene.giesen,lucas.davi}@uni-due.de
[3] Örebro University, Örebro, Sweden

Abstract. Smart contracts have become essential to decentralized applications and enable secure, transparent automation of agreements. However, their transparency and immutability also make them vulnerable to attacks. Traditional ransomware attacks encrypt data to demand a ransom, but such direct manipulation is impossible with smart contracts due to their immutability. This paper introduces *Extortionware*, a novel ransomware-inspired attack method that exploits vulnerabilities in smart contracts to demand a ransom without directly withdrawing assets. We explain the Extortionware framework and demonstrate its relevance in practice with three case studies in which attackers could have locked over $465,000 worth of assets. To mitigate this threat, we developed an analysis approach to detect potential Extortionware-relevant vulnerabilities. We evaluate our approach by demonstrating its effectiveness on these real-world case studies and applying it to a dataset of 20,137 Ethereum smart contracts, where the analysis uncovers three distinct instances of Extortionware-like behavior in audited projects.

Keywords: Smart Contracts · Ethereum · Extortionware · Ransomware · Static Analysis · Vulnerability Detection

1 Introduction

Smart contracts have become essential for decentralized applications (DApps) and blockchain-based services because they can self-execute, self-verify, and are tamper-resistant. These features make smart contracts ideal for automating agreements securely and transparently. Thus, smart contracts are frequently used by multiple untrusted parties to make publicly verifiable agreements. However,

R. Preatoni and C. Scholz—Contributed equally to this work.

S. Nadjm-Tehrani et al. (Eds.): ARES 2026, LNCS 16898, pp. 415–437, 2027.
https://doi.org/10.1007/978-3-032-36874-4_21

this transparency allows anyone to access, read, and inspect the smart contract's code, which enables attackers to identify and exploit vulnerabilities.

In general, smart contracts are vulnerable to various issues, each with a different impact on the system's or users' security and privacy [2]. Despite efforts by researchers and industry experts to improve vulnerability identification and mitigation, publicly deployed smart contracts remain exposed to security threats. Perez et al. [28] have shown that many contracts deployed on the Ethereum blockchain still have well-known vulnerabilities. However, some of these vulnerabilities are considered minor because they do not allow attackers to withdraw funds, while most attackers' motivation is financial gain. Although these vulnerabilities are frequently deprioritized in audits for their seemingly low impact, some have proven capable of locking contract assets or disrupting key functionalities. These vulnerabilities are generally referred to as griefing vulnerabilities [15]. Notably, some of these issues were initially labeled as "informational" or "low severity", highlighting a dangerous underestimation of their exploitability [33].

Because smart contracts are computer programs, they are also prone to vulnerabilities that often occur in traditional computer systems, such as integer bugs and privilege escalation flaws. These types of vulnerabilities have been extensively studied in the field of smart contract security [3,14,17,31,37].

However, other types of threats against computer systems are more subtle and, to date, have not been considered in the smart contract domain. A prominent example is ransomware, which has caused significant financial losses in traditional systems, with individual payments reaching up to $75 million [35].

The usual assumption is that neither smart contract code nor data can be tampered with—therefore, the core ransomware primitive (encryption) does not apply. However, the general principle of exploiting vulnerabilities for financial gain still holds. Crucially, we observe that vulnerabilities often considered minor—because they do not enable direct asset extraction—can evolve from accidental denial-of-service into deliberate extortion mechanisms. The attacker does not steal funds, but she locks them in place, gaining exclusive control over their release and creating economic leverage over the victim. Unlike traditional ransomware, everything occurs on-chain: the ransom contract is publicly verifiable, and its effect can be simulated in advance, offering a paradoxical form of trustless extortion.

Contribution. In this paper, we present the first investigation of ransomware-based attacks in the domain of smart contracts. As we describe in Sect. 4, we develop an attack methodology, referred to as Extortionware, that enables attackers to exploit smart contract vulnerabilities and generate financial gain by demanding a ransom, even if the vulnerability does not permit direct asset withdrawal. We provide an in-depth analysis by describing (Sect. 5) three real-world smart contract case studies that could have been exploited by Extortionware, resulting in more than $465,000 in losses. Lastly, we present an approach to detect vulnerabilities in smart contracts to analyze whether they are potentially susceptible to Extortionware (cf. Sect. 6). Our approach, based on static analysis, successfully detects all three case studies and is further evaluated on a dataset of 20,137 Ethereum smart contracts, where it identifies three additional instances of Extortionware-like vulnerabilities in audited contracts.

2 Background

Smart contracts are susceptible to a wide range of vulnerabilities, as documented in frameworks such as the Smart Contract Security Verification Stan- dard (SCSVS) [7]. In this section, we review the vulnerability classes most relevant to Extortionware attacks and provide a brief overview of traditional ransomware as a conceptual baseline.

Access Control Vulnerabilities. These occur when contracts fail to restrict access to sensitive functions, allowing unauthorized users to execute critical operations [16]. In Solidity, functions are public by default, meaning that any external account or contract can call them unless the developer explicitly adds access restrictions. Common manifestations include missing modifiers (e.g., `onlyOwner`), improper role management, and privilege escalation paths. When left unprotected, administrative functions that modify state variables (persistent data elements within a smart contract) become exposed to any external caller, potentially enabling attackers to alter the contract's behavior.

Unexpected Revert and Denial of Service. A separate class of vulnerabilities arises when a contract makes external calls without properly handling failures. Ethereum smart contracts can call other contracts, for example, to transfer Ether or interact with token interfaces. In Ethereum, an execution *reverts* when it aborts and undoes all state changes made so far, returning the contract to its prior state; reverting is the standard way to signal a failed or invalid operation. If the callee reverts, the caller's execution is blocked as well, unless the call is wrapped in appropriate error handling. An attacker who controls the callee address can therefore cause the calling function to always fail, effectively preventing asset transfers or other critical operations from completing.

Locked Ether. Ether can become permanently locked inside a contract in several ways [26]. A common case occurs when a contract can receive Ether but lacks any function to send it out, or when all withdrawal paths depend on external calls to a configurable address. If that address is replaced by a contract that always reverts, all funds become inaccessible. Locked Ether can also result from the destruction of a dependent contract or from logic errors that leave no viable withdrawal path. In all cases, the lock persists indefinitely and cannot be resolved without the cooperation of whoever controls the blocking condition.

Re-entrancy. External calls to untrusted contracts can be exploited to re-enter the calling contract before its state is updated [2]. This occurs because Ethereum processes external calls synchronously: the caller's execution pauses until the callee returns, but the caller's state may not yet reflect the ongoing operation. A malicious callee can use this window to invoke the caller again, leading to repeated withdrawals or unauthorized state changes. The DAO hack of 2016 is one of the most prominent examples of this vulnerability class, resulting in the loss of approximately $60 million in Ether [24].

Ransomware Attacks. In traditional ransomware [4], an attacker infiltrates a victim's system, encrypts critical data using strong cryptography, and demands payment for the decryption key. To maximize pressure, the attacker typically destroys backups and shadow copies, leaving the victim unable to recover without the key. The victim cannot restore operations independently, as breaking the encryption is computationally infeasible. Ransomware has caused substantial damage in recent years, with individual payments reaching up to $75 million [35]. While smart contracts cannot be encrypted in the same way, we draw on the ransomware model as a conceptual baseline for the Extortionware attack presented in the following sections.

3 Threat Model

This section presents and discusses the threat model relevant to Extortionware attacks on smart contracts.

We consider a smart contract deployed on a public blockchain, such as Ethereum, where the contracts' bytecode and state are available to all users inspecting the blockchain. We further assume the attacker is knowledgeable about smart contract development, has full read access to the public blockchain, and uses tools such as blockchain crawlers (e.g., Etherscan [12]) and vulnerability scanners to identify targets. Once a suitable victim is identified, the attacker initiates an Extortionware attack as detailed in Sect. 4.1. We distinguish two adversarial models based on whether the attacker controls a privileged role in the target contract at the time the Extortionware condition is triggered.

3.1 Unprivileged Attacker

In the first model, the attacker holds no special role in the target contract. We assume that the contract contains at least one exploitable vulnerability that remains undiscovered by its owner at deployment time. This assumption is realistic given the rapidly evolving blockchain ecosystem and the pressure to deploy quickly [28]. In this setting, Extortionware arises when an external party can trigger a contract state in which asset transfers or withdrawals are no longer possible, despite having no legitimate authority over the contract. The resulting threat is particularly significant because an outsider can lock value in a contract with which they have no trusted relationship. In this model, the attacker relies on weaknesses internal to the smart contract, such as missing or flawed access control on externally reachable functions, rather than on any previously acquired privileged role.

3.2 Privileged Attacker

In the second model, the attacker has effective control over a privileged role at the time of the attack (e.g., owner, admin, or governance participant). Importantly, this model is defined by the attacker's privileges at the time the attack is executed, not by how those privileges were originally obtained. Such control may stem either from a legitimate privileged position or from a prior compromise, such as key compromise [25], insider abuse [1], social engineering [25,34], or a governance takeover [19].

In this setting, Extortionware does not rely on gaining additional permissions during the attack. Rather, it arises when an actor who already controls a privileged role can abuse an existing contract capability to induce a lock on a critical operation, while still being unable to withdraw the locked assets directly.

A natural question is why a legitimate privileged actor would attack their own contract. The reason is economic: the extortion payoff may exceed the legitimate revenue associated with that role (e.g., royalties or fees). In such cases, Extortionware becomes attractive precisely because the attacker cannot monetize the attack through direct theft and instead uses the induced denial of functionality as leverage to demand a ransom (cf. Case Studies 2 and 3, Sects. 5.2 and 5.3).

4 The Extortionware Framework

In this section, we provide a detailed description of the steps of the Extortionware attack and discuss the most relevant smart contract vulnerabilities that Extortionware might exploit.

4.1 Extortionware Life-Cycle

The fact that smart contract code is publicly available gives malicious users unique opportunities to exploit potential vulnerabilities. In fact, it is reasonable to assume that a malicious user exploits the identified vulnerability to attack the smart contract. Figure 1 shows the steps of an Extortionware attack.

As with traditional ransomware, we assume the attacker possesses essential information and returns it to the victim only upon payment of a ransom. Unlike ransomware, we do not assume that the attacker can hide information on the victim's side (e.g., by encrypting it). Instead, we assume that the attacker identifies a vulnerability in a publicly available smart contract and exploits it, while the victim remains unaware of this vulnerability, allowing the attacker to demand a ransom.

Extortionware begins with an individual or company creating a smart contract to transfer funds and goods. The attack then includes the following five phases.

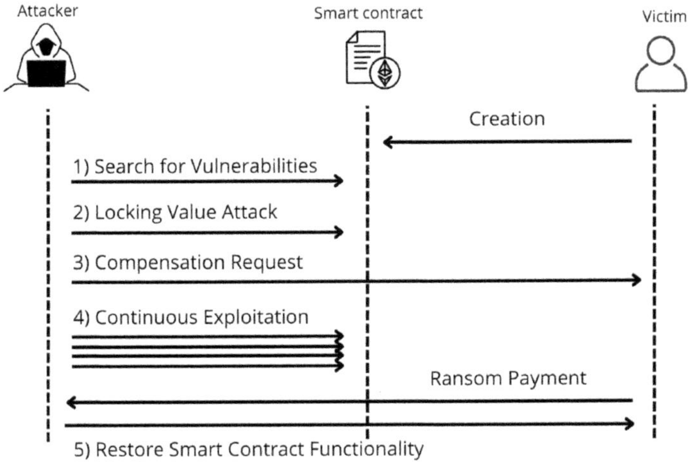

Fig. 1. Life-cycle of the Extortionware attack.

1. **Scouting for Vulnerable Smart Contracts.** The attacker first crawls the blockchain to identify vulnerable smart contracts belonging to potential victims. Since smart contract code is publicly available, attackers can identify potential vulnerabilities.
2. **Locking Attack.** The attacker executes a specific operation within the victim's smart contract that compromises the contract. This is achieved by performing a Denial of Service (DoS) attack, making the smart contract or essential functions unusable. To achieve this, the attacker can alter a state variable that references an external contract. By replacing this address with a malicious contract under their control that reverts any call, they effectively disable the functionality that depends on it, resulting in a denial-of-service attack.
3. **Compensation Request.** The attacker requests a ransom to restore the functionality of the victim's smart contract. The request is controlled through the injected contract, which automatically blocks all operations until the ransom is paid. As a result, a trustless environment is created for the interaction between the attacker and the victim, in which the contract guarantees the unlocking of functionality upon payment.
4. **Continuous Exploitation.** As long as the ransom remains unpaid, the smart contract's functionalities will remain blocked, potentially causing severe consequences. This includes the risk of funds becoming locked or inaccessible, which can lead to significant financial losses and disrupt critical business operations.
5. **Ransom Payment.** Once the ransom is paid, the malicious contract automatically stops reverting transactions, unlocking the smart contract's functionalities, and restoring normal operations. The company can then move the assets and rewrite the smart contract code to prevent similar attacks in the future.

4.2 Necessary Conditions and Enabling Vulnerabilities for Extortionware

The core mechanism that enables Extortionware is an attacker-induced *value lock*: digital assets—fungible tokens (e.g., ETH, ERC-20) or non-fungible tokens (NFTs)—become trapped within the contract, preventing their transfer or use. We define an Extortionware vulnerability through the following three necessary conditions:

1. **Asset Locking (C1).** The attacker can trigger a state change that causes all asset-transferring functions to revert, locking the contract's value.
2. **No Direct Theft (C2).** The vulnerability does not allow the attacker to withdraw or redirect the locked assets. The only way to monetize the attack is through a ransom demand.
3. **Exclusive Unlock Control (C3).** The attacker retains sole ability to restore normal operation. No other party—neither the victim nor a third party—can independently reverse the lock.

These conditions distinguish Extortionware from related but distinct threats. *Griefing* vulnerabilities can satisfy C1 and C2, yet they are traditionally considered low-severity because the attacker has no apparent path to monetization. When such a vulnerability additionally satisfies C3, the attacker gains full control and can offer to restore normal operation only in exchange for payment, turning an otherwise unprofitable disruption into a viable economic attack. Contrarily, when a privileged actor can both lock *and* withdraw funds (e.g., in a rug pull), C2 is violated, and extortion is unnecessary. However, not all privileged roles grant withdrawal rights. When a contract's design allows an admin to disrupt operations but not to extract assets, all three conditions can be met, and Extortionware becomes the only viable monetization path, as we show in Case Studies 2 and 3 (Sects. 5.2 and 5.3).

We note that C3 may also be approximated *probabilistically* rather than satisfied deterministically. If the locking function is publicly callable, an attacker can monitor the blockchain for the victim's unlock transaction and immediately re-lock the assets before the victim can withdraw them. By repeatedly exploiting transaction ordering in this way, the attacker can maintain effective control over the locked state, even without an exclusive lock. Our evaluation identifies two contracts that exhibit this pattern Sect. 7.3.

Having defined the conditions that characterize Extortionware, we now discuss how these conditions can arise in practice from known smart contract weaknesses, including combinations of vulnerabilities that are not rare in real-world deployments. Our goal is not to define Extortionware as a new low-level bug class, but as a higher-level attack condition that can emerge from the interaction of existing vulnerabilities and design weaknesses. To illustrate one representative path through which this condition may arise, we highlight the following combination:

- **Access Control Vulnerabilities:** These allow the attacker to modify contract state variables that reference external contract addresses. By redirecting

these references to a malicious contract that reverts, the attacker disrupts the normal execution flow and disables critical operations, enabling an Extortionware scenario. Such vulnerabilities arise when sensitive state-changing functions—such as those that update contract dependencies, token interfaces, or external references—lack appropriate access restrictions. This pattern has been observed in real-world audits [33] and discussed in vulnerability frameworks, such as the SCSVS [7].
- **Unexpected Revert Vulnerabilities:** By exploiting flaws in how the smart contract logic handles failed transactions, the attacker leverages these vulnerabilities with calls to the injected contract to revert operations unexpectedly. This reversion prevents asset transfers, locking them within the contract.

We note that this vulnerability combination is mainly representative of the unprivileged attacker model. In the privileged attacker model, an access-control vulnerability may not be necessary, since the attacker may already have legitimate authority to modify sensitive contract references or operational parameters. In such cases, the locking mechanism may still rely on unexpected-revert vulnerability, but the attack is enabled by the abuse of existing privileges rather than by missing access restrictions.

Together, these vulnerabilities create a scenario where an attacker can block the flow of assets without being able to steal them directly. This locked value makes Extortionware unique, shifting the attacker's focus from theft to extortion, requiring a ransom to unlock the assets.

5 Real-World Case Studies

In this section, we analyze known vulnerabilities found in previous versions of real-world smart contracts that could have been exploited using Extortionware attacks [20,27,33]. We present the end-to-end implementation of three case studies based on real-world vulnerabilities to demonstrate the impact of our attack. In these case studies, Extortionware represents the only possible method for the attacker to achieve economic gain. The shared steps of the exploits are illustrated in Fig. 2.

5.1 Case Study 1: Talent Protocol Case

Background. Talent Protocol is a decentralized platform for professional networks where talents can build an on-chain resume. One of its admin functions, `swapStableForToken`, permits the retrieval of the stablecoins stored in the contract, depositing an equivalent amount of the platform's token (TAL) in exchange. The transfer functions related to the token TAL are managed by the token contract, which can be set **only once** by the `setToken` function. This function was designed to be used once the token contract was developed, allowing the TAL token to be used for staking instead of stablecoins. Once set, the contract transitions permanently from staking stablecoins to staking TAL tokens, making the function single-use, as the `stablePhaseOnly` modifier prevents it

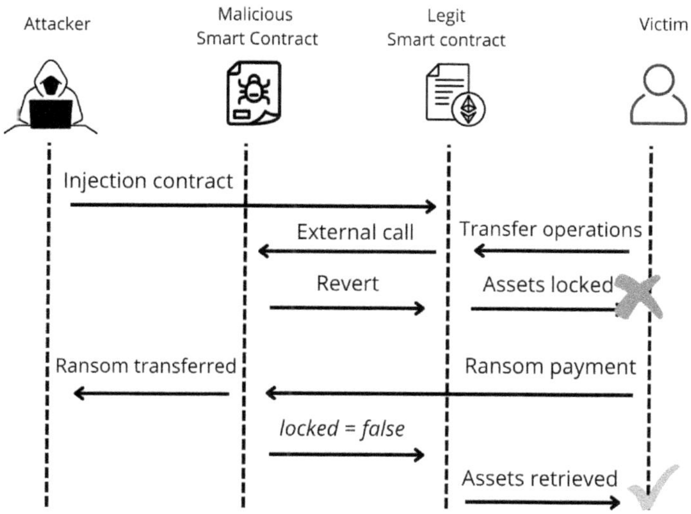

Fig. 2. Detailed life-cycle of the Extortionware attack in the exploits.

from being called once the TAL token is set. However, an **access control vulnerability** found in the `setToken` function allowed anyone to call the function and set an arbitrary contract address, as long as the token's name was "TAL" and it followed the ERC20 standard.

The vulnerable implementation of the `setToken` function is shown in Listing 1.1:

```
function setToken(address _token) public stablePhaseOnly {
    require(_token != address(0), "Address must be set");
    require(ERC20(_token).symbol() == "TAL", "Token must be TAL");

    token = _token;
}
```

Listing 1.1. Vulnerable `setToken` function (Talent Protocol)

Exploitation. In this scenario, an Extortionware attack could exploit the vulnerability to inject a malicious contract that reverts token transfers, including the deposit function. As a result, the `swapStableForToken` function would become unusable, and the stablecoin funds would be locked until the ransom is paid, as there are no other functions to move the funds out. Since the `setToken` function is single-use, the attacker's modification becomes irreversible, granting them exclusive control over unlocking the funds, which is a key condition for Extortionware attacks.

Outcome. When the vulnerability was discovered, the contract held about $465,000 in stablecoins, and the token contract still needed to be set since the developing team was still working on it. An Extortionware attack could have locked almost half a million dollars, and the only way for the victim to unlock the funds would have been to pay the ransom to the contract address.

5.2 Case Study 2: Charged Particle Case

Background. Charged Particles is a decentralized NFT marketplace where users can deposit ERC-compliant tokens into any NFT. Within the Charged Particles protocol, a “Proton” denotes an ERC-721 contract representing an NFT that can be “energized” by integrating interest-bearing assets. This allows the NFT to act as a container for other assets, generating additional value over time. As is common practice in NFT transactions, the sales of these NFTs include the payment of **royalties** to the original creator. In particular, the buy function, which enables the transfer of the NFT from the current owner to the buyer, also includes the payment of royalties through an external call to the creator’s address. The main vulnerability of this function is the presence of an external call within the buying process, which could lead to an unexpected revert and prevent the sale from being finalized.

Exploitation. In this scenario, an Extortionware attack could be carried out by the creator of an NFT or by an attacker who has gained access to the creator’s privileges. The attack would involve setting a malicious contract as the creator’s address, causing the royalties payment to revert until a ransom is paid. This address is saved as a state variable in the contract storage, and the creator can modify it, redirecting the external call to any chosen address. As a result, the buy function would become unusable, and the NFT would be locked.

Outcome. The vulnerability would have allowed a malicious creator to lock the asset transfer from one user to another. This would create a scenario where a user would have to pay bribes larger than the typical royalties to buy or sell an NFT. Since NFTs can often hold considerable value, this could prevent users from accessing or trading high-value assets, significantly increasing the financial consequences of the attack.

5.3 Case Study 3: Masterchefv2

Background. Masterchefv2 is the second version of the smart contract used in Decentralized Finance (DeFi) platforms like SushiSwap and PancakeSwap to manage liquidity provision and reward distribution. The functions `withdraw` and `emergencyWithdraw` allow the users to retrieve their tokens from the contract. One key advantage of the original MasterChef smart contract is that the owner could never block users from withdrawing the tokens they initially deposited, even if the owner was malicious. However, in the second version, both withdrawal functions include an external call to the `rewarder` address, which could be set by the owner at any time, including after users have deposited tokens.

Exploitation. In this scenario, an Extortionware attack could be carried out by the contract owner or by an attacker who has gained access to the owner's privileges. The attacker could set a malicious contract as the rewarder's address, causing the revert of the withdraw functions until a ransom is paid.

Outcome. As a result, any attempt by the user to withdraw would result in a reverted transaction, locking the tokens and potentially a significant amount of value inside the contract. This is especially concerning given that many platforms use forked versions of this contract.

6 Extortionware Detection

Now that we have a clear understanding of the Extortionware attack and a grasp of three specific case studies, we aim to provide a static analysis tool to identify this specific nuance of Extortionware in other smart contracts. We implement our detector as a custom plugin for Slither [13], a static analysis framework for Solidity. Our detector consists of multiple stages and employs a bottom-up approach. Before checking for preconditions, we verify code locations that may potentially allow Extortionware. To provide a clear understanding, we first provide a high-level overview of the detector's workflow, followed by a detailed explanation of each stage.

High-Level Overview. The detector aims to identify smart contracts that could be targeted by Extortionware, as described in Sect. 4. In particular, we focus on a specific nuance of Extortionware, where an attacker can manipulate a state variable—a persistent data element within a smart contract—to cause critical functions to revert, thereby disrupting the contract's regular operation.

As illustrated in Fig. 3, the analysis involves the following stages:

1. **Potential Sink Identification.** Locate all calls to contracts whose addresses are stored in writable state variables.
2. **Revertable Functions Identification.** Find all functions that can be reverted if all sinks revert (we denote this set of functions as R).
3. **Asset-Specific Sending Functions Identification.** Identify all functions capable of transferring a specific type of asset (we denote this set of functions as T).
4. **Vulnerability Condition Check.** Check if all sending functions are susceptible to reversion by verifying if $T \subseteq R$.

If the condition $T \subseteq R$ holds, the contract may be vulnerable to Extortionware attacks, as an attacker controlling the identified state variables can revert *every* sending function. To prevent recompromise, the setter of the global variable should also be included in the revertable functions.

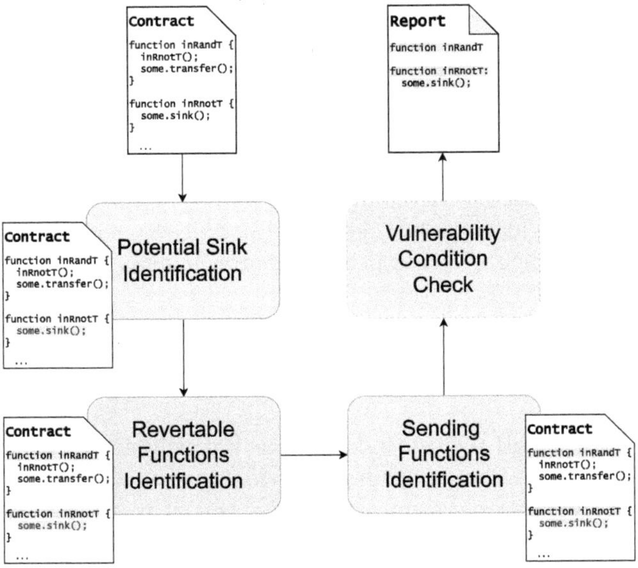

Fig. 3. Workflow of our detector processing a smart contract.

6.1 Potential Sink Identification

In this context, a *sink* is a point in the code where a function makes an external call (either high-level or low-level) that depends on a state variable.

These state variables need to be *writable by the attacker*, meaning any user can modify them without access restrictions (i.e., without proper access control) or through other vulnerabilities that allow the attacker to gain control over them. To achieve this, the detector iterates over all functions in the contract. It examines their Slither Intermediate Representations (SlitherIRs) to identify operations that involve external calls that depend on state variables. For each of these state variables, we need to determine if it is publicly writable. To do this, we perform a taint analysis and propagate taint from every attacker-writable assignment to any related calls and assignments. If any taint reaches the state variable (and if the state variable is a mapping or array, it must match the corresponding index or member), we flag it as attacker-controlled.

6.2 Revertable Functions Identification

After identifying the sinks, we can compute the set R, which contains all functions that can be reverted due to interactions with the sinks. To achieve this, we first flag every function containing a sink as revertable. Furthermore, we assume that a reverting sink will cause its enclosing function to revert. Therefore, we build a call graph and flag all functions that lead to a sink as well as revertable functions.

6.3 Asset-Specific Sending Functions Identification

At this stage, we compute the set T of functions that can transfer a given asset. The goal is to conservatively approximate all externally callable functions that may move value, either directly or via internal calls.

Ether. For *Ether* transfers, we proceed as follows.

1. *Instruction collection.* We locate every SlitherIR instruction that can send value (e.g., high-level calls, low-level calls, *transfer*, *send*, contract creation). This is not limited to the current contract. We also include reachable functions in inherited contracts and contracts called by the current contract, as these can affect the asset flow.
2. *Non-zero feasibility.* For each instruction, we symbolically trace the *amount* parameter backwards to its sources. If the backward slice shows the value must be zero, we drop the instruction.
3. *Call-graph propagation.* We propagate the remaining sending instructions over the call-graph so that functions indirectly transferring *Ether* via calls are included. During propagation, we keep only paths where the *amount* cannot be proven to be zero, and we iterate until no new candidates are added.
4. *Filter functions.* We intersect the resulting set with the contract's *public* and *external* functions.

Tokens. Although our implementation focuses on Ether transfers, we adapt the same procedure to other assets by detecting token-transfer interfaces via function signature matching.

1. *Instruction collection.* We match common names: *transfer*, *approve*, *transferFrom* and *safeTransferFrom* (ERC20/ERC721, see Sect. 8).
2. *Non-zero feasibility and propagation.* We apply the same non-zero slice to the *amount* and the same call-graph propagation. For *safeTransferFrom*, we additionally require that the recipient is not the contract itself before treating the call as a sending candidate.

Our approach does not rely on exhaustively identifying every custom-named transfer function. If such a function is not recognized, the detector may raise additional false positives, but it does not miss actual Extortionware cases. In practice, analysts can refine the interface specification by adding project-specific function names, which further reduces noise without compromising detection soundness.

6.4 Vulnerability Condition Check

The final step involves checking if all asset-transferring functions are at risk of reverting by verifying if $T \subseteq R$. Suppose this condition is met for the asset type under consideration. In that case, an attacker can potentially revert all asset-transferring functions by manipulating the writable state variables identified earlier.

7 Evaluation

The goal of this evaluation is to assess whether Extortionware-related patterns can be observed in real-world smart contracts when analyzing a large corpus. To this end, we conduct a feasibility study that combines a curated dataset of audited decentralized applications with the three real-world case studies presented in Sect. 5.

We structure our evaluation around two analyses, each grounded in a distinct adversarial model:

- **Analysis 1: Unprivileged Extortionware Scan.** This analysis assumes the attacker has no initial privileges. We therefore only consider setting functions that lack any access-control modifiers (e.g., `onlyOwner`). This models a stricter scenario in which Extortionware can emerge only if the contract already contains a known vulnerability, such as a missing access control.
- **Analysis 2: Privileged Extortionware Scan.** In this broader model, we lift the access-control restriction and include all setting functions, regardless of whether they are protected. This reflects a threat model in which the attacker is assumed to hold contract-level privileges, enabling a broader class of Extortionware behaviors.

7.1 Dataset

This study focuses on audited DApps drawn from the DAppSCAN [38] dataset, a public collection of smart contracts aggregated from leading security firms (e.g., Trail of Bits, ConsenSys Diligence, and PeckShield). Each DAppSCAN project contains professionally reviewed contracts annotated with known vulnerabilities. This makes the dataset particularly suitable for our feasibility study, as Extortionware attacks aim to make griefing financially lucrative.

To ensure complete and reproducible builds, we obtained the full DAppSCAN corpus from the dataset maintainers, including all `node_modules` dependencies required for successful compilation. Since the dataset does not contain compilation entry points, we compile all Solidity files in these projects separately, excluding files in `node_modules`. These directories hold third-party library dependencies (e.g., OpenZeppelin) that are needed only as compilation context and are not part of the audited project's own logic; analyzing them would inflate the corpus with duplicated library code and yield findings outside each project's scope.

In total, our evaluation covers 20,137 Solidity contracts. Among these, 7,484 contracts result in analysis errors due to unresolved dependencies or compilation failures. In comparison, the remaining 12,653 contracts are compiled successfully and used in both analyses described in Sect. 7.3.

7.2 Tooling and Setup

We run all analyses using *Slither* together with *CryticCompile*, which automatically resolves the correct Solidity compiler version for each contract. All evaluations are executed inside isolated *Docker* containers to ensure consistent `solc-select` behavior across parallel jobs. The complete analysis is performed on a server equipped with 32 virtual CPUs and 64 GB of RAM, running Ubuntu 22.04 LTS on an `x86_64` architecture. All contracts flagged by the detector are manually validated to confirm whether the reported patterns correspond to Extortionware-relevant behavior.

7.3 Results and Manual Validation

Analysis 1: Unprivileged Extortionware. In the first analysis, we consider only setting functions that lack access control (i.e., functions without modifiers such as `onlyOwner`). If a function is protected, we stop the search for Extortionware patterns. This models an unprivileged attacker and allows us to detect cases where Extortionware emerges from known weaknesses, such as missing access control. Across the 12,653 successfully compiled contracts, the detector reports 17 candidates for Extortionware-related behavior. We manually inspect all detections and classify them as follows:

- **Mocks and test artifacts (8 cases).** These detections originate from test or mock contracts included in some DAppSCAN projects. The contracts are not part of deployable contract logic.
- **False positives (5 cases, including two duplicates).** After deduplication, these detections stem from non-standard authentication patterns (e.g., multi-signature governance or specific Access Control List pattern) that fall outside the current detector's access-control model. Supporting these cases would require additional pattern modeling.
- **True positives (4 cases, including two duplicates).** These contracts contain asset-locking logic that an unprivileged caller can manipulate. After deduplication, only two distinct cases remain, and both correspond to a variant of Extortionware rather than the classical pattern based on exclusive unlock privileges. These two cases are analysed in detail below.

While our Extortionware detector was primarily designed to detect contracts in which an attacker holds exclusive unlock privileges, we identified two vulnerabilities in the DAppSCAN dataset that vary from the strict pattern. In these cases, the contracts lack a strictly exclusive unlock mechanism. However, upon closer examination, both exhibit a related vulnerability pattern that still facilitates Extortionware. Specifically, the identified contracts contain a vulnerability that allows any actor with sufficient transaction priority to repeatedly reinvoke asset locking. An adversary could exploit this behavior by continuously relocking the asset immediately after it is unlocked, potentially through front-running or by rapidly resubmitting lock transactions.

We interpret these findings as evidence of a previously unmodeled variant of Extortionware. Rather than relying on exclusive control, this variant leverages competitive transaction ordering and repeated state modification to achieve a comparable effect. This suggests that Extortionware may encompass a broader class of vulnerabilities than initially hypothesized, in which the threat arises not only from exclusive locks but also from strategic exploitation and execution timing.

Analysis 2: Privileged Extortionware. Across the 12,653 successfully compiled contracts, the detector reports 141 candidates for Extortionware-related behavior. We manually inspect all detections and classify them as follows:

- **Mocks and test artifacts (20 cases).** These detections stem from mock or test contracts included in several DAppSCAN projects. Since these files are not meant for deployment, they fall outside the scope of Extortionware analysis.
- **False positives (120 cases, including 64 duplicates).** The majority of false positives arise in systems that assume administrative trust as an explicit design assumption. We group the root causes into several categories:
  - *Economically irrational attack surfaces.* In many cases, privileged roles can technically trigger an Extortionware-style action, such as blocking user transfers or withdrawals. However, exercising such power would immediately undermine market confidence and collapse the token's value, eliminating any realistic prospect of extracting profit. The same capability can still constitute a realistic threat in a different adversarial model. Specifically, preventing users from exiting their positions can be exploited as a *soft rug pull*, in which the attacker sells their own shares and then degrades the project's functionality. Thus, although these cases match the syntactic Extortionware pattern, the attack is economically self-destructive and therefore considered a false positive.
  - *Benign owner privileges.* Other contracts expose patterns, such as owner-controlled reserve withdrawals or token minting. Although these cases technically fit our pattern, the owner could prevent the transfer of assets, making this approach illogical. The owner already has simpler and more explicit methods to access the underlying assets without resorting to Extortionware. Therefore, we categorize these alerts as false positives.
  - *Self-limiting attacker roles.* A small subset includes cases where the owner could, in principle, block flows, but doing so would restrict only the owner's own assets. These detections, therefore, do not constitute a meaningful threat.
  - *Asset-Type Misalignment.* Our detector conservatively treats functions as reversible, even when control flow for asset-specific operations prevents this in practice. For example, Ether-related alerts may be raised even when the corresponding sink is used exclusively for non-Ether assets.
  - *Inline assembly limitations.* Three contracts implement Ether transfer logic using inline assembly, which prevents Slither from correctly detecting the value transfer. As a result, these contracts appear vulnerable even though they merely expose limitations of the analysis framework. Extending Slither's assembly support would resolve this issue.

- **True positives (one case).** The alerts contain a single instance that satisfies our definition of Extortionware when the privileged role is modeled as an adversary. In the *yDelegatedVault* contract, the governance entity can unilaterally redirect the vault's controller to an arbitrary contract. Since the controller mediates all transfer-related operations and determines whether withdrawals succeed, a malicious governance actor can intentionally induce withdrawal failures and re-enable them under specific conditions. This gives the privileged actor effective control over the users' ability to reclaim their assets and enables Extortionware without compromising the underlying assets. We therefore classify this behaviour as an Extortionware-style attack carried out by a privileged adversary.

As expected, the privileged analysis yields more detections than the unprivileged case, reflecting the broader search space. Manual validation indicates that most alerts, while technically allowing asset-locking as defined in Sect. 4, are economically illogical or the owner already has rights that provide more direct access to the assets. Nonetheless, manual validation confirms that one contract exhibits privileged locking behavior that could support an Extortionware scenario.

7.4 Case Study Validation

To complement the large-scale evaluation, we test the detector on the three real-world contracts analysed in Sect. 5. We run two configurations: (1) the Ether–sending-function detector and (2) the Token–sending-function detector.

Under the Ether configuration, the detector flags the case study whose sending path transfers native Ether. The remaining two case studies do not surface in this setting because their sending logic handles ERC-20 tokens rather than Ether. When we enable the token-based configuration, the detector correctly identifies the remaining two contracts. Overall, using the combined configuration, the detector identifies all three real-world case studies. The difference between the Ether and token results reflects the asset type involved in the sending path and is not a limitation of the analysis.

8 Discussion

Exclusive Unlock Control Vulnerabilities. The case studies presented in this paper highlight the real-world applicability of Extortionware through three examples involving actual smart contracts. These cases demonstrate not only the viability of the attack but also the potential impact, as substantial funds or valuable digital assets could be locked. A key peculiarity of the vulnerabilities exploited by Extortionware is the attacker's exclusive ability to unlock the assets: the action required to release them can only be performed by a single entity, the attacker, who has gained privileged control. In our case studies, this privileged status is achieved through manipulated access control mechanisms within the smart contract, as seen in Sects. 5.2 and 5.3, or by being the first to exploit a one-time function (Sect. 5.1). However, this privileged control can be obtained in various ways, making it challenging to identify the vulnerability of exclusive unlock control.

Detection Challenges. Despite rigorous testing, our detector exhibited false positives on a curated dataset of security-audited smart contracts from real-world DApp projects. This reflects the inherent challenge of generalizing detection: differences in contract architectures and assets complicate a universal solution despite the consistent attack pattern. Our detector focuses on detecting Ether-sending functions and is not a comprehensive detector for Token-sending functions. This is because many tokens do not strictly adhere to the standard ERC20 or ERC721 function names and interfaces. Instead, they often implement custom or non-standard methods for token transfers. Detecting generic token transfer functions is a significant challenge, as highlighted by recent research [6,18]. Therefore, our token detection remains minimalistic, focusing on standard token interfaces. While this approach was sufficient for our case studies, it may not be transferable to the broader tokens ecosystem with varying implementations. Improving the detector to accurately identify token transfer functions that do not conform to standard interfaces is an important area for future work.

Expanding Extortionware to Ownership Control. An alternative application of Extortionware exploits ownership control rather than focusing on asset locking. In this scenario, an attacker transfers the contract's ownership to a malicious smart contract after compromising the owner's private keys or exploiting vulnerabilities in access control mechanisms. Crucially, as in asset-locking scenarios, the attacker must be unable to withdraw funds directly, ensuring that extortion remains the only viable method to monetize the attack. The ransom contract is programmed to return ownership to the original owner only once a ransom payment has been made. This perspective demonstrates that Extortionware is a broader threat, extending beyond asset-locking to include other vectors, such as direct manipulation of contract ownership.

Evolving Threats in Smart Contract Security. The relevance of this attack is amplified because these vulnerabilities have so far been largely underestimated in traditional smart contract security analysis, where most attention has focused on vulnerabilities that allow the direct theft of funds. However, Extortionware shifts the focus from theft to extortion by locking assets and forcing victims to pay a ransom to regain access. A notable strength of this extortion mechanism is that the ransom payment is implemented directly within the smart contract, which is effective given the trustless environment between attacker and victim. Unlike traditional ransomware, the victim can verify the malicious contract code and simulate outcomes before deciding, adding a layer of transparency that could increase the likelihood of payment. This overlooked attack vector demonstrates the need for a broader approach to smart contract security that considers not only theft but also extortion and the economic impact of locked assets.

To reduce the attack surface and limit the impact of Extortionware, contracts should restrict updates to external dependency addresses and avoid push-based payment flows in critical asset-transfer paths. The latter can be achieved through pull-over-push payment patterns, where funds are recorded as claimable balances and withdrawn separately by recipients, preventing external payment failures from blocking core contract functionality. Additional safeguards such as timelocks or multi-signature approval can further reduce the risk of abuse in privileged settings.

Future work should expand detection methods and investigate additional Extortionware variants.

9 Related Work

In this section, we review the literature on smart contract vulnerabilities and their exploitation, particularly in the context of extortionware attacks. As our work is the first to address how smart contract vulnerabilities can be exploited to demand a ransom, we focus on related work in these areas.

Smart Contract Vulnerabilities. Multiple studies have investigated vulnerabilities in smart contracts and the tools used to detect them. Atzei et al. [2] provide an early survey of smart contract vulnerabilities, including the King of the Ether and GovernMental Ponzi scheme contracts, cataloging several vulnerability types that are still relevant today.

Building on this, Dika et al. [10,11] extend the taxonomy to 22 vulnerabilities, assign severity levels to each, and evaluate automatic analysis tools such as Mythril [8], Oyente [24], and Remix [30]. Rameder et al. [29] further classify the vulnerabilities and analysis tools for smart contracts and provide an updated overview of the documented vulnerabilities and detection methods.

Perez et al. [28] analyze vulnerabilities in Ethereum smart contracts and show that only a few contracts pose a significant risk relative to the total amount at stake. This does not diminish the relevance of our contribution: we aim to raise awareness of this new threat before it causes losses.

Krupp et al. [22] propose *thEther*, a tool that automatically generates exploits for vulnerable contracts, emphasizing the practicality of attacks on smart contracts.

More recently, Chaliasos et al. [5] and Sendner et al. [32] have conducted extensive evaluations of automated vulnerability detection tools, highlighting their limitations. Chaliasos et al. [5] reveal that current tools, despite years of development, could only prevent 8% of the attacks studied, leaving a significant proportion of vulnerabilities undetected. Similarly, Sendner et al. [32] underscore the high rates of false positives and negatives in existing tools, noting that no single scanner consistently performs across vulnerability categories. Both studies emphasize the urgent need for improved detection capabilities to address the evolving complexity of smart contract vulnerabilities effectively.

Smart Contract use in Ransomware Attacks. Research also examined the overlap between smart contracts and ransomware. Karapapas et al. [21] propose a model in which smart contracts enable ransomware-as-a-service by using them as a mediator to automate ransom payments and key exchanges. In this way, the confidence that victims will receive the decryption keys after payment is increased.

Similarly, other works [9,23] discuss leveraging blockchain and smart contracts to regulate ransomware attacks, allowing attackers to manage the exchange of cryptographic keys and increase the granularity and automation of attacks.

Torres et al. [36] study malicious smart contracts on the blockchain, focusing on honeypots designed to lure users into traps. While their work centers on detecting such honeypots, it highlights the broader issue of malicious smart contracts within the blockchain ecosystem.

While prior work has extensively studied smart contract vulnerabilities and the use of smart contracts to improve ransomware attacks, our work is the first to show how vulnerabilities in smart contracts can be exploited to demand ransom from contract owners—a new class of attacks that we refer to as extortionware.

10 Conclusion

In this paper, we introduced Extortionware, a novel class of attacks that enables attackers to exploit smart contracts for financial gain even when they cannot directly withdraw funds. Extortionware exploits minor vulnerabilities—traditionally considered low-risk because they do not enable direct theft—to lock up valuable assets within a contract, forcing victims to pay a ransom and turning seemingly insignificant issues into significant threats. Using three real-world case studies, we demonstrated the feasibility and impact of Extortionware. In each case, the attackers exploited access-control vulnerabilities and leveraged unexpected reverts to gain exclusive control over the release of assets. Beyond detecting all three real-world case studies, our evaluation of 20,137 audited Ethereum smart contracts uncovered three additional instances of Extortionware-like vulnerabilities. Our work highlights the need for greater awareness by showing how attackers can exploit minor vulnerabilities to create major financial threats.

Acknowledgments. This work has been partially funded by the European Union ERC CONSEC under grant No. 101042266 and the Deutsche Forschungsgemeinschaft (DFG, German Research Foundation)—SFB 1119 (CROSSING) 236615297 within project T1. The views and opinions expressed are those of the authors only and do not necessarily reflect those of the European Union or the European Research Council Executive Agency. Neither the European Union nor the granting authority can be held responsible for them.

Disclosure of Interests. The authors have no competing interests to declare that are relevant to the content of this article.

References

1. Agarwal, S., Atondo Siu, J., Ordekian, M., Hutchings, A., Mariconti, E., Vasek, M.: DeFi deception–uncovering the prevalence of Rugpulls in cryptocurrency projects. In: Baldimtsi, F., Cachin, C. (eds.) Financial Cryptography and Data Security, FC 2023. LNCS, vol. 13950. Springer, Cham(2023). https://doi.org/10.1007/978-3-031-47754-6_21
2. Atzei, N., Bartoletti, M., Cimoli, T.: A survey of attacks on Ethereum smart contracts (SoK). In: Maffei, M., Ryan, M. (eds.) POST 2017. LNCS, vol. 10204, pp. 164–186. Springer, Heidelberg (2017). https://doi.org/10.1007/978-3-662-54455-6_8
3. Boi, B., Esposito, C., Lee, S.: Smart contract vulnerability detection: the role of large language model (LLM). SIGAPP Appl. Comput. Rev. **24**(2), 19–29 (2024). https://doi.org/10.1145/3687251.3687253
4. Brewer, R.: Ransomware attacks: detection, prevention and cure. Netw. Secur. **2016**(9), 5–9 (2016)
5. Chaliasos, S., et al.: Smart contract and defi security tools: do they meet the needs of practitioners? In: Proceedings of the IEEE/ACM 46th International Conference on Software Engineering, ICSE '24 (2024)
6. Chen, T., et al.: TokenScope: automatically detecting inconsistent behaviors of cryptocurrency tokens in Ethereum. In: Proceedings of the 2019 ACM SIGSAC Conference on Computer and Communications Security (CCS '19), pp. 1503–1520 (2019)
7. ComposableSecurity: Smart contract security verification standard. https://github.com/ComposableSecurity/SCSVS. Accessed 2025
8. ConsenSys: Mythril: Security analysis tool for EVM bytecode. https://github.com/ConsenSys/mythril. Accessed 01 Oct 2024
9. Delgado-Mohatar, O., Sierra-Cámara, J.M., Anguiano, E.: Blockchain-based semi-autonomous ransomware. Futur. Gener. Comput. Syst. **112**, 589–603 (2020)
10. Dika, A.: Ethereum smart contracts: security vulnerabilities and security tools. Master's thesis, NTNU (2017)
11. Dika, A., Nowostawski, M.: Security vulnerabilities in Ethereum smart contracts. In: IEEE International Conference on Internet of Things (iThings) and IEEE Green Computing and Communications (GreenCom) and IEEE Cyber, Physical and Social Computing (CPSCom) and IEEE Smart Data (SmartData), pp. 955–962 (2018)
12. Etherscan: Etherscan: The ethereum blockchain explorer. https://etherscan.io. Accessed 2025
13. Feist, J., Grieco, G., Groce, A.: Slither: a static analysis framework for smart contracts. In: 2019 IEEE/ACM 2nd International Workshop on Emerging Trends in Software Engineering for Blockchain (WETSEB). IEEE, May 2019
14. Ferreira Torres, C., Baden, M., Norvill, R., Fiz Pontiveros, B.B., Jonker, H., Mauw, S.: ægis: shielding vulnerable smart contracts against attacks. In: Proceedings of the 15th ACM Asia Conference on Computer and Communications Security, ASIA CCS '20, p. 584–597. Association for Computing Machinery, New York, NY, USA (2020). https://doi.org/10.1145/3320269.3384756
15. George, W.: An analysis of griefs and griefing factors. Front. Blockchain **6**, 1137155 (2023)
16. Ghaleb, A., Rubin, J., Pattabiraman, K.: AChecker: statically detecting smart contract access control vulnerabilities. In: 2023 IEEE/ACM 45th International Conference on Software Engineering (ICSE), pp. 945–956. IEEE (2023)

17. Grieco, G., Song, W., Cygan, A., Feist, J., Groce, A.: Echidna: effective, usable, and fast fuzzing for smart contracts. In: Proceedings of the 29th ACM SIGSOFT International Symposium on Software Testing and Analysis, ISSTA 2020, pp. 557–560. Association for Computing Machinery, New York, NY, USA (2020). https://doi.org/10.1145/3395363.3404366
18. He, Z., et al.: TokenAware: accurate and efficient bookkeeping recognition for token smart contracts. ACM Trans. Softw. Eng. Methodol. (2023)
19. Immunefi: Hack analysis: Beanstalk governance attack, April 2022 (2022). https://medium.com/immunefi/hack-analysis-beanstalk-governance-attack-april-2022-f42788fc821e. Accessed 09 Mar 2026
20. Immunefi: Charged particles bug report. https://medium.com/immunefi/charged-particles-griefing-bug-fix-postmortem-d2791e49a66b. Accessed 2025
21. Karapapas, C., Pittaras, I., Fotiou, N., Polyzos, G.C.: Ransomware as a Service using Smart Contracts and IPFS. In: 2020 IEEE International Conference on Blockchain and Cryptocurrency (ICBC), pp. 1–5. IEEE (2020)
22. Krupp, J., Rossow, C.: {teEther}: gnawing at Ethereum to automatically exploit smart contracts. In: 27th USENIX Security Symposium (USENIX Security 18), pp. 1317–1333 (2018)
23. Kumar, A.S.L., Mishra, S.: Ransomware criminal smart contract. In: 2024 IEEE International Conference on Blockchain (Blockchain), pp. 219–226. IEEE (2024)
24. Luu, L., Chu, D.H., Olickel, H., Saxena, P., Hobor, A.: Making smart contracts smarter. In: Proceedings of the 2016 ACM SIGSAC Conference on Computer and Communications Security, pp. 254–269 (2016)
25. Ronin Network: Back to building: Ronin security breach postmortem (2022). https://roninchain.com/blog/posts/back-to-building-ronin-security-breach-6513cc78a5edc1001b03c364. Accessed 09 Mar 2026
26. Nikolic, I., Kolluri, A., Sergey, I., Saxena, P., Hobor, A.: Finding the greedy, prodigal, and suicidal contracts at scale (2018). https://arxiv.org/abs/1802.06038
27. Onewayfunction: MasterChefV2 bug report. https://mirror.xyz/onewayfunction.eth/J6mp8FmcEPBj3Q4e64GA48zmiqYoB9BobMNFgXdPJXQ. Accessed 2025
28. Perez, D., Livshits, B.: Smart contract vulnerabilities: vulnerable does not imply exploited. In: 30th USENIX Security Symposium (USENIX Security 21) (2021)
29. Rameder, H., di Angelo, M., Salzer, G.: Review of automated vulnerability analysis of smart contracts on Ethereum. Front. Blockchain **5** (2022)
30. Remix Team: Remix - Ethereum ide & community. https://remix.ethereum.org. Accessed 2024
31. Rodler, M., Li, W., Karame, G.O., Davi, L.: EVMPatch: timely and automated patching of Ethereum smart contracts. In: USENIX Security Symposium (USENIX Security 2021) (2021)
32. Sendner, C., Petzi, L., Stang, J., Dmitrienko, A.: Large-scale study of vulnerability scanners for Ethereum smart contracts. In: 2024 IEEE Symposium on Security and Privacy (SP), pp. 2273–2290 (2024)
33. SkidsDAO: Talent protocol bug report. https://mirror.xyz/0xCf39521413F8De389771e35bB4C77b4bb827b7B3/HdSq7TVvk-s7DzQgN3u0pV8UFiVkaDft18HgmePTag4. Accessed 2025
34. Sygnia: Bybit – what we know so far (2025). https://www.sygnia.co/blog/sygnia-investigation-bybit-hack/. Accessed 09 Mar 2026
35. Zscaler ThreatLabz: Threatlabz 2024_ransomware report. https://www.zscaler.com/resources/industry-reports/threatlabz-ransomware-report.pdf. Accessed 2025

36. Torres, C.F., Steichen, M., State, R.: The art of the scam: demystifying honeypots in Ethereum smart contracts. In: 28th USENIX Security Symposium (USENIX Security 19), pp. 1591–1607 (2019)
37. Zhang, Z., Zhang, B., Xu, W., Lin, Z.: Demystifying exploitable bugs in smart contracts. In: 2023 IEEE/ACM 45th International Conference on Software Engineering (ICSE), pp. 615–627 (2023). https://doi.org/10.1109/ICSE48619.2023.00061
38. Zheng, Z., Su, J., Chen, J., Lo, D., Zhong, Z., Ye, M.: DAppSCAN: building large-scale datasets for smart contract weaknesses in DApp projects. IEEE Trans. Softw. Eng. (2024). https://doi.org/10.1109/TSE.2024.3383422

Should Miners Be Worried? Detecting Pool-Based Cryptocurrency Mining Under Anonymity Preserving Tools

Richa Gupta(✉), Rachit Bhandari, S. Jithin, Bhargav Jani, Vinayak Sharma, and Sambuddho Chakravarty

Indraprastha Institute of Information Technology Delhi, New Delhi, India
{richa,rachit23413,jithins,bhargav24115,vinayak21574, sambuddho}@iiitd.ac.in

Abstract. As governments increasingly regulate/restrict cryptocurrency mining due to financial, environmental, and policy concerns, detecting mining activity at the network level has become an important problem. In practice, miners can evade traditional deep packet inspection by tunneling pool communication through encrypted channels such as VPNs, *Tor*, or proxies. However, it is unclear whether these mechanisms meaningfully reduce the detectability of mining activity in network traffic. In this paper, we present the first systematic evaluation of whether pool-based cryptocurrency mining remains detectable at the network level under realistic deployment scenarios. Specifically, we investigate whether *Stratum*-based mining traffic—the de facto standard for pool mining—remains detectable when routed through anonymity-preserving channels such as VPNs and Tor. To answer this question, we design an evaluation methodology that operates exclusively on flow-level metadata and analyze mining traffic across 10 major cryptocurrencies and several widely used public mining pools. Our study includes plaintext traffic, VPN-tunneled traffic (*OpenVPN* TCP/UDP and *WireGuard*), and Tor-routed traffic in a realistic campus-gateway environment containing over 20 million background flows. Our results show that mining activity remains distinguishable from background traffic even when encrypted, achieving up to 0.85 precision and 0.88 recall under VPN tunneling, and 0.95 precision and 0.99 recall under Tor. Moreover, the underlying cryptocurrency can be identified with high accuracy under VPN encryption (0.96 precision and recall), though it becomes significantly more challenging under Tor. These findings suggest that encrypted tunneling does not eliminate detectability risk and may provide miners with a false sense of invisibility.

Keywords: pool mining · stratum protocol · censorship · cryptocurrencies · blockchain

S. Nadjm-Tehrani et al. (Eds.): ARES 2026, LNCS 16898, pp. 438–460, 2027.
https://doi.org/10.1007/978-3-032-36874-4_22

1 Introduction

Cryptocurrencies were introduced as an alternative to traditional fiat currencies backed by governments, enabling peer-to-peer transfers without reliance on intermediaries. Beginning with *Bitcoin* in 2009 [24], cryptocurrencies promised greater transparency and the ability to transfer value globally without restrictions or surveillance [20]. Over time, they evolved beyond a medium of exchange into an investment asset, with individuals seeking profits through buying, holding, and trading. There are two primary ways to acquire cryptocurrencies: (1) purchasing them using fiat currency through exchanges such as *Binance* [1], and (2) mining, which involves contributing computational power to validate transactions and secure the blockchain network in exchange for newly minted coins.

As demand for popular cryptocurrencies like Bitcoin (BTC) and *Ethereum* (ETH) increased, acquiring them through exchanges became more expensive, making mining an attractive alternative. Cryptocurrency mining uses specialized hardware to solve computational puzzles that validate blockchain transactions in exchange for newly minted coins. However, rising mining difficulty, particularly for networks such as Bitcoin, combined with high hardware and electricity costs has made solo mining economically risky for individuals. To address these challenges, pool mining emerged as the dominant model [16], allowing miners to aggregate computational resources and share rewards proportionally. Large pools such as *SlushPool*, *F2Pool*, and *Antpool* enable miners to participate and earn steady returns without operating large-scale mining infrastructure.

While mining pools have lowered the technical and financial barriers to cryptocurrency mining, the growing adoption of decentralized and privacy-focused cryptocurrencies has introduced significant regulatory challenges. Several countries have responded with restrictive measures. Japan [33] and South Korea [31] directed exchanges to remove privacy-enhancing cryptocurrencies such as *Monero* (XMR) and *ZCash* (ZEC). China provides another prominent example. Once responsible for over 65% of global Bitcoin mining power [32], it initiated a large-scale crackdown in 2021 by shutting down mining operations and withdrawing electricity support, citing concerns over financial stability, fraud prevention, and consumer protection [27,37]. Although these actions vary in scope, they collectively reflect increasing state-level efforts to curb cryptocurrency mining.

Beyond financial considerations, the environmental impact of proof-of-work (PoW) based cryptocurrencies has emerged as a major concern. The high energy consumption and associated carbon footprint of large-scale mining operations have prompted several governments to view mining as a threat to environmental sustainability goals [30,35]. Together with broader regulatory pressures, these concerns continue to shape the evolving landscape of cryptocurrency adoption and governance. The adversary in such a scenario could attempt to identify the mining traffic using network traffic inspection tools like DPI. In response to such concerns, miners frequently rely on encrypted and anonymity preserving tools – such as VPN and *Tor* to conceal their communication with mining pools, believing to be shielded from network-level monitoring. However, several studies [6,17,28] have shown that traffic analysis attacks on these anonymous systems can still reveal communication patterns by examining flow metadata. This raises a fundamental question: Should miners be worried whether their activity can be detected even when routed through VPNs or Tor? Our work examines whether network-level mechanisms can effectively detect and regulate pool-based cryptocurrency mining under realistic adversarial conditions, while also highlighting the implications of such mechanisms for miners and regulators. By understanding potential regulatory tactics and technological countermeasures, miners can better prepare for possible disruptions that could impact their operations and investments in the future.

The closest existing work addressing such questions involves detecting cryptojacking. *Cryptojacking* is the unauthorized use of someone else's resources to mine cryptocurrency without their knowledge or consent. Such approaches largely focus on identifying unauthorized activity in localized or controlled settings. However, prior works such as [38] and [10] exhibit several practical limitations. These approaches lack comprehensive evaluation across multiple cryptocurrencies making their robustness in real-world, multi-coin environments difficult to assess. The methodology is tested just for 2–3 cryptocurrencies without using any anonymity tool. Moreover, techniques that depend on correlating observed mining traffic with actual block generation time face fundamental scalability limitations as the ecosystem grows. Finally, the existing methods treat cryptojacking detection as a binary classification problem, without attempting to identify the specific cryptocurrency being mined. In contrast, enforcement and regulatory scenarios often require fine-grained identification of the specific cryptocurrency involved [31,33]. Existing literature does not address this question, leaving unclear whether reliance on VPNs or Tor meaningfully reduces cryptocurrency detection or identification risk.

To address these challenges, we formulate and empirically evaluate the above question from the perspective of a powerful network-level adversary, such as a national regulator or internet service providers capable of observing flow-level metadata at scale as considered in [4,6]. Importantly, we do not introduce a fundamentally new detection algorithm. Instead, we conduct a systematic measurement study to assess the resilience or fragility of encrypted mining traffic under realistic adversarial observation much like [4].

Building on these concerns, this paper aims to investigate the answer to the following questions: RQ1: Does pool-based cryptocurrency mining remain distinguishable from background traffic using only flow-level metadata? RQ2: To what extent do anonymity-preserving tools such as VPNs and Tor reduce the detectability of cryptomining traffic? RQ3: Even under encrypted tunneling, can an adversary identify the specific cryptocurrency being mined and with how much accuracy? RQ4: What observation duration is required for reliable detection under realistic traffic conditions?

To answer these questions, we develop *Mining Under Radar (MUR)*, an evaluation methodology that operates solely on packet-level metadata (e.g., packet sizes and inter-arrival times) without inspecting payload contents. We analyze *Stratum*-based mining traffic across 10 major proof-of-work cryptocurrencies and multiple widely used mining pools. Our evaluation uses a realistic campus-gateway dataset containing over 20 million background flows, allowing us to assess detectability under highly imbalanced and noisy conditions. MUR accurately identifies the cryptocurrency mining under both encrypted and unencrypted traffic, achieving precision of 0.85 and recall of 0.88, while with Tor precision is 0.95 and 0.99 respectively. The primary contributions of this work are as follows:

1. A first systematic study examining whether pool-based cryptocurrency mining remains detectable at the network level even when miners employ privacy-preserving tools like as VPNs and Tor. For this, MUR is a designed as a lightweight two-staged evaluation methodology consisting of – Phase 1: Detecting mining traffic amidst volumes of background flows. Phase 2: Identifying the specific cryptocurrency being mined.
2. Evaluation of MUR in a realistic campus gateway deployment, involving mining traffic routed through VPN and Tor tunnels. Our results show that mining remains distinguishable from background traffic even when tunneled through VPNs (precision of 0.85, recall of 0.88) and Tor (precision as 0.95 and recall as 0.99), with just 20 min of monitored traffic, due to characteristic packet structures. The cryptocurrency detection accuracies with unencrypted and encrypted traffic achieves precision and recall of 0.96 in 10mins of observation window. With Tor, it is around 50%.
3. Description of internals of stratum protocol showing its idiosyncrasies. This proved useful while designing features of MUR.
4. A discussion on the practical implications of our findings for network operators/regulators, highlighting trade-offs between detection accuracy, false positives, and monitoring duration.

2 Background and Related Work

2.1 Background

Pool Mining. Pool-based cryptocurrency mining allows multiple miners to combine computational power to increase the probability of solving a *Proof-of-Work* (PoW) puzzle. In most cryptocurrencies, miners search for a nonce (random number) that, when combined with the block header, produces a hash (e.g., SHA-256 in Bitcoin) below a target threshold defined by the network's difficulty.

Rather than mining independently, miners connect to a mining pool that coordinates the process. The pool constructs a block template containing the previous block hash, current transactions, coinbase information, and other metadata, and distributes smaller mining tasks (jobs) to connected miners. Each job assigns a portion of the nonce or extranonce search space, partitioning the overall search space to avoid overlap and enable parallel work.

Miners submit partial solutions, called *shares*, which satisfy the pool's lower difficulty threshold and serve as proof of contributed work. Shares allow the pool to track each miner's contribution. If a miner discovers a hash satisfying the network-wide difficulty target, the pool submits the block to the blockchain network for validation. Once accepted, the pool distributes the block reward among participating miners according to their submitted shares, using common reward schemes include *Pay-Per-Share* (PPS), *Proportional*, and *Pay-Per-Last-N-Shares* (PPLNS), balancing fairness, variance, and risk.

Stratum Protocol. Mining pools commonly use Stratum [34], a lightweight TCP-based protocol that defines how mining jobs are issued, shares are submitted, and connections are maintained. Mining traffic typically consists of long-lived TCP connections with low data volume but high regularity, as miners periodically receive job updates and submit shares. Messages are exchanged in plaintext using the JSON-RPC format. Stratum replaces earlier protocols such as *getwork* and *getblocktemplate.* Although implementations vary across cryptocurrencies, the overall workflow remains largely consistent (Fig. 2b).

Prior work [39] identifies three major Stratum protocol implementations used by most cryptocurrencies. A next-generation version, *Stratum v2*, is currently under testing by its developer, *Braiins Pool* [2]. Due to its limited adoption, we exclude it from the scope of this study.

2.2 Related Work

Prior work on detecting illicit cryptocurrency mining using network measurements broadly falls into three categories: (i) traffic behavior analysis using network metadata, (ii) payload or protocol inspection techniques, and (iii) approaches that discover hidden mining infrastructure. While these systems demonstrate promising results, most assume direct visibility into mining traffic and do not consider adversaries who intentionally obscure communication through anonymity-preserving overlays such as VPNs or Tor.

Network-Traffic Based Mining Detection. Several works detect mining activity by analyzing statistical or temporal patterns in network traffic without inspecting payloads. *MineHunter* [38] correlates mining job timestamps with blockchain's block creation events to identify mining activity, but relies on stable timing and synchronized nodes, making it sensitive to network jitter and tunneling effects. *CJSniffer* [10] applies statistical tests on packet inter-arrival times followed by hashrate fluctuation analysis to distinguish mining traffic from cryptojacking, which may be distorted by encrypted tunnels.

DeCrypto combines deep packet inspection (DPI), TLS fingerprinting, and machine learning-based classification to detect mining traffic, but relies heavily on DPI and evaluations containing largely unencrypted mining traffic. Enhancing DeCrypto further exploits periodic communication patterns in mining protocols using time-series analysis, but requires long mining flows to reliably detect periodicity, which may not hold in practice due to reconnections or pool switching.

Payload and Protocol Inspection Approaches. Some studies detect mining activity through inspection of raw or lightly obfuscated traffic. For example, [23] identifies mining protocols in unencrypted traces using techniques such as deep packet inspection. However, such approaches assume direct access to plaintext traffic and therefore do not reflect modern deployments where encryption is widely used. *CryptoMakesNoise* [3] studies mining detection across a limited set of cryptocurrencies but provides limited evaluation details, making it difficult to assess its generalizability.

Mining Infrastructure Discovery. Other work focuses on identifying hidden mining pools rather than detecting mining traffic itself. For example, [39] aims to discover stealthy mining pools whose domains are not publicly advertised. While this work reveals covert mining infrastructures, it does not address the problem of detecting mining activity at the network level.

Summary and Research Gap. Existing work primarily focuses on binary classification of mining activity and assumes direct network visibility. Few studies evaluate adversaries that deliberately route traffic through anonymity-preserving overlays such as VPNs or Tor. Consequently, it remains unclear whether mining traffic remains detectable under such conditions, or whether the specific cryptocurrency being mined can still be inferred from obfuscated network flows. Our work addresses this gap by empirically evaluating mining detectability under VPN and Tor routing and by examining whether cryptocurrency-level classification remains feasible in such environments.

3 Adversarial Model

Several countries have imposed restrictions on privacy preserving cryptocurrencies such as Monero (XMR) and ZCash (ZEC) [31,33]. While these actions often involve delisting such currencies from exchanges, mining remains a potential mechanism for generating new coins. In other cases, governments have taken stronger measures; for example, China has previously imposed large-scale restrictions on Bitcoin mining [11]. These developments indicate growing regulatory interest in identifying and controlling cryptocurrency mining activities.

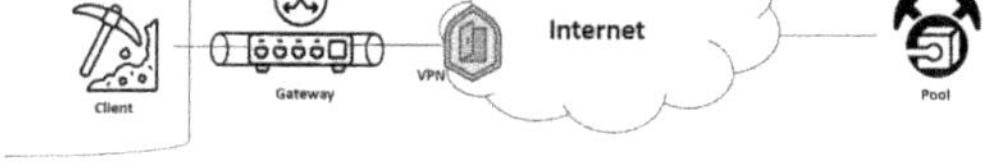

Fig. 1. Threat Model: Adversary between mining client and stratum pool server.

Motivated by this context, we consider an adversary whose objective is to identify and block or throttle pool-based cryptocurrency mining that violates regulatory or policy constraints, such as financial regulations or environmental concerns [30,31,33,35,37]. As illustrated in Fig. 1, we model a nation-state level adversary (e.g., a governmental agency or network regulator) capable of passively monitoring network traffic at ISPs. We consider a nation-state adversary, that can throttle, block or monitor the traffic between client and VPN/Tor nodes using mechanisms such as DPI, traffic fingerprinting [7,8,12].

We assume the adversary has access to flow-level metadata, including IP addresses, port numbers, timestamps, protocol types, flow durations, packet size statistics, *etc.*, and can exploit these to employ traffic analysis techniques such as statistical feature extraction, heuristic classification, and supervised model training to identify characteristic patterns of pool-based mining [4]. Prior work shows that deep packet inspection (DPI) can detect illicit mining activity, particularly in the context of cryptojacking [23]. To evade such monitoring, mining platforms such as *HiveOS* [15] support routing mining traffic through VPNs or encrypted proxies to obscure traffic patterns and evade network-level detection.

In this work, we therefore assume an adversary capable of detecting mining activity using only flow-level metadata without inspecting packet payloads. Specifically, the adversary attempts to identify encrypted mining traffic and infer the cryptocurrency being mined by exploiting persistent long-lived connections, timing regularity, and statistical characteristics typical of mining protocols.

4 Evaluation Methodology (MUR)

To systematically evaluate whether encrypted tunneling reduces mining detectability, we construct an evaluation methodology called Mining under Radar (MUR). The goal of MUR is not to introduce a new detection algorithm, but to provide a structured way to evaluate mining detectability and cryptocurrency identification across different deployment scenarios like plaintext, VPN and Tor.

MUR follows a two phase approach using statistical flow features like packet sizes, inter-arrival times, flow duration. The first phase – *Mining Detection* – performs coarse-grained classification to determine whether a network flow is pool based mining traffic or regular background traffic. The second phase – *Cryptocurrency Detection* – takes only those flows identified as mining-related from fomer phase and attempt to determine which cryptocurrency is being mined. This fine-grained classification allows us to evaluate whether encrypted mining traffic can determine the underlying cryptocurrency, necessary for selective enforcement [31,33]. The overall design of MUR is depicted in Fig. 2a.

Before detailing the methodology, we first describe characteristics of Stratum-based mining traffic observed during experiments. These empirical observations guided the design choices in MUR and helped us to determine the features used in both phases.

4.1 Characteristics of Stratum Pool Traffic

Pool-based mining traffic exhibits distinct temporal and statistical characteristics. These include stable inter-packet delays, regular upstream/downstream

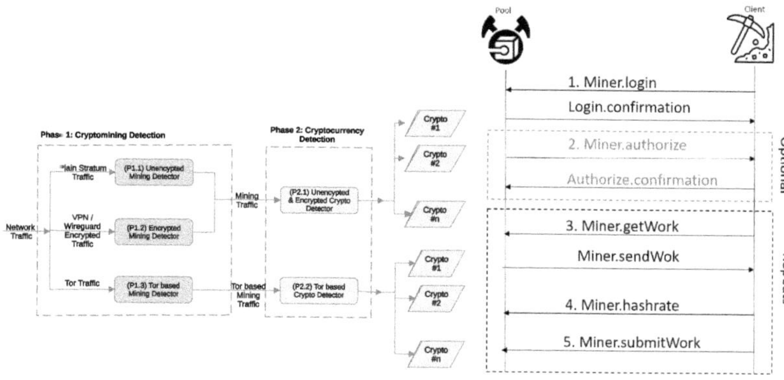

(a) High level design of MUR

(b) Stratum protocol flow.

Fig. 2. High level design of MUR and stratum protocol

packet exchange, and minimal variance in packet sizes, making them suitable targets for flow-level traffic analysis and fingerprinting. We highlight the protocol-level attributes intrinsic to Stratum which are leveraged by MUR to detect cryptomining traffic, differentiating it from conventional encrypted traffic.

1) Periodicity of Messages: Referring to Fig. 2b, the Stratum protocol follows a broadly similar communication sequence across its various implementations [39], for communication between the mining pool and the client.

The messages from the client to the pool are majorly of three types – *registration*, *submit hashrate* and *submit job* messages. The registration message *i.e.*, miner login is a one-time process carried out at the time a miner joins a pool. Following this, only in STRATUM-ETC, the miner advertises its computing capability by sending the hashrate it can provide. This message is sent periodically, and works as a keep-alive message. Other Stratum flavors do not have a separate keep alive message. The last message sent from a client to the pool, in outgoing direction, is to submit a job (solution) message. The frequency of this message is highly dependent on the computing capabilities of the miner. Higher miner hashrate would mean a greater number of puzzles could be solved per unit of time, as compared to miners having a lower hashrate. This has also been illustrated in [10]. Thus, the periodicity of traffic sent from mining client to pool varies, which makes it less viable to be used in classification.

On the other hand, the pool sends two kinds of messages to the client–*viz.*, *job* and *response*, following the registration confirmation. The job message is a periodic message sent from mining pool to the mining client, in incoming direction, containing information about the puzzle that needs to be solved by the miners. Independent of a client's computing capabilities, pool provider keeps sending job messages, so that at no point a miner solves a stale puzzle. The job packet contains a unique signature (as discussed further) for each cryptocurrency. Hence, in our approach the statistical features in the incoming direction from pool to client are considered important.

2) Analysis of Job Packet Generation Timing: In Stratum based pool mining protocol, the time of job packet generation is governed by three primary events: (i) detection of a new block on network (T_{block}), (ii) a periodic refresh interval configured by the pool (T_{refresh}), and (iii) exhaustion of the miner's nonce space requiring new work (T_{nonce}). The earliest of these events determine the rate at which job packets reaches the client, *i.e.*, IATs of the job packets reflect how the pool manages job updates. This information is collated from the open-source mining pool servers like MiningCore [26] and *open-etc-pool* [9].

Since pool-specific parameters such as T_{refresh} are not publicly disclosed, we conduct a black-box empirical analysis. To that end, we deploy controlled mining clients and connect them to multiple public mining pools across ten cryptocurrencies. From the captured traffic, we extract bidirectional temporal and statistical flow features, discarding TCP ACKs and infrequent control messages (e.g., login acknowledgments) to isolate job-related communication.

Figure 3a shows that job packet inter-arrival times differ across cryptocurrencies but remain consistent within each one. Coins with shorter block intervals like CFX tend to show consistently lower and less variable IATs, whereas coins with longer block intervals like ETC and ZEC exhibit higher mean IATs and greater dispersion. In some coins, we observe broader IAT variability across pools, suggesting flexible configuration policies at the pool level. Although the timing varies across coins and pools, mining traffic consistently exhibits bursty and somewhat regular communication patterns rather than random behavior.

These findings are directly relevant to the design of MUR. Overall, IAT based statistics serve as key discriminative feature. As later confirmed by feature importance, these features play a critical role in both mining detection and cryptocurrency attribution.

3) Distribution of Packet Sizes: Communication between miners and pools in Stratum-based protocols is typically structured in JSON format. While most pools follow standard protocol fields, some implement customized variations, which can lead to differences in job packet sizes. These variations arise from differences in job template structure and protocol configuration.

To study this effect, we analyzed the sizes of job packets sent from pools to miners across multiple cryptocurrencies and pools. Using the same experimental setup described earlier, we extracted packet size statistics from job-related messages. Figure 3b presents the average job packet sizes observed across the selected cryptocurrencies and mining pools. Our measurements show that job packet sizes differ noticeably across cryptocurrencies. For example, some cryptocurrencies like BTC, LTC consistently generate larger job packets, while others produce relatively compact templates like CFX, ETC, ZEC. In certain cases like with ZEC, ETC, CFX, packet sizes overlap across coins, indicating that size alone may not uniquely identify a cryptocurrency. However, when combined with timing and flow-level statistical features, packet size characteristics contribute additional discriminative power. Overall, these results show that packet size patterns differ across cryptocurrencies, although they are not as distinctive as timing patterns. This observation further motivates the inclusion of size-based features in MUR and aligns with the feature importance analysis presented later. **4) Developer Fee Mechanism in Mining Client:** Many widely used mining clients, such as *nanominer*, *cgminer*, and *lolMiner*, incorporate developer-fee mechanisms as part of their monetization model. We believe, this could impact the traffic structure, thus affecting the detection accuracies. These mechanisms work by redirecting a small fraction of mining effort to wallets controlled by the software developers. This typically occurs in one of two ways. First, some clients implement a developer-fee (DevFee) session, in which the miner's connection to the primary mining pool is intermittently terminated and temporarily redirected to a developer-controlled pool or wallet address. During this brief interval—often lasting only a few seconds and occurring approximately once every two hours—the miner effectively mines on behalf of the developer before reconnecting to the original pool. As a result, mining flows in such configurations may appear as short-lived sessions rather than persistent, long-duration connections. Second, certain clients establish a parallel TLS-encrypted connection to a developer-controlled endpoint while maintaining the primary mining pool session. In this case, the developer-fee traffic coexists with the main mining stream, producing concurrent flows associated with different destinations.

These mechanisms introduce additional variability in traffic patterns. In scenarios involving intermittent DevFee sessions, mining traffic may not manifest as continuous long-term flows, complicating simplistic detection assumptions based solely on session duration. Conversely, when parallel encrypted connections are present, the aggregate traffic profile may be further obfuscated—particularly when routed through anonymity-preserving overlays such as VPNs or Tor—potentially masking coin-specific characteristics.

From the perspective of our study, these client-level behaviors are important because they influence the observable traffic structure and therefore affect the packet size and IAT of packet (except in Tor), which in turns affects both detection and cryptocurrency attribution under encrypted routing conditions.

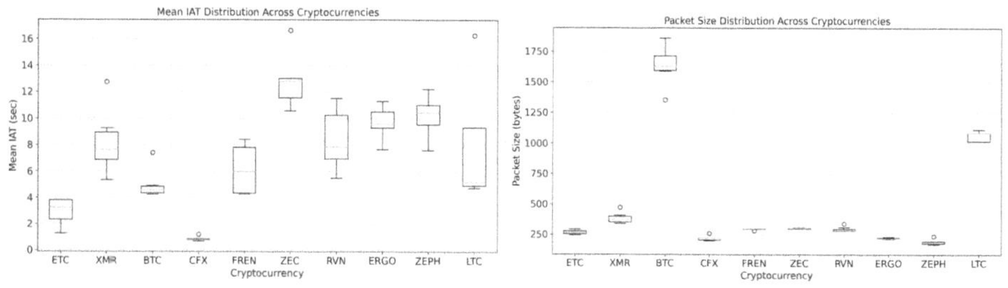

(a) IAT distribution

(b) Packet Size Distribution

Fig. 3. Distribution of IATs and job packet sizes for traffic sent from mining pool server to client.

4.2 Data Pre-processing

MUR uses six fields from the captured packet headers for detection: the source and destination IP addresses, port numbers, protocol type, packet size, besides the recorded packet arrival time. MUR does not require any payload information. To preserve users' privacy, only network and transport headers (up to Layer 4) (and never the payloads), are captured and processed. The IP addresses of the background traffic are pseudonymized using well-established tools like *Crypto-Pan* [19]. Additionally, the following pre-processing steps are also employed.[1]

Discarding Irrelevant Packets. Our analysis of stratum traffic, in Sect. 4.1, shows that majority of messages exchanged between pool and client in incoming direction are periodic in nature. Those that aren't include messages like *miner authorization* Fig. 2b are communicated only once. Considering such non-periodic messages may have a negative impact on the model training, as they typically appear only at the beginning of well established mining sessions. Therefore, these are excluded from the analysis. Additionally, we also discard TCP ACKS in this pre-processing phase as they may negatively influence the statistical features.

Discarding Irrelevant Flows. We discard internal flows (*i.e.*, flows having both the end points within the institute's boundary), flows with multicast and broadcast addresses, and certain oblivious protocols' packets, *e.g.* DNS, since real-world miners would likely hide all their traffic, including DNS messages, through encapsulation and encryption, *e.g.* via VPNs and Tor.

We discard flows where incidentally the derived statistical feature values, *e.g.* mean IAT, packet size *etc.*, are recorded as zero, conveying no meaningful information. File uploads and video streaming, where bulk traffic is mostly transmitted in one direction, with mostly acknowledgments arriving in the opposite direction, are some such application scenarios.

Discarding Short-Lived Streams. Mining traffic is generally characterized by persistent, long-lived connections between the miner and the mining pool, as sustained participation is required to generate meaningful rewards. Very short-duration flows are unlikely to correspond to productive mining activity and are more commonly associated with background application traffic. Accordingly, we discard flows whose duration is shorter than the observation window under consideration. We consider the observation window of 10mins, 15mins, 20mins and 30mins. This filtering step aligns with the pool's behavior and helps eliminate around 98% of background traffic. As a result, the subsequent analysis becomes more robust while legitimate mining sessions remain unaffected.

[1] Most aren't applicable to Tor. It segments data into fixed-size 512-byte cells, exhibiting modified traffic patterns, making packet-size based preprocessing difficult, as also explained in Sect. 4.4.

4.3 Feature Selection

Based on the characteristics of Stratum protocol studied in Sect. 4.1, feature selection was carried out to identify the most discriminative network behavioral attributes for effectively distinguishing mining activity from background processes.

Discarding Port Number. After a detailed analysis of the Stratum's de facto protocol, it was observed that no standardized port numbers are associated with its communication. Consequently, port numbers do not provide any discriminative information and have therefore been excluded from further consideration. Furthermore, when traffic is relayed through anonymity-preserving tools (such as VPNs or Tor), port numbers lose their distinguishability, reinforcing their limited relevance as a distinguishing feature in such contexts.

Packet Size and Timing Based Features. As discussed in Sect. 4.1, packet size and timing are the most important features in identification of the crypto-mining traffic. We henceforth, extracted all statistical features (mean, median, standard deviation and max) based on these two primary features for traffic in inbound direction. Apart from these, we also extracted the total packet count, total bytes and throughput for inbound traffic. In total, 10 features were used for proposed approach.

Features Relevant to MUR, Compared to Other Scenarios. In traditional traffic fingerprinting applications such as website fingerprinting—a broad range of features such as features including packet-level, burst-level, TCP-level, port-level, and IP-level have been proposed to capture distinctive communication patterns [4,21]. Burst-oriented features, *i.e.*, those used for website fingerprinting, are not applicable to Stratum-based mining traffic, which exhibits continuous, low-volume, bidirectional exchanges between the mining client and pool server.

4.4 Phase 1: Mining Detection

In this phase, MUR aims to segregate mining pool traffic from background flows. The network traffic is mix of crypto and background traffic flows. In case, the mining traffic is unencrypted, MUR uses straightforward DPI based detection. To hide mining footprints, further miners may choose to join pool servers using tunneling protocols like VPN, Tor. In such a case MUR uses ML based technique.

To understand the impact of such obfuscation techniques on detection methodology, we selected ten Proof-of-work based cryptocurrencies, namely *Bitcoin* (BTC), *Ethereum Classic* (ETC), *Monero* (XMR), *Conflux* (CFX), *ZCASH* (ZEC), *Frencoin* (FREN), *Ergo* (ERGO), *Ravencoin* (RVN), *Litecoin* (LTC) and *Zephyr* (ZEPH) as they ranked among the top 30 popular cryptocurrencies by market capitalization as of Jan 2025 [22]. The rationale behind this strategic selection is that nation-state adversaries would likely prioritize targeting cryptocurrencies that are both highly active and economically significant with BTC, XMR and ZEC already under the government's radar [31,33,37]. ETC and CFX were chosen due to their ongoing relevance in terms of market activity and on-chain transaction volumes. To capture realistic miner behavior, we identified the popularly used mining pools for each cryptocurrency based on their hashrate, using data from [22]. These selected pools primarily operate using the Stratum protocol, the de facto standard for mining communication. By focusing on these dominant cryptocurrencies and pools, our analysis is rooted in the real-world dynamics of mining traffic. This phase is designed as three independent detection approaches with – first stage (P1.1) working on unencrypted traffic, second (P1.2) on encrypted traffic and third (P1.3) on traffic going via Tor.

(P1.1) Unencrypted Mining Detector: Following the footprints of several prior works, an adversary can use a DPI-based heuristic to detect plaintext Stratum traffic. This involves scanning packet payloads for protocol-specific keywords such as "mining", "blob", "stratum", "mining.notify", "job". The goal is to assess whether simple keyword matching could reliably distinguish unencrypted Stratum communication from background traffic.

(P1.2) VPN-Based Mining Detector: To counter straightforward detection, a miner may route his/her traffic to the pool via anonymization tools like VPNs. Even while using them, we believe the network level features like IATs and packet sizes reveal the nature of underlying traffic. To that end, we adopt a ML-based binary classification approach capable of distinguishing mining traffic from background traffic. We employ RandomForest and XGBoost classifier, which generally perform well over unbalanced dataset.

(P1.3) Tor Based Mining Detector: Tor [5] is a low-latency overlay network providing anonymity by routing traffic through a cascade of volunteer operated relays. Tor ensures that none of these relays knows the complete path. Although not widely adopted for cryptomining, there are instances where Tor has been employed for anonymous mining [25,36].

In Tor, application payloads are segmented into fixed 512-byte *cells* [5], which are encrypted in layers, and then transported through a TCP connection between the client and the *guard* node [5]. The guard subsequently forwards it through the *circuit* to the intended destination. An adversary passively monitoring the traffic on the client-guard TCP connection carrying the cryptomining traffic, observes TLS packets that are frequently $\approx$ 602bytes. This occurs because Stratum messages, typically under 300bytes, fit entire within a 512-byte cell without being segmented. Consequently the outer encrypted packet ($\approx$602 bytes, accounting for TLS header and packet framing overheads), contains exactly one Tor cell that in turn encapsulates a full Stratum message.

Furthermore, the low volume of Stratum traffic, compared to web, reduces the likelihood that Tor batches multiple cells into a single TLS packet. As a result, Stratum messages tend to appear as a sequence of regular, single-cell TLS packets, forming a distinctive network-level signature, exploitable for detection.

4.5 Phase 2: Cryptocurrency Detection

The phase 2 of our approach further extends Phase 1 by incorporating a broader adversarial scenario in which a state or network-level adversary seeks to monitor, throttle, or entirely block traffic associated with specific cryptocurrencies. Motivated by such developments [31,33,37], our work advances the initial framework by proposing a machine learning (ML)-based approach to accurately identify cryptocurrency mining traffic under these restrictive conditions. This allows us to simulate miner's perspective, assessing how effectively could adversary detect and differentiate mining activity, even when mining traffic is tunneled through anonymity networks such as Tor or VPNs.

This phase is divided into two approaches – first (P2.1) working on encrypted and unencrypted mining traffic, and the second (P2.2) on mining traffic going via Tor. For this phase, we retain the same set of features used in Phase 1 for both training and testing our ML models, ensuring consistency in feature space while evaluating the performance of various classifiers across different coins.

(P2.1) Unencrypted and Encrypted Crypto Detector: While spotting unencrypted stratum traffic is trivial, employing DPI to search specific keywords in the packets' payloads, identifying which particular cryptocurrency is being mined is not straightforward. The underlying Stratum protocol exhibits detectable variations – such as STRATUM-BTC, STRATUM-ETC, or STRATUM-XMR as also mentioned in [39]. These protocol "flavors" seldom reveal the actual cryptocurrency. Like most PoW cryptocurrencies—such as LTC, RVN, ERGO, and ZEC – adopt the STRATUM-BTC style communication protocol primarily because of its simplicity, low resource consumption, and widely supported design originally built for UTXO (Unspent Transaction Output) based coins. In contrast, ETC inherits Ethereum's JSON-RPC and ETH-Stratum job format, which includes Ethash-specific fields (like seedhash), while XMR employs a RandomX-specific Stratum dialect containing additional metadata (like seedhash, algo). As a result, ETC and XMR mining traffic are seldom transported using STRATUM-BTC protocol. Importantly, BTC-style Stratum messages do not reveal the actual cryptocurrency; they only convey generic job templates and share submissions. Only a small subset of coins – such as Conflux (CFX)—explicitly embed the coin identifier in their handshake or authorization messages, making them rare exceptions.

Furthermore, the problem becomes even more complex in the presence of encrypted mining traffic, where protocol-level identifiers and message contents are completely hidden. In such cases, classical DPI techniques lose effectiveness, leaving only coarse statistical properties – often insufficient for distinguishing closely related mining algorithms or coins. To overcome these limitations and enable accurate per cryptocurrency identification, we introduce a ML-based classification model trained exclusively on mining flows. By learning subtle behavioural differences, such as those highlighted in Sect. 4.1, the ML model can differentiate between mining algorithms even when the traffic is encrypted. This approach allows us to generalize beyond protocol fingerprints and reliably detect the cryptocurrency being mined across diverse network conditions.

(P2.2) Tor Based Crypto Detector: When mining traffic is routed through the Tor network, its observable characteristics undergo a fundamental transformation. Tor encapsulates application data into fixed-size 512-byte cells, altering their original sizes and timing patterns. As a result, the statistical fingerprints that characterize conventional (encrypted or unencrypted) mining traffic, may not be completely preserved. Consequently, a model trained on non-Tor mining flows cannot generalize to Tor-routed traffic.

To address this divergence, our methodology employs a dedicated machine learning classifier specifically trained on Tor encapsulated mining data. By isolating Tor traffic as a separate domain, the model is able to learn Tor-specific flow-level properties such as altered inter-arrival dynamics while still distinguishing mining activity from background Tor traffic.

5 Evaluation

We assessed MUR within campus network environments using real-world traffic data. This section outlines our methodology for gathering labeled cryptomining traffic as well as real-world background (non-mining) traffic for comparison.

5.1 Data Collection

For longitudinally studying cryptomining traffic patterns, we curated a labeled dataset by emulating real-world mining scenarios, using clients deployed in our campus network. The clients utilized both CPUs and GPUs and were configured to connect to multiple mining pools, mining various cryptocurrencies.

According to the threat model considered in this paper, the mining stream was routed through OpenVPN and Wireuard gateways deployed at geographically distinct locations. The mining traffic was captured using tcpdump on a 10 Gbps campus backbone link, ensuring the presence of significant background traffic characteristic of medium-sized enterprise networks. These background flows included website visits, video streaming, voice calls and numerous other flows. To make sure enough diversity in background traffic, we also pooled in over 2 h traffic from *MAWI* database, a publicly available dataset [14]. To ensure user privacy, IP addresses within the captured traffic flows are anonymized using Crypto-PAn [19]. This redaction step preserves the structure of the traffic while preventing identification of any individual users or endpoints. Moreover, MUR requires only first 64 bytes to build the approach.

The traffic captured serves as the training and testing set and was used to derive flow-level features for each cryptocurrency. The data collection effort was carried out intermittently over a period of approximately five months, from July to Nov 2025. During this time, we captured network traces for nearly 600 distinct mining scenarios, covering diverse cryptocurrencies, pool servers, tunneling configurations, and protocol variations. To ensure consistency, the maximum mining session duration per client was restricted to 2 h per cryptocurrency-pool pair across both phases. The background data collected all this while comprised around 21M flows, *i.e.* mining traffic as compared to background traffic always remains in minority as seen in most of the related work in literature [3,10].

Unencrypted Mining Traffic. To inspect the possibility of detecting mining traffic from unencrypted mining flows, as previously described in Sect. 4.4(P1.1), we collected mining traffic generated by different cryptocurrencies across multiple mining pools. For this, we deployed mining clients for the cryptocurrencies considered by us and connected them to their respective mining pools. The traffic generated during these mining sessions was captured. Each mining session was executed for a maximum duration of 2 h, allowing sufficient time to observe multiple job assignment and share submission cycles. We generated around 600 mining flows. The collected dataset provides a representative view of unencrypted mining traffic and will be used for evaluating the detection performance of MUR in this phase.

Mining Traffic Through Anonymity Tools. As mentioned, miners may use anonymisation tools to conceal both their identity and the characteristics of their traffic. To evaluate the robustness of our proposed approach under such obfuscation, we assess how well it detects mining flows routed through VPN tunnels. We consider three widely deployed VPN technologies: OpenVPN operating over both TCP and UDP, and WireGuard—representing configurations commonly used by commercial VPN providers.

For OpenVPN, we set up two tunnels using a standard certificate-based authentication framework and contemporary encrypted transport over a routed TUN interface. Aside from the difference in underlying transport (TCP vs. UDP), both configurations follow the same security practices used in real deployments [29]. For WireGuard, we configured a typical client–server tunnel using its built-in lightweight key-exchange mechanism and integrated authenticated encryption, with the client forwarding all traffic through the VPN interface. Routing-related system settings were adjusted to ensure smooth operation without altering system's main routing table. These VPN environments provide realistic scenarios to test whether mining activity remains identifiable even when encapsulated within encrypted, privacy-preserving tunnels.

Using these configurations, we collected nearly 1500 VPN-encapsulated mining flows across all the three tunnel configurations for 2 h of duration. The metadata of the flows was extracted and models were evaluated.

Mining Traffic Through Tor. Tor, The Onion Router, is a low-latency overlay network providing anonymity by routing traffic through volunteer operated relays. Its layered encryption design ensures that no single relay knows the complete data path. Though not widely used, there are instances where Tor has been employed for anonymous mining [25,36]. Mining clients may leverage Tor to conceal their pool affiliation, geographic location, or operational identity—particularly in jurisdictions where cryptocurrency mining is regulated, monitored, or subject to targeted network scrutiny.

To evaluate the impact of Tor on Stratum communication, we configured mining clients to route *only* the mining-related traffic through Tor by specifying Tor's local SOCKS proxy within the miner configuration. This setup enables selective anonymization, ensuring that only Stratum job and share submission flows traverse the Tor circuit, while all other system traffic continues to follow the default network routing path. We collected around 584 mining flows for 7 cryptocurrencies – ETC, XMR, ZEC, ERGO, RVN, CFX, ZEPH across different mining pools for 2 h of duration each.

5.2 Efficacy of Proposed Approach

We implemented MUR to be able to answer the following questions – Is pool based cryptomining traffic distinguishable from background traffic?, Can someone spot the traffic when it is routed through different anonymity tools? With how much confidence can the underlying cryptocurrency be identified? How much observation time is required for reliable detection? To evaluate the efficacy of our evaluation model *w.r.t* above questions, we present the results for each phase separately.

Time Window Analysis. MUR is proposed as a near real-time approach, aiming to identify cryptomining traffic as early as possible using only metadata. To evaluate its responsiveness and detection efficiency using low volume of data, each network flow is further subdivided into smaller time windows of fixed durations—specifically, 10 mins, 15 mins, 20 mins and 30 mins – resulting in 12, 8, 6 and 4 flows, respectively, for every two hour-long mining session. These subdivisions allow us to evaluate MUR under varying window sizes and identify the minimum observation window necessary for reliably detecting mining traffic. Accordingly, we present result from each phase of MUR *w.r.t* these window sizes.

Phase 1: Cryptomining Detection. The aim of this phase is to detect cryptomining flows among background traffic. To evaluate the detection capability of MUR in this scenario, we report results from all the stages. This would help us gauge the efficacy of proposed methodology which we believe could be exploited by adversary to discover cryptomining traffic.
P1.1: Unencrypted Mining Detector: As described in Sect. 4.4 we employed DPI on following stratum related keywords – "mining", "blob", "stratum", "mining.notify", "mining.submit", "eth_getwork" and got 100% accuracy in detecting mining flows with FP = 0 and FN = 0 while varying time window analysis. In other words, every mining flow containing these identifiable protocol markers was correctly classified as mining traffic, while no background traffic was classified as mining. These results indicate that plaintext stratum implementations expose highly distinctive markers, making them trivially detectable.
P1.2: Encrypted Mining Detector: We trained two models – Random Forest and XGBoost, using a labeled dataset curated by combining mining and background cross traffic. To evaluate the efficacy of our proposed approach in

detecting pool-based cryptomining, we supplied 70% of total data (from each label) for training. The train and test dataset had a mix of mining traffic, spanning multiple cryptocurrencies and background traffic. To assess how quickly the system can identify mining traffic, we conducted a time window-based analysis.

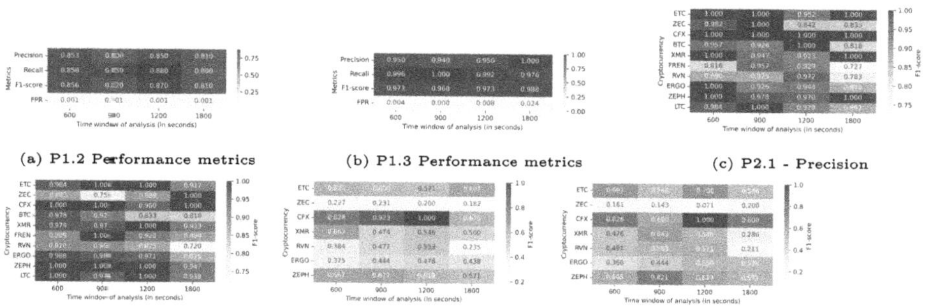

(a) P1.2 Performance metrics (b) P1.3 Performance metrics (c) P2.1 - Precision

(d) P2.1 - Recall (e) P2.2 - Precision (f) P2.2 - Recall

Fig. 4. Evaluation Results of different phases of MUR with varying time window

From Fig. 4a, we see that MUR can reliably detect encrypted cryptomining activity with only 20 min of traffic snapshot. The dataset had around 175K background flows and 692 mining flows, respectively. XGBoost classifier gave the best results with precision, recall, and F1-score for identifying mining flows from background traffic as 0.85, 0.88, and 0.87 respectively with FPR as 0.06%. These results demonstrate that MUR is capable of distinguishing mining traffic despite use of tunneling protocols. A detailed inspection of False Negatives (FNs) – *i.e.*, mining flows that were not detected – reveals an uneven distribution across cryptocurrencies. Most of the missed flows belong to ZEPH, ERGO, and RVN, suggesting that their protocol behaviors or pool implementations introduce traffic patterns that appear closer to background traffic. Importantly, the classifier does not fail uniformly – only some flows for a given coin–pool pair are missed, while others were correctly identified.

On analyzing the falsely classified background flows, we found these flows predominantly used port 443 and were likely associated with encrypted web services However, these instances were very limited in number and constituted only a negligible fraction of the overall background traffic. We did not investigate these flows further due to ethical considerations related to user privacy and the anonymized nature of the dataset.

The most influential features were `std_size`, `std_iat`, `mean_size`, and `median_size`. As observed in Sect. 4.1, Stratum-based mining communication exhibits structured packet exchanges due to periodic job notifications and share submissions between miners and pools. This interaction results in relatively consistent packet size characteristics, as job notification messages tend to have similar payload structures. Consequently, packet-size based statistics exhibit stable distributions across mining flows, making features such as mean, median, and standard deviation of packet sizes highly informative for distinguishing mining traffic from benign network activity.

P1.3: Tor based Mining Detector: The experimental setup mirrors that of P1.2 (Sect. 5.2), with the sole difference that mining traffic in this case is routed through the Tor network. MUR was able to detect this Tor tunneled mining traffic within 20mins of observation window. The dataset comprised around 43K background flows and 418 mining flows. XGBoost classifier gave the best performance. We achieved precision, recall, and F1-score of 0.95, 0.99 and 0.97, respectively, in distinguishing Tor-tunneled mining flows from background traffic as also evident from Fig. 4b. The most contributing feature were again median_size and mean_size, which exhibit a unique pattern in case of mining traffic as described in Sect. 4.4. These results demonstrate that Tor does not fully obfuscate mining behavior, and that mining activity remains detectable at the network level with high confidence.

Phase 2: Cryptocurrency Detection. The aim of this phase is to detect cryptocurrency involved in the process. To determine the identification capabilities of MUR, we further present the results from each stage.

P2.1: Unencrypted and Encrypted Crypto Detector: We use two ML models – RandomForest and XGBoost trained with data from all 10 cryptocurrencies. This phase had around 2252 flows for a window size of 10 mins, with nearly uniform representation from each cryptocurrency. The dataset includes both encrypted and unencrypted mining flows. The best performing results are obtained with XGBoost classifier. MUR attains average precision, recall and F1-score of 0.96 as depicted in Fig. 4c and d respectively. Major misclassifications among these are between RVN and ZEC. The most influential features for detecting underlying cryptocurrency were volume and size related statistical attributes, such as the mean and median packet sizes, packet counts, and throughput.

P2.2: Tor based Crypto Detector: Here as well we use ML models – RandomForest and XGBoost trained with data from 7 cryptocurrencies – ETC, ZEC, CFX, XMR, RVN, ZEPH and ERGO with around 418 flows from seven categories, of 20mins duration each. 70% of this data is used for training the models and remaining 30% for testing. From Figs. 4e and f, it is evident that MUR finds it challenging to detect individual coins using anonymity preserving tools like Tor. MUR obtains precision, recall and F1-score of 0.56, 0.58 and 0.56 respectively for window size of 20mins. In that case, accurate detecting of cryptocurrencies using Tor might not be achievable. The most important feature were mean_size, std_size, mean_iat and median_iat. As noted earlier, Tor transmits data in fixed size cells, size-related features alone no longer played a significant role when the traffic was routed through Tor. Here, inter-arrival-time (IAT) features played an equally important role.

To conclude, our study provides affirmative answers to all three research questions asked in Sect. 1. First, from results of Phase 1, it is evident that pool-based cryptocurrency mining activity is detectable via network-level traffic analysis (RQ1). Second, the use of VPNs and Tor does not prevent such detection (RQ2). Third, results from Phase 2 show that, with suitable training, the underlying cryptocurrency being mined can also be identified despite the use of anonymity mechanisms like VPNs (RQ3). Finally, results reveal that as low as 10–20 mins of mining traffic is sufficient to spot the cryptomining and cryptocurrency with great efficacy (RQ4).

6 Limitations and Future Work

Despite our efforts, there are certain challenges that still linger. We discuss those challenges and propose potential solutions.

1. Currently, MUR displays a limited performance while using TLS encrypted mining traffic in Phase 2. We plan to strengthen the approach by using TLS based mining data while training our models, to help it train better.
2. While MUR relies on strong statistical features (IATs, packet sizes, throughput), its accuracy drops for certain edge cases – short flows (<15 min), cryptocurrencies with overlapping statistical patterns Fig. 4a. The current feature set can be further improved to include other features like percentiles.
3. Under Tor, MUR's performance declines notably in Phase 2. This probably is due to the changes in latency of the packets when routed through Tor. These effects suppress natural variations in mining traffic, causing overlaps with other coins and sometimes background-like behavior, ultimately resulting in substantially lower precision and recall.
4. MUR uses MAWI dataset for training [14], along with the flows captured at the institute gateway. However, for MAWI, the ground truth labels of the underlying protocols are unavailable. While it is not an imperative to use this dataset, other labeled ones could be used as well.
5. The future defenses against MUR may involve utilizing intelligently crafted and injected cover traffic, that makes it hard to differentiate mining flows from oblivious ones [13,17,18], without significantly impacting mining gains.

7 Ethical Considerations

To ensure ethical integrity, all experiments are designed in accordance with the Belmont Report's principles of respect for persons, beneficence, and justice. Importantly, the traffic analyzed is generated using self-hosted mining clients within a controlled lab environment, and no real user data or third-party mining traffic is collected. To preserve privacy, only network headers (up to Layer 4) are captured—never the packet payloads—and all IP addresses in background traffic are pseudonymized using established tools like Crypto-Pan [19].

We obtained formal approval from the Institutional Review Board (IRB) to ensure that our research complies with ethical standards concerning data privacy, informed consent, and responsible experimentation. The approval is registered under the IRB Registration Number $EC/NEW/INST/2024/DL/0440$/File Number $IRB - IIITD/FR/04/2025/01$.

8 Conclusion

This paper examined whether pool-based cryptocurrency mining can evade detection when miners employ anonymity-preserving tools such as VPNs and Tor. Our results show that mining traffic remains identifiable even under such tunneling mechanisms. Using only flow-level metadata—specifically packet inter-arrival times and packet sizes, mining flows can be distinguished from background traffic with as little as 20 min of network captures.

Under VPN tunneling, mining detection achieves 0.85 precision and 0.88 recall, while Tor-based tunneling improves detection to 0.95 precision and 0.99 recall. For cryptocurrency identification, VPN-tunneled traffic achieves 0.96 precision and recall over a 10-minute observation window. However, Tor degrades performance because latency-induced timing variations add noise and increase false positives. Overall, these findings show that anonymity-preserving tools alter traffic characteristics but do not fully obscure mining activity – VPN-routed mining remains highly detectable, whereas Tor's variability complicates precise cryptocurrency identification. Thus, miners cannot entirely rely on such tools to evade traffic-based detection.

Disclosure of Interests. The authors have no competing interests to declare that are relevant to the content of this article.

References

1. Binance: Binance (2025). https://www.binance.com/en-IN
2. Braiins: Past and future of bitcoin mining protocols: Stratum V2 overview (2025). https://braiins.com/blog/past-and-future-of-bitcoin-mining-protocols-stratum-v2-overview
3. Caprolu, M., Raponi, S., Oligeri, G., Di Pietro, R.: Cryptomining makes noise: detecting cryptojacking via machine learning. Comput. Commun. **171**, 126–139 (2021)
4. Cherubin, G., Jansen, R., Troncoso, C.: Online website fingerprinting: evaluating website fingerprinting attacks on tor in the real world. In: USENIX Security Symposium (USENIX Security 22), Boston, MA, USA, pp. 753–770 (2022)
5. Dingledine, R., Mathewson, N., Syverson, P.: Tor: the second-generation onion router. In: USENIX Security Symposium (USENIX Security 04), San Diego, CA, USA (2004)
6. Draper-Gil, G., Lashkari, A.H., Mamun, M.S.I., Ghorbani, A.A.: Characterization of encrypted and VPN traffic using time-related. In: Proceedings of the International Conference on Information Systems Security and Privacy (ICISSP), Rome, Italy, pp. 407–414 (2016)
7. Dunna, A., O'Brien, C., Gill, P.: Analyzing China's blocking of unpublished tor bridges. In: 8th USENIX Workshop on Free and Open Communications on the Internet (FOCI 18), Baltimore, MD (2018)
8. Ensafi, R., Fifield, D., Winter, P., Feamster, N., Weaver, N., Paxson, V.: Examining how the great firewall discovers hidden circumvention servers. In: Proceedings of the Internet Measurement Conference, IMC '15, New York, NY, USA, pp. 445–458 (2015)

9. Etclabscore: Openetcpool (2020). https://github.com/etclabscore/open-etc-pool/blob/master/config.example.json
10. Feng, Y., Li, J., Sisodia, D.: CJ-Sniffer: measurement and content-agnostic detection of cryptojacking traffic. In: Proceedings of the 25th International Symposium on Research in Attacks, Intrusions and Defenses, RAID '22, New York, NY, USA, pp. 482–494 (2022)
11. Freemman Law: China and Cryptocurrency (2022). https://freemanlaw.com/cryptocurrency/china/
12. Vijaya, G., Dhiyanesh, M.S., Hashmi, M.D., Junaith Rehaan, K., Kavennesh, B.V.: Robust technique for detecting and blocking of VPN over networks. In: 2024 Ninth International Conference on Science Technology Engineering and Mathematics (ICONSTEM), pp. 1–5 (2024)
13. Gong J., Wang, T.: Zero-delay lightweight defenses against website fingerprinting. In: 29th USENIX Security Symposium (USENIX Security 20), Boston, MA, USA, pp. 717–734 (2020)
14. MAWI Working Group Traffic: MAWI working group traffic archive (2025). https://mawi.wide.ad.jp/mawi/
15. HiveOs: HiveOs (2025). https://hiveon.com/os/
16. Investopedia Team: Mining Pool: Definition, How It Works, Methods, and Benefits (2024). https://www.investopedia.com/terms/m/mining-pool.asp
17. Jithin, S., Gupta, R., Ranjan, R.K., Nagpal, S., Maity, M., Chakravarty, S.: VoIP Vanguard: a practical front line defense against VoIP identification attacks in Tor. In: International Conference on Network and System Security, Abu Dhabi, UAE, pp. 319–346 (2024)
18. Juárez, M., Imani, M., Perry, M., Dıaz, C., Wright, M.: WTF-PAD: toward an efficient website fingerprinting defense for Tor. CoRR abs/1512.00524 (2015)
19. Jun, X., Jinliang, F., Mostafa, A., Moon, S.B.: On the design and performance of prefix-preserving IP traffic trace anonymization. In: Proceedings of the First ACM SIGCOMM Workshop on Internet Measurement, San Francisco, California, USA, vol. 31, p. 263 (2001)
20. Kaspersky: What is Cryptocurrency and how does it work? (2025). https://www.kaspersky.com/resource-center/definitions/what-is-cryptocurrency
21. Lashkari, A.H., Gil, G.D., Mamun, M.S.I., Ghorbani, A.A.: Characterization of Tor traffic using time based features. In: International Conference on Information Systems Security and Privacy, Porto, Portugal, vol. 2, pp. 253–262 (2017)
22. MiningPoolStats: MiningPoolStats (2025). https://miningpoolstats.stream/
23. i Muñoz, J.Z., Suárez-Varela, J., Barlet-Ros, P.: Detecting cryptocurrency miners with NetFlow/IPFIX network measurements. In: IEEE International Symposium on Measurements & Networking (M&N), Catania, Italy, pp. 1–6 (2019)
24. Nakamoto, S.: Bitcoin: a peer-to-peer electronic cash system (2008)
25. The Hacker News Logo: Hackers exploit misconfigured docker APIs to mine cryptocurrency via Tor network (2025). https://thehackernews.com/2025/06/hackers-exploit-misconfigured-docker.html
26. Oliver Weichhold: MiningCore (2022). https://github.com/oliverw/miningcore/blob/master/examples/ethereum_pool.json
27. People's Bank of China: Notice on Further Preventing and Resolving the Risks of Virtual Currency Trading and Speculation) (2021). http://www.pbc.gov.cn/en/3688110/3688172/4157443/4353814/index.html
28. Rahman, M.S., Sirinam, P., Mathews, N., Gangadhara, K.G., Wright, M.: Tik-Tok: the utility of packet timing in website fingerprinting attacks. In: Proceedings on Privacy Enhancing Technologies, vol. 2020, Montreal, Canada, pp. 5–24 (2020)

29. Rajore, T., et al.: VPN or Vpwn? How afraid should you be of VPN traffic identification? In: Network Traffic Measurement and Analysis Conference (TMA), Copenhagen, Denmark, pp. 1–11 (2025)
30. Reuters: Iran bans cryptocurrency mining for 4 months amid power cuts (2021). https://www.reuters.com/technology/iran-bans-cryptocurrency-mining-4-months-amid-power-cuts-2021-05-26/
31. Sanction Scanner: New crypto regulations in South Korea (2025). https://www.sanctionscanner.com/blog/new-crypto-regulations-in-south-korea-445
32. SCMP: Bitcoin was once dominated by China, but the Trump bump is shifting momentum to US (2025). https://www.scmp.com/tech/blockchain/article/3288731/bitcoin-was-once-dominated-china-trump-bump-shifting-momentum-us
33. Shobhit Seth: Japan's FSA Bans Private Cryptocurrencies (2019). https://www.investopedia.com/news/japans-fsa-bans-private-cryptocurrencies/#:~:text=Japan
34. Startum: Startum mining (2022). https://github.com/stratum-mining
35. Telegrafi: Panic as Kosovo bans cryptocurrency mining to save electricity (2022). https://telegrafi.com/en/panik-ndersa-kosova-ndalon-mihjen-e-kriptovalutave-per-te-kursyer-energjine-elektrike/
36. Torry: Can you mine cryptocurrency on the dark web? the hidden mining pools of Tor (2021). https://www.torry.io/blog/can-you-mine-cryptocurrency-on-the-dark-web/
37. Wired: China's sweeping cryptocurrency ban was inevitable (2020). https://www.wired.com/story/chinas-sweeping-cryptocurrency-ban-inevitable
38. Zhang, S., et al.: MineHunter: a practical cryptomining traffic detection algorithm based on time series tracking. In: Proceedings of the Annual Computer Security Applications Conference, New York, NY, USA, pp. 1051–1063 (2021)
39. Zhang, Z., et al.: Under the dark: a systematical study of stealthy mining pools (ab)use in the wild. In: Proceedings of SIGSAC Conference on Computer and Communications Security, New York, NY, USA, pp. 326–340 (2023)

SoK: The Illusion of Additive Security: Censorship Resistance Across the Bitcoin Ecosystem

Marc Schreiner and Pascal Tippe(✉)

FernUniversität in Hagen, Hagen, Germany
marc.schreiner.science@proton.me, pascal.tippe@fernuni-hagen.de

Abstract. While Bitcoin is fundamentally designed as a censorship-resistant payment network, its operational reality faces increasing jurisdictional pressure from state-level sanctions. Current academic research evaluates these vulnerabilities in isolation: analyzing base-layer mining, Layer 2 routing, and federated sidechains using incompatible metrics. This methodological fragmentation obscures how censorship risks cascade across the protocol stack. To bridge this gap, we present a Systematization of Knowledge that introduces a unified, 17-indicator framework to systematically quantify censorship resistance across the Bitcoin ecosystem. Synthesizing 43 academic sources and additional data from January 2026, we demonstrate that censorship resistance inherits hierarchically. We find that while higher-layer protocols offer internal privacy mitigations like onion routing, their ultimate systemic security depends on the unilateral exit-option to a neutral base layer, which federated sidechains currently lack. Furthermore, we identify a critical gap: while advanced cryptographic mitigations like Stratum V2 and trustless rollups exist, operational friction and the pursuit of liquidity efficiency might slow down their adoption. Consequently, transaction flow remains bottlenecked by highly identifiable, centralized corporate entities acting as single points of coercion. We conclude that systemic resilience is currently limited by intermediary vulnerabilities and requires both base-layer upgrades (e.g., covenants) and the broader economic adoption of trust-minimized technologies.

Keywords: Censorship Resistance · Bitcoin Ecosystem · Off-Chain Protocols

1 Introduction

Bitcoin is widely characterized as a censorship-resistant payment network, built on the premise that valid transactions will invariably be processed according to uniform consensus rules [34]. However, in operational reality, this property is increasingly challenged by regulatory interventions and state-level sanctions. The vulnerability of decentralized protocols to jurisdictional pressure was starkly

S. Nadjm-Tehrani et al. (Eds.): ARES 2026, LNCS 16898, pp. 461–483, 2027.
https://doi.org/10.1007/978-3-032-36874-4_23

demonstrated by the U.S. Office of Foreign Assets Control (OFAC) sanctions against the Tornado Cash protocol in August 2022. Following the sanctions, the protocol experienced a severe and sustained decline in transaction volume and network liquidity, proving that legal and reputational risks are sufficient to suppress participation and effectively filter transactions, even when the underlying open-source code remains fully functional. Within the Bitcoin ecosystem, this threat vector is particularly critical because transaction processing is not an abstract, automatic function. It is heavily mediated by the economic and operational decisions of concrete actors. Block production on the base layer is dominated by large mining pools, while the scaling of transaction throughput is facilitated by secondary layers, such as the Lightning Network's routing hubs and the institutional federations of sidechains. These architectural layers introduce distinct intermediaries that operate as functional gatekeepers. Consequently, censorship resistance cannot be treated as a guaranteed, monolithic system property. It is the fragile result of interacting technical, economic, and organizational constraints.

The academic discourse surrounding blockchain censorship resistance has historically evaluated these vulnerabilities in isolation. Existing literature predominantly focuses on specific technical layers, analyzing mining pools via game-theoretic thresholds and empirical hash rate measurements [13,56], the Lightning Network via topological centrality and traffic fingerprinting [36,60], or federated sidechains by evaluating architectural trust assumptions and formalizing censorship as economic cost functions [15]. While these siloed analyses offer deep layer-specific insights, they utilize fundamentally incompatible measurement metrics. This methodological fragmentation obscures systemic interdependencies and makes it impossible to compare censorship resilience across the protocol stack. Crucially, the literature fails to capture how the foundational security guarantees of a secondary layer (such as the unilateral exit mechanism) might be entirely undermined by the jurisdictional capture of a base-layer intermediary.

Our Contributions: To bridge this methodological gap, this paper presents a Systematization of Knowledge (SoK) evaluating the censorship resistance of the Bitcoin ecosystem against sanction-induced transaction filtering. We shift the paradigm from isolated protocol analysis to a holistic, cross-layer evaluation. Specifically, our contributions are threefold:

- **A Unified Evaluation Framework:** We develop a multi-dimensional SoK coding framework comprising 17 distinct indicators across six core categories (Decentralization, Permissionlessness, Transparency, Protocol Design, Economic Incentives, and Social & Geopolitics). This taxonomy translates incompatible technical metrics into a unified evaluation grid.
- **Cross-Layer Synthesis:** We systematically apply this framework to 43 existing academic studies, formal verifications, and architectural models spanning Layer 1 (Mining Pools), Layer 2 (The Lightning Network), and Federated Sidechains (Liquid and RSK).

- **Empirical Baseline (2026):** Because theoretical literature frequently lags behind operational market dynamics, we augment our synthesis with additional collected data collected in January 2026. This includes the evaluation of dominant mining pool configurations, Terms of Services (ToS), and sidechain governance structures.

Key Findings: Our systematization reveals a discrepancy between theoretical protocol security and operational centralization. We demonstrate that censorship resistance within the ecosystem is not additive, but inherits hierarchically. While technologies like onion routing and confidential transactions provide strong in-flight privacy, they do not currently achieve absolute anonymity against sophisticated network analysis. Consequently, the ultimate security of these higher layers relies heavily on the *exit-option*: the ability to bypass gatekeepers and fall back to the base layer. Because major intermediaries across all three layers are highly identifiable corporate entities concentrated in specific geopolitical blocks, they represent highly vulnerable *single points of coercion*. We conclude that the ecosystem suffers from a critical gap: the cryptographic tools to mitigate these chokepoints (such as Stratum V2 and trustless peg-outs) already exist, but operational convenience, technical friction, and the economic pursuit of liquidity efficiency currently hinder their widespread adoption.

2 Background and Related Work

To systematically evaluate censorship resistance across the Bitcoin ecosystem, it is necessary to decouple the monolithic concept of *the blockchain* into its constituent architectural layers. Transaction processing traverses distinct infrastructural levels, each introducing unique technical bottlenecks and trust assumptions.

2.1 Technical Foundations: Architecture and Control Points

Potential censorship mechanisms do not emerge abstractly within the protocol. Instead, they manifest at specific decision-making bottlenecks. We classify these control points across three operational layers:

Layer 1: Proof-of-Work and Pool Coordination. The lifecycle of a Bitcoin transaction operates as a multi-stage filtering process. Transactions utilizing the Unspent Transaction Output (UTXO) model are propagated via a peer-to-peer gossip network. Ultimately, miners act as auctioneers, selecting transactions from the mempool based on fee rates to maximize the profitability of their blocks [34]. However, the economic necessity of variance smoothing has driven individual miners into large mining pools [49]. Under the dominant Stratum V1 protocol, the pool operator retains exclusive authority over block template construction [39]. This hierarchical architecture centralizes decision-making power, theoretically allowing a pool operator to filter or censor specific transactions before distributing the hashing tasks to individual miners.

Layer 2: Off-Chain Routing and State Channels. The Lightning Network (LN) shifts transaction validation from a global consensus mechanism to a network of localized, bilateral micro-payment channels secured by 2-of-2 multisignature addresses. Payments are routed across multiple intermediaries (hops) using Hashed Timelock Contracts (HTLCs) [45]. Consequently, the vector for censorship on Layer 2 shifts from the exclusion of transactions in a block to the deliberate refusal to route payment packets. The vulnerability to this routing censorship is inextricably linked to the network's topology and the availability of alternative liquid paths.

Layer 3: Federated Sidechains and Two-Way Pegs. Federated sidechains introduce a hybrid architecture designed to enhance scalability and expressiveness while anchoring security to the Bitcoin mainchain via a two-way *peg* [3]. Crucially, because the Bitcoin base layer intentionally restricts its scripting language and currently lacks expressive *covenants* (the ability to natively enforce constraints on future transaction outputs) or the ability to cheaply verify zero-knowledge proofs, the mainchain cannot unilaterally enforce a mathematical state transition from a secondary network. Consequently, unlike trustless rollups on more expressive blockchains, dominant Bitcoin sidechain implementations like the Liquid Network and RSK must rely on a *strong federation* of designated functionaries [37]. To execute a *peg-out* (withdrawing assets back to the mainchain), a defined multi-signature quorum of these functionaries is strictly required. This reliance on institutional gatekeepers fundamentally shifts the censorship risk model, as the protocol does not currently provision a unilateral exit mechanism without the federation's collective authorization.

2.2 Threat Model: Defining Censorship and the Exit-Option

In the context of this SoK, we do not model censorship as a global denial-of-service attack against the network's liveness. Instead, we define censorship as the *selective suppression or delay of valid transactions* contrary to standard protocol rules. The overarching security assumption of the Bitcoin ecosystem relies on the ability to *permissionlessly bypass* censoring intermediaries. On the base layer, this assumes that if one mining pool censors a transaction, the user can bypass them because another economically rational miner will eventually include it. However, on higher infrastructural layers (Layer 2 and sidechains), this resilience also depends on the economic principle of the *exit-option*: the cryptographic guarantee that a user can unilaterally withdraw their funds back to the neutral base layer without requiring the intermediary's permission or cooperation.

2.3 Related Work: The Fragmentation of Censorship Research

The scientific discourse surrounding censorship resistance has historically evaluated vulnerabilities within isolated architectural domains. This has led to diverse but fragmented research directions tailored to the specific technical realities of each layer.

Layer 1: Structural, Game-Theoretic, and Empirical Analyses Research concerning the base layer encompasses a wide spectrum of methodologies. Early structural analyses identified the economic necessity of mining pools for variance smoothing, highlighting the inevitable centralization of hash rate [49]. This structural view is heavily complemented by game-theoretic security models. Foundational studies demonstrated that the protocol is not perfectly incentive-compatible, modeling how attackers can leverage strategies like Selfish Mining to gain disproportionate rewards even with a minority of the hash rate [13]. Recent works have expanded these formal threat models to include Partial Selfish Mining via zero-knowledge proofs, creating trust-minimized incentives for miner collusion [59]. Parallel to these theoretical models, empirical research evaluates censorship resistance under real-world network conditions. These studies demonstrate how attackers can exploit scaling mechanisms to delay block propagation [19] and how high stale block rates physically fragment the honest network's effective hash rate, thereby lowering the threshold for censorship attacks [19].

Layer 2: Topological Centralization and Protocol Verification In contrast to the base layer, research on the Lightning Network investigates censorship primarily through the lens of network topology and active traffic manipulation. Extensive empirical measurements of the network graph reveal a persistent hub-and-spoke centralization, with Gini coefficients for channel capacity frequently exceeding 0.90 [60]. This topological fragility has prompted research into active censorship vectors. Recent studies have demonstrated that despite the protocol's use of end-to-end encrypted Sphinx routing, intermediaries can selectively filter payments by fingerprinting TCP metadata (such as timing and packet sizes) [36]. Furthermore, a growing body of literature employs formal verification methods to evaluate the payment protocol itself, successfully identifying structural vulnerabilities such as congestion attacks and payout-race scenarios that compromise payment liveness [53,57].

Layer 3: Trust Assumptions and Economic Cost Functions Research on federated sidechains largely focuses on the tension between scalability and trust minimization. While early designs aimed for trustless two-way pegs, their reliance on vetted functionaries and hardware security modules reduces the trust. To formalize these risks, recent theoretical work defines censorship resistance on sidechains as a quantifiable economic cost function: calculating the exact financial capital an attacker must expend to suppress a transaction against competing, rational block proposers [15].

2.4 Identifying the Gap: The Need for Systematization

While the aforementioned studies offer rigorous insights into specific attack vectors, their methodological fragmentation prevents a holistic understanding of the ecosystem's systemic resilience. Currently, censorship resistance is operationalized using fundamentally incompatible frameworks: game-theoretic thresholds for mining, topological and traffic-analysis metrics for off-chain routing, and formal economic cost functions for sidechain federations. This methodological divide obscures how vulnerabilities interact across the protocol stack. For instance, the literature lacks a unified approach to evaluate how the topological censorship of a Layer 2 routing hub might be exacerbated by the jurisdictional capture of a Layer 1 mining pool. To bridge this gap, this paper introduces a Systematization of Knowledge (SoK). The objective is not merely to aggregate existing literature, but to establish a multidimensional framework that synthesizes disparate technical, economic, and regulatory findings. By translating these diverse research directions into a unified comparative taxonomy, this SoK enables the systematic evaluation of cumulative censorship risks, thereby illuminating how technical safeguards on one layer may be compromised by socio-economic or regulatory dependencies on another.

3 Methodology

To address the fragmentation of current research on censorship resistance, this paper adopts a Systematization of Knowledge (SoK) methodology. Rather than evaluating censorship resistance as a monolithic or purely theoretical property, we introduce a multidimensional coding framework designed to systematically quantify and compare vulnerabilities across the different architectural layers of the Bitcoin ecosystem.

3.1 Scope of Analysis

To systematically evaluate censorship resistance within the Bitcoin ecosystem, this Systematization of Knowledge (SoK) adopts a component-oriented taxonomy. Rather than analyzing the blockchain as a monolithic entity, the investigation isolates specific technological and organizational control points across three distinct infrastructural layers. This stratification is necessary because potential censorship mechanisms do not emerge abstractly within the protocol, but at specific decision-making bottlenecks that vary fundamentally across the network architecture.

First, the analysis examines the base layer (Layer 1) by focusing on mining pools. Mining pools are critical intermediaries directly responsible for block template construction and the inclusion or filtering of pending transactions. Evaluating this layer establishes the foundational baseline for censorship resistance, determining the extent to which valid transactions can bypass external restrictions during initial block production. Second, the scope includes the Lightning Network as a representative Layer-2 scaling solution. This off-chain network introduces distinct architectural and economic characteristics, particularly regarding routing topologies and liquidity concentration. These structural properties manifest entirely different vectors for transaction censorship, specifically the refusal of payment routing, compared to the broadcast mechanisms of the base layer. Third, federated sidechains are evaluated as an alternative architectural model. Unlike permissionless mechanisms, implementations such as Liquid and RSK [31] rely on explicit trust assumptions and governance rules, utilizing designated federations to secure the two-way peg. This design fundamentally shifts the censorship resistance dynamic from open competition toward institutional trust and gatekeeping. By analysing the ecosystem as these three components, the methodology ensures that censorship resistance is measured not as a uniform, theoretical property, but as a practical resilience metric subjected to sanction-induced filtering attempts across varying infrastructural layers.

3.2 Data Collection and Search Strategy

The data collection strategy utilized a multi-stage approach. The initial phase established a baseline using foundational protocol whitepapers and recent case studies on sanction-induced filtering, specifically the OFAC interventions concerning Tornado Cash [55]. A systematic database search was then conducted across the ACM Digital Library, IEEE Xplore, and the specific security venues IEEE S&P, NDSS, USENIX Security, and ESORICS, using keywords such as *censorship resistance*, *transaction filtering*, *sanctions*, *mining pools*, *lightning network*, *federated sidechains*, and *permissionlessness*. To capture developments beyond peer-review publication lag, the corpus was extended via arXiv and targeted web searches, supplemented by forward and backward snowballing. Academic publications were included only if they provided original empirical measurements, formal protocol verifications, or architectural simulations. Pure surveys and reviews were excluded. Because essential protocol specifications and governance rules often bypass peer review, official developer documentations, API specifications, and provider Terms of Service were also treated as primary data sources, as were real-time network metrics from specialized platforms (e.g., mempool.space). The research methodology of each source is recorded in the evidence map (Table 2, column **M**), spanning five paradigms: Empirical Network Analysis (E), Mathematical & Game-Theoretic Modelling (G), System Design & Protocol Architecture (D), Simulation & Algorithmics (S), and Systematization of Knowledge (K); sources may employ multiple methods. We use **G** narrowly for theoretical constructs that calculate actor behaviour or evaluate incentive structures, such as Markov decision processes, game-theoretic analyses, probabilistic behavioural models, cost-benefit functions, difference equations, or economic case studies. Formal cryptographic proofs and protocol verification are therefore coded as **D** unless they also model actor incentives.

3.3 Iterative Framework Development

The coding framework was developed iteratively by two coders with backgrounds in IT security through a deductive-inductive approach, ensuring methodological rigor and inter-coder reliability. In the initial deductive phase, one coder derived six fundamental evaluation criteria from foundational security and blockchain literature, aiming to capture abstract concepts of censorship resistance such as decentralization and economic incentives. These criteria were subsequently refined with the second coder to establish a robust theoretical baseline. One author then conducted a literature assessment to map the six abstract criteria onto the specific technical, architectural, and operational realities of the three analyzed subsystems, generating a detailed set of layer-specific categories. The second coder audited this categorization and several metrics were substantially revised to better reflect real-world adversarial models. A notable outcome of this phase was the refinement of the geographic indicators. The coders determined that counting different jurisdictions was inadequate for measuring the risk of regulatory capture. Consequently, the metric was overhauled into a geopolitical block model (Block A: West-Alliance, Block B: Eastern Block, Block C: Neutral) to more accurately assess the vulnerability to coordinated, cross-border sanctions. To validate the framework's practical applicability and ensure consistent interpretation, both coders subsequently conducted a test coding, independently analyzing and coding a representative subset of the gathered literature. Discrepancies, such as the initial conflation of technical participation barriers with economic costs, were discussed and resolved. This process resulted in the finalization of the codebook, which contains 17 defined and operationalized indicators distributed across the six base categories.

3.4 Structure of the Coding Framework

The finalized evaluation framework encompasses three principal artifacts designed to ensure the systematic and reproducible synthesis of heterogeneous literature: the codebook, the score matrix, and the evidence matrix. The codebook constitutes the core of the methodology, defining six primary categories of censorship resistance: decentralization, permissionlessness, transparency, protocol design, economic incentives, and social incentives. Across these six categories, the framework operationalizes 17 distinct indicators (see Table 1). To enable cross-layer comparability despite fundamental architectural differences, the master codebook defines these indicators at an abstract, systemic level. This theoretical abstraction is subsequently translated into layer-specific technical metrics within three specialized sub-modules tailored to mining pools, the lightning network, and federated sidechains. Evaluations are quantified using an ordinal scale ranging from 1 to 3. A score of 3 indicates high resilience, characterizing a system component that is decentralized, permissionless, and robust against external intervention. A score of 2 denotes moderate resilience, where centralization tendencies or barriers exist that render censorship possible under specific conditions, though not trivially enforceable. A score of 1 reflects low resilience, identifying components with severe centralization, explicit control mechanisms, or single points of failure that facilitate effective third-party censorship. Additionally, the designation *n.a.* (not available) is assigned when the analyzed literature lacks sufficient empirical or theoretical data to derive a reliable evaluation for a specific indicator. To process the extracted data, findings are aggregated into a score matrix, which maps the evaluated papers and their respective findings against the 17 indicators, allowing the identification of cross-layer patterns and research gaps. Crucially, to guarantee intersubjective traceability, every assigned score is paralleled by a corresponding entry in the evidence matrix. This matrix captures a comprehensive evidence layer for each evaluation unit, documenting the evidence type, the underlying data basis, the specific operationalization metric, a confidence assessment of the paper's methodological rigor, and an explicit citation. Furthermore, synthesis rules govern the coding application to prevent the overestimation of theoretical system capabilities. For example, adhering to the *Default over Possibility* principle, technical countermeasures are awarded high resilience scores solely if they are active by default or exhibit proven practical adoption, rather than existing merely as optional theoretical features. Additionally, to methodologically distinguish deliberate censorship from transient technical latency, disruptions are only classified as permanent blockades if transactions are verifiably suppressed for a continuous period of at least four weeks.

3.5 Grounding of the Categories

While Table 1 details the operationalized indicators, the selection of the six primary categories is grounded in foundational blockchain and security literature to ensure a complete measurement of censorship resistance. First, we evaluate **(1) Decentralization** politically, focusing on the distribution of autonomous decision-making power regarding transaction inclusion and routing. Second, the system must exhibit **(2) Permissionlessness**, meaning the absence of central gatekeepers, which we measure through the technical and financial barriers to entry and the ability to unilaterally withdraw assets without third-party approval. Third, a system's resilience is fundamentally weakened if censorship cannot be distinguished from benign technical latency. Therefore, **(3) Transparency** evaluates the network's observability and the ability to attribute malicious filtering to specific actors. Fourth, **(4) Protocol Design** assesses inherent technical implementations, such as whether the protocol enforces privacy by default or offers automated failover mechanisms to circumvent blockades. Fifth, because censorship must be economically punitive in competitive networks, **(5) Economic Incentives** analyzes the direct opportunity costs of filtering valid transactions and the system's resilience against out-of-band bribery. Finally, because censorship is frequently induced by external state actors, **(6) Social Incentives & Geopolitics** measures the vulnerability to regulatory capture by assessing the jurisdictional concentration of gatekeepers across geopolitical blocks and their legal accountability.

Table 1. The Master Codebook: Abstract Indicators and Ordinal Evaluation Scale

Category	ID & Indicator	Abstract Definition	High Resilience (3)	Moderate Resilience (2)	Low Resilience (1)
1. Decentralization	1A Decision Power	Who determines the core action (e.g., block/route)?	Participant decides autonomously	Central entity proposes, participant can reject	Central entity dictates completely
	1B Power Concentration	Number/diversity of control points.	Very large, globally diverse group	Manageable, diverse group	Single entity/homogeneous group
2. Permissionlessness	2A Compliance-Gate	Formal/identity requirements for participation.	No identity checks (permissionless)	Registration/light hurdles (no strict ID)	Formal approval/Strict KYC
	2B Capital-Gate	Material/financial entry costs.	Negligible costs	Significant investment required	Prohibitive costs
	2C Exit-Gate	Can an actor exit without third-party consent?	Unilateral, permissionless exit	Exit possible but with limits/delays	Exit permissioned/blockable
3. Transparency	3A Observability	Can external observers detect censorship?	Deterministically provable	Statistically probable	Indistinguishable from technical failures
	3B Attribution	Can misbehavior be tied to a specific actor?	Censorship & actor clearly identifiable	Censorship visible, but actor unclear	Neither detectable nor attributable
	3C Auditability	Resource barrier for detection/monitoring.	Low resources; many actors can audit	Moderate resources	High resources/requires central entity
4. Protocol Design	4A Countermeasures	Inherent anti-censorship technical safeguards.	Explicit anti-censorship features by default	Neutral, but favors centralization	None; system design aids filtering
	4B Privacy	Difficulty of transaction linkability.	Privacy by default (strong)	Pseudonymity; analysis possible	Identity/cleartext is part of the design
	4C Circumvention	Availability of failover/alternative routes.	Automated failover mechanisms	Manual/inefficient alternatives	No circumvention possible
5. Economic Incentives	5A Revenue Loss	Direct financial cost to the censor.	Direct and significant	Minor/compensable	Neutral/negligible
	5B Bribery Resilience	Censor identity & required collusion threshold.	Anonymous/Dynamic; $\geq 2/3$ required	Pseudonymous; $< 2/3$ required	Known entities; simple minority can censor
	5C Indirect Costs	Reputation and market share risks.	Strong (high skin in the game)	Mixed incentives	Low skin in the game
6. Social & Geopolitics	6A Exit-Friction	Switching costs for users leaving a service.	Immediate, cost-free switching	Switching involves costs/delays	Severely restricted (Lock-in effect)
	6B Capture Risk	Jurisdictional concentration of gatekeepers.	High diversity; no single block $> 50\%$	Pol. Block $> 50\%$, but no single country	Single country (or EU) $> 50\%$
	6C Accountability	Legal identifiability and sanctionability.	Anonymous/Shadow actors (untargetable)	Pseudonymous (partially targetable)	Clear identity: legally sanctionable

4 Layer-Specific Vulnerability Analysis

To avoid the siloed perspectives prevalent in prior research, we synthesize our findings using the framework defined in Sect. 3. Rather than treating the Bitcoin ecosystem as a monolith, we evaluate the censorship resistance of specific technological and organizational control points across three distinct infrastructural layers: the base layer (mining pools), Layer 2 (the Lightning Network), and federated sidechains. Table 2 presents the comprehensive evidence map resulting from our coding process. It bridges the gap between theoretical protocol capabilities and operational realities by mapping 43 analyzed sources (comprising formal verifications, empirical measurements, and architectural simulations) against our six core evaluation categories (C1-C6). Crucially, because academic literature frequently lags behind operational market dynamics, the row *Empirical (Jan 2026)* aggregates primary data collected by the authors. This empirical baseline includes the manual evaluation of mining pool terms of services (ToS), lightning service provider network topologies, and the governance structures of the Liquid and RSK federations.

Table 2. Comprehensive Evidence Map: Mapping of Literature and Primary Data to SoK Categories. A bullet (•) indicates that the evaluated source provided sufficient empirical, architectural, or theoretical evidence to assign a valid resilience score (1, 2, or 3) for at least one indicator within the respective category. It does not imply a positive assessment of censorship resistance. Bullets may also denote negative or contrastive evidence, such as centralization, permissioning, weak privacy, or accountable gatekeepers. The row *Empirical (Jan 2026)* represents primary data collected by the authors to bridge the gap between academic theory and current operational reality. This includes the manual evaluation of Mining Pool Terms of Service (ToS) and ASIC firmware configurations (Layer 1), Lightning Service Provider (LSP) network topologies and jurisdiction mapping (Layer 2), and the governance structures of the Liquid and RSK federations (Layer 3). **Categories mapped: C1**: Decentralization, **C2**: Permissionlessness, **C3**: Transparency, **C4**: Protocol Design, **C5**: Economic Incentives, **C6**: Social, Operational & Geopolitical Factors. **M**: Research methodology—**E**: Empirical Analysis, **G**: Mathematical & Game-Theoretic Modelling of actor behaviour, incentives, or cost-benefit functions, **D**: System Design & Protocol Architecture, **S**: Simulation & Algorithmics, **K**: Systematization of Knowledge; sources may employ multiple methods.

Analyzed Source	Categories Coded						
	C1	C2	C3	C4	C5	C6	M
Layer 1: Mining Pools							
Rosenfeld [49]	•	•			•	•	G
Carlsten et al. [8]	•		•	•	•		GS
Gervais et al. [19]	•			•	•	•	EGS
Harrigan et al. [23]			•	•		•	E
Narayanan et al. [35]	•	•	•	•	•	•	DGK
Zolotavkin et al. [63]					•	•	GS
Gencer et al. [18]	•		•		•		E
Pontiveros et al. [44]	•		•		•		E
Romiti et al. [47]	•		•	•		•	E
Huang et al. [24]	•				•	•	ES
Wang et al. [56]	•		•		•		EG
Zhang et al. [62]	•		•	•		•	E
Tran et al. [54]	•		•	•	•	•	ED
Papathanasiou et al. [40]	•	•	•	•		•	D
Chee et al. [10]	•	•	•	•	•	•	D
Empirical (Jan 2026)	•	•		•	•	•	EK
Layer 2: Lightning Network							
Poon et al. [45]	•	•		•			D
Danezis et al. [11]	•			•			D
Hüttel et al. [26]	•			•			D
Atmanavičiūtė et al. [2]	•			•	•		E
Zabka et al. [60]	•				•		E
Ndolo et al. [36]	•		•	•	•	•	ES
Kappos et al. [27]	•			•			ES
Layer 2: Lightning Network (cont.)							
Rohrer et al. [46]	•	•		•	•		ES
Saraswathi et al. [50]	•	•		•			S
Carotti et al. [9]	•			•	•		EGS
Guasoni et al. [20]	•	•				•	G
Pickhardt et al. [42]	•			•			S
McCorry et al. [33]			•	•		•	D
Leinweber et al. [29]		•	•	•	•		DS
Empirical (Jan 2026)	•	•		•	•	•	ED
Layer 3: Federated Sidechains (Liquid/RSK)							
Dilley et al. [12]	•	•	•	•	•	•	D
Lerner et al. [31]	•	•	•	•	•	•	D
Kiayias et al. [28]		•	•	•		•	D
Zamyatin et al. [61]	•	•	•	•	•	•	DK
Baldimtsi et al. [4]		•	•	•		•	D
Garoffolo et al. [17]		•	•	•			D
Yin et al. [58]	•	•	•	•	•	•	DS
Bespalov et al. [5]		•			•		GS
Guo et al. [21]		•	•	•		•	DS
Hwang et al. [25]	•	•	•	•	•	•	DS
Haeberlen et al. [22]			•			•	DES
Poelstra et al. [43]			•	•			D
Noether et al. [38]		•	•	•			D
Pathak et al. [41]	•	•	•	•	•	•	DS
Empirics: Liquid & RSK	•	•		•	•	•	E

4.1 Layer 1: Mining Pools (Base Layer)

Data Basis: The evaluation of the base layer synthesizes 15 academic publications, focusing on hash rate concentration metrics (e.g., Romiti et al. [47], Wang et al. [56]) and theoretical incentive modeling [8,49]. Because academic literature frequently lags behind operational market dynamics, we augmented this corpus with a primary empirical analysis (January 2026). We used real-time network topology data from *mempool.space* [52] and evaluated the ToS, imprints and documentations of the five largest mining pools.

Decision Power and Centralization: The empirical data demonstrates a severe structural vulnerability rooted in the dominant network architecture. The literature extensively criticizes the Stratum V1 protocol for centralizing block template construction at the pool server [35,54,56]. We empirically validated this vulnerability: our 2026 interface analysis confirmed that the market leaders (controlling ~54% of the global hash rate) do not offer Stratum V2 Job Negotiation to miners by default. Consequently, the decision power over transaction inclusion (**1A: Score 1**) rests entirely with a highly concentrated oligopoly (**1B: Score 2**), creating an effective choke point.

Erosion of Permissionlessness and Privacy: While mining pools economically democratize participation by smoothing reward variances and eliminating prohibitive capital barriers for individual miners (**2B: Score 3**), our ToS analysis reveals a strict operational erosion of permissionless access. To mitigate legal exposure, large pools implement explicit compliance gates (**2A: Score 1**) and exit gates (**2C: Score 1**). For instance, Foundry USA Pool restricts access to authorized users subject to background screenings and identity validation via authoritative data sources [14]. Similarly, AntPool and F2Pool require the provision of accurate personal information [1,16] and retain the contractual right to freeze accounts or enforce ex-post KYC verification upon the detection of "unusual or unauthorized" activities [1] or conduct deemed "objectionable" by the operator [16]. This regulatory compliance is exacerbated by a lack of inherent protocol-level safeguards against filtering (**4A: Score 1**) and poor on-chain privacy, as transparent payouts and frequent address reuse create deanonymizable clusters (**4B: Score 1**) [23,47].

Economic Resiliency and Failover Mechanics: Despite the centralization of power, the base layer maintains systemic resilience through strong economic and geopolitical countermeasures. Rational pools follow a feerate-first strategy, meaning censorship incurs a direct revenue loss (**5A: Score 3**) [8,56]. While many large pool operators are registered corporate entities with high legal accountability (**6C: Score 3**) and correspondingly low bribery resilience (**5B: Score 1**), they face an asymmetric threat from their users. A universal market shift to FPPS (Full Pay Per Share) models has effectively eliminated exit friction (**6A: Score 3**). Combined with automated failover mechanics in modern ASIC firmware (**4C: Score 3**), many configurations allow miners to instantly migrate their hash rate to alternative pools [6,7,32]. This threat of hash rate migration enforces severe indirect reputational costs (**5C: Score 3**). Finally, synchronized regulatory capture is mitigated by a diversified geopolitical distribution (**6B: Score 3**), with over 53% of the hash rate operating in geopolitically neutral or fragmented jurisdictions (Block C), preventing a single legal framework from monopolizing the network.

Transparency and Attribution: Unlike Layer 2's stealth censorship, the public nature of the base layer ensures that censorship is highly visible. The persistent exclusion of profitable transactions from the mempool deviates significantly from natural network latency, making censorship statistically observable (**3A: Score 2**) [44]. Furthermore, attribution is often possible (**3B: Score 3**) because pools voluntarily tag their blocks in the coinbase transaction to build reputation [47]. However, auditing these occurrences requires moderate resources (**3C: Score 2**), as it demands running full nodes and specialized mempool crawlers to provide statistical proof [56].

4.2 Layer 2: Lightning Network (Routing Layer)

Data Basis: The evaluation of the Lightning Network (LN) synthesizes 14 academic publications, ranging from foundational protocol specifications to recent empirical topology measurements. We augmented this with a primary analysis (from January 2026) mapping the most liquid lightning service providers to their legal jurisdictions and ToS.

The Topological Mismatch (Decentralization & Geopolitics): The power dynamics within the LN are characterized by a fundamental dichotomy between protocol design and network reality. At the protocol level, the LN enforces strict source routing, granting the sender complete technical autonomy over path selection (**1A: Score 3**) [45]. However, recent measurements confirm an extreme hub-and-spoke structure where the top 10% of nodes control approximately 96.5% of the total network capacity, resulting in a Gini coefficient exceeding 0.97 (**1B: Score 1**) [2,60]. This liquidity concentration creates unavoidable "chokepoints". Furthermore, our 2026 geographic mapping exposes severe regulatory capture risks (**6B: Score 1**): over 95% of the analyzed top-tier liquidity resides within the west-alliance (block A), with roughly 60% concentrated specifically in US jurisdictions. Because these dominant routing hubs are frequently operated by registered corporate entities and exchanges (e.g., Bitfinex, Binance), they exhibit high legal accountability (**6C: Score 3**) and correspondingly low resilience against state-level coercion or bribery (**5B: Score 1**).

Stealth Censorship and Plausible Deniability (Transparency): Unlike the base layer, where censorship is publicly visible in the mempool, censorship on Layer 2 can operate silently. The LN suffers from a critical lack of observability (**3A: Score 1**). If a routing node drops a payment packet, the sender cannot deterministically distinguish this malicious filtering from a benign technical failure, such as a temporary lack of channel liquidity [36]. This plausible deniability allows intermediaries to engage in stealth censorship without suffering the reputational damage (**5C: Score 2**) that normally disciplines malicious actors. Despite these vulnerabilities, the LN offers a native circumvention mechanism via Multi-Path Payments (MPP) (**4C: Score 2**). If an intermediary censors a specific route, Multi-Path Payments (MPP) allows the sender's client to automatically fragment the payment and route it through alternative channels, provided sufficient parallel liquidity exists. However, Saraswathi et al. [50] show that MPP is currently not widely used.

Protocol Safeguards and Exit Friction: The LN attempts to mitigate routing censorship through Sphinx onion routing (**4A: Score 3**), ensuring intermediaries only know their immediate predecessor and successor [11]. However, experimental studies show this privacy is fragile (**4B: Score 1**), as traffic and timing analyses can reliably de-anonymize payment flows [27,36]. If a user's transactions are consistently filtered, the ultimate economic corrective is the unilateral exit (Force Close). While the protocol guarantees this right, allowing users to settle their funds on the base layer without counterpart approval (**2C: Score 2**), it is hindered by mandatory timelocks (Settlement Delays) [45]. Consequently, assets can remain locked and exposed to market volatility for days during a censorship event, representing a significant friction compared to the instant failover mechanics of mining pools.

4.3 Layer 3: Federated Sidechains

Data Basis: The evaluation of Layer 3 synthesizes 12 academic publications. To bridge the gap between abstract models and operational reality, this literature is augmented by a systematic documentary analysis of the official protocol specifications and governance guidelines of two dominant sidechains: the Liquid Network [12,51] and Rootstock (RSK) [31,48] (as of January 2026). Because both systems rely on federated two-way pegs rather than purely permissionless consensus, we evaluate their censorship resistance by analyzing their institutional trust models and architectural constraints.

Architectural Dichotomy: Block Production vs. Privacy: While both networks aim to scale Bitcoin, they adopt divergent architectural philosophies that result in different censorship vectors. RSK utilizes merged mining, allowing the open Bitcoin mining network to dynamically and competitively create blocks (**1A: Score 3**). However, it inherits an Ethereum-compatible account model, resulting in complete plaintext transparency of transactions. This visibility maximizes linkability (**4B: Score 1**) and makes granular, targeted censorship based on addresses or smart contract calls technically trivial (**4A: Score 1**). Conversely, Liquid relies on a closed, deterministic Round-Robin consensus among 15 designated functionaries (**1A: Score 2**). To mitigate the risk of targeted filtering by these centralized gatekeepers, Liquid natively implements Confidential Transactions (CT) (**4A: Score 3**). By cryptographically blinding transaction amounts and asset types, the protocol prevents functionaries from effectively discriminating against specific value transfers. Yet, this obfuscation creates a trade-off in transparency: it becomes highly difficult for external observers to distinguish malicious censorship by a functionary from benign technical latency (**3A: Score 1**). Furthermore, while CT provides strong amounts privacy, the transaction graph remains public, limiting absolute unlinkability (**4B: Score 2**).

The Exit-Gate and Emergency Circumvention: A fundamental vulnerability across both evaluated sidechains is the friction and trust required for asset withdrawal. Liquid users are entirely dependent on a supermajority (11 of 15) of the federation to authorize a peg-out (**2C: Score 1**), effectively trapping funds if the functionaries comply with an external censorship mandate. RSK attempts to automate this process via its "PowPeg" smart contracts, allowing users to initiate a peg-out permissionlessly, albeit with a mandatory security delay of 4,000 blocks (approximately 33 h) (**2C: Score 2**). However, this automation still fundamentally relies on the federation's Hardware Security Modules (HSMs) to execute the final signature on the base layer. If these HSMs are coerced to censor a transaction, the user requires an automated circumvention mechanism. Because the Bitcoin base layer currently lacks the expressivity to verify complex remote state transitions trustlessly, neither network offers a true, unilateral emergency exit (**4C: Score 1**). Our analysis of RSK's fallback protocol (RSKIP-201 [30]) reveals that its emergency mechanism merely defaults to another trusted multisig controlled by designated parties after one year of HSM inactivity, rather than granting the user cryptographic sovereignty over their funds. Furthermore, RSK enforces a strict minimum peg-in of 0.005 BTC (**2B: Score 2**), imposing significant capital barriers for regular users compared to Liquid's lack of protocol-enforced minimums (**2B: Score 3**).

Governance and Regulatory Capture: Ultimately, the security of current federated sidechains devolves from cryptography to institutional governance. Becoming a Liquid functionary or an RSK "Pegnatory" is strictly permissioned (**2A: Score 1**). Both federations consist mainly of heavily vetted, registered corporate entities, such as exchanges and institutional banks (**6C: Score 3**). While this high accountability provides strong indirect economic deterrence against malicious theft, as these entities would destroy their core business reputation (**5C: Score 3**), it simultaneously maximizes their vulnerability to state coercion (**5B: Score 1**). Our documentary analysis reveals that over 50% of the validators in both networks are domiciled within the West-Alliance geopolitical block (**6B: Score 2**). Consequently, rather than acting as decentralized safe havens, these federations represent highly identifiable, geographically concentrated single points of coercion.

5 Discussion and Synthesis

The isolated evaluation of the base layer, Layer 2, and federated sidechains reveals a significant discrepancy between technological protocol architecture and institutional reality. While the technical protocols differ fundamentally, their socio-economic vulnerabilities, particularly their susceptibility to state coercion, converge significantly.

5.1 The Illusion of Additive Security and Cumulative Vulnerabilities

A fragmented view of the ecosystem might lead to the fallacy that security mechanisms are additive. However, the synthesis demonstrates that censorship resistance is inherited hierarchically. Ultimately, a transaction on Layer 2 is never more secure than its finalization on Layer 1. If the base layer fails as a neutral arbiter, the security models of the overlying layers collapse. This hierarchy creates a severe domino effect concerning the network's exit options (2C). Layer 2 solutions and sidechains legitimize their intermediaries by guaranteeing users the ability to retreat to the base layer via a force close or peg-out. However, this safety net assumes a censorship-resistant base layer. While off-chain Lightning transactions are obfuscated via Sphinx routing, the ultimate settlement relies on the base layer. If a user needs to force-close a channel, they are entirely dependent on mining pools to include that specific transaction. Because operators of major pools possess high accountability (6C: Score 3) and are legally reachable, they could be coerced into ignoring the closing transactions of sanctioned addresses. In such a scenario, the user is effectively expropriated, as they cannot rescue their values onto the main chain. For federated sidechains, this dynamic is even more critical as an exit requires not only the tolerance of miners but also the active signature of the federation.

5.2 Theoretical Improvements Vs. Operational Realities

Our analysis exposes a profound paradox: while theoretical protocols already provide advanced tools for high censorship resistance (potential Score 3), the operational status quo frequently remains in centralized structures (Score 1). This gap is not caused by a lack of cryptographic innovation, but rather by economic incentives. Efficiency, convenience, and established power structures currently hinder the broad implementation of more secure alternatives. The literature discusses several mature concepts to mitigate these specific layer vulnerabilities:

Mining (Base Layer): The vulnerability of Stratum V1 centralizing block composition at the pool server creates a single point of failure for censorship. Theoretical solutions like Stratum V2 and its Job Negotiation protocol return decision-making power to individual miners, making central filtering by pool operators technically impossible.

Lightning Network (Layer 2): While the protocol technically allows for the avoidance of censoring hubs via MPPs, the network exhibits an extreme concentration of power, with a Gini coefficient exceeding 0.97. The driver of this gap is liquidity efficiency. Large central hubs offer the cheapest and most reliable routes. The widespread adoption of probabilistic routing and MPPs is required to shift the network away from its vulnerable hub-and-spoke topology.

Federated Sidechains (Layer 3): Systems like Liquid and RSK currently rely on federations of known institutional companies for their exit gates (2C: Score 1). This reliance is not merely an arbitrary design choice, but a systemic limitation imposed by Bitcoin's current base-layer consensus rules, which lack the expressive covenants required to enforce trustless state transitions. While theoretical concepts like Zendoo or NIPoPoWs demonstrate that trustless peg-outs are achievable, implementing them natively on Bitcoin requires bridging this systemic gap. Emerging paradigms such as proposed base-layer covenant soft-forks offer a mature theoretical pathway. These solutions could effectively upgrade current trusted federations into true, trust-minimized rollups, replacing institutional multi-signature quorums with mathematical guarantees.

5.3 The Accountability Paradox and Geopolitics

A comparison of our evaluation matrices identifies Accountability (6C) as a cross-layer primary vulnerability. This reveals a security ambivalence: high accountability functions as a necessary condition for detecting and socially punishing censorship, yet simultaneously presents a systemic risk. Contrary to the assumption of decentralized anonymity, the central gatekeepers across all three evaluated layers are predominantly identifiable legal entities. Leading mining pools (e.g., Foundry, AntPool) exhibit high accountability (6C: Score 3). This legal tangibility makes them susceptible to state coercion, even as it allows the network to attribute censorship and sanction it through hash rate migration. This identical pattern is visible in the Lightning Network, where routing nodes are operated by regulated exchanges, and in federated sidechains like Liquid, whose security model explicitly relies on known functionaries. Consequently, these entities create a clear *single point of coercion* where sanctions can be enforced without technical protocols immediately preventing it.

5.4 Future Research Directions

The most pressing cross-layer gap is *real-time censorship detection*: current studies are retrospective, and online systems distinguishing deliberate filtering from benign latency would substantially reduce the detection window for state-induced suppression. At the **base layer**, game-theoretic models study Selfish Mining and Undercutting in isolation. Combined adversarial strategies may lower the effective censorship threshold below classical majority levels. The economic viability of non-custodial pool models in a fee-only regime also remains open with direct implications for pool decentralization. For the **Lightning Network**, routing models omit on-chain channel management costs, which may erode the apparent advantage of central hubs under realistic settlement assumptions. Verifiable metrics distinguishing deliberate filtering from routine failures are needed to operationalize the stealth-censorship threat identified in Sect. 4. For **federated sidechains**, realizing trustless exits requires applying ZKPs as chain relays for light-client verification without covenant soft-forks, and constructing formal security proofs under fully adaptive corruption, ensuring protocols hold against adversaries who corrupt members after observing transcripts.

6 Conclusion

By applying a unified 17-indicator framework across the base layer, the Lightning Network, and federated sidechains, this paper evaluated the Bitcoin ecosystem's resilience against sanction-induced transaction filtering, bridging the methodological fragmentation in existing research.

Three findings emerge from our synthesis. First, censorship resistance inherits hierarchically rather than additively: the exit-option guarantees of Layer 2 and sidechain protocols are entirely dependent on base-layer neutrality, making mining pool compliance the ecosystem's critical bottleneck. Second, the adoption gap between mature cryptographic mitigations (Stratum V2, MPP, trustless peg-out designs) and operational deployment is driven by economic incentives, not by a lack of technical solutions. Third, intermediaries at all three layers are legally identifiable, geopolitically concentrated corporate entities that constitute single points of coercion no in-protocol obfuscation fully neutralizes. Until trust-minimized block production and trustless two-way pegs achieve broad economic adoption, the ecosystem's resilience rests on minority hash-rate defection and reputational deterrence rather than cryptographic guarantees. The technologies for robust censorship resistance exist, but the obstacle is market internalization.

Acknowledgments. The authors used generative AI-based tools to revise the text, improve flow and correct any typos, grammatical errors, and awkward phrasing. These tools were additionally used to assist with LaTeX source code, and support brainstorming of initial ideas. The authors remain responsible for the content, analysis, and conclusions of the paper.

Disclosure of Interests. The authors have no competing interests to declare that are relevant to the content of this article.

References

1. ANTPOOL: ANTPOOL user service agreement (2026). https://www.antpool.com/protocal/copyRight1
2. Atmanavičiūtė, L., Vanagas, T., Masteika, S.: Quantitative analysis of centralization in the bitcoin lightning network through centrality metrics. IEEE Access **13**, 168761–168781 (2025). https://doi.org/10.1109/ACCESS.2025.3614085
3. Back, A., et al.: Enabling blockchain innovations with pegged sidechains. Technical report, Blockstream (2014). https://blockstream.com/sidechains.pdf
4. Baldimtsi, F., Miers, I., Zhang, X., Garcia-Alfaro, J., Muñoz-Tapia, J.L., Navarro-Arribas, G.: Anonymous sidechains. In: Soriano, M. (ed.) Data Privacy Management, Cryptocurrencies and Blockchain Technology, pp. 262–277. Springer, Cham (2022). https://doi.org/10.1007/978-3-030-93944-1_17
5. Bespalov, Y., Kovalchuk, L., Nelasa, H., Oliynykov, R., Garoffolo, A.: Game theory analysis of incentive distribution for prompt generation of the proof tree in zk-SNARK based sidechains. In: 2022 IEEE International Carnahan Conference on Security Technology (ICCST), pp. 1–7 (2022). https://doi.org/10.1109/ICCST52959.2022.9896484
6. Bitmain Support: Connect ANTMINER D3 to pools - Antpool (2022). https://support.bitmain.com/hc/en-us/articles/115002909233-Connect-ANTMINER-D3-to-Pools-Antpool
7. Braiins Academy: Configuration — Braiins OS (2026). https://academy.braiins.com/en/braiins-os/configuration/
8. Carlsten, M., Kalodner, H., Weinberg, S.M., Narayanan, A.: On the instability of bitcoin without the block reward. In: Proceedings of the 2016 ACM SIGSAC Conference on Computer and Communications Security, CCS '16, pp. 154–167. Association for Computing Machinery, New York, NY, USA (2016). https://doi.org/10.1145/2976749.2978408
9. Carotti, A., Sguanci, C., Sidiropoulos, A.: Rational economic behaviours in the bitcoin lightning network. In: 2024 IEEE International Conference on Blockchain and Cryptocurrency (ICBC), pp. 594–601 (2024). https://doi.org/10.1109/ICBC59979.2024.10634468
10. Chee, R., Chitturi, K., Dufour-Sans, E., Soska, K.: OCEAN: a built-in replacement for mining pools. Cryptology ePrint Archive, Paper 2019/1081 (2019). https://eprint.iacr.org/2019/1081
11. Danezis, G., Goldberg, I.: Sphinx: a compact and provably secure mix format. In: 30th IEEE Symposium on Security and Privacy, pp. 269–282 (2009). https://doi.org/10.1109/SP.2009.15
12. Dilley, J., Poelstra, A., Wilkins, J., Piekarska, M., Gorlick, B., Friedenbach, M.: Strong federations: an interoperable blockchain solution to centralized third-party risks (2017). https://arxiv.org/abs/1612.05491
13. Eyal, I., Sirer, E.G.: Majority is not enough: bitcoin mining is vulnerable. Commun. ACM **61**(7), 95–102 (2018). https://doi.org/10.1145/3212998
14. Foundry Digital LLC: Terms and conditions (2023). https://foundrydigital.com/terms-and-conditions/
15. Fox, E., Pai, M., Resnick, M.: Censorship resistance in on-chain auctions (2023). https://arxiv.org/abs/2301.13321
16. Fram Farm Inc.: F2Pool terms of service (2026). https://www.f2pool.com/terms
17. Garoffolo, A., Kaidalov, D., Oliynykov, R.: Zendoo: a zk-SNARK verifiable cross-chain transfer protocol enabling decoupled and decentralized sidechains. In: 2020

IEEE 40th International Conference on Distributed Computing Systems (ICDCS), pp. 1257–1262 (2020). https://doi.org/10.1109/ICDCS47774.2020.00161
18. Gencer, A.E., Basu, S., Eyal, I., van Renesse, R., Sirer, E.G.: Decentralization in Bitcoin and Ethereum networks. In: Meiklejohn, S., Sako, K. (eds.) FC 2018. LNCS, vol. 10957, pp. 439–457. Springer, Heidelberg (2018). https://doi.org/10.1007/978-3-662-58387-6_24
19. Gervais, A., Karame, G.O., Wüst, K., Glykantzis, V., Ritzdorf, H., Capkun, S.: On the security and performance of proof of work blockchains. In: Proceedings of the 2016 ACM SIGSAC Conference on Computer and Communications Security, CCS '16, pp. 3–16. Association for Computing Machinery, New York, NY, USA (2016). https://doi.org/10.1145/2976749.2978341
20. Guasoni, P., Huberman, G., Shikhelman, C.: Lightning network economics: channels. Manage. Sci. **70**(6), 3827–3840 (2024). https://doi.org/10.1287/mnsc.2022.01664
21. Guo, J., Gai, K., Zhu, L., Zhang, Z.: An approach of secure two-way-pegged multisidechain. Presented at the Algorithms and Architectures for Parallel Processing (2020). https://doi.org/10.1007/978-3-030-38961-1_47
22. Haeberlen, A., Kouznetsov, P., Druschel, P.: PeerReview: practical accountability for distributed systems. SIGOPS Oper. Syst. Rev. **41**(6), 175–188 (2007). https://doi.org/10.1145/1323293.1294279
23. Harrigan, M., Fretter, C.: The unreasonable effectiveness of address clustering. In: 2016 International IEEE Conferences on Ubiquitous Intelligence & Computing, Advanced and Trusted Computing, Scalable Computing and Communications, Cloud and Big Data Computing, Internet of People, and Smart World Congress (UIC/ATC/ScalCom/CBDCom/IoP/SmartWorld), pp. 368–373 (2016). https://doi.org/10.1109/UIC-ATC-ScalCom-CBDCom-IoP-SmartWorld.2016.0071
24. Huang, C.Y., Wen, Y.F., Chen, Y.W.: Analyzing on reward and fee effect on the size of mining pools - a case of bitcoin system. In: 2023 International Conference on Consumer Electronics - Taiwan (ICCE-Taiwan), pp. 213–214 (2023). https://doi.org/10.1109/ICCE-Taiwan58799.2023.10226748
25. Hwang, G.-H., Chen, P.-H., Lu, C.-H., Chiu, C., Lin, H.-C., Jheng, A.-J.: InfiniteChain: a multi-chain architecture with distributed auditing of sidechains for public blockchains. In: Chen, S., Wang, H., Zhang, L.-J. (eds.) ICBC 2018. LNCS, vol. 10974, pp. 47–60. Springer, Cham (2018). https://doi.org/10.1007/978-3-319-94478-4_4
26. Hüttel, H., Staroveski, V.: Secrecy and authenticity properties of the lightning network protocol. In: Proceedings of the 6th International Conference on Information Systems Security and Privacy - ICISSP, pp. 119–130. INSTICC, SciTePress (2020). https://doi.org/10.5220/0008974801190130
27. Kappos, G., et al.: An empirical analysis of privacy in the lightning network. In: Borisov, N., Diaz, C. (eds.) FC 2021. LNCS, vol. 12674, pp. 167–186. Springer, Heidelberg (2021). https://doi.org/10.1007/978-3-662-64322-8_8
28. Kiayias, A., Zindros, D.: Proof-of-work sidechains. In: Bracciali, A., Clark, J., Pintore, F., Rønne, P.B., Sala, M. (eds.) FC 2019. LNCS, vol. 11599, pp. 21–34. Springer, Cham (2020). https://doi.org/10.1007/978-3-030-43725-1_3
29. Leinweber, M., Grundmann, M., Schönborn, L., Hartenstein, H.: TEE-based distributed watchtowers for fraud protection in the lightning network. In: Pérez-Solà, C., Navarro-Arribas, G., Biryukov, A., Garcia-Alfaro, J. (eds.) DPM/CBT -2019. LNCS, vol. 11737, pp. 177–194. Springer, Cham (2019). https://doi.org/10.1007/978-3-030-31500-9_11

30. Lerner, S.D.: Time-locked Emergency Multisignature. Rootstock Improvement Proposal RSKIP201, Rootstock (2021). https://ips.rootstock.io/IPs/RSKIP201.html
31. Lerner, S.D., et al.: RSK: a bitcoin sidechain with stateful smart-contracts. Cryptology ePrint Archive, Paper 2022/684 (2022). https://eprint.iacr.org/2022/684
32. Luxor Technologies: Hashrate splitting (2026). https://docs.luxor.tech/firmware/features/hashratesplit
33. McCorry, P., Bakshi, S., Bentov, I., Meiklejohn, S., Miller, A.: Pisa: arbitration outsourcing for state channels. In: Proceedings of the 1st ACM Conference on Advances in Financial Technologies, AFT '9, pp. 16–30. Association for Computing Machinery, New York, NY, USA (2019). https://doi.org/10.1145/3318041.3355461
34. Nakamoto, S.: Bitcoin: a peer-to-peer electronic cash system. Technical report, Bitcoin.org (2008). https://bitcoin.org/bitcoin.pdf
35. Narayanan, A., Bonneau, J., Felten, E., Miller, A., Goldfeder, S.: Bitcoin and Cryptocurrency Technologies: A Comprehensive Introduction. Princeton University Press, Princeton, NJ, USA (2016)
36. Ndolo, C., Tschorsch, F.: Payment censorship in the lightning network despite encrypted communication. In: Böhme, R., Kiffer, L. (eds.) 6th Conference on Advances in Financial Technologies (AFT 2024). Leibniz International Proceedings in Informatics (LIPIcs), vol. 316, pp. 12:1–12:24. Schloss Dagstuhl – Leibniz-Zentrum für Informatik, Dagstuhl, Germany (2024). https://doi.org/10.4230/LIPIcs.AFT.2024.12
37. Nick, J., Poelstra, A., Sanders, G.: Liquid: a bitcoin sidechain. Technical report, Blockstream, May 2020. https://blockstream.com/assets/downloads/pdf/liquid-whitepaper.pdf
38. Noether, S., Mackenzie, A.: The Monero Research Lab: ring confidential transactions. Ledger **1**, 1–18 (2016). https://doi.org/10.5195/ledger.2016.34
39. Palatinus, M.: Stratum mining protocol specification. Slush Pool/BitcoinTalk Forum (2012). https://en.bitcoin.it/wiki/Stratum_mining_protocol
40. Papathanasiou, A., Kyriakidou, C.N., Pittaras, I., Polyzos, G.: Smart contract-based decentralized mining pools for proof-of-work blockchains. In: 2024 IEEE International Conference on Blockchain (Blockchain), pp. 227–234 (2024). https://doi.org/10.1109/Blockchain62396.2024.00037
41. Pathak, A., Al-Anbagi, I., Hamilton, H.J.: SATI: sidechain-based access control & trust mechanism for IoT networks. IEEE Trans. Netw. Serv. Manage. **21**(5), 5888–5903 (2024). https://doi.org/10.1109/TNSM.2024.3438621
42. Pickhardt, R., Richter, S.: Optimally reliable & cheap payment flows on the lightning network (2021). https://arxiv.org/abs/2107.05322
43. Poelstra, A., Back, A., Friedenbach, M., Maxwell, G., Wuille, P.: Confidential assets. In: Zohar, A., et al. (eds.) FC 2018. LNCS, vol. 10958, pp. 43–63. Springer, Heidelberg (2019). https://doi.org/10.1007/978-3-662-58820-8_4
44. Pontiveros, B.B.F., Norvill, R., State, R.: Monitoring the transaction selection policy of bitcoin mining pools. In: 2018 IEEE/IFIP Network Operations and Management Symposium, NOMS 2018, pp. 1–6 (2018). https://doi.org/10.1109/NOMS.2018.8406328
45. Poon, J., Dryja, T.: The bitcoin lightning network: Scalable off-chain instant payments. White paper, January 2016. https://cdn.nakamotoinstitute.org/docs/lightning-network.pdf, draft Version 0.5.9.2
46. Rohrer, E., Malliaris, J., Tschorsch, F.: Discharged payment channels: quantifying the lightning network's resilience to topology-based attacks. In: 2019 IEEE Euro-

pean Symposium on Security and Privacy Workshops (EuroS&PW), pp. 347–356 (2019). https://doi.org/10.1109/EuroSPW.2019.00045
47. Romiti, M., Judmayer, A., Zamyatin, A., Haslhofer, B.: A deep dive into bitcoin mining pools: an empirical analysis of mining shares (2019). https://arxiv.org/abs/1905.05999
48. Rootstock: Bitcoin Smart Contracts - Build on Bitcoin | Rootstock (RSK) (2026). https://rootstock.io/
49. Rosenfeld, M.: Analysis of bitcoin pooled mining reward systems (2011). https://arxiv.org/abs/1112.4980
50. Saraswathi, S., Kümmerle, C.: An exposition of pathfinding strategies within lightning network clients. In: 2025 IEEE International Conference on Blockchain and Cryptocurrency (ICBC), pp. 1–17 (2025). https://doi.org/10.1109/ICBC64466.2025.11114515
51. The Liquid Network: The Liquid Network: The Financial Layer for Bitcoin Capital Markets (2026). https://liquid.net/
52. The Mempool Open Source Project: Mempool - Bitcoin Explorer (2026). https://mempool.space/
53. Tikhomirov, S., Moreno-Sanchez, P., Maffei, M.: A quantitative analysis of security, anonymity and scalability for the lightning network. In: 2020 IEEE European Symposium on Security and Privacy Workshops (EuroS&PW), pp. 387–396 (2020). https://doi.org/10.1109/EuroSPW51379.2020.00059
54. Tran, M., von Arx, T., Vanbever, L.: Routing attacks on cryptocurrency mining pools. In: 2024 IEEE Symposium on Security and Privacy (SP), pp. 3805–3821 (2024). https://doi.org/10.1109/SP54263.2024.00254
55. U.S. Department of the Treasury: U.S. treasury sanctions notorious virtual currency mixer tornado cash. Press Release, August 2022. https://home.treasury.gov/news/press-releases/jy0916
56. Wang, C., Chu, X., Qin, Y.: Dissecting mining pools of bitcoin network: measurement, analysis and modeling. IEEE Trans. Netw. Sci. Eng. **10**(1), 398–412 (2023). https://doi.org/10.1109/TNSE.2022.3210537
57. Weintraub, B., Kumble, S.P., Nita-Rotaru, C., Roos, S.: Payout races and congested channels: a formal analysis of security in the lightning network. In: Proceedings of the 2024 on ACM SIGSAC Conference on Computer and Communications Security, CCS '24, pp. 2562–2576. Association for Computing Machinery, New York, NY, USA (2024). https://doi.org/10.1145/3658644.3670315
58. Yin, L., Xu, J., Tang, Q.: Sidechains with fast cross-chain transfers. IEEE Trans. Depend. Secure Comput. **19**(6), 3925–3940 (2022). https://doi.org/10.1109/TDSC.2021.3114151
59. Yu, J., Gao, S., Song, R., Cai, Z., Xiao, B.: Mining attack with zero knowledge in the blockchain. In: Proceedings of the 20th ACM Asia Conference on Computer and Communications Security, ASIA CCS '25, pp. 890–905. Association for Computing Machinery, New York, NY, USA (2025). https://doi.org/10.1145/3708821.3733906
60. Zabka, P., Foerster, K.T., Decker, C., Schmid, S.: Short paper: a centrality analysis of the lightning network. In: Eyal, I., Garay, J. (eds.) Financial Cryptography and Data Security, pp. 374–385. Springer, Cham (2022). https://doi.org/10.1007/978-3-031-18283-9_18
61. Zamyatin, A., et al.: SoK: communication across distributed ledgers. In: Borisov, N., Diaz, C. (eds.) FC 2021. LNCS, vol. 12675, pp. 3–36. Springer, Heidelberg (2021). https://doi.org/10.1007/978-3-662-64331-0_1

62. Zhang, Z., et al.: Under the dark: a systematical study of stealthy mining pools (ab)use in the wild. In: Proceedings of the 2023 ACM SIGSAC Conference on Computer and Communications Security, CCS '23, pp. 326–340. Association for Computing Machinery, New York, NY, USA (2023). https://doi.org/10.1145/3576915.3616377
63. Zolotavkin, Y., García, J., Rudolph, C.: Incentive compatibility of pay per last n shares in bitcoin mining pools. Presented at the Decision and Game Theory for Security (2017). https://doi.org/10.1007/978-3-319-68711-7_2

Author Index

S. Nadjm-Tehrani et al. (Eds.): ARES 2026, LNCS 16898, pp. 485–486, 2027.
https://doi.org/10.1007/978-3-032-36874-4